HEROIC MEXICO

Books by William Weber Johnson

KELLY BLUE

MEXICO

THE ANDEAN REPUBLICS

HEROIC MEXICO

BAJA CALIFORNIA

FORTY-NINERS

CORTÉS

UNITED STATES

Tijuana
Mexicali
Nogales
Cananea
Agua
Prieta
Columbus
El Paso
Ciudad
Juárez
Hermosillo
Casas Grandes
Guaymas
Ojinaga
Chihuahua
Ciudad Obregón
Navojoa
Piedras Negras
Sabinas
Parral
Jiménez
Cuatro Ciénegas
Nuevo Laredo
Monclova
Hacienda
Canutillo
San Pedro
Hacienda
Guadalupe
La Paz
Culiacán
Torreón
Monterrey
Saltillo
Durango
Mazatlán
Ciudad Victoria
Zacatecas
Aguascalientes
San Luis
Potosí
Tepic
León
Guanajuato
Guadalajara
Irapuato
Querétaro
Celaya
Jiquilpan
MEXICO
CITY
Manzanillo
Morelia
Toluca
Puebl
Cuernavaca
Anenecuilco
Cuautla
Chilpancingo
Acapulco

PACIFIC

OCEAN

N

0   Miles   500
palacios

HEROIC
MEXICO

The Narrative History
of a Twentieth Century Revolution

by WILLIAM WEBER JOHNSON

Harcourt Brace Jovanovich, Publishers
San Diego   New York   London

- San Antonio
- Matamoros

GULF OF
MEXICO

- Tampico
- Mérida
- Córdoba • Veracruz
- Campeche
- Orizaba
- Tehuacán
- Ciudad Chetumal
- Oaxaca
- Villahermosa
- Tehuantepec
- Tuxtla Gutiérrez
- BRITISH HONDURAS

CARIBBEAN SEA

GUATEMALA

HONDURAS

EL SALVADOR

NICARAGUA

Copyright © 1984, 1968 by William Weber Johnson

Library of Congress Cataloging in Publication Data

Johnson, William Weber, 1909-
  Heroic Mexico.

  Bibliography: p.
  Includes index.
  1. Mexico—History—1910-1946. I. Title.
F1234.J78 1984   972.08   83-22856
ISBN: 0-15-640080-4

All Rights Reserved
Printed in the United States of America
First Harvest/HBJ Edition 1984

To E.A.J. for her help and encouragement,
and to J.J.J., P.W.J., and R.McM.E.
for their patience and understanding.

FOREWORD

FRANCISCO VILLA HAD BEEN DEAD for forty-three years when the Mexican Congress decided recently that he was, after all, a hero of the nation. This came about only after a long and bitter debate in which the famous northern guerrilla leader was loudly denounced as a murderer and bandit and, alternately, warmly praised as a military genius and protector of the humble.

With this difficult decision made it was ordered that Villa's name be inscribed in gilt letters on the walls of the Chamber of Deputies, along with the names of Francisco Madero, Venustiano Carranza, Alvaro Obregón, Emiliano Zapata, and others who had long since been officially declared heroes.

It is one of the peculiarities of recent Mexican history that the men who led the Revolution sooner or later became enemies. Madero, to his misfortune, loved and trusted almost everyone. He was scorned by Carranza, ignored by Obregón, disavowed by Zapata and, finally, killed by men who had sworn to protect and obey him. Carranza was fought by Villa and Zapata and, finally, was abandoned and driven to his death by Obregón. Zapata was disappointed with both Madero and Villa; he hated Obregón and Carranza and was betrayed and killed with the latter's knowledge. Obregón was several times nearly killed by Villa and was once sentenced to death by Carranza. Villa never wavered in his loyalty to Madero, but he became disillusioned with most of his revolutionary colleagues and killed many of them personally—and wanted to do the same for Carranza and Obregón.

All of them were heroes, all were martyrs by assassination, and almost all were mutually antagonistic and incompatible. Their only common ground was service to the Revolution, that upheaval that rocked Mexico for thirty years and came close to destroying it.

In the modern, progressive Mexico that emerged from all this torment it is strange to find that these old antipathies live on among survivors and descendants of survivors. One man's hero is another's scoundrel. What is truth for a Carrancista is untruth for a Villista. What is holy for the one is abomination for the other. What is fact in one document becomes fiction in another and vice versa. It greatly complicates the task of putting together a narrative history of modern Mexico. It is reasonable to ask why—with all the confusion and contradiction—such a project was undertaken.

While the acknowledged heroes of the Revolution were sometimes less than heroic—at least in each other's eyes—the true heroism of this mighty struggle belonged to the Mexican people, the unsung, faceless thousands who fought through a terrible present to escape an intolerable past and reach an uncertain future. Non-Mexicans know very little of what Mexico has suffered. Nor is it certain that the suffering has ended. When the first edition of this book was published, Mexico was preparing for its role as host to the 19th Olympic Games, an ambitious gesture of nationalism and pride in its achievements. But on the very eve of the games, students demonstrating against one-party rule, detention of political prisoners, and police brutality were shot down by police and military in the Plaza of Tlatelolco. The shocking event was the beginning of a period in which the purpose and accomplishments of the Revolution came seriously into question. The Revolution had, it is true, found, through heroic measures, cures for some of Mexico's ancient and persistent ills. But in Mexico as elsewhere, social, political, and economic health remains elusive. By understanding something of Mexico's travail, non-Mexicans may perhaps gain insight into the revolutionary processes at work in much of Latin America and elsewhere—and, with that insight, possibly patience and sympathy as well.

W.W.J.

San Diego, California
October 1983.

HEROIC (hi rō′ ik) adj . . . having or involving recourse to boldness, daring, or extreme measures. *Heroic surgery saved his life* . . .

The Random House Dictionary
of the English Language

CONTENTS

HEROIC MEXICO

CHAPTER I

MAN OF STONE

"General Díaz's ideal was the petrifica-
tion of the State . . . a death's head had
taken the place of the living man . . ."

Francisco Bulnes, *The Whole
Truth about Mexico*

WHEN SEPTEMBER COMES to the high central plateau of Mexico the rains
that have fallen every afternoon of the summer months are ending. The
air is fine and clear. The maize has grown tall. The spikes of maguey,
marching to the horizon in ranks of jagged symmetry, are a fresh gray-
green. The mountain slopes above the valley, wastelands through much
of the year, now have, faintly, the color of life. The cumulus clouds
that towered over the old City of Mexico are gone. The white peaks of
Popocatepetl and Ixtaccihuatl seem to float in deep blue space. And
there is an air of expectancy, of hope.

In the times when the ancient city of the plateau was known as
Tenochtitlan, capital of the Aztec empire, it was a season of the year
called Teutleco, the homecoming of the gods. The temples were richly
adorned, and rooftop gardens cascaded flowers. Wooden drums throbbed,
clay flutes trilled and conch shell trumpets blared. There was much
drinking of pulque, the fermented juice of the maguey, and the cele-
brants, normally abstemious, explained their heavy drinking as "washing the feet of the gods."

September of 1910 in Mexico City was also a time of festival. The
nation was celebrating, at a cost of twenty million pesos (and twenty
carloads of imported champagne) the one hundredth anniversary of
Mexico's declaration of independence from Spain. There were parades
and feasts, pomp and ceremony, and many honors for the heroes of the
independence movement, Miguel Hidalgo y Costilla and José María

Morelos y Pavón, who began the fight for freedom and who were martyrs in its cause.

But Mexico was celebrating more than the centennial of the war for independence and the deeds of Hidalgo and Morelos in the remote past. The true center of attention was General José de la Cruz Porfirio Díaz, better known as Don Porfirio, the strong man who had ruled Mexico for more than a third of a century. It was in no sense a home-coming for him. To most Mexicans it seemed that he had been there forever—in the National Palace, in the summer palace of Chapultepec, in the town house at 8 Calle Cadena. He was the most permanent fixture in a nation noted for impermanence. With only one significant interruption he had ruled the country since 1876 and might well go on governing it forever. September 15, the eve of Independence Day, was celebrated as his birthday, and in this September of 1910 he was eighty years old. He had spent most of his long life in the service of his nation, had fought forty-odd battles and had, as perennial president, imposed *la paz porfiriana,* the Porfirian peace. He was a magnificent man for any age, erect, strong, and an excellent horseman still. On his broad chest he wore, on occasion, twenty-seven medals and decorations, thirteen of them from admiring foreign nations—Britain, France, Russia, China, Japan, Venezuela, Holland, Persia, and so on. His beautiful second wife, thirty-five years his junior, had taught him elegant social deportment and fine table manners (he no longer used toothpicks in public) and had converted him to the aristocracy. His name, Porfirio, Spanish for porphyry, fitted his rocky mien. Although he had recently become quite deaf it mattered little, for he did the speaking; others listened. He was a figure of stern dignity, tall for a Mexican, with piercing eyes, flaring nostrils, strong square jaw, and the extended ear lobes that are said to promise longevity. People whispered about him, as they always do about great men; that he aped the British in his formal attire and the Texans in his country clothes; that he employed a French cosmetologist to whiten his cheeks and lighten his lips and make him look less like a Mixtec Indian. Critics whispered that he was senile, and they called him *el llorón,* the great weeper. For he had a tendency to weep on emotional occasions—a schoolgirl reciting a patriotic poem, a father pleading futilely to save his son from the firing squad. His defenders, and most of the *gente decente* were his defenders, main-tained that this was not a sign of senility but only of great heart.

Whatever the state of his heart and mind, Don Porfirio was now, in 1910, recognized around the world as the maker of modern Mexico, the man who had somehow brought stability and progress to a land that had before him been a country of chaos and confusion. Count Tolstoi had called him a "prodigy of nature." Andrew Carnegie had praised his "wisdom and courage and commanding character" and urged that he "be held up to the hero-worship of mankind." Theodore Roosevelt had admired him as "the greatest statesman now living . . . [who] has done for his country what no other living man has done for any country"—which was interesting since many of T.R.'s political foes had openly wished that the United States could be governed by someone less like Roosevelt, the trust-buster, and more like Díaz, an unswerving friend of big business. An American writer compared him, favorably, with Washington, Lincoln, Robert E. Lee, with Peter the Great and Frederick the Great, with Bismarck and Hannibal. Subsidized biographies, ground out by Mexican government presses in many languages in preparation for the Centennial, dwelt heavily, and in capital letters, on the Illustrious President, his Intrepid Moral Character, his Distinguished Statesmanship and Devoted Patriotism.

All nations of the world with which Mexico enjoyed relations had been invited to send missions to help Don Porfirio (and Mexico) celebrate the Centennial, "this never-to-be-forgotten occasion which is to us of so vast importance." Most of them did. Thirty-seven foreign journalists also came—Samuel Bowles of the *Springfield Republican,* Victor Murdock of the *Wichita Eagle,* Victor Rosewater of the *Omaha Bee,* Hamilton Holt of *The Independent,* Arthur W. Page of *World's Work,* and others. All came at the expense of the Mexican government, which had systematically suppressed newspapers at home, imprisoning, even assassinating unfriendly editors and writers and rewarding the lickspittles; only three newspapers in the country were said to be without government subsidy and control, one each in Veracruz and Yucatán and one in Mexico City. The junketing journalists had their attention directed to other matters. They and the special ambassadors, envoys, and ministers were taken on deluxe tours to observe the accomplishments of the Díaz regime. They inspected railroads, port works, industries. They dined sumptuously and frequently and drank fine wines. And they were carefully steered away from the products of poverty and misery which, in a curious way, seemed to multiply just as rapidly as the nation's material gains.

Public works—institutions, factories, schools, monuments—had been rushed to completion in time for the celebration. For those only projected a first stone would be laid. For those completed earlier, much earlier in some cases, there could, at least, be dedicatory ceremonies. One of the events of the Centennial month was the celebration of the "founding" of the National University, an institution which had been established in 1553 and was one of the most venerable of the New World —although it had been closed for the past sixty years. There was a new— really new—insane asylum at Mixcoac, a jail at San Jerónimo Atlixco, additions to the penitentiary, a gunpowder factory, a new ministry of foreign relations, a new Municipal Palace, a YMCA, the new park at Balbuena, tramlines to Xochimilco and Tizapán. One newspaper speculated whether the automobile might not someday replace the tramcar as it already was replacing the horse-drawn carriages in progressive Mexico. There was a new seismological station and there were improvements to the tunnel of Tequixquiac. The first stone was laid for a grand legislative palace. New 1200-candlepower street lights were installed in the streets of San Francisco, 5 de Mayo, and 16 de Septiembre, and in the Alameda. The fine new Italianate postoffice was in use and much admired. The famous 22-ton glass curtain from Tiffany was in place in the new National Theater but the building itself was not yet complete and already the massive structure was beginning to sink into the unstable subsoil of Mexico City. Nor was there time for the projected razing of the pestilential prison of Belem which, one enthusiast said, would be replaced with "a garden among whose trees the passing wind will sing": there was no place else to put the political prisoners.

Monuments were dedicated to certain aspects of Mexico's history and to illustrious foreigners—Washington, Pasteur, Garibaldi, and Alexander Humboldt, the great explorer and Mexicanist. There appeared to be less interest in the nation's Indian past than in its Spanish antecedents. Two bronze statues of Aztec warriors—people of the capital affectionately called them "the green Indians"—marking the end of the Paseo de la Reforma had, some time before, been deemed unsuitable and carted off to a poor barrio. Now a monument to Isabel the Catholic, queen of Spain, was begun in Chapultepec Park, and a principal downtown street, Espíritu Santo, was renamed Isabel la Católica. A plaque was installed at the Ciudadela, the mid-city arsenal, marking the spot where the great Morelos had been a prisoner just before facing a firing squad. A huge monument to Benito Juárez was dedicated in the Alameda with the solemn (and tearful) participation of Porfirio Díaz who had at first been a disciple and ally of Juárez and later his bitter enemy and an opponent of almost everything Juárez had stood for. And there was the grand monument to Independence in the Paseo de la Reforma: a broad base with symbolic figures of War, Peace, Law, and Justice; at the top of a column 65 feet high was a giant angel of gilded bronze holding a laurel wreath in her right hand, a broken chain in her left.

A group of political malcontents attempted during the Centennial observance to pay homage to the heroes of the independence at the new monument and at the same time to protest the most recent "election" of Porfirio Díaz. Mounted police under the command of their much-hated chief, Ramón Castro, rode them down and hauled two dozen of them off to Belem. Demonstrators who escaped the police made their way to the Calle Cadena and threw rocks and oranges through the windows of Don Porfirio's house. It was the one discordant note in an otherwise festive month. The police had been given strict instructions to avoid such disturbances; nothing was to mar the beauty and tranquillity of the celebration. The city's 1200 beggars had been warned to stay off the streets. Barefoot, pajama-clad Indians were discouraged from even entering the city, capital of a nation which was at least one-third Indian. Five thousand tons of corn were imported from Argentina to eliminate the distressing sight of the hungry poor people waiting in queues to buy scarce grain. There was also a distribution of free clothing.

The distinguished visitors meanwhile admired foreign-owned industry, sat on European gilt furniture, drank French wines and Spanish brandy, attended Italian opera, listened to small talk of French and Spanish novels, or of English sports—cricket, lawn tennis, fox hunts, and pigeon shoots.

Day after day Don Porfirio received visiting dignitaries in the National Palace, accepting their gifts, listening gravely to their repetitious compliments. Said U. S. Congressman David J. Foster of Vermont, chairman of the House Committee on Foreign Relations: "Don Porfirio Díaz is the most prominent figure of the contemporary world." Curtis Guild, former Massachusetts governor and Special Ambassador of the United States, observed that Díaz was "the greatest statesman in the world." Brazilian Ambassador Antonio da Fontoeira Xavier: "General Díaz has made of his nation a great country. He is a man whom all admire . . . one of the most extraordinary men in the world."

No envoy attracted so much attention as Don Camilo Polavieja, ambassador extraordinary of Alfonso XIII of Spain. Polavieja, a marquis and one of the four captains-general of the royal Spanish army, was a stooped and bandy-legged little man of seventy-two, with a huge white mustache, stiff with wax. His dress uniforms, even in this assemblage of extravagant ceremonial dress, were beyond compare, heavy with medals won in Europe, Africa, Cuba, and the Philippines. His air was that of an hidalgo and he was widely entertained at functions given by the many Spanish social clubs and by upper-class Mexicans whose emotional loyalties to Spain were strong. Polavieja attended the ceremonies honoring Isabel the Catholic, presided at the opening of an exhibition of Spanish art and, in the name of his monarch, decorated Don Porfirio with the great cross and chain of the order of Carlos III, an honor usually reserved for royalty.

But of all the gestures proclaiming the warm rapprochement between Mexico and the country she was so bitterly fighting just a century before, the grandest involved José María Morelos y Pavón, the most stalwart and unrelenting enemy the Spaniards had faced in Mexico. The Spanish troops had captured Morelos' dress uniform, sword, baton, plumed hat, and pectoral cross. For nearly a century these souvenirs had rested in the Artillery Museum in Madrid. Now in the name of Alfonso XIII, Polavieja presented them as a gift to President Díaz.

The French, not to be outdone in gestures of affectionate reconciliation, brought, in a round, glass-topped case the great silver keys to the City of Mexico which Mexican conservatives had given to the commander of the invading French forces in 1863. These too were presented to Don Porfirio who had achieved his greatest military glory in fighting the French and in so doing had become a figure to reckon with in Mexican history.

At a banquet for the visiting delegations Díaz said: "Centennial Mexico is in a position to show the world that it is a country worthy of taking a place among the civilized nations, that it is a people regenerated by work . . . We want to celebrate with works of peace and progress. We want humanity, gathered in our country as our guests, to pass judgment on the capacities of a people and a government impelled by the same motive, the love of country, and guided by one inspiration—unlimited national progress." The official bulletin of the Federal District echoed: "Depositing our heart on the altar of the nation we Mexicans should today swear to maintain the work of Hidalgo, Morelos, Guerrero, and Iturbide, all gloriously crowned by the energetic labor of Porfirio Díaz which has permitted Mexico to enter fully into the congress of prestigious and cultured nations." There was no mention of Benito Juárez, Mexico's Lincoln.

There was gaiety as well as solemnity—parties, receptions, banquets, balls, bullfights dedicated to the Centennial, dramatic spectacles—including *Aida* at the Teatro Arbeu, and a special Centennial lottery. A young army lieutenant and a shoemaker, both from Mazatlán, held portions of ticket number 3396 and won 125,000 pesos apiece. The prettiest girls from all parts of the Republic had been brought to the capital to help entertain the distinguished guests. Colorful regional costumes and splendid dress uniforms added brilliance and charm to the crowds.

One of the largest crowds gathered in the Zócalo, the historic square fronting the National Palace and the cathedral, the heart of Mexico, on the eve of Independence Day—and also of Don Porfirio's birthday. There was music and fireworks, and at 11 P.M. Don Porfirio appeared on the central balcony of the palace. He rang the bell of Father Hidalgo—the bell the idealistic priest had used to signal the beginning of the struggle, just one hundred years before. And with a voice somewhat flattened by his increasing deafness Don Porfirio shouted out the traditional *grito* or cry: "Long live liberty! Long live independence! Long live the heroes! Long live the Mexican people!"

These were not quite the words of Father Hidalgo. He had summoned his Indian parishioners with the same dull-toned old bell and told them: "My children, this day comes to us a new dispensation. Are you ready to receive it? Will you be free? Will you make the effort to recover from the hated Spaniards the lands stolen from your forefathers three hundred years ago?" Then he shouted: "Long live independence! Long live America! Down with bad government!" And his parishioners, who may not have understood his words at first, now grasped them and roared back "Death to the gachupines [Spaniards]."

But if history, manners, and politics had somewhat altered the words, the response in the Zócalo on the night of September 15, 1910, was nevertheless emotional and exciting. The cathedral bells rang out, massed choruses sang the national anthem and fireworks lit up the sky. The people laughed, wept, embraced, and kissed.

Of all the festivities the most spectacular was the grand ball in the National Palace on the night of September 23, with Don Porfirio host to the diplomatic corps, visiting dignitaries, members of the government and Mexican society. New red velvet carpet covered the stairs from the Gate of Honor. The great central patio of the palace was converted into a ballroom. Thousands of electric stars twinkled overhead. Arches surrounding the patio were decked with flowers and the air was heavy with the scent of roses and gardenias. The corridors were furnished with rich carpets, fine paintings, bronze and marble sculpture and decorative urns. A banquet room was set up on the east side of the patio. Huge tables were loaded with delicacies—oysters from Guaymas, shrimp from Campeche, red snapper from Veracruz, hams, turkeys, sides of beef, roast kid, suckling pig. Five hundred liveried waiters poured champagne into crystal goblets, and 150 musicians played waltzes from a flowered platform. At 10 P.M. Don Porfirio made his entry with the wife of the Italian ambassador on his arm, followed by Special Ambassador Curtis Guild escorting Señora Díaz. Then came other ambassadors, chiefs of mission, and members of the president's cabinet. Finally the dancing began and lasted until dawn. It was, one journalist reported in breathless prose, "like a fairy tale."

There were, of course, parades. There was a procession in honor of the Mexican flag, with children from all the primary schools of the capital marching to the National Palace and there, before the approving eyes of Don Porfirio, reciting: "Flag! Tricolor flag! Flag of Mexico! In this year and in this month in which the Republic completes its first century of independent life we promise with all our souls to be always united around you as a symbol of the fatherland in order that Mexico may be perpetually free and victorious."

There were parades of "allegorical cars" representing commerce, banking, industry, agriculture, mining, and the press—that part of the press that had survived. There was a stirring military parade. Visiting sailors from Argentina, Germany, Brazil, and France marched smartly. Mexican charros with silver saddles rode by, followed by Díaz's own special force of *rurales* in dove-gray jackets, tight trousers, and big sombreros. Then came the cadets from the Military College in dress uniforms and plumed helmets, and ten thousand soldiers of the Mexican army under the command of General Francisco A. Vélez, a revered veteran of the war with the United States in 1846–48 and with the French in 1862–67. But the most elaborate of the parades was the one devoted to Mexico's history. Moctezuma, the ill-starred Aztec emperor was carried in a palanquin and guarded by "tiger warriors." There was Doña Marina, the high-born Aztec maiden who became interpreter for and mistress to the Spanish conqueror and a betrayer of her own people; and Hernán Cortés himself, riding a white horse and followed by his principal captains, his soldiers and Indian allies. In front of the palace the encounter between Moctezuma and Cortés was reenacted, the latter placing a string of glass beads around the neck of the Indian ruler. There were richly garbed viceroys, priests, and Inquisitors representing the colonial era; there was the somber figure of Father Hidalgo who began the struggle with Spain, and the gaudy man who ended it—Agustín de Iturbide and his army of the Three Guarantees.

And there the pageant ended—just at the beginning of Mexico's most eventful century. No hint of Iturbide's attempt to create a New World monarchy with himself as Emperor Agustín. Nor of the valiant but hopeless efforts of those dedicated old guerrilla fighters, Vicente Guerrero and Guadalupe Victoria, to make Mexican independence a reality. No suggestion of the villainous but picturesque Antonio López de Santa Anna who had cost Mexico so much. Nothing of the Emperor Maximilian whose alien sponsorship, good heart and confused mind made him one of the most pathetic figures in Mexican history. And, most remarkably, no portrayal of Benito Juárez, the solemn Zapotec Indian who led Mexico in the War of the Reform—a struggle more meaningful in some ways than the War of Independence.

One obvious reason for the omission was that the long life and colorful career of Porfirio Díaz—instigator of and chief spectator at this pageant—spanned most of the history of Mexico since independence. Anyone unfamiliar with recent Mexican history had only to study him. He had donned a uniform and carried a gun in the war with the United States. He had defied the dictator Santa Anna and become a fugitive and guerrilla fighter, an able warrior for the cause of the Reform. He had become a national hero in the war against the French invaders, a paladin for Juárez. Then, strangely, he had become an enemy of Juárez. Gaining power he had created a Mexico wholly different from the one envisioned by Juárez, wielding authority far greater than Juárez had either had or wanted.

CHAPTER 2

FIFTH SUN

> ". . . this is our sun . . . it moves and follows its path. And as elders continue to say, under this sun there will be earthquakes and hunger and then our end shall come."
>
> Miguel León-Portilla, *Aztec Thought and Culture*

SHIFTS IN ALLEGIANCE AND POWER—some of them slow, evolutionary, and logical but more of them bewilderingly rapid, haphazard, and treacherous —had marked the whole history of Mexico.

The Aztecs, whose gods demanded human sacrifice, forcibly put together an empire that extended from the Panuco River in the north to Central America in the south. They held it together in a system that demanded regular tributes in wealth and human lives. It was a politico-social pattern that was to be repeated in Mexico: at the top, despotic power; at the bottom, resentful deprivation; and between them a void in which the winds of destruction would rise. The Aztecs lived with a foreknowledge of disaster. According to their mythology, the earth had known four earlier epochs, each governed by a sun. The period of the first sun ended when the earth's inhabitants were eaten by ocelots. The world of the second sun was destroyed by wind, the third by a rain of fire, the fourth by water. The fifth sun—the one under which the Aztecs were living when the Spaniards came to the New World—was pre-destined to end with earthquakes, famine, and terror. The instability of the Aztec empire was such that Cortés and his ridiculously small band of Spanish adventurers in 1519 found willing allies among the Aztec-oppressed peoples, the Totonacs and the Tlaxcalans. Indian fighting Indian became the decisive factor in the Spanish Conquest. As was so often to be the case in the future, the result was quite different from that hoped for by the rebels. The Totonacs and the Tlaxcalans rid themselves of the Aztec oppression and became, along with the Aztecs and all other Indian peoples, victims of Spanish domination.

The three centuries of colonialism in Mexico were, in comparison with the violence of the Conquest that had gone before it and the violence that was to follow it in the nineteenth century, a period of peace. Great cities were built—with fine palaces, magnificent churches, seminaries, colleges, universities. Roads were pushed through the mountains, jungles, and deserts where there had only been footpaths before. The Indians were given a new religion and put to work. They mined silver, to which they had never before attached any particular importance. They worked on the broad plantations and ranches which had once been their own communal land. Horses and wheeled vehicles carried freight, although in many cases it was still more economical to have burdens carried by Indians. Missions and military outposts enforced peace and brought a measure of European culture to remote corners of the New World.

Where the Indian civilization had made distinctions between royalty, priests, warriors, and workers, the Spaniards created a new and more complicated multi-layered society. At the top were the Spaniards, the natives of Spain, sometimes called *peninsulares,* i.e. from the Iberian Peninsula, but more often, and hatefully, referred to as *gachupines,* from the Aztec *catzopini,* a man with spurs. These were the important people, the viceroys, the military commanders, the high ecclesiastics and bureaucrats who came out from Spain to govern and reap the harvest of conquest.

Below them were the creoles, people of pure European blood who were born in the New World. Whether they became soldiers, colonial administrators, priests, scholars, professionals, merchants, planters, or ranchers they were, no matter how successful, inferior in esteem and privilege to the *gachupines.*

Within nine months of the Conquest, a new class was created in Mexico, the mestizos, or people of mixed blood. Mexico is today a mestizo nation and proud of it. A plaque marking the site of the last great battle of Tenochtitlan where the fate of the Aztec empire was sealed says: "It was neither triumph nor defeat but the dolorous birth of the mestizo people who are Mexico today." In the three centuries of colonization no more than 300,000 Spaniards came to Mexico from Europe, comparatively few of them women. Spanish authorities later recognized sixteen different grades of crossbreeding of European, Indian, and Negro blood. They were well below the *gachupines* and creoles in the social structure but above the pure Indian population. The mestizos became servants, artisans, shopkeepers, soldiers, even professionals and priests—and at the time of the Inquisition were conceded the distinction of being considered *gente de razón,* or people of reason who, unlike the Indians, were responsible creatures and therefore subject to punishment.

At the bottom of the social scale were the Indian masses. Unlike the Indians of North America, who were pushed back and reduced until they became an inconsequential minority, the Indians of Mexico were, ironically, preserved, protected in a limited way, and regarded as a valuable natural resource. They were needed to mine the silver and raise the crops that would be sent to Spain. At the end of the colonial era Mexico was providing two-thirds of Spain's revenues; without the Indians it could not have been done. Most of them were landless peasants, chattels attached to Spanish landholdings and, more often than not, no more than slaves.

Throughout the colonial era there had been rebellions by Indians, mestizos and, on occasion, creoles, but the Spanish authorities had put them down with no great difficulty. But by the beginning of the nineteenth century the creoles, who were to provide most of the intellectual leadership in the war of independence, were being stirred by the political and ideological currents of the American and French revolutions. Meanwhile Spain, which had been a world power, was brought to the edge of destruction. Charles IV abdicated, Ferdinand VII was imprisoned and Napoleon put his brother, Joseph Bonaparte, on the Spanish throne. Independence movements sprang up in all parts of Spanish America.

In Mexico Father Hidalgo, the priest of Dolores in the intendancy of Guanajuato, had long been disobedient to colonial authority—teaching his Indian parishioners to speak Spanish, encouraging them to plant grapevines and olives, helping them to develop new home industries— all in defiance of colonial law. Now he urged his Indians to strike for freedom.

With no experience or knowledge of military matters Hidalgo was soon at the head of a horde of 80,000—mostly Indians and mestizos with a sprinkling of freedom-minded creoles. Armed with little more than arrows, clubs, knives, and stones they marched across Mexico. Royalist forces melted before their savage attack. They very nearly took Mexico City itself, but at the last moment Father Hidalgo turned back, appalled by the bloodshed and destruction. He withdrew to Guadalajara where he attempted to form a government, promising freedom to the Indians and restoration of ancestral lands to the peasants. He was soon decisively beaten by royalist forces, driven into flight, betrayed by a former follower, captured, and executed. His head, placed in a cage, was hung on the walls of Guanajuato.

Hidalgo's position of leadership in the independence movement was taken over by José María Morelos y Pavón, a short, swart mestizo, a one-time mule driver who had struggled for an education. He had studied under Hidalgo and had become a priest, assigned to undesirable parishes in the *tierra caliente* of Michoacán. He was an earthier man than his mentor. Like many priests of the period, he fathered a number of illegitimate children, three by his own count, four by other calculations. He was also thoughtful, determined, and a brilliant guerrilla commander, and came very close to creating an independent Mexico. But he interrupted his military campaign to set up a revolutionary congress in Chilpancingo, and, later, at Apatzingán, to draw up a constitution for the nation that was taking shape. Sovereignty rested with the people. All men were equal, and slavery would be outlawed. Lands would be restored to the Indians. The special privileges of the clergy and the military—privileges which exempted them from the laws that governed everyone else—would be abolished. Properties of the wealthy and of the Church would be confiscated and divided between the government and the poor. These revolutionary concepts clarified the division—already existing but ill-defined—between liberal and conservative thought in Mexico. The division was to be fought over for more than a century to come. While Morelos was occupied with these matters the royalist forces gathered strength. Morelos, after a heroic campaign, was defeated, tried, officially degraded, condemned, and executed.

Mexican independence was finally achieved by a man who had none of the ideals, principles, or liberal sympathies of Hidalgo and Morelos: Agustín de Iturbide. A mestizo—although he claimed to be creole—Iturbide was a royalist officer noted for wholesale execution of his captives and for a decisive victory over Morelos in the field. He was suspended for a time for stealing silver from convoys he was supposed to guard, but through the intercession of conservative friends he was reinstated. By this time both he and his conservative backers had begun to think in terms of an independent Mexico, free of the reforms which the new Spanish constitution prescribed. In a switch of loyalties—the sort of switch that was to become increasingly familiar in Mexico—he formed an alliance with the surviving revolutionists. At the town of Iguala he drew up his "three guarantees" plan for independence. His three guarantees: independence of Mexico under a monarch—possibly Ferdinand VII; preservation of the authority and privileges of the Catholic Church; and equality between the native-born creoles and the Spaniards in Mexico. On August 24, 1821, Iturbide persuaded the Spanish viceroy, Juan O'Donojú, to recognize the Plan of Iguala, and Mexico was, at last, free and independent—under Iturbide, who soon arranged to have himself declared Emperor Agustín I of Mexico.

"Emperor" Agustín ruled the new nation for less than a year. He went into exile, then attempted a comeback and was executed. He was the first of a procession of oddly assorted characters who were to govern Mexico in the post-independence confusion—confusion that was perhaps normal since the Mexicans had had, under Spanish rule, no experience in self-government. Some of the emerging leaders were simple, idealistic, dedicated men who floundered in the complexities of government; some were power-crazed egotists who almost destroyed the country in its infancy.

Most bizarre of the lot was Antonio López de Santa Anna who was to be ruler of Mexico eleven different times between 1833 and 1855. His political sympathies ranged from conservative to liberal and back again. He had been a royalist officer, a supporter of Iturbide, and then a plotter against Iturbide. He was a man of stony expression, of extravagant and licentious behavior. He insisted on being addressed as "Most Serene Highness," and fancied himself as the "Napoleon of the West." His lavish tastes helped bankrupt the nation and his military ventures usually led to disaster. His misadventures in Texas, the bloody slaughter at the Alamo and his ignominious defeat at the battle of San Jacinto, were directly responsible for Mexico's loss of Texas. This, coupled with the expansive territorial ambitions of Mexico's neighbor to the north, led to the war with the United States in 1846–48. Through the peace treaty and Santa Anna's subsequent sale of the Mesilla valley of Arizona and New Mexico—for only $10,000,000—Mexico lost more than half its national territory.

Out of the disorder, bankruptcy, and confusion that Santa Anna brought to Mexico there emerged the second of Mexico's revolutions— the War of the Reform—and one of Mexico's truly great leaders, Benito Juárez. A pure-blooded Zapotec Indian from the mountains of Oaxaca, he was, like Morelos, barely five feet tall. He had the single-mindedness and solemnity of an Indian. He was as plain in dress and manner as Iturbide and Santa Anna had been gaudy. He had a passionate regard for the rule of law—which until then had been almost wholly lacking in Mexico's life as a nation—and played a key role in the formulation of the reform laws which became part of the Constitution of 1857. The new constitution was related in spirit to the now almost-forgotten constitution which Morelos' followers had adopted at Apatzingán in 1814.

The new constitution proclaimed the inviolability of individual rights to liberty, equality, property, and security. It called for a representative republican form of government. But its most controversial aspects were those aimed at the Catholic Church; ordering the Church and other corporations to divest themselves of landholdings; establishing freedom for all religious beliefs; legalizing civil marriages; permitting priests and nuns to renounce their vows; and calling for free public schools—a provision close to the heart of Juárez who had struggled mightily to acquire his own education. The constitution outraged both the Church and the conservatives allied with it. Opponents carried banners with the legend "*Death to Tolerance.*" The Archbishop of Mexico denied the sacraments to anyone who swore to uphold the constitution. Pope Pius IX declared the constitution null and void. The incumbent President refused to enforce it and Juárez, who was chief justice of the supreme court, became President of Mexico. It was the beginning of the bloody three-year War of the Reform, during which Juárez was the head of a fugitive government. When the conservative opposition was finally overcome Juárez took over a nation that was crippled and hard-pressed by foreign creditors. France, Spain, and Britain demanded payment of the debts and the French landed an expeditionary force in Mexico. The French troops marched inland, were welcomed to the capital by the anti-Reform conservatives and Juárez once more became a fugitive President. The conservatives then, negotiating with Napoleon III, arranged for Archduke Maximilian of Austria to come and rule Mexico—the second time in the nation's short life that it had been declared an empire. Maximilian was a strange ruler in a country that had become accustomed to strange rulers. Tall and blond with a full forked beard, he loved Mexico and Mexican ways, ate spicy Mexican food and on occasion dressed as a charro. And, to the consternation of his conservative backers, he showed interest in social reform and even expressed admiration for Juárez. When Napoleon III withdrew his support, Maximilian was doomed. With the few troops he could muster Maximilian made a last stand on the Hill of Bells at Querétaro. Before his execution by a firing squad he exclaimed: "May my blood be the last ever shed for the redemption of this unfortunate country. Viva Mexico!"

Maximilian's blood was not the last to be shed, nor was redemption near at hand. Juárez became President again in fact as well as title, and upon returning to the capital, July 15, 1867, issued a conciliatory statement that included his most famous and oft-quoted words: "The people and government must respect the rights of all. Among individuals, as among nations, peace is respect for the rights of others." It was a noble and magnanimous statement to come from a country which had suffered so much at the hands of others. Juárez began rebuilding the country, erecting schools, constructing railroads and trying to find solutions to the country's grave financial woes. He was reelected in 1867 and again in 1871, but the country was far from peaceful. The armed forces were reduced and unemployed soldiers, unprepared either by experience or temperament for peacetime labors, roamed the country. There were armed rebellions in Veracruz, Yucatán, Sonora, Puebla, San Luis Potosí, Zacatecas, and Aguascalientes. Some were acts of banditry. Others were ill-organized political movements. Many of them were in the name of a man who had been Juárez' friend and disciple, his most stalwart soldier in the War of the Reform and the war against the French invaders, a man who had retired from military life to grow sugar cane on his farm in Oaxaca (and secretly manufacture gunpowder and cannon): Porfirio Díaz.

This, then, was the man who presided over the Centennial festivities in Mexico City in September 1910.

This was the man who had broken with his old leader, Benito Juárez, on the question of reelection, who had said, in his declaration of La Noria in 1875: "Indefinite reelection . . . of the federal executive has placed national institutions in danger . . . I do not aspire to power . . . No citizen should impose and perpetuate himself in the exercise of power, and this will be the last revolution." It was the same man who, having seized power in 1876, had controlled the country ever since, manipulating elections, amending the constitution and adjusting the laws of succession to fit his ambitions. Sycophants—many of whom remembered when the mere rumor of Don Porfirio's indisposition had dropped the price of Mexican bonds a sickening eleven points—had convinced him of his indispensability. He had deliberately chosen as his Vice-President Ramón Corral, the most-hated man in the country. Corral had grown rich and powerful on the smuggling of Chinese immigrants in his home state of Sonora and also on the enslavement of Yaqui Indians and seizure of their lands. He was regarded as the protector of commercialized vice in Mexico City and suffered from a far advanced social disease. So whole-heartedly was he disliked that no one would willingly accept him as President in preference to Don Porfirio, oppressive though the latter's power might be. It was an ingenious Díaz maneuver to make his own tenure secure.

On September 27, 1910, as an appropriate climax to the Centennial celebration, the federal congress declared Porfirio Díaz and Ramón Corral re-elected as President and Vice-President of the Republic of Mexico for the period 1910–16. It would be an eighth term for the old enemy of "indefinite reelection."

Mexico, in large part because of the long and unyielding reign of Don Porfirio, was on the brink of its third and ultimate revolution— the first of the great national upheavals that would in the twentieth century change the face and nature of the world. Apparently this ominous fact was sensed by none of the spectators in the Centennial carnival.

Throughout the year, and since the beginning of the century for that matter, there had been warning signs of the coming storm. The one-third of the nation that was Indian existed in misery. The growing industrial working class was little better off, for hours were long, wages low (12½ cents a day) and prices high. A Mexican laborer had to work twelve times as long as his U.S. counterpart to buy a measure of corn, almost twenty times as long to buy a piece of cheap cloth. Workers who tried to improve their lot were shot down by stony-faced soldiers. Peasants who did the same thing were shot, usually in the back, by Díaz's *rurales,* one-time bandits whom the dictator had put into uniform. Political democracy existed only in Don Porfirio's index finger; a man to whom he pointed was declared elected. Intellectuals who protested faced exile if they were lucky, prison or death if they were not.

If anyone could have read the storm signals correctly it should have been Porfirio Díaz, the man against whom the storm would soon break. He was an old revolutionary himself, well-versed in the shaping of human unrest to political ends. But his memory of the violence and force that misery and oppression can beget had become dim. His hearing, once sharply attuned to the cries of discontent, had in the years of applause and flattery, almost completely gone. The growing murmur of coming violence was, for him, a meaningless jumble of sound.

CHAPTER 3

THE AGITATOR

> "I have, in short, lost everything except my honor as a fighter . . ."
>
> Ricardo Flores Magón

PORTENTS OF THE STORM came with increasing frequency in 1910, the Centennial year.

The Anti-Reelectionist party had attracted wide popular support in its effort to overthrow Díaz by legal means, at the polls. The government had circumvented this threat by jailing the leaders and 60,000 members of the party. It then ignored the ballots.

A group of intellectuals and workers who met secretly in the Mexico City suburb of Tacubaya and plotted rebellion was betrayed to the government and easily dissolved.

In the remote southeastern state of Yucatán, where slavery on the henequen plantations was a way of life, some 1500 peasants, Maya Indians for the most part, seized hunting rifles and machetes and stormed the town of Valladolid. They captured the hated *jefe politico* of the town, Luis Felipe de Regil, and murdered him. They assaulted the police headquarters, set prisoners free, took over the municipal palace and published a revolutionary "plan" proclaiming individual liberty and the end of political abuses. They held the town for six days. Then federal troops moved in, shot down all the leaders and sent the others either to jail or back to the henequen plantations—there was little difference.

Federal soldiers broke up a demonstration of rebellious peasants in Tlaxcala by firing into the massed demonstrators, killing many.

In the state of Veracruz, Santana Rodríguez Palafox, otherwise known as Santanón, or Big Santana, had become a dangerous anti-government guerrilla. Earlier, as a peaceful citizen, he had supplied meat to a German *hacendado,* Robert Voigt. Voigt had cheated him of seven hundred pesos. When Santanón protested, the German stole his wife and arranged, through the local *jefe politico,* for Santanón to be forced into military service. Santanón escaped, and organized a group of rebels in the mountains. He began, with a small group of followers, raiding haciendas —particularly German-owned ones, frequently meeting and defeating greatly superior numbers of *rurales.* On June 6, 1910, he seized a large hacienda in southern Veracruz and shortly thereafter took over the town of San Andrés Tuxtla. The government sent out a punitive expedition headed by the quixotic, hot-tempered poet, Salvador Díaz Mirón, who was also a federal deputy in the Díaz government. Santanón played a cat-and-mouse game with his pursuer among the cane fields and the jungles. When the poet complained loudly that he had exhausted his supply of cigars, Santanón stepped out of a thicket, gave him a handful of excellent cigars and disappeared again without Díaz Mirón realizing what had happened. The government, pressed by the German minister, finally sent more capable soldiers in pursuit of Santanón, among them Francisco Cárdenas, who was to become famous as an executioner. Santanón was run to earth on the banks of the Huasuntán River, near Acayucán, Veracruz, and killed. As was the custom, his bullet-riddled body was placed on exhibition in the plaza of Acayucán. The authorities found in his pocket a five-peso note and a recently dated document identifying him as a recognized representative of the junta of the Mexican Liberal party of Los Angeles, California.

The Liberal party, which had reached out and commissioned the obscure Santanón as "Military Commander of those forces which he organizes and Special Delegate in charge of unifying revolutionary elements" was the most militant of the various foes of the Díaz government. Its founder and leader was Ricardo Flores Magón, a journalist who had been fighting the dictatorship for almost two decades.

Flores Magón had recently been silent, serving a term in the federal penitentiary at Florence, Arizona, for violation of the U.S. neutrality laws. He was, finally, released, and was welcomed to Los Angeles with an emotional meeting in the Labor Temple, a meeting in which $414 was collected to finance the reappearance of *Regeneración.* Now, in September 1910, he resumed publication of this fugitive paper which, in its ten years of intermittent life, had been hounded from Mexico City to San Luis Potosí, to San Antonio, Texas, to St. Louis, Missouri, and finally Los Angeles.

The dedicated revolutionist sat in a sparsely furnished second-floor office at the corner of Fourth Street and Towne Avenue in a shabby section of downtown Los Angeles and, hour after hour, put furious words on paper.

"Here we are," he wrote, "with the torch of the Revolution in one hand and the program of the Liberal party in the other, declaring war. The weapons of Caesar's mercenaries will not harm the citizen who heeds his responsibility. The bayonets of the rebels will answer, blow for blow . . . Mexicans: to war!"

He went on: "Workers, listen: The infamous peace which we Mexicans have suffered . . . will soon be broken. Today's calm conceals the violence of tomorrow's insurrection. Revolution is the logical consequence of the thousand crimes of a despotism . . . It has to come, unfailingly, fatefully, with the punctuality of the sun banishing sorrowful night. You will see, you workers, the force of revolution. Your hands will grasp the gun . . . The revolution must come, irrevocably, and better still, it will triumph. By blood and fire it will come to the den where the jackals who have been devouring you for thirty-four years are holding their last feast . . . Proletarians! keep in mind that you are the nerve of the revolution. Go to it, not like cattle to the slaughterhouse, but as men conscious of all their rights. Go to the fight. Knock resolutely on the doors. Glory waits impatiently . . . Break your chains on the heads of your executioners."

The fiery, florid, richly figured style was peculiarly his own. Whether it carried his signature or not, readers of scarce copies of *Regeneración* in the arid plains of Chihuahua and Coahuila or the sierras of Jalisco and Oaxaca, the jungles of Veracruz and Tabasco, would know it was the work of Ricardo Flores Magón. This was a man who counseled them that the riches they created with their labor all belonged to them, the ones who wove cloth and yet went unclothed, who sowed grain and still went hungry, who dug precious metal from the earth only to be poorer than before. This was a man who fought the bosses—who fought the greatest boss of all: Don Porfirio Díaz. He was—or at least promised soon to be—the avenger of all the wrongs of Don Porfirio, his soldiers, his *rurales.* He would punish the Yankee mine owners, the *hacendados,* the political chiefs who stole land and did Don Profirio's bidding, the *científicos,* the rich and the evil old men who advised Don Porfirio. He would bring to justice the slave traders who took the Indians' land, drove them from their villages and sold them at twenty-five pesos a head. And he would end the system in which peasants, conscripted into military service, were forced to shoot down strikers and strikers' wives and children—their own kind.

"I exhort you," Flores Magón wrote, "be not dismayed. I see among you the firm resolution to overthrow this shameful, hateful despotism which has weighed so heavily on the Mexican race, this despotism of Porfirio Díaz. Your attitude merits the applause of all honorable men. But I repeat: take with you in combat the knowledge that the revolution is made by you and you alone, that the insurrection will be sustained with your blood and that the fruits of this struggle will belong to your families if you uphold with integrity your right to enjoy all benefits of civilization."

The little paper containing these words would be smuggled into Mexico. Magonistas would get Sears Roebuck catalogs, tear out some sections, insert copies of *Regeneración,* and mail them to Mexico. Mexican railroad workers would hide bundles on their trains, to be dropped off in remote spots. In El Paso one enthusiast had joined the Salvation Army so that he could, without question, cross the border to Juárez, presumably to save souls in that sinful border town, but really to distribute copies of *Regeneración.* There were, in all of Mexico, forty-odd Liberal clubs, from Tamaulipas to Guerrero, from Sonora to Yucatán—lawyers, schoolteachers, miners, industrial workers, and peasants who could not read but who would listen carefully while the burning words of Ricardo Flores Magón were read to them. Few of them knew Ricardo Flores Magón personally: he had long been in exile. Much of the time he had been in jail or prison, but his words, thanks to a devoted and ingenious group of fellow-conspirators, kept getting through to the Mexican people. In the last ten years of the *Porfiriato* his was the loudest, clearest, most unequivocal voice urging the Mexican people to revolution, redemption and, as the nameplate of his paper proclaimed, to regeneration.

He did not look the part of a revolutionist; a lawyer, perhaps, or a scholar or teacher. He was of medium height—five feet eight inches, and heavy: 225 pounds. The severe black suits which he always wore stretched tightly across the shoulders and the bulky torso. His black hair was long and thick, arching up from a broad forehead, curling at the ends, as did his large but carefully trimmed mustache. His appearance was that of the mestizo intellectual. His intense dark eyes were myopic behind rimless glasses. People were to say later that he personally avoided the combat he urged on others. There were reasons. He could not see to aim a gun. He was too portly to run. And although he advocated bloodshed he personally had an aversion to it.

Before a crowd his deportment could be as violent as his prose. Otherwise his manners were subdued, almost gentle. The door of his office, when he had an office, was always open; he would interrupt his precious work to talk with anyone. While most of his words, spoken or written, were polemic, hortatory, conspiratorial, he could speak or write just as effectively in a nostalgic vein of the natural beauties of his own *tierra* in Oaxaca. And the letters which he wrote from prison to María Talavera, sometimes described as his companion, sometimes as his *amiga,* sometimes as his wife, were full of tenderness and passion.

He was thirty-six years old. He had been born (on Independence

Day, 1874) shortly after the death of the great Benito Juárez, and just before the beginning of the long reign of his archenemy, Porfirio Díaz. All three men were from the mountain state of Oaxaca: Juárez from the village of Guelatao, Díaz from the state capital, and Flores Magón from the village of San Antonio Eloxochitlán, a name that in the ancient tongue meant land of corn and flowers. It was near Teotitlán del Camino, a district that had for a thousand years or more been a principal crossroads in Mexico, on the centuries-old route from the mountains and plateaus of central Mexico down into the hot countries of the east and south. It was a route that had been traversed in forgotten times by the mysterious Olmecs. The Mayans, the Zapotecs, and Mixtecs—who still dwelt there—the Aztecs and, finally the Spaniards, had all passed here. It is a high, dry country, a land of brilliant colors and strange shapes: mountains that, as the sun turns, change from pink to gray-blue to mauve; earth that is red, brown, and green, shaped into grotesque forms by centuries of erosion. In the lower valleys where there is more warmth and moisture there are tidy plots of corn and groves of coffee trees. And in the cool, dark places grow the magic mushrooms which produce weird and wonderful visions.

Flores Magón's father, Don Teodoro, was an Aztec Indian. His ancestors had been among a group of Aztec warriors sent from Tenochtitlán long before the Spanish Conquest to guard the conquered Mixtec people. This garrison of Aztecs established a community in the Mixtec country, a community which remained Aztec. Don Teodoro Flores was chief of the tribal group. He was also a professional soldier who had served in the war against the United States in 1846–48, for the Juárez government in the War of the Reform, and against the French at the Battle of Puebla—where he, incidentally, served under the command of Porfirio Díaz. He was with Díaz in the Tuxtepec rebellion, and during Ricardo's childhood held the rank of colonel in the Díaz army. But he remained faithful to Indian customs and beliefs. He taught his sons the primitive sort of Indian socialism in which he believed: land held and worked in common, with the produce of able men being distributed among all members of the community according to their needs.

Ricardo Flores Magón was the second of three sons. The eldest, Jesús, was to become a lawyer and later a government official in the post-Díaz government. Ricardo and his younger brother, Enrique, were to be lifelong revolutionists.

The mother, Margarita, had a fraction of Spanish blood (one great-grandfather had come from Cartagena, Spain). She was ambitious and eager for her children to be educated, a difficult thing in rural Oaxaca. She took her three sons to Mexico City. There they lived in near-poverty in the Plaza of San Juan, and the boys went to school. Ricardo was a superior student from the first. He followed his elder brother, Jesús, into law school, and in 1892, was arrested for the first of many times. He and some sixty other students were seized for protesting against the coming reelection of President Díaz for his fourth term. The students were herded into the National Palace and, had the demonstration not attracted so much attention, they might have been executed.

Díaz by this time was no longer trying to hide the methods by which he ruled and intended to go on ruling. Three potential rivals for the presidency had in recent years been assassinated. In 1886 General Trinidad García de la Cadena had been killed in Zacatecas on orders of Díaz. Three years later General Ramón Corona, governor of Jalisco, was similarly killed. Dr. Ignacio Martínez had been forced to go into exile in Brownsville, Texas, where he published an anti-Díaz periodical; Díaz agents, crossing the border from Matamoros, successfully assassinated him on their third attempt.

Suppression of the press was becoming general. The press had become free under Juárez—although much of it was critical of him. This freedom was maintained under Juárez' successor, Sebastian Lerdo de Tejada, continued through Díaz's first term in office, 1876–80, and through the presidency of Díaz's hand-picked successor, Manuel González. The press was active in exposing the abundant corruption in González' administration—exposure that Díaz was believed to have encouraged, since it helped pave the way for his own return to the presidency.

But early in his second term Díaz began a war with the press. At the end of the first year fifty newspapermen were in prison—some on such inconsequential charges as having written critically of the King of Italy. Not only were editors and writers jailed; so were printers and news vendors. Journalists took leave of each other, half-jokingly, with *"hasta Belem,"* or "I'll see you in jail." The Belem Prison in Mexico City, and the ancient fortress of San Juan de Ulúa at Veracruz which had been converted into a prison, were vile places: dark, unventilated cells with rats, lice, spiders, scorpions, pestilential air, floors covered inches deep with mud and excrement. Some journalists spent most of their lives in such places. Filomena Mata, editor of the conservative *Diario del Hogar,* was imprisoned more than thirty times by Díaz because, editorially, he favored constitutionalism, freedom of the press, equal rights for women and opposed presidential reelection. Other journalists fared worse. Emilio Ordoñez was seized and burned in a lime kiln on the orders of the Díaz-appointed governor of Hidalgo, Rafael Cravioto. In Puebla another Díaz appointee, Governor Mucio P. Martínez, who had become rich through corruption, ordered the assassination of Jesús Olmos y Contreras, a curious and persistent reporter. In the state of

Morelia the editor of *El Explorador,* Luis González, met a similar end.

It was in this atmosphere of political and journalistic suppression that Ricardo Flores Magón abandoned the study of law and became a militant journalist. Between 1892 and 1900 he worked for a series of opposition papers, most of them short-lived. In 1900 he came into his own as an editor. His older brother, Jesús, who had completed his legal education, began, with another lawyer, a legal journal called *Regeneración,* devoted to reporting irregularities in judicial proceedings and other matters of interest to lawyers. Since the judicial system was completely dominated by the Díaz government, the paper quickly evolved into a political organ; within a few months Ricardo Flores Magón was installed as editor and had declared *Regeneración* to be "an independent journal of combat" opposed to "centralism and autocracy." He soon published a review of the promises Díaz had made at the beginning of each of his presidential terms, and the way in which the promises had been broken or forgotten. As a delegate to the first congress of Liberal clubs in San Luis Potosí he made a speech in which he denounced the Díaz administration as "a den of bandits." Within two months the government had thrown both Ricardo and Jesús Flores Magón into Belem Prison. From prison the brothers wrote articles for *Regeneración* and had them smuggled out. One of these, published on August 6, 1901, demanded that Díaz resign, whereupon the government closed down the printing shop of *Diario del Hogar,* where *Regeneración* had been printed. *Regeneración* reappeared in San Luis Potosí but only for a few issues and then was suspended. Ricardo Flores Magón was on his way as a revolutionary journalist.

Many years later one of his fellow revolutionists, Juan Sarabia, was to say: "The publication of a revolutionary paper is equal to the taking of a city; the proclamation of a political plan is the same as the bloodiest of combats—they form equal parts of a rebellion and are inherent in it . . . I have never seen, nor, probably, will I ever see a revolution without the propagation of ideas as a preliminary and the shedding of blood as the inevitable means of deciding the outcome . . ."

These were words that Ricardo Flores Magón might have spoken. Ricardo and Jesús were released from Belem on April 30, 1902. Their beloved mother had died while they were in prison. Jesús thereafter moderated his revolutionary feelings, but Ricardo's were stronger than ever. By July of that year he had taken over the editorship of *El Hijo de Ahuizote,* a journal devoted to caricatures and cartoons; by September he was in trouble—and prison—again for criticizing the Minister of War. By January he was out again and asking editorially, "Why hide the black reality? The constitution is dead." By mid-April, Ricardo, this time with his younger brother Enrique, was back in Belem. The presses they had used were confiscated and stored away in the Ciudadela. All publications were threatened with prosecution if they printed so much as a word written by Ricardo Flores Magón. Ricardo learned through a friendly jailer that if he attempted to resume his career in Mexico it was an automatic sentence of death. When he regained his freedom at the end of 1903 he and Enrique fled the country.

Regeneración reappeared in San Antonio, Texas, November 5, 1904. Within a month a man they could identify only as "a Díaz agent," broke into the rented house the two brothers occupied and attacked Ricardo. The assailant was overcome by Enrique and taken away by the police. But by the next day the unidentified man had been set free and Enrique was fined $40 for disturbing the peace. Ricardo thought, probably correctly, that this might be the first of many troubles in a city so near Mexico and the long-armed power of the Díaz government. He decided to move, and on February 5, 1905, *Regeneración* resumed publication in St. Louis. St. Louis was an agreeable place. There were many Russian, German, and Spanish anarchist refugees there. Among Flores Magón's friends were Emma Goldman and the Spanish anarchist Florencio Bazora. The office of *Regeneración* at 107 North Avenue was a gathering place for radicals of all sorts. Into the paper's postoffice box, number 584, poured a steady stream of gifts, loans, and subscriptions. Within seven months the paper's circulation had climbed to 20,000. With the subscriptions came letters from Liberal clubs in Mexico. The Club Benito Juárez in Parral, Chihuahua, according to its director, Antonio Balboa, had raised a war fund of eight and one-half pesos ($4.25 U.S.). Encarnación García, Encarnación Ogaz, Jesús Zubía, Jesús Ogaz, J. M. Asúnsolo, and Nicolás Montejano had each contributed twenty-five centavos. Ramón Delgado of Tlanchinol, Hidalgo, reported that while few of his municipality's 2000 citizens were ready to seize arms and rebel, almost no one liked Díaz and once armed rebellion had broken out nearly everyone would contribute to the cause. So it went from club to club, from town to town, all over Mexico.

What neither Flores Magón nor Balboa nor Delgado nor any of the other conspirators knew was that much of their correspondence was being monitored by Díaz authorities. Enrique Clay Creel, governor of Chihuahua, a rich landowner himself and married to a daughter of the even richer landowner, Don Luis Terrazas, was functioning as head of an espionage service for Díaz. Creel was later to serve as Díaz's ambassador to Washington and as his foreign minister, positions from which he could more effectively enlist the official assistance of the United States in observing and controlling the exiled revolutionists. Now, in 1905, in addition to making an impressive collection of copies of Magonista correspondence, Creel had secured the cooperation of various

U.S. authorities and had employed a St. Louis private detective named
Thomas Furlong. Furlong and his men watched every move made by
the Mexican radicals in St. Louis. One of his undercover operatives,
Ansel T. Samuels, was working as an advertising solicitor for *Regeneración*. Furlong was to boast, years later, that through his various
operations 180 anti-Díaz Mexican expatriates had been sent back to
Mexico, either through the legal processes of extradition or the much
simpler method of physically pushing them across the border where
they could be seized by Mexican authorities.

Late in 1905 Manuel Esperón de la Flor, Díaz's *jefe politico* from
Pochutla, Oaxaca, arrived in St. Louis and filed charges of defamation
against *Regeneración*. Ricardo and Enrique Flores Magón and Juan
Sarabia were arrested, and the presses stopped. The refugee community
in St. Louis raised bail for the three, and friendly sources within Mexico,
notably *El Colmillo Publico,* an opposition paper which had managed
to keep publishing by disguising its opposition with an air of frivolity,
produced $2000 for a defense fund. *Regeneración* resumed publication
in February 1906, only to become embroiled in difficulties with U.S.
postal authorities who maintained that because most of its circulation was
in Mexico it was not entitled to fourth-class mailing privileges.

In addition to the chronic problems of *Regeneración,* Flores Magón
and his comrades were concerned with drafting of a revolutionary
manifesto. On July 1, 1906, the "organizational junta of the Mexican
Liberal party," with Ricardo as president, Juan Sarabia as vice-president,
Antonio I. Villareal secretary, and Enrique Flores Magón treasurer,
published their program. Insofar as the coming Mexican Revolution was
to have a master plan, this was it. Many aspects of it are reflected in the
Mexican Constitution of 1917—which is the cornerstone of present-day
Mexico.

THE CONSPIRATORS

"Mexicans: Join hands with those who fight for justice, who speed the coming of that bright day when tyranny will fall forever and democracy will rise."

Program of the Mexican Liberal party. St. Louis, Missouri, July 1, 1906

EACH OF THE FIFTY-TWO PROVISIONS of the 1906 program of the Liberal party was aimed at a specific aspect of the Díaz dictatorship.

The presidential term was to be reduced to four years and there was to be no reelection of either the president or state governors.

(Díaz, who had come to power with the slogan of "no reelection," had amended the constitution not only to permit reelection, but also increasing the presidential term to six years.)

Obligatory military service was to be suppressed.

(Forced service in the army had become a Díaz weapon. Recalcitrant Indians, rebellious landless peasants and troublesome industrial workers were put into uniform for indefinite periods and subjected to military discipline.)

Freedom of the press was to be restored and strengthened, with restrictive penalties to be imposed only for deceitful untruthfulness, blackmail, and violations of the law regarding morals.

(By this time no one could keep count of the journalists who had been either imprisoned or assassinated, nor of the number of publications that had been suppressed.)

Enough primary schools must be built to meet the country's need, teachers must have adequate pay, there would be compulsory instruction in arts, crafts, military training, and civics, all children would be required to attend school until the age of fourteen, and no children under that age could be employed.

(*Only a fraction of Mexico's children had access to schools. Many of them were put to work in the field or factory before they even reached school age.*)

The Laws of the Reform, as embodied in the Constitution of 1857, were to be strengthened and enforced with severe penalties for infractions. Schools operated by the Catholic clergy were to be suppressed. Churches would be considered business enterprises and taxed accordingly. Real estate held by the clergy would be nationalized.

(*The anticlerical provisions of the Constitution of 1857 had been tacitly forgotten. Subsidized newspapers editorialized that the Laws of the Reform were not "adaptable to our environment." Díaz, who had fought against the conservative-Catholic forces in the War of the Reform, now conceded that while as President he could profess no religion, he was, as a private citizen, a Catholic. His young wife, Carmen, was an ardent Catholic. One Mexican prelate, Bishop Ignacio Montes de Oca y Obregón, had declared that the Church in Mexico no longer needed to fear application of the Laws of the Reform, since it had the support of the women of the country and the tolerance of President Díaz. The Church had again begun to acquire vast properties. Priests offered the best education there was to be had and, for Díaz, played a useful role in keeping the repressed masses from rebelling against the dictatorship.*)

A whole series of laws would ameliorate the conditions of labor. There was to be an eight-hour day and a minimum daily wage of one peso or four times the then prevailing rate, to apply to piecework as well as regular employment. Domestic servants were to be protected by the labor laws. Conditions of work must be hygienic, food must be provided for workers in rural areas, indemnity must be paid for work accidents. Wages must be paid in legal currency, all debts of workers to employers would be nullified, and the infamous *tiendas de raya,* or company stores, would be abolished. Foreign workers must be kept in a minority, and there would be no difference in wages for Mexican and foreign workers. Sunday was to be a day of rest.

(*Each of these provisions was aimed at abuses that had come to be considered normal. Perhaps the gravest of these abuses was the employment of slave labor, a common thing on the henequen plantations of Yucatán which bought dispossessed Indians at twenty-five pesos a head, and the use of* enganchado *("hooked") or contract labor. Professional recruiters lured workers with promises of high wages, gave them a paltry advance against a future income, and delivered them to the employers. Wages, far lower than promised, were withheld entirely* until the advance had been settled, by which time the laborer was so in debt to the company store that he could not leave.)

The Indians were to be protected.

(*The Díaz regime had made systematic warfare against the Maya Indians of Yucatán, the Tarahumaras of Chihuahua, the Yaquis and Mayos of Sonora. Indians who occupied desirable land were goaded into rebellion, bloodily suppressed, physically removed from their land and, in many cases, sold into slavery.*)

Landowners must make their land productive; those who did not would be deprived of the land. The land thus acquired by the government would be given, in suitable parcels, to citizens who needed and wanted it, with the provision that it be used for agricultural production and that it not be sold. Exiled Mexicans would be welcomed back to their country and given parcels of land. The state would form an agricultural bank to make low-interest, long-term loans to finance these new landowners. In order to own land in Mexico foreigners must become Mexican citizens.

(*Land ownership was one of the key problems—perhaps the most basic one. Concentration of land in a few hands was as old as the Spanish Conquest—but under Díaz the concentration had been intensified. Under a series of surveying and colonization laws vast parcels of public land, sometimes measured in degrees of latitude rather than hectares or square kilometers, had been given to favored individuals and speculative land companies. More than a fourth of the area of the Republic was thus given away during successive Díaz administrations. Communally owned village lands were ordered divided up and sold to individuals—who almost immediately resold to large landowners, with the result that ancient community lands disappeared into large private holdings. Land to which there was no clear title—although it might have been held and worked by one community or family for centuries, was subject to acquisition by "denouncement"—and the denouncer usually was the nearest large landowner. Manipulation of water rights—of vital importance in an arid country—destroyed the usefulness of many small holdings. The result was the creation of great private holdings and a multitude of landless peasants who either worked as feudal peons or were set adrift. Luis Terrazas of Chihuahua—the saying was current that "Terrazas is not of Chihuahua but Chihuahua is of Terrazas"—and his son-in-law, Enrique Creel, between them owned 14,000,000 acres. Vice-President Corral owned a considerable part of the state of Sonora, and the Escandón family owned much of the rich sugar cane land in Morelos. Less than one percent of the families of Mexico controlled 85 percent of the nation. Foreigners, both individuals and land companies, were among the largest owners.*)

William Randolph Hearst's Babícora covered more than a million acres; the W. C. Greene holdings in Sonora amounted to more than 600,000 acres; the Colorado River Land Company more than 700,000 in Baja California.)

The proposals of the Liberal party went on and on—everything from the suppression of *jefes politicos* and restoration of municipal self-government to the granting of rights and privileges to illegitimate children. It was a much more far-reaching document than anything projected by Hidalgo in his Guadalajara proposals, by Morelos in his constitution of Apatzingán, or by the Constitution of 1857.

Although the Flores Magóns had taken the name of Juárez' Liberal party, it was more radical than liberal; its ends could be achieved only by total destruction of Mexico's political, social, and economic structure as it existed in the first decade of the twentieth century.

But even before the program of the Liberal party was completed, published and smuggled into Mexico, the revolution which *Regeneración* had been urging appeared to be taking shape. In June 1906 there was a serious strike at the copper mines of Cananea in the state of Sonora, just below the Arizona border. It was soon followed by other strikes which proved that the Mexican workers were an explosive element in Porfirio Díaz's supposedly peaceful Mexico.

The Consolidated Copper Company of Cananea, property of an American, Colonel William C. Greene, employed 5360 Mexicans and 2200 Americans. Although wages were well above national averages, Mexican workers received three pesos (about $1.50 U.S.) for a work day of ten to eleven hours, while American mine workers received seven pesos for a shorter work day. The Mexicans organized and demanded a standard eight-hour working day, a minimum wage of five pesos, a system of promotion and a stipulation that the number of foreign employees would be held to 25 percent. They were ignored, and on June 1, 1906, a strike was declared. Some 2000 strikers marched toward the mine lumberyard, where most of the employees were American, intending to invite them to join the strike. They were met with a burst of rifle fire. A riot broke out in which both Americans and Mexicans were killed. Armed Americans pursued the strikers through the streets and into the mountains—the retreating strikers set fire to buildings as they fled—even their own company-supplied homes, and the flames of Cananea could be seen in Douglas, Arizona, fifty miles away. The American consul in Cananea, W. J. Galbraith, appealed to President Theodore Roosevelt to send American troops. Colonel Greene, the owner, was well-connected in Mexico. He appealed to his friend, Rafael Izábal, governor of Sonora and a close friend of Vice-President Ramón Corral. Izábal dispatched state troops and federal *rurales,* and, in a move of questionable protocol and policy, asked the U. S. State Department for aid. The governor then went to Naco, Arizona—on the border just below Bisbee. There he found a force of high-spirited, gun-toting American volunteers—a group he estimated at about two hundred; other sources figured it as high as four hundred. The group had been warned by the Arizona territorial governor to stay out of Mexico, but at Izábal's invitation they went anyway. This impromptu and unofficial American intervention was to give the Cananea strike much more importance in Mexican revolutionary history than it might otherwise have had. Martial law was declared, peace restored, and Colonel Greene, wearing six-shooters, was back in charge of Cananea. There were twenty-three killed and twenty-two wounded, most of them Mexican strikers, and there was great damage to the physical plant of the mining company. Fifty accused strike leaders were shipped off to the dungeons of San Juan de Ulúa in Veracruz.

The Cananea strike set off a whole series of labor upheavals, principally among the textile workers in the states of Puebla, Tlaxcala, Querétaro, Jalisco, the Federal District, and in Veracruz. In December 1906 many mill owners, sensing trouble, closed their plants, putting 25,000 laborers out of work. Workers in the textile mill district of Orizaba, Veracruz, had formed a Circle of Free Workers, demanding improvements in wages, hours, and working conditions, and abolition of the company stores—through which the workers were kept in perpetual debt to their employers. The management refused and the workers appealed to President Díaz to settle the dispute. Far from solving the problem, Díaz aggravated it by ruling that individual workers with complaints should submit them in writing to the management, and if they were not satisfied with the employer's decision they must leave. The workers must promise not to go on strike. He also decreed that the mill owners must not employ children under the age of seven.

The Díaz ruling brought on the famous Rio Blanco strike of January 7, 1907. Workers, their wives and children formed an angry mob. They blocked entrances to the mills, wrecked the hated company stores, freed prisoners from the jails, set their company-owned houses ablaze. Federal troops were rushed in from the cities of Veracruz, Jalapa, and Mexico City. Soldiers fired point-blank into the massed strikers. More than two hundred strikers and their dependents were killed. One lieutenant, Gabriel Arroyo, refused to order his company to fire into a crowd containing women and children; he and his company were summarily executed. Other strikers, as they were rounded up, went before firing squads. Corpses that could not be buried immediately were stacked on railroad cars, taken to Veracruz and dumped in the Gulf of Mexico for the sharks. The mill owners gave a banquet for General Rosalino Martínez and his officers.

In addition to the labor upheavals there were minor rebellions inspired by local leaders in various parts of the republic—Miguel Alemán in Veracruz, Juan Alvarez in Torreón, Angel Barrios in Oaxaca, Andrés Sánchez in the state of Mexico, Antonio Cebada in Puebla, Antonio Carvajal in Tabasco. But such movements were isolated, unsuccessful, uncoordinated. The only planned, articulated revolutionary leadership came from the exiled Ricardo Flores Magón and his fellow journalistic revolutionists. Their leadership was zealous but haphazard.

By the time the program of the Liberal party was completed, Ricardo Flores Magón had jumped bail in the St. Louis libel case and fled to Canada, first to Toronto, then to Montreal. In August 1906, he and his brother Enrique, and Juan Sarabia furtively made their way to El Paso, Texas, and continued their plotting. They sent a proclamation to the various Liberal clubs in Mexico: "We rebel against the dictatorship of Porfirio Díaz on September 2." But every move they made was carefully watched by agents of the Mexican government. One Liberal club, made up of miners in Douglas, Arizona, planned to seize the custom house of Agua Prieta, Mexico; but one of the club members, Trinidad Gómez, was in the pay of Governor Izábal of Sonora, and they were arrested by U.S. authorities. In El Paso, Ricardo and other plotters laid their plans in the home of Modesto Díaz, east of the city. Arms were being smuggled to the Mexican side of the Rio Grande. A striking force of a hundred men would cross the river, recover the arms, overcome the garrison and free prisoners from the jails—and Juárez, one of the most important Mexican ports of entry, would be theirs. Meanwhile, the Mexican consul in El Paso, Francisco Mallen, had enlisted the help of El Paso police, who kept a close watch over the conspirators.

The revolution was delayed and rescheduled for September 26, 1906. On that date a group of thirty rebels crossed the border, seized and briefly held the town of Jiménez but then was forced to retreat to the U.S. side of the border where they were arrested.

The main strike against Juárez was scheduled for the same time but was delayed because of the shortage of arms and ammunition. It was postponed until October 19, and then participated in by only five men— two of them the Mexican army spies. The three revolutionists—Juan Sarabia among them, were immediately arrested by Mexican authorities. Ricardo Flores Magón managed to escape a trap that had been set for him. With difficulty—because of his weight and nearsightedness—he climbed on a freight train and headed for California.

These were the beginnings of the Mexican Revolution—fervid and ambitious but also inept, beset by treachery and played out in obscurity.

A young man who fell in the raid on Jiménez on September 26, 1906, may have been the first victim of the Revolution, but historians do not know whether his name was Alvarez or Almarez.

Ricardo Flores Magón after reaching California had, at first, gone into hiding in Sacramento. The Díaz government had placed a price of $20,000 on his head. Finally he came to Los Angeles and, with Antonio I. Villareal and Librado Rivera, rented a house at 113 East Pico Boulevard. On the night of August 23, 1907, four detectives, headed by the Magonistas' old enemy, the St. Louis detective, Thomas Furlong, accompanied by two Los Angeles newspapermen, broke into the house. The three revolutionists were finally subdued and taken to a police station where they were booked for "resisting arrest." Their attorney, a Socialist named Job Harriman, questioned Detective Furlong at the preliminary hearing. Furlong admitted that he had entered the house and seized the men without warrant, that he had taken their papers without authority and that he was in the pay of the Mexican government. But by this time the charges had been expanded to include robbery, homicide (of a John Doe), criminal libel, and conspiracy to violate the neutrality laws. They were, after two years, tried and convicted on the last charge and sentenced to eighteen months in the federal penitentiary in Arizona.

The case of the accused Mexicans attracted wide interest in leftist circles in the United States. The International Workers of the World and the Western Federation of Miners gave what support they could, and so did the Socialists and Socialist sympathizers such as a Los Angeles bank employee named Primrose Noel, and a Boston heiress, Elizabeth Darling Trowbridge. The latter gave freely to the cause of the Mexican liberals and finally married one of them—Manuel Sarabia. But the most effective of the sympathizers was a newspaperman, John Kenneth Turner. He was intrigued with the strange way in which U.S. justice was being administered and, because of that, became interested in conditions in Mexico which had produced the revolutionary sentiments. With the help of one of the Mexican liberals, Lázaro Gutiérrez de Lara, he made a trip into Mexico, posing as an investor interested in the henequen plantations of Yucatán and tobacco production in the Valle Nacional. His wife, Ethel Duffy Turner, remained in California, working for *Regeneración*. Upon Turner's return he wrote a series of articles in the best muckraking tradition. Some of them appeared in the *American* magazine and all later appeared in book form as *Barbarous Mexico,* a passionate and horrifying account of conditions under Díaz. The appearance of the magazine articles inspired many journalistic defenses of Díaz—in the newspapers controlled by William Randolph Hearst and Harrison Gray Otis—both of whom were substantial property owners in Mexico, in *Sunset* magazine, the *Overland Monthly, Moody's Magazine, Cosmopolitan, Banker's Magazine, World's Work,* and *Mining World.* Despite the Díaz defenders, Turner's reportage helped spread disenchantment with Díaz in the United States.

Meanwhile Ricardo Flores Magón, with notes smuggled from prison in his laundry, directed a second attempt at launching a revolution in Mexico. It was more ambitious than the 1906 attempt, but equally ill-starred. The uprising was scheduled for the night of June 25, 1908. Forty-six Liberal clubs in all parts of Mexico were alerted. But, as before, the Mexican government was forewarned. On June 23 and 24 the government rounded up members of Liberal clubs all over the Republic, locked them up and confiscated arms and ammunition. On June 24 Mexican government agents, operating freely on the American side of the Rio Grande, surprised three revolutionists, including Enrique Flores Magón, in a house in El Paso. The three escaped, but the agents seized a quantity of dynamite, several thousand cartridges and much correspondence. On the following day, June 25, a group of Magonistas fell on the town of Viesca, Coahuila, posted their party program, freed prisoners from the jail and, before being driven off into the mountains by federal troops, took over 20,000 pesos from the local branch of the Banco de Nuevo León—a bank founded by the Maderos of Coahuila, a wealthy family which would soon become deeply involved in the Revolution. Most of the fugitives were captured. Some were sent to the prison of San Juan Ulúa, and some, including one of the leaders, José Lugo, were shot. On the night of June 26 another group of forty men struck at the town of Las Vacas, Coahuila—the present-day Villa Acuña, just across the river from Del Rio, Texas. Eleven of the attackers were killed, including one of the leaders, Benjamín Canales, and the federal forces lost nine men before the revolutionists, their ammunition exhausted, were driven back across the river. Still another striking force headed for Palomas, Chihuahua, by way of Columbus, New Mexico, but was met by a superior force of federal troops and had to retreat into the desert.

Out of prison once more, Ricardo Flores Magón was, in 1910, planning his third attempt at revolution. His political philosophy had changed in the years of agitation, frustration, and persecution. It was no longer the simple, primitive socialism of the Mexican Indians that he had learned from his father. He had studied Kropotkin, Bakunin, and Marx. He had learned much from European refugees in St. Louis—and had borrowed from them the slogan of "Land and Liberty," which, as *Tierra y Libertad* was to echo through the revolutionary years that lay ahead in Mexico. For him it was no longer enough just to oppose the dictatorship of Porfirio Díaz. The whole of the old political, social, and economic structure must be pulled down. Revolution had become an end in itself. He had become, in short, an anarchist, and he had nothing but scorn for the men of more moderate views who agreed that Díaz must go but disagreed on what should happen then. These more moderate men were now planning a revolution of their own for November 20, 1910, and, on November 19, Ricardo Flores Magón wrote:

"Be not confused, you proletarians, you disinherited ones. The conservative and bourgeois parties speak to you of liberty, of justice, of law, of honorable government. Be not deceived. What you need is the assurance of well-being and daily bread for your families. No government can give you that. You must seize them. Take possession of the land, which is the source of all riches. No government can give you the land. Understand this well. The law defends the 'rights' of the usurpers of this wealth. You must seize it in spite of the law, in spite of the government, in spite of the so-called rights of property. You must seize it yourselves in the name of natural justice, in the name of the right of all humanity to live . . ."

If Flores Magón had prevailed the history of Mexico and the world might have been quite different. But more moderate men were the ones who would shape the immediate course of the Mexican Revolution, borrowing liberally from the principles formulated by Flores Magón in his 1906 program.

In 1910 no one took Flores Magón and his followers very seriously. An advertisement in Mexico City newspapers for a mattress manufacturer showed a cartoon of a full-bearded, wild-eyed man with the verse:

> I am a furious anarchist
> And I will take terrible vengeance
> Against everyone save those I find
> Sleeping in a Mestas bed.

CHAPTER 5

THE APOSTLE

"To our national heroes, to independent
journalists, to all good Mexicans."
Dedication of Francisco I. Madero's
La sucesión presidencial en 1910

WHEN REVOLUTION CAME to Mexico, violent, bloody, and destructive, it
was launched not by a firebrand like Ricardo Flores Magón but by a
mild man who abhorred violence and who, until he was forced into it,
opposed the very notion of armed rebellion.

His name was Francisco Ignacio Madero,* a member of a powerful
and wealthy clan of the state of Coahuila in northern Mexico. Everything
about him was at variance with the accepted notion of a revolutionist.
His background was not one of oppression, hunger, and yearning but,
instead, of comfort, culture, and respected authority. Hatred was alien
to his nature; his tendency to forgive his enemies came to be the despair
of his friends and allies. In neither temperament nor physique was he the
sort of giant out of whom folk heroes are made. His manners were gentle, modest, and considerate. He was an excellent horseman, a skilled
swimmer, a tireless dancer and, on occasion, displayed great stamina
and courage, even heroism, but he was still a small, insignificant man
physically, less than five feet three inches tall and weighing no more than
140 pounds. He had a broad, domed forehead, intense dark eyes. His
hair was dark brown, almost black; his mustache and beard were a
somewhat lighter shade of brown; they were short and carefully trimmed,
concealing a receding chin and elongating his otherwise round face.
His voice was high-pitched, sometimes shrill, and his manner of

* Most American and Mexican sources give his middle name as Indalecio, and
some, more fanciful, give it as Inocencio (innocence). His marriage license and
other legal documents bearing his signature give it as Ignacio.

speaking was quick and nervous. The gestures he made with his hands repeated the broken rhythms of his speech.

He believed in democratic principles, had confidence in the ability of people to govern themselves, and hated the bossism and militarism which had characterized Mexican government for most of its one hundred years of uneasy independence. He was unfamiliar with the radical ideologies of his time and knew almost nothing of the intellectual forces that had helped Flores Magón evolve from an anti-Díaz journalist to a practicing anarchist. Madero's intellectual preparation was a hodgepodge of practical bookkeeping, stenography, commercial law, banking, progressive agriculture, Goethe, Macaulay, Napoleon, Byron, Shakespeare, Alexandre Dumas, and Victor Hugo. His knowledge of his own country's history was precarious and his understanding of the basic problems of the nation was hazy. He had great faith in education and political democracy as Mexico's best hope for the future.

He was a vegetarian. He shunned tobacco and alcohol, although he had used both as a young man. He became a practitioner of homeopathic medicine and, at a time when many Mexican intellectuals were dabbling in theosophy, a devotee of spiritualism. According to one story he learned, as a child, through the manipulation of a planchette, that he would one day be President of Mexico. In 1906—after he had already been initiated in the rough and tumble of practical politics—he wrote to a noted French spiritualist interpreting the coming struggle in Mexico in spiritualistic terms. As late as 1909, when he had become the leader of the anti-reelectionist movement and a probable candidate for the presidency in the election of 1910, he was deeply involved with spiritualism. Under the pen name of "Bhima" he wrote a manual of spiritualism and expressed his faith in telepathy: "An individual finds himself in a distressing situation and communicates his distress to a loved one, no matter how far away. Thus when a serous mishap occurs to a person, the image which represents the mishap is transmitted to some of his relatives or friends who perceive the image with great precision. These cases are much more frequent in the moments of death. There are many cases of families that have been apprised of the disappearance of one of their members by this process."

Because of his role in the Revolution Mexicans—who love descriptive titles—came to call him the Apostle, the Redeemer, the Immaculate, the Incorruptible, the Savior, even the Bridegroom of Mexico; but at the same time, for his strangeness, he was given many less flattering titles— *el chaparrito* (the little runt), the monkey of Coahuila, the lunatic of Parras. And Porfirio Díaz whose downfall Madero was to bring about, disdainfully referred to him as *el loquito* (the little madman).

The true Madero was neither saint nor lunatic, but he was strange, and even his family at times seemed somewhat puzzled by him. His grandfather, the patriarch Evaristo, who was to die one month before Madero's great revolutionary triumph, scolded him for dereliction of family duties and warned him that crusaders more often than not ended up as martyrs. His father, Francisco, Sr., long suspected that Madero's book which caused such a stir, *La sucesión presidencial en 1910,* must have been written by someone else. And even Gustavo, the most devoted of his brothers, a man who would, later, lay down his own life in Madero's cause, was once quoted as saying, "of a family of clever men the only fool was President."

Madero's brief, intense political life, which began in obscurity in 1905, reached its climax in 1911 and ended tragically in 1913, was marked by ambivalence. On the one hand he was driven by the imperatives of revolution, the desperate need for change in Mexico, and by his idealism. And he was at the same time inhibited by loyalty to the Madero clan, and its ties to the old regime, to the landed aristocracy to which it belonged, and the traditional Mexico that had made it prosperous and important. At the age of thirty-five he was to write to his father, "in spite of my age I do not wish to disobey you."

The Maderos were and are one of the important families of Mexico, although their history was somewhat obscure. The brothers Joaquín and José had come from Cádiz in 1786. They may have been Jewish—friends of Madero such as the brilliant journalist Juan Sánchez Azcona thought so—but they became Mexican and Catholic. They were hard workers in the hard country of northern Mexico. The northern states—particularly Sonora, Chihuahua, Coahuila, and Nuevo León—produced industrious people, in sharp contrast to the luxury-loving landowning classes of central and southern Mexico. It was the North that would produce the most extraordinary figures of the coming revolution.

The Maderos prospered in Mexico and became vastly wealthy under the leadership of Francisco's grandfather Evaristo, who was a grandson of Joaquín. Evaristo traded in Texas cotton during the Civil War in the United States, bought land, grew cotton, acquired textile mills, planted vineyards, built wineries and distilleries, mined copper and coal, produced guayule rubber, went into banking, and served as governor of Coahuila from 1881 to 1884. By 1911, the year of his death and of his grandson's triumph, he was reckoned to be worth $15,000,000 (U.S.), owning 1,728,000 acres, much of it bought at eight to ten cents an acre. His children—there were fourteen of them living, plus thirty-four grandchildren and fifty-six great-grandchildren—had accumulated their own fortunes, and the cumulative Madero holdings were among the most impressive in Mexico. The Madero men had a wide reputation for energy, sobriety, and business sense; the women were handsome and wholesome if not beautiful.

Francisco—the family called him Panchito—was born October 30, 1873, in Parras de la Fuente, Coahuila, the eldest of fifteen children born to Francisco, Sr., and his wife Mercedes. As a small child he ate poorly, was quiet and pensive. He early developed a love of the land, riding on horseback about the vast Madero properties. He thought for a time of entering the priesthood but gave it up. As were most young men of his class, he was sent abroad for education, first to a seminary in Baltimore, later to Paris. There he specialized in commercial studies and, according to Sánchez Azcona, indulged his love of dancing at the student dances of Bullier and "the less innocent ones of Moulin Rouge." He also developed his interest in spiritualism. Later he and Gustavo briefly attended the University of California in Berkeley.

From 1894 to 1905—when politics became an absorbing interest—he was a cotton planter and a successful one, specializing in advanced methods, in improved seeds, in irrigation. He helped develop the great and rich cotton-raising district of Laguna, on the border of southern Coahuila and Durango. He built up a fortune of his own—possibly as much as a quarter of a million dollars. He married a spirited little woman, Sara Pérez, who was later to accompany him on his turbulent political campaign trips, confident that she could take care of herself in any disturbance by using her hatpin. There were no children, and Madero showered kindness on the children of men who worked for him, feeding them at his own table—often as many as fifty at a time—building schools, and giving scholarships. For their families, in time of drought and depression, he set up free community dining rooms. He administered homeopathic medicines to anyone who would take them.

Various factors contributed to his entry into politics. He, along with many other Mexicans, was outraged in 1903 when General Bernardo Reyes, governor of the neighboring state of Nuevo León, bloodily suppressed an opposition political manifestation in Monterrey. Reyes, the former Minister of War, was beginning to be talked about as a possible rival of Díaz for the presidency. His actions in Monterrey indicated that in the unlikely event of his succeeding Díaz, Mexico would still be ruled oppressively. Reyes' path in politics was to cross Madero's more than once, to the very end.

Another was the reelection of Díaz in 1904. At the same time Díaz had increased the length of the term from four to six years, and had selected the unpopular Ramón Corral as his Vice-President. There was a high-handedness about it, a brazen disregard for public sensibilities that rankled Madero and many others.

Madero concluded that perhaps the time had come for a genuine democratic movement in Mexico. With friends he formed a Benito Juárez Democratic club in San Pedro, Coahuila. The club attempted first to elect a municipal president of San Pedro, and somewhat later to elect a governor of the state. Municipal and state elections in the Díaz regime were held, as a matter of form, but the results were always predetermined in favor of the candidate the Díaz regime had selected. If balloting was permitted at all the ballots were ignored.

While these efforts were futile, they gave Madero his initiation into politics. He gained experience in political organization and in opposition journalism: he financed and directed two political journals. They were eventually suppressed and the editors forced to flee the country. The doughty Señora Madero hid the fleeing journalists in her home and courageously stood off police until they could escape.

Madero was an early contributor to Ricardo Flores Magón's Liberal party and, at least for a while, a member of it. When Flores Magón, a fugitive in San Antonio, decided to transfer *Regeneración* to St. Louis there was friendly correspondence with Madero, and Madero, in addition to sending funds for subscriptions, loaned the shaky publication 2000 pesos to help with the expenses of reestablishment. When the Liberal party set up its organizing junta in St. Louis in 1905, membership credential No. 4 was issued to Francisco I. Madero. But Madero's relationship with the Magonistas ended when the Liberal party program was published in the following year. The program called for a social revolution, and all Madero had in mind was some political reforms. Madero and Flores Magón were in agreement on the need for changes in Mexico and in their hatred of political oppression. But Flores Magón was, almost from the outset, a true revolutionist who wanted to destroy the old order entirely in order to build anew—and his insistence on cataclysmic change grew with the passing years. Madero was, at first, not a revolutionist at all—and later only a reluctant one. He did not take part in the Magonistas' abortive attempts at revolution in 1906 and 1908, but instead, deplored them. Prisciliano Silva, one of Flores Magón's henchman, called on Madero in the early fall of 1906 to ask his help in obtaining four hundred carbines for use in launching the revolution in Torreón. Silva reported that Madero told him that Díaz was "not a tyrant—somewhat inflexible perhaps, but not a tyrant. I will never give aid to a revolution—I have a true horror of the shedding of blood." A week later, after the Magonistas' attack on Jiménez, Chihuahua, Madero wrote his grandfather Evaristo Madero, assuring him that he had had no part in it and adding that this attempt at revolution was "out of place, and at present I believe that a revolution is more harmful to the country than toleration of the bad government which we have, because in spite of it we are making progress—although possibly not as rapidly as might be desired." Somewhat later, in his book, *La sucesión presidencial en 1910,* Madero was to write: "When a man . . . takes the fatal road of revolution we should suspect all his acts and distrust all his promises."

La sucesión was Madero's first attempt at formulation of a political philosophy. It was produced in response to an external event. That event was an article in the American publication, *Pearson's Magazine,* for March 1908. An American journalist, James Creelman had, a few months earlier, traveled to Mexico and interviewed Porfirio Díaz at Chapultepec Castle. A Mexican journalist later reported that Díaz had told him that the government paid Creelman 50,000 pesos for the job. Whether the reportage was subsidized or not, it was highly favorable—almost slavishly so—to both Díaz and Mexico—but it contained an explosive element. Creelman reported that Díaz, folding his arms over his deep chest and speaking with great emphasis, said: "I welcome an opposition party in the Mexican Republic. If it appears, I will regard it as a blessing, not as an evil. And if it can develop power, not to exploit but to govern, I will stand by it, support it, advise it and forget myself in the successful inauguration of complete (ly) democratic government in the country. It is enough for me that I have seen Mexico rise among the peaceful and useful nations. I have no desire to continue in the presidency. This nation is ready for her ultimate life of freedom. At the age of seventy-seven years I am satisfied . . ." And author Creelman, conceding that although Díaz had converted a republic to an autocracy, added: ". . . it is impossible to look into his face when he speaks of the principles of popular sovereignty without believing that even now he would take up arms and shed his blood in defense of it."

This was news of the first magnitude. The Mexico City newspaper, *El Imparcial,* regularly subsidized by the Díaz government (at the rate of 5400 pesos monthly) and properly worshipful, translated the Creelman article and reprinted it in full; so did provincial papers throughout Mexico. And there was a flurry of political activity—the most meaningful, perhaps, in the long history of Díaz rule. Backers of General Reyes, the strong man of Nuevo León, began booming his candidacy for the 1910 election. The *científicos,* the old men around Díaz, looked at José Yves Limantour, the canny Minister of the Treasury and most capable member of Díaz's official family, as the man of the future. The Magonistas, inside Mexico and abroad, began plotting still another armed uprising. Nonrevolutionary political parties came to life. And there was a flood of political pamphlets and books.

Madero, suffering from an eye ailment which he was doctoring himself, had retreated to the little second-floor library which he had added to his house at San Pedro de las Colonias and began writing a book, scribbling it out on the lined gray paper of children's school notebooks, his handwriting varying from bold and clear to cramped and nervous. As a political document it was mild, particularly when compared with the explosive stridency of Flores Magón. He reviewed Mexico's tragic history and critically examined the current political scene. He did not denounce Díaz personally, but only the absolutism of the Díaz regime and the resultant atrophying of the nation's democratic institutions and of Mexicans' ability to govern themselves in democratic fashion. In fact Madero later was to send a copy of the book to Díaz with a courteous explanatory letter.

He finished the book in October 1908 and had it printed. But it was nearly four months before it was made available to the public, a period during which Madero engaged in an involved correspondence with his father over the question of whether it should be released. Although some of his siblings, especially brother Gustavo, had become devoted partisans of Francisco's political ideas, the family was still committed to the status quo and fearful (1) that Francisco was making a fool of himself, and (2) that he would imperil the family fortune (the financial crisis of 1907 had hurt the Maderos as it had hurt most of Mexico). Francisco's pleading letters to his father were loyal and dutiful, but insistent.

The book was bland and inoffensive. It reiterated Madero's opposition to revolution. The country had suffered from militarism since the war for independence, and militarism had produced the dictatorship of General Díaz. "To seek a change by force of arms would aggravate our internal situation, prolong the era of militarism and bring grave international complications," Madero wrote. He proposed the creation of "The Anti-Reelectionist party" with two fundamental principles: "liberty of suffrage and no reelection." This phrase, subsequently altered to "effective suffrage and no reelection," became the rallying cry of the Madero revolution. They are sacred words in Mexico today, used in official correspondence and pronouncements and in the naming of streets and parks.

Even with this slogan, Madero had no objection to another reelection of Díaz *if* it were a free election and if the Anti-Reelectionists could be represented in the vice-presidency, the national legislature and the state governorships.

Despite its mildness the little book was popular. It went into second and third editions. And it projected Madero into a position of leadership of the opposition. By June of 1909 he and his wife were off on a speaking tour in behalf of the new political movement—*antireeleccionismo*.

It would have been no great surprise if he had found himself speaking in a vacuum. The concept of political parties had never been strong in Mexico, and now it had all but disappeared. There had been, since independence, liberal and conservative political elements in Mexico. But they were not parties so much as groupings by tendency, given form only by the personality of a leader. Then came Porfirio Díaz, who raised personality-politics to new heights. He took over the presidency as a super-liberal, and then, in the intervening years, became more conservative than the conservatives. In the end the old political differences, liberal and conservative, had been merged and destroyed in the personality of one man, a national hero.

Now Madero, in no sense heroic, was trying to restore political consciousness and civic vitality to the Mexican people. He was attempting to do it on a basis of principle, not personality. He was not projecting himself as a candidate for the presidency, but as the advocate of a reawakening. The odds were great, almost impossible. But several things were to aid him. One was the book he had published. People were curious to see the man who had had the courage to raise his voice in opposition. And there was also a national uneasiness. A pro-Díaz writer and legislator, Francisco Bulnes, had noticed it some years before. "There is," he wrote, "peace in the streets, in the casinos, the theaters, churches, on the public roads, in the garrisons, schools and in foreign affairs—but still no peace of conscience." Madero was to make his appeal to this uneasy conscience.

He went from Mexico City to Orizaba, to Veracruz, across the Gulf to the Yucatán Peninsula. Wherever Anti-Reelectionist clubs had been formed there were large crowds. Where there was no such club Madero installed one. When the authorities made public meetings impossible—as they did in Tampico on his return from Yucatán—he would move on to the next place. There were big and enthusiastic meetings in Monterrey and in his home state at Parras and Torreón. Straining his own resources and those of his relatives who were willing to help, he was soon supporting two political newspapers in Coahuila and a daily, *El Antireeleccionista,* in Mexico City. Later in the year he made another speaking tour to the west and north: Querétaro, Guadalajara, Colima, Mazatlán, Culiacán, Navajoa, Alamos, Guaymas, Hermosillo, Chihuahua, and Parral. When there was trouble with the police Madero would improvise—speaking on a deserted beach, from his carriage, from a hotel balcony, in a cockfight ring or at a dance. He gained in confidence and eloquence and proved his courage. In Chihauhua the Benito Juárez Anti-Reelectionist club announced that it wanted to support Madero for the presidency.

But Madero insisted that the choice of candidates must be made in open convention. Accordingly, a convention was scheduled for April 15, 1910. In preparation for it he published a pamphlet outlining his party's aims, hoping to attract wider support. Where his book had been largely confined to political considerations, he now touched—although lightly—

on social problems, improvements of the lot of labor and division of national lands among small proprietors. Other opposition groups, including the one that had been supporting the possible candidacy of General Reyes, were invited to take part in the convention.

Madero won his party's nomination for the presidency—without attending the convention. He was in hiding at the time. A warrant had been issued for his arrest in connection with a land dispute—which actually had been settled. The warrant was canceled and Madero came out of hiding. The next day he had an interview with Porfirio Díaz, arranged by the popular governor of Veracruz, Teodoro Dehesa, who may have hoped for a compromise helpful to his own political ambitions.

There were no witnesses to the hour-long interview. But Madero was struck by the old man's vagueness and his seeming unawareness of what was going on. According to indirect reports Díaz scoffed at Madero's candidacy, compared him with Nicolás de Zúñiga y Miranda, an eccentric who, for many years, had aspired to the presidency and had become a national political joke. And, Díaz is supposed to have said to Madero, whose sincerity and idealism he must have sensed, "Señor, a man must be more than honest to govern Mexico."

It apparently was at this point that Madero began, unwillingly, to concede that the Díaz regime could never be peacefully overcome, that there must, instead, be a revolution. And he worried about how, once started, it could end. Some of his collaborators—notably the young intellectual José Vasconcelos—had already expressed impatience with his nonrevolutionary attitudes.

Nevertheless he proceeded to campaign vigorously throughout the country, despite difficulties of transportation and legal obstacles placed in his way by authorities. Crowds were huge—10,000 in Guadalajara, 25,000 in Puebla, 20,000 in Orizaba, more than 30,000 in Mexico City. His emotional and devoted followers had begun to call him "the apostle of democracy," and he was, without quite knowing it, forming the shock troops of the upheaval that was soon to come. Unrest was growing fast. Even among the illiterate masses who had no very clear notion of what Madero was talking about there was a sense of fateful excitement. The appearance of Halley's comet on May 4, 1910, was widely interpreted as a sign of approaching war. Somewhat later a *corrido,* one of those Mexican popular songs based on current events, was written about it:

> Oh comet, if you had but known
> What it was you prophesied,
> You never would have come out that way,
> Lighting up the sky . . .
> Mother Guadalupe,
> Give us your blessing . . .

CHAPTER 6

RELUCTANT REBEL

"It is very easy to put a country into combustion when it possesses the elements of discord . . ."

Lorenzo de Zavala, *Ensayo historico de las revoluciones de Méjico desde 1808 hasta 1832* (Vol. I, 1831)

FINALLY the Díaz government had had enough of Francisco Madero and his Anti-Reelection party. On June 6, 1910, Madero was arrested in Monterrey, accused falsely of inciting to rebellion and insulting the person of the President, and shortly thereafter he was taken to the state penitentiary in San Luis Potosí where the offense was alleged to have occurred.

By the time of the primary election day, June 21, some five thousand Anti-Reelectionists around the country were also in jail, and when the secondary and final election was held July 8 there were an estimated 60,000 behind bars. In prison Madero discussed with his brother Gustavo and with Dr. Rafael Cepeda of San Luis Potosí the advisability of an uprising and even considered a tentative date, July 14. But with so many of the party workers in jail it was an impossibility—and Madero was still reluctant anyway. The election results were, of course, declared to be overwhelmingly for Díaz and Corral—an outcome which was to be officially proclaimed by the Chamber of Deputies the following October 4.

Through the efforts of his family and of Dr. Cepeda, Madero was released on 8000 pesos bail on July 19, with the proviso that he stay in San Luis Potosí. He worked on the only remaining legal means of protest against the "election"—a compilation of evidence of irregularities in the voting and a petition to the congressional electoral committee to nullify the results. Although he could not have had much hope for a change, he waited for the official declaration of Díaz's reelection. Also as a patriotic and nationalistic Mexican he did not want to offer any distraction to the month-long celebration of Mexico's Centennial in September. But each day he took longer walks in San Luis Potosí, wandering farther and farther from the house which police had under surveillance. On October 4 the congressional committee made its ruling. That day Madero did not return from his walk, but stayed overnight in the home of a servant. The next day, dressed in a railroad laborer's clothes, with a straw sombrero pulled low on his head and a red bandanna concealing the pear-shaped beard, he fled. He walked to El Peñasco, a railroad flag stop eight miles north of San Luis Potosí, boarded a northbound train, hid in a baggage car and headed for the border, for freedom—and for the rebellion which was no longer avoidable.

There had, meanwhile, been uprisings around the country, in Yucatán, Tlaxcala, Veracruz, Sinaloa, some near the capital itself. Some had been inspired by the Magonistas but more were spontaneous. There was, as yet, no effective plan for revolution.

This Madero was soon to remedy. Reaching San Antonio, Texas, he stayed, at first, in the home of a friend, Ernesto Fernández Arteaga, at 8 West Macon Street. There he met with friends, fellow members of the Anti-Reelection party who also had fled Mexico—Sánchez Azcona, the journalist whose paper, *México Nuevo,* had been suppressed by the government; Roque Estrada, who had been arrested with Madero in Monterrey; Gildardo Magaña, who was later to become hostile to Madero; Francisco J. Múgica, a journalist from Michoacán, and Juan Andrew Almazán, "the schoolboy revolutionist," both of whom were to become important generals; and Aquiles Serdán, a bald-headed young merchant and political activist from Puebla.

By October 25 Madero and his friends had drawn up the 2500-word "Plan of San Luis Potosí," a proclamation of revolutionary principles and, in effect, a declaration of war on the Díaz government. The election of the previous July was declared null. The presidency of Díaz was not recognized. Instead, Madero was declared provisional President of Mexico, to serve until free elections could be held. In terms of political philosophy and purpose it was not as far-seeing and comprehensive as had been the program of the Liberal party, published four years earlier. It was, on the other hand, more specific as to the immediate steps. All citizens were called upon to take up arms at 6 P.M. on Sunday, November 20, 1910, to overthrow the "illegitimate" government of Porfirio Díaz.

The plan was deliberately backdated to October 5, 1910, Madero's last day in San Luis Potosí, in the hope of avoiding any allegation of violation of the United States neutrality laws by a conspiracy against a friendly government.

Madero and his fellow plotters were to have very little difficulty with U.S. authorities. There was certainly nothing like the troubles encountered by Ricardo Flores Magón and his Liberal party. The Maderistas were not dangerous radicals. Many of them—as did Madero himself— came from important families with good connections in the United States. In addition, the United States was beginning to be disillusioned with Porfirio Díaz. He had granted important oil concessions to the British firm of Pearson & Son, to the distinct annoyance of Standard Oil and other U.S. business circles (it was to be suggested later—and subsequently disproved—that Standard Oil had contributed heavily to Madero's war chest). U.S. mining interests were eager for more concessions than the Díaz government was willing to give them. He had refused to renew the U. S. Navy's lease on its base on Magdalena Bay in Baja California, an important coaling station, and was thought to be favoring the Japanese navy. He was giving aid and comfort to José Santos Zelaya, the anti-U.S. president of Nicaragua, and had even sent a Mexican gunboat to bring him safely to exile in Mexico. His Secretary of the Treasury, José Yves Limantour, was strengthening Mexico's European financial connections. All of these things eased matters for Madero and his fellow conspirators.

Madero's temporary headquarters was attacked by some unidentified men—supposedly Mexican secret service agents; and on two occasions there were warrants for his arrest. But on the whole he had little trouble. The journalist Sánchez Azcona was to write: "Our actions had the sympathy of the people of the southern part of the U.S. . . . At their own risk some lower authorities of the administration of that country, close to us in friendship and sympathetic with our aims, voluntarily neglected the vigilance which their positions obligated them to exercise over us. In this way we could acquire and transfer supplies to Mexican territory . . ."

In addition, Madero was tactfully cultivating U.S. public opinion, explaining at every opportunity—and in careful, moderate terms—the conditions in Mexico against which they were struggling, the injustices that had occurred, the reasons for his position. He would, somewhat later, advise the U. S. State Department and the various foreign embassies in Washington of what was happening: "The national insurrection is just and necessary because the Mexican people have exhausted in vain all legal and pacific recourses, first by voting freely in the election and later by denouncing and nullifying the scandalous electoral fraud; patriotic because it has no other aim than the reestablishment of a constitutional regime; and finally necessary because for many years there has been no justice—the Mexican people live without the guarantees provided by law." He promised that the revolutionary forces would honor treaties with and debts to foreign countries when victory came.

But victory was still far in the future. The high-minded Madero was one of the most ill-prepared revolutionists in history. He had had no military experience. He had some knowledge of Napoleon's campaigns, but this was hardly applicable to the terrain of Mexico and the temperament of Mexicans. Violence and bloodshed were equally distasteful to him. But, in desperation, he had called for an armed rebellion, and he was the leader. He had to take to the field. He set up a general headquarters in the Hutchins Hotel. From a shoe dealer in Commerce Street of San Antonio he ordered a pair of yellow leather riding boots, suitable for campaigning, and prepared to go to war. He would cross the border at Eagle Pass on the night of November 19. His uncle, Catarino Benavides, promised to recruit at least five hundred, perhaps even eight hundred men, and to meet him. At the head of this group Madero would then fall on the Mexican border city, Ciudad Porfirio Díaz (Piedras Negras) and seize it as a beachhead of the revolution. He would then have a source of revenue—customs receipts—and a channel for the importation of arms, ammunition, and other supplies.

Madero and a few companions stole out of San Antonio, bought horses at Carrizo Springs, headed for the border and camped at a ranch called El Indio. On the black, starless night of the 19th the north wind, bitterly cold, was sweeping down over the plains of Texas. Madero and his friends became lost, but finally found and waded across the shallow Rio Grande. They shivered through the night, waiting for dawn and the recruits that Catarino Benavides would bring. Dawn came, but Uncle Catarino did not. He did not arrive until late in the afternoon of November 20, and instead of five hundred armed men he brought only four, and federal troops were not far behind. Disappointed, Madero returned to San Antonio.

Meanwhile his father, unaware of what was happening, had told a newspaper reporter that his son was now on Mexican soil, that the revolution had begun, that Francisco Jr. would set Mexico free or die in the attempt, and that the revolutionary movement was supported by some of the best and wealthiest people of Mexico. In the past six months Francisco Sr. and the rest of the family, vastly pleased by Francisco Jr.'s nomination for the presidency, had wholeheartedly joined his cause.

Up and down the border and as far away as Washington and New York newspapers carried brief, fragmentary—and not very accurate— reports of the activities of the "insurrection." There was heavy buying of arms and ammunition in Phoenix, Tucson, Benson, Nogales, and Naco. Stealthy departure of many Mexicans from border towns was noted. Reports of outbreaks came from Cananea, Hermosillo, and Guaymas in Sonora. Rioting was said to be taking place in Puebla. Hundreds were reported killed in a battle at Zacatecas. There were disturbances in Coahuila. In Ciudad Porfirio Díaz a Mexican had made the mistake of shouting "Viva Madero" near the federal barracks; an officer ran his sword through him. Madero's wife was reported to have organized a corps of nurses and was headed for the border. The news was uncertain, unreliable.

After the frustration at Eagle Pass, Madero held worried conferences with members of his family in San Antonio. What money he had—and his personal resources were nearly exhausted by this time—he divided among his revolutionary colleagues in San Antonio, and then left for New Orleans. Critics said that, in accordance with the advice of the Madero family, he was planning to flee to Europe and to ask Díaz for amnesty for his fellow revolutionists and, naturally, for the Madero family.

He was both disappointed and distressed. And he was greatly saddened by the death of Aquiles Serdán in Puebla. Serdán, after conferring with Madero in San Antonio, had made his way back to Puebla disguised in widow's weeds. Weapons for the November 20 uprising were stockpiled in the Serdán house at 4 Calle Santa Clara. On the 18th the house was raided by police and federal soldiers, and in the fighting Serdán, his brother Máximo and a young student, Jesús Nieto, were killed, the first martyrs of the Madero-led revolution.

Loyal Maderistas denied that Madero had even considered suing for amnesty or fleeing to Europe. Instead, he went to New Orleans where he stayed with a friend from his Paris days. He spent part of his time in New Orleans public parks, commiserating with frustrated revolutionists from Honduras. He also was darning his own socks—having no money for new ones. With a few friends he talked of a new invasion attempt by way of Veracruz, where revolutionary sentiment was vigorous. But by the end of December the plans for a Veracruz invasion had been abandoned and he was back in San Antonio. There was another abortive attempt at invasion at Las Vacas, Coahuila (now Villa Acuña, opposite Del Rio, Texas) in which Madero took no active part. After two weeks he moved to Dallas, spent a week there, then went to El Paso and hid in the home of a schoolteacher, Braulio Hernández, where he spent three weeks (at the end of which he and his brother Raul promised Hernández's wife that they would pay for their laundry as soon as there was a change in their fortunes). A warrant for Madero's arrest for violation of the neutrality laws had been issued; U.S. authorities were apparently less friendly than they had been. It was also clear by now that the huge northern state of Chihuahua, just across the river, would be one of the main theaters of revolutionary operations. Madero's call to rebellion of the previous November 20 had had effect there; there were risings by Pascual Orozco in San Isidro, by José de la Luz Blanco in Santo Tomás, by Doroteo Arango, alias Francisco "Pancho" Villa, in San Andrés—very near the state capital of Chihuahua City, and by Guillermo Baca in Parral—and fighting had been going on ever since.

There were sparks of rebellion not only in Chihuahua but all over Mexico, and the wind was rising. The Díaz government was busy stamping out the sparks, but the fires were spreading, disorganized and undirected but effective. Peasants, ranchers, schoolteachers, lawyers, students, and merchants were oiling their rifles, strapping cartridge belts across their chests and stealing off to join self-constituted *jefes* of the revolution. Some had been active in Flores Magón's Liberal party, some in Madero's Anti-Reelectionist party, but many of them had heard neither of Flores Magón nor Madero, and hadn't the least notion of the program of the Liberal party or Madero's Plan of San Luis Potosí. The time had come to strike a blow at the dictatorship which in one way or another had touched all of them. There were furious, bloody skirmishes throughout the northern two-thirds of the republic. Federal troops and the hated *rurales* were rushed from one place to another, trying to find and fight an elusive enemy that would strike and then fade away, into the sierra or the desert. The respected federal colonel, Martín Luis Guzmán (whose son, of the same name, was to become one of the greatest chroniclers of the Revolution) was sent with a troop train to reinforce the forces of General Juan J. Navarro at Pedernales, west of Chihuahua City. At the canyon of Malpaso the train was ambushed by revolutionists. Colonel Guzmán, mortally wounded, angrily shouted at the guerrillas to come out of hiding and fight like soldiers—but the guerrillas continued to shoot with devastating accuracy from well-concealed positions, and then disappeared.

It was that kind of war. The most successful of the *guerrilleros* in the early stages in the north was Pascual Orozco, a tall, thin, unsmiling man with the sinister good looks of a Western movie villain. As a muleteer and wagon master hauling metals from the mines of western Chihuahua he had learned guerrilla warfare by fighting off bandits—some of whom subsequently became his followers. He was less angry at Porfirio Díaz than he was at a nearby landowner—but the landowner was in league with the powerful Terrazas-Creel clan of Chihuahua and therefore was linked with the Díaz regime. After obeying the call to arms on November 20 he confided to a friend "I am not going to fight for Madero but for the rights of the people." At other times he sneered at Madero as "the dwarf of Parras."

By early December 1910, Orozco had besieged and captured Ciudad Guerrero, a hundred miles west of Chihuahua City on the Northwestern Railroad—the first important military victory of the Revolution. He held it for a time, successfully fighting off federal attempts to retake it, and in the process became a battlefield hero, as had Francisco Villa, a former bandit. After a time Orozco abandoned Ciudad Guerrero and captured two railroad trains to carry his troops, their horses, and equipment. He then moved north toward Ciudad Juárez. The Juárez garrison had been reduced. On the El Paso side of the river the Maderistas were hoping Orozco could capture Juárez on February 5 so that Madero could make his entry into Mexico on the anniversary of the signing of the Constitution of 1857. Orozco had some success in the settlement of Bauche, but was unable to take Juárez.

Madero by this time not only had to get out of the United States; he also had to catch up with the rebellion which was going on without him. He shaved off his beard in an effort at disguise and on February 13 he crossed the Rio Grande at Isleta, fifteen miles southeast of El Paso. At the village of Zaragoza on the Mexican side he met a small party of revolutionary troops commanded by José de la Luz Soto. With a total of 137 men Madero moved south in Chihuahua, living on canned beans and soda crackers and scraps of tough beef broiled over smoky fires. They went first to Ahumada on the Central Railroad, then west across the desert to San Buenaventura, where the townspeople put on a gala welcome and where he was joined by more troops, increasing his force to five hundred. Madero, wearing his yellow boots, riding breeches, a Norfolk jacket, and a Texas-style hat looked like a Coahuila *hacendado* out for a day in the fields except for the tricolor hatband—red, white, and green—which had been adopted as a badge of the revolutionary forces. It was a motley group. There were men in simple ranch clothes, in business suits, Indians shrouded in multicolored sarapes, miners in overalls, a few men in the brocaded jackets and tight trousers of charros, some in odd parts of captured federal uniforms. There were visored military caps, high-crowned sombreros of heavy felt with gilt adornments, wide-brimmed straw hats, artillerymen's helmets, and the putty-colored Stetsons of those who lived near the border. Some wore cowboy boots, others buttoned shoes, thigh-high brush-riders' boots of soft leather, miners' brogans, Indian *guaraches*—and there were many bare feet, particularly among the *soldaderas,* the women who followed their men to war, carrying food and infants on their backs.

Madero was told that the town of Casas Grandes, farther to the west, was held by only a reduced federal garrison, and he ordered an attack. He divided his force into three columns and marched into battle. He himself occupied an exposed position among the mysterious pre-Hispanic ruins that overlooked the town. The approach of his troops was under full observation and under heavy fire. But the fight continued—and the Maderistas might have carried the day except for the unexpected arrival of federal reinforcements under the very able Colonel Samuel García Cuellar. It ended in a complete rout for the Madero forces. Madero had shown little talent as a battlefield commander, and his losses were heavy in men and matériel. Of his five hundred men he had lost a hundred, either dead or captured; and eight valuable freight wagons were gone with badly needed supplies of ammunition and equipment. But he had also displayed great physical courage. Although he was wounded in the right arm he had stoutly resisted all advice to withdraw until the engagement became completely hopeless.

Madero retreated, on foot at first, dirty, weary, his beard only partially grown out again. He established an encampment at Bustillos, about thirty miles west of Chihuahua City. Here he was joined by Orozco, Villa, and scores more of independent leaders, and he began planning strategy for the capture of Juárez, the key border city. Here also he began to get reports on the revolutionary outbreaks throughout the Republic. His brother Gustavo estimated that by April 1911 there were more than 18,000 men bearing arms for the Revolution: 5200 in Chihuahua, 1000 in Coahuila, 4000 in Sonora, 2000 in Sinaloa, 800 in Zacatecas, 200 in Nuevo León, 1500 each in Puebla, Veracruz, and Guerrero, and 1000 in Yucatán.

Just to the south of Mexico City in the rich sugar cane growing state of Morelos, Emiliano Zapata, a young rancher from Ayala with an inscrutable Indian face and a deep resentment of the encroachments of *hacendados* on traditional Indian lands, had long been preparing for rebellion. With a group of like-minded men from Ayala he seized the local garrison, cut telephone and telegraph wires and was soon at the head of an army of eight hundred, blowing up trains, burning haciendas, and seizing towns almost at will.

Both in Morelos and in the adjacent state of Guerrero Juan Andrew Almazán, the young medical student who had been with Madero in San Antonio was campaigning, now with Zapata, now with the Figueroa brothers.

In the northwestern state of Sonora there were sharp skirmishes between federal and rebel forces at Hermosillo, at Colorado, and at Ures.

Below Sonora, there were half a dozen uprisings between January and April—at Culiacán, Palma Sola, Cosala, Llano Grande, El Palmar, and finally at Tepic—all directed by Madero's personal friend, Manuel Bonilla, an engineer.

In Zacatecas a singularly daring rebel, Luis Moya, had been fighting federal forces since early February and, early in April, made a bold raid to the very heart of the city of Zacatecas.

Venustiano Carranza, a landowner who had been a federal deputy, senator, and state governor under Díaz and who had joined the Madero forces in San Antonio, promised after various delays that he would soon take command of the revolutionary forces in his (and Madero's) home state of Coahuila.

The reports, some strange and seemingly disconnected, came from all parts of Mexico—from Veracruz, Yucatán, Tabasco, but the strangest ones came from the territory of Baja California. In the Mexicali-Tijuana area there was an entirely separate revolution going on. It was the work of the Liberal party, the followers of Ricardo Flores Magón.

When Flores Magón had been released from the U.S. federal penitentiary at Florence, Arizona, August 3, 1910, he had been approached by a Madero emissary, asking his aid in the coming struggle. Flores Magón put a price of $5000 on his cooperation. Madero ignored the demand and the breach between them became still wider. Flores Magón urged his followers on in a separate revolutionary movement, ignoring Madero's "bourgeois and capitalist" leadership. "Madero," he wrote in the spring of 1911, "is a millionaire who has increased his fabulous fortune with the sweat and tears of peons on his haciendas. The Maderista party is fighting to . . . establish a bourgeois republic like that of the United States."

Small Magonista groups had been fighting in Sonora, Veracruz, and Chihuahua completely independent of the Maderistas. One of Flores Magón's closest collaborators, Praxedis Guerrero, a young poet who came from an aristocratic family in Guanajuato, was killed in a raid on the small Chihuahua town of Janos. Others of Flores Magón's followers considered their leader's position ridiculous and went over to the Madero camp, most notable of them being Antonio I. Villareal.

The Baja California revolution was undertaken without consultation with the Maderistas. The Magonistas would, for a while, control much of the northern part of the peninsula, hoping for the establishment of a separate socialist state. Before their venture ended they would be fighting not the forces of the old Díaz regime but forces representing the Madero revolution—revolutionist against revolutionist.

CHAPTER 7

RISING TIDE

"The movement will continue so long
as there are tears to dry, griefs to comfort . . ."

Alberto Morales Jiménez, *1910, biografía de un año decisivo*

ON MARCH 7, 1911, while Madero, disheartened, his right arm in a sling,
the new yellow boots soiled with dust and blood, was retreating across
the bleak wasteland of Chihuahua after his defeat at Casas Grandes,
a French liner docked in New York. A distinguished Mexican, tall,
poised, perfectly groomed, disembarked and, with his wife, who was not
feeling well, went to the Hotel Plaza. From the moment of their arrival
in their suite the telephone began ringing. In recent days a number of
important Mexicans had arrived in New York and they all wanted to
talk to the man who had just returned from France.

The man in the Plaza was José Yves Limantour, secretary of the
Mexican treasury and the ablest man in the *científico* circle that surrounded Porfirio Díaz and ran his government. Limantour, a man with
cold gray eyes deeply recessed under an impressive forehead, was the
one who always had to explain to Don Porfirio how many ciphers it
took to make a million (Díaz was as weak in arithmetic as he was in
grammar and spelling). Limantour knew all about millions. His French-
born father had, in the 1850s, pressed a legal claim to 600,000 acres of
land which included the site of the city of San Francisco. Failing in that
suit he had built up tremendous holdings of real estate in Mexico. His
son, a skilled lawyer and prudent investor, built a huge fortune of his
own. As Díaz's financial genius, Limantour had devised Mexico's banking system, stabilized the peso (at 2.01 to the dollar), worked out a
merger of the national railroads. In France on this trip he had negotiated

a refunding of Mexico's national debt at four percent with a 200,000,000 peso loan.

While in France he had been in correspondence with Evaristo Madero, patriarch of the Madero clan and grandfather of Francisco I. Madero. Don Evaristo, one of Limantour's early law clients, was eager to see order restored to Mexico. The vast Madero properties had been placed under embargo. Their varied products could not be sold. Accounts receivable could not be collected. The properties themselves could not be mortgaged or sold to raise needed cash. The family-owned bank in Monterrey had been placed under government control. Limantour had an affection for Evaristo, whom he addressed as "dear old friend," and was himself concerned over what was happening in Mexico. He was particularly worried over the massing of 20,000 U.S. troops in San Antonio, fearing U.S. intervention if disorder continued. He agreed to meetings in New York with Francisco, Sr., and Gustavo Madero. He also would meet with Díaz's ambassador to Washington, Francisco León de la Barra, and with Francisco Vázquez Gómez. The last was Madero's confidential agent in Washington. Vázquez Gómez had been the candidate for vice-president on the Anti-Reelectionist ticket with Madero in 1910, but had opposed revolution, had frequently disagreed with his running mate. He was at this point resentful because the Maderos were not providing him with sufficient funds. He was forced to stay in the unimpressive Imperial Hotel while the Maderos lodged in a fourth-floor suite at the Astor.

Even if they could afford a suite at the Astor, the Madero family as a whole was hard-pressed financially, and the plight of Gustavo Madero was worse than the others. He, more than any other member of the family, had adopted the cause of Francisco, Jr., as his own. When "Panchito" was imprisoned the previous year, Gustavo had gone on with the work of organizing Anti-Reelectionist clubs. He had purchased a newspaper for propaganda purposes and was arrested and imprisoned briefly on a trumped-up charge of attempting to subvert an army officer. He had joined Madero in San Antonio, where the Revolution was plotted, and took on the difficult assignment of raising funds for the coming struggle. He tried, unsuccessfully, to borrow on Madero properties. He then tried to sell a series of old Mexican bonds to U.S. interests. The bonds had a face value of $5,000,000, but they had been repudiated almost a half century before, in the Juárez administration. Gustavo offered the lot for $1,000,000 with the promise of redemption at face value when the Revolution was won. There were no takers. He then resorted to more desperate measures. He held a concession for construction of a railroad across the state of Zacatecas, connecting Mexico's two trunk lines, and had interested a French banker in underwriting the bond issue. The banker, Henri Rochette, had advanced 750,000 pesos as first payment on the issue—and Gustavo had proceeded to use the funds for the Revolution. More than 300,000 pesos had gone for arms and ammunition. Fat fees had been paid to lawyers and "confidential agents" in New York, Washington, San Antonio, and El Paso. Substantial sums had been paid out for pro-Madero propaganda, for travel, and other expenses. Now, in March 1911, only some 3000 pesos remained and Gustavo was in trouble. The French banker had begun legal proceedings against him, and Gustavo was having to spend much of his time hiding in a friend's apartment in 69th Street.

Of all the male members of the Madero clan (one contemporary source estimated that there were 173 of them, counting sons, brothers, uncles, and cousins) Gustavo was the most dashing and, as the Mexicans say, the most *vivo,* or sharp. Most of the Madero men were dour, humorless, thrifty, and cautious. Gustavo was gregarious, voluble, dressed in high fashion, and had the instincts of a gambler. He was tall, well set up, fair-skinned, clean-shaven, and one of his bright blue eyes (the right one) was glass. Because of this he was often called *Ojo Parado* (Fixed Eye); and because of his energy, his enthusiasm, and his ability to get things done one way or another, legal or not, he was also called "the muscle of the Revolution." He was also a man of great courage.

In the various conferences which Limantour had in New York with the Maderos, with Vázquez Gómez and De la Barra, the suave finance minister's position began to emerge. He conceded that Francisco Madero, Jr., had attracted a strong following among the Mexican people, that the demand for reforms posed a real threat to the peace of Mexico and might have to be met in some measure. He refused to discuss the possibility of President Díaz being forced to resign. This was unacceptable. But at the same time he agreed that Díaz could not live forever and might not be able to finish out the term of office to which he had recently been reelected. He knew that the prospect of Vice-President Corral succeeding to the presidency was not a happy one for Mexico. He also knew the precarious state of Corral's health, and that Corral probably would not live long enough to step into the presidency if and when Díaz did leave it. Some rearrangement of Díaz's cabinet to provide an acceptable successor might be the answer. Francisco Madero, Sr., suggested that Limantour himself was the man best suited to succeed Díaz. Limantour would have none of it, but pointed out that Francisco León de la Barra, the Ambassador to Washington, would be a wise choice. A secret code with which Limantour could communicate with Francisco Madero, Sr., was agreed upon. Such messages would bear the cable address "Wardnot" and would be delivered to Edward Ward, a clerk in the office of some Madero friends at 69 Wall Street.

Limantour returned to Mexico City on March 20, apparently committed to work for changes that would ease the revolutionary pressures. Four days later most of Díaz's cabinet resigned, obviously by request. Of the resulting changes the most significant was the appointment of Ambassador De la Barra as Minister of Foreign Relations, putting him first in line of succession to the presidency after Corral. A week later President Díaz addressed the opening of the 25th Legislature in the new Chamber of Deputies building, and promised laws which would provide more effective suffrage, would make reelection impossible and would give some autonomy to local government. He also promised steps toward division of land and judicial reform. A few days later Vice-President Corral was granted an eight-month leave of absence and sailed for Europe, never to return. The changes all seemed clearly aimed at calming the popular unrest stirred up by the Maderista movement.

But the movement was not to be so easily stopped. From his temporary "capital," the hacienda of Bustillos, Chihuahua, provisional President Madero made tentative, probing military movements toward the state capital, the city of Chihuahua—just enough to guarantee a concentration of federal troops there, and then moved north toward Juárez on the border which was thus left with a reduced garrison. A military novice, Madero had learned much of strategy and tactics in a few weeks from the 3000 self-taught soldiers who now surrounded him. He knew now that the federal army, supposedly 30,000 strong and invincible, was much less than that. Greedy commanders had kept their rosters padded and pocketed supply money. The effective strength of the army was perhaps no more than 14,000 and it was spread thin now, coping with insurrections in all parts of the republic.

By April 19 Madero and his revolutionary army had moved north and were camped outside of Juárez. Madero moved into a tiny adobe house on the Las Flores ranch, on the bank of the Rio Grande just to the west of the town, across from the Guggenheim smelter. This was his temporary presidential residence, called the "Gray House." He was joined by his loyal and stouthearted wife, Sara. Nearby there was a temporary wooden bridge across the Rio Grande. He crossed to the American side and, in the Sheldon Hotel, he was able to bathe and change to civilian clothes, which he greatly preferred to his improvised battlefield gear.

Immediately upon his arrival Madero had sent a message to the federal commander in Juárez, General Juan Navarro, demanding his surrender. Navarro refused, but within three days a ten-day armistice had been arranged in order to permit negotiations with envoys who had just arrived in El Paso from Mexico City. The envoys, Oscar Braniff and Toribio Esquivel Obregón, had no official capacity but had come at the suggestion of Limantour to explore the possibility of settlement.

The armistice was repeatedly extended. The negotiations that went on for the next month were marked by confusion, misunderstanding and, occasionally, by violent interruption. Madero's position in the negotiations seemed to shift from firm insistence on Díaz's resignation to a more conciliatory position in which he would demand only the establishment of the principles of effective suffrage and no reelection, on appointment of revolutionary governors in approximately half of the Mexican states, and withdrawal of federal troops from northern Mexico.

The negotiations with Braniff and Esquivel Obregón were inconclusive. But on May 3 an authorized representative of Díaz arrived, the eminent jurist and justice of the supreme court, Francisco Carvajal. It began to be clear that Díaz needed peace and needed it quickly. Carvajal had his first meeting with Madero seated in an automobile on the outskirts of Juárez, and got the impression that Madero did not demand the resignation of President Díaz. But the next day when he met with Madero's peace commissioners the Maderistas insisted upon the resignation of both Díaz and Corral; Madero himself would resign from his "provisional presidency" and an interim President acceptable to both sides would hold office until elections could be held to select a constitutional President.

Madero appeared to be vacillating between his family's eagerness for peace and the insistent demands of his revolutionary followers for a clean sweep of the old regime. Restlessness was growing—and among the most restless were Orozco and Villa, the guerrilla warriors who, by now, had been inactive for more than a fortnight while the confusing negotiations went on. On May 5, the anniversary of the Battle of Puebla in 1862, Madero summoned the revolutionary troops, made a speech commemorating the national holiday, and announced promotions for many of the *jefes,* Orozco to the rank of brigadier general, Villa and others to the grade of colonel. He was generously applauded.

The May 5 celebration in Mexico City was different. The annual parade was canceled; the government wanted no crowds, and in addition the armed forces who would normally make up much of the marching column were otherwise engaged. Díaz, who always before had taken part in the celebration, stayed home; a wreath in his name was laid on the tomb of Ignacio Zaragoza, hero of the Battle of Puebla.

After the Battle of Casas Grandes, Díaz had confidently predicted an early end to the insurrection. Now he conceded its seriousness and on May 7 addressed a manifesto to the Mexican people, saying "the President . . . will retire from power when his conscience tells him that, upon retiring, he will not turn the country over to anarchy, and he will do it in a decorous fashion becoming to the nation and befitting an executive who may have committed many errors but who also had known how to defend his nation and serve it with loyalty."

The public was confused. Did this mean Díaz really would resign? Soon? Ever? Would the insurrection become a widespread civil war? The newspapers were of little help. Defeats of revolutionists in obscure places were displayed prominently, their victories largely ignored. A report that rebels in the surrounding mountains would soon sweep down on the capital was branded as a vicious canard, but in the same breath the correspondent said that the city was ready for whatever might befall it. A dispatch from El Paso said that in the rebel camp outside of Juárez the manifesto of President Díaz had caused "jubilation." A dispatch from Paris quoted Vice-President Corral: Peace would prevail and he would be back in Mexico by fall. There was a rash of advertisements for Dr. Miles' Nervina and Dr. Richards' pills for nervous people. For sturdier souls the Tampico News Company, located only a block away from Díaz's town house, offered a complete stock of "Winchester and Marlin carbines of all calibers, double action and automatic pistols and genuine American cartridges."

But neither the sturdy souls nor the timid ones could take much comfort from the news that filtered through government censorship. In the nearby states of Morelos and Puebla, Emiliano Zapata was marauding with a thousand men behind him, seeming to take towns and villages at will—Jonacatepec, Yautepec, Izucar de Matamoros. When federal troops arrived the hard-riding Zapatistas simply faded away, only to reappear later to take another village, burn another hacienda or blow up another train. In Veracruz, San Andrés Tuxtla was in Maderista hands and other towns were threatened. Hermosillo, the capital of Sonora, and Saltillo, capital of Coahuila, were both menaced by insurrectionists. The Arrieta brothers had taken the city of Durango, lost it, and then placed it under a crippling siege. In Guerrero the Figueroa brothers had seized Acapulco and Chilapa.

In the north there was uneasy tension. Colonel Edgar Z. Steever, commander of the U. S. 4th Cavalry at Fort Bliss, Texas, warned both Madero and the federal commander at Juárez, General Navarro, that if fighting broke out and bullets fell on the American side—as they inevitably would—U.S. forces would intervene. The armistice negotiations with Carvajal had come to an impasse and Madero, fearful of U.S. intervention, announced to his troops that instead of making the final assault on Juárez they would withdraw to the south and prepare for an advance on Mexico City. In Mexico City newspapers printed a somewhat hysterical El Paso dispatch saying that Madero would move to the south with 100,000 troops—roughly thirty times the number actually under his command.

Madero's troops were rough, unlettered men for the most part. They knew little of military discipline and order, and there was little organizational structure. Benjamin Viljoen, a veteran of the Boer War who had become a New Mexico rancher and, later, joined forces with Madero, referred to his troops as commandos. Giuseppe Garibaldi, another foreign-born Maderista, grandson of the Italian patriot—described the men he commanded as a "group." Most of the Mexicans referred to military units simply as *gente* or people—the *gente* of Orozco, the *gente* of Villa.

The loyalties of these *gente* were to their immediate leaders. Ever since Madero took the field there had been a strong tendency to insubordination. Madero's commissioning of the presumptuous Garibaldi, who wore a tan riding suit and a green velour hat with the narrow brim turned down, had caused mutinous resentment. Garibaldi was widely regarded as a filibuster. There were also among Madero's troops many Liberal party adherents, followers of Flores Magón. Madero, who said they were not Liberals but Socialists, had trouble controlling them. They resisted orders and wore red ribbons on their hats instead of the Maderista tricolor. During the advance toward Juárez six of their leaders announced their intention of separating themselves from the Maderista forces. Madero ordered them thrown into jail, and the resentment continued.

The armistice and peace negotiations had kept the rebel troops in an uneasy state of suspension. In the various camps on the outskirts of Juárez there was much grumbling. The revolutionary soldiers were without pay, poorly clad—and on the northern plains of Chihuahua the nights can be bitingly cold, even in May. They had little food and no opportunity to live off the country as they had while actively campaigning.

And there was, finally, the ill-concealed animosity of the tall, hard-muscled Orozco for Madero. He had under his command at least 1500 effectives. The federal forces in Juárez, including the regular garrison, the Navarro brigade and the *rurales,* amounted to about seven hundred. Although Juárez was said to be well fortified and entrenched, odds were heavily on the side of the rebels, and Orozco and his men were eager for a victory that appeared easy. Orozco, 30-30 Winchester in hand and speaking in the laconic Chihuahua drawl, told his men repeatedly that Juárez could be taken *con puro fusil,* with nothing but a rifle. Madero's proposal of a move to the south to avoid the possibility of U.S. intervention heightened the unrest. There was much muttering and repetition of the old *dicho,* "Poor Mexico, so far from God and so close to the United States."

Insults were exchanged continually between rebels and federals. Colonel Manuel Tamborel often shared a bottle of brandy with the El Paso newspaperman, Tim Turner, and used such occasions to issue deliberately insulting statements. One was that the rebels, not being men enough to take Juárez, were raiding defenseless ranches and stealing chickens. Such slurs infuriated Orozco.

With the connivance of Villa and other leaders Orozco plotted to break the peace. A small detachment of rebels led by Captain Reyes Robinson exchanged first insults and then shots with a federal outpost at El Molino at 10 A.M. on May 8. Orozco and Villa had absented themselves in El Paso at the time, and Orozco was sitting in a barber chair being shaved when the expected news was brought to him. Pretending surprise, he left, half-shaven, and with Villa crossed back to the Mexican side and innocently asked Madero what had happened. Madero ordered them to halt the fighting—and meanwhile sent a message to Navarro saying he was ordering a cease-fire. Orozco and Villa, instead of obeying Madero, threw more troops into the fray and reported back to their worried commander-in-chief that the fighting was too widespread to be contained—as indeed it was by this time. It blazed all over Juárez—at the international line, with Orozco advancing from the west, on the south side of the town where Villa took command, and on the east where José de la Luz Blanco was striking.

The attackers had two pieces of artillery. One was a small, muzzle-loading brass cannon, a relic of the Mexican-American war of 1846–48. It had been stolen from the lawn of the El Paso City Hall. It was effective at short range, firing charges of scrap iron, nails, and stones. The other was a long-barreled, small-bore, unrifled cannon which the rebels themselves had manufactured in the machine shops of a logging camp at Madera, Chihuahua. Its first shot whistled high and away from the battle. The second struck and punctured the water tank which supplied the federal troops in Juárez. With the third shot the makeshift cannon blew up.

Navarro's troops were well entrenched, but their water and electricity were cut off, and the rebels advanced under cover, dynamiting their way from one building to another.

The revolution was running away from Madero again. He vacillated, ordering a cease-fire, following it up with an order to attack, then again ordering a cease-fire, then still another order for attack. The attack went on without interruption. In the course of it the sharp-tongued Colonel Tamborel and many of his men were killed. Two days after the outbreak General Navarro surrendered with all his troops—big, strapping cavalrymen with red-trimmed uniforms and black varnished kepis and the little foot soldiers in shoddy blue uniforms with shaven heads. The first major battle was over—won by the forces of the Revolution.

VICTORY AT JUAREZ

"The Revolution was not the work of
saints but of men of flesh and bone, men
of passions and of many defects."

Francisco L. Urquizo, *Origen del
ejército constitucionalista*

MADERO ACCEPTED THE VICTORY that he had really not wished for, set up
his headquarters in the prefecture of Juárez, and organized his government, beginning with a provisional cabinet. His appointment of Venustiano Carranza as Secretary of War caused immediate trouble. Carranza
was not a popular man. He had repeatedly delayed taking an active
part in the Revolution. He was known to have been a partisan of General
Reyes, the former governor of the state of Nuevo León. For these
things and for his complacency Carranza was disliked generally by the
active revolutionists, particularly by Orozco who had hoped to be Minister of War himself. Orozco sneered at all of Madero's ministers and
other close advisers as *músicos* (musicians) who had done nothing to
further the Revolution.

There were other irritants. Díaz's negotiators, Oscar Braniff and
Toribio Esquivel Obregón, had slyly been working on Orozco's pride,
assuring him that he was the real hero of the Revolution and suggesting
that he was being ignored and, worse, snubbed by Madero and the
Madero family. Orozco was soon complaining that his troops were still
hungry, while Madero and his circle were enjoying victory banquets
across the river in El Paso.

Finally there was the question of the captured federal commander,
Navarro. Orozco and most of his men wanted to shoot him. Navarro
had bayoneted his prisoners, and in the retaking of Cierro Prieto a few

months earlier had executed a score or more of innocent civilians as well.

Three days after the fall of Juárez there was a showdown. Very early in the morning Orozco had a conference in the Sheldon Hotel in El Paso with Toribio Esquivel Obregón. Then, with an armed escort, Orozco, followed by Villa with more armed men, went to Madero's headquarters, where he demanded that the captive general, Navarro, be turned over to him. Madero refused. Orozco seized the smaller man by his lapels, brandishing a pistol in his left hand.

"I am the President . . ." Madero exclaimed.

"But you are not going out of here, Señor Madero," said Orozco, and raised his pistol. At this point Abraham González and Gustavo Madero, the latter also armed with a pistol, grappled with Orozco. In the struggle Madero managed to free himself and made his way to the door and the street where he faced a hundred of Orozco's armed men. He climbed on the rear seat of an open automobile and spoke to the troops.

"I am the President of the republic," he shouted. "I initiated this libertarian movement and I have sustained it with my sincerity and my fortune. I am the chief of the Revolution, and Orozco is no more than one of its generals. They [meaning, apparently, the Díaz envoys] have deceived Orozco. I hold no rancor toward him. I offer him my hand as a friend and colleague, and I invite him to continue to fight under my government."

Orozco, who had followed Madero out the door and into the automobile, pistol still in hand, ignored Madero's outstretched right hand. He appeared ready to say something, but words had never come easily to him, and he said nothing. Madero continued, his voice rising:

"Here I am. Kill me if you wish. Either with me or with Orozco. Who is the President of the republic?"

Someone shouted "Viva Madero" and the cry was taken up by most of the men in the street. Orozco looked at his feet, holstered his gun, and this time when Madero extended his hand Orozco took it. Villa, who had betrayed Madero once in the attack on Juárez and had been, with Orozco's urging, prepared to do it again, shouldered his way through the crowd, grimacing with emotion. He grasped the side of the automobile and pleaded: "Shoot me, Señor Madero, punish me, punish me." Madero smiled and reassured him: "Why shoot you, a brave man? Go, calm your boys and get them ready to continue the fight."

In the showdown with the troops in front of his headquarters Madero had again—just as he had at Casas Grandes—exhibited great personal courage. Nor was this all. Knowing the volatile tempers of most of his revolutionary troops, their tendency to insubordination and their hatred for General Navarro, he next loaded the defeated federal general into his car and personally escorted him to the international bridge and saw him safely on the American side under a pledge not to take up arms against the Revolution. Madero then returned to his headquarters and did his best to erase the evidence of disunity that the struggle with Orozco had revealed. Conciliatory statements were issued, money, supplies, and equipment were issued to the restless troops. A little later arrangements were made for the discreet withdrawal to the interior of Chihuahua of both Orozco and Villa. Peace negotiations were then resumed.

The fall of Juárez was quickly followed by news of other impressive rebel victories. Tehuacán, a spa in northern Puebla much favored by wealthy people of Mexico City, fell to the revolutionists. The Arrieta brothers retook Durango after a fifteen-day siege. Federal forces were compelled to evacuate Hermosillo, capital of Sonora. Cananea, the mining town in northern Sonora which had been the scene of the bloody strike in 1906, fell to revolutionists under Juan Cabral. Federal forces evacuated Torreón under Maderista pressure, but before revolutionary forces could reestablish order the townspeople, sympathetic with the Revolution, had murdered two hundred Chinese residents for supposed cooperation with the federals (all they had done was complain that the revolutionists had robbed the local Bank of China). Pachuca and Tulancingo in the state of Hidalgo, just to the north of Mexico City, were seized by the rebels, as was Saltillo, capital of the northern state of Coahuila. Just to the south of Mexico City, Zapatistas seized Cuautla, another resort town favored by people from the capital; they burned the municipal palace and the principal hotel. Farther to the south in the state of Guerrero an army of 4000 Indians, armed with machetes and arrows and carrying a banner of the Virgin of Guadalupe—just as had the followers of Father Hidalgo a century before—helped the Figueroa brothers take Chilpancingo. In far away Baja California the anti-Madero Magonistas consolidated their position in Tijuana and prepared to advance on Ensenada.

On May 21 Cuernavaca, capital of the state of Morelos, was evacuated by federal troops and taken over by the Zapatistas—an event that normally would have been of cataclysmic importance in view of its proximity to Mexico City. But as things were it was almost overlooked. For in Juárez on that day the representatives of Madero and Díaz finally agreed upon peace. At 10:30 at night they met in front of the Juárez customs house—which by now had become the headquarters of the Revolution—and by the light of automobile headlamps signed the six-point peace pact.

The treaty of Juárez provided for the resignation of Díaz and Corral before the end of May, and for the succession, as interim President, of

Francisco León de la Barra, recently the ambassador to Washington and now Minister of Foreign Relations. De la Barra would call national elections in which a constitutional President would be chosen. The interim government would be obedient to public opinion and would indemnify damages resulting from the Revolution. Hostilities would cease, and revolutionary troops would be discharged, once steps had been taken to guarantee peace and public order; telegraph and railway lines would be restored.

Communication facilities were meager under the best of circumstances and worse now after the months of fighting, and it was to be many weeks before news of the peace treaty would reach some isolated areas where rebels and federal troops were locked in combat. But the news reached Mexico City almost immediately. Government censorship had been eased and there was surging excitement. Shops along the Calle San Francisco and the Avenida Juárez pulled down their steel shutters. Throngs of blue-clad laborers and white-clad Indians, students and office workers linked arms and marched through the streets, waving banners with the revolutionary slogans of Effective Suffrage and No Reelection. They beat on tin chamber pots, shouted *vivas* for Madero and *mueras* for Díaz, and chanted the revolutionary jingle,

> Little work, lots of *dinero*,
> Beans for all—Viva Madero!

It was a gibe at Díaz's favorite toast, "long live work," as well as a salute to the Revolution.

Don Porfirio had been little seen since May 7 when he made his last appearance before the Chamber of Deputies and offered his conditional resignation. On that occasion he had ridden alone in his open coach through the Calle Bolívar. In his black suit and silk hat he had seemed more somber and austere than usual. Twelve outriders in blue uniforms and silver helmets preceded and followed his carriage to keep back the crowds—but there were no crowds. Passers-by glanced casually at the dignified old man in the carriage and went on their way, no longer awed, no longer excited by the presence of greatness. After his message to the Chamber—words calculated to bring a warm and grateful response from the Mexican public—there was open scoffing at Díaz and his "conscience."

More and more the old man stayed in the town house in the Calle Cadena, hearing only faintly the cheers for Madero, the "little madman" from Coahuila whom he had so grossly underestimated. He saw few of his advisers: Limantour, who kept him posted on negotiations at Juárez; his Minister of War, General Manuel González Cosío, who brought him distressing news of successes of the "bandits" in Morelos and Hidalgo. González Cosío was also still trying to explain why the federal army could field so few troops—less than half the number carried on the rosters. At this point General Reyes was on his way back from Europe; when he arrived Díaz planned to reinstall him as Minister of War—if there was time. Sometimes he saw Don Guillermo Landa y Escandon, governor of the Federal District, and remembered the bird shooting they had enjoyed on the old hacienda of the Conde de Regla, that fabulously wealthy man who had owned the Real del Monte mines and had been able to loan the King of Spain a billion pesos. And he saw General Fernando González, governor of the state of Mexico and son of the man he, Díaz, had installed as President in 1880—the only time he had allowed the presidency to get out of his hands. He would see his son, Porfirito, who now lived in the house with pink cupolas in the Calle Humboldt into which the fifty-four-year-old Díaz and his nineteen-year-old wife had moved in 1884, the year he was elected to the presidency for the second time. He did not see his daughter Luz, who was with her husband, Francisco Rincón Gallardo, on their hacienda of Santa Maria in Aguascalientes, nor Amada, who was married to Ignacio de la Torre, owner of great estates in Morelos and who had, for a while, employed as a groom that *bandido,* Emiliano Zapata.

The old man was suffering from an ulcerated molar, and his wife, Carmen, a handsome woman of forty-five, would allow few people in to see him. Between rare visits the old man had ample time for reflection—and for puzzlement. He was the same Porfirio Díaz he had always been—or was he? He could still command, he still had the old authority. His physical strength was faltering, but his spirit was still strong, the spirit that had carried him through forty-six battles. He was still a man much admired, much respected, and he could recall with pleasure all the honors that had been heaped on him at the time of the Centennial celebration, only eight months ago; and in January he had received still another foreign decoration—the Collar of the Red Eagle, sent to him by Kaiser Wilhelm II of Germany and presented by Baron Hartmann von Richthofen. He had not changed. He was the same Porfirio Díaz, but Mexico had changed. Many of the changes were of his doing, the millions in foreign trade, the billions in foreign investments, the railroads, the port works in Veracruz, Coatzacoalcos, Salina Cruz, Manzanillo, the postal and telegraph system—so efficient until recently. All this and still a surplus of 11,000,000 pesos in the treasury. These changes were good; but the 15,000,000 people of Mexico had changed. They were no longer grateful, faithful, obedient, afraid of punishment. They no longer knew what was good for them and for Mexico. They wanted him to leave.

Soon after the peace treaty was signed in Juárez, Díaz drafted his statement of resignation. It lay on the broad table in the first-floor library of the house in Calle Cadena—unsigned.

On May 24 rumors flooded the city that Don Porfirio's resignation would be presented that day to the Chamber of Deputies. The public galleries of the new chamber at the corner of Doncelos and Bolívar, five blocks from Díaz's house at Cadena and Bolívar, were crowded with would-be spectators of the historic event—and the crowd overflowed into the streets outside, where still other crowds marched turbulently and noisily. Mounted policemen were on patrol, clubs in hand, pistols at their side.

When it became apparent that the expected resignation was not to be delivered that day the disappointed crowds withdrew and—more by instinct than by plan—moved toward the Zócalo, the heart of the city and the nation. On one side stood the National Palace, on another the cathedral, on another the Municipal Palace. The great and historic square had once been the principal plaza of Tenochtitlan, the center of the empire of Anahuac, a place of palaces, pyramids, treasure houses, and temples tended by priests with blood-clotted hair who tore the still-beating hearts from the heaving chests of their victims. Here Moctezuma, a prisoner in one of his own palaces, had been slain. Here, on the rubble of palaces, temples, and pyramids, Cortés had begun building a Spanish city in the New World, a city that was to be magnificently Spanish in appearance but never wholly Spanish in spirit. Here, in the National Palace, there had been a motley collection of powerful men, viceroys and grand inquisitors, the gaudy Iturbide, the sinister Santa Anna, the perplexed Maximilian, the solemn Juárez. Here, for so many years, Porfirio Díaz had ruled, and here, once each year, he had tolled the liberty bell and repeated Father Hidalgo's *grito* of independence—words that had become almost meaningless in his strict regime. Here, finally, came the people of Mexico, clamoring for the end of *porfirismo*.

The air was threatening. It was the end of the dry season that had begun at the time of the Centennial celebration the previous fall. Gusty winds from the east swept dust and grit from the plateau and sent it flying through the streets of the city, irritating eyes and tempers. Late in the afternoon great inky clouds billowed up, concealing the Sierra of Ajusco to the southwest and the snow peaks of Ixtaccihuatl and Popocatepetl to the southeast. Still the crowds came, shouting, beating on tin pots, waving improvised banners, streaming in from all directions. By dusk the streets leading into the Zócalo were massed with people— San Francisco and 16 de Septiembre on the west, Relox and Empedradillo on the north. And the Zócalo itself was massed with a crowd that no one could count—estimates ran as high as 75,000. Although they did little more than make noise, wave their banners and shout for the delayed resignation, they seemed menacing. At 9 P.M. mounted police rushed from the gates of the National Palace and charged the crowd, wielding the flat sides of their sabers, shouting orders to disperse. The people retaliated by striking at the horses with their banner staves. Many police were thrown and members of the crowd were trampled. The police charged the mass three times and failed to break it up. On the fourth charge the angered mob, screaming with rage attacked the police in earnest, pulling them from their horses, fists and staves flying. Machine guns opened up from the roof of the National Palace, and riflemen fired from the towers of the cathedral on the north, from the roof of the Municipal Palace on the south and from the commercial buildings and the National Pawnshop on the west. Still the crowd did not disperse. Then, suddenly the rain that had threatened since midafternoon, poured down. The mob that had stood up to sabers and gunfire, melted away, seeking shelter from the storm. Newspapers loyal to the Díaz regime reported the toll of the disorder as seven killed and forty wounded. But eyewitnesses said at least two hundred had died.

While the mob had surged through the streets in the afternoon Porfirio Díaz, in agony with his infected jaw and dazed by opiates, had made his way from his second-floor bedroom to the first-floor library. He sat at the desk staring at the resignation which awaited only his signature and the date. Without signing it he fell asleep in the chair and slept there until early evening. Then Doña Carmen helped him back upstairs and the old dictator slept soundly through the stormy night. The next morning, early, he was back at the desk and, with his wife steadying his shaky hand, signed the document. It was addressed to the Chamber of Deputies.

"The Mexican people who have heaped honors on me," it said, ". . . have rebelled . . . claiming that my exercise of the supreme power is the cause of their insurrection. I know of no act of mine which would motivate such a social phenomenon; but acknowledging, without conceding, that I may be unconsciously at fault, I am unable to rationalize or judge my culpability . . . Respecting, as I always have respected, the will of the people . . . I come before the supreme representation of the nation to resign without reservation the position of constitutional President of the republic . . . I do it with good reason, when to retain it would mean the shedding of more Mexican blood, impairment of the national credit, destruction of . . . its resources and exposing its policies to international conflict. I hope that when the passions that accompany any revolution are calmed that a conscientious and thorough investigation will render to the national conscience a correct judgment which will permit me to die, taking with me in the depth of my soul the esteem which I have always and will always devote to my countrymen." The president of the Chamber of Deputies arrived in the Calle Cadena to receive the historic document from the old man's hands. The new Minister of Foreign Relations, De la Barra, who would become interim President, also called.

That day and part of the following night Díaz spent in the completion of arrangements that had already been begun. At the old San Lázaro station, the terminal of the narrow gauge Interoceanic road to Veracruz, a special train had been waiting for three days. At 2 A.M. of May 26 automobiles began to arrive at the station, driving slowly and quietly through the empty moonlit streets of the capital. Doña Carmen and her relatives, Porfirito and his family and servants, accompanied by scores of trunks and valises, arrived first. Then at 2:30 A.M. the long yellow automobile of General González arrived, its lights dimmed. Out of it stepped Porfirio Díaz, muffled to the eyes. Then the old man entered the Pullman car reserved for him and started on the road to exile. He spent a few days in Veracruz, holding court for the admirers who came to call and muttering "They've turned the mares loose—let's see who can corral them again." He then boarded the German ship *Ypiranga* and sailed for Europe where he would spend the last four years of his life. On shipboard he gave an embrace to General Victoriano Huerta, who had commanded the guard train escorting Díaz from Mexico City to Veracruz. Huerta, a bullet-headed little Indian with weak eyes and a rumbling bass voice, was profuse in his expression of sorrow and loyalty. Díaz's last words to him: "Now they will be convinced, by hard experience, that the only way to govern the country well is the way I did it." Huerta was to remember the words.

On the same night that Porfirio Díaz sailed from Veracruz, Francisco I. Madero attended a victory banquet in the Toltec Club of El Paso, just across the border from the scene of his triumph. El Paso businessmen were the hosts. The U. S. 4th Cavalry Band played. There were liquors and wines, fillet of sole *ravigotte,* sweetbreads *à la Madero,* beef tenderloin with mushrooms. Madero nibbled at his potatoes and asparagus. At his left hand sat Mayor C. E. Kelly, the toastmaster. At his right was General Navarro, the federal commander whose life Madero had saved. There was much oratory, much talk of military glory and freedom. When it was Madero's time he spoke modestly, thanking his largely American audience for the sympathy and hospitality. And he added that he felt very sorry that his men had stolen the old cannon from the El Paso City Hall lawn to use in the attack on Juárez. And he promised that Mexico would replace it with another cannon if the original could not be found.

THE TRIUMPH

"Our Revolution has been like an earthquake, a cataclysm . . ."
Antonio Díaz Soto y Gama

EARLY IN THE MORNING of June 7, 1911, a severe earthquake struck Mexico City, shattering windows, tumbling walls and piling rubble in the streets. Two hundred seven persons were killed.

A little later in the day Francisco I. Madero, victorious chief of the Revolution, made his triumphant entry into the capital. The horror and sadness of the one event were diminished by the joy and exuberance of the other. Before the day was over the people of the capital were singing a jingle:

"Some say yes and some say no,
But when Madero arrived even the earth trembled."

Madero's four-day journey from the northern frontier had been a festive procession. Unable to move directly south from Juárez because of railroad destruction, the Apostle of the Revolution had gone over to the American side and traveled down to Eagle Pass. Here he crossed the bridge over the Rio Grande, saluting a floral arch that had been erected for the day. He entered the Mexican border town which under the dictatorship had been known as Ciudad Porfirio Díaz but which now, in honor of the occasion, had resumed its pre-dictatorship name of Piedras Negras.

Madero stood on the balcony of the Municipal Palace in Piedras Negras and spoke. He remarked on how much easier it was now to enter his native land; only two hundred days earlier he had failed here in his first effort to launch the Revolution on Mexican soil. He paid tribute to the American people "who were with us in the moment of trial." And he spoke on the theme that was dearest to him: "In winning our liberties we have achieved a new era. It is the era of the vote. Live it bravely, and do not forget that it will bring you victories more fruitful and important than those we have won on fields of battle."

A special train was made up and Madero started south. At each stop his official party grew. Other revolutionists boarded the train; so did increasing numbers of the vast Madero family.

No village was too small for a stop, and no hour inconvenient. At the tiny Coahuila settlement of Hipólito there was a great throng with a band and fireworks at 4 A.M. In Madero's home town of San Pedro de las Colonias 10,000 people waited at the railroad station, and a sumptuous two-hour lunch was served in the Casino Olegario Molina. In Torreón there were 15,000 in the crowd and much passionate oratory, including references to Madero as "the Hidalgo of 1910," which was reasonably accurate, and "the Mexican Napoleon," which was not. At León the train arrived at 6 A.M., and 20,000 people were waiting. At Silao there were even more, and Madero embraced and wept over twelve-year-old Ricardo Taboada who had been blinded in one eye by a federal soldier for shouting "Viva Madero." Everywhere there were masses of people; revolutionary soldiers in an astonishing variety of uniforms and pretty girls in fiesta dresses. There was more oratory, patriotic recitations by bright, shining-faced children, fireworks, flowers, bands, and choruses.

Madero's train was due in Mexico City at 7 A.M. but did not arrive until noon. The station platforms—cracked in many places by that morning's earthquake, were packed with people and the crowd continued to grow—women carrying flowers, men wearing tricolor revolutionary hatbands. When the train crept into the station the locomotive's whistle could hardly be heard above the din—cheers, band music, anthem-singing choruses, and shouts of "Viva Madero." Madero, his normally sallow face deeply tanned by the strong sun of the northern plains, and his wife, Sara, pale under a large hat, left the last car of the train and inched their way through the crowd. They took seats in an open carriage with Eduardo Hay, a companion in arms who had lost an eye in the battle of Casas Grandes, and Giuseppe Garibaldi, the Italian soldier of fortune, and began a slow journey through the streets of the capital. Veterans of the Revolution marched beside the carriage with wreaths of flowers on their rifles. They were followed by tens of thousands of enthusiasts, cheering wildly. The procession moved through the broad Paseo de la Reforma where spectators clustered like flies on the monuments to Columbus and Charles IV of Spain. The main thoroughfares and side streets of the business district were jammed with people, all the way to the National Palace.

At the palace Madero and his wife were ceremoniously received in the Salon of Ambassadors by the interim President, Francisco León de la Barra. Outside in the broad Zócalo massed crowds waved flags, placards, and handkerchiefs, and screamed for Madero to appear. When he finally did make an appearance on a balcony of the palace he waved both his arms but his words were lost in the cheers from the historic square below.

Late in the afternoon Madero and his wife returned by automobile to his parents' house at the corner of Liverpool and Berlin, an ornate brick chalet. A gentle rain had begun to fall and continued to fall intermittently long after dark. Nevertheless, thousands stood in the streets outside the Madero house, shouting vivas—for Madero, for the Revolution, for the fatherland, and for democracy. It was said that many were uncertain as to what or who *la democrácia* was, and that some thought it was the lady who had ridden at Madero's side.

If there was some confusion and misunderstanding they in no way curbed the extravagance of the welcome. There had been no reception like it in Mexico since the entry of Iturbide and his army at the end of the war for independence. Such ostentation seemed to fit the arrogant and pompous Iturbide, a man who sought the adulation of the crowd. Madero, a small, plain man who had rocketed from obscure political eccentricity into the position of a national hero, seemed ill-cast for the role. His triumphant entry into the capital was made just a year to the day after Díaz's authorities had ignominiously arrested him and sent him to prison like a common criminal. Only six months before he had been a disheartened, penniless, frustrated, and indecisive exile, wondering where to turn. Now he was idolized in a fashion the politically cynical Mexicans normally lavished only on famous bullfighters such as Rodolfo Gaona (who that week was having notable success with bulls of Tres Palacios at Caceres, Spain).

There was, for a time, great and novel happiness. The interim government appeared to be living up to the provisions of the peace pact. Amnesty was granted to the political prisoners who had crowded the cells at Belem, the penitentiary, and the fortress-prison of San Juan Ulúa at Veracruz. The government accepted Gustavo Madero's itemized expense account and reimbursed him for the 642,195 pesos he had spent on the Revolution, thereby saving him from almost certain prosecution for embezzlement. There were representatives of the Revolution in De la Barra's cabinet—although not as many as some revolutionists thought there should be. And De la Barra had called for an election in the fall to choose a President in the free manner prescribed by the long-ignored Constitution of 1857. De la Barra also announced that he would not be a candidate himself.

It was clear that Madero would be a candidate and, barring a miracle, a successful one. Large crowds of followers gathered each day around the house in the Calle Liverpool. The words the short, bearded man spoke to these admirers were regarded as revelation, whether they were understood or not. There would have been no hindrance if Madero had seen fit to declare himself President immediately. He might have saved both himself and Mexico much trouble had he done so. Taking power at the high tide of his popularity might have brought peace and stability. His idealism, sincerity, and quite literal belief in his political pronouncements would have tempered an otherwise undemocratic seizure of power and might have freed him for the sort of decisive action which was needed.

But Madero intended to lead his country only if duly elected to office. He set up political headquarters in an old mansion on the Paseo de la Reforma, reorganized the political party he had founded and began campaigning as though Mexico were a well-established and smoothly functioning democracy, which it was not.

The stubborn purity of Madero's political intentions was admirable. But it was also impractical. He had insisted from the outset that "restoration" of political democracy would solve all of the nation's perplexities. But democracy had never been firmly rooted in Mexico, and in the long years of the Díaz dictatorship the few roots had withered and died. There was nothing to restore. The nation's chronic problems of social and economic justice and political representation had become so grave that they were unresponsive to mild treatment. The demand for their correction had given potency to the revolutionary movement of which Madero was the leader—a leader who never quite understood either the urgency of the demand or the explosive power that had been handed to him.

His first serious error, perhaps, had been the treaty of Juárez. His position had been strong. The Díaz regime was near collapse and the old and ailing dictator was looking for an honorable way to withdraw. Madero could have dictated the terms of settlement. Yet the treaty was one that might have been drawn between two contending groups that had fought each other to a stalemate. Madero gave up the provisional presidency. The man named to the interim presidency, De la Barra, had no sympathy for the Revolution and the aims of the revolutionists. The great and powerful bureaucracy of the Díaz regime remained almost intact, running the government. The federal army, defeated in the field, was preserved. Its officer corps, tough and reactionary almost to a man, survived with a lively hatred for the nondescript revolutionary army that had beaten it. The revolutionary soldiers, meanwhile, were told to lay down their arms, to go home and go to work, to obey the government that seemed to differ little from the one they had fought to overthrow.

The discharge of these revolutionary troops was to cause much trouble. More often than not it became entangled in the agrarian problem, the demand for restoration of land to the Indians who made up so much of Mexico's population. This, for many of them, was what the Revolution was about. Why should they put down their arms until their lands had been given back to them?

Madero had taken note of the land problem in his Plan of San Luis Potosí. In Article 3 he had promised that lands illegally taken from their owners would be given back to them by legal means. But, with characteristic caution and moderation, he had begun to modify his views. Almost immediately after signing the treaty of Juárez he had issued a manifesto in which he said that it would be impossible to satisfy at once the hopes aroused by Article 3. But, he added, any disappointment occasioned by the delay was preferable to a prolongation of the civil war.

To many of Madero's followers this sounded at best like foolishness and at worst like betrayal. One of his first visitors after his arrival in Mexico City was Emiliano Zapata, the peasant leader who had been fighting in Morelos, Puebla, and Guerrero. Zapata, unlike most revolutionists, cared little about politics and had no personal ambitions. All he wanted was for ancestral lands to be given back to the villages that had owned them communally for centuries.

When he came to see Madero in the house in the Calle Liverpool, Zapata, dressed in the tight trousers and short jacket of a charro, kept his broad-brimmed hat on his head and his carbine in his hand. He took off his hat during the midday meal but refused to part with his carbine.

To Zapata's reiterated demand for restoration of land Madero gave what was fast becoming a stock answer to all the problems that were pressing in on him: "Everything will be done, but in due course and according to law, for this is a delicate matter and cannot be resolved superficially at the stroke of a pen."

Zapata stared at the heavy gold watch chain stretched across Madero's vest.

"Look, Señor Madero," he said slowly, gesturing with the tightly held carbine, "if I, having the advantage of being armed, robbed you of your watch and kept it, and then some time later we met again but with both of us equally armed, wouldn't you have the right to demand the return of the watch?"

"Of course, General," said Madero, "and I would have the right to ask for payment for the use you had of it."

"This is exactly what has happened in Morelos," said Zapata. "Some *hacendados* have taken the land of the villages. My soldiers, armed peasants, urge me to say to you that they want to proceed right away with the restitution of the land."

Madero again promised that everything would be done in time. He also accepted Zapata's invitation to come to Morelos and see the problem firsthand.

Madero's reluctance to take decisive action brought criticism from many other friends and allies. Roque Estrada, one of the men closest to him in the early days of the Revolution, wrote: ". . . if you continue this weakness and complacency they [the enemies of the Revolution] will destroy the ideals of the Revolution . . . To leave the federal army standing while disbanding revolutionary forces is to open the road to victory for the reaction."

The brilliant lawyer Luis Cabrera published an open letter to Madero making an apt analogy. "Revolutions," he wrote, "are always painful operations for the social body. But the surgeon has, above all, the responsibility not to close the incision until the gangrene has been cleaned out. The operation, whether it was necessary or not, has begun. You opened the wound, and you must close it. But woe to you if, frightened by the sight of blood or the cries of pain, you close the wound without having disinfected it or removed the source of trouble. The operation will have been useless and history will curse your name—not because you operated but because the fatherland continues to suffer . . . and will be subject to relapses, each more dangerous than the last, each more painful and exhausting."

There was crueler criticism, on personal rather than political-philosophical grounds. Most of it came from what had been the Díaz aristocracy and the hangers-on of that aristocracy. A few of their leaders had followed Díaz into exile but many remained behind, their lives little changed. They scoffed at "Maderito" (Little Madero) and made jokes about his strange ways, the vegetarianism, the homeopathy, the communion with the spirits. They criticized him for taking a ride in an airplane. They hinted that he was mentally unstable and, perhaps because he occasionally had a facial tic, that he was an epileptic. They referred to his mother, a strong-minded, fearless woman, as the she-devil. The name of Madero's devoted wife, Sara P. de Madero, was punned into *sarape de Madero* (Madero's blanket). All of the Madero women, wholesome, plain-looking women from the provincial North, were subjected to sniffing scorn by the stylishly dressed women of the capital, who called them *sinverguenzas* (shameless ones); they hissed at them on the street and instructed their servants to do the same. A diplomatic wife observed the Madero women at a reception and wrote in her memoirs that "mostly the women comprising the Madero phalanx wore beetling, towering toques and tight-waisted, dull dresses, or very big picture hats and impossible high-necked spangled gowns with trains, reminding one of King Edward's remark to Lord H. when he appeared in a frock coat and pearl-gray trousers in a country house in the morning: 'Good God, when will you learn to dress?'"

The political affections of many of the surviving *porfiristas* were now directed at Bernardo Reyes, the old soldier from Nuevo León, a picturesque, quixotic man whose long blond beard, unruly forelock, and piercing blue eyes made work easy for cartoonists. Reyes was a dandy. When in uniform he wore bells on his spurs. In civilian dress he frequently had a red carnation in his lapel. The red carnation became the symbol of *reyismo,* and red carnations were to be seen in the lapels of the best-tailored sack coats in Mexico City.

Reyes had been a first-rate soldier and commanded the loyalty of many of the top officers of the federal army. He had, years earlier, virtually wiped out brigandage in northeastern Mexico. Intellectually he was a romantic, a delver into history and a lover of poetry, some of it considered quite advanced and daring at the time. Politically he was a curious mixture. Although as governor of Nuevo León he had been the author of some of the earliest labor legislation in Mexico he had also been a hard-fisted ruler who did not hesitate to shoot down political opposition. Porfirio Díaz had at first admired Reyes, then distrusted him as a likely political rival. In his last troubled days Díaz ordered Reyes home from Europe in an effort to shore up his crumbling empire.

Reyes did not reach Mexico City until Díaz was gone. His only public statement was that he intended to work for the pacification of the country, but it was clear that he still wanted to be president—and the promised free elections gave him a chance. Madero, who had arrived in the city just ahead of him, invited the old general to a conference. He offered him the portfolio of Ministry of War in his own cabinet, once he had been elected. In return Reyes disavowed his presidential ambitions. The disavowal, however, did not halt the activity of Reyes' followers. More and more red carnations appeared. Soon there would be street fights between Reyistas and Maderistas. Finally, in September, charging that the election would be unfair, Reyes left the country again, making vaguely threatening statements which Madero interpreted correctly as a threat to rebel.

That Reyes should be against Madero surprised no one. But that the Vázquez Gómez brothers should become his bitter enemies was something else again; they had been important members of the revolutionary hierarchy. The brothers, Francisco the doctor and Emilio the lawyer, were natives of Tamaulipas. They were short, stocky men, alike in appearance as Tweedledum and Tweedledee, and were of almost pure Indian blood. Coming from a background of poverty they had struggled for education and had won distinction in their professions. Francisco had for a time been personal physician to Porfirio Díaz. Politically he was a liberal—although a discreet and moderate one—and the Anti-Reelectionist party nominated him for the vice-presidency on the ticket with Madero in 1910. He was an even more reluctant revolutionist than Madero. When the latter urged him to join the armed rebellion scheduled for November 20, 1910, he declined a belligerent role and became, instead, the Maderos' confidential agent in Washington. The schism with Francisco Madero was widened by Vázquez Gómez' dislike and distrust of the various Madero relatives. He felt that the Maderos were fighting for themselves and their business interests instead of for the Revolution. He nevertheless served as one of Madero's peace negotiators in Juárez and became Minister of Education in the cabinet of the interim President, De la Barra. His brother Emilio, more radical politically, served briefly as Minister of Government in the same cabinet. In this post he was given the responsibility, among other things, for the discharge of revolutionary troops, one of the provisions of the Juárez treaty which his brother helped negotiate. Emilio was opposed to liquidation of the rebel troops and instead obstructed it. He was forced to resign.

Meanwhile Madero had dissolved the old Anti-Reelectionist party—which had nominated him and Francisco Vázquez Gómez with him in 1910—and created a new one, the Constitutional Progressive party. The new party would certainly nominate Madero, its founder, but it was not obligated to renominate Francisco Vázquez Gómez for the vice-presidency—and this was apparently what Madero hoped to avoid. Instead it chose José María Pino Suárez, a Yucatecan lawyer, journalist, and poet who had been an ardent—although somewhat unimpressive—Madero supporter from the outset. The move alienated the followers of Vázquez Gómez. There were complaints that Madero had imposed Pino Suárez on the party, but there was little evidence of it. The proceedings of the convention were open and democratic. An American diplomat described it as "the first untrammeled political convention ever held in this country . . . really free and open . . . an admirable temper displayed . . . Sessions, while turbulent at times, were well conducted, and each plank of the party platform was fully discussed before being incorporated." The platform included provisions for freedom of the press, judicial reform, Mexicanization of the railroads (largely operated by U.S. personnel), return of uprooted Indians to their homelands and restoration of their property, and aid for small farmers.

CHAPTER 10

MEN OF MORELOS

> ". . . the lands, woods and water which have been usurped . . . will be restored immediately . . ."
>
> Plan of Ayala, November 27, 1911

THE ALIENATION of the Vázquez Gómez brothers, while it was to cause future trouble, was not so pressing a problem as was the stubborn belligerence of the Zapatista troops in the South who refused to lay down their arms. Zapata's irregular army was for the most part made up of illiterate peasants who were suspicious and distrustful of outsiders by nature. Theirs was a small world—they called it the *patria chica* (little fatherland). Their dominant passions were love of the land and hatred of the landowners who had stolen it from them.

They had a few friends and many enemies. What the outside world regarded justifiably as Zapatista terrorism and brigandage was, for them, a holy war. They attached little importance to human life, their own or others, and their favorite song, sung in throat-catching fashion around smoky fires at night in the mountains of the South, ended with the refrain:

> "If they are going to kill me tomorrow,
> Why, let them kill me today."

The only important thing was the land.

These attitudes had been bred into Zapata and his followers. Zapata's own village, Anenecuilco—where he was born August 8, 1879—had been involved in land disputes for nearly five centuries. In a way it was a classic case of Mexico's troublesome, complicated land question. It had long divided Mexico in halves: on one side an Indian peasantry with a mystical attachment of the earth and to growing things and no clear concept of private property—the land belonged to everyone; on the other a white or mixed blood minority with a highly developed sense of property, attached to the land as a means to an end, not as an end in itself.

An ancient people—they were later labeled Tlahuicas, although that was not their name—were living in the warm, well-watered, and lush valleys of Morelos centuries before the power-hungry Aztecs moved into central Mexico and began building their empire. The Tlahuicas were peaceful farmers, who in their leisure, liked to walk about with bouquets of roses in their hands. With the rise of the Aztecs in the fifteenth century the Tlahuicas became a subject people, ceding part of their ancestral lands to the new overlords and paying regular tribute in cotton and grain.

Anenecuilco ("place where the water moves like a worm") was named for the meandering little river that divided it, the banks thickly grown with willow, wild fig, coral trees, and casahuate, the "stupid tree," whose sap was said to produce imbecility. To the west of the river the land was rough and rocky, hospitable only to mesquite and cactus; to the east the land was rich, flat enough for irrigation, broad and friendly.

Anenecuilco endured the Aztecs and later it endured the Spaniards. It was part of the 25,000 square mile tract awarded to Hernán Cortés for his conquest of New Spain. Sugar cane was introduced into a climate that was ideal for it. The Indians learned how to grow cane as well as corn and cotton. They also acquired certain obligations: to work for the new landlords and to give a share of their own crops to the crown and the church. But they retained their land—the village itself and the ejido or communally owned land around it. They continued to live as a *calpulli,* "a precinct of known people of ancient lineage who have long held their land." The inviolability of their property was established by royal decree as it was for other Indian pueblos in New Spain.

In the late sixteenth century the people of Anenecuilco made an innocent mistake. They generously ceded to a group of Dominican fathers the right to plant crops on a part of their communal land which was not then in use. The Dominicans continued to use it, and the borrowed land became, in time, the powerful and privately owned Hacienda de Coahuistla. Another parcel of land ceded for the establishment of a hospital became, in later years, the privately owned Hacienda de Hospital.

These and other haciendas, with the help first of the unfortunate Lerdo laws (by which Indian village lands could be "denounced") and, later, through Porfirio Díaz's cessions of supposedly vacant land, continued to grow—the growth invariably at the expense of the Indian communities. The people of Anenecuilco were put in the position of proving that they did in fact exist as a village. In 1887 Coahuistla was owned by Manuel Mendoza Cortina. Mendoza Cortina, eager to extend the boundaries of his hacienda, ordered his workers to destroy the barrio of Olaque, adjacent to Anenecuilco. The chapel was pulled down and its building stones made into a wall. The houses were leveled. The orchards of mango, mamey, avocado, and coffee were uprooted and burned to make way for sugar cane.

The event was a traumatic one in Anenecuilco and one which according to local legend made an indelible impression on Emiliano Zapata, then eight years old. The boy is said to have found his father, Gabriel, weeping over the destruction of Olaque.

"But why don't you fight?" asked the boy.

"Because they are powerful," the father said.

And in the pattern of most such legends, Emiliano vowed someday to fight the *hacendados*.

The Zapatas lived in a tiny rubblework and thatch hut in the southwestern part of Anenecuilco. The father had once worked for the Hacienda de Hospital; the mother, Cleofas Salazar, came from a family that had been in Anenecuilco for generations. There were ten children. Emiliano—invariably called 'Miliano both as a child and as a man—was next to the youngest. He had the barest sort of education—and never learned to read. But he learned much of Mexican history and of local lore. Two uncles had fought in both the War of the Reform and the war against the French intervention and they liked to talk of their experiences, both then and in fighting the notorious Plata bandit gang in later years. The people of Anenecuilco, unlike the poor in many parts of Mexico, had no sympathy for bandits—which made later allegations of banditry against Zapata particularly ironic. From his uncles Emiliano also learned expert use of the rifle; his expert horsemanship he picked up on his own.

When Zapata was sixteen his father and mother died. He and his brother Eufemio supported what was left of the family. That same year the Hacienda de Hospital began to appropriate the little remaining land that the village still held—more of the good land on the east side of the river, and even the rough, unusable land on the west side. The people of the village, farmers by tradition, were now reduced to either farming in shares on land that once belonged to them, paying three measures of corn out of each one hundred to the *hacendado,* or to stock raising. Stock could be grazed on untillable land, but the animals invariably strayed onto hacienda land, and hacienda guards began shooting them. When the villagers came to claim the dead stock—nothing could be wasted—the guards started shooting at the villagers. Animals which were not shot were held in hacienda corrals, without food or water; to reclaim them the villagers had to pay a ransom.

That Emiliano was resentful of the *hacendados* was certain (as a child he had been beaten by hacienda guards for helping himself to hay on hacienda land, hay which otherwise would have been burned). The authorities apparently regarded him as a trouble maker, and in 1908 he was conscripted into the army and assigned to the 9th Cavalry Regiment in Cuernavaca. His military service was brief. Ignacio de la Torre y Mier, a powerful *hacendado* who was well-connected politically, knew of Zapata's great skill with horses. He arranged for him to be released from the army and to serve as a groom for the stable of thoroughbreds at the De la Torre mansion in Mexico City. Firsthand observation of the rich and idle life led by *hacendados* deepened Zapata's feeling against the wealthy. He also developed a dislike of the city itself; never thereafter, even at the peak of his career as a revolutionist, would he stay in the city a minute longer than he had to.

Zapata was slender but well-muscled. His hair and his large mustaches were blue-black. His eyes were dark, luminous, and brooding, and when he was fatigued they seemed to be circled with purple. His skin was normally dark and burned darker still by the hot sun of Morelos. He was an accomplished and enthusiastic performer in country rodeos, a trick rider and he bore a number of scars from country-style bullfights. He liked cockfights, drank ample quantities of aguardiente and mezcal and enjoyed women. His amorous attachments were numerous and usually casual. But even when these involvements were of only one night's duration his demeanor was one of gentleness, even tenderness and he was always solicitous of the future welfare of both the woman and any off-spring that might result.

In 1909 Zapata was back in Anenecuilco with little time for rodeos, liquor, or women. The government had, that year, passed a reevaluation law which would determine disputed property boundaries. The villagers of Anenecuilco foresaw that this would be an opportunity for the *hacendados* to legitimatize their land claims against the villages. The older men of Anenecuilco who had been fighting the property war for so many years wearily suggested that younger men take it up. Zapata, then thirty, was elected president of the defense junta of Anenecuilco. Locking himself in the village church with a friend who could read he studied the little bundle of tattered documents that told of the village's ancient history and its legitimate right to the lands which surrounded it. The villagers emptied their thin purses for a defense fund. Lawyers went to work in Cuautla, Cuernavaca, and Mexico City to try to clarify the village's status; they accomplished little but did stir up the resentment of the *hacendado* of El Hospital. In the spring of 1910 the hacienda announced that the villagers could not plant corn on hacienda land, even as sharecroppers.

The villagers wrote to the Governor of Morelos asking for help: "The season of rains is coming and we, the poor farmers, should be preparing the land for corn planting." Couldn't the governor, they asked, do something to help them against the *hacendado* of El Hospital? They outlined the history of the village's struggle against the encroachment of the hacienda.

A minor functionary of the state government replied casually, asking for more details.

The men of Anenecuilco pored through their old documents and maps once more and wrote another letter, desperately this time, for the clouds that presaged the summer rains and the growing season were piling up in the sierra. They sent off their letter on May 8. On May 16 the secretary of the state governor replied: he was turning over their complaint to the proprietor of the Hacienda de Hospital. They would, in short, get no help from the state government but were, instead, left just where they had been before, at the mercy of the *hacendado*.

The *hacendado* sent them a message making his position clear: "If the people of Anenecuilco want to plant corn let them plant it in a flower pot, because not even on the hillsides are they going to have the use of my land."

The summer rains in 1910 were scant and the crops raised on the little land that did still belong to Anenecuilco were poor. The corn failed to produce ears. The cane was stunted and dry. Everyone in the village was bitter and some, including Zapata, were talking armed rebellion. The talks continued.

In the fall Francisco Madero, as a fugitive in Texas, issued his Plan of San Luis Potosí. Article 3 of the plan, dealing with Indians who had been dispossessed of their lands, struck a responsive chord in many parts of Mexico—including Morelos. What was left of the defense fund of Anenecuilco was used to send Pablo Torres Burgos, a shopkeeper of Villa Ayala, to San Antonio to confer with Madero. Torres Burgos returned with a commission to lead the revolutionary forces in Morelos. Zapata, followed by seventy men, became an active revolutionist on March 11, 1911.

When Torres Burgos was brutally killed by government troops a short time later Zapata became head of the movement. From the outset he displayed courage and gifts as a guerrilla commander, never hesitating to do the unusual. In one of his early engagements he commandeered a locomotive, loaded it with his men, drove it on the narrow gauge tracks that connected the various haciendas and crashed it through the gates of the Hacienda de Huichila to seize a valuable booty of rifles, ammunition, and horses. Isolated as they were in the heart of Mexico the Zapatistas, unlike the revolutionists in the northern states who had access to the markets of the United States, had to be self-supporting, getting weapons and supplies from their victims.

It was not a pleasant war. Government troops in Morelos were merciless—a favorite method of execution was to hang a man and build a fire under him so that he suffered the agonies of strangulation and flames at the same time. The Zapatistas quickly demonstrated that they could be just as cruel, although Zapata himself tried to exercise restraint.

On the night of May 6, 1911, Zapata and his men were in Jonacatepec, which they had just taken and celebrated the news of Madero's victory at Ciudad Juárez. One of Zapata's lieutenants, Abraham Martínez, lurched to his feet, belched loudly and, with slurred words, said: "General, I want to toast your health and wish that for once and all you would get rid of this notion that we should kill only Spaniards and rich *hacendados,* that this way you'll fulfill your mission. Get rid of these cowards who are always preaching that we shouldn't rob, shouldn't kill, shouldn't violate women—because this is the only way the people can get even for the outrages they've suffered under the dictatorship."

But if Zapata was more moderate than his followers he was just as insistent that there must be a settlement of the land question before his irregular army disbanded. Because of the ambiguity of the treaty of Juárez, Madero's inability to act decisively and the reactionary nature of the interim government the Zapatistas continued on a war footing. Morelos landowners, terrified, hysterically reported their sometimes real but often imagined atrocities to the Mexico City press. The newspapers exaggerated both fact and fiction and referred to Zapata as "the Attila of the South." The interim government sent more and more troops to restore order; the more troops that were sent the more stubbornly unyielding the Zapatistas became. They raided, burned buildings and crops, drove away stock, attacked towns, wrecked trains and fought the federal detachments that were sent against them.

All through the summer and fall of 1911 Madero tried to find a solution to the Zapatista problem. In mid-June he went, at Zapata's invitation, on a trip to Cuernavaca and other Zapatista strongholds. In Cuernavaca he was given an extravagant welcome. Roses and gardenias pelted the high-wheeled Packard touring car that carried him from the railroad station to the Palace of Cortés. Pajama-clad sandal-shod Zapatista troopers stood at respectful attention; Zapatista horsemen, trussed in cartridge belts and bristling with rifles, sidearms, and knives rode at his side as a guard of honor. Madero's exchanges with Zapata were cordial and there was mutual respect between the two men. While Zapata was impatient with the delay in distributing land he recognized Madero's honesty and good will. And Madero, while well aware of the horrors the Zapatistas had committed, admired the peasant leader's dedication to a single, unselfish end. Of all the *jefes* who had rallied to Madero's cause Zapata was probably the most dedicated, the least devious. The two men, the optimistic, trusting little man from the North and the distrustful Indian from the South in time might have reached an accord which could have been the salvation of both of them. But misunderstandings, mistakes, bad judgment, and downright betrayal were to make their efforts futile.

Shortly after the Cuernavaca trip Madero was invited to Puebla, a city in which there was still many sympathizers with the old Díaz regime. *Poblanos* (people of Puebla) have, in Mexican regional folklore, a reputation for deceitfulness and treachery. Soon there were rumors that there would be an attempt on Madero's life. Zapatistas in Puebla began rounding up supposed enemies of Madero. The De la Barra government intervened and ordered the Zapatista leader jailed for his presumption. A little later the Zapatista troops, camped in the Puebla bullring, were attacked by federal troops under Colonel Aureliano Blanquet; more than eighty were killed and some two hundred wounded. Madero, upon his arrival, publicly praised Colonel Blanquet for his valor and loyalty in restoring order. The gesture helped complicate the already difficult Zapatista question.

Another military man was to be even more instrumental in alienating the Zapatistas. General Victoriano Huerta, the soldier who had sorrowfully told Porfirio Díaz goodbye in the port of Veracruz, was sent to Morelos with instructions to control the Zapatista disorders. He was also told to work in accord with Madero, who was still trying to reach a peaceful solution of the Zapatista problem. Huerta's manner was ingratiating. He took meals and went for walks with Madero in the cobbled, tilted streets of Cuernavaca, repeatedly assuring him of his friendship, admiration and loyalty. Yet, when Madero would set off for peace talks with Zapata, Huerta, under the guise of military exercises, would order his troops forward in menacing fashion, exciting the suspicious Zapatistas and placing Madero's life in jeopardy. It was conjectured that Huerta hoped to provoke the Zapatistas into either capturing or killing Madero. Madero later denounced Huerta, whom he knew to be an admirer of both Díaz and Bernardo Reyes, for his "inexplicable conduct," and Huerta was put on the army's inactive list.

The Zapatista problem, meanwhile, seemed farther from solution than ever despite Madero's repeated efforts to work out a peace plan acceptable to both the guerrilla fighters and the interim government of De la Barra. Conservative elements in the capital and much of the press, reveling in its new-found freedom, were bitterly critical of Madero for negotiating with a "bandit." Madero, in a speech to Zapata's followers at Cuautla, referred to this criticism. "Our enemies do not rest," he said. "They would like to make it appear that I have no control over the chiefs who aided me in the Revolution . . . They say that I am a great patriot and a sincere man but that I lack energy, that I lack the abilities to govern because I have not ordered General Zapata shot . . . such an act would not require either bravery or energy. One needs only to be an assassin and a criminal to shoot one of the most valiant soldiers of the Liberating Army."

Madero's friendly words and peace-making gestures came to nothing. Zapata, unlettered and unsophisticated as he was, must have sensed their positions could not be reconciled. He would not compromise his demand that land be restored to his peasant followers; and although he several times seemed ready to disarm them it was never done because his conditions could not be met. Inevitably they drifted apart. By November 1911, Zapata had publicly broken with Madero and disavowed him.

On November 27, camped in the Sierra of Ayoxustla, Zapata published his Plan of Ayala, which said:

". . . the land, woods and water which have been usurped . . . through tyranny and venal justice will be restored immediately to the villages or citizens who have the corresponding titles to them . . . They shall maintain such possession at all cost with their arms. The usurpers who think they have a right to such property may present their claims before special courts to be established after the triumph of the Revolution . . . The great majority of Mexicans own nothing more than the soil they stand upon . . . unable to engage in industry or agriculture because lands, woods and water are monopolized by a few. Therefore such properties shall be expropriated . . . in order that the villages and citizens of Mexico may obtain ejidos, colonies, townsites and tillable lands . . . The properties of those . . . who may oppose this Plan, directly or indirectly, shall be seized . . ."

Aside from the vigorous denunciation of Madero, which was probably the work of the schoolteacher Otilio Montaño, one of Zapata's intellectual advisers, the document was as simple and direct as Zapata was. Zapata and his men believed in it with passionate sincerity and thereafter insisted on its acceptance as a prerequisite to any alliance with other revolutionary elements.

Nor was it an empty promise, to be honored only in revolutionary oratory. When haciendas fell to his army Zapata turned them over to his soldiers and to the peasants who had been working the land. It was straightforward and effective, not complicated by any legal rigmarole of expropriation and division. In between armed clashes his followers were expected to till their newly won fields, with a rifle close at hand in case it was needed.

CHAPTER II

UNEASY APOSTOLATE

> "It is true. My government has not
> achieved peace. But the rights, liberties
> and guarantees which we are winning in
> all sectors of the nation are worth more
> than peace."
>
> Francisco Madero

MADERO EASILY WON the presidency of Mexico. In the first free election in many years there were random votes for bullfighters, barbers and bandits, and even some for the ex-dictator, Díaz—but Madero won 99 percent of the vote (the old guard distributed handbills saying "even the spirits vote for Madero"). Because the country was in such a state of turmoil De la Barra was eager to turn over the office to his successor. This he did on November 6, more than three weeks before the official date for transfer of power. The official bulletin of the Federal District government urged: "Let us gather around Citizen Francisco I. Madero . . . leaving behind hatreds, rancors, partisan animosities, sorrows of past struggles, and in close fraternal embrace let us demonstrate to the world that we know how to be true patriots and Mexicans of the heart."

The sentiment was fine—and futile, for Madero's 15½ months of administration were to be marked by one upheaval after another—from regional disturbances to serious rebellions that threatened to sweep the entire nation into civil war. Zapata's break with the Madero administration was soon followed by an abortive revolution led by Bernardo Reyes—the rebellion that Madero had been certain he was planning. Old, blind in one eye, paralyzed in one hand, Reyes crossed the border from Texas with a few followers on December 13, 1911, counting on a nationwide response to his call to rebellion. There were a few Reyista uprisings scattered around the country, but nothing like the revolution

Reyes had hoped for. The old man wandered aimlessly in northern Mexico and finally, on Christmas Night, surrendered to a military outpost. He sent a note to the commanding officer, saying candidly: "I called the army and the people [to revolt] and nobody answered. I consider this attitude a protest and I have resolved not to continue this war against the government. I place myself at your disposition." In an earlier day he would have been executed promptly. Instead he was taken to Mexico City and placed in comfortable quarters in the military prison of Santiago Tlaltelolco.

The apparent end of the Reyes rebellion did not mean that Mexico was peaceful. The American Ambassador, Henry Lane Wilson, who seldom bothered to conceal his animosity toward Madero, reported to Secretary of State Philander C. Knox: ". . . Mexico is seething with discontent." The Reyista rebellion, he added, might have succeeded under a "more daring, popular and able leader."

Madero's immediate troubles were to come from his friends, ex-friends, and one-time followers. There were disturbances in all parts of the Republic, with the greatest uneasiness in the North.

Three days after Madero's inauguration Emilio Vázquez Gómez declared, in San Antonio, Texas, that he was the chief of "the revolution which is to raise me to the presidency." A little later he predicted that "Señor Madero's downfall will be achieved with astonishing speed." By early 1912 there were a number of Vazquista revolutionary movements in Sinaloa, Zacatecas, and particularly in the large northern state of Chihuahua—where one of the leaders was Braulio Hernández, in whose El Paso home Madero had hidden a year earlier and whose wife the penniless Madero had promised to send money to pay for his laundry.

But the man who was destined to be the principal figure in the counterrevolutionary movement in Chihuahua was Pascual Orozco. The saturnine Orozco had been the ablest of the irregular commanders in the early stages of the Madero revolution, a battlefield hero, and had been frustrated ever since. He had wanted to be Minister of War in Madero's provisional cabinet, but had been passed over. He had wanted to execute the federal commander at Juárez but was stopped by Madero himself. He had attempted to lead a mutiny against Madero, and failed. He had asked 50,000 pesos for his services in the Madero movement and received only 5000. He had hoped for an important military command but was, instead, put in charge of irregular forces in the military zone of Chihuahua. He had hoped to be elected governor of Chihuahua but was not. Madero tried to comfort the one-time mule driver's sensibilities. He was invited to Mexico City and a large delegation was sent to meet him at the train. But Orozco, with his country manners and diffidence, was not recognized; he walked unnoticed through the crowd and made his way to his hotel alone. He served as one of the escorting officers when Madero assumed the presidency. At a banquet for Madero the President pointedly referred to him as "my right arm"—but to this and other compliments Orozco responded with only grim silence.

In January 1912, Orozco submitted his resignation from his military command to return, he said, to private business. The resignation did not take effect immediately and for a time Orozco was—or appeared to be—engaged in combating various anti-Madero movements in Chihuahua. To help him in this effort the central government sent him additional supplies of rifles and ammunition. Then on March 3 Orozco openly rebelled against Madero.

Orozco had an irregular army of about six thousand men, well equipped and with plenty of money to buy more arms and ammunition. Money and encouragement had come to him from conservative elements in Chihuahua, principally the vastly wealthy Terrazas and Creel families whose members were fearful of whatever steps the Madero government might take to expropriate and divide large land holdings. They had showered gifts and flattery on the resentful Orozco, knowing—just as Porfirio Díaz's envoys at Juárez had known—that he was susceptible to such blandishments.

At the outset of his rebellion Orozco was allied with the movement led by Emilio Vázquez Gómez. But Orozco's conservative backers regarded the radical Vázquez Gómez with no more favor than they did Madero. In addition, both Orozco and Vázquez Gómez wanted the same thing: the presidency. Vázquez Gómez retreated into political oblivion and Orozco marched south toward Mexico City.

In the capital General José González Salas, Minister of War and a relative of Madero's by marriage, resigned his cabinet post to take command of the federal army and meet the Orozco threat. Like Madero himself and other Madero relatives, González Salas had been the victim of much journalistic abuse, and the field command was an opportunity to redeem himself.

It was, instead, a disaster. González Salas prepared to meet the Orozquistas on the arid plains of southern Chihuahua, but his advance was turned into a rout. First a "wild locomotive," carefully charged with dynamite by the Orozquistas, roared down the tracks and, near Rellano station, crashed head-on into the train carrying forward elements of the federal troops. The train was wrecked, much track destroyed and the surviving federal troops were at the mercy of the hard-riding, straight-shooting rebels, who attacked in the rear. One battalion of federal troops mutinied and was fired on by other federals. González Salas, wounded and remorseful, ordered a retreat to Torreón and then committed suicide.

In Mexico City there had been widespread nervousness when Orozco rebelled. With the Rellano debacle and the arrival in the capital of trains carrying wounded and dying men the uneasiness grew. Under pressure from his cabinet Madero chose a new commander for the northern campaign: Victoriano Huerta, the man whom he had ordered to inactive duty for sabotaging his efforts to make peace with Zapata. Madero both disliked and distrusted Huerta, but he was an able commander and this was what was needed.

Huerta reassembled and reorganized the federal troops, ordered railroad tracks repaired so that his troops could be transported, and went north to Chihuahua to direct the campaign in person. Huerta seemed to move with maddening slowness and there was criticism of him within Madero's government. There also was friction with the irregular troops who were fighting for Madero. Francisco Villa, the colorful *guerrillero* who had recently been promoted to brigadier general, fell out with Huerta in a dispute over a horse and was sentenced to death for insubordination. He was saved at the last moment on Madero's orders and was taken back to Mexico City for imprisonment.

Despite the slowness and dissension in the ranks Huerta went from victory to victory—at Rellano, Bachimba, Bermejillo, Chihuahua City, Juárez. Finally, in early September, Pascual Orozco and his remaining followers were badly beaten at the border town of Ojinaga and took refuge in the United States.

The most ambitious and threatening of the uprisings against the Madero government was over. Meanwhile there had been a significant shift in power. The federal army, defeated in the Madero revolution and unable to cope with the rebellious Zapatistas in the South, had, under Huerta, redeemed itself in the field. Madero, with many of his old revolutionary allies either alienated or openly rebellious, was thrust into a position of dependence upon the federal army.

The next movement against the Madero government came within weeks of the end of the Orozco revolution. Its leader was Felix Díaz, nephew of the old dictator, and according to one story it was financed with 50,000 pesos sent from Paris by Don Porfirio's wife. It was certain, however, that he had backing from powerful conservatives.

Felix Díaz was plump and vain and had the reputation of a lady's man. Due more to his uncle's influence than his own talents he was a career army man with the rank of brigadier general, and he had served as police inspector of Mexico City. His political intrigues frequently got him in trouble from which Porfirio Díaz had to extricate him. He survived his uncle's resignation, occupied a seat in the Chamber of Deputies and tried to win the governorship of the state of Oaxaca. When he failed to win the election his followers launched an abortive uprising. Felix Díaz moved on to Veracruz where there was a substantial

amount of anti-Madero feeling. He resigned his commission in the army
to make himself a free agent. With the support of one army battalion and
part of another he took command of the city of Veracruz and declared
himself in rebellion against Madero. He called for an "era of peace and
concord," "order in the economy, calm and impartial justice for all."
The plan, which called for the installation of Felix Díaz as interim
President of Mexico, was designed to attract the conservative elements
of Mexico and the military. He sought recognition by the United States
as a belligerent, and his activities were viewed with sympathy by W. W.
Canada, the U.S. consul in Veracruz.

Díaz was overconfident, and the armed forces which he had expected
to come over to his side did not. Instead, within a week Díaz and his
staff were captured. A military tribunal condemned Díaz to death.
Madero, although implored to do so by some of the most fashionable
women of the capital, refused to interfere with the verdict. But before
the death sentence could be carried out the federal supreme court ruled
that Díaz, having resigned his commission, was not subject to military
justice. Pending a trial as a civilian he was locked up in the island
fortress of San Juan Ulúa at Veracruz. Rumors circulated that a jailbreak
would be arranged and the federal government transferred him to the
penitentiary in Mexico City—which was what the authors of the rumors
had hoped for. Here, in cell 71, he waited, as did Bernardo Reyes in the
military prison of Santiago Tlaltelolco for what both knew would come:
a better planned and better executed blow against the Madero government.

In one year the Madero administration had survived three major
rebellions and perhaps a dozen minor ones. The Zapatista war went on
and on, sometimes almost in the suburbs of the capital. In December
Madero held a secret meeting with Zapata, trying once more to reach
an agreement. A key factor was the money needed to buy, legally, the
land to distribute to Zapata's *agraristas*. This could not be done until the
government straightened out its finances. The cost of combating the
rebellions had been heavy. Madero's Minister of the Treasury, Ernesto
Madero—also his uncle—was seeking authorization for a loan of
100,000,000 pesos, but the national legislature was obstructive. Whatever
agreement Madero may have had with Zapata was nullified by the
delay.

Madero had made some progress toward achieving the aims of the
Revolution. He had made electoral reform a reality, and he had been
elected to office in the first free election in living memory. He had taken
the first steps—slowly and cautiously—toward land and labor reform,
and was reconstructing and extending roads and railroads. He had also
established freedom of the press—and suffered for it. The Mexican press,

completely unaccustomed to freedom and independence, took advantage of it by attacking its benefactor mercilessly—"biting the hand that removed the muzzle," Gustavo Madero said. On almost any day Madero could read unbridled denunciations of himself, his administration, his family ("Señor Madero, you lack the qualifications necessary for the high position which you occupy . . . the fall of the fatherland is the consequence"). Day after day political cartoonists portrayed him as a grotesque dwarf swaddled in outsize clothing, as a dog in a silk hat, as a figure flattened into the pavement by a steamroller labeled "Public Opinion." Some of the bitterest cartoons came from the pen of a man who would, later, be recognized as one of the great artists of the Revolution—José Clemente Orozco.

Madero was subjected to constant criticism for the nepotism in his administration. An uncle was Secretary of the Treasury. A cousin was Secretary of the Government. There were perhaps ten Madero relatives scattered through the governmental bureaucracy, but nepotism had always been common in Mexican politics. Much of the resentment of the Madero clan was the result of the activity of the President's beloved and trusted brother, Gustavo. Practical and tough where Francisco was idealistic and gentle, Gustavo had taken over the operation of Madero's Constitutional Progressive party. When a show of force was needed he would take to the streets with a mob of political followers called *La Porra* (The Bludgeon). He was criticized for the irregular way in which he had raised funds for the Revolution and for reclaiming his expenses from the government. He was gossiped about as a grafter, although there was no evidence of it. His nickname, *Ojo Parado,* was an epithet of hatred and fear. He realized that his presence was increasingly an embarrassment to his brother. Toward the end of 1912 he asked for and received an appointment to a special diplomatic mission to Japan.

Between the crises which kept his administration on an emergency footing Madero tried to cultivate a climate of tolerance and respect in a nation which had known little of either. When *porfirista* legislators passed a bill making a national holiday of April 2, the date of Porfirio Díaz's greatest military victory, Madero gladly signed it into law. When his own partisans tried to establish restrictive controls on the press—which was maltreating him daily on personal as well as political grounds—he blocked them.

If he failed to make any substantial progress toward solving the nation's chronic problems he showed in many small ways the goodness of his heart and his love of Mexico and Mexicans. He built rural schools and provided free lunches for schoolchildren—just as he had on his hacienda back in Coahuila. Although he was accused of fiscal mismanagement, taxes were being collected impartially, and government

revenues were running 20 percent higher than ever before. He prohibited the exhibition in public offices of portraits of living persons, himself included—a blow against the political iconography which has always
been a characteristic of Mexican political life. He granted pensions to
poets and historians to get on with their work and provided funds for a
Mexican scholar to attend an archaeological congress in Switzerland.
He established a museum in Apatzingán where, in times more troubled
than Madero's own, the first Mexican congress had been called together
by Morelos, another man who tried to reform Mexico.

Madero had the vision of Morelos but less zeal, just as he had the
humanity of Hidalgo and the trust of Juárez in righteousness and law.
But he did not fit the pattern of leadership in his time. He was no hero,
nor a general, nor even a soldier. He had none of the faults—gambling,
womanizing, violent behavior—that so many Mexicans thought made
for *machismo* (excessive maleness), a quality they expected in their
leaders. He was not an assassin, nor could he be a tyrant. He was, instead,
an affable little man who was loyal and loving with his family and
friends, courteous to his enemies. He rode horseback, played tennis on
the courts at Chapultepec and liked to go to the Club Campestre for
dancing on Sunday afternoon. He affected a hand-worked vest of pea-
cock blue with his severely plain business suits, and he was always ready
to smile at times when circumstances seemed to call for a stern if not
menacing demeanor. He was, perhaps, living in the wrong age or in the
wrong country—or both.

THE TRAGIC TEN

"On that day dust will cover the earth . . .
plague will cover the face of the land . . .
a cloud will arise . . . a strong man will
seize the country . . . the houses will fall
in ruins . . ."

Chilam Balam (Mayan prophecies)

EVEN BEFORE Francisco I. Madero assumed the office of the presidency there had been frequent rumors of conspiracies to either prevent him from taking office or overturning the government once he had taken charge of it.

One name cropped up persistently in the rumors: Victoriano Huerta. As early as October 6, 1911, the U. S. State Department was informed that plans were being made for a *coup d'état* and that Huerta was involved in it.

There were grounds to suspect Huerta. He was a Díaz man. He had impeded Madero's efforts to negotiate with Zapata. But he had redeemed himself in the campaign against Orozco. His series of successes in this campaign raised him to the position of a military hero, particularly in conservative circles. A *Bachimba March* and a *Rellano Waltz* were composed in honor of his victories. By the time Huerta reached Juárez in his northward pursuit of Orozco the Mexico City papers were printing reports that he would on Independence Day, September 16, 1912, capitalize on his current popularity by declaring himself President of Mexico. In an interview Huerta damned the press for its "penny ambitions," and added: "I am not an Orozco . . . further bloodying of the soil of the Fatherland. I am an old soldier . . ."

The old soldier was soon in trouble with Madero again and back on the inactive list. The reason officially given was chronic eye infection which had been aggravated by the dust of the northern campaign. More important, he was unable to produce vouchers for some million and a half pesos in expenses. To inquiries he would shrug and say, "I am no bookkeeper." Huerta's *Memoirs,* written not by Huerta but by some- one who knew him very well, said his personal savings as a result of the Orozco campaign amounted to 30,000 pesos which he invested in rental houses.

Huerta had on at least one occasion publicly taken Madero to task for friction between them. Somewhat tipsily—he was reputed to be the hardest drinker in a hard-drinking army—he had made a little speech to the President at a banquet in Bucareli Hall: "Señor Madero, you are wrong to doubt the army. Doubt is the greatest insult one can offer to an honorable and loyal army—and the Mexican army has few equals. You are wrong . . ."

Madero had ample reason to suspect the army. The Mexican army had never liked civilians, whom they described as *catrines* (dudes)— the same word some Mexican Indians used to describe non-Indians. In particular they disliked civilians in a position of supreme authority— and before Madero there had been only two others, Benito Juárez and Sebastian Lerdo de Tejada, both in the previous century. On the occasion of the election of the latter, an old line general, Donato Guerra, had voiced army sentiments frankly. The army, he said, would never tolerate as President anyone but a military man. The temperament of the Mexican people, he said, was heroic and demanded a hero as leader— and only military men qualified as heroes. Porfirio Díaz came to power soon after.

Almost all of the rumors of conspiracies that made the rounds during Madero's short administration involved military men. There were, of course, some soldiers who were loyal. One such was Felipe Angeles. Angeles was relieved of his duties as head of the Military College at Chapultepec, Mexico's West Point, to take command of federal troops in the state of Morelos. Here he dealt with the rebellious Zapatistas as fairly and justly as possible under quasi-wartime conditions.

Early in January, Angeles crossed into the neighboring state of Mexico to observe operations of elements of the 29th Battalion against guerrilla elements led by one of Zapata's lieutenants named Genovevo de la O. The 29th was commanded by General Aureliano Blanquet who had, somewhat earlier, put Madero in a difficult position by killing eighty Zapatistas in the bullring at Puebla.

Angeles found that on their newest mission Blanquet's troops had indiscriminately set fire to fields and crops along their route, presumably to deprive De la O of supplies but working a hardship on innocent peasants. He was also told the story of a woman in the village of Ocuila.

She had been accused of being the lover of Genovevo de la O. This she admitted, but said she had done it only in order to protect her younger sisters from violence of other Zapatistas. The interrogating federal officer said that if she would sleep with him he would provide her and her sisters with a safe-conduct out of the trouble area. She agreed, and while she was performing her part of the bargain her younger sisters were raped by other officers of the 29th.

These were typical misfortunes of war. Angeles was far more disturbed by something else. A 29th Battalion engineer, Rafael Izquierdo, who had been a student with him at the Military College, approached Angeles in the village church at Malinalco and whispered: "If you only knew about this conspiracy and who is in it you would be amazed." Angeles deduced—correctly—that General Blanquet and other officers of the 29th were involved in a plot to overthrow Madero.

A few weeks later Gustavo Madero received more concrete information. An army colonel who was in financial straits approached Gustavo Madero at his home in the Calle Londres, borrowed five hundred pesos and, in gratitude, turned over a list of twenty-two conspirators, himself among them, who were planning to overthrow the government. Gustavo hurried to Chapultepec Castle and showed the list to Madero.

To no one's surprise both Bernardo Reyes and Felix Díaz were on the list. But since both had already attempted rebellion and failed and were in custody charged with treason they were not to be taken too seriously. The only civilian on the list was Reyes' son, Rodolfo, who had been involved in many intrigues in the interest of his father's political ambitions. There were also some top army officers. One was General Manuel Mondragón, an able artilleryman and a notorious malcontent who, since his return from a European mission, had been on the inactive list. There was General Blanquet who commanded 4000 troops stationed at Toluca, forty miles west of the capital. There was General Joaquín Beltrán who had captured Felix Díaz at Veracruz and who now commanded infantry units garrisoned at Tacubaya, only four miles from Chapultepec Castle, the presidential residence. General Guillermo Rubio Navarrete, in charge of artillery units at Tacubaya, was also on the list. The commands of all the alleged conspirators totaled about 14,000 troops in or near the capital. The most significant name on the list was that of General Victoriano Huerta, but after his name there was a question mark.

President Madero laughed at his brother's concern. It seemed clear to him that Gustavo had been gullible, that he had been sold a spurious document fabricated for the purpose. The most doubtful aspect of the list, Madero thought, was the uncertainty about Huerta, indicated by the question mark after his name. If anyone was likely to rebel, it was

Huerta. There would be no uncertainty about it; therefore the entire list was fraudulent. It was one of his major miscalculations.

One of the President's aides, Colonel Rubén Morales, also heard rumors of the coming *cuartelazo* (garrison revolt). He tried to report his findings to Madero, failed, and instead told Señora Madero. For this he was reprimanded by the incredulous President.

Juan Sánchez Azcona, Madero's secretary, picked up threads of the story. So did the Vice-President, José María Pino Suárez, who tried to convince the Minister of War, Angel García Peña, of the impending danger. "If you have no confidence in the army and no faith in its men then you are ill-equipped to govern," General García Peña told him. Somewhat later the Inspector of Police in the capital, Emiliano López Figueroa, heard the story and he, too, went to the Minister of War with the information that "the generals" were about to strike. "What generals?" asked García Peña. "Bernardo Reyes and Felix Díaz are prisoners. Nobody would follow Mondragón. Huerta? Huerta is a drunkard who only chases money. One can't believe it . . . Go to sleep and let me do the same."

The plotters were able to work openly. Mondragón went from one garrison to another, subverting and enlisting. So did Cecilio Ocón, a prosperous civilian who had worshiped Porfirio Díaz and now had transferred his loyalty to Felix Díaz. Ocón bought the Majestic Hotel, just across the Zócalo from the National Palace, and undertook major "remodeling." Wagons and carts daily delivered lumber, bags of cement, and other building supplies—all concealing rifles, sidearms, and ammunition.

There was uncertainty as to the zero hour. According to some sources the coup had been planned for January 1, for February 5 or 11, and as late as March 16. But if the date was uncertain, the existence of a plot was apparent to almost everyone except the man it most concerned, Francisco Madero. His brother Gustavo was genuinely alarmed and postponed his diplomatic mission to Japan. He began investigating, trying to determine the extent of the conspiracy and the best way of meeting it. On Saturday night, February 8, Gustavo was dining in the Sylvain Restaurant with some political friends. Police Inspector López Figueroa, fresh from his unproductive meeting with the Minister of War, found him there and told him what he knew. Gustavo hastily left and cruised the neighborhood of the Tacubaya garrison in an automobile, noting signs of activity. Inside the garrison the leaders of the conspiracy had met to eat and drink. Knowing that they were by now being closely observed they decided to strike at dawn the next day. Felix Díaz, whose delivery from the penitentiary was part of the plan, was unaware of the decision. When his deliverers arrived a few hours later he refused at first to leave his cell, not knowing for certain that the rebellion was under way.

Chapultepec Castle stands on a steep hill in the west-central part of the city surrounded by a grove of huge *ahuehuete* (cypress) trees that had been old and much venerated by the Aztec rulers who came to Chapultepec for rest and meditation. One of the forest guards charged with the protection of these ancient trees was awakened at 2 A.M., Sunday, February 9, by noise in Chapultepec Avenue below the castle. Peering through the darkness he made out a column of soldiers, full equipped, accompanied by cavalry and horse-drawn cannons moving east along the avenue toward the center of the city. The guard communicated his information to Adolfo Bassó, a one-time navy officer who was superintendent of the National Palace.

At about the same time the six hundred cadets of the military school at Tlalpan, fifteen miles south of the center of the city, commandeered tramcars on the Xochimilco line and headed for the palace which was to be the scene of the insurrection which they had agreed to support.

Meanwhile the column from Tacubaya divided. One section marched to the old military prison of Santiago Tlaltelolco, a thick-walled building where Fray Bernardino de Sahagún had once taught Spanish to the sons of Aztec nobles and, in the process, learned much of the ancient culture that Spain had destroyed. Here Bernardo Reyes was liberated from his cell. The old general had been waiting for his deliverers, dressed in his finest uniform. His favorite horse was saddled and waiting for him, along with a pair of pistols and a saber. Reyes joined General Gregorio Ruíz at the head of the column and they advanced toward the Zócalo and the National Palace. As they left the ancient prison the remaining inmates rioted and set fire to the building; several hundred of them died —the first victims of the reign of terror that was about to begin.

The other column, led by General Mondragón, had gone to the penitentiary, less than a mile east of the National Palace. A cannon manned by Cecilio Ocón, the militant civilian, was wheeled into place, ready to blast open the main gate of the prison if necessary. Felix Díaz, somewhat confused and not yet finished with his shaving, was permitted to join his liberators, and the column turned and marched toward the Zócalo.

The rebel forces now amounted to about three thousand men, armed with six cannons and fourteen machine guns. The Mondragón-Díaz group halted before reaching the Zócalo. The other column, led by General Ruíz, a large, heavy-jowled man with sweeping white mustaches, and by General Reyes, advanced directly on the National Palace. According to plan it should by now be in the hands of the young cadets from Tlalpan. But Bassó, Gustavo Madero, and General Villar had regained control of the palace and were now in charge with a body of about five hundred loyal troops, who confronted the Ruíz-Reyes column. Villar, old and arthritic but completely fearless, approached Ruíz, seized the reins of his horse and ordered him to dismount and surrender as a prisoner. Ruíz complied, but Reyes continued to advance. The palace guard opened fire and Reyes, the old romantic who had so often said he wanted to fight for the pacification of his country, was one of the first to fall, a pistol shot in his head and machine-gun bullets in his body.

The fighting lasted no more than ten minutes—and some three hundred were dead, many of them curious civilians who had gathered to see what was going on. The palace was still in the hands of the government. The remainder of the rebel force, now greatly diminished, withdrew from their reserve position near the palace. Led by Mondragón and Díaz they moved somewhat aimlessly through the streets of Mina and Rosales and into Bucareli. Seeking a place to rest, regroup and reconsider, they attacked the Ciudadela, the mid-city arsenal. They easily overcame the small custodial force and barricaded themselves inside the four-foot-thick walls. The first steps in their planned *golpe* had been disastrous, but here they were secure for the time being and were in possession of an ample supply of arms and ammunition.

Meanwhile Madero, at Chapultepec Castle, decided that his place was in the National Palace. Swinging into an English saddle on a fine toast-colored Arabian horse he started out on the most direct route to the Palace, through the beautiful Paseo de la Reforma and into Avenida Juárez. Dressed in civilian clothes and serenely confident, he might have been going for one of his regular Sunday morning rides, except that he was accompanied, on foot, by loyal cadets of the Military College. As the group moved through the Paseo they were joined by hundreds of cheering civilians. At the end of Avenida Juárez, in front of the still incompleted Palace of Fine Arts, the irregular column was forced to halt. There was sporadic firing in the street and one shot, apparently fired by a sniper from the Palace of Fine Arts, killed a bystander within a few feet of Madero. Madero was persuaded to dismount and take shelter in the Daguerre photographic studio. Here he received firsthand reports on the fighting at the Zócalo, including the disturbing news that the loyal General Villar, commander of the plaza—a man whose skill with firearms had brought him the army nickname of "Remington"—had been seriously wounded and would have to be replaced. By a strange twist of fate one of the people who joined him in the photographic studio was General Victoriano Huerta, in civilian dress. Huerta was again on inactive duty—because of the difficulty over his military vouchers—and once more, as he had so often in the past, he effusively and abjectly assured Madero of his loyalty. Madero then committed one of the greatest of his many errors. Although he neither liked nor trusted Huerta, he appointed him commander of the plaza to replace the disabled Villar. Villar, on hearing of the appointment, remarked "Be very careful, Victoriano, very careful." Madero intended it only as a temporary arrangement, to stand only until a more trustworthy officer could be installed in the critical post.

When there was a lull in the street disturbances the party left the photographic studio and moved through the Calle San Francisco toward the National Palace. Here Huerta performed his first act as newly appointed commander of the plaza. He ordered the immediate execution of his old friend and military colleague, Gregorio Ruíz. The sentence was carried out in the patio of the palace before a firing squad. Ruíz had, of course, been caught red-handed in an act of treason. But the speed with which the execution took place was unusual. Huerta may have been eager to demonstrate his new loyalty to Madero and willing to prove it at the cost of a friend's life. Or he may have been afraid that Ruíz would talk and disclose that he, Huerta, was a party to the conspiracy or was, at least, familiar with its details. Huerta, in his zeal, also wanted to execute some of the rebellious youngsters from the officer candidate school, but Madero prevented it.

Madero, after reestablishing himself in the palace, took off for Cuernavaca by automobile. Here he consulted with the loyal Felipe Angeles and ordered him and his one thousand troops to return to the capital. There was no interference from the Zapatistas. They were taking no part in the new rebellion. Although they had lost faith in Madero and disavowed his leadership, they had no sympathy with the military clique that was seeking to overthrow the President. Zapata had, in fact, recently resumed negotiations with Madero.

Madero intended to give Angeles the key military post to which he had temporarily assigned Huerta. But Angeles was Huerta's junior in the military hierarchy, having been advanced only recently from colonel to brigadier, and military seniority was strictly observed, even in this emergency. Instead Angeles was named chief of staff of the ministry of war and assigned by Huerta to a sector northwest of the rebel-held Ciudadela. Angeles was an accomplished artilleryman, one of the best in the Mexican army, and it was perhaps significant that the position to which he was assigned was almost useless from an artilleryman's point of view. For one thing there was no clear range for aiming and firing on the Ciudadela. The intervening territory was closely built up with residential and commercial buildings and heavily populated with noncombatants. In addition, his post was close to both the American Embassy and the British legation. If his artillery pieces drew fire from the Ciudadela there would certainly be protests from the two diplomatic establishments, with consequent international complications which the government wished to avoid.

This was only one of the many strange things about the *Decena Trágica* (the tragic ten days) which followed.

On Monday, February 10, the first day after the outbreak, the city was ominously quiet. People stayed off the street. Few newspapers were published. Tramcars did not run and there was almost no traffic save for improvised ambulances which, with white flags flying, moved about picking up the wounded from the previous day's fighting. On the second day an artillery duel began, the rebels firing from the Ciudadela, the government forces from the area around the National Palace. The range between the two bases was the most closely settled in the entire city. Effective fire was impossible for both sides—but the firing was heavy and continual. Gun crews, apparently knowing the impossibility of hitting their targets, were shooting at random. When an artillery piece recoiled and changed position the artillerymen would not bother to reposition and aim it, but would simply load and fire again. Machine-gun crews, unaccustomed to the use of that tricky weapon, sprayed shot in all directions. In all the shelling that followed there were only two direct hits on the National Palace—one of which destroyed the Mariana Gate—and only one on the Ciudadela. Meanwhile the buildings between the two strongholds suffered heavy damage—and so did the non-combatants. At the end of the first day's firing five hundred were dead; at the end of the ten-day period the toll had risen to approximately 5000—the majority of them civilians.

The government forces commanded by Huerta numbered some 6000 and additional troops supposedly loyal were on the way. The forces of Felix Díaz and Mondragón inside the Ciudadela amounted to only 1800. Once, many years before, a rebel force which had barricaded itself inside the Ciudadela had been overcome by government forces in a matter of hours. The Ciudadela now was even more vulnerable than it had been then; many windows had been opened in the thick walls, and it should have been easier to take. But it apparently was not. Huerta sent columns of soldiers known to be loyal, marching in the open down the streets leading to the Ciudadela where they were mowed down easily by the rebels' machine guns. He positioned his artillery to the northeast, north, and northwest, neglecting almost entirely the south side which was unobstructed and from which artillery fire could have been effective. Only an infantry attack was attempted from the south; in repelling it with artillery the rebels blew up the northwest corner of Belem Prison, liberating many prisoners, some of whom joined the forces in the Ciudadela.

There was much skirmishing. The rebels seized the sixth district police station at the corner of Victoria and Revillagigedo and the government troops recaptured it. The rebels left their stronghold, seized the old colonial chapel of Campo Florido and lost it again to an assault by government troops. There was much talk of reinforcements arriving but uncertainty as to which side was being reinforced. Soldiers stationed outside one of the legations were asked which side they were on. "Well señor," said one of the soldiers, "our officer will be back soon and then we'll know."

As a battle it was spurious, fraudulent, a grand deception—like the strategy of a pickpocket who jostles a victim from one side to distract his attention and then picks the pocket from the other side. The purpose, which did not become immediately apparent, was to create a scene of such havoc and frightfulness that any solution, no matter how dishonorable, would become preferable to present horror.

Corpses lay in the street where they fell, bloating in the February sun. Persons dying of natural causes could not be buried; their bodies lay in the gutters, putrefying along with the battle victims. Government troops tried to collect the corpses. Some were loaded on two-wheeled carts, taken to Balbuena Park, piled in huge mounds and burned. Others were doused with kerosene where they lay and burned in the street. Still they accumulated faster than these primitive methods could dispose of them. Garbage was piled on the sidewalks. All city services had ceased. No food supplies came into the city and people barricaded in their homes were starving. Electric lines came down in the cannonading and the nights were dark and terrifying, lighted only by the funeral fires and the flames from houses set ablaze by looters or vandals. On the night of the 14th the Madero home in the Calle Liverpool was put to the torch by a group of "aristocratic cretins" as one commentator described them. The Madero family, except for the President, who was in the National Palace, took refuge in the Japanese legation.

At one point a cease-fire was arranged. Dwellers in the danger zone took advantage of the respite to flee—carrying the odd assortment of belongings which people seize at such times—bird cages, family portraits, party dresses, and prized pieces of china. The firing was resumed without warning and more corpses littered the streets.

Meanwhile a strange series of parleys had gone on, so complicated, so seemingly contradictory, so twisted in loyalty and purpose that Mexican historians are still in disagreement on many details.

On Monday, February 10, Felix Díaz left the Ciudadela to meet an emissary of Victoriano Huerta in the centrally located El Globo pastry shop. A meeting between Díaz and Huerta was arranged. This second meeting took place the next day, Tuesday the 11th—the same day on which the aimless but devastating artillery duel began. Huerta and Díaz met in the Calle Nápoles home of Enrique Cepeda, an engineer and close friend of Huerta. What was said is not known, but the fact that the meeting took place was observed by Cepeda's next-door neighbor, Jesús Urueta, a pro-Madero member of the Chamber of Deputies. He immediately reported it to Gustavo Madero. Gustavo, in turn, reported to his brother the President this overt instance of fraternization between supposed enemies, possible proof of the treacherous disloyalty of Huerta. The President did nothing.

During the armistice on Sunday, February 16, Colonel Rubén Morales, the aide who had vainly tried to warn Madero of the conspiracy, observed eighteen carts loaded with provisions moving into the "besieged" Ciudadela with no interference from federal troops. Morales reported his observation to the President, and Madero called for an explanation from Huerta. The wily general at first shrugged off the report as nonsense, but when confronted with Morales' detailed description of the event he finally conceded that it was true. But, he said, he had planned it that way. Without provisions the rebels would leave the Ciudadela and scatter through the city to seek food and supplies. It might be wise, he added slyly, to send both wine and women to the besieged rebels to make certain they stayed together. And again he made one of his extravagant protestations of fidelity and dedication to his leader, embracing Madero and telling him "You are secure in the arms of General Huerta"—a grimly ominous assurance. Madero accepted it innocently.

By the evening of the next day, Monday the 17th, Gustavo Madero, who had none of his brother's innocence, decided matters had gone far enough. He enlisted the help of Jesús Urueta, his friend who had reported to him the secret meeting between Huerta and Díaz. Urueta joined Huerta in the command post at the National Palace, armed with cognac which the general liked so well (it was said that the only foreigners Huerta tolerated were Hennessy and Martell). After much drinking and idle talk between the two of them, Gustavo stepped into the room, pistol in hand, disarmed Huerta and placed him under arrest. At 2 A.M. Tuesday Huerta was taken before President Madero and once more accused of disloyalty. Huerta dismissed the meeting at the Cepeda house as "a matter of skirts," i.e. an assignation. As for the lack of progress in the campaign against the rebels, he reminded Madero that he had been criticized for slowness in his campaign against Orozco in Chihuahua; yet he had in the end soundly defeated Orozco and given the government a great triumph.

Madero once more seemed to be taken in. Upon Huerta's promise that he would seize all the rebels of the Ciudadela within the next twenty-four hours Madero not only released him but personally returned to him the pistol Gustavo had confiscated.

For Huerta the time for decisive action had come. The disastrous sham war could go on no longer. The conspiratorial machinery which had been slowly assembled now took visible shape and began to move. Blanquet, with the four thousand troops of his 29th Battalion, had been ordered from his garrison at Toluca to the capital to reinforce the federal troops early in the rebellion. It took him almost a week to reach the capital, a march which could have been made in a few days. Now he left his troops outside the city, at Tlaxpana, and held a meeting with Huerta who told him: "We have on our hands a very grave situation and we must resolve it," to which Blanquet simply answered "Whatever you order." Elements of the 29th were then assigned as guards at the National Palace, replacing the Carabineros of Coahuila, troops known to be loyal to Madero.

Now, on the morning of February 18, Huerta met with a group of anti-Madero federal senators, who agreed with him on the need for decisive action. The senators had already made one suggestion to Madero that he resign, giving as their reason the danger of intervention by the United States in Mexico's turmoil—an idea that the American ambassador planted and cultivated. Madero had rebuffed them the first time but had wired President William Howard Taft for a clarification of the U.S. position. Now the senators, after their conference with Huerta and apparently encouraged by it, called on Madero again and once more suggested that he resign.

To this Madero replied with unusual heat. "I am here by mandate of the Mexican people," he said, "and I will leave the National Palace only by death or by mandate of that same people." And he showed them a reply he had received from President Taft. While Taft admitted grave concern over the Mexican situation he stated flatly that reports of plans to send American forces into Mexico inaccurate and that "fresh assurances of friendship to Mexico are unnecessary . . . This nation sympathizes deeply with the afflictions of the Mexican people." Madero asked the senators to convey this information to Huerta in his presence, and Huerta, for the last time, vowed his loyalty to Madero and promised a major attack on the Ciudadela that afternoon.

A little later both Huerta and Gustavo Madero, who had handled him so roughly the night before, were guests at a luncheon in the Gambrinus Restaurant, a deluxe establishment in the Calle San Francisco. The unpleasantness of the previous night seemed forgotten. Gustavo politely asked Huerta what he would take, meaning to drink—a rhetorical question since Huerta always took cognac. "The Ciudadela," replied Huerta. A spirit of camaraderie seemed to prevail. When Huerta excused himself to go outside and make a telephone call he asked for and received the loan of Gustavo's pistol, having, he said, forgotten his own. Huerta was no sooner gone than a squad of soldiers stormed into the room, took Gustavo prisoner and locked him in a cloakroom.

It was 1:30 P.M. At the same time a climactic scene was played out at the National Palace. Madero and some of his ministers had been discussing the problem of provisions for both troops and civilian population, meeting in an antechamber of the cabinet room, a grand *sala* with yellow brocade walls, draperies of green broadcloth and fleur-de-lis embossed on the ceiling—a relic of the days when the room had been used by the Emperor Maximilian. Their discussion was interrupted by the sudden appearance of Lieutenant Colonel Jiménez Riveroll of Blanquet's 29th Battalion. The colonel said he had a message from General Huerta: that General Manuel Rivera and his troops had arrived from Oaxaca and had immediately rebelled against the government; that the President must accompany Jiménez Riveroll to a safer place. Madero interjected that he knew of Rivera's certain loyalty (actually Rivera was loyal and had, upon arrival in the capital, been removed from his command and placed under arrest by Huerta). As Madero spoke there was a disturbance in the next room. A company of soldiers in battle gear with rifles at the ready and led by Major Rafael Izquierdo—the same one who had hinted to General Angeles of the conspiracy—appeared. Madero ordered the soldiers out of the room. Jiménez Riveroll now spoke the truth. He had come, he said, on the orders of General Blanquet, acting jointly with General Huerta, to arrest the President. Madero protested, and the colonel turned to the soldiers, barked out an order to take aim, but before he could complete the command he was dropped by a shot from one of Madero's aides. Another aide shot Izquierdo. The company of soldiers, confused, fired anyway—and in the hail of shot Madero's cousin, Marcos Hernández, was killed. There were sounds of commotion outside the palace. Madero went to a window overlooking the Zócalo and shouted to the troops below that he was all right and would be with them in a moment. Followed by his cabinet members he descended to the ground level of the palace. There he was met by General Blanquet, resplendent in a black uniform trimmed in gold braid. Blanquet had only a few days before sent Madero a telegram acknowledging reports of his disloyalty and assuring the President of his faithful adhesion. Now, pistol in hand, he approached the President and in a parade ground voice announced "You are my prisoner." To this Madero retorted "I am the President and you are a traitor." But he was surrounded by disloyal troops. With his Vice-President and members of his cabinet he was made prisoner. The group was marched to the intendancy, a suite on the south side of the second patio of the palace, once the repository of the national archives but now the office of the superintendent of the palace. Somewhat later the cabinet members were released, but Madero and Pino Suárez remained, to be joined by General Angeles. Angeles had refused to obey a cease-fire order and was arrested for insubordination. Just across the Zócalo the bells of the cathedral began, on Huerta's orders, to ring wildly to announce to the tormented people of Mexico City that the ten days of terror were over. Victoriano Huerta dispatched a message to the foreign embassies and legations and to President Taft announcing: I HAVE THE HONOR TO INFORM YOU THAT I HAVE OVERTHROWN THIS GOVERNMENT. THE ARMED FORCES SUPPORT ME AND FROM NOW ON PEACE AND PROSPERITY WILL REIGN.

Huerta and Felix Díaz, the two supposed enemies, went to the American Embassy where they drew up the "pact of the Ciudadela," which Mexicans forever after were to refer to as the "pact of the Embassy." Huerta, the dark, beady-eyed Indian, and the plump, dandified Díaz, divided up Mexico between them. Huerta would become provisional President and would name, with Díaz's approval, a new cabinet. In the next election Díaz would, with Huerta's support, be chosen President of Mexico.

Huerta also agreed to turn Gustavo Madero, still held prisoner in the Gambrinus Restaurant, over to Díaz's men, along with Adolfo Bassó, superintendent of the National Palace, a stout-hearted, loyal Maderista who was suspected of having fired one of the shots that killed Bernardo Reyes. The two prisoners were carried to the Ciudadela by automobile. Cecilio Ocón, the civilian who had been active in fomenting the rebellion, struck the first blow against Gustavo Madero. Soon others in a mob of several hundred closed in on the President's brother. A soldier used a bayonet to gouge out Gustavo's one good eye. Another, with a badly aimed pistol, shot away the lower part of his face. Gustavo fell to the ground at the base of a monument to Morelos. He was repeatedly shot and stabbed and, finally, quite literally torn apart by the mob. The day of Gustavo's death was the same day on which he had been scheduled to leave for Japan. Later the grounds were searched in vain for two days in an effort to find enough of his remains to be given burial. His glass eye survived as a souvenir of the night of horror. It was displayed, handled and discussed in many cantinas and barracks rooms until, in time, it became unsafe to admit any connection with the event.

A little after Gustavo's end Adolfo Bassó was, with somewhat more consideration, placed against a wall of the Ciudadela in front of a firing squad. The one-time sailor gazed at the sky, complained mildly that he could not locate Ursa Major, a constellation he had often used for navigation, and calmly gave the order for his own death: ". . . *apunten . . . fuego!*"

That Francisco Madero did not immediately meet a similar death was due to Huerta's insistence on legal steps to validate an extra-legal, amoral series of events. Madero and Pino Suárez must first be forced to resign their offices so that the usurpation could wear the trappings of constitutionality.

A Huerta emissary called on the imprisoned President early the next day. His message was bluntly clear: resign and go freely into exile, or face the consequences—a threat of death.

Madero realized the hopelessness of his present situation. He wanted, if possible, to escape into exile so that he could, in time, return to Mexico to lead a new revolutionary movement. He wanted his associates, his family, his supporters, friends, and sympathizers to be spared. He also knew, finally and at great cost, the utter unreliability of anything Huerta might say, offer, or promise. By resigning he might save them. He specified that the resignations would be handed to neutral diplomats who would hold them until they had Huerta's written guarantees in hand. The ministers of Japan and Chile, both of whom had displayed friendly concern for the deposed President, would, as representatives of the diplomatic corps and of world opinion, accompany him and his party to Veracruz to see them safely embarked toward exile. Huerta's emissary indicated that this agreement was acceptable. Madero and Pino Suárez then drafted their joint statement of resignation, making a simple statement of fact and avoiding the temptation to make it a polemic. The resignations were handed to Pedro Lascuráin, Madero's Foreign Minister and the only cabinet member who had not, by this time, been forced to resign. Lascuráin was expected to place the resignations in the hands of the friendly diplomats.

The Chamber of Deputies had already been called into session, preparatory to receiving the resignations. Lascuráin presented the resignations directly to the chamber. The disinclination of some Maderista deputies to act was overcome by their fear for Madero's safety, and the resignations were accepted. With the presidency and vice-presidency vacant, the Foreign Minister, Lascuráin, then automatically became interim President. He remained President long enough to do just three things. He ended one session of the chamber and convened a new one. He appointed Victoriano Huerta to the vacant Ministry of Government—next in line after the Foreign Ministry in the order of succession to the presidency. And he then resigned, after an administration of less than an hour.

At San Lázaro station a special train had been made up and was waiting to take the deposed leaders and their families to Veracruz where they would be placed aboard a Cuban gunboat and start the journey into exile. Now members of the train crew were told they could go home. The train was not leaving.

In the intendancy of the National Palace Francisco I. Madero paced the floor, walking between a mirror at one end of the room and the sentry-guarded door at the other. As he walked he examined his watch fob with great attention; one of the decorative stones was missing. And he talked with Manuel Márquez Sterling, the Cuban minister who had assumed his post in Mexico only the previous month but who had become a steadfast and faithful friend. It was he who had arranged for the Cuban ship at Veracruz and who was now spending much of his time with Madero, whom he knew to be in grave danger.

Madero spoke in rambling fashion. A President constitutionally elected for a full term who was overthrown in only fifteen months, he said, should blame no one but himself. "The reason is—and history—if it is just, will confirm it—that he did not know how to sustain himself." With curious detachment he was referring to himself in the third person. Now he switched to the first person: "If I govern again I will gather around me men of resolution . . . I have made grave errors . . . But it is already late . . ."

THE AMBASSADOR

> "In Mexico the word [*chingar*] also
> means to injure, to lacerate, to violate . . .
> to destroy."
>
> Octavio Paz, *The Labyrinth of Solitude*

THE AMERICAN AMBASSADOR to Mexico, Henry Lane Wilson, was inextricably involved in the fate of Francisco Madero. Victoriano Huerta and Felix Díaz had met at the American Embassy, at Wilson's invitation, to negotiate their pact, and had agreed upon it with Wilson's smiling approval. The ambassador, a dry, thin, sharp-featured man whose toupee was carefully parted in the middle of his forehead, had suddenly become a key figure in the events of that tragic February.

Wilson, an exponent of "dollar diplomacy," was a peevish, aggressive man with the air of a moderately successful small-town lawyer. He came from a well-to-do family of Scotch-Irish ancestry. His father had been a congressman from Indiana, a veteran of the war with Mexico, a lieutenant colonel of volunteers in the Civil War and United States Minister to Venezuela. Wilson grew up in the pleasant, elm-shaded town of Crawfordsville, Indiana, and was graduated from the local college, Wabash. He read law in the office of Benjamin Harrison in the state capital, Indianapolis, and was active in Harrison's 1888 campaign for the presidency—an election in which Harrison lost the popular vote to Grover Cleveland but won in the electoral college. Later Harrison was to offer Wilson appointment as Minister to Venezuela, the post his father had occupied (coincidentally the Venezuelan government was a client of Harrison's law firm), but Wilson declined. He became involved in journalism, was for a time publisher and editor of the Lafayette (Indiana) *Journal,* moved to Spokane, Washington, where he was, in succession, a lawyer, a banker, and a speculator in real estate. In the last occupation he was badly hurt financially in the panic of 1893. He managed the campaign of his brother, John Lockwood Wilson, for the U. S. Senate and in 1896 worked for the nomination and election of William McKinley to the presidency. As a reward he was appointed to the U.S. foreign service with the rank of minister, serving first in Chile and later in Belgium. Early in 1910 he was transferred to Mexico with the rank of ambassador.

Wilson was ultraconservative and was well-connected in U.S. business circles, particularly through his brother. John Lockwood Wilson, after serving in the United States Senate, was regarded as Republican boss of the state of Washington. When he decided to buy controlling interest in the Seattle *Post-Intelligencer* the money was made available to him by James J. Hill, the railroad magnate. He was closely associated with Richard Achilles Ballinger, the former Mayor of Seattle, in handling political matters for the Guggenheim mining and smelting interests. Ballinger became Secretary of the Interior in William H. Taft's cabinet and the target of bitter criticism from conservationists who charged that his policies on public lands and resources favored private interests, notably the Guggenheims. As a member of Taft's cabinet he was instrumental in securing the appointment of Henry Lane Wilson to the embassy in Mexico City. The Guggenheims' American Smelting & Refining Company had substantial interests in Mexico and was an industrial rival of the powerful Madero clan, which also had important mining interests. The connection may have been circumstantial, but it was well-fixed in the minds of members of the American colony in Mexico. When Arnold Shanklin, an American consular officer who frequently disagreed with Ambassador Wilson, was posted back to the United States his friends saw him off at the railroad station and shouted "Don't be smelted or refined!"

Wilson, fifty-three years of age on his arrival in Mexico, was given to nervous gestures and a quick-paced short-stepped walk. His mustache was gray and drooping. He wore pince-nez glasses suspended from a broad black ribbon. Behind the crotchety appearance there was a strong will, a minimum of patience and a complete dedication to American business.

Wilson was not, at first, pleased with the government of Porfirio Díaz. The fact that it was a dictatorship was not bothersome; he was to say that a "mailed fist" was needed to govern Mexico, a country given to "anarchy and revolution," and, later he came to regard the Díaz regime as Mexico's golden age. But at the time of his arrival relations between the United States and the Díaz government were strained. Not only did U.S. oil companies feel that they were being discriminated against; the

American railroad magnate E. H. Harriman was being thwarted in his attempt to consolidate—and control—the Mexican railroads. Secretary Limantour—a friend of the Madero family—had blocked the Guggenheims in their attempt to acquire the Real del Monte silver mines.

Ambassador Wilson busily pushed claims against the Díaz government on behalf of U.S. interests, and if he was, at times, antagonistic, he still found the old dictator "remarkable" and "alert" and admired his "true monarchical dignity."

He was never to use such admiring words for Francisco I. Madero, whose revolutionary movement was to lead to the collapse of the Díaz regime. On the day of Madero's triumphant entry into Mexico City, June 7, 1911, Wilson predicted the "ultimate downfall of the Madero government." A little later, in a letter to Secretary of State Knox, Wilson told of having met Madero. ". . . He is insignificant in appearance, of diffident manners, hesitating in speech and seems to be highly nervous and uncertain in his course . . ."

At a dinner given to Madero at the University Club by the American colony the ambassador was the principal speaker. Wilson was tactless, blustering, and condescending, telling Madero how he should run his government once he had taken office. Madero, normally the soul of amiability, scowled and tugged nervously at his beard, and at the end of the tasteless performance, left the club in anger.

The ambassador's descriptions of Madero grew progressively more severe. Soon he was describing Madero as ". . . a dreamer, more of a mountebank than a messiah . . . a disorganized brain." His references to the Madero government, when it came to power, were loaded with invective: it was corrupt, impotent, inept, truculent, dishonest, insincere, capricious, tyrannical. He criticized Madero's program as being unrealistic and Utopian and at the same time criticized him for not carrying it out. He accused the Maderistas of interfering in state elections, forgetting that under Díaz state elections had been a farce. He complained that Madero was hampering freedom of the press although he, Wilson, had, during the Díaz administration, succeeded in getting several newspapers suppressed for expressing views he considered inappropriate.

Even more vigorously than he had done with the Díaz government, Ambassador Wilson pressed constantly for settlement of claims against Mexico at times when patience might have produced more substantial results. Not content with American claims, he also undertook those of other nations. He was very active in the suit of the Tlahualilo Land Company, a British-owned concern, on the grounds that some shares in the firm were American-held. He also participated in the Chinese government's suit for damages in the deaths of some Chinese nationals during the Madero revolution. His only connection here was that one of his Mexico City cronies, Lebbens Redman Wilfley, was, among other things, an attorney for the Chinese government.

Friends and relatives of Madero told a story which, they said, helped to explain Ambassador Wilson's animosity. Early in the Madero administration, they said, Wilson approached Rafael Hernández, Madero's cousin and one of his cabinet ministers, and asked that Madero be persuaded to assign him a "decorous" monthly subsidy similar to one he said that ex-President Díaz had given him to supplement the inadequate allowance provided by the United States government. Also, the story went, the ambassador's wife approached Señora Madero, asking her help in getting Madero's support for a business venture by which Wilson could make 50,000 pesos (approximately $25,000 U.S.) a year to help meet his expenses. Rafael Hernández favored such a concession or subsidy, believing it would tend to curb the ambassador's aggressiveness. Whatever the truth of the story—and it is repeated by at least four Mexican chroniclers of the period—Madero did nothing of the sort.

Instead Madero became more and more firm in his resistance to the American ambassador. He was confident that the change from a Republican to a Democratic administration in the United States in March 1913 would bring a change in diplomatic assignments, including Henry Lane Wilson's removal. He had already sent a confidential note to the Democratic President-elect, Woodrow Wilson, telling him that Ambassador Wilson was persona non grata. On one of his Sunday horseback rides in Chapultepec Park he told the Mexican intellectual José Vasconcelos: "You cannot imagine the impertinences [of Ambassador Wilson] . . . Now the American ambassador no longer runs the country. At least he hasn't much time left. In a few months Woodrow Wilson will become President of the United States and he is my friend. The first thing I will ask him is to change ambassadors. This Henry Lane Wilson is an alcoholic . . ."

The charge of overindulgence, which Mexicans often leveled at Wilson (one writer said that Wilson practiced "saloon diplomacy") was a comparatively minor matter. The important thing was that his ideas and attitudes, which otherwise might have been regarded as nothing more than peculiar, were given great importance because of his position. Not only was he the representative of Mexico's powerful neighbor—a neighbor that Mexico traditionally distrusted; he was also ex officio dean of the diplomatic colony, the only full-fledged ambassador in a corps of ministers. Although some of the ministers, mainly those of Cuba, Chile, and Japan, were kindly disposed toward the Madero government, most of the others were inclined to follow Wilson's lead.

Confident from the outset that the Madero administration could not endure, Wilson was equally convinced that the government was unable to protect the lives and property of foreigners, Americans and others. After the government's early setback in the Orozco rebellion Wilson predicted that the government would soon collapse. He organized a foreigners' defense league and demanded that the State Department ship him a thousand rifles with a million rounds of ammunition. When, somewhat later, the Orozco rebellion was crushed he advised the State Department: "These victories and this recovery of territory, while lending a temporary prestige to the national government, have apparently produced no other substantial results."

His reporting on Mexican affairs had led the State Department to caution him to "observe the strictest neutrality, interfering in no wise between contending forces." The Secretary of State, Philander Chase Knox, the chief practitioner of "dollar diplomacy," thought it advisable to warn President Taft of Ambassador Wilson's "increasing pessimism . . . [which] appears to the department to be unjustified if not, indeed, misleading." The department also found that Wilson frequently based his official dispatches on highly unreliable stories that had appeared in the *Mexican Herald,* a shaky English language newspaper which was consistently lavish in its praise of Ambassador Wilson, and doing so without bothering to check their accuracy.

His communications, written or oral, contained frequent, admiring references to "the higher and educated classes who in the final analysis must rule this country either through a gradual conversion of the present administration or by open revolution." The rest of the Mexican population he lumped together as "disorderly elements of society." This imprecise method of description was illustrated in his reference to the lynching and burning of an itinerant Mexican worker in Texas. He was, said Wilson was seeming indifference, "hung or boiled or something like that."

From the outbreak of the Mondragón-Díaz rebellion Wilson tended to exaggerate the potency and popularity of the rebel forces and to belittle the strength of the forces loyal to Madero as well as Madero's personal popularity. For Felix Díaz he had nothing but admiration: "A man of fine and independent . . . unblemished character, of physical courage, brave in war, moderate in peace." At the end of the *Decena Trágica* when Felix Díaz arrived at the American Embassy to sign his peace pact with Victoriano Huerta the ambassador made no effort to hide his enthusiasm and greeted him with "Long live General Díaz, savior of Mexico." In addition to displaying partiality the ambassador's attitude revealed somewhat faulty judgment. Díaz was neither a strong nor a particularly popular figure. In the uprising of February 9 it was General Manuel Mondragón who organized the rebel forces and directed the fighting from the Ciudadela. Díaz, however, sensed the American ambassador's susceptibility to flattery and used it. Wilson, after a visit to the Ciudadela during the ten-day siege, reported with pleasure: "General Díaz received us with the full honors of war."*

The ambassador may have been a frustrated military man, remembering his father's distinguished career in both the Mexican War and the Civil War. Shortly after the outbreak of the ultimate rebellion against Madero the United States ordered navy vessels into the ports of Veracruz, Tampico, Acapulco, and Mazatlán "to observe and report . . . without bias" the degree of protection being given foreigners and, presumably, to evacuate them if it became necessary. Ambassador Wilson jumped at the opportunity to become a combat commander in what he apparently hoped would be an American intervention. I REQUEST IMMEDIATE INSTRUCTION, he wired the Secretary of State, AS TO THE MEASURE OF CONTROL I WILL BE PERMITTED TO EXERCISE OVER THE AMERICAN SHIPS AND MARINES WHICH SHOULD ARRIVE TOMORROW AT VARIOUS MEXICAN PORTS. IN REGARD TO MEXICO CITY [200 miles from the nearest seaport] AND VERACRUZ I RECOMMEND THAT I BE CLOTHED . . . WITH POWER TO ACT IMMEDIATELY IN CRISES WITHOUT FURTHER INSTRUCTION. THE SITUATION IS HOURLY BECOMING MORE DANGEROUS. The State Department replied that while it appreciated his anxiety IT WOULD BE INADVISABLE TO INSTRUCT YOU IN THE WAY YOU SUGGEST.

Horrible as were the results of the intracity war during the *Decena Trágica,* Ambassador Wilson magnified it to even more cataclysmic proportions. He cruised the battle zone in an automobile waving an American flag aloft. He shepherded frightened Americans and other foreigners into the embassy and at the same time complained to Madero that they were all endangered because the embassy was within artillery range of the contending forces. Madero immediately offered him the use of a mansion in suburban Tacubaya, well away from the fighting. Wilson scorned the offer. The Secretary of State advised him: "If . . . the position of the embassy becomes really dangerous you should evacuate the premises rather than risk casualties . . . It would perhaps be best for you and other Americans to take up temporary quarters beyond the range of fire." Still the ambassador refused to move; to do so would have robbed him of his principal reason for frequent complaints to

* During the same visit to the Ciudadela Wilson pointedly ignored the plea for help of John Kenneth Turner, the American writer. Turner, whose *Barbarous Mexico* had graphically portrayed conditions in Mexico under the Díaz dictatorship, was being held by the Mondragón-Díaz force under sentence of death for "spying." Although Turner pleaded with Wilson in person the ambassador did nothing. Turner, after his escape, made a formal complaint to the State Department.

President Madero—complaints which seemed to place the blame for the battle on the government rather than on the rebels who started it.

Early in the conflict Wilson had mentioned to Madero the possibility of intervention by U.S. forces if the fighting were not ended immediately —presumably by the government surrendering to the rebel forces in the Ciudadela. Madero showed no fright. Wilson next went to work on Foreign Minister Pedro Lascuráin in what he described as a "man to man" talk. As a result of it, Wilson reported, Lascuráin "is profoundly impressed with what he believes to be the threatening attitude of our government." The ambassador's hints had the desired effect. Lascuráin conveyed his fears regarding intervention to a group of senators, meeting not as senators but as individuals. The senators, most of them opponents of Madero of long standing, agreed that the only hope was to end the conflict by persuading Madero to resign.

While the senators were deliberating Wilson had called into consultation the German, Spanish, and British ministers—the last, Francis Stronge, was a Belfast Irishman who frequently went about with a parrot on his shoulder. Wilson reported to the State Department on their meeting: "The opinion of the assembled colleagues was unanimous and clear that we should at once, even without instructions, request President Madero to resign in order to save further bloodshed and possible international complications, the idea being that the executive power should be turned over to Congress."

In the space of an hour on Saturday, February 15, Madero was confronted with two suggestions for his resignation—one from the senators and one from the three diplomats—both stemming from the activities of the American ambassador. Later in the day Wilson himself saw Madero. Madero showed him the text of the wire he had sent to President Taft, asking for clarification of American intentions regarding armed intervention. In a separate message, transmitted through Mexico's Washington Embassy, Madero complained of foreign diplomats meddling in the internal affairs of Mexico.

Wilson was furious. Madero's complaint, he told the State Department, was "irregular, false, and misleading." But he did not despair. He had, meanwhile, finally met Victoriano Huerta, a man whose loyalty to the government had long been open to question. Huerta found a kindred soul and took the ambassador into his confidence. Enrique Cepeda, who had been instrumental in setting up the meetings between Huerta and his supposed enemy, Felix Díaz, now became a courier between the office of the American ambassador and Huerta's command post. The ambassador was kept well informed on developments as the plot played out. Thus, at 4 P.M. on February 17 almost twenty-four hours before

Madero was finally overthrown, Wilson was able to advise the State Department that it was soon to occur.

This message was to become a key element in the bitter disputes Henry Lane Wilson later had with the American press and with President Woodrow Wilson over the role he played—or did not play—in the overthrow of Madero. An American newspaperman in Mexico, Robert Hammond Murray, published in *Harper's Weekly* in the spring of 1916 a six-part series of articles entitled *Huerta and the Two Wilsons*. Murray, highly critical of the former ambassador, cited Wilson's dispatches. Henry Lane Wilson complained that Murray had used "mutilated" and "garbled" versions of the dispatches, and that later Woodrow Wilson, in criticizing the ambassador, had also used the "garbled" version of the dispatch of 4 P.M., February 17, 1913.

The official version, according to both Henry Lane Wilson in his memoirs and *Foreign Relations of the United States 1912/1913*, was: "Huerta notifies me to expect some action that will remove Madero from power at any moment; plans fully matured, the purpose of delay being to avoid any violence or bloodshed. I asked his messenger no questions and made no suggestions beyond requesting that no lives be taken except by due process of law. I am unable to say whether or not these plans will materialize; I simply repeat to the government the word sent to me, which I feel bound to listen to as it so intimately concerns our nationals."

The version of the dispatch cited by Murray—and supposedly quoted by Woodrow Wilson—was: "General Huerta has just sent his messenger to me again to say that I may anticipate some action which will remove Madero from power at any moment, and that plans were fully matured, the purpose of the delay being to avoid any violence or bloodshed. I asked no questions beyond requesting that no lives be taken except by due process of law. I am unable to say whether these plans will come to anything or not. I simply repeat to the government the words sent to me, which I feel bound to listen to, as it so intimately concerns the situation of the nationals in the city."

The wording was different, but the sense was not. The ambassador clearly had prior knowledge of the plan to unseat Madero. He made no effort to communicate his information to the Madero government to which he was accredited. He did, however, suggest to an Associated Press correspondent that it would be well to be at the National Palace the next day at noon.

As a man well versed in power politics and as a close—although sometimes jaundiced—observer of Mexican revolutionary turmoil over the past three years Wilson must have known that from the moment of the overthrow Madero's life would be in jeopardy. A regime whose origins were as suspect and whose tenure was so narrowly based as that of the Huerta-Díaz coalition could not afford the risk of a living Madero. Madero's administration may have been inept, but his personal popularity with the masses of Mexico was still strong.

But after Madero's forcible removal Ambassador Wilson, who until the coup had played a vigorously aggressive role in directing Mexico's tortured destiny, displayed a cautious manner, almost a horror of the notion of meddling in the affairs of the unhappy nation.

On the day after the overthrow Wilson reported that "Huerta asked my advice as to whether it was best to send the ex-president out of the country or place him in a lunatic asylum. I replied that he ought to do that which was best for the peace of the country." Somewhat later he recommended that the Huerta government not take the lives of Madero and Pino Suárez "without due process of law."

The State Department, "dollar diplomacy" or not, was becoming alarmed: GENERAL HUERTA'S CONSULTING YOU AS TO THE TREATMENT OF MADERO TENDS TO GIVE YOU A CERTAIN RESPONSIBILITY IN THE MATTER, the State Department wired. IT MOREOVER GOES WITHOUT SAYING THAT CRUEL TREATMENT OF THE EX-PRESIDENT WOULD INJURE, IN THE EYES OF THE WORLD, THE REPUTATION OF THE MEXICAN CIVILIZATION, AND THIS GOVERNMENT HOPES TO HEAR OF NO SUCH TREATMENT AND HOPES TO HEAR THAT HE HAS BEEN DEALT WITH IN A MANNER CONSISTENT WITH PEACE AND HUMANITY.

The following day the State Department, having by this time received Wilson's tardy report of the murder of Gustavo Madero, wired again: the killing of Gustavo had CAUSED A MOST UNFAVORABLE IMPRESSION HERE and again expressed hope that THERE IS NO PROSPECT OF INJURY TO THE DEPOSED PRESIDENT OR VICE-PRESIDENT OR THEIR FAMILIES.

The State Department was not alone in expressing concern to Ambassador Wilson. The ministers of Cuba and Japan, on the day after the coup, delivered to Wilson, as dean of the diplomatic corps, a letter the Madero family had addressed to the corps asking for intercession to save Madero's life. Wilson, who had had no hesitation in suggesting Madero's resignation in the name of the diplomatic corps (although he had consulted only three ministers), now balked. Individual diplomats, he said, could, if they liked, intercede with Huerta but they could not do it in the name of the corps.

Prominent Mexicans such as José Vasconcelos appealed to the ambassador. So did the head of the Masonic lodge in Mexico City—Madero was a Mason and so were both Ambassador Wilson and President Taft. Members of the Texas state legislature appealed to the State Department. And finally Madero's wife, Sara, and his sister, Mercedes, called on the ambassador on February 20. Señora Madero later told an interviewer that the ambassador was barely civil. He complained to her of Madero's "peculiar ideas" and said that the former president did not know how to govern and that he neither sought nor listened to the advice of the American ambassador. As for interceding to protect Madero, he said, it was "a responsibility which I do not wish to undertake." Señora Madero had brought with her a message written by Madero's mother, addressed to President Taft, pleading for his help. The ambassador said that this was not necessary but finally accepted the telegram and put it in his pocket. Late on the following day Wilson advised the State Department: "I have just received a letter from the mother of President Madero asking me to intercede with General Huerta to spare his life and that of Pino Suárez . . ." There was no indication that he had taken any action. Madero's mother received no reply or acknowledgment. A letter inquiring, ten days later, whether the original message had been received also went unanswered.

On the day after his interview with Señora Madero, Ambassador Wilson led the diplomatic corps to a reception given by Victoriano Huerta at the National Palace. It was Huerta's first formal appearance since assuming the presidency. Ambassador Wilson served as spokesman for his colleagues, offering felicitations to Huerta and expressing the hope that "your excellency will dedicate all your efforts, your patriotism and knowledge to the service of the nation and obtain the complete reestablishment of tranquillity . . ."

The new President responded cordially and led the diplomats to a table loaded with pastries, wines, and liquors. The American ambassador, normally a stern-faced man with a piercing gaze, seemed to be bubbling with joy. Taking a glass of pale sherry he offered a toast to Huerta, "that your government may bring back peace to the Mexican people." Huerta nodded amiably. The ambassador went on: The next day, in honor of the birthday of George Washington, he invited the President, his cabinet, and his diplomatic colleagues and their wives to a reception at the American Embassy.

On the evening of the 22nd Huerta and his party were late in arriving at the huge thirty-room medieval-style American Embassy at the corner of the Calles Puebla and Veracruz. The ambassador anxiously kept looking at his watch. The other diplomats chatted. Riquelme Hevia, the Chilean minister, whispered to the Cuban minister, Márquez Sterling, that he had heard that Madero and Pino Suárez had been transferred from the National Palace to the penitentiary. Márquez Sterling said he doubted it. Someone else whispered that Madero had been wounded. Still another commented: "Alive or dead, yes; wounded, no." The Chilean minister said he intended to raise the question of expatriation of the prisoners. He was asked: "Wouldn't this make you non grata to the present government?" The Chilean minister replied: "Absurd. We are ministers of friendly sister nations. We don't act against anyone but for everyone. We are doing a service to Mexico." The Cuban, Márquez Sterling, who had been doing more than any of his colleagues to save Madero and Pino Suárez, nodded approval. He handed the Chilean a message he had just received from his government: "The president and government congratulate you for your noble and humanitarian efforts to aid the government of Mexico in resolving the present situation and in saving the lives of the ex-president and the ex-vice-president . . . The Cuban people, as all others, would be overjoyed by respect for the life of Madero and his companions in proof of the magnanimity of the Mexican nation." The Chilean minister, impressed, said he would like to make mention of this in a note he intended to address to the Foreign Minister the next day.

The discussion of the fate of Madero was interrupted by the late arrival of General Huerta, followed by a large party of cabinet ministers, aides, and political hangers-on. Huerta bobbed his close-clipped head to left and right, constantly readjusting his slipping spectacles. Mrs. Wilson approached him. The old general bowed from the waist, and then, led by the ambassador's wife, went through the crowd acknowledging introductions with soft-spoken but elaborate Spanish pleasantries—"I kiss your feet . . . much pleasure . . . your servant." Finally Huerta was escorted to the table. Here the ambassador raised a champagne goblet and offered a toast to George Washington. Huerta, staring fixedly, gravely imitated him.

As the reception broke up and the diplomats and government officials filed out of the embassy they noticed the ambassador and the President seated in a small room at one side of the entrance hall, the same room in which, a few nights earlier, Huerta and Felix Díaz, the supposed enemies, had exchanged an embrace with the ambassador as a happy witness. Now the ambassador sat on a sofa, elbows on knees, his head moving back and forth to punctuate his words. Huerta slouched in an easy chair, only his bullet head and bronze face out of the shadow, listening closely. The departing guests could not hear what was said.*

---

* *The New York Times* of the next morning, Sunday, February 23, reported under a Mexico City dateline of February 22 that Madero and Pino Suárez "were transferred today from the National Palace to the penitentiary. A member of the provisional cabinet said that probably no decision as to their fate would be made for some days." In the next column the *Times* correspondent reported that "President Huerta is getting the situation well in hand."

CHAPTER 14

THE ASSASSINS

"It's an error to judge the execution of Madero as a crime," interupted Father Jeremiah. ". . . you can injure, wound, kill, do anything you like, in short, if it redounds to your own good and *ad majorem Dei gloriam.*"

Mariano Azuela, *Los Caciques*

WHILE Ambassador Wilson and General Huerta conferred at the embassy, Madero and Pino Suárez were preparing to go to bed on army cots in the intendancy of the National Palace. Pino Suárez was pessimistic, almost hopeless. He had written, with a yellow pencil on a sheet of cheap white paper, a farewell letter to a close friend. Madero showed signs of having wept. He had been visited by his mother and had learned of the terrible end of his brother, Gustavo. He had, on his knees, begged his mother's forgiveness.

A few hours earlier three young men had innocently become involved in a series of events which would terrify them for years to come.

At 5:30 in the afternoon nineteen-year-old Ricardo Romero was summoned by Alberto Murphy, who employed him as chauffeur. Murphy, whose wife was a niece of Porfirio Díaz, lived at 52 Calle San Agustín, and was the owner of a new Protos limousine of which he was very proud. He asked Romero if the car was ready for use. Romero said it was. In that case Romero was put at the orders of Cecilio Ocón, the grim-faced businessman who had been close to Felix Díaz all through the *Decena Trágica* and had struck the first blow against the unfortunate Gustavo Madero a few nights earlier. Ocón emerged from an office in the Murphy house and ordered Romero to drive him to the National Palace. The short winter day was over and there were many lights in the palace. Romero parked and waited for an hour and a half. Ocón then reappeared and ordered Romero to drive him to the home of Felix Díaz in the Calle Artes. Here he disappeared for a few minutes, then came out and ordered Romero to drive him to the Ministry of War at the National Palace. Then they returned to the Felix Díaz residence, where Ocón remained for a half hour. After this Romero drove him once more to the National Palace and was ordered to park the Protos limousine outside the intendancy. Nearby was parked the presidential car and a third one, a Peerless touring car which Romero, with a chauffeur's eye, noticed had been somewhat altered by use of Packard parts. It was managed by another young chauffeur, Ricardo Hernández, about Romero's own age, and a helper, Génaro Rodríguez.

Hernández worked for Frank Doughty, operator of the Garage Inglés. On the late afternoon of February 22 he and his helper were in the car at a taxi stand on the Alameda, waiting for business. They were approached by a tall black-clad man whom Hernández later identified as Francisco Alanís, butler in the household of Ignacio de la Torre y Mier, a son-in-law of Porfirio Díaz. Alanís arranged for the hire of the car on an extended basis and then ordered Hernández to drive through the Calle San Francisco to the central gate of the National Palace. There he left him waiting for almost four hours. Then a major of the *rurales,* later identified as Francisco Cárdenas, approached the car and ordered Hernández to drive inside the palace and park the car outside the intendancy. Here Hernández and his helper, Génaro Rodríguez, and the other chauffeur waited.

A small man wrapped in a military cape and with a black felt hat pulled low on his head emerged from the intendancy. It was Francisco Madero, until a few days before President of Mexico. Madero started for the presidential car but was motioned back by Cárdenas and told, instead, to get in the closed Protos, driven by Romero. Cárdenas ordered a soldier into the front seat with Romero with instructions not to allow him to talk. Pino Suárez, the former Vice-President, now came out, also wrapped in a military cape, accompanied by two more men in the uniforms of *rurales.* He was ordered into the Peerless, and the *rurales* got in on either side of him. Cárdenas and still another officer of the *rurales,* a fat man with olive skin who addressed Cárdenas with the familiar *tu,* now got into the rear seat of the Protos with Madero. On Cárdenas' orders the two cars moved out of the palace, into the Calle Moneda, past the San Lázaro station of the Interoceanic Railroad—by which Madero had vainly hoped to be taken to Veracruz and exile—and finally to the penitentiary in the Calle Lecumberri.

It was now approximately 11 P.M. and the penitentiary was brightly lighted at an hour when it usually was dark. The two cars approached it slowly. The first car, carrying Madero, stopped near the main en-

trance, and the second car stopped close behind it. Madero made a move
to get out of the car but was ordered to sit still. Cárdenas got out. As he
did so he unholstered his pistol and placed it in the waistband of his
trousers. He went to the penitentiary gate, spoke briefly with a guard. He
then returned to the car, accompanied by the guard, and climbed back
in beside Madero. The guard stood on the running board of the car and
ordered the driver to turn and proceed along the north wall toward the
rear of the penitentiary. A turn was then made along the east wall, and
the cars stopped before a small rear door to the prison.

"Get out," Cárdenas ordered. He addressed him as *carajo* (prick).
As the little ex-President stepped to the ground Cárdenas pulled the gun
from the waistband of his trousers and shot him in the back of the head.

Pino Suárez was forced from the second car. He opened his mouth to
say something, but before it was said he too was shot. The fallen man
sighed deeply and his body twitched. "The sonofabitch moved," said
someone, and more shots were pumped into the ex-Vice-President. The
lights of the penitentiary went out.

A watchman in one of the octagonal crenellated towers of the penitentiary had watched the scene with astonishment. He rushed to a telephone to call the prison director, Colonel Luis Ballesteros, a new man
from the army who had been appointed to the post only that afternoon.
The watchman blurted out what had happened. The new director told
him: "It is nothing. Forget it."

The young chauffeurs had backed away from their cars and stood
together. "Are they going to shoot us?" Romero asked Hernández. "Shut
up so you don't get us in trouble," said Hernández.

Now Cárdenas and the others aimed their guns at the two automobiles and started shooting, shattering windows and headlights and
puncturing the metal panels but not shooting at the motors or gasoline
tanks.

Hernández and his helper were ordered to get back in their car and
to drive back to the National Palace with the two *rurales* who had
accompanied Pino Suárez. The two young men were told that if they
talked about what they had seen their heads would be in danger. They
then returned the car to the garage, noticing that in addition to the
bullet damage the seat cushions were stained with blood. Hernández,
with his employer's permission, went into hiding, emerging only long
enough to be taken to the National Palace the next day where he was
asked to sign a document which he was not permitted to read.

At the rear of the penitentiary the two bodies were tumbled into the
rear seat of Romero's car, Madero's body on top of that of Pino Suárez.
The latter's legs hung out the door and were broken in the rough handling. Romero was warned by Cárdenas that if he did not obey orders

the same thing would happen to him. They then returned to the front entrance. Here the bodies were dragged by the feet from the car and dropped on a coarse gray blanket, after which they were carried into the penitentiary. In the process a silver chain and watch, engraved with initials, and a yellow pencil fell from Pino Suárez' pocket. Cárdenas picked them up and stared at them curiously.

Somewhat later an ambulance from the Military Hospital drew up at the main gate of the prison and unloaded four corpses. These too were carried inside the prison walls.

Romero drove Cárdenas and his fat fellow officer back to the National Palace, leaving them at the Mariana Gate, where Cárdenas cautioned him that if he spoke a single word about what had happened his life would be in danger. The major added that Romero would be required to come to the National Palace to make a declaration; all he had to do was sign a piece of paper. Everything would be arranged. Romero then drove to Murphy's house, put the car in the courtyard and was directed by the porter to see Señor Murphy. He went to Murphy's bedroom where his employer asked him what had happened. "Don't be afraid," Murphy said. "Nothing will happen to you. I will give you a gift to keep your silence." Romero said he wanted no gift, that he just wanted to keep from being killed. He thought, unhappily, that it being a Saturday he would normally have gone to a dance that night. A few days later Cecilio Ocón, the man with whom he had begun the evening's grim adventure, came for him and took him to the National Palace where he, like Hernández, signed a document which he was not permitted to read. Afterward Major Cárdenas, who was in the office, came out with Ocón to look at the damages to the car.

It was Cárdenas who would, ultimately, provide other details of what had happened that night. Cárdenas was quickly advanced to the rank of general, and, in April 1913, two months after the Madero murder, was defeated by anti-Huerta revolutionists in a battle at Tacámburo in the state of Michoacán. He then fled Mexico and made his way to Guatemala, where he let his beard grow and disguised himself as a mule trader.

But the disguise was penetrated and President Estrada Cabrera of Guatemala ordered his arrest. For a time Cárdenas remained at liberty under bond provided by a friendly Mexican. He made an attempt to escape but was captured near the border of El Salvador and returned to Guatemala City. There, finally, he made a confession, in June 1915, that filled in many of the gaps in the story that had already been partially told in statements by the young chauffeurs.

Cárdenas' story: That at about 1 P.M. on the afternoon of February 22 an aide of General Aureliano Blanquet came to his hotel room. Cárdenas was ordered to appear immediately before Blanquet at the

National Palace. There Blanquet told him brusquely that the Mexican nation required a great service of him: that he must kill Francisco Madero. Cárdenas objected that this could be a matter of grave consequences, but Blanquet assured him that the decision had been reached by President Huerta's cabinet. To clarify matters he took him to the office of General Mondragón, Minister of War. Here they met Mondragón, Felix Díaz, and Cecilio Ocón. Neither Díaz nor Ocón were members of the cabinet, but Mondragón was, and he confirmed the mission for which Cárdenas had been chosen. He added that in such matters they must rely on people of confidence and there were not many such people available. Cárdenas felt complimented by the trust but still feared the responsibility, and asked how and where the execution should take place. At this point Ocón, the civilian, broke in to say that it would not be a formal execution. Instead, he said, there would be a simulated attack on the escort taking the victims to the penitentiary, and that in the skirmish between the escort and the "attackers" Madero, Pino Suárez, and General Angeles would be killed. Cárdenas, a veteran of many killings in rural Mexico, objected again that such a matter would be hard to bring off in the capital of the nation.

Mondragón told him not to be fussy; this would not be the first time he had killed a man.

Cárdenas agreed that this was true, but he had never killed a man of this stature.

Felix Díaz said that Madero was really quite small, which was not what Cárdenas had meant.

Ocón said that if Cárdenas was a coward he himself had been ready ever since February 18, the day of Madero's arrest, to kill him at any time the order was given.

Mondragón, in response to a question from Blanquet, said the sentence of death had been approved by all members of the Huerta government.

Cárdenas agreed to do it, but a little later had a recurrence of his uneasiness. He returned to Blanquet, saying it was a very serious matter and that he would like to speak with the President.

Blanquet, in a bad humor, then escorted Cárdenas through the palace to the presidential suite. They found Huerta in the dining room, where Blanquet explained the problem. Huerta poured cognac for the visitors and then took Cárdenas by the arm, leading him into a corridor where, as Cárdenas remembered, there was a barber chair. Huerta told him that the cabinet had taken this resolution for the good of the fatherland and that he, being one of the few trusted men available, had been designated for the mission. Cárdenas asked the President if all three men should die. "Let Angeles alone," said Huerta, "but the other two must be killed, this very day without fail."

Cárdenas returned to Blanquet's office. Ocón provided more details. He, Ocón, would lead the "attacking" force of ten disguised police-men. They would avoid shooting in order not to wound the escorting soldiers. Cárdenas was given to understand that he himself must kill Madero, and that another officer of the *rurales* would kill Pino Suárez. For this secondary task Blanquet recommended Rafael Pimienta.

With this Cárdenas went in search of a Corporal Pimienta, who was to be his accomplice. After having some drinks with Pimienta, they went to the home of Ignacio de la Torre y Mier and arranged for the automobile.

From this point on the Cárdenas story did not differ markedly from that told by the young chauffeurs. But in conclusion Cárdenas insisted that as a soldier he was obliged to obey orders, and that in this case the order came from President Huerta and the order was with the approval of Huerta's ministers. He said that after the murders he had himself heard General Blanquet telephone several ministers and inform them that the deed had been done.

The president of Guatemala was prepared in 1915 to extradite Cárde-nas, but by this time there was so much revolutionary confusion in Mexico it was uncertain as to who was running the country. Cárdenas remained in Guatemala. For four years he was a prisoner, until a Guate-malan revolution tumbled the government of Estrada Cabrera, during which all prisoners were set free. In 1920 it appeared that Mexico would finally succeed in having Cárdenas extradited for trial. Sitting on a park bench in Guatemala City, Cárdenas put a pistol to his head and shot himself. Before dying he was reported to have confessed once more, this time to a Mexican journalist who happened to be there, that it was he who killed Francisco Madero. There was much uncertainty about the whole matter including the rumor that circulated in Mexico that Cárdenas died with two bullets in his head.

His supposed accomplice, Rafael Pimienta, who was a corporal in the *rurales* on the night of the assassination, advanced quickly in the ranks of the Mexican army and, in time, switched sides, joining the anti-Huerta revolutionary forces in the state of Sonora and rose to the grade of general. In the same year as the suicide of Cárdenas he was formally charged with the murder of Pino Suárez. In his preliminary statement he conceded that he was present at the time but that the killing had been done by another officer of the *rurales* who by this time could not be found. Pimienta was indicted but later absolved by a military court. Three years later he was once more in rebellion against the government, was captured and executed.

By now Victoriano Huerta had been dead for many years, the facts of his guilt or innocence in the deaths of Madero and Pino Suárez still not clearly established. The only thing that was certain was that he had been the head of a government which either had authorized the murders or knowingly allowed them to be committed.

As to Huerta's cabinet having authorized the murders there was doubt. Some ministers seem to have been in the dark as to what was going on. Huerta, who had had no experience in governmental routine, was quite informal in holding cabinet meetings. They were held at irregular times. Some ministers might not even be informed of the meeting. Huerta might or might not attend; if he did attend he might not stay, or might not listen to what transpired. Nor were the meetings confined to members of the cabinet—hence the occasional appearance of such non-ministers as Felix Díaz and Cecilio Ocón.

Without their prior knowledge, the ministers were summoned by Huerta to a post-midnight meeting of the cabinet on the night of the murders. The meeting lasted until nearly dawn and during the course of it an "explanatory" statement was sent out to newspapers, diplomats, and Mexican embassies abroad. The message to the Mexican Embassy in Washington, sent over the signature of Foreign Relations Minister Francisco León de la Barra, said:

"Last evening while Señores Francisco I. Madero and José María Pino Suárez were being taken from the National Palace to the penitentiary as prisoners for trial on various charges, two groups of armed men attempted to release the prisoners and twice attacked the escort. There was a fight in which five persons [someone had lost count of the corpses; counting those brought from the Military Hospital there were six], among them Señores Madero and Pino Suárez, lost their lives. The government marked the event for a thorough judicial investigation so as to clear up every circumstance. The late functionaries will be buried with the honors due the offices they held. The federal government is recognized and supported by nearly all governors, including former Maderistas; general yearning and well-founded hopes for restoration of peace. Representatives of foreign nations manifest sentiments friendly to the government. Public opinion tranquil and optimistic."

The leading figure of the various representatives of foreign governments who manifested friendly sentiments was, not surprisingly, the American ambassador, Henry Lane Wilson. He had already, without formal instruction from his government, extended what amounted to de facto recognition to the Huerta government, congratulating Huerta formally on his new position, entertaining him at the American Embassy, and sending a message to all U.S. consular offices in Mexico instructing them to "urge general submission and adhesion to the new Government."

On the day after the murder Ambassador Wilson gave the government's statement regarding the assassination to the Associated Press and asked the State Department to "accept it as emanating from this embassy." Later he wired the State Department: I AM DISPOSED TO ACCEPT THE GOVERNMENT'S VERSION OF THE AFFAIR AND CONSIDER IT A CLOSED IN-CIDENT, IN SPITE OF ALL THE CURRENT RUMORS. He urged the department to INFORM THE AMERICAN PUBLIC OF THE FRIENDLY DISPOSITION OF THIS [Huerta's] GOVERNMENT and added that THE COOPERATION OF THE DE-PARTMENT IN THIS DIRECTION WILL BE OF INFINITE VALUE.

The United States government apparently did not know quite what to think of (1) the assassinations, (2) Huerta, or (3) the behavior of its ambassador in Mexico. Newspapers in the United States and elsewhere expressed outrage and were critical of Ambassador Wilson.

The Taft administration, which was to leave office within a few days, took no action to recognize the Huerta government as Ambassador Wilson urged—and as, indeed, the ambassador himself had already done without authorization. The State Department advised Wilson that the press regarded as "inadequate" the official explanation of the killing of the ex-President. The *New York World* said that Madero and Pino Suárez "were shot to death by cowards acting in behalf of other cowards whose false excuses can only add to their guilt." The *New York Tribune* said that "the official account . . . staggers credulity . . ." The *Philadelphia Press* said "the cold-blooded assassination will shock the civilized world." *The Times* of London said "civilized nations will place their own construction upon the lame and halting story which the successful conspirators who now rule Mexico have chosen to put out to us. It is by no means convincing."

Madero and Pino Suárez were not buried with the honors promised in the Foreign Minister's message. Instead their bodies were wrapped in prison bedclothes and dumped into shallow graves at the penitentiary. Humble people from throughout the capital trudged to the spot behind the prison where the two men had been killed. They scraped the blood-soaked earth for a memento of the man who had pledged them his help. They built a cairn of stones and on it placed candles that guttered in the February night.

On the day after her husband's death Señora Madero went to the penitentiary to claim the body so that it could be given proper burial. The prison authorities were evasive. The Cuban minister, Márquez Sterling, who accompanied her, suggested that only the American ambassador could help. "No, no," Señora Madero said, "I want nothing from the ambassador . . . He is to blame, the same as the others."

After many requests from other members of the diplomatic corps the bodies of Madero and Pino Suárez were released to their families. Madero's coffin was placed aboard a black-draped tramcar and taken to the

Panteón Francés. After the services the surviving members of the Madero family fled Mexico.

In the United States the administration of Woodrow Wilson succeeded that of William Howard Taft. To the new Secretary of State, William Jennings Bryan, Ambassador Wilson wrote a long letter taking note of newspaper criticism of the relations between the American Embassy and the Huerta regime. Wilson wrote that he had "never for a moment believed the lives of Madero and Pino Suárez were in danger from the government." But a few paragraphs later he said that he had "personally visited different members of the cabinet for the purpose of expressing my deep concern for the preservation of the ex-president's life." Regarding the facts of the assassination Wilson thought that "history will undoubtedly straighten out this tangle." He himself had accepted the official version of the killing as "the surest method of arresting hasty judgment and of allaying that singular and perverse sentimentality which frequently leads to the commission of greater crimes as punishments for lesser ones." And since "those two Mexicans" had been "relegated to private life by their resignations" he was somewhat puzzled that their deaths should cause such "expressions of popular disapproval in the United States."

Woodrow Wilson's government neither accepted the official version of the deaths of Madero and Pino Suárez nor did it recognize the Huerta regime. And Ambassador Wilson was not kept in his post much longer. On August 4, 1913, the State Department said Wilson's resignation had been accepted and added that "the part which he felt it his duty to take in the early stages of the recent revolution in Mexico would make it difficult for him to represent the views of the present administration." A well-organized campaign by American businessmen residing in Mexico failed in its effort to retain him as ambassador. Wilson, although his pride was involved, probably would not have liked working for Woodrow Wilson and William Jennings Bryan. President Wilson's views of foreign policy seemed strange to Henry Lane Wilson. The President, in his *History of the American People,* had condemned the United States' war against Mexico in 1846–48—in which the ambassador's father had fought—as "inexcusable aggression," and spoke of General Winfield Scott's troops fighting "men as brave as themselves, a subtile, spirited race, tenacious to the last of all that it could hold." Views like this were incompatible with the ambassador's disregard for Mexico's sovereignty and his contempt for most Mexicans. For Bryan, the ambassador had nothing but scorn. Bryan, he said, "ran the Department of State like the back kitchen of a restaurant." Bryan did little to improve the relationship. Shortly after he had taken office the State Department sent to Ambassador Wilson a wire of commendation for his services during the Mexican disorders. It was sent over the signature of Secretary Bryan, but apparently was the work of a lesser official. The ambassador joyfully released it to the press. Secretary of State Bryan then publicly denied any knowledge of the wire, clearly indicating that he in no way endorsed the activities of the ambassador.

Wilson retired to Indianapolis, fulminating at every opportunity against the President and the Secretary of State. The accumulating evidence of treason and deliberate murder in the Mexican coup did nothing to modify his views of the victim, Francisco I. Madero. In his memoirs, published fourteen years after his mission to Mexico, Wilson was still describing Madero as "unsound . . . of imperfect education and vision . . . [who] came into power as an apostle of liberty but he was simply a man of disordered intellect who happened to be in the public eye at the psychological moment. The responsibilities of office and the disappointments growing out of rivalries and intrigues shattered his reason completely, and in the last days . . . his mental qualities, always abnormal, developed into a homicidal, dangerous form of lunacy . . . Clothed with the chief power of the nation, dormant evil qualities in the blood or in the race came to the surface and wrought ruin."

The fall of Madero might have occurred without the interference of Henry Lane Wilson, but most people in Mexico at the time thought otherwise. One of them, Edward I. Bell, a newspaperman in Mexico throughout the period, described Wilson as "an ambassador who should not have been there . . . lamentably misplaced, unsympathetic, injudicious, and disastrously harmful. Knowing, as I do, how narrowly Madero missed a triumph over the extraordinary difficulties and deadly enemies that beset him, I am constrained to believe that the least value that can be assigned to the unfortunate influence of the American ambassador is still sufficient to have turned the scale. The right man in the place, tactful, well-disposed, keenly discerning, a man who earnestly desired the established government to continue because he had the foresight to perceive what must follow its violent overthrow—such a man as dean of the diplomatic corps and representative of the most influential nation could have lent enough support to Madero to keep him up until the wave of violence had subsided and the revival of prosperity had turned the minds of the masses toward peaceful means of living. And he could have done it without offensive interference, without going beyond the bounds of diplomatic propriety."

THE USURPER

> "There are no problems in my father-
> land . . ."
>
> *Memorias de Victoriano Huerta*

VICTORIANO HUERTA CAME TO POWER with the promise to restore peace to
Mexico, and the promise won him the adherence of many Mexicans who
might otherwise have been appalled by his methods. But instead of peace
the Huerta regime initiated a period of senseless violence and terror. Ten
days after Huerta assumed the presidency his troops had machine-
gunned one hundred alleged Maderistas in the suburb of Santa Julia. It
was, said José Vasconcelos, "one of the most confused, perverse, and destructive periods in the life of our nation."

Soon after taking office he appointed an old crony and drinking
companion, Enrique Cepeda, to the post of Governor of the Federal
District, the governmental unit which contains the national capital.
Cepeda, who had served Huerta in many confidential missions, was
variously described as an engineer, a doctor, sometimes as Huerta's
nephew and sometimes as his illegitimate son. During the *Decena
Trágica,* he had arranged the Huerta-Díaz meeting and had also served
as Huerta's messenger to Ambassador Wilson. The appointment of
Cepeda was made over the objections of many members of Huerta's
cabinet.

Cepeda was, like Huerta, a hard drinker, but he did not handle
it as well. As governor he celebrated nightly. On the night of March
25 he had been making the rounds of cantinas and restaurants with
a group of companions. Sometime after midnight he issued orders
from the Sylvain Restaurant for a company of police to report for
duty. Thirty armed men reported, and Cepeda, a loaded pistol in one
hand, led them to the penitentiary. Roaring drunkenly and pounding

on the door with his pistol butt he demanded that three Maderista state governors, held there on political charges, be delivered to him.

The warden of the penitentiary courageously replied that such an order could be issued only by the judges who had committed the three governors. Cepeda, mumbling and staggering, finally retreated and led his company of men to the old prison of Belem, and demanded admittance. The warden here was less firm, and Cepeda was allowed to enter. He made his way to cell No. 60, occupied by twenty-four-year-old Gabriel Hernández. Hernández, an enthusiastic Maderista revolutionist from the state of Hidalgo, had quickly risen to the rank of general in charge of a corps of *rurales* and had steadfastly supported the Madero government. On Madero's fall he had been thrown into Belem.

The young revolutionist was awakened by the drunken governor, hauled from his cell and taken to a bullet-scarred wall of the prison courtyard. There Cepeda took command of the firing squad and had him shot. His followers then built a pyre of scrap lumber in the courtyard, doused the body with gasoline and burned it while prisoners in the surrounding cells howled protests.

Cepeda was removed from the governorship and made to stand trial. He was acquitted, but shortly thereafter disappeared. The story was current that he had been seized by some of Huerta's executioners, taken forcibly to Veracruz and placed in the old island fortress of San Juan de Ulúa. There, while taking a stroll in the patio of the fortress, he was mysteriously shot down, and his body thrown into the Gulf of Mexico where, presumably, sharks destroyed the evidence of one of Huerta's mistakes. Many more were to follow.

For nearly a year and a half Huerta ruled the desolation he had helped create in Mexico. He was sly, vengeful, and distrusting. Many people referred to him as *el chacal* (the jackal). He jealously guarded the presidency from real or imagined rivals and systematically eliminated old friends and fellow conspirators from positions of authority. But aside from the power that went with the office Huerta seemed to have little interest in it. He rarely kept appointments, or, having kept them, might walk out before there could be any conclusion. He chose and dismissed cabinet ministers like a child arranging a row of pebbles.

Members of his cabinet, diplomats, brother generals, and foreign investors pursued him about the capital in automobiles, guessing at his whereabouts. He might be found sitting in El Globo or El Colón or another of his favorite cafes, with the inevitable *copita* of cognac in front of him. Or he might be in the humble hideaway house in the suburb of Popotla where an Indian crone, fanning a charcoal fire with a turkey wing, prepared the simple dishes that he liked, hot with chile.

If he went to a banquet at the plush and gilt Sylvain, whose chef was said to have once worked for the Russian czar, he would let the food go untasted while he drank glass after glass of brandy. He seemed unaffected by the quantities of alcohol he consumed; his eyes would seem beadier, his manner more withdrawn and his nerves, if anything, steadier. The only indication of tenseness was the rapidity with which he puffed at the small black cigarettes which he liked. Although a new brand of European-style cigarettes had been introduced with Huerta's laurel-wreathed portrait on the package, Huerta still preferred the cheap brand he had always favored. He was also believed to be a steady user of marijuana.

He was regarded as eccentric, deceptive, and unpredictable. He also was personally fearless. He was shaved daily by a barber whose brother he had condemned to death before a firing squad.

He moved his large family from a modest home in the Calle Liverpool to a more elaborate one in the Calle Alfonso Herrera. He managed rental property which he had recently acquired, and he owned a chain of gambling places, centavo houses for the poor and five-peso establishments for the wealthy. One son, Jorge, handled arms and ammunition contracts for the army; another, Victoriano, Jr., dealt in military uniforms. Huerta bought his wife an impressive diamond and arranged a marriage for his daughter, Luz, with a promising young captain on his staff. But he himself was not ostentatious. He did not occupy the presidential apartment at Chapultepec Castle, and went there only for state occasions. For these and other solemn events he bought an ill-fitting frock coat and a silk hat. These, he said, he meant to wear when he was invited to Washington so that the Yankee politicians could see for themselves that he was not a half-naked, blood-stained savage with a machete in one hand and a bottle of aguardiente in the other. But relations with Washington became steadily worse and the invitation never came. The frock coat and silk hat saw less and less use. Huerta seemed more at ease in a baggy gray sweater and a slouch hat. His shoulders were broad; his arms were long and swung loosely from his short body. He had the small hands and feet and flat features of an Indian, but unlike the soft-spoken Indians his voice was deep and resonant, booming rhythmically like a drumbeat. His eyes were weak and he constantly adjusted and readjusted his glasses.

Orators sometimes referred to him as "a new Cuauhtémoc," linking him with the last great chieftain of the Aztec empire who was treacherously killed by Hernán Cortés in 1525. It was complimentary but inaccurate. Cuauhtémoc had remained stoically and heroically Indian until the end. Huerta was, in fact, an Indian—a Huichol, from the village of Colotlán in northern Jalisco. The Huichol are a superstitious people who celebrate religious rites with god-eyes, prayer arrows, and the hallucinogenic peyote buttons. Huerta inherited the sharp senses and quick mind for which the Huichol were noted, but there were few other similarities and he was said to be both distrusted and hated in his native village. Because he could read and write he was, as a youth, singled out by General Donato Guerra—the one who said that the heroic Mexican people could only be governed by heroes, i.e. military men—and given a position as his secretary. Huerta rapidly adapted to the white man's world in the federal army. Through the patronage of Porfirio Díaz he was appointed to the Military College. Early in his career he demonstrated, usually against Indian outlaws, the sort of tough ruthlessness and willingness to use treachery that was highly regarded in Díaz's army. He went on to fight the Maya Indians in Yucatán, the Magonista rebels in Veracruz, the Zapatista rebels in Morelos both before and after the success of the Madero revolution. He also excelled in staff work, was a skilled surveyor, cartographer, engineer, and a railroad specialist. He carefully studied the career of Napoleon, both the military campaigns and the political maxims.

Sometimes, as President, he spoke with great candor. He would describe himself as "suspicious as a rat—because I have to be." Mexico he characterized as a "country of illusion, falsehood, and error." He spoke openly of the various opportunities he had had to overthrow the Madero government before the one he finally seized upon. One of his many criticisms of his legally elected predecessor was that Madero, for want of energy or purpose, was reluctant to take human life. Yet, Huerta would complain, inconsistently, Madero twice tried to kill him, once with a sharpshooter in the National Palace and again by putting cyanide in his wine.

His only unswerving loyalty was to the army. The decision that officers of the *rurales*—as distinguished from career army officers—should be the executioners of Madero and Pino Suárez was said to have been Huerta's. He did not want the reputation of the army sullied. He distributed military decorations with a liberal hand. The Cross of Military Merit—a medal of which soldiers had always said "you have to die three times to get it"—was handed out in wholesale lots. He created two new grades of superior rank in the army, including the top designation of "general of the army," a position to which he advanced Porfirio Díaz, Aureliano Blanquet, and himself.

His only purpose as President appeared to be an attempt at restoration of the hard-fisted peace of Díaz. Early in the Huerta administration the former dictator, now eighty-two years old and sight-seeing in Egypt, was invited to come home and take an active command in the Mexican army. The old man sensibly declined. Busts and portraits of Don

Porfirio, removed during Madero's rule, were, nevertheless, restored to the National Palace and other public buildings, and in the homes of the wealthy and pious, portraits of the stern-faced Don Porfirio were back up on the walls, sharing honors with the Virgin of Guadalupe.

Huerta's public utterances were variations on a single theme: Laws are unimportant when the fate of the nation is at stake; he intended to save the fatherland, whatever the cost.

It was clear that the cost of pacification would be high—if it could be achieved at all. The government levied troops in unprecedented numbers and sent them to the far-flung and ill-defined fronts. Pascual Orozco whom Huerta had so badly punished in his northern campaign, joined his former enemy and was given a combat command. So did Juan Andrew Almazán, who had been called "the schoolboy general" when he had fought for Madero. So did Jesús (One Eye) Morales, one of Zapata's generals.

Huerta wheedled donations from bankers, businessmen, landowners, and clergy, almost all of whom were kindly disposed toward him and his government, hoping for a return to the golden age of Díaz. When these well-wishers seemed reluctant he would remind them, pointedly, of the number of trees in Chapultepec Park suitable for hanging. But even with their support the financial position of the government became steadily more precarious. Payments on the national debt were suspended. The peso drifted in value from 49 cents (U.S.) to 29, and Huerta had to buy desperately needed military supplies with cheapened money.

The government had political as well as financial problems. No sooner had the Huerta government come to power than the conspiracy on which it was based began to come apart. General Manuel Mondragón, the mastermind of the Ciudadela forces, was the first to go. He was relieved of the portfolio of Minister of War and sent into exile. Before embarking from Veracruz he addressed a bitter letter to his fellow conspirator, Felix Díaz, accusing him of faithlessness. Felix Díaz himself, who, by the "Pact of the Embassy" was supposed to succeed Huerta in the presidency, was soon put out of the way. He was sent off on a diplomatic mission to express the Mexican government's appreciation to the Emperor of Japan for the latter's cooperation in the celebration of the Mexican Centennial three years before (the same mission for which Francisco Madero had designated his brother Gustavo). Díaz did not complete the mission. He returned to Mexico from Europe, bent on pressing his claim on the presidency, and then was forced to take refuge in Havana, where he denounced Huerta as having been guilty in the murder of Madero. He also was to offer his services to the anti-Huerta revolutionary forces, but they wanted no part of him.

The degree of Huerta's dissatisfaction with or distrust of his political allies could be seen in the high turnover rate of his ministers. In eighteen months of administration he had four Foreign Ministers, four Ministers of Government, four Ministers of Commerce, three Ministers each in Treasury and Education, and two each in War, Communications, and Justice.

There was an unprecedented wave of political assassinations. Governor Abraham González of Chihuahua, who had been a member of Madero's cabinet, was arrested and placed on a train for Mexico City. At the lonely station of Mápula his guards seized him and threw him under the wheels of the moving train. In Oaxaca the Huerta-appointed governor was said to have executed without trial more than three hundred persons, many of them children. Solón Argüello, a young Nicaragua-born poet and journalist who had been an enthusiastic Maderista, was seized and shot without a hearing.

The toll was particularly heavy among members of the Chamber of Deputies and the Senate. Deputy Nestor Monroy was accused of fomenting a plot against the Huerta government and, with his followers, workers for the most part, was executed at Tlalnepantla. Serapio Rendón, a lawyer and close friend of the late Vice-President (he was the recipient of the letter Pino Suárez had written in the last hour of his life) was assassinated after making an anti-Huerta speech in the Chamber of Deputies (his trigger-happy executioner shot him in the back of the head while he sat at a table writing a farewell letter to his wife). Deputy Edmundo Pastelín disappeared and was presumed dead. Deputy Adolfo Gurrión was shot in Juchitán, Oaxaca, on orders of Huerta's Minister of Government, Dr. Aureliano Urrutía, an Indian from Xochimilco whose principal qualification for office was that he had treated Huerta for an eye ailment.

Only rarely were political prisoners given a trial. Some were shot outright. Many were killed by application of the *ley fuga,* the law of flight. The prisoner would be taken to some lonely place, a cemetery, an outlying railroad station, or a rural road and shot there for allegedly attempting to escape.

Of all the assassinations the one of most consequence was that of Dr. Belisario Domínguez, a federal senator from the state of Chiapas. Normally the members of the Senate—unlike the Chamber of Deputies in which there was much anti-Huerta feeling—abstained from criticism of the Huerta regime. Not Senator Domínguez. On September 23, 1913, he delivered to the president of the Senate the text of a speech which he proposed to deliver. The Senate president refused permission for him to deliver it on the grounds that it contained "no concrete proposal." The text of the undelivered speech circulated widely however. It was a daring denunciation of Huerta and his government, and its proposals were very concrete indeed, calling for Huerta's ouster.

Huerta, Domínguez said, had done nothing toward pacification of the country and the present situation was worse than ever before. Other nations, formerly friends of Mexico, had refused to recognize its illegal government. Mexican currency was depreciating. The public credit was suffering. The press was gagged. Fields had been abandoned, villages leveled, and famine was spreading throughout the country.

The reason, Domínguez said, was that the Mexican people "cannot resign themselves to accept as president a soldier who seized power through treason and whose first act on assuming the presidency was to assassinate the president legally chosen by popular vote, a president who had heaped promotions, honors and distinctions on him, the same Victoriano Huerta who had publicly sworn loyalty and unshakable fidelity."

Huerta, he said, must be repudiated. "You will say to me, gentlemen, that the attempt is dangerous because Victoriano Huerta is a bloody and ferocious soldier who does not hesitate to kill when obstructed. It is not important, gentlemen. The fatherland demands that you fulfill your obligations, even in danger, even with the certainty of losing your lives. Would you, for fear of death, permit him to continue in power? Look within yourselves and answer this question: What would you say of the crew of a great ship which, in a violent storm and a perilous sea, chose as its pilot a butcher who had no knowledge of navigation in the first place and whose only qualification was that he had betrayed and assassinated the captain of the ship? The world is waiting and the fatherland expects you to honor it before the world by casting out the shame of having as first magistrate a traitor and assassin."

Huerta indignantly ordered Domínguez arrested. On October 8 the senator was seized in his room at the Hotel Jardín, taken to the cemetery in the lovely old colonial suburb of Coyoacán and there in the shade of the ancient laurel trees shot and dumped in a grave.

Domínguez' brother senators, who for the most part had placidly followed Huerta's orders, did nothing about it. But members of the lower house, the Chamber of Deputies, were not so tractable. They demanded an investigation and appointed a commission to carry it out. Huerta ordered them to cease interfering with the executive power of the government. The deputies stood their ground. Huerta sent troops of the 29th Battalion—the military unit which by switching loyalty, had sealed Madero's fate—to surround the chamber. The soldiers had a list of 110 unfriendly deputies. They managed to catch eighty-four of them —the rest having either gone into hiding or escaped from the capital on their way to join the revolutionary forces that were by now active in almost all parts of the country. The unlucky eighty-four were marched off to the penitentiary and locked up. Huerta then dissolved both legislative bodies. He had also closed the courts so that he now controlled the judicial and legislative branches of the government as well as the executive; he had also personally assumed the power and authority of the Ministries of War, Finance, and Government.

The presidential election which Huerta had promised on taking the interim presidency had originally been scheduled for April 1913. This was postponed and another election was set for October 26. The names of a half-dozen candidates, including Felix Díaz, Federico Gamboa, and others appeared on the ballot. The public, totally disillusioned by Huerta's repressive measures, hardly bothered to vote. "Unpopularity of the candidates forcefully demonstrated," said a newspaper headline. Fewer than half the polling places reported. The electoral commission ruled the presidential election void, but new members of both the Senate and Chamber of Deputies were declared elected. Thus, with an obedient congress and the authority of the principal branches of the government in his own hands Huerta had become an absolute dictator, a harsher and more arbitrary one than his idol, Porfirio Díaz, had ever been.

The excuse for his political excesses, of course, was the gathering strength of the revolutionary forces being mounted against him. Francisco Madero had been ineffective as a live and functioning revolutionary leader, addicted to debilitating compromises; but as a martyr, betrayed and slain by the forces of reaction, Madero was more powerful and persuasive than he had ever been in life. Rebellion flared from the remote vastness of Sonora, Chihuahua, and Coahuila in the north, down into the hot country of Guerrero, Michoacán, and Morelos in the south, and the jungle and savannas of Veracruz and Tabasco. In the northwest Yaqui and Mayo Indians fought with bows and arrows until they could seize firearms from fallen federals. Vaqueros in the northern ranch country outrode and outshot the government's cavalry. Workers from mines and mills manufactured grenades and cannons and became skilled artillerymen. Railroad workers wrecked government troop trains.

The government denounced the revolutionists as bandits (one observer said the Revolution was planned by intellectuals and executed by bandits and after a while they could not be told apart). "Bandits" by the hundreds were strung up on trees and telegraph poles to die of strangulation, their bodies left to swing in the wind and dry in the sun. But the insurrection continued and grew, sometimes with purposeful intensity but just as often with a furious sort of aimlessness. Juan Sánchez, a soldier, told the newspaper correspondent John Reed, "Why, it is good fighting—you don't have to work in the mines." Demetrio Macías, one of Mariano Azuela's revolutionary characters, in trying to explain to his wife why he goes on fighting, tosses a pebble into a deep canyon and says "Look at that stone, how it keeps on going." Like the falling stone, the Revolution had developed a terrifying momentum.

In addition to the internal turmoil which was rapidly becoming a full-scale civil war, Huerta had vexations abroad. The United States refused to recognize him or his regime. Huerta had every reason to be confused. He had staged his *coup d'état* with the blessing and encouragement of the U.S. ambassador. Ambassador Wilson personally recognized Huerta as President of Mexico and urged his government to follow his lead. He had even ordered American consular offices in Mexico to urge adhesion to the new regime in their respective areas. Huerta appreciated it. The ambassador, he said, "served us as if he were one of the San Patricios," a reference to the American deserters in the Mexican army during the war of 1846–48.

But Wilson received no support from the Taft administration with which he was politically allied. When the Republican administration was succeeded, in a few weeks, by the Democratic administration of Woodrow Wilson the ambassador's position was even less tenable. The new President exemplified the American political axiom that Republican Presidents preside over things as they are while Democratic Presidents concern themselves with things as they ought to be.

Wilson, scholarly, idealistic—and quite inexperienced in practical foreign affairs—was appalled by "dollar diplomacy" in general and the course of events in Mexico in particular. Although he was a man of greater intellect and tougher fiber, he had many of the same qualities that had marked the unfortunate Madero.

Soon after taking office Wilson addressed a statement to his cabinet saying that one of his administration's principal objectives would be to "cultivate friendship and deserve the confidence of" the various Latin American nations. But, he warned, cooperation would be "possible only when supported at every turn by orderly processes of just government based upon law, not upon arbitrary and irregular force."

This statement and subsequent ones caused alarm in professional diplomatic circles, both in the United States and abroad. It was a denial of the time-honored practice of recognizing de facto governments. In Mexico it was correctly interpreted as a blow at Huerta.

Somewhat later President Wilson said in an interview that his sympathies were with the "submerged 85 percent of the people of that [Mexican] Republic who are now struggling toward liberty."

President Wilson privately referred to Huerta as "that scoundrel . . .

so false, so sly, so full of bravado," and feared he "would not let go till he pulls the whole house down with him."

Nevertheless the President tried to make Huerta let go without wrecking the house. Pressures were strong, particularly from the U.S. business community, for some kind of settlement of the Mexican question—either recognition and support for the Huerta regime so that peace—and good business—could be restored, or direct aid to the anti-Huerta revolutionists to bring a quick resolution of matters.

Distrusting the reports of Ambassador Wilson, whom he soon removed from office, President Wilson began sending personal representatives into Mexico to advise him of the situation. One was William Bayard Hale, former clergyman who had become a Hearst journalist and Wilson's biographer (and was later a paid propagandist for the imperial German government). Another was John Lind, former congressman and governor of Minnesota. Through Lind, President Wilson transmitted specific proposals to Huerta: that all fighting in Mexico should cease; that there be an "early and free" election in which all contending elements would take part; that Huerta agree not to be a candidate in such an election; and that all parties abide by the results of such an election. The proposals made no mention of recognition, even temporary recognition of the Huerta presidency.

Lind delivered the proposals to Foreign Minister Federico Gamboa on August 14, 1913. They were, of course, rejected. Huerta's formal position was that to agree to these suggestions would amount to recognition of the rebel movement, which he would not concede. Instead he made his own demands: that rebel forces be prevented from arming themselves in the United States, and that a new ambassador be sent to replace Henry Lane Wilson, i.e. that recognition be extended to the Huerta government. Privately Huerta blustered that he was of a mind to march his army all the way to St. Louis, Missouri, as a defiant show of force against the unfriendly neighbor.

When Huerta imprisoned the eighty-four congressmen, dissolved the legislature and took most of the powers of government in his own hands U.S.-Mexican relations worsened. Secretary of State William Jennings Bryan dispatched a message to the Mexican Foreign Minister warning that "any violence done to the legislators will shock civilized world and raise serious questions . . . Government, to be deserving of respect, must conform to established laws and usage . . ." This was quickly followed by a message from President Wilson: "The President, shocked at the lawless methods employed by General Huerta and as a sincere friend of Mexico, is deeply distressed by the present situation. General Huerta's course in dissolving Congress and arresting deputies the President finds it impossible to regard otherwise than as an act of bad faith toward the United States. It is not only a violation of constitutional guarantees but it destroys all possibility of a free and fair election . . . An election held at this time and under conditions as they now exist would have none of the sanctions with which the law surrounds the ballot, and its results could therefore not be regarded as representing the will of the people. The President would not feel justified in accepting the result of such an election or in recognizing a president so chosen."

From this point on Huerta's relations with the Wilson administration, never good, steadily deteriorated. He had won recognition from most of the great powers. Indeed the new British minister, Sir Lionel Carden, presented his credentials on the day after the dissolution of the Congress—seeming thereby to underscore Britain's already granted recognition and to give approval to Huerta's harsh action. Recognition by Britain, important to any new regime, had at least in part been the work of the British oilman, Lord Cowdray, whose holdings in Mexico, through ownership or lease, amounted to more than a million and a half acres of oil-producing land. The British fleet, recently converted from coal to oil, badly needed Lord Cowdray's Mexican petroleum.

But without recognition by its powerful neighbor, the United States, Huerta's government labored under a crippling handicap. Arms and ammunition needed to fight the rebel forces could not be obtained from the United States. Loans to pay for war matériel, wherever obtained, were hard to negotiate so long as the Huerta regime's credit rating was impaired by non-recognition. A loan from French financial sources to the Huerta government, negotiated and agreed upon, was at the last minute canceled because of U.S. opposition. President Wilson worked hard trying to persuade Britain, Germany, and France to withdraw recognition of Huerta. His Mobile address on October 27, 1913, with many Latin American businessmen in his audience, was aimed directly at those foreign powers which let selfish business concerns determine foreign policy. "It is a very perilous thing," he said, "to determine the foreign policy of a nation in terms of material interest. It not only is unfair to those with whom you are dealing, but it is degrading as regards your own actions." He denied that the United States had any annexationist intentions toward Mexico. His own foreign policy, he said, was aimed at "the development of constitutional liberty in the world."

It was clear that the sympathies of President Wilson were with the anti-Huerta rebels—the so-called Constitutionalist movement led by Venustiano Carranza, the governor of Coahuila. Through his confidential agents Wilson assured Carranza that the arms embargo—which hampered but did not wholly prevent the revolutionists from obtaining arms in the United States—would be lifted.

The embargo actually was lifted early in February 1914 without Carranza making any commitment to President Wilson's Mexican policy. The Huerta government felt with reason that the United States was aiding the insurrection both materially and morally. The stage was set for a crisis, and it was soon triggered by a seemingly simple incident at the oil port of Tampico. The port was held by federal troops but was under siege by revolutionists. The U. S. Navy kept the port of Tampico under surveillance because of the importance of foreign oil holdings there—warning both federal and revolutionary troops to stay away from oil wells, supplies, tanks, and other foreign-owned property. On the night of April 9 Mexican federal troops, enforcing siege regulations, arrested the paymaster of the U.S.S. *Dolphin* and seven unarmed sailors who were loading gasoline supplies in a whaleboat at a dock in the city. Two of the sailors had not even left the boat, which, naturally, flew the U.S. flag. The Americans were shortly released and returned to their ship with an apologetic note from the Mexican commander, explaining that the Mexican soldiers had simply been carrying out orders that no one was to be allowed to land at the dock. The American admiral, Henry T. Mayo, would not let the matter rest. He insisted on a more formal apology, punishment of the responsible officers, plus the raising of the American flag on shore and a 21-gun salute by the Mexicans.

At almost the same time another American admiral, Frank F. Fletcher, who was keeping Veracruz under surveillance, also became embroiled with Mexican authorities. One of the admiral's mail orderlies was arrested by a Mexican soldier who mistakenly believed him to be an AWOL seaman for whom a reward had been posted.

To further complicate matters, cables from the American Embassy in Mexico City to the State Department in Washington were held up by a Mexican censor—just when it was urgent that the State Department be fully and promptly informed regarding negotiations to straighten out the Tampico and Veracruz incidents.

Huerta, before whom the matter was laid, agreed to a formal apology to Admiral Mayo and to the disciplining of the Mexican officer involved in the Tampico dockside incident. But he balked at the demanded salute to the American flag—as would any other nationalistic Mexican, including his archenemy, Venustiano Carranza.

The U. S. Atlantic Fleet was ordered to Tampico, and it was understood that until Huerta ordered the salute the warships would prevent unloading—either at Tampico or Veracruz—of the arms and ammunition which Huerta was importing from Germany. Huerta suggested first that the matter be submitted to the International Court of Arbitration at the Hague. Then he agreed to order the firing of the 21-gun salute but only under conditions which the United States found unacceptable; to agree to them would have been tantamount to recognition of Huerta as the legal spokesman for Mexico. President Wilson conferred with his special agent, John Lind, who argued for intervention; he also had learned that it would be impossible to seize the arms destined for Huerta until they actually had been landed on Mexican soil. The German ship *Ypiranga*, the same ship on which Porfirio Díaz had sailed for Europe, was approaching Veracruz with a cargo of two hundred machine guns and 15,000,000 rounds of ammunition for Huerta. The *Ypiranga* could not be seized, but the port facilities of Veracruz could. Accordingly an order for the seizure of Veracruz was dispatched to Admiral Fletcher early on the morning of April 21. At first the landing was peaceful; but in the afternoon a group of Mexican naval cadets from the Veracruz academy led a poorly armed group of civilians in trying to repel the Americans. In the fighting that followed nineteen American sailors and marines and more than three hundred Mexicans were killed—most of them civilians. Meanwhile the *Ypiranga* turned around, sailed south and without hindrance unloaded its cargo at Puerto Mexico (now Coatzacoalcos).

The United States, without intending to do so, appeared to have gone to war with Mexico in a somewhat confused effort to help that poor country solve its problems. Huerta was furious. He militarized his cabinet officers, ordering them to wear gold-embroidered green sashes of office at all times. He appealed for volunteers to fight the Yankee invaders (and sent most of them off to fight Francisco Villa in the North and Alvaro Obregón in the Northwest). His expressions of nationalistic outrage won him the admiration of many who had heretofore regarded him as an ogre. He sent peace feelers to Zapata and Obregón. Even Carranza denounced the action of the United States—although he was careful to point out that it was all Huerta's fault. The official press railed at Wilson as "a wicked puritan with horse teeth" and "an exotic and nauseous Carrancista pedagogue." Only Villa, the reckless warrior of Chihuahua, expressed indifference. He did not care what the *yanquis* did so long as they did not do it in his territory.

Official embarrassment in the United States was eased three days later when Argentina, Brazil, and Chile offered to mediate the Mexican-American dispute—an offer which President Wilson promptly accepted, as did Huerta. The ABC mediation conference opened on May 18, 1914, at Niagara Falls, Ontario, and deliberated for six weeks. The protocol adopted called for a neutralist provisional government recognized by all contending groups in Mexico. The results were disappointing to President Wilson, unacceptable to Carranza and immaterial to Huerta whose time was running out. The revolutionary armies were pressing closer and closer. Villa had taken the key city of Torreón again and had won a smashing victory at Zacatecas. The army of the Northwest under Obregón had pushed down into central Mexico. The army of the Northeast had seized the port and oilfields of Tampico and the northern industrial city of Monterrey. San Luis Potosí, Guanajuato, León, and Querétaro had fallen. Federal forces were crippled and diminished, short of rifles, artillery, and ammunition. The railroads were wrecked. The port city of Veracruz—whose custom house had always been a principal source of revenue—was occupied by the Americans. The treasury was almost empty, the currency nearly worthless.

At 6 P.M. on July 10, 1914 Huerta summoned his cabinet to the Yellow Salon of the National Palace. There the oath of office as Minister of Foreign Relations was administered to Francisco Carvajal, a respected jurist who had, a few years earlier, served as Porfirio Díaz's official envoy in the peace negotiations with Madero. His new post put him in line for succession to the presidency once Huerta was gone—and it was obvious Huerta soon would be; he and his faithful henchman, Aureliano Blanquet, were said to have removed the last 2,000,000 pesos from the national treasury (the treasury had had a balance of 33,000,000 pesos when Huerta seized the presidency).

Five days later Huerta delivered his resignation. After sly references to Woodrow Wilson and his "puritanical conscience" and the "so-called Democratic party" of the United States, he concluded: "God bless you—and me too." On July 20 he arrived in Puerto Mexico and boarded the German ship *Dresden*. Huerta sailed for Spain leaving behind a Mexico far more chaotic than it had ever been before.

CHAPTER 16

THE FIRST CHIEF

"The Revolution which compromises is lost."

Venustiano Carranza

THREE MEN—two soldiers and a politician—were the authors of Huerta's downfall. The soldiers—Alvaro Obregón in the Northwest and Francisco Villa in the North—achieved their ends with blood and fire, as chroniclers of the Revolution said. The politician, Venustiano Carranza, achieved his with complicated maneuvers and manipulations which would, in time, turn most of his followers against him.

For seven years Carranza was to be the gray eminence of the Mexican Revolution, a serene, patriarchal, and autocratic figure who appeared to have little in common with his heterogeneous revolutionary followers. He was a tall, big-bellied man of aristocratic bearing who sat a horse well, who enjoyed fine food and elegant tailoring and seldom revealed his emotions. His eyes were always concealed by blue-tinted spectacles, his mouth by a white beard which he continually combed with the hooked fingers of his left hand.

He came from a substantial and conservative landowning family of Coahuila. Coahuila and its neighbors to the west, Chihuahua and Sonora, all fronting on the U.S.-Mexican border, are the three largest states in Mexico. Remote from the capital, they have always displayed a spirit of tough independence and self-reliance, and the Carranzas were products of this environment. Like most of their friends and associates, they were of European descent but had long been a fixture in Coahuila. The father, Jesús Carranza, had been an Indian fighter and a soldier for Benito Juárez. He retired from military life and became one of the great Coahuila landowners, with the family base at Cuatro Ciénegas, a village in the arid country west of Monclova. Venustiano was one of fifteen children. He was born in 1859, was educated first in Cuatro Ciénegas, later in the state capital, Saltillo, and finally in the National Preparatory School in Mexico City. He was a sober, close-mouthed youth and a diligent student. He was well read in Mexican history and liked to quote Plutarch and Cervantes. He probably would have become a professional man had it not been for his eyes which were sensitive to light. They watered copiously and continued to do so for the rest of his life. Doctors prescribed complete rest, so he returned to Coahuila and learned the ranching and farming business. He entered politics at the age of twenty-eight as municipal president of Cuatro Ciénegas. When the state governor, José María Garza Galán, a Díaz appointee, moved to have himself "reelected" Carranza and his brothers, Emilio, Sebatián, and Jesús, became leaders in a local rebellion against authority. When Porfirio Díaz learned that the resistance to his man Garza Galán was being led by *gente decente* instead of bandits he asked General Bernardo Reyes, governor of nearby Nuevo León and boss of northeastern Mexico, to settle matters. Reyes installed a governor more to the liking of the Carranzas. It was the beginning of a long friendship between Carranza and Reyes.

With this change in his fortunes Carranza became a deputy in the state legislature, then, with the blessing of Reyes, a federal deputy and finally a federal senator. As a legislator of the Díaz era Carranza was in no way remarkable; the old dictator did not want remarkable legislators, and Carranza, as one fellow legislator said, was a "political nonentity." In 1908 Carranza was appointed provisional governor of his home state, Coahuila, to replace a man who had fallen from Porfirian grace. The following year Carranza became a formal candidate for the governorship; but Reyes, his mentor, had fallen out with Díaz and Carranza had no official support for his candidacy. Help came from his fellow Coahuilan, Francisco I. Madero, who had recently formed his Anti-Reelection party. It was unexpected—and possibly unwanted. Carranza, writing a letter to Porfirio Díaz in connection with a dispute over irrigation water from the Nazas River—a dispute in which Madero interests were involved—said, "I have arranged for the syndicate to withdraw the representation of Francisco I. Madero who might be able to take advantage of this circumstance to add a new element to his campaign against the government . . . I hope this action will meet with your approval and will serve as proof of my unvarying adhesion to the good progress of your government—today criticized by a person of no political significance."

Díaz was not impressed and did not support Carranza's candidacy; his opponent was installed as governor. Carranza then began to cultivate his relations with Madero, the "person of no political significance." By

September of 1909 he was holding meetings with Madero and talking about the possibility of an armed rebellion against the dictatorship. A curious sidelight was that Carranza tried to interest his old political benefactor, Reyes—whom Madero hated—in joining the Anti-Reelectionist group, or possibly in leading it. Reyes declined.

When Madero was imprisoned in San Luis Potosí in 1910 Carranza paid him a visit at the prison, according to one of his biographers, "without fear of official anger," and when Madero was released under bond Carranza wrote him a congratulatory note. But he showed no eagerness to become an active revolutionist. On November 20 of that year when Madero's first attempt at armed rebellion aborted there was a minor uprising in Cuatro Ciénegas, Carranza's home town. It was not led by Carranza but by Cesareo Castro, who later was to become one of his lieutenants. Carranza did send emissaries to Madero's headquarters in San Antonio, one of them being his brother, Jesús. The fact that Carranza was communicating—and perhaps conspiring—with Madero was duly reported to Díaz. Carranza found it advisable to leave the country. Finally, in January 1911, long after the first attempt at rebellion, Carranza went to San Antonio and established himself in a residence of 501 South Presa Street. The following month Madero named Carranza provisional governor of Coahuila and commander in chief of the Third Military Zone, consisting of Coahuila, Nuevo León, and Tamaulipas. Carranza apparently did little about it; revolutionary activity in Coahuila remained minimal.

Madero, campaigning in Chihuahua, received reports from his brothers of Carranza's lassitude. He wrote his brother Alfonso: "It is very important that Carranza should get busy, without further delays . . . If I gave him an important assignment it was in confidence that he could carry it out . . . I am told that he is again talking of the return of Reyes and this is the reason for the vacillation . . . If this is true I may be forced to withdraw my confidence and even his appointment; the loyalty I have shown him does not deserve such a response."

Later Carranza wrote to Madero from San Antonio admitting that there had been unavoidable delays but saying that in recent weeks he had begun organizing the revolutionary forces in Coahuila and Nuevo León and that "I will soon be at the head of the movement in Coahuila . . . and we will be able to fight the government forces with success." Madero received the letter at the hacienda of Bustillos where he was regrouping his troops and recovering from the wound he had suffered at Casas Grandes.

Carranza was no firebrand, and throughout his career friends complained of his slowness. Older than most of the revolutionists (Madero was fourteen years his junior), he had an air of imperturbable rectitude and deliberation; confronted with a question or a crisis, he would carefully comb his beard, stare through the tinted spectacles, and more often than not, do nothing.

Nevertheless when Madero's revolutionary forces were besieging Juárez in the spring of 1911 Carranza appeared on the scene and was named Minister of War in the provisional cabinet—an appointment which infuriated front line fighters and led to the Orozco-Villa mutiny against Madero.

When Madero began peace negotiations with Díaz's representatives, Carranza was loud in his objections to the soft line that Madero seemed inclined to take. "Great social reforms can be brought about only by decisive victories," he said. "If we take advantage of the opportunity to enter Mexico City leading a hundred thousand men and try to guide the revolution along a path of positive legality, we will quickly lose our prestige. The friends of the dictatorship will react. Revolutions must be implacable if they are to triumph in a definitive manner. What do we gain with the resignations of Díaz and Corral? Their friends will remain in power. The corrupt system which we are fighting will remain. The interim government would be vicious, anemic, and sterile prolongation of the dictatorship . . . The clean element of the revolution will be contaminated. There will come days of grief and misery for the republic and the people will curse us because, for an unhealthy humanitarianism, to save a few drops of guilty blood we will have wasted the fruit of so much effort and so much sacrifice. The revolution which compromises commits suicide!"

These fiery words—so out of keeping with anything anyone had seen in Carranza's character thus far—were prophetic, but they did not change the direction of negotiations. In due course the resignation of Díaz and the installation of the De la Barra government were agreed upon, and Madero the successful revolutionist became Madero the civilian aspirant to the presidency. His cabinet was disbanded. Madero appointed Carranza interim governor of Coahuila, a position he had held earlier under Díaz. The state legislature of Coahuila did not like the idea, but it acquiesced and Carranza was installed, news of which, according to one of his biographers, "caused profound enthusiasm in all social classes." He occupied the provisional governorship for only a few months, then resigned to become a regular candidate for the governorship in the coming elections. He was elected for the period of December 22, 1911, to December 14, 1913.

Carranza had higher ambitions. During the first year in office one of his young confidants prepared a booklet on Carranza which bore all the earmarks of a campaign biography. The governor was also paying two hundred pesos a month to a Mexico City journalist, Ignacio Herrerias, editor of *La Prensa,* to see to it that the governor was frequently and favorably mentioned in the columns of newspapers in the capital. There began to be friction with Madero. When Pascual Orozco rebelled against the government Coahuila state troops were sent to the front in Chihuahua, supported and directed by the federal government. Carranza, back in the state capital, Saltillo, tried to maintain control himself, issuing orders which federal commanders, with Madero's backing were forced to countermand. Late in 1912 Carranza sent an intermediary to Mexico City to suggest to Madero Carranza's appointment as Minister of Government, the second ranking position in the cabinet.

"But man," Madero was said to have replied, "how can you recommend Don Venustiano . . . a sluggish old man [*pachorrudo*] who stands on one foot and asks permission to put the other one forward?"

Old and sluggish though he may have been, Carranza was apprehensive about Madero's administration. A few weeks later he invited the governors of the neighboring states of Chihuahua, Sonora, San Luis Potosí, and Aquascalientes to a hunting party at Ciénega del Toro in the sierra of Arteaga above Saltillo. Only one of the governors—Dr. Rafael Cepeda of San Luis Potosí—attended; the others sent representatives. Carranza did not take part in the hunt himself but afterward entertained his guests at a banquet in the Hotel Universal in Saltillo where, in an after-dinner speech, he spoke gravely of the dangers facing Madero and suggesting that the state governors should act together. There was widespread suspicion that Carranza might be planning to take action against Madero himself. His disagreements with Madero were well known. So was his long time loyalty to General Reyes, now a prisoner of the Madero government for his attempted rebellion.

That Carranza knew something was coming was clear. It was said that the theatrical artist Fanny Anitúa, who was appearing in Saltillo in early February 1913, was urged by Carranza to remain in Saltillo rather than proceed to Mexico City because of the trouble brewing there. Gustavo Madero received a letter from Carranza telling details of the planned revolt, with names and dates. A little later, shortly after the anti-Madero uprising had begun, Carranza sent an envoy to Madero to suggest that he move his person and his government to Saltillo, out of harm's way and, presumably, close to the sage advice of the man from Cuatro Ciénegas. Madero, optimistic as ever, declined.

When Madero and Pino Suárez were forced to resign from the presidency and vice-presidency Victoriano Huerta sent a form telegram to all state governors: THE PRESIDENT AND VICE-PRESIDENT BEING PRISONERS, I, AUTHORIZED BY THE SENATE, HAVE ASSUMED THE EXECUTIVE POWER. Carranza knew and distrusted Huerta. He called a group of friends, many of them deputies in the state legislature, into his office, read them the telegram from Huerta, and commented: "Gentlemen: the constitution, which should be the guide of all Mexicans, authorizes neither the Senate nor the Chamber of Deputies to name a President who has not been elected by the people. It is the obligation of the government of Coahuila, if it functions according to law, to refuse to recognize these acts." The state legislature was hastily convened and accordingly refused to recognize Huerta and at the same time gave extraordinary powers to Governor Carranza to "arm forces for the purpose of sustaining constitutional order in the republic." Carranza then sent out a message to other state governors and military men, urging them to "put themselves at the head of national sentiment, justly indignant, and unfurl the flag of legality in order to sustain the constitutional government chosen in the last election . . ." In all of Carranza's utterances there was strong emphasis on the constitution and upon constitutionality. The armed movement of which he was to assume the leadership would be known as Constitutionalist.

Carranza's behavior was confusing. On the one hand he bristled with indignation and seemed ready to go to war. On the other he seemed to be seeking some sort of accommodation with Huerta. It was perhaps natural. He had only a few hundred troops. He had no way of knowing whether other state governors had received his message or, having received it, whether they were sympathetic. On February 21 the U.S. consul in Saltillo, Philip E. Holland, reported to the State Department that Carranza had changed his mind and decided that possibly Huerta's elevation to the presidency had been constitutional after all.

Carranza sent two representatives to the capital to speak with Huerta of the possibility of a settlement of Coahuila's (and Carranza's) differences with him, and sent an introductory message to Huerta: "I hope that the matters which these gentlemen will discuss with you will be arranged satisfactorily." The envoys reported back that the interview was cordial and suggested that Governor Carranza express "the harmony which exists between the state and the republic."

Nothing came of the suggestion, but Ambassador Wilson advised the State Department that the Huerta government refused to accept Carranza's adhesion and was sending troops into Coahuila to restore order.

Carranza also exchanged messages with General F. Trucy Aubert, who commanded three thousand federal troops at Torreón, trying, unsuccessfully, to arrange a discussion of their differences. He also conferred with the American consul, Holland. He understood from Holland, through an interpreter, that the U.S. government had recognized Huerta and that the usurper was supported not only by the federal army but also by state governors and various dissident groups, even including Emiliano Zapata. Holland apparently was relying on inaccurate information supplied by Ambassador Wilson.

Later the same day Carranza received messages from Governor José María Maytorena of Sonora and Governor Matías Guerra of Tamaulipas indicating that they intended to recognize Huerta. Carranza was angry. He dictated a telegram to President Taft: THE HASTE WITH WHICH YOUR GOVERNMENT HAS RECOGNIZED THE SPURIOUS GOVERNMENT WHICH HUERTA IS TRYING TO ESTABLISH BY TREASON AND CRIME HAS BROUGHT CIVIL WAR IN THE STATE OF COAHUILA WHICH I REPRESENT, AND VERY SOON IT WILL SPREAD TO THE ENTIRE NATION. THE MEXICAN PEOPLE CONDEMN THE VILLAINOUS UPRISING WHICH HAS DEPRIVED IT OF ITS CONSTITUTIONAL GOVERNMENT; BUT THEY KNOW THAT ITS INSTITUTIONS ARE INTACT AND WILL SUSTAIN IT. I HOPE THAT YOUR SUCCESSOR WILL ACT WITH MORE CIRCUMSPECTION IN REGARD TO THE SOCIAL AND POLITICAL INTERESTS OF MY COUNTRY. The message was considerably toned down by the alarmed supervisor of the telegraph office in Saltillo, but it was still clear that Carranza was furious with the United States for the supposed recognition of Huerta—which had not occurred except in the wishes of Ambassador Wilson.

Two days later, on the 27th, Carranza left Saltillo at the head of a small column of armed men and set up headquarters in the town of Arteaga. The tentative negotiations with the federal government were at an end; Carranza, it appeared, had only been borrowing time to set his revolutionary house in order. From this point on his attitude toward the Huerta government was one of unswerving enmity. On the 28th from Arteaga he sent a wire to the American ambassador in Mexico City stating his terms for peace: Huerta, along with his fellow conspirators and all others who supported them, must leave the country and remain away until legal elections had been held; Pedro Lascuráin, Foreign Minister under Madero, should take over as interim president, governing with a cabinet which Carranza would help choose; revolutionary forces would garrison Mexico City. It was a bold demand, made by a man who had very few troops, for unconditional surrender before the war had even begun.

On authority that had been granted by his state legislature Carranza began a series of forced loans from bankers and businessmen to raise the funds that would be needed. He made arrangements for arms and ammunition to be manufactured in the industrial centers of Monclova and Piedras Negras. With Saltillo in imminent danger of occupation by federal troops Piedras Negras was made the revolutionary capital of the state. A large sign, PALACIO DE GOBIERNO, was erected on the customs house in Piedras Negras, clearly seen from the American side where, among the border dwellers, there was friendly sentiment for the Carrancistas. Carranza also shipped his family off to San Antonio, Texas.

At his temporary headquarters in Arteaga, Carranza met with a group of old friends who came to try to dissuade him from rebellion and what they considered his own certain fate. He explained: "The attitude I have assumed is not one of rebellion. The rebels are those who have taken over the government of the republic in a hasty *cuartelazo*. I have no other course . . . I know how to honor my state and the high office I occupy by the will of its people. If this means that I die, I will know how to die as honorable citizens and patriots do."

With his small group of followers Carranza moved from Arteaga to Monclova, in the center of the state. En route they were involved in several skirmishes with federal troops. Carranza also received word that Governor Abraham González of the neighboring state of Chihuahua had been assassinated despite his surrender to the federal government. It made a deep impression on Carranza. It seemed to prove beyond doubt that there was no retreat.

Meanwhile, more troops had joined him, and although his force was still small he turned back toward Saltillo. Once again in Arteaga he prepared to attack the government forces occupying the state capital. Carranza reached the federal commander by telephone and suggested that bloodshed be avoided. The federal commander said it would be dishonorable for him not to defend Saltillo against any attack, whereupon Carranza reportedly told him: "What do you know of honor? Don't speak of it. You know only how to live off the government without responsibility. I will repeat in person what I am telling you by telephone. Wait for me if you will. We will withdraw our troops and meet in any place you choose, just the two of us." The personal confrontation did not come off. Instead, Carranza's meager forces attacked Saltillo in three slender columns. After two days of fighting, they were forced to withdraw because of lack of ammunition.

On the retreat from Saltillo, Carranza, astride his favorite black horse, seemed silent and thoughtful. On the night of March 25 the party stopped at the hacienda of Guadalupe, about midway between Saltillo and Monclova. It is lonely country with chalky soil and sparse vegetation—mesquite, cactus, agave, desert willow, creosote bush, and the snaky stems of ocotillo. To the north and west lay high mountains. The hacienda house was a large, plain building of plastered adobe and red brick, U-shaped and looking toward the south where, beyond the tilted planes of low mountains, lay Saltillo and, beyond that, the heart of Mexico. Carranza and his men were made welcome by the caretaker, Francisco Parada. The next morning Carranza and his staff were served a staggering breakfast of barbecued kid, beef, beans, chiles, coffee, and corn tortillas. Carranza gave his troops two hundred pesos with which to buy a cow to slaughter for their own breakfast. Afterward he withdrew to a small office with his secretary, Alfredo Breceda. Sitting in a rickety chair, staring at the floor and, thoughtfully combing his beard with his fingers, he began dictating what was to become known as the Plan of Guadalupe, the charter of the Constitutionalist movement. Some of the things he had said before: Huerta was not recognized as President. The legislative and judicial powers under his control were also disavowed. So were all state governors who, thirty days from that date, still recognized the authority of Huerta. But something new was added: Venustiano Carranza was nominated, by Venustiano Carranza, as "First Chief of the army which will be Constitutionalist." When the Constitutionalist army occupied the national capital executive power would be exercised by First Chief Carranza until elections could be held.

At 11 A.M. of that hot and dusty March morning Carranza had a bugler summon his followers to the patio of the hacienda. The group did not look like an army. Few had uniforms. Most were dressed in country clothes, high soft leather boots, blankets over their shoulders, rifles in their hands or pistols in their belts, but with cartridge belts noticeably empty. Breceda, the secretary, read Carranza's document to them, and asked that they sign it.

Some of the men—many of whom had fought in the Madero revolution and remembered how inadequate Madero's Plan of San Luis Potosí had been as a revolutionary charter—had some reservations. Madero had paid too little attention to the social-economic problems that underlay the revolutionary movement, and had aimed principally at political goals. Carranza's plan seemed to do the same thing, with more brevity. Its target was the usurper, Victoriano Huerta, and its goal the reestablishment of legal government. It was brief, bare, and plain, and, many thought, too simple.

When Carranza heard their comments, he addressed them: "Do you want the war to last two years or five? The landowners, the clergy, and the industrialists are even stronger and more vigorous than the usurping government. We must finish with it first and then attack the problems which justly concern you."

Younger men in the group interjected that they were willing to fight not only two years or five years but even ten years if necessary. But older men sided with Carranza and urged the signing of the document in its present version, promising that once the immediate objective had been won they would proceed to draft a program for the social revolution. The younger men agreed and the Plan of Guadalupe was signed. It was one of the pivotal events, just as had been the signing of the treaty of Juárez, at which the Mexican Revolution might have taken a different and possibly more decisive course. But the personality of Venustiano Carranza—stubborn, idealistic, authoritarian, and conservative—had prevailed.

In conferring upon himself the quasi-military title of First Chief Carranza acted arbitrarily. He assumed supreme authority over revolutionary forces throughout Mexico but left responsibility in the hands of others. His civilian status—and he was passionately a civilian, distrusting military men to the end of his life—was one reason he was acceptable. Madero had permitted the federal army to continue in existence and had been destroyed by it. Professional soldiers were in disrepute. The revolutionary movement had to be led by a civilian. Only two others might have qualified for the position. But Governor González of Chihuahua had been assassinated on Huerta's orders, and Governor Maytorena of Sonora had shown himself to be indecisive. Rather than take sides for or against Huerta he had asked for a leave of absence and gone to Tucson, Arizona, to recover his health.

Meanwhile more militant revolutionists had taken the field—Francisco Villa, the Herrera brothers and Rosalío Hernández in Chihuahua, Manuel Chao, Tomás Urbina, the Arrieta brothers, Calixto Contreras, and Orestes Pereyra in Durango. There were scattered uprisings in Sinaloa, Tepic, Colima, San Luis Potosí, Tamaulipas, Michoacán, and Guerrero. In Morelos Emiliano Zapata, who had fought the forces of Díaz and Madero, had never left the field and was now fighting Huerta.

Most of these rebels knew little about Carranza and nothing about the Plan of Guadalupe. Carranza undertook to correct this. He sent his secretary, Breceda, to Sonora with copies of the Plan of Guadalupe. Breceda met with the interim governor, Ignacio L. Pesqueira, members of the state legislature and the state military leaders, Alvaro Obregón, Juan G. Cabral, and Salvador Alvarado.

A week later, in Monclova, Carranza welcomed delegates from both Sonora and Chihuahua. Monclova, an old stock-raising town in a region of iron and coal deposits, had been capital of the combined states of Coahuila and Texas a century before. Now it was a quiet, provincial town with few accommodations for visitors. The delegates were put up in a hotel a few kilometers east of town. Carranza sat up most of the first night with his guests, discussing his views. The views seemed to have little bearing on the problems at hand. He favored freedom for municipalities to govern themselves, and a divorce law—which seemed to have no connection with anything under consideration at the moment. He thought labor cooperatives might be preferable to unions and syndicates. He thought mineral subsoil rights must be reserved to the nation as they had been in colonial times.

If Carranza seemed somewhat vague on the social issues, he was, nevertheless, recognized as the most acceptable leader for the revolutionary movement. Chihuahua was in a state of chaos and had no effective leadership. In Sonora the interim governor and the governor-on-leave hated each other, and there was jealousy among the military leaders. At the conclusion of three days of discussion at Monclova the delegates signed a resolution endorsing Carranza's Plan of Guadalupe. It was also decided to send one of the Sonora delegates, Roberto Pesqueira, to Washington, D.C., as a confidential agent to seek recognition of the Constitutionalists.

The other Sonora delegate, De la Huerta, held a long conversation with Carranza about the military aspects of the movement. Carranza recalled the mutiny of Orozco and Villa against Madero at Juárez. Orozco was now with Huerta, but Villa was in Chihuahua, fighting federal forces with his guerrilla band and doing it effectively. Carranza did not trust him and was eager to learn about the military leaders in Sonora—since one of them might have to be used as a counterweight to the dashing, picturesque Villa. De la Huerta explained as well as he could. There was Juan G. Cabral, son of a Portuguese father and a Mexican mother; he was a good leader and spoke English well, a useful thing in the border country. There was Salvador Alvarado, also a talented leader of men; he had been a druggist, strongly inclined toward philosophy, quite radical in his social ideas. There also was Benjamín Hill, very cultured, educated in Italy, polished, and an able soldier. All three had fought against the Díaz dictatorship, had been ardent Maderistas. Finally there was Alvaro Obregón. Obregón had been a farmer in Huatabampo during the Madero revolution and had taken no part in it. He had later fought for Madero in putting down the Orozco rebellion, but he was not a Maderista, as the others were, and he was not a cultured man as Hill was. But, said De la Huerta, he was a man of much intelligence, very engaging as a person, jovial, very adaptable, and in military actions thus far had shown himself to be a soldier of great promise.

Carranza was impressed. "He will be our military chief," said Carranza, and asked that De la Huerta inform Governor Pesqueira of this decision. De la Huerta, with some curiosity, asked Carranza if he had anything against old line Maderistas.

The First Chief answered: "I don't like those who caused the ruin of Pancho Madero."

Carranza was urged to make a visit to Sonora to become acquainted firsthand with the revolutionary forces at work there and he agreed to do so, but he postponed it for the time being to attend to matters of state.

He had already published a "Manifesto to the American People," in which he reviewed the Díaz dictatorship, the Madero revolution, Madero's election and his betrayal and the usurpation of Huerta. "I ask the American people and the governments of their states: If the events of Mexico City had occurred in Washington, if an army chief had seized the President and Vice-President and assassinated them and then by force had assumed the first magistracy of the nation, would you have followed any other course than the one we, the people of Sonora and Coahuila, have followed? I believe not. The usurping President would have been thrown out within twenty-four hours. I hope, then, that the American people will find our present fight against the so-called government of General Huerta justified and will forgive us whatever harm we may unavoidably cause to their interests during the struggle in which we are involved."

At the suggestion of his Washington agent, Pesqueira, Carranza later took another step aimed at winning American sympathy. He drew up a decree promising adjustment of foreign claims based on damages suffered in the Revolution from 1910 onward, the claims to be judged, after the conclusion of the Revolution, by a mixed commission of Mexicans and foreigners. The draft of the decree was sent off to the Washington agent for whatever use he could make of it. When Carranza's colleagues objected that the use of a mixed commission might infringe on Mexico's sovereignty, Carranza reassured them: "You are right . . . At the first opportunity we will modify it. Meanwhile, it has not been published. It remains in my desk. We will make all possible advantage of it until the time comes to modify it."

Carranza's agents did their best to block efforts of Huerta to borrow money both in London and Paris. Carranza needed money too, but he did not want to borrow it abroad. Instead he decreed an issue of 5,000,000 pesos of paper money and ordered that it must be accepted by the public. The bills, well-printed, had the heading "Constitutionalist Army of Mexico," bore the seal of the First Chief, and the information that they would be redeemed by an unspecified treasury. It was the first of a flood of paper money. By the end of the year Carranza had raised the limit from five to 20,000,000 pesos. Soon everyone was printing money —the Constitutionalist army, the various state governments, private banks, the army of the Northwest, the army of the Northeast, the Division of the North and smaller military groups. Only the unsophisticated peasants led by Emiliano Zapata remained fiscally sound and honest; they melted bars of solid silver and cast their own money. The deluge of paper money continued. By 1915–16 it was estimated that some 500,000,000 pesos in paper had been printed. None of it had any guarantee and the bills were disparagingly called *bilimbiques,* no matter who issued them or for what purpose.*

In another decree the First Chief declared in effect the Juárez law of January 25, 1862, a move which caused alarm among some of his associates. The Juárez law had originally been aimed at the French invaders and their collaborators, imposing the death penalty for "crimes against the nation, the order, the public peace and individual guarantees." On May 14, 1913, Carranza wired a Mexico City newspaper, *El Imparcial,* that he had issued a decree putting in effect the Juárez law BY WHICH HUERTA, HIS ACCOMPLICES IN THE MILITARY MOB AND SUSTAINERS OF HIS SO-CALLED GOVERNMENT WILL BE JUDGED. The nature of the law was such that it was susceptible to broad and flexible interpretation and it was to lead to widespread violation of the usually accepted rules of warfare in the coming struggle; those who surrendered were shot.

Carranza also tried to line up additional support for the Plan of Guadalupe and his First Chieftainship. He wrote letters to Governor Nicolás Cámara Vales of faroff Yucatán and to Governor Manuel Castilla Brito of Campeche, explaining his movement and inviting them to join. He also sent, by messenger, a somewhat brusque letter to Emiliano Zapata in Morelos: "This will be delivered to you by Señor Alfredo Quesnel who also will deliver to you a copy of the Plan of Guadalupe and other decrees issued by the First Chief of the Constitutionalist Army. Señor Quesnel will explain fully the propositions which motivate us and with which we are fighting for the reestablishment of constitutional order in the republic. If you are in agreement . . . I hope that you will second our plan and make public the adhesion of yourself and the chiefs and officers of your army and put yourself in communication with me."

Carranza trusted Zapata no more than he did Villa. But he also knew that until Huerta was disposed of the Zapatistas and the Villistas could be valuable allies. After that they might be a problem, particularly if they ever got together.

Partially to avoid any such union he issued a decree on July 4 reorganizing the revolutionary forces, either real or imagined, into seven army corps—corps of the Northeast, East, West, Center, South, Southeast,

* One version of the origin of the slang word *bilimbique* for paper money was that in the state of Durango there had been an overseer of a mine named William Vique. Vique paid his workers, not with money but with vouchers bearing his signature, redeemable only in merchandise at the company store. The workers gave the vouchers the name of the overseer, William Vique, which they mispronounced *bilimbique.* When Francisco Villa began circulating his currency in Durango the bills were called *bilimbiques,* and the name soon spread to all revolutionary currency.

and Northwest. There was no mention of Zapata in connection with the army corps of the South, the area in which he was operating. And the North—Villa's territory—was not even to have a corps of its own. Instead, the army corps of the Northwest would include not only Sonora, Sinaloa, and the territory of Baja California, which was natural, but also Chihuahua and Durango, the theater in which Villa and his friends were operating very successfully. Each corps would be commanded by a general in chief to be named later by Carranza. In a letter to Governor Pesqueira of Sonora Carranza suggested that the Sonoran forces be sent to Chihuahua to capture Juárez and Chihuahua City, after which they should advance on Torreón, where they would be joined by troops from Coahuila. There was no mention of Villa and his troops and the important victories they had already won.

It was both rude and presumptuous. The Constitutional forces under Carranza's immediate authority had performed in lackluster fashion. Only Lucio Blanco, a dashing cavalry commander, had shown any talent. He had attacked the border town of Matamoros and driven the federal troops across the river into the United States. But except for Blanco's victory the campaign in the Northeast had been a succession of failures.

Carranza decided to visit Sonora where the revolutionary forces commanded by Obregón were going from victory to victory. Leaving General Pablo González in charge of operations in Coahuila, Nuevo León, and Tamaulipas, he took off, barely ahead of federal troops commanded by General Joaquín Maass. In the Laguna region he paused to witness an unsuccessful attempt of revolutionary forces to take Torreón (and it began to be said that no victories were ever won if Carranza were in the vicinity).

He went on to Durango, met many of the revolutionary leaders there and installed Pastor Rouaix as governor of the state. He left Durango on horseback with an escort of 120 men and made his way up through the towering Sierra Madre Occidental and down into the Pacific coast state of Sinaloa—an arduous trip which could be made only by an accomplished horseman, which Carranza was, despite his considerable girth.

A friend wrote to Carranza that back in Coahuila the cause was suffering for lack of leadership: "The revolutionists, without resources, are obliged to commit acts of banditry, thus discrediting their chiefs. This explains why the people in the villages arm themselves when the rebels approach instead of opening their doors and welcoming them with music as they did in 1910."

But Carranza was now more concerned with Sonora, which was to be his base of operations for the next six months.

THE CENTAUR

> ". . . For me the war began when I was born. God brought me into the world to battle."
>
> Martín Luis Guzmán, *Memoirs of Pancho Villa*

FRANCISCO VILLA WAS a bandit. There might be arguments whether he was a villain or a hero, a madman or a genius, but everyone agreed that he was a bandit. His pre-Revolution career had been one of unashamed outlawry and violence, in sharp contrast to Venustiano Carranza's staid respectability.

He was a rebel by nature, and had been for most of his life. When he was still a child, son of a sharecropping family, he was in almost constant trouble with authority, whether that authority was the *hacendado* for whom his family toiled, or the *rurales* who maintained peace on the landowner's terms. Bandits were his childhood heroes, as they were for most of the long-suffering poor of Mexico. Bandits were the only ones strong enough and daring enough to fight against an oppressive system. There was a distinction between bandits and thieves. Thieves stole for themselves, from rich and poor alike. Bandits stole only from the wealthy and often, shared their gains with the poor. Their feats were chronicled in *corridos,* the ballads which served to keep an illiterate people informed as to what was going on in their unhappy world. The heroes were such men as Heraclío Bernal, Macario Romero, Valentín Maceres, Manuel Reyes, Benito Canales. In time Francisco Villa would have more *corridos* composed about him and his exploits than all the others. As a folk hero he was an expression of the stored-up resentments and frustrations of the Mexican people. Such feelings are better expressed by a man of extremes and excesses than they are by a man of moderation. He was both picturesque and picaresque. Villa knew it and made the most of it. He was a natural story teller and loved to tell tales about himself, his voice high-pitched, his pronunciation slurred and careless, his language full of sharp, visual images (and strangely lacking in both profanity and obscenity). Whether it was true or not did not matter. The result of it all—the ballad-making, the colorful newspaper stories about him, and the imaginative stories Villa told about himself—created a larger-than-life image with somewhat indistinct outlines, a myth that contradicted itself constantly but never ceased to cause astonishment, amusement, or sheer horror.

He came from Durango, a state noted for fragrant yellow roses and white scorpions, the deadliest of their kind. Villa was born Doroteo Arango, eldest of five children, on June 5, 1878, in Rio Grande, municipality of San Juan del Rio. He was the legitimate child of Agustín Arango and Micaela Arámbula and was said to have weighed twelve pounds at birth. Later the family moved to the Rancho Gogojito in the municipality of Canatlán. His father died early and Doroteo was the head of the family while still a child. He had worked in the fields almost since infancy and was, by all accounts, an able and hard worker. But he also had wanderlust. At times he would go away by himself into the Sierra Madre Occidental, the monstrous and complex mountains that separate Durango and Chihuahua from the Pacific littoral. Again he would go off with *arrieros,* drivers of mule trains, hauling market goods to Parral or Durango City and bringing back needed supplies for people in the back country. Keeping track of these orders— a paper of pins for this neighbor, a packet of spice for another—helped develop the phenomenal memory that was to be so useful to him in his military campaigns. Although he learned to read later in life he could never write more than his name; he kept things in his head instead of on scraps of paper.

That he soon became an outlaw was certain. But the circumstances of it are hazy. Most explanations concern one of his sisters, Martina, who was raped. The story came, originally, from Villa himself, but the versions vary radically in detail. The girl's assailant was either the landowner, Don Agustín López Negrete, or the landowner's son, or the landowner's major-domo, or an officer in the *rurales*. Whichever of the four it was, Villa, an outraged elder brother, shot the assailant either once or three times, either killed or wounded him, and was either seized on the spot or escaped. But escape he did, ultimately, into the remote sierra which, by this time, he knew well.

He joined an outlaw band headed by Ignacio Parra and changed his name from Doroteo Arango to Francisco (Pancho) Villa. Most outlaws changed their names, even when they weren't saddled with a feminine-sounding name like Doroteo. The name of Francisco Villa had belonged to various bandits, one of them a recently deceased member of the Parra gang. Villa's own explanation of the name was fanciful. He said that Villa was the name of his paternal grandfather, while his grandmother was an Arango. His father, being illegitimate, took the maternal name, Arango. Therefore what he, Francisco Villa, had done was merely reclaim a name that was rightfully his. But the records of the state of Durango identify the paternal grandfather as Antonio Arango (not Villa) and the grandmother was Faustina Vela (again, not Villa, but somewhat closer). If Villa had really cared he could have had the record altered to support this explanation—or he could have had the record destroyed, as he often did, particularly in his subsequent polygamous "marriages." But he didn't care—and no one ever dared question him very closely about anything.

The Parra gang robbed and stole when they could, but their principal business was cattle rustling which was regarded as semi-legitimate. For centuries past cattle had run wild on unfenced land in Durango, Chihuahua, and nearby states. While they all presumably belonged to someone, more often than not they became the property of whoever was enterprising enough to find them, butcher them or drive them to market. But under Porfirio Díaz great grants of land were made to favorites, and people like the Terrazas in Chihuahua, the López Negretes in Durango and others began keeping count of their herds and killing—or ordering killed—anyone who preyed on them.

As an outlaw Villa became not only a skilled horseman and marksman, with rifle or pistol (in either hand); he also became a first-rate backwoods butcher, killing beeves, cutting them up, drying meat in the sun, and peddling it to miners and woodcutters. By 1910 he was living in Chihuahua City—in a three-room house of whitewashed adobe in the Calle Diez, trading in horses and working in his own butcher shop, cutting and selling meat of uncertain origin. He also hung around the stockyards, listening to the gossip of cattlemen and cowboys. He would relay information on big cattle drives to outlaw accomplices who could then raid them and take over the herds for themselves.

In 1910 at the age of thirty-two he was a big (six feet, 200 pounds) man, indescribably graceful on a spirited horse—he came to be called the Centaur of the North—but awkward and ambling on the ground, walking with the rolling, pigeon-toed gait of a horseman, his arms thrust outward by the great thickness of the chest. His hair was reddish brown and tousled, almost kinky, and his mustache was thick. His mouth, in a state of repose, was usually open, giving him an adenoidal appearance. His teeth were strong, crooked and stained brown, as are the teeth of many people from Durango because of iron oxide in the water. But the feature most people remembered was his eyes. They were prominent, light brown and friendly; however, in an instant of temper they could change. The lids would draw together, the open, pop-eyed look would be replaced by a squint, and the color shifted from soft brown to blazing topaz, dangerous and foreboding. Some observers compared his rages with epileptic seizures.

That he was, or at least had been, an outlaw and murderer was generally known, but he had lived at peace in Chihuahua City and stayed out of trouble until shortly before the outbreak of the Madero revolution, when he shot down a one-time friend in the streets. He then disappeared into the Sierra Azul.

But before this he had become a friend and admirer of Abraham González, a large, gentle man, a provincial intellectual and organizer of the Anti-Reelectionist movement. In the fall of 1910 he was recruiting for the revolution that Madero would attempt to launch on November 20, looking for men who could fight, who had friends who could fight, who knew their way around the country—the villages and ranchos as well as the cities, the mountain trails and passes as well as the main-traveled roads. Villa filled all counts, and González spent long hours talking with the rough man from Durango, explaining Madero's political ideas, expounding on the injuries and injustices from which the Mexican people had so long suffered under Porfirio Díaz. Villa, having his own burden of injuries and injustices—at least by his lights—was a willing disciple. But there was something else. Although he was a ruffian who had lived by violence and crime, he was always susceptible to the goodness and sincerity of men completely unlike himself. It was this way with Abraham González. When Villa left Chihuahua City for the Sierra Azul it was not to resume his career as a bandit but to become a fighter for González and Madero, good men who promised to bring goodness to Mexico. And it was a convenient time to get out of Chihuahua City anyway.

Villa took fifteen men with him. Hidden away in the mountains he began to recruit followers, choosing men who were well-mounted and well-armed, men who were willing to lead a rough life. Soon after receiving word from González to launch the revolution Villa and his troop, by now numbering 375, fell on the town of San Andrés, Chihuahua, took it easily and held it. In their exuberance Villa's men rode back and forth through the town, firing their guns in the air—like fireworks to celebrate a fiesta—until he cautioned them to save their ammunition for when it was needed.

At a time when Madero, after his first unsuccessful effort, was despairing of the revolution which he had hoped to start, Villa and his men and other groups like them were carrying on a lively guerrilla war in the state of Chihuahua. Villa had begun to evolve as a military commander instead of the leader of a gang of outlaws. He made mistakes, some of them costly—usually hopeless attacks on greatly superior federal forces, and he was wounded once in a battle on the outskirts of Chihuahua City, barely escaping. But he learned from each mistake, and he shaped his troop of followers into a disciplined force. When he joined Madero at Bustillos the following March he had a well-trained little army of five hundred, and he was commissioned a colonel.

Villa was as overwhelmed by the goodness of "little Señor Madero" as he had been by González. He said, according to his devoted biographer, Martín Luis Guzmán, "Here is one rich man who fights for the people. He is a little fellow but he has a great soul. If all the rich and powerful in Mexico were like him, there would be no struggle and no suffering, for all of us would be doing our duty. And what else is there for the rich to do if not to relieve the poor of their misery?"

Shortly after that Madero issued a decree extending a full pardon to Villa for crimes that had been attributed to him. The abuses of the dictatorship, said the decree, had forced Villa to commit "certain acts" for which he was persecuted. The pardon was granted "in view of the great services he had rendered to the cause of national independence."

A few weeks later Madero wrote a letter to the *El Paso Times*—which, like most U.S. papers, had found the colorful Villa very good copy. Madero argued, with somewhat shaky logic, that it was wrong to call Villa a bandit, that persecution had prevented him from following peaceful pursuits, that he had never robbed or killed except in self-defense. Villa would agree later that his disobedience of orders in the unauthorized battle for Juárez and the subsequent mutiny against Madero was a betrayal of his leader, adding that "when I think of the evil I wanted to do to Señor Madero I feel my heart between two stones." But he excused himself in part because it had been "a great and beautiful battle."

At the conclusion of the mutiny Villa resigned his command under the pretext of going on a secret mission for Madero. Madero's brother Raul was placed in command of Villa's men and the outlaw-turned-soldier, with a 10,000 pesos subsidy from Madero in his pocket, returned to civilian life.

He never thereafter trusted Pascual Orozco. He informed Madero of this when he visited with the newly installed President in December of that year, fidgeting uncomfortably in the gilt and plush splendor of Chapultepec Castle. Orozco, he told Madero, was consorting with the Terrazas and other great landowning families in Chihuahua, all enemies of the Madero administration, and was almost certainly planning a rebellion. He promised Madero that he, Villa, would remain loyal.

Later, Villa claimed, Orozco's father offered him 300,000 pesos if he would desert the Madero cause. By the time Orozco actually rebelled against the Madero government Villa was once more in the field, fighting him. With only sixty men he overcame, in Parral, a garrison of four hundred Orozco men. Many of them decided to follow Villa; with these and other recruits he once more had an army of five hundred men. He forced the wealthy men of Parral to "loan" him 150,000 pesos and with this he bought supplies and ammunition for his new army.

When Victoriano Huerta was appointed by President Madero to take command of the campaign against Orozco, Villa was ordered to attach his force to the federal army under Huerta. As a result his men were better outfitted and armed, getting Mausers to replace the nondescript rifles most of them used. Villa was elevated to brigadier general, a promotion he was reluctant to accept since he knew that officers in the regular army would resent it. He felt uncomfortable and knew that some of his fellow officers laughed at the way the ill-fitting uniform seemed to exaggerate his awkwardness. He had to spend much time extricating his followers—such as his old friend and fellow bandit Tomás Urbina—from difficulties with the many rules and regulations of the regular army. He wondered at Huerta, who seemed to be drunk much of the time, but he followed his orders as closely as he could, and he began to understand the operational intricacies of a trained military force, the ways in which cavalry, infantry, and artillery could best be balanced and used. His tactics before this had always been simple: with as many men as possible, well-mounted and well-armed, to deliver a *golpe* (blow) against the enemy. Now he learned ways to advance methodically, protecting his flanks, softening up the objective and taking measures to hold gained ground permanently instead of just for a few bloody, glorious minutes. He and his troops fought brilliantly at Tlahualilo, Conejo, and Parral. Colonel Guillermo Rubio Navarrete, a federal artilleryman, became a collaborator and friend and their two skills blended well. To Rubio Navarrete's knowledge of heavy weapons Villa added an intimate knowledge of the terrain and possible ambushes. Rubio Navarrete later saved Villa from death before a firing squad.

Victoriano Huerta did not like Villa. As a regular army man he disliked all irregulars, and Villa in particular. Villa was rough and wild, passionate rather than disciplined, instinctive rather than calculating, an effective leader of his own kind of men but difficult to control. He had helped inflict the embarrassing defeat on the federal forces at Juárez and had thus contributed to the downfall of Huerta's old idol, Díaz.

Soon after Villa's victory at Parral on June 1, 1912, Huerta found the excuse he apparently was looking for. A fine mare had been seized as booty by Villa's men. Such thefts were so common they usually went unnoticed. Huerta's staff limousine had been similarly acquired. But a complaint was made to Huerta and Huerta issued orders for Villa to return the mare to the owner.

Villa, suffering from chills and fever in a room in Charley Chi's hotel in Jiménez, refused. Wrapped in a blanket and shivering he was seized, disarmed and escorted to the execution wall where he was to be shot for insubordination, with no semblance of the court martial to which he was entitled.

The sergeant of the firing squad marked an X on the wall with his bayonet and ordered Villa to stand in front of it. Villa emptied his pockets, gave his watch and money to the men who would shoot him, and prepared to die. His new friend, Rubio Navarrete, had become alarmed and sought the aid of Colonel Raul Madero, brother of the President. Colonel Madero telegraphed his brother. Just as the firing squad was ready to shoot Villa a telegram came from the President, sparing Villa's life and ordering that he be taken to Mexico City for trial.

Huerta obeyed the President's orders and sent Villa to the capital along with a note to Madero: "Personally I consider Villa a useful man in combat. But I, as a general in command of a division, believe he is a dangerous man. With each step he tends to debauch discipline . . ."

In custody in Mexico City, first in the penitentiary and later in the military prison of Santiago Tlaltelolco, Villa seemed to become aware for the first time of the deficiencies in his education. While awaiting trial for insubordination he worked hard at trying to learn to read, mumbling his way through *Don Quixote* (he was fascinated to learn that part of it had been written while the author, like himself, was a prisoner), and *The Three Musketeers*. He tried to learn to write, even buying a typewriter in the hope that this might make it easier. He discussed revolutionary philosophy with a fellow prisoner at the penitentiary, Gildardo Magaña, one of Emiliano Zapata's intellectual disciples. Villa applauded Zapata's agrarian views but disapproved of Zapata's rebellion against the Madero government. He was still loyal, even though he remained in prison on the orders of the government of his beloved "little Señor Madero." To make the time pass more agreeably he painted his cell, bought a good bed and received regular visits from a young woman, Rosita Palacio, Mexican penal regulations being very permissive in such matters.

General Bernardo Reyes was a prisoner in Santiago Tlaltelolco and was involved in the conspiracy that was to explode in February 1913. Villa was invited to participate in the plot. Instead he escaped. A young court clerk, Carlos Jáuregui, provided a file to cut the bars of Villa's cell and brought a disguise: a bowler hat, a Spanish cape, dark trousers and canvas shoes. In this garb, with his mustache shaved off and with the cape wrapped around his face, Villa walked away from the prison in Jáuregui's company on the day before Christmas 1912. They hired an automobile to take them to Toluca, went on from there to Guadalajara, to Colima and to the seaport of Manzanillo where they boarded a northbound steamer. Disembarking at Mazatlán, Villa and his companion made their way overland to Nogales on the U.S. border and thence to El Paso where he stayed in a cheap hotel. With Jáuregui's help he plodded his way through the newspapers for the increasingly alarming reports that were coming out of Mexico City.

He also sent word to his old friend and patron, Governor González of Chihuahua: "Don Abraham—I am safe and sane in El Paso. Here I am, at your orders. I am the same Pancho Villa you have known in times past, suffering from misfortune but with no bad thoughts. Please tell the president of the republic about me and tell him . . . that if I am considered a bad man in my own country I am disposed to remain here in the United States. Tell him also that there is going to be a *cuartelazo*, because they offered to set me free if I would join their movement, but wanting no part of treason I decided to win my liberty at risk to my life, by escaping. Tell him that the men of his cabinet do not favor him and that I am faithful and that time covers up as much as it uncovers. And of you, Don Abraham, I beg that I be permitted to take charge of the volunteer forces of the state, because we are losing. I believe what I am telling you. Francisco Villa."

González urged him to stay where he was, but Villa began buying horses, pasturing them on the Juárez side of the international border, and recruiting men.

On the same day in early March 1913 on which Abraham González, whom he loved as a father, was thrust under the wheels of a moving train, Villa and eight followers crossed the border at Isleta and returned to Mexico, resolved to fight the Huerta regime. There was Carlos Jáuregui, who had helped him escape from prison; also Juan Dozal, Miguel Saavedra Pérez, Pedro Sapién, Dario Silva, Manuel Ochoa, Pascual Alvarez Tostado, and Tomás Morales. From this small seed the great Division of the North, most awesome of the various revolutionary armies, was to grow.

The little party crossed the Rio Grande at 9 P.M., traveled through the night, lunched at Samalayuca, below Juárez, and moved on south, avoiding the larger towns. In seven days they reached San Andrés, sixty miles southwest of Chihuahua City. Here Villa had many friends and also a wife. Now instead of eight men he had twenty-three, including his two brothers Hipólito and Antonio. He dispatched a telegram to General Antonio Rábago, who had been his companion in arms in the Orozco campaign, when they both were under Huerta's command. Huerta had installed Rábago as governor of Chihuahua. Villa told him: KNOWING THAT THE GOVERNMENT YOU REPRESENT WAS PREPARING TO EXTRADITE ME, I DECIDED TO COME HERE AND SAVE YOU THE BOTHER. HERE I AM IN MEXICO RESOLVED TO MAKE WAR UPON THE TYRANNY WHICH YOU DEFEND. FRANCISCO VILLA. He then went on with his recruiting: 60 men from Ciénega de Ortiz, 180 from San José and Santa María de Cuevas, 250 from Pilár de Conchos and Valle de Rosario, 400 from Carretas and San Lorenzo. Occasionally they would find valuable booty—such as 122 bars of silver on a passenger train they raided near Chavarría, and there were frequent skirmishes with federal troops. At Casas Grandes they overcame a federal force of 400, killed 40 of the enemy during the fight, captured 60 more. The 60 were lined up in files of three and shot, three at a time to save ammunition. The bodies were dumped in a deep well. Villa and his growing army moved on.

Villa set up a headquarters in the town of Ascención in northwestern Chihuahua and proceeded to equip his men. Some help in the way of arms and ammunition came from the revolutionary garrison in the border town of Agua Prieta, across the mountains to the west, where Colonel Plutarco Elías Calles was in charge. But this was not enough. Villa and his men stole herds of cattle and drove them north to Columbus, New Mexico, where Samuel Ravel, a merchant, served as broker for their sale. The funds went for more arms and ammunition.

CHAPTER 18

THE DIVISION OF THE NORTH

"Everybody follows them, but to where?
Nobody knows. It is the Revolution, the
magical word, the word that is going to
change everything, that is going to bring
us immense delight and a quick death."

Octavio Paz, *Labyrinth of Solitude*

WHILE HE WAS BASED at Ascención, Villa was visited by emissaries
from Venustiano Carranza of Coahuila. The visitors, Juan Sánchez
Azcona and Alfredo Breceda, explained Carranza's views, the details
of the Plan of Guadalupe, and the way in which the Constitutionalist
forces would be organized.

Villa, somewhat contemptuous of the First Chief's lack of military
success in his own state, Coahuila, objected to Carranza's plan to place
the revolutionary forces of Chihuahua under the command of those
of Sonora. He insisted on complete freedom of movement in his own
theater of operations, Chihuahua. He said to tell Carranza that he
accepted the Plan of Guadalupe, but that he would permit no outside
interference in his operations. If he needed more generals he would
appoint some himself.

Sánchez Azcona and Breceda also relayed Carranza's disapproval of
robbery and mistreatment of women. Women, Villa replied, do what
they like. As for robbery—his men needed horses, saddles, arms, money,
and beef to eat, and they would take them wherever they found
them. This was not robbery but warfare. Carranza's representatives
promised to secure for Villa some artillery pieces from Sonora.

After six weeks in Ascención Villa was ready to move south again.
He now had seven hundred men under his command. They were
joined by other revolutionary groups as they advanced on San Andrés,

held by a superior federal force of 1300 commanded by General Felix Terrazas. They were temporarily slowed down by the federal artillery, but Colonel Juan Medina, an ex-federal officer who had joined Villa at Ascención, captured two 75-millimeter cannons and a store of ammunition. With the help of these weapons Villa's troops won their first important victory on August 26, 1913. The federal commander, Terrazas, fled toward Chihuahua aboard a locomotive. More than a hundred federals died in the battle—compared with Villa's loss of 32—and 236 captured soldiers were executed by Villa's men immediately after the battle. Villa had been shooting prisoners long before he heard of Carranza's revival of the Juárez law of 1862, and he continued to do so. At San Andrés he also used the ammunition-saving practice he had begun at Casas Grandes. The prisoners were lined up in files of four and shot.

Most important result of the battle for Villa was the loot. He captured seven railroad trains, great supplies of food and clothing, 421 7-millimeter rifles and 20,000 cartridges. He was now equipped for a major campaign.

Villa hoped to clear federal troops out of the state of Chihuahua, including strong garrisons at the capital, Chihuahua City, and the border city of Juárez. In order to cut these forces off from Mexico City he headed for Torreón, an important railroad junction and the heart of the rich Laguna cotton district, on the boundary between Coahuila and Durango.

Villa incorporated the troops of Rosalío Hernández and Maclovio Herrera into his own growing army and, once more, moved south. At Jiménez he was again joined by his old friend and fellow bandit, Tomás Urbina. Urbina was accompanied by Rodolfo Fierro, a former railroad worker with a reputation as a cold-blooded brute. They had just come from Durango where Urbina won some victories and much loot (he was said to have taken 539,000 pesos in cash from the Durango branch of the Banco de Londres). He also had a tale to amuse Villa. Carranza had visited the Durango revolutionists recently, preaching unity. Before leaving for his trip through the mountains toward Sonora the First Chief, knowing of the considerable booty Urbina had taken, had asked him for a contribution toward the expenses of the journey. "I gave him sixty pesos and an old broken saddle for which I had no use," said Urbina. "Did I do right, *compadre?*" Villa roared with laughter and nodded his head in agreement.

Other revolutionists were joining the advance on Torreón. Some were former federal officers who had turned against Huerta: trim, well-uniformed men who were precise in their manners and slept in the field at night wearing cloth masks to train their mustaches. But most of them were armed rabble, ragged, dirty, and indescribably fierce.

At the hacienda of La Loma, on the banks of the Nazas River, the various leaders, each with his personal following, held a council of war.

Carranza during his visit to Durango, had authorized Manuel Chao, a former schoolteacher, to take command of the revolutionary forces in Chihuahua. It was an arbitrary exercise of his authority and another affront to Villa who was by far the most successful of the various rebels operating in Chihuahua. In the La Loma meeting there were, at the outset, harsh words between Chao and Villa, each man reaching for his gun. But Chao, a man of milder disposition than Villa, gave in, and the other *jefes* unanimously agreed on Villa as their leader. It was also decided that the massed force which he now headed would be known as the Division of the North. Thus, little more than six months after crossing the border with eight followers, Villa was now the commander of some 10,000 men, randomly equipped but fearless and willing to gamble everything in an assault on the strong federal forces in Torreón.

With the advice of the former federal officer, Colonel Medina, Villa divided his force for the attack. Villa would lead his own brigade in an advance on Aviles along the right bank of the Nazas River. Maclovio Herrera and the Juárez brigade would march against the twin towns of Lerdo and Gómez Palacio, advancing along the left bank of the river. The Morelos brigade led by Tomás Urbina would protect Villa's right flank. Within four hours of the beginning of the engagement Villa and Urbina had overcome the federal defenders of Aviles. The fighting in Gómez Palacio and Lerdo went on for two days, but the Juárez brigade finally crushed resistance. Villa personally led the final assault on Torreón, fighting both night and day. The federal forces lost at least eight hundred dead—and the losses in the Division of the North were considerable—among them Pedro Sapién, one of the eight men who had crossed the border with Villa. The revolutionists took 120 prisoners and shot all the officers.

The victory at Torreón was important. There was tremendous booty in arms and supplies. Communication between federal troops in the north and the center of the country was severed. The defeat hurt government morale (Huerta's most repressive measures were launched almost immediately afterward). It relieved pressure on the revolutionary troops fighting under Pablo González in the Northeast and under Alvaro Obregón in the Northwest. And it changed Francisco Villa's reputation. He was no longer just a foolhardy, bloodthirsty, and lucky guerrilla commander. He had demonstrated a masterful command of strategy and tactics—worthy of a graduate of the Military College at Chapultepec.

Villa established his Torreón headquarters in the Hotel Salvador. An orchestra was set up on the sidewalk in front of the hotel, and at 4 A.M. on the first day of occupation played *Las Mañanitas* over and over again, with bystanders singing the lovely, inappropriate words:

Awake, my love, awake;
Look, the dawn is here.
All the birds are singing
And the moon will disappear.

A band of trumpets marched through the streets blaring noisily. That night a banquet was held in the Casino de la Laguna. Officers of the revolutionary army, bewhiskered and dressed in a strange variety of uniforms, drank, ate, shouted at one another and danced. Young women brought garlands of flowers and presented them to General Villa.

Villa was smitten with one of the girls, a dark-eyed beauty named Juana Torres, an employee of a tailor's shop. Within days he had "married" her. Villa, temperate in such uninteresting things as tobacco and alcohol, had an insatiable appetite for women. But he did not satisfy it with rape or routine seduction. If the woman wanted to be married—and he preferred such women—he married her, conveniently forgetting his other marriages (the first and most permanent one was to Luz Corral). He once said, with an air of disbelief, "There may be women who do not love me." One of his biographers, Pere Foix, described his taste in women as "always Mexican, with dusky Indian skin and large black eyes and breasts hard as rocks." To another biographer, Martín Luis Guzmán, Villa said: "You must never do violence to women. Lead them all to the altar. You know that church marriages don't mean a thing. That way you don't have to lose good time, and you don't make them unhappy. Just look at me. I've got my legal wife . . . but I've got others that are legitimate too in the sight of God or of the law that means most to them, which is the same thing. That way they are not ashamed or embarrassed, because whatever slip or sin there may have been is mine. And what could be better than an easy conscience and a nice friendly understanding with the women you take a notion to? Don't pay any attention if the priest objects . . . just threaten to put a bullet through him." He claimed he had lost count of the women he had loved after counting up to seventy-five, and no one knows how many marriage ceremonies there were; sometimes they came so close together that one wife would find herself forced to serve breakfast in bed to Villa and a more recent wife.

Villa delivered needed surgical supplies to Torreón's civil hospitals and made free-handed distribution of captured food to Torreón's poor. He also imposed a forced loan on the city's businessmen, Spaniards for the most part, to provide funds for his further operations. Then, leaving a garrison in Torreón, he turned north and headed for Chihuahua City, using the captured trains. Villa traveled in a caboose which was especially equipped for his comfort and privacy. The most recent Señora Villa had made flowered curtains for the windows. She had also seen to it that the general's linen was immaculate and that his tunics had, for once, a full complement of buttons.

From Santa Rosalía de Camargo he sent a telegram to the federal troops defending Chihuahua City—headed by his one-time friend but now bitter enemy, Pascual Orozco—demanding the surrender of the city. The reply was terse: "Come and get it." Villa tried repeatedly, launching one fierce attack after another, and then settled down for what the federals assumed to be a siege. But Villa left only a fraction of his troops as besiegers. With the rest he moved north of Chihuahua City. There he seized a coal train proceeding south from Juárez. He forced the conductor to telegraph the dispatching office in Juárez that because of the revolution he could not get his train into Chihuahua. He was ordered to return to Juárez. Villa had his men unload the coal from the cars. They then climbed aboard and started for Juárez. At each station along the line the conductor, with a pistol at his head, was forced to give a telegraphic report on his progress. During the night of November 15 the steam-driven Trojan horse moved into the unsuspecting city of Juárez, and within an hour Villa had taken complete control. Some of his troops he sent to take over the unwary federal garrison while others went to the city's many gambling halls confiscating the money—both pesos and dollars—that was on the tables. By the morning of the 16th the most brilliant surprise maneuver of the Revolution was an accomplished fact. With the money seized from banks and gambling rooms Villa had a tremendous war chest which he proceeded to spend, buying more guns, ammunition and clothing for his troops, all readily available there on the border. He also advised Carranza of the fall of Juárez and asked him for additional troops plus 300,000 pesos of the money the First Chief was printing.

Villa had become a famous man. Newspaper correspondents from all parts of the world swarmed around his headquarters in Juárez. To the question "Do you speak English?" he would reply "*Si,* American Smelting and Refining *y* sonofabitch." He tried to behave with dignity and circumspection. He heeded the advice of Colonel Medina and of Brigadier General Hugh L. Scott, the American commander from across the river with whom Villa had become friendly. Instead of shooting his prisoners he gave them a choice of joining the Division of the North or crossing the bridge to asylum in the United States. But he was unable to change the ways of his followers, some of whom executed prisoners in wholesale lots. Rodolfo Fierro was said to have personally executed three hundred men, pausing only long enough to cure a cramp in his trigger finger.

A week after his victory at Juárez Villa received word that the federal troops who had successfully defended Chihuahua City against him were now advancing toward Juárez. He sent Fierro and a train with wrecking equipment south along the Central Railroad to destroy tracks and bridges and thus slow the approach of the 5500 federal troops long enough for Villa to prepare to meet them. Villa deployed his forces, 6200 strong, on a line twelve miles long between Bauche and Tierra Blanca, south of Juárez, occupying high ground looking over a sandy wasteland which would slow the attacking federals.

The battle began on November 23 and lasted for two days. Villa's direction of the revolutionary army was just as masterful as it had been at Torreón. The federals left nearly a thousand dead on the field. They then withdrew, not toward Chihuahua City, where a garrison of only two hundred men had been left, but toward Ojinaga, a border town opposite Presidio, Texas, southeast of Juárez. Villa first sent three thousand troops under the command of Pánfilo Natera late in December. When this force failed to overcome the federals Villa again took the field himself and overwhelmed Ojinaga in a battle that lasted only sixty-five minutes. The last of the federal troops in Chihuahua fled across the Rio Grande, among them Villa's old enemy Pascual Orozco. Villa had a friendly conference with the general in charge of American troops at Presidio, John J. Pershing, thanked him for providing refuge for the defeated federal soldiers. Chihuahua, largest of the Mexican states, was now free of federal troops.

Villa went to Chihuahua City and established a military government. The problems were large and complex, but Villa met them in his own way. He would listen gravely to the advice of his staff, but then would wag a forefinger back and forth and say *"no sirve"* ("it won't work") and go ahead and do as he had planned. He issued decrees in rapid succession. No one could impose forced loans, "except by order of General Headquarters or under the signature of the under-signed general in chief" (Villa); no soldier had the right to requisition horses or other private property "unless he has a written order with the seal and signature of the Citizen First Chief" (again, Villa).

He persuaded the garrison of two hundred federal soldiers who had been left behind as a police force to surrender their arms, after which he gave them a safe-conduct to the border. He assigned his own troops to police duty. He also put them to work running the electric plant, the tramways, the bakeries, the slaughterhouse. Meat and bread were put on sale at low, controlled prices. The sale of liquor was banned; any soldier found drunk was summarily shot.

In the space of a few weeks Villa, an uneducated man with a love of children and a passion for education, had ordered construction started on forty schools and the list kept growing. He would say "this morning I saw some children at the corner of such and such street doing nothing; we will build a school there." He ordered regimental bands formed and there were band concerts daily. He had the mangled remains of his old patron and political mentor, Abraham Gonzáles, exhumed and placed in a tiny coffin which he personally carried in his arms at memorial services.

He met with various foreign consuls and promised that the lives and property of their nationals would be respected—except for Spaniards, whom he hated and blamed for much of Mexico's woe. All Spaniards had to be out of Mexico within ten days. He confiscated the vast estates of the Terrazas family and sent their great herds of cattle to the slaughterhouse or to the border for sale in the United States. The younger Luis Terrazas, only one to remain behind when the clan took refuge in El Paso, was tortured until he disclosed where the gold reserves of the Banco Minero were hidden. Then Villa held him for a 500,000 peso ransom.

All this money, along with the bounty he had taken in Juárez and the paper money sent to him by Carranza, was still not enough for his plans. He decreed establishment of a state bank and put the state government presses to work turning out two million paper pesos of his own, guaranteed by nothing but his own signature. He used it to give his soldiers their back pay and to distribute to the poor at Christmas time. It was decreed to be the only legal tender. Anyone refusing to accept it was imprisoned. Those who had hoarded the old hard money—now declared illegal—were ordered to turn it in for the new—and Villa's coffers bulged some more.

Confiscated farms and ranches were handed over to Villa's favorites, and the large landholdings of the Terrazas family and others were divided up into 25-hectare (61.8 acres) plots and distributed to disabled veterans and to widows and orphans of the Maderista revolution. William Benton, a stubborn Scotsman who had acquired a great area of ranching land in northern Chihuahua, came to Villa and, in considerable temper, complained that his fences were being cut and his cattle stolen by Villa's men. When the angry Benton made a motion which might have been a reach for his gun, Villa had him seized and taken away. Of the fact that Benton was killed there was no question. But circumstances and even the place of burial remained uncertain, and there was a great diplomatic outcry. Mass meetings were held in El Paso. The British government, which had no contact with Villa, made representations by way of the U. S. State Department. Villa later said that Benton had not been formally executed by a firing squad but, standing on the edge of his own grave, at Samalayuca, south of Juárez, was clubbed to death with a gun butt by Fierro, the killer.

The Benton affair helped to strain relations between Villa and Carranza. It reflected unfavorably on the Constitutionalist cause. Representations from foreign governments were being made directly to Villa instead of to the First Chief, who was now in Nogales. Indeed, all the publicity that had attended Villa's victories at Torreón, Juárez, Tierra Blanca, and Ojinaga and now the unwelcome interest in the Benton affair made it appear, in the eyes of the outside world, that Villa was the Revolution. Carranza, in faraway Sonora, was almost entirely overlooked.

Villa probably would not have liked Carranza even if the First Chief had not slighted him and his Division of the North. Carranza was withdrawn, aristocratic, and conservative, a representative of everything that Villa disliked. He was the kind of a man Villa called either *perfumado,* smelling of scent rather than sweat and dust, or *chocolatero,* a drinker of chocolate instead of strong Mexican coffee, a man's drink.

There were ideological differences as well. In the lull between the capture of Juárez and the Battle of Tierra Blanca, Villa had been considering the question of distributing land. An inquiry had been sent to Carranza, and the latter had replied: "Not only am I in disagreement with the distribution of land to the people, but tell General Villa he must return to the owners lands which were distributed during the regime of Abraham González." To a visiting Zapatista, Gildardo Magaña, whom he had met a year before while in prison in Mexico City, Villa said: "This is impossible, no matter what Señor Carranza wants. To return the lands . . . would necessitate taking them away from widows of men who lost their lives in defense of the Revolution." He soon went ahead with his own plans for expropriating and dividing farm land.

Carranza, in an effort to establish liaison, sent one of his cabinet members, Francisco Escudero, a bibulous and argumentative lawyer, to see Villa. It was an unfortunate choice. At a banquet Escudero became drunk and insulted Villa: "My general, I am a better man than you . . . It takes more courage to face and overcome arguments than to exchange fire on the battlefield." Villa restrained his temper until Escudero predicted that Villa would become another Pascual Orozco, a deserter to the cause. At this point Villa said: "Señor, you are nothing but a sot . . . if you were not Carranza's representative I would shoot you on the spot."

He then left, more suspicious than ever of Carranza and the *perfumados* with whom he surrounded himself.

Carranza, having failed in his effort to install Manuel Chao as field commander of the Chihuahua forces before the Battle of Torreón, now indicated that Chao should become provisional governor of Chihuahua. Villa, who was functioning as military governor of the state, was against Chao. He wrote a polite letter of explanation to Carranza: "The time is coming when I will have to abandon the government of this state to continue military operations toward the interior; you must think of someone to substitute for me. Because of what you told in your letter and from what I have also been told by my esteemed companion, General Chao, I believe you are inclined toward this worthy soldier as my substitute. Permit me to tell you with all frankness—without this indicating the slightest lack of understanding and harmony between General Chao and me—that although I consider him one of the best elements in the state he seems inappropriate to take charge under the present circumstances because he lacks the energies needed for dominating the situation . . . The work of our enemies continues. To control this we need a well-informed man with energy to maintain the peace and tranquillity which we are winning at the cost of so much sacrifice."

Carranza was unmoved. He still insisted on Chao as governor, and Villa obediently gave in. He continued to correspond with Carranza, urging him, as chief of the revolutionary movement, to transfer his headquarters to Chihuahua. The state of Chihuahua, he wrote, "is entirely dominated and is the most rapid and convenient route to the interior of the country, and it seems to me the time has come for the transfer of the supreme powers of the republic to this place. If, as I hope, you think the same, I pray that you will advise me of your early arrival. I have a special interest in seeing this being made the provisional capital of the republic. Here you would be more in contact with the general movement of the Revolution. Moreover, I need you . . . to guide me with your advice."

Villa was well aware of Carranza's distrust and jealousy and tried to avoid them. To the newspaper reporters who referred to him as leader of the Revolution and who were persistently curious about his intentions he declared: "I have no ambition to be president of the republic if our cause wins. They say that the victories of Chihuahua and Ojinaga have attracted attention to me. I do not have the least desire to take over the role of Señor Carranza, whom I recognize as the supreme chief of our cause. In case Señor Carranza becomes president I will continue giving him my aid and obeying his orders. As proof of my adhesion I declare myself ready to abandon the country should he order me to do so. I have always been in perfect agreement with

Señor Carranza. I have never had personal ambitions. I have fought as a good citizen for the liberty of my country and not to improve my situation. I am a soldier under the orders of my chief . . . We do not fight in favor of personalities but to liberate the country from the clutches of tyranny and the ambitions of usurpers."

It is doubtful whether such declarations of loyalty had any effect on Carranza. But the First Chief gladly made one concession to Villa: He sent him Felipe Angeles, one of the most respected men in Mexico both for his military skills and his integrity (he had remained loyal to Madero to the end).

Angeles had been released from custody by the Huerta regime after Madero's murder and sent on a study mission to Europe—the usual procedure for getting rid of a professional soldier without executing him. Angeles had abandoned his mission in France and made his way to Sonora to join the revolutionary forces. He was welcomed enthusiastically and Carranza appointed him Secretary of War in his cabinet. The appointment caused trouble, just as had Madero's appointment of Carranza to the same post in his provisional cabinet in Juárez in 1911. The presence of a professional soldier was resented by the amateur soldiers who dominated the revolutionary forces of the Northwest. None resented it more than the ablest amateur soldier of the lot, Alvaro Obregón. Obregón complained to Carranza that they were supposed to be fighting against, not with federal officers (actually there were other ex-federals serving under Obregón's command and doing so brilliantly). Secondly, Obregón said, Angeles was too deliberate in his speech; he probably was hiding something.

Carranza gave in immediately, demoting Angeles to "Subsecretary of War in charge of the office," explaining to Obregón that Angeles' role would be strictly limited, and that he, Carranza, would make all decisions and issue all orders. Angeles' frankness and honesty did nothing to improve his status. He did not hesitate to disagree with the First Chief when the latter seemed to be talking nonsense. Others in Carranza's devoted retinue were aghast at his daring; soon none would speak to him or be seen in his company.

From a distance Angeles had followed Villa's campaign in Chihuahua with astonishment. After the final battle against the federals at Ojinaga he wired Villa, expressing his admiration and wishing that he could take part in Villa's next engagement. Villa was flattered and delighted. He immediately wired Carranza asking if Angeles could be assigned to his forces. When Carranza agreed Villa was ecstatic. He considered turning over the command of the Division of the North to Angeles and taking a subordinate command for himself. He was dissuaded from doing this. But he made Angeles' arrival in Chihuahua an occasion for celebration. There were reviews and parades, banquets, music, and oratory. Villa, a *pelado* (nobody), uncouth, slovenly in his dress, coarse in his speech, was full of respect and affection for this hidalgo, an officer and gentleman, a great man, precise and proper in everything. They ate meals together and Villa unabashedly asked for guidance in his table manners. After meals they would sit for hours while Angeles, in his best military academy manner, described the classic campaigns of history, but he was always careful to add that he could teach Villa nothing, that battles like Tierra Blanca were masterpieces of tactics and that he, Angeles, was proud to place himself at Villa's orders.

Villa gave Angeles command of his artillery. He had by now accumulated a huge supply of heavy weapons—some taken from defeated federals, some purchased new in the United States. Together they planned the campaign to the South. The division now had trains—flatcars for artillery and staff automobiles, boxcars for troops, cattle cars for horses, cabooses for the generals. There were well-equipped hospital trains. And there were many officers, some graduates of Chapultepec, like Angeles, some unschooled but seasoned guerrilla fighters like Villa. And there were 12,000 troops. First Torreón must be taken again; it had been recaptured by the federals. It would be a difficult task. Beyond Torreón there lay Zacatecas, Aguascalientes, León, Celaya—and the capital itself—all along the central avenue to the heart of the country. It would be a bitter and costly campaign, but it would also be the ultimate one. On the first anniversary of Madero's assassination Villa said: "In a few days we will meet the enemies of Madero and the enemies of the Mexican people, in Torreón. That's where we will break the spine of the Huertistas and the cursed spirit of despotism. We will take Torreón, with our teeth if need be."

MEN OF THE NORTHWEST

"I asked a trooper with a photo button
of Madero pinned to his coat who that
was. *'Pues, quien sabe, señor,'* he replied.
'My captain told me he was a great saint.
I fight because it is not so hard as to
work.' "

John Reed, *Insurgent Mexico*

THAT CARRANZA, who had thus far achieved little distinction as a revolutionary leader, could deal imperiously with Angeles, the distinguished soldier, and with Villa, who had won so many battlefield victories, was a tribute to the older man's managerial skill.

Long before leaving Coahuila, Carranza had arrived at several accurate conclusions. One was that the revolutionary movement in the northwestern state of Sonora was impressively vital. The other was that the most important man in Sonora was Alvaro Obregón.

Shortly after drawing up the Plan of Guadalupe Carranza had received a message from Obregón: "I beg to present my respects to Señor Carranza and suggest, solely on my own initiative, that there be issued a decree disqualifying all the military chiefs who take part in the armed movement from occupying public office, since all of our national misfortunes have been due to the unbridled ambitions of military men."

Carranza the unconditional civilian knew already from the reports of Adolfo de la Huerta that Obregón was the ablest of the revolutionary military leaders who had arisen in Sonora. Here, then, was a successful soldier, one capable of leading the Constitutionalist forces to the ultimate victory, and one who would not stand in the way of Carranza's political ambitions. Obregón was not a troublemaker.

Obregón was on hand to meet Carranza when the latter and his party completed their crossing of the Sierra Madre Occidental on September 14, 1913. The meeting took place at the village of El Fuerte, Sinaloa. Obregón was a short, stocky man, thick-chested, broad-shouldered and with the fair skin and green eyes that suggested Spanish descent. His bearing was military—stiffly erect, unsmiling, attentive—but his appearance was not. He wore a rumpled and soiled uniform of white duck, scuffed leggings, a visored military cap that was too small, and several days growth of beard. He was deferential in his manner and said little but watched Carranza closely, noting how he concerned himself with such matters as the stabling of his horse and the cleaning of his uniform and seemed only mildly interested in reports on the campaign in the Northwest. Later Obregón confided to a friend that he found Carranza "a great man for little things and a small man for great ones . . . persistent and dogmatic as well." He sensed the sort of things Carranza would like to hear, and he told him: "Here in Sonora we don't have any agrarians, thank God! All of us here are in this business because of patriotism and to avenge the death of Señor Madero."

Obregón, Carranza, and the latter's escorting party started north for Hermosillo. En route they stopped at the hacienda of Santa María to inspect the main body of Obregón's troops and the great stores of military supplies Obregón had captured from the federals.

"What an army!" Carranza exclaimed. Then, tactlessly, he added: "If we had had all this in Coahuila we would by now be in Mexico City." Carranza apparently did not intend it as a slight to Obregón and his troops. For when the party reached Hermosillo one of Carranza's first official acts was to name Obregón "chief of the army corps of the Northwest." He had already defined the corps theater as Sonora, Sinaloa, Durango, Chihuahua, and the territory of Baja California. Somewhat later he enlarged it to include the states of Jalisco, the territory of Tepic (now Nayarit), Colima and Aguascalientes—more than 40 percent of Mexico's area.

Obregón, who came to be called *El Invicto,* the unconquered, was not the spectacular, colorful military commander that Francisco Villa was. His tactics were less daring, more calculated, depending as much on his opponents' mistakes as on his own skills. But that Obregón should be a military leader at all, let alone a phenomenally successful one, was somewhat surprising. He was a farmer and mechanic and a small-town politician.

Obregón had been the youngest in a family of eighteen children—there was a thirty-year span between eldest and youngest—growing up on the hacienda of Siquisiva in the old silver mining district of Alamos, Sonora. His grandparents were Spanish—and it was thought the family name might have been a Spanish version of O'Brien. Unlike most *gachupines* in Mexico they had not prospered and Obregón's parents were, if not impoverished, in very modest circumstances. As a young man Obregón, who loved dancing, once rode on horseback from Siquisiva to Huatabampo—a distance of about twenty-five miles—to attend a dance. Because he lacked the fifty centavos admission he was thrown out. According to local folklore he declared, "Someday I'll be president of the republic, and you'll be sorry." He went to school in Huatabampo where his eldest brother, José, was the village schoolmaster, an argumentative agnostic in a Catholic society. Obregón's subsequent anticlericalism may have stemmed from the brother's influence. Or it may have come from reading smuggled copies of Flores Magón's *Regeneración.* Whichever it was, he would declare, in later years, that the woes of Mexico were due to clericalism, capitalism and militarism, and adding, with a typical Obregón touch, "we militarists can take care of clericalism and capitalism, but who is going to take care of us militarists?"

His life was not easy. By the time he was thirteen he was raising tobacco and manufacturing cigarettes on a small scale; he worked as a mechanic on an hacienda and later in a sugar refinery at Navolato, Sinaloa. By the time he was twenty-three he was married and farming on his own at Huatabampo—a farm he called Quinta Chilla (Poor Farm). His principal crop then and later—he remained a landowner and farmer throughout his military and political career—was garbanzos (chick-peas). To make his 200 hectares (494 acres) more efficient he invented and built a garbanzo planting machine. Huatabampo is near the delta of the Mayo River; the soil is rich, deep, and a dark chocolate in color, producing substantial crops of cotton, wheat, and vegetables. The place names—Huatabampo, Etchojoa, Bocobampo are Mayo, as are most of the natives. Obregón had a deep affection for the Mayo, could speak their language and named one of his sons Mayo.

His wife died young, leaving him with two small children. This and the struggle to make a living out of Quinta Chilla kept him out of the Maderista uprising, although his sympathies were with Madero. In 1911 he was elected municipal president of Huatabampo and displayed both promise and ambition as a politician. He had easy manners, good humor, practicality, and an amazing memory. It was said that he could listen to a list of fifty numbered objects given in random order and immediately recite them back in correct numerical order. Such gifts are particularly useful for politicians, military men, and gamblers.

When the Orozco rebellion broke out in the spring of 1912 the state of Sonora issued orders for municipal presidents to recruit volunteers in their communities. Obregón raised a company of three hundred men, most of them Mayo Indians, and became their commander. There were only two rifles among the three hundred men. The rest carried bows and arrows. They marched to Navajoa where the municipal president gave them six more rifles, with ten cartridges each, and with a total of eight firearms Obregón's company set out for war.

At Hermosillo, Obregón and his men were given equipment and the rudiments of military training and formed into the Sonora column which, under the command of Agustín Sanginés, prepared to march against the Orozquistas in Chihuahua. Obregón was given the rank of lieutenant colonel in command of cavalry.

In his first military action Obregón displayed both skill and daring. At Ojitos, Chihuahua, where the Sonora column was attacked by Oroz-quistas, he was ordered to detail one of his officers and fifty men to capture an enemy cannon which had become stuck in a ditch. Instead he took the assignment himself. By the time he and his men reached the scene the enemy had pulled the cannon out of the ditch and was retreating with it and two other artillery pieces. Although ordered to rejoin the main force of the Sonora column, Obregón and his men, first on horseback and then on foot, pursued the retreating Orozquista column, overwhelmed them in hand-to-hand fighting and captured the cannon.

In this and other actions in the Orozquista campaign Obregón served with distinction. General Sanginés—who was his only teacher in military science—asked him how long he planned to remain in the army. Obregón replied that he would remain only as long as his country needed him. "You had better prepare then to stay in for four or five years," said Sanginés, "because this Indian, Huerta, is going to give us a headache." Obregón was shocked at the time by the general's attitude toward Victoriano Huerta, the general-in-chief of the government forces. Later, at Sabinal, Huerta came to inspect the Sonora column and Sanginés introduced the principal officers individually to "this Indian, Huerta." When he came to Obregón, he said "Lieutenant Colonel Obregón is the one who captured the artillery at Ojitos." Huerta peered at Obregón through his glasses, grasped his hand and said in his deep voice: "I hope this officer will be a promise for the fatherland."

After additional duty in northern Sonora—important only in that it familiarized him with terrain over which he would be fighting at a later date, Obregón and his men returned to Hermosillo. He was raised to the rank of colonel in recognition of his services and, after some delay, allowed to resign. He returned to Huatabampo and had been in his home little more than an hour when an urgent telegram summoned him back to Hermosillo. Returning to Navajoa, which he had left only a few hours before and where he would take the train for Hermosillo, he met with friends in the Hotel Ortiz and discussed the alarming news from Mexico City: Madero and Pino Suárez had been arrested and Huerta was taking over the government. The reaction to the news was immediate and unequivocal. They must all be prepared to fight Huerta. His friends decided to accompany Obregón to Hermosillo and offer their services.

Ignacio Pesqueira, the interim governor, named Obregón head of the state military establishment. Benjamín Hill, a trained soldier, and Salvador Alvarado, an impassioned and militant druggist, were given commands and sent off to the southern and central parts of the state. Others were sent to cut the bridges in the area of Guaymas, where the strongest federal garrison was located. Obregón prepared to go to the northern part of the state where many revolutionary groups were already in arms. His first objective was the border town of Nogales, important because of the munitions and supplies that were available in the United States.

Before leaving Hermosillo, Obregón staged a parade of his troops and issued a manifesto to the people of Sonora. The document was remarkable for its purple prose. Sonorans were told that the nation was writhing in the hands of a matricide, who, having thrust a dagger into the country's heart, now threatened all the entrails and that history would recoil from recording such monstrosities. Huerta and his cohorts were described as a wolf pack with blood-stained jaws, howling and threatening to dig up the remains of Cuauhtémoc, Hidalgo, and Juárez—and a moment later as an octopus whose tentacles clutched the bloody tatters of the Mexican constitution.

He also addressed a letter to his son, who was in the care of Obregón's three sisters back in Huatabampo. The son, Humberto, was advised that his father was marching "for the northern frontier with my battalion at the call of the fatherland which is having its vitals destroyed; good Mexicans cannot ignore this call, and it is my only regret that you are too young to come with me [the boy was five]. If I have the glory of dying in this cause, bless your orphanhood for you can proudly call yourself the son of a patriot."

If Obregón was somewhat high-flown in his language he was, fortunately, also practical, vigorous, well-coordinated, and a skilled organizer. His phenomenal memory, with which he had once played parlor games, was now put to good use, keeping track of troop dispositions and supplies. He also had a chess player's skill in foreseeing cause and effect far in advance. His experience in the Orozco campaign had been brief but he had learned much from the professional soldiers with whom he had served—and had forgotten nothing. With a combination of dignity, authority, ease, and good humor he was a natural leader.

At the outset the revolutionary forces in Sonora were outnumbered by federal troops by about two to one. But they were eager to fight, and the federals were overconfident, refusing to take the enemy seriously. There was also a confusion of loyalties. A few months before they had been fighting to uphold the Madero regime; now they were called upon to support the man who had overthrown Madero.

Obregón's assault on the four-hundred-man federal force in Nogales on March 14, 1913, while well enough done, was in no way remarkable. Obregón said later that his success there "was due to the enemy's laziness more than to our ability . . . our march from Hermosillo took six days, and in less than a day they could have fortified Nogales so that it would have been very difficult for us . . . but they attached no importance to my advance and this confidence cost them their first loss."

Obregón then moved to link up with other revolutionary forces in northern Sonora. In the copper mining town of Cananea, to the east, Manuel M. Diéguez, a veteran of the Cananea strike of 1908 was now the municipal president and had declared himself in rebellion against Huerta. So had Aniceto Campos, municipal president of Fronteras. The town of Nacozari had been taken over by revolutionary forces headed by Pedro Bracamontes, and in Agua Prieta, the police commissioner, Plutarco Elías Calles, was at the head of a small rebel force. Calles and Bracamontes joined forces for an attack on large federal forces under General Pedro Ojeda in Naco. Obregón ordered them to wait until he could join forces with them—but the message did not arrive in time and the revolutionists suffered their first defeat.

Obregón joined Diéguez at Cananea; by mid-April, after heavy fighting at Naco and Agua Prieta they had wiped out Ojeda's federal forces all along the northern border of the state. Obregón now moved south, first to the capital, Hermosillo, and then down the coast to within a short distance of the strong federal garrison at Guaymas. Here he could observe the port city being heavily reinforced—three warships, two freighters, three thousand additional men. It was clear that the central government had ordered a counteroffensive, probably aimed at Hermosillo. Obregón and his troops withdrew, figuring, sensibly, that if there was to be a clash with the federal troops the revolutionists' chances would increase in direct proportion to the distance from the Guaymas stronghold. At Ortiz station he received orders from Governor Pesqueira to retreat no further, that his withdrawal was causing alarm in the state capital. Obregón accordingly turned and prepared to fight. There followed two battles, one at Santa Rosa on May 13, 1913, and one at Santa María, a month later. The federals were beaten, driven back into Guaymas where they were besieged and immobilized. Obregón captured huge quantities of artillery, hand weapons, ammunition, and other stores. Except for the section of railroad in Guaymas itself, under federal control, there was now a clear way to the south. Obregón's next move would be into Sinaloa, where he hoped to take control of the coastal towns in order to prevent supplies from being shipped to the besieged federals in Guaymas. He had been promoted to brigadier general and was the most successful revolutionary chief of the Northwest.

Even the federals were impressed. A federal officer whom Obregón had known during the Orozco campaign wrote to him on behalf of the commander of the besieged port of Guaymas, General Ojeda, whom Obregón hated. It was suggested that Obregón desert to the federal cause; they would give him a general's rank and other honors.

Obregón once more indulged in bombast. He replied: "If through some monstrosity I should be dragged to such a degradation I would still refuse to place myself at the orders of a man who, lacking military skills, has led his troops only to disaster and shame, leaving them abandoned in their hour of danger, showing them only his back. I have beaten him before and I will beat him again. I express my regret that you, a man whom I esteem, fight in an army which, for the national honor, has no right to exist."

But if Obregón tended to be sententious in his pronouncements, his political instincts were sound and practical. He had no liking for José María Maytorena, the governor of Sonora who, unable to make up his mind about Huerta, had taken a leave of absence and fled to Arizona at the early, critical stage of the Sonora revolution. In the summer of 1913 Maytorena, impressed with the victories being won in his home state, announced from his refuge in Tucson that he intended to return and resume the governorship and the command of the revolutionary forces in Sonora. Both Obregón and the interim governor, Pesqueira, were opposed. Maytorena took his case to Carranza in Coahuila. Maytorena, who looked like a prosperous shoe clerk, had much in common with Carranza. Both were prosperous, conservative landowners, and both were governors, and they were old friends. Carranza agreed that Maytorena should be allowed to resume the governorship. His reasoning may have been legalistic, or it may have been dictated by the fact that Carranza would soon be visiting Sonora and it would be convenient to have an old friend in the governor's chair.

Maytorena returned to Sonora late in July and met in Nogales with

Pesqueira and the principal military leaders, including Obregón. The revolutionists were at first unanimous in their opposition to Maytorena. But Carranza's secretary, Alfredo Breceda, was there to voice the First Chief's support of Maytorena. Obregón then switched over to Carranza's position and argued that since Maytorena had been legally elected and had been given his leave in a legal manner there was nothing to bar his resumption of the office which was rightfully his. The other revolutionists followed Obregón's lead.

It was the first of many instances in which Obregón was to follow Carranza's dictates, even when they ran counter to his own judgment. Carranza was a difficult man to follow, his position seeming to shift without warning. He was known to be opposed to the more radical elements in the revolutionary movement, to distrust the visionaries who had been enthusiastic supporters of Madero. His Plan of Guadalupe had espoused nothing more than the overthrow of the usurper Huerta and a return to constitutional government. He had stubbornly resisted any social program, and he opposed any hurried steps in this direction—as Lucio Blanco found out.

Blanco, a man of theatrical good looks and engaging manners, had provided Carranza with the one victory of any consequence in the Northeast, the capture of Matamoros. But Blanco was not content with his military victory. In August 1913 Blanco seized the hacienda of Los Borregos, property of Felix Díaz. With bands playing and flags flying, Blanco, seated at a sarape-draped table in an open field, began dividing the Díaz property among peasants in the Matamoros area. And he issued a manifesto: "Finally, after many efforts and three years of fighting and sacrifice, the Revolution is beginning to orient itself toward solution of one of the great problems of our country, the equitable distribution of land."

Word of what Blanco had done reached Carranza just as he was ending his long horseback trip to Sonora. He was not pleased. He sent a message to Blanco telling him that (1) in distributing land he had assumed authority that was vested only in the First Chief; (2) he must report to the First Chief in Sonora for reassignment; and (3) he must turn over his command to General Pablo González. The last was the cruelest blow. González was probably the most inept of the commanders in the Northeast. Nevertheless Blanco obeyed, reported to Carranza in Sonora and was assigned a subordinate command under Obregón.

This seemed to make Carranza's attitude perfectly clear. Yet, shortly after arriving in Hermosillo, Carranza made a speech which seemed to reverse his position. "The people of Mexico should know," he said, "that when the battle is over they must begin the majestic and formidable social struggle, the struggle of the classes. For, whether we want it or not, and no matter who opposes it, new social ideas must be implanted in our masses. It is not just a matter of dividing the lands and the national riches, of securing effective suffrage, of opening more schools. It is something greater and more sacred: to establish justice, to seek equality, to eradicate the powerful ones, to establish an equilibrium of the national conscience."

Perhaps because he sensed the urgency and militancy of the revolutionary spirit in Sonora he had changed. He appeared to accept the necessity for land distribution and to be insisting on much more. Heretofore he had always ended his letters and decrees with "Liberty and Constitution." Now they ended with "Constitution and Reforms."

Carranza's headquarters for most of the stay in Sonora was in the dingy, overcrowded Hotel Escobosa in Nogales, only two blocks from the international border and an escape to safety should it ever become necessary. Here, *el viejo* (the old man)—he was just fifty-four but his companions were much younger—held court, sitting in a rocking chair, dressed in the peculiar sort of uniform he had adopted as his own. These suits, well tailored in either field gray or brown gabardine, were of a semi-military design. The tunic had no epaulets, but there were metal buttons, without insignia, all the way to the collar. They added to his already impressive dignity. He wore dark glasses indoors and out and maintained a monumental calm in the presence of strangers, particularly in meeting foreign correspondents who came to see the great man and learn of the progress of the Constitutionalist campaign. His aides, especially Isidro Fabela, the acting Secretary of Foreign Relations, tried to prevent questions being asked directly of the First Chief. When the questions did get through to Carranza the reply might be either irrelevant or false. Asked about his relations with Zapata Carranza replied that Zapata had placed himself at Carranza's orders. Reminded that Zapata had published a letter disavowing Carranza's leadership and the Plan of Guadalupe, Carranza insisted that such a document must be apocryphal.

Foreign representatives were also puzzled by his attitude. When a confidential agent of President Woodrow Wilson asked him if he intended to assume the presidency of Mexico when the Revolution was won, Carranza parried the question by denouncing foreign nations meddling in the affairs of Mexico. But he also criticized them for failing to deal with him as a head of government, and he had his own staff of diplomatic agents, housed in the Burlington Hotel in Washington, D.C., working for recognition.

Such problems seemed to cause him little concern. Every morning he took a canter on his horse, and every afternoon a brief siesta.

Stores on the American side of the border provided ample creature comforts. Good wines were served at his staff dinners. When his money ran low he increased the "internal debt" and speeded up the presses that produced his paper money. When he traveled he had a private three-car train—an old-fashioned Pullman car with a buffet-kitchen at one end for himself, a second car for his escort, a third for horses. He was gallant with the ladies, liked to give dancing parties in towns where there was a plentiful supply of beautiful girls, and issued stern instructions to his staff as to their deportment. His social manners were benign and paternalistic and everyone was quick to learn how he responded to flattery.

While his usual attitude was one of fatherly kindness and lofty amiability he did not hesitate to reveal his prejudices. An Hermosillo journalist was severely scolded by the First Chief in person for writing too frequently and favorably of the military victories of Francisco Villa. He also showed a growing antipathy for the memory of Francisco Madero—the man whose death most of the revolutionists thought they were fighting to avenge. When it was suggested that the first anniversary of Madero's death be declared a day of mourning and marked by memorial services, Carranza objected: "Madero and Pino Suárez and their partisans with their stupidity were responsible for what happened and because of this the memory should not be glorified." The memorial services were held anyway, in the Noriega Theater in Hermosillo. Carranza attended with Governor Maytorena, but he said nothing. When ardent Maderistas such as the González Garza brothers, Roque and Federico, volunteered their services Carranza rejected them coldly.

The military campaign in the Northwest had, meanwhile, in late 1913 and early 1914, made great strides. All of Sonora except for the besieged port of Guaymas, was under control of the revolutionists. By late November, after a fierce battle for Culiacán, most of Sinaloa, also, was in rebel hands. The surviving federal troops in Sinaloa had been driven into the port city of Mazatlán; here they, like their comrades at Guaymas, were put under siege while the revolutionary troops moved farther south.

On March 3, 1914, from Nogales, Carranza sent Obregón a lengthy letter of "instructions" for his operations. Aside from expanding Obregón's theater of operations the letter largely amounted to authorization to do things that Obregón had already done—recruit troops, requisition money and other necessities, hold Guaymas and Mazatlán under siege, appoint and promote officers as needed. If the letter struck Obregón as strange and unnecessary he concealed it and continued to treat Carranza with deference. He noted in his memoirs that "I immediately began to make preparation to obey the superior orders of the First Chief."

In March 1914 Carranza prepared to leave Sonora for Chihuahua. What he had accomplished during six months in Sonora was difficult to assess. The armed rebellion in the Northwest had achieved impressive momentum before he arrived and it continued with little assistance from him; he merely approved what others had done. He had, perhaps, with his great dignity, given the revolutionary movement an air of respectability. But in an area where he could have been of genuine service, establishing unity among dissident revolutionary factions, he had not only failed but often made the dissension more acute. He had seen to it that Maytorena was reinstated as governor of Sonora, deepening a schism that was already grave. In the neighboring state of Sinaloa he supported Felipe Riveros in his claim to the governorship, thus offending many Sinaloa revolutionists who thought he should be disqualified for having briefly recognized Huerta. Later Carranza was to arouse the antipathy of Riveros by trying to install some of his own men in Riveros' state government.

These schisms, occasionally the result of differing ideologies but more often coming from the clash of personalities and ambitions, were to mark the course of the revolution, not only in Sonora and Sinaloa but throughout Mexico. Carranza's insistence on his own infallibility, his jealousy and his susceptibility to flattery tended to aggravate rather than alleviate the differences.

Finally, accompanied by a battalion of Sonora troops as an escort, Carranza and his staff proceeded to Naco and Agua Prieta. Then, on horseback, they climbed up into the Sierra Madre Occidental, traversed the great Púlpito canyon, and came down into Chihuahua.

His most significant accomplishment was the alliance with Alvaro Obregón, an alliance that was to shape the destinies of both men and of the Mexican nation.

CHAPTER 20

TORREON AGAIN

> "Señor, what a profound thing war is . . .
> only at the cost of slaughter can the cause
> of the people progress."
>
> Martín Luis Guzmán, *Memoirs of
> Pancho Villa*

WHEN CARRANZA ARRIVED in Chihuahua he took care to do it properly. He halted his column outside of Juárez, had a bath, a haircut and massage, had his uniform sponged and pressed, his boots polished. Then, with the 4th Sonora Battalion as an escort, he made a formal entry into the border city, appearing, observers said, as a conquering hero in a city that had been conquered and pacified months before.

Meanwhile the man who had conquered and pacified Juárez—and all of the state of Chihuahua for that matter—was moving south, determined to take the much-fought-over city of Torreón once more. Villa was now the general-in-chief of a huge and powerful army. While there was still no standard uniform, the troops were well-armed, well-supplied with ammunition. There were fewer *soldaderas,* the ragged women who followed their men to war to cook for them, dress their wounds and nurse them (and often to barter with enemy *soldaderas,* trading cartridges for food). Instead, there were efficient commissaries to dish out nourishing meals, and hospital trains, well-staffed with doctors and trained nurses and amply supplied with bandages and medicines. There were cars for troops and horses, flatcars for artillery, and even automobiles. Villa now used a Packard touring car instead of a horse, and his agents in El Paso sent him a steady stream of spare parts and tires. Villa also wore a uniform, a carefully buttoned tunic and a visored military cap in place of the *vaquero* garb he had worn before—high leather boots, drill pants, *guayabera* shirt, and a

Texas hat. He was trying to be more decorous. He worried about the outbursts of raging temper that had always been—and continued to be—part of his character; on the advice of one of his military doctors he was eating less meat in the hope that this would help him control himself. To a visiting doctor who commented on the fact that Villa did not drink Villa replied: "If Pancho Villa drank what a terrible man he would be."

He was inordinately proud of his great army and prowled endlessly from brigade to brigade, battalion to battalion, inspecting equipment, talking to the troops. Instead of eating with his staff in the comfort and formality of his headquarters car, he liked to eat with the men, borrowing a tortilla here to scoop up a few beans, then taking—despite his doctor's advice—chunks of meat in his fingers, borrowing soldiers' lighted cigarettes for a few puffs. It was said that he feared poison in his food, and in this random method of eating he could avoid it. Or he may have suffered the loneliness of a man who had risen far above his origins. He talked about "when times change and I have to return to the sierra," but his outward air was one of eagerness to get on with the fight.

His phenomenal military reputation had brought more and more men into his army. Former federal soldiers—Felipe Angeles the foremost among them—were eager to serve under him. Unruly guerrilla leaders like Tomás Urbina and Maclovio Herrera obediently fitted themselves into the hierarchy of the Division of the North. Inexperienced young men came to offer their services. So did old enemies. Felix Díaz, one of the authors of the *cuartelazo* that overthrew Madero, had now fallen out with Huerta. He sent an envoy, José Bonales Sandoval, to offer his services in the fight against Huerta. Villa refused, and would have shot Bonales Sandoval on the spot except for Carranza's advice to the contrary; he did not shoot him until some time later.

The trains moved south over the dusty plains of Chihuahua under the brilliant March sun, train after train, the locomotives laboring with the heavy load. It was a more disciplined army than Villa had ever had before. Still troops rode on the tops of boxcars, spread sheets of tin for cooking fires on the cartops and wasted good ammunition shooting at jackrabbits or, lacking targets, just shooting in the air and yelling like coyotes.

At Escalón, Villa stopped the trains and marshaled his troops. He had nine brigades of infantry and cavalry plus two regiments of artillery under General Angeles. Advance units repaired railway track so that the military trains could follow. Villa set up his headquarters at an hacienda south of Bermejillo. General Angeles suggested that they give General José Refugio Velasco, the federal commander in

Torreón, an opportunity to surrender and spare lives on both sides. General Velasco was a respected federal; at the time of Madero's overthrow he had, for a while, maintained his loyalty to Madero despite Huerta's orders. But he was a career army man, and remained faithful to the army which was now serving Huerta. Angeles found a functioning telephone and called Velasco in Torreón. The conversation was courteous, almost courtly.

"Good afternoon, Señor General Velasco," said Angeles.

"Good afternoon, Señor General Angeles," said Velasco. "Where are you speaking from?"

"From Bermejillo, Señor General," said Angeles.

"Have you taken Bermejillo already?"

"Yes, Señor General."

"I congratulate you."

"Thank you, Señor General."

"Were there many casualties?"

"Hardly any, Señor General. That is why I am calling you. You will save the lives of many Mexicans by bringing your useless resistance to an end and surrendering the places you occupy."

"Señor General, permit me to take issue with you," replied Velasco, and handed the telephone to a Colonel Solórzano who informed Angeles that it would be the revolutionists who surrendered.

A little later the telephone rang and Villa answered. The exchange was less courtly this time.

"Who is speaking?" The voice was that of another federal commander.

"Francisco Villa, Señor."

"Francisco Villa?"

"Yes, Señor. Francisco Villa. Your servant."

"Fine, because we are coming for you in just a moment."

"Come on, Señores, you will be welcome."

"Good. Fix supper."

"We'll have something warm for you."

"We'll be there."

"Good, Señor, but if that's too much trouble, we'll come and get you. We have traveled a long way just for the pleasure of seeing you, and we are getting tired of looking for you everywhere."

"Are there many of you?"

"Not so many, Señor. Just a couple of regiments of artillery and ten thousand men."

Villa was fighting over territory he had fought over before, but this time he had more troops, better trained and armed, supported by Angeles' well-directed artillery fire. Sacramento fell; so did Lerdo and Gómez Palacio. From Gómez Palacio Villa sent a polite message to

General Velasco, expressing admiration for Velasco's attitude in the immediate aftermath of the Huerta coup, but adding: "Our troops increase from day to day and our cause is favored by public opinion throughout the republic except for those privileged classes who want to maintain a dictator to protect their interests; since our ultimate triumph is certain, you, if you continue to fight against the people, will go down to personal disaster and history will record your name along with those generals who have supported the executive power of the nation even when that power has been usurped by means of crime and scorn for the national honor . . ." There was no answer.

At the same time Villa sent a message to Carranza on the first anniversary of the Plan of Guadalupe: "Señor, on this memorable day, a happy date for the rights of the people, you unfurled the flag of liberty against the enemies of legality and the Constitution. I express my joy and that of my troops, and hope for the early triumph of the cause for which we fight and of which you are the chief." Carranza, who had just arrived in Chihuahua, did not bother to answer.

The story is told that while the preparations for the final assault on Torreón were under way a handful of poor Indians from the district stood on a nearby hill. From here they watched all the seemingly confused movement, the troops and cavalry being deployed, the artillery pieces being wheeled into place. A Villista officer noticed them and warned them that they would be in the line of fire and that they should, for their own safety, withdraw. "But, Señor," said one of the Indians, "this is where we always stand when there is a battle for Torreón." Torreón had been attacked unsuccessfully by the revolutionists with Carranza as a non-participating witness, in July 1913. It had been taken by Villa in November 1913. In December the federals, greatly reinforced, had retaken it. Now Villa was getting ready to take it again.

Federal resistance was stubborn; points that the revolutionists had taken were never entirely secure from counterattack. Infantry advances and cavalry charges went on day and night, Villa leading one of the charges himself. Finally on the afternoon of April 2 the federals began withdrawing; there was hand to hand fighting in the streets between the revolutionists and the federals, equally exhausted, and by 10 that night the Division of the North held Torreón and controlled the important Laguna district. Villa estimated his losses at five hundred dead and fifteen hundred wounded, and, he advised Carranza, "the cost has been great and painful." To a newspaper correspondent he said "You may say I feel the kind of joy you think proper, but I am not happy, because we pay for the victory in the blood of our comrades." Federal losses were far heavier.

There had been much destruction in the city, and there was none of the gaiety of Villa's first truimph in Torreón—no marching bands, no singing of *Las Mañanitas*. There were thousands of dead to burn or bury, thousands of wounded to be treated, and little rest for the troops. Most of them were sent on in pursuit of the retreating federals. There was another fierce battle at San Pedro de las Colonias, the home of Francisco Madero, resulting in another victory for the revolutionists, also a costly one. Many of the cavalry horses had, by this time, been ridden so long and hard that their blankets stuck to their raw backs like scabs. The victory here—over some 12,000 federal troops commanded by twenty-two generals—and a later one at Paredón were anticlimactic. The great battle for Torreón was a high point in Villa's military fortunes; here Huerta had sent his best troops and officers, the best of his equipment, and, although they were not yet militarily destroyed, the central government could never again make such an effort.

Villa began putting the railroads back in running order—Torreón offered rail communication to all points on the compass. He took inventory of captured federal arms and ammunition and other booty—notably 100,000 bales of cotton, already loaded on freight trains and ready for shipment to the U.S. border to be traded for still more war matériel. He imposed taxes, appropriated the revenue of gambling houses and searched out herds of cattle and hoards of gold. As he had done in Chihuahua, he ordered the Spaniards in Torreón to leave Mexico and go into exile, but, instead of ten days, gave them only forty-eight hours.

He found time to amuse himself. As he usually did, he took up with a woman, this time Otilia Meraz. Otilia was completely unlike the virginal Juana Torres whom Villa had "married" after his first Torreón battle. She was experienced, a professional and a trouble maker. She insisted on dining with Villa and his staff. She took sly pleasure in pointing out those of Villa's officers with whom she had slept, knowing it would infuriate him. Villa would order the offending officer to perform menial tasks such as serving food to himself and his new mistress. But in time he wearied of Otilia and her provocations and he turned his attention to more serious matters.

One of the most troublesome problems involved General Pablo González, Carranza's appointee as chief of the army corps of the Northeast. In the early stages of the battle for Torreón, Villa had seized control of the rail line running eastward from Torreón to Monterrey. Between the two points there were substantial numbers of federal troops which could reinforce Torreón. He twice asked González to destroy the rail line and prevent such reinforcements but González had done nothing. After the battle of San Pedro de las Colonias Felipe Angeles, who still held—at least technically—the title of Subsecretary of War in Carranza's cabinet, wrote to the First Chief urging that General González, then in Monterrey, be instructed to advance and meet the retreating federal troops—that such a movement could end the campaign. Nothing happened, and the federal troops were able to concentrate and regroup in Saltillo. Villa's financial agent in Chihuahua City, Lázaro de la Garza, had also approached the First Chief in Villa's behalf, urging that González be ordered to act. To this Carranza testily replied that he had not ordered Villa's attack on Torreón in the first place.

Clearly there was something wrong, and Villa left Torreón for Chihuahua to find out what it was.

Villa's encounter with Carranza in Chihuahua was not a happy one. "My first impulse was a feeling of respect toward this old man who represented the honor and justice for which our people were fighting," Villa is reported to have said. "I embraced him emotionally, but after a few words my blood turned cold because I understood that I could not open my heart to him because for him I was not a friend but a rival. He never looked at me directly, and his entire conversation was reduced to reminding me of the differences of our origins, pointing out to me all the offices he had held—municipal president, political chief, governor, senator, and finally First Chief, and in explaining to me decrees and laws which I did not understand . . . I believed then, that this was not a popular leader but a court clerk, the owner of an hacienda instead of the interpreter of the hopes of the peasants. There was nothing in common between that man and me, one a politician and the other a humble fighter. He wanted, at whatever cost, the presidency of Mexico, and I wanted many things for my country which he could not understand."

Villa commented on the activity of other revolutionary generals, praising the success of Obregón in the West, and then bringing up the sensitive question of the inactivity of Pablo González in the Northeast. Carranza's comment was evasive. He said that circumstances had not been favorable for González as they had been for Obregón, but he indicated that additional resources being made available to González would increase his effectiveness. For Villa, who had created a powerful and successful army with little or no help from the First Chief, the answer must have been less than satisfying. He then took off for the border city of Juárez to make arrangements for war matériel to replenish the supplies expended in the battles of Torreón, San Pedro and Paredón.

In the meanwhile the American forces had landed in Veracruz. From Chihuahua, Carranza addressed a stern note to President Wilson regarding the "highly offensive" act. It was all Huerta's fault, and the United

States' demands for satisfaction from Huerta were useless since Huerta did not represent the Mexican people. But, he added, "the invasion of our territory and the stay of your forces in the port of Veracruz, violating the rights that constitute our existence as a free and independent sovereign entity, may indeed drag us into an unequal war . . . which until today we have desired to avoid."

Villa's attitude toward the United States was quite different—an attitude that may have been spontaneous or may have been assumed deliberately to embarrass the man who had just embarrassed him in Chihuahua City. In Juárez he had dinner with George Carothers, special agent of the State Department. He had a multicolored Saltillo sarape which he wanted Carothers to present to his old friend, General Hugh L. Scott, and he told Carothers he had come to Juárez for the purpose of restoring confidence between the United States and the Constitutionalists. As far as Villa was concerned he welcomed the U.S. troops' possession of the port of Veracruz so that nothing could get through to "the little drunkard," Huerta. "Villa's attitude," Carothers reported, "is that Carranza may write pretty notes from Chihuahua, but that he is here to do the work . . . I have hope of establishing the neutrality of the Constitutionalists through Villa."

Villa addressed a formal note to President Wilson: "The great majority of the Mexican people . . . believe in the sincerity of the declarations of President Wilson that no war with Mexico is desired . . . They are sure that the difficulties between the United States of America and the United Mexican States have originated in the deliberate attempt of the usurper Huerta to force a war between the two countries . . . It is true that the situation has been aggravated by the form of the note of the Constitutionalist Governor of Coahuila, First Chief of the Constitutionalist Army; but this note was entirely personal, and the attitude of one person, whatever his momentary authority, cannot carry such weight as to bring on a war . . . Señor Carranza in his note has only endeavored to defend the dignity of the republic, without in the least intending his attitude to be considered as a hostile act against the government of the United States, a country from which we have received such great demonstrations of consideration and sympathy."

CHAPTER 21

THE BREAKUP

"Wherever Carranza went discord, hesitation and slowness inhibited the revolutionary movement."

José Vasconcelos, *A Mexican Ulysses*

UNTIL NOW Villa had been an obedient subordinate to Carranza; the First Chief's arbitrary decisions had baffled him at times, but he followed them as well as he could, and when there were no orders he acted on his own and reported dutifully to Carranza. Now he had become insubordinate. He not only had presumed to speak to the head of another nation on behalf of all Mexicans. He also had injected an almost apologetic interpretation of what the First Chief, in his legalistic jargon, had really meant to say. That there was not an immediate and decisive break in relations between the First Chief and his most successful, most unruly general, was probably due to Carranza's addiction to a waiting game.

Villa knew that Carranza was angry with him. But when he returned to Chihuahua City, Carranza treated him politely and suggested, mildly, that it might be wise for Villa to refrain from comment on international matters. Carranza may have assumed that, given time, Villa himself would provide an even better excuse for the inevitable break.

Villa provided the excuse almost immediately. He ordered the arrest and execution of Manuel Chao, the governor of the state of Chihuahua whom he had reluctantly installed in office on Carranza's orders. The grounds were somewhat vague—a dispute over a trainload of cattle, a quarrel over Chao's occupancy of a mansion belonging to one of the Terrazas clan, his disregard of military orders Villa had given him, or simply the fact that Chao was a "politician" a description which Villa used contemptuously, who was "running the government without

due respect for my authority." He insisted later that he had never intended to shoot Chao but only to assert his authority. Whatever the
reason, Chao was spared at the last moment.

Carranza summoned Villa to discuss the Chao incident, and then
invited both men to have breakfast with him, Villa on his right, Chao
on his left. Carranza made a little speech on the necessity of harmony.
Villa once more demonstrated the rapidity with which he could shift
from black anger to expansive good nature. He responded warmly to
Carranza's conciliatory gestures and arranged for a banquet that night
in honor of Chao and "as a mark of my insubordination and affection
for the good person of the First Chief." At the banquet Villa spoke
effusively of his devotion to Carranza and ended his speech by giving
the First Chief a bear-like embrace.

Carranza, shortly afterward, was approached by a group of generals
from Villa's Division of the North, each of whom had a complaint
against Villa for the way in which he had commanded them during
the Torreón campaign. They were, they said, tired of Villa's excesses
and did not want to be identified with them. They proposed to shoot
Villa. Once more Carranza played the role of peacemaker, this time
in defense of Villa. He reminded the generals that they were Villa's
subordinates and if they took any action against Villa he, the First
Chief, would regretfully have to punish them.

But, if Carranza considered Villa worth saving from a mutiny of
his own followers, he did not intend to let Villa have his way. Villa,
back in Torreón, was ready to resume his military campaign. His
troops were rested and his supply of munitions had been replenished.
The federal troops that had survived the battles of Torreón, San Pedro,
and Paredón had been driven into the territory of Pablo González and
were concentrated at Saltillo where González, based on Monterrey,
should be able to annihilate them. Villa planned to move south and
attack the federals at Zacatecas, the next strong point on the road to
Mexico City. Carranza was invited to visit Torreón. Villa welcomed him
ostentatiously with parades, a military review and a banquet. Carranza,
asked to speak on his revolutionary aims, declared that the Constitutionalist program was not a revolutionary movement nor was he himself a revolutionist. He discussed at length the need for revision of
laws governing the postal service, the budget and the tariff structure.
His audience, hoping for inspiration, listened dully. Afterward Villa
informed Carranza of his plans for an attack on Zacatecas. The First
Chief shook his head and combed his beard. The next mission of the
Division of the North, he said, would be to attack the federal troops
in Saltillo, to the east of Torreón.

The Villistas groaned. This would be a lateral movement of 170 miles, most of it through an area they had already conquered once instead of an advance of more than 300 miles into enemy territory. It would be an action against troops that the Division of the North had already beaten, instead of against the fresh federal troops that held Zacatecas. It was an operation which Carranza's man Pablo González, who had done little enough to date, should be able to handle with ease. Villa's generals, notably Felipe Angeles, objected, but Carranza stood firm and Villa finally agreed. Saltillo was, after all, the capital of Carranza's home state of Coahuila; perhaps with Saltillo liberated the First Chief would be more content to let Villa get on with more serious military matters.

Carranza, having laid down orders for the Division of the North, left Torreón for Durango for a visit with the revolutionists who controlled that state. He courteously invited Villa to accompany him, but Villa declined. If Saltillo had to be taken, he preferred to direct his troops in person. Besides, the leading revolutionists in Durango, the Arrieta brothers, Domingo and Mariano, were unfriendly; they had given only minimal and grudging support during the battle for Torreón. So Villa bade a cool farewell to the First Chief and marched against Saltillo.

It was not a difficult operation. The federal troops in Saltillo were weary, short of ammunition and disorganized—General Velasco had been wounded at the battle of San Pedro and his subordinates were second-rate. They resisted as well as they could, but by May 20 Villa and his men had control of the Coahuila capital. Villa obeyed Carranza's orders and installed Jesús Acuña as provisional governor of the liberated state (Carranza's own legal term as governor had expired) although he did it with some misgiving. Villa felt that Acuña was one of Carranza's *perfumados;* he had seemed on the verge of fainting when Villa, lying on the ground and eating his lunch under some mesquite trees, had casually ordered the execution on the spot of two captured federal officers who had been brought before him. He had had to remind Acuña that these were, after all, the orders of First Chief Carranza. Villa established order in Saltillo, forbade his men to drink and sedately attended a dance given in his honor in the patio of the Madero Institute, a normal school, asking the band to play a favorite tune, *Jesusita en Chihuahua,* over and over again.

He also became acquainted with Pablo González, whom he had often reviled. González, the chronic loser, had finally won the port of Tampico after a long siege and had occupied Monterrey. Now he appeared in Saltillo to relieve Villa. Villa found González to be a likable man "of a gentle character that would help him little in the field." And, again obedient to Carranza's orders, he prepared to turn over military custody of Saltillo to González. The two, the fierce Villa and the mild González, took evening walks through the streets of Saltillo. Groups of Villa's soldiers would see them and shout "Viva Villa, Viva Pancho Villa!" González listened to them nervously, but was assured by Villa that it was a good thing, between battles, to allow the troops to be somewhat disorderly. More seriously, Villa spoke of his plans for taking Zacatecas after which he and his Division of the North should join with González and his army corps of the Northeast and Obregón and his army corps of the Northwest for a triumphant advance on the capital.

When the time came for Villa's departure for Torreón he and González parted on a basis of friendship and understanding. And he had genuine admiration for one of González' generals, Antonio I. Villareal. Villareal, a big, burly former schoolteacher who had been a close associate of Ricardo Flores Magón both in the publication of the fugitive paper, *Regeneración,* and in the Magonistas' various abortive attempts to start a revolution. He and Flores Magón had parted when Villareal decided to fight for Madero in the Revolution of 1910. Now, in González' corps, he had proven himself an able field commander and was, in addition, just as daring and radical as González and his protector, Carranza, were cautious and conservative. Villa made a mental note to keep track of Villareal.

Carranza, meanwhile, had waited in Durango for Villa to take Saltillo. He now permitted his feelings toward Villa and toward Villa's idol, Madero, to come into the open. He told the journalist Heriberto Barrón: "These Maderistas believe that I am going to deliver myself into their hands. The shortcomings of Madero and Pino Suárez were the cause of the disaster of their administration. I will seek new men, not stained with the responsibility of that disaster, to help me and we will advance by new routes which will not end in disaster." He predicted that it would not be long before Villa rebelled against him, and whatever Villa might say to the contrary were "hypocrisies of that bandit."

In addition to speaking rancorously of Villa and Madero, Carranza was issuing military orders that he must have known would infuriate Villa. He ordered Pánfilo Natera and the Arrieta brothers to mount an attack on Zacatecas, the objective Villa had been so anxious to take when Carranza ordered him to turn back and take Saltillo. He could not have made a more irritating choice. It was Natera whom Villa had sent in the previous December to take Ojinaga; Natera failed and Villa had to take charge himself. The Arrietas had long been enemies of Villa.

Having made these arrangements Carranza prepared to return to his old state capital, Saltillo, which now, due to Villa's efforts, was in friendly hands. He made a stopover in Torreón. Villa, angry because of Carranza's decision on Zacatecas and knowing that relations between himself and the First Chief were near the breaking point, had purposely left Torreón. His generals, however, entertained the First Chief at a banquet. There was a noticeable coolness toward the First Chief.

Barrón, the journalist who had spoken with Carranza in Durango, had followed him to Torreón, and here Barrón had an interview with Felipe Angeles regarding Carranza's attitude. The strained relations between Villa and Carranza, said Angeles, could be blamed only on the latter "with his dictatorial and absolutist tendencies and his Porfirian antecedents." Those loyal to Madero, Angeles continued, had, at first, enthusiastically followed Carranza and recognized his leadership, but Carranza had rejected them, giving them to understand that he had no use for the memory of Madero nor for Madero's followers. The rejected Maderistas had—as he himself had done—gathered around Villa. This was the beginning of the schism, and it had been aggravated, Angeles thought, by Carranza's devotion to the Machiavellian maxim of "divide and rule." Wherever Carranza had gone—in Sonora or Chihuahua —he had caused disunity among the revolutionists. So great was his jealousy of the victories Villa had achieved with his Division of the North, he was now planning to prevent Villa from winning more honors. The sending of Natera and the Arrieta brothers against Zacatecas was part of the plan. These forces Carranza planned to later form into a Division of the Center which would then advance toward the capital, Angeles said, leaving Villa and the Division of the North behind.

Carranza, finally back in Saltillo, which he had last seen almost a year before, received a letter from Toribio Ortega who, with his troops, was in Gómez Palacio, near Torreón. Ortega was a veteran revolutionist who had taken up the cause in Ojinaga six days before Madero's call to arms in November 1910 and had been fighting ever since. He was stubbornly faithful to revolutionary aims and had carefully avoided involvement in the many factional disputes. Ortega was disturbed by the present crisis between Villa, his immediate commander, and Carranza, the head of the Constitutionalist cause. He was, he told Carranza, against *personalismo,* the glorification of one personality at the cost of others, and if Villa were guilty of this, as his critics said, he, Ortega, would be the first to protest. But, he continued: "General Villa is a patriot. I don't pretend that he is perfect. He has defects—perfection doesn't exist in humans. But these defects are obscured by relevant qualities and meritorious action. Villa an ambitious man? I don't believe it. His ambition is to see his country free of tyrants and despots, in seeing it great and progressive, in breaking the chains . . . Personal ambition? None. Today he is chief of the Division of the North, a position he won with his merits and military deeds; tomorrow he will be a simple citizen." Ortega concluded by saying that dissension could be disastrous, that he and other chiefs of the Division of the North would always obey the First Chief and that Villa always had been and always would be the most faithful of his subordinates.

Carranza had little time to think about Ortega's letter. The news from Zacatecas—the campaign that he himself had planned and ordered—was bad. Pánfilo Natera was not only making no progress; he was in grave danger of a crippling defeat. Dispatches from the battlefront were being watched closely by Carranza and his staff in Saltillo and by Villa and his generals gathered around the telegrapher's desk at the railroad station in Torreón.

At 5:25 P.M., June 10, Carranza had his telegrapher tap out a message to Villa: GENERAL NATERA INFORMS ME THAT TODAY HE BEGAN OPERATIONS AGAINST THE PLAZA OF ZACATECAS AND THAT HE HAS GOOD REASON TO EXPECT A TRIUMPH. NEVERTHELESS, ORDER TROOPS . . . TO BE READY TO REINFORCE NATERA . . . IN CASE IT SHOULD BE NECESSARY.

Villa replied that he was ready to obey any orders.

The next morning Carranza wired: YESTERDAY I ORDERED YOU TO SEND REINFORCEMENTS TO GENERAL NATERA . . . IF YOU HAVE NOT DONE SO I ORDER YOU TO SEND 3000 MEN AND TWO BATTERIES OF ARTILLERY.

Villa replied: PERMIT ME TO SUGGEST THE MOVEMENT OF THE ENTIRE DIVISION AT MY COMMAND TO ASSURE THE SUCCESS OF THE OPERATION AND MINIMIZE THE SUFFERING OF THE TROOPS . . . I WOULD TAKE ALL MY ARTILLERY. IF YOU AGREE I SUGGEST YOU ORDER GENERAL NATERA TO SUSPEND HIS ATTACK UNTIL MY ARRIVAL IN ORDER TO AVOID THE USELESS SACRIFICE OF LIVES, SINCE I HAVE INFORMATION THAT HIS FIRST ATTACKS HAVE BEEN BEATEN OFF . . . Villa, apparently expecting agreement, ordered his troops to prepare for a move south.

Carranza's reply, which did not come until the following day, the 12th, appeared to ignore Villa's suggestion: VERY URGENT. YESTERDAY I ORDERED YOU TO SEND 3000 MEN WITH ARTILLERY TO REINFORCE THE TROOPS ATTACKING ZACATECAS. TODAY GENERAL NATERA INFORMS ME HE HAS OCCUPIED MAGNIFICENT POSITIONS AND NEEDS ARTILLERY AND AMMUNITION TO HOLD THEM. I THOUGHT YOU WOULD HAVE SENT THE TROOPS I ORDERED. IF THEY HAVE NOT GONE SEND THEM IMMEDIATELY UNDER THE COMMAND OF GENERAL JOSE ISABEL ROBLES . . . WITH A LITTLE EFFORT THE CITY WILL BE OURS. INSTEAD OF 3000, SEND 5000 TROOPS, AND IF POSSIBLE ALSO SEND 30-30 AND MAUSER AMMUNITION. Carranza was signing his tactical messages EL P.J. DEL E.C. (*el primer jefe del Ejército Constitucional*—the First Chief of the Constitutional Army).

Villa did not reply until that evening. Then : I AM SORRY TO REPORT THAT GENERAL ROBLES IS UNABLE TO GO BECAUSE HE HAS BEEN ILL FOR SOME TIME [he had been wounded in the battle of Torreón]. I WANT VERY MUCH TO MOBILIZE THE FORCES AT MY COMMAND BUT BECAUSE OF HEAVY RAINS THERE HAVE BEEN NUMEROUS WASHOUTS ALONG THE RAILROAD LINE. I HAVE ORDERED IMMEDIATE REPAIRS IN ORDER TO FULFILL YOUR ORDERS.

The following morning Villa sent another wire to Carranza and his temper was beginning to show: IT WILL BE FIVE DAYS BEFORE I CAN SEND HELP TO GENERAL NATERA. SENOR, WHO ORDERED THESE MEN INTO THIS ACTION WITHOUT ANY ASSURANCE OF COMPLETE SUCCESS? YOU AND THEY KNOW THAT WE HAVE WHAT IS NEEDED FOR IT. THE PROBLEM YOU POSE FOR ME IS DIFFICULT. FIRST, ROBLES IS SICK. SECOND, IF URBINA WERE SENT HE WOULDN'T GET ALONG WITH THE ARRIETAS [the Urbina-Arrieta feud was of long standing], AND NOTHING WOULD BE ACCOMPLISHED. NOW TELL ME, SENOR, IF I WENT WITH MY DIVISION WOULD I BE UNDER THE ORDERS OF THE ARRIETAS OR NATERA, TAKING THE CITY IN ORDER FOR THEM TO ENTER? He went on: if the Natera-Arrieta troops committed disorders in the captured city he, Villa, would discipline them; there would be trouble and the Revolution would suffer. PLEASE, he said, TELL ME WHAT WE ARE GOING TO DO. IF YOU THINK I WOULD BE A HINDRANCE . . . AND YOU WANT SOMEONE ELSE TO TAKE COMMAND OF MY FORCES, I WANT TO KNOW WHO IT IS SO THAT I CAN JUDGE WHETHER THEY ARE APT AND CAPABLE OF CARING FOR THEM AS I DO MYSELF . . . I MAKE THIS OBSERVATION ONLY WITH THE END OF TAKING CARE OF MY SOLDIERS . . .

Carranza's reply was wordy. He told of the assurances he had received from Natera and the Arrietas that they could take Zacatecas. He reviewed the positions the attacking forces had taken and minimized their reverses—and again reminded Villa that he had been ordered to send reinforcements. This was no time, he said, to censure Natera and his men because they had attacked without assurance of success, and he reminded Villa that between the first battle of Torreón and the capture of Juárez he, Villa, had been unsuccessful in his attack on Chihuahua City. Nor, he said, would Villa have taken Torreón the second time if it had not been for the help of other generals whom he, Carranza, had ordered to fight under Villa's command (an inaccuracy since the Torreón campaign had been planned and begun before Carranza came to Chihuahua from Sonora). He was not ordering Villa to place himself under Natera's command; only that part of his troops should help Natera. IT IS, he said, NEITHER NECESSARY NOR CONVENIENT FOR YOU TO SEPARATE FROM THE COMMAND OF YOUR TROOPS, BUT IF YOU INSIST ON DOING THIS I MUST PROCEED FOR THE GOOD OF THE CAUSE AND FOR THE CONSTITUTIONALIST ARMY WHICH I HAVE THE HONOR TO COMMAND. And he again ordered reinforcements to be sent to Natera, who would be able to hold out in his present position only two more days.

Villa's reply was curt: I HAVE DECIDED TO RESIGN FROM THE COMMAND OF THE DIVISION. TELL ME TO WHOM I SHOULD TURN IT OVER.

Carranza answered: I AM TRULY PAINED TO BE OBLIGED TO ACCEPT YOUR RESIGNATION. I THANK YOU IN THE NAME OF THE NATION FOR THE IMPORTANT SERVICES YOU HAVE RENDERED OUR CAUSE, AND I WOULD LIKE FOR YOU TO TAKE CHARGE OF THE STATE GOVERNMENT OF CHIHUAHUA. He requested that Villa call into a telegraphic conference all the generals of the Division of the North to help him make a decision as to who should take Villa's place.

The generals gathered in the telegraph office the next day, read the messages that had been exchanged, and sent a suggestion to Carranza: that he reconsider his acceptance of Villa's resignation, since his separation from the command would cause grave disturbances. Carranza said he had taken possible disturbances into consideration in making his decision and ordered them to get on with the choice of a successor to Villa so that the needed reinforcements could be sent to Natera.

The discussion among the generals became heated. Back went a wire to Carranza: WE COULD, FOLLOWING THE EXAMPLE OF GENERAL VILLA, RESIGN THE COMMANDS OF OUR RESPECTIVE TROOPS, THUS DISSOLVING THE DIVISION OF THE NORTH, BUT WE SHOULD NOT DEPRIVE OUR CAUSE OF SUCH A VALIANT MILITARY ELEMENT. CONSEQUENTLY, WE ARE GOING TO PERSUADE THE CHIEF OF THIS DIVISION TO CONTINUE THE FIGHT AGAINST THE HUERTA GOVERNMENT AS THOUGH NOTHING DISAGREEABLE HAD OCCURRED AND WE URGE YOU TO PROCEED IN A SIMILAR MANNER WITH THE OBJECT OF CONQUERING THE COMMON ENEMY.

This was getting close to insubordination. Back came a message from Carranza: I AM SORRY TO INFORM YOU IT IS IMPOSSIBLE FOR ME TO CHANGE THE DECISION I MADE IN ACCEPTING GENERAL VILLA'S RESIGNATION; THE DISCIPLINE OF THE ARMY, WITHOUT WHICH THERE WOULD BE ANARCHY IN OUR FILES, DEMANDS IT. THREE DAYS AGO I ORDERED GENERAL VILLA . . . and he told again of the need for reinforcements. Now he urged them to make their decision—and to reach it without Villa being present at their deliberations.

The generals replied: WE HAVE IRREVOCABLY RESOLVED TO CONTINUE FIGHTING UNDER THE COMMAND OF GENERAL FRANCISCO VILLA . . . [this decision] WAS CAREFULLY CONSIDERED IN THE ABSENCE OF THE CHIEF OF THE DIVISION OF THE NORTH. OUR PROPOSALS TO THE CHIEF HAVE BEEN SUCCESSFUL. WE WILL MARCH PROMPTLY TO THE SOUTH.

Carranza: WHEN I ASKED YOU TO DESIGNATE A CHIEF TO REPLACE GENERAL VILLA I DID IT ONLY TO AVOID POSSIBLE DIFFICULTIES IN CASE WHOEVER I MIGHT NOMINATE MIGHT NOT BE THE MOST APPROPRIATE CHOICE. AS YOU KNOW, MAKING SUCH A DESIGNATION IS ONE OF THE FUNCTIONS OF

THE FIRST CHIEF. IN VIEW OF YOUR MESSAGE TODAY I COULD MAKE SUCH A CHOICE, BUT BEFORE DOING THIS I WANT TO PROCEED IN ACCORD WITH YOU. And then he ordered six of the generals to come to Saltillo for a conference with him.

The generals' reply to this: YOUR LAST TELEGRAM MAKES US SUSPECT THAT YOU EITHER DID NOT UNDERSTAND OR DID NOT WANT TO UNDERSTAND OUR PREVIOUS MESSAGES . . . WE ARE IGNORING YOUR ORDER TO GENERAL VILLA TO ABANDON HIS COMMAND, AND IT IS IMPOSSIBLE FOR US TO TAKE ANY OTHER ATTITUDE IN VIEW OF THIS IMPOLITIC, UNCONSTITUTIONAL AND ANTI-PATRIOTIC DECISION. WE HAVE CONVINCED GENERAL VILLA THAT HIS COMMITMENTS TO THE FATHERLAND OBLIGE HIM TO CONTINUE IN COMMAND AS THOUGH YOU HAD NEVER TAKEN THE MALEVOLENT RESOLUTION TO DEPRIVE OUR CAUSE OF ITS MOST PRESTIGIOUS LEADER . . . The language grew stronger. The First Chief was defrauding the Mexican people, sowing a crop of disunity among revolutionary elements, was courting trouble in his handling of foreign relations. They knew of Carranza's distrust of anyone who put him in the shade, and of his insistence that there be no one in a position of importance in the Revolution who was not an unconditional Carrancista. BUT MORE IMPORTANT THAN THESE DESIRES OF YOURS ARE THOSE OF THE MEXICAN PEOPLE FOR WHOM THE PRESTIGIOUS AND VICTORIOUS SWORD OF GENERAL VILLA IS INDISPENSABLE. THE GENERALS WHOM YOU SUMMONED TO SALTILLO CANNOT COME BECAUSE WE ARE MARCHING TO THE SOUTH.

The message bore the names of Calixto Contreras, Tomás Urbina, Mateo Almanza, T. Rodríguez, Severiano Ceniceros, Eugenio Aguirre Benavides, José E. Rodríguez, Orestes Pereyra, Martiniano Servín, José Isabel Robles, Felipe Angeles, Rosalío G. Hernández, Toribio Ortega, Maclovio Herrera, M. García. Two of them, Maclovio Herrera and Rosalío Hernández, were among the group that had approached Carranza a short time before proposing to kill Villa.

Manuel Chao, the man Carranza had designated as governor of Chihuahua against Villa's opposition and the man whom Villa had ordered shot, arrived in Torreón en route to Saltillo where he had been ordered by Carranza. Informed of the generals' message to the First Chief, he sent one of his own: I AM IN COMPLETE AGREEMENT WITH THE MESSAGE SENT TO YOU BY THE GENERALS OF THIS DIVISION AND I MAKE IT MY OWN.

Maclovio Herrera, a rough fighting man who had had more than his share of quarrels with Villa, was not content with the message he and his colleagues had sent. He told the telegrapher he had a personal message to send to the First Chief. The telegrapher hesitated. Herrera pulled his revolver and pointed it at the telegrapher's head. "Send this message. Don Venustiano Carranza, Saltillo. You are a sonofabitch. Signed Maclovio Herrera."

CHAPTER 22

ZACATECAS

"Hah! You drunkard Victoriano,
Your evil heart will skip a beat,
When you hear of Zacatecas
Where your troops have met defeat."

Corrido on the taking of Zacatecas

THE BATTLE OF ZACATECAS in June 1914 was to be the cruelest of the Revolution. It also was to make certain the end of the Huerta regime.

The little city is an old and rich one. It was established in 1548, soon after the conquering Spaniards found veins of silver and gold in the nearby mountains. In the next three centuries the mines produced almost 700,000,000 pesos worth of silver bullion. Much of the silver coinage that circulated in Mexico was minted in the Casa Moneda in Zacatecas. It was a town with fine houses and elaborate churches squeezed into a narrow canyon running roughly north and south. Because of the scarcity of level ground many of the houses were built with multiple stories, unlike the classic one-or-two-level Mexican house. Some of the streets rose so steeply that they could be negotiated only by stairs. Surrounding the town are hills and uplands—La Bufa, El Grillo, La Sierpe, Loreto, Las Bolsas, Los Clérigos, rising a thousand or more feet above the town; the town itself is approximately a mile and a half above sea level. The climate is brisk and the air fresh. The soil—except for its minerals—is poor, and water almost non-existent. An aqueduct built by the Spaniards never brought enough water for the community's needs. Water was dipped from abandoned mines, carried into the city in horse-hide bags and sold from door to door. Drainage was always a problem. From time to time Zacatecas suffered from epidemics.

To the north of Zacatecas is Fresnillo; beyond it to the northwest lies Durango, and to the northeast Torreón. Leading out of Zacatecas to the south is the road to Aguascalientes. Zacatecas is a halfway point between northern Mexico and central Mexico. It also is at a point where the continent, like a funnel, begins to narrow sharply. On the southwest lies Jalisco, the great and powerful state of which Guadalajara is the capital, and to the east lies San Luis Potosí.

In the late spring of 1914 Zacatecas was in the center of the war zone. Alvaro Obregón's army corps of the Northwest was sweeping down into Jalisco, leaving federal troops bottled up in the ports of Guaymas and Mazatlán. In the Northeast, Pablo González' army corps was headed for San Luis Potosí. To the North was Francisco Villa's huge and spectacular Division of the North, seemingly invincible, based on Torreón. Villa's victory at Torreón and the clean-up operations which had followed it had crippled Huerta's federal forces—but the federals were not dead yet. The *coup de grâce* was still needed, and it could be delivered at Zacatecas. After that the three revolutionary groups—the Northwest, the Northeast, and the North—could join for the final drive on Mexico City. But the action at Zacatecas would not be quick, easy, and merciful. It would, instead, become the bloodiest clash of the war.

Zacatecas was no stranger to the Revolution. In the spring of 1911 Luis Moya, a rebel against the Díaz dictatorship, had taken the town and held it briefly (he was killed a short time later by a stray bullet). In June 1913 Zacatecas was taken again, this time by Pánfilo Natera from Durango. Natera, a tall thin man with the swarthy skin, acquiline nose and wispy mustache of an Indian, had seized a position on La Bufa and annihilated the defending federal garrison. Natera controlled Zacatecas for two weeks and then returned to campaigning in Durango and Chihuahua.

A year after his first capture of Zacatecas, Natera once more attacked the mining town. This time he was not acting on his own, as he had been in 1913. Now he was at the orders of Carranza. Carranza's knowledge of military tactics was slight, almost non-existent; his main consideration was long-range political strategy. He did not want Francisco Villa to add another victory to his already impressive string. Nor did he want him to win a position from which he could advance quickly and easily to become the liberator of Mexico City—an honor Carranza wanted to preserve for either Obregón or González or both. Nor did he want Villa to link up with Emiliano Zapata, the peasant leader of the South who had stubbornly refused to recognize Carranza's leadership and authority.

Natera could muster no more than six thousand men, mainly cavalry, unsupported by artillery and could accomplish little against the strong positions which the federals had by this time established around Zacatecas. Badly beaten in his first attack, he withdrew to Fresnillo, forty miles to the north, and waited while Villa and his generals in Torreón argued by telegraph with Carranza.

Natera personally felt no enmity toward Villa. Villa had raised him to the rank of brigadier general, and, although there were occasional frictions, they had worked well together. Some of Natera's generals, notably the Arrieta brothers, hated Villa. But on the whole Natera and his troops desperately hoped for help not only from the Division of the North but from Villa himself. Villa and his division had an awesome reputation. And there was excited talk among Natera's men of the magnificent equipment of the Division of the North—the artillery, the good rifles and ammunition, the splendid horses, the hospital trains, the unlimited resources—and even the wearing apparel of the men who followed the Centaur of the North—Texas hats and four-dollar American-made shoes. There was a feeling of relief when the impasse was broken—not resolved in agreement but in disobedience—and the Division of the North was on its way to Zacatecas.

The 12,000 or so troops in Zacatecas commanded by General Luis Medina Barrón, prepared for the showdown. They had eleven fieldpieces and ninety machine guns. Funds were collected from the wealthy men of the town and from the clergy, both of whom were friendly to the Huerta regime. Stores of food and drink were placed in the hilltop fortifications. Horses, mules, and fodder were taken from haciendas and farms. Scouting patrols were sent out (on one of them General Medina Barrón's brother, Javier, was killed). Urgent messages were sent for reinforcements. Some four thousand men under Pasual Orozco were supposedly on their way from Aguascalientes. The *soldaderas,* left behind in the city, lighted candles on the steps of churches and prayed for victory.

Villa's massive forces began moving south from Torreón on June 16. First came Villa's *compadre,* Tomás Urbina, with a strong cavalry force. Then, on the 17th, came the artillery under Felipe Angeles, as urbane and proper as Urbina was crude and ruthless. The bulk of the Division of the North followed, day after day. Infantry and cavalry units took up positions to the east of Zacatecas at Guadalupe, to the southwest and south, driving the advance federal units back to their fortified hilltops. Angeles placed his main artillery batteries at Veta Grande, an abandoned mining property due north of the city with a clear range for the federal strongpoints guarding the northern approaches to Zacatecas, the hill of El Grillo on the west and that of La Bufa on the east. Secondary batteries were placed south of the city. By the time Villa arrived, on the afternoon of the 22nd the forces under his and Natera's command, some 25,000 in all, were in place on all sides of Zacatecas, ready to begin the battle. They had been harassed by federal artillery fire in assuming their places, but losses had been minor and they did not attempt serious retaliation, waiting for Villa's command to begin the attack, set for 10 A.M. on the 23rd.

Villa made his reputation as a leader of furious cavalry charges and critics said this was all he could do. But, while cavalry charges fitted his stormy character, Villa was capable of more sophisticated warfare. Actually the attack on Zacatecas was a complicated and well-coordinated military maneuver. In part it was due to Villa's almost instinctive mastery of battlefield tactics and in part to the counsel of the highly skilled Angeles. Federico Cervantes, a major in artillery at the Battle of Zacatecas (and later a biographer of both Villa and Angeles), wrote: "It was . . . the nearest thing to a complete battle . . . It presented all phases: preliminary reconnaissance and contact with the enemy, encirclement for a siege, orderly distribution of the troops, well-considered selection of artillery positions, effective employment of artillery to support the other arms, selection of a principal front of attack plus a reserve position, regular and predetermined development of the battle, a methodical assault on the enemy strongpoints, and the final effort and follow-up, so effective that the reserves annihilated the retreating enemy troops."

With cavalry and infantry ready to advance against the federal hill positions, Villa's artillery units deliberately drew federal fire on themselves—they had fifty artillery pieces and could afford to lose some—so that the attacking forces could move forward. The foot soldiers reached the hills and began to climb the steep, rocky slopes under rifle fire that was, at first, thick and deadly. Early losses were heavy, but the momentum of the huge attacking force was great. As they continued to scramble forward, the fire from the federal guns diminished, became erratic and, finally, panicky. While the federals had had plenty of time to prepare their defenses, the trenches they had tried to dig in the flinty soil were too shallow; although they had many rolls of barbed wire on hand they had made little use of it. By 1:30 P.M., three and a half hours after the start of the battle, the revolutionists had swept the summit of El Grillo. Within another hour they held the heights overlooking the south end of the city. By 4 P.M. the attackers had overwhelmed the strongest federal position, La Bufa, and a wild, disorganized retreat began. Federal soldiers dashed through the streets of Zacatecas. Many of them tried to take refuge in the barricaded houses of the poor—most of the wealthy people had left the city—but were turned away, even when they offered wads of currency. Many of the householders were genuinely sympathetic with the revolutionists and others feared reprisals if they offered shelter. At 4:30 P.M. the withdrawing troops dynamited the federal building, which also served as their arsenal, and three hundred people, most of them women and children, were killed. A few minutes later a second explosion wrecked the state building and there were more civilian casualties. A captured federal officer saved his own life and probably the lives of hundreds more by informing his captors that other dynamite charges were set to go off when the city's electric current was turned on—the generators were used only for four hours each evening.

Revolutionists were by now pouring into the city from all directions and the federals fled toward the south and the road to Guadalupe. Here the canyon narrowed. The revolutionists set up machine guns on the canyon's sides overlooking the crowded road and raked the retreating column. The movement—of men running on foot or riding, often two to a horse—slowed, and the road became choked with bodies of men and animals, as were the narrow streets of Zacatecas behind them. A few— possibly no more than a few hundred—managed to escape. The federal commander, General Medina Barrón, wounded in the left leg, reached the town of Soledad, farther to the south, with only fourteen followers. At least three of his subordinate generals were dead. Although an accurate count was impossible, between five and eight thousand federals were dead and another twenty-five hundred wounded. More than three thousand were taken prisoner—some to be shot, some to be incorporated into Villa's army, others to be turned free since they had been forced into military service.

Constitutionalist losses, dead and wounded together, amounted to about four thousand men. General Trinidad Rodríguez, one of Villa's most trusted collaborators, was killed on the battlefield. General Toribio Ortega, who had defended his leader in the letter to Carranza, was mortally wounded. Villa ordered that they both be buried in a mausoleum in Chihuahua which he intended to also serve as his own burial place.

Disposing of the dead in and around Zacatecas was a gigantic problem —and a serious one, the city being susceptible as it was to epidemics. Some bodies were shoveled into shallow trenches and covered over. Others by the thousands, were thrown into abandoned mine shafts. Still more were stacked on railroad flatcars, hauled out into open country and dumped. Still others, by the hundreds, were piled in the city's plaza, doused with gasoline and burned (one Zacatecan, then still a boy, recalled later how he watched with horrified fascination the way in which the bodies, reacting to the flames, would jerk and twitch spasmodically as if still alive). A decree was issued compelling property owners to dispose of any corpses found within three meters of their property.

There were other horrors. Acting on a rumor that some unwounded federal officers were sheltered in the local civil hospital, Villa demanded information from the hospital staff. When the nursing sisters and doctors refused to talk he ordered them to be marched off to the cemetery and shot. The order was rescinded at the last moment. Some priests of the Christian Brothers' San José College were not so lucky. The entire staff was arrested. Three, the director, principal, and chaplain, were taken to La Bufa and shot. The rest were loaded on top of a freight car and sent north into exile in the United States. Other priests in the city were taken in custody, then released long enough to raise 100,000 pesos in ransom money, then rearrested and shipped north to the U.S. border. The chaplain of another Catholic institution, the Teresiano College for Young Women, was shot because he tried to bar revolutionists from the school. A priest in the nearby town of Calera was ordered to raise 50,000 pesos for his ransom. Unable to do so, he too was shot. The Bishop of Zacatecas, Miguel M. de la Mora, was absent at the time; the revolutionists had to be satisfied with looting his palace. The harsh measures against the clergy were based on the aid which some of them had given to Huerta's troops.

The treatment of prisoners below the officer rank was for the most part humane. Wounded men were treated in Villa's field hospitals—staffed with fifteen surgeons and sixty nurses. Those able to travel were loaded on trains and taken north to Torreón for either discharge or incorporation into the Division of the North. But the hunt went on for federal officers. A few were found. Some were shot as soon as discovered; some were brought before Villa for sentencing. One of these was Rafael Ancheta, who had been commissioned a captain only recently before the Zacatecas action. Before that he had been a wine salesman and a talented musician in Mexico City. He had been forced into service and commissioned, not because he had any military talents but because he was an educated man and the federal army was desperate for officers. After the battle he had put on a peasant's clothes and tried to hide. Taken to the railroad car Villa used as his headquarters, he told the general he was a poor farmer, out looking for some corn and beans to buy—food was very scarce.

"Let me see your hands, little friend," said Villa.

Ancheta extended his smooth, uncallused hands and Villa looked at them.

"These aren't the hands of a farmer," said Villa. "They belong to a *perfumado.*"

Ancheta protested that he was indeed a farmer.

Villa pointed to some sacks of corn in the corner of the car. One of them, he said, contained *pepitilla* (seed corn) which any farmer would recognize. He ordered Ancheta to pick the correct sack.

Ancheta gave up. "I am an artist, Señor General, who was forced into the federal army."

"What kind of an artist?" asked Villa. Ancheta told him—a cellist and pianist.

"Well, then," said Villa, "play something for me." And he pointed to a looted piano, standing in the car and ordered some women hangers-on to dust it off. Ancheta seated himself at the piano and began to play.

"What is that?" Villa interrupted.

Ancheta replied that it was a composition by Meyerbeer.

"I don't know the lady," said Villa. "Play me something Mexican, play me '*Las Tres Pelonas*,' and you"—indicating the women hangers-on —"dance."

The shaken Ancheta began playing the revolutionary jingle over and over again and the women danced, raising dust from the floor of the railroad car, and singing the chorus—

> "There were three whores
> Sitting in a *silla*
> Saying to each other,
> Viva Pancho Villa."

Villa kept Ancheta at his musical punishment for five hours, then turned him free.

The piano was a small part of the loot the Constitutionalists took in Zacatecas. Villa said later that he had issued orders against looting; if they were issued they were ignored. Generals and other high-ranking officers appropriated houses for themselves, packed up furniture, silverware, china, kitchen utensils, pictures, and clothing and sent them back to northern Mexico, leaving only the bare essentials for their own temporary comfort. Paintings were stripped from gilt frames—the frames looked valuable. Locks were shot off closets, cabinets and desks. Books, ledgers, correspondence were used for fires. Horses were stabled on lower floors, trampling manure into parquet floors and carpeting. *Soldaderas* donned bridal dresses and ball gowns that had belonged to Zacatecas society, and with their broad, callused feet crammed into satin slippers, moved into the upper floors with their friends. Common soldiers picked up whatever they could, regardless of its utility. Mariano Azuela, the novelist who was a doctor in Villa's army tells in *The Underdogs* of an Oliver typewriter one soldier had taken for himself in Zacatecas although neither he nor any of his companions knew how to use the machine. As they withdrew the typewriter grew heavier and heavier. The first soldier sold it to a companion for ten pesos. This purchaser, tiring of it, sold it to a third for eight pesos. The typewriter went on changing hands, the price dropping with each transaction until the final owner bought it for twenty-five centavos just for the pleasure of smashing it against a stone wall.

The looting was at first haphazard and capricious. Later it became more methodical, and witnesses described columns of horse-drawn wagons moving through the streets toward the railroad station, loaded with furniture, wearing apparel, implements, musical instruments, sewing machines, even bird cages. A survey by consular officials some time after the battle produced an estimate of 3,750,000 pesos worth of loot taken from Zacatecas, the bulk of it from the homes of the wealthy. Some forty automobiles were taken, along with every other kind of vehicle, plus all horses and mules.

It was reckoned also that at least 250,000 pesos had been raised in payment of ransoms to avoid the death penalty. Even payments of the demanded sum did not insure safety. One of Natera's underlings, General Tomás Domínguez, a one-time cowboy, tried to locate Juan Zesati, a rancher with whom he had once, long before, had a disagreement. Unable to do so, he arrested Zesati's brother, Francisco, and Francisco's eighteen-year-old son. He demanded a thousand pesos of his prisoners. Zesati could raise only two hundred, which he turned over to his captor—but was still held. A friend went to see General Natera, obtained an order for Zesati's release. Domínguez glanced at the order, laughed and tore it up. Meanwhile he had arrested and held for 20,000 pesos ransom one Jacinto Carlos and his son Salvador, and also Manuel Gómez, held for 5000 pesos ransom. In both the latter cases the full amount demanded was paid, but then all five—Gómez, the two Carlos men, and the two Zesatis—were stripped of their clothing and shot at close range.

The execution of Salvador Hernández, operator of the Calderón Theater, and his son Enrique, was, at first, something of a mystery. Hernández was not a member of the anti-revolutionary oligarchy of Zacatecas but was, instead, regarded as a friend of the poor. He regularly admitted penniless children to his theater when there were seats to spare. But it was remembered that Hernández and his son both had a number of gold teeth. When the bodies were recovered the teeth were missing.

Villa had gone back to Torreón soon after the battle and Pánfilo Natera was in charge of Zacatecas. He made an effort to maintain order. He forbade the sale of alcoholic spirits (and reserved for himself a monopoly of beer sales). He ordered the execution of one federal officer who, tiring of the Zacatecas girl he had made his mistress, killed her and mutilated her face in an effort to avoid identification. He ordered looting stopped, but he installed his father, Colonel Francisco Natera, in the mansion of the Ibarguengoytia family and the older man had soon stripped the place. Natera himself occupied a room—decorated in delicate blue—that had once belonged to a daughter of the Gómez Gordon family. He was aware of the excesses committed by his men but in many cases could do nothing about them. In the specific case of the outrageous General Tomás Domínguez he was powerless to act since Domínguez commanded approximately five thousand troops; a showdown would be dangerous.

Aside from the grisly aspects there was a certain air of fiesta about Zacatecas, at least for the occupying troops and their officers. Much of the loot went into lavish charro outfits that became almost a standard uniform among revolutionists in Zacatecas—finely worked boots, tight-fitting trousers, short jackets embroidered with gold and silver thread, brightly colored silk handkerchiefs, broad-brimmed heavy sombreros loaded with ornaments of silver and gold, saddles decorated with silver *conchos.* To show off all this splendor successful revolutionists often rode their horses into saloons (which remained open despite Natera's orders); and General Santos Bañuelos, whose outfit was more elaborate than most (his black velvet trousers had a double row of silver buttons down each leg) once rode his horse into the Calderón Theater and sat on his fine saddle throughout a performance. Bands were organized and offered regular concerts in the parks, the program being limited to airs popular with the Villista troops—*Adelita, La Cucaracha,* and *Tierra Blanca,* the last composed in honor of one of Villa's great victories. Children were given lapel buttons bearing a portrait of Villa superimposed on the tricolor of Mexico.

One of the observers of the scene in Zacatecas was Leon J. Canova, recently appointed a special agent for the U. S. State Department. Canova was a former newspaperman who had served in Cuba and spoke Spanish. Early in his mission he had spent some time in Saltillo with Carranza, whose dignity he admired. He arrived in Zacatecas early in August. He was predisposed to view the activities of the Villista forces with both suspicion and alarm. His long, rambling dispatches to the State Department on what he saw and heard in Zacatecas were burdened with turgid words—pandemonium, chaos, debauchery, brutality, gore—all of it a "grewsome" sight. What happened in Zacatecas, he reported, all in capital letters, was like the "sacking of Europe by the invading hordes of barbarous Huns; the pitiless conquest of Spain by the fanatical Moors; the debauchery of Constantinople by the Turks when Constantine's defense failed, or the plundering of Panama by Morgan's freebooters. Lust for blood, gluttony for loot and a fierce thirst for vengeance . . . a litany of crime."

Canova found General Natera "not a bad man . . . as Indians go. He is uncouth, ignorant, and easily misled. He has no moral courage and under some conditions no physical courage . . . He is not a disciplinarian and the men under him ignore his orders and scoff at him . . ." He also observed that Natera liked to laugh and joke, was addicted to liquor and bawdy houses, but the principal problem was his lack of control over his subordinates. The Constitutionalist slogan of "Viva la Constitución," Canova reported, had been replaced with "viva la prostitución." In the same connection he said "there are no authentic accounts of rape, but this is easily accounted for by the small value put upon virtue by the majority of the people here. Rape was quite unnecessary."

Canova, in trying to reconstruct what had happened in the aftermath of the Battle of Zacatecas, became acquainted with the most important revolutionary figures in the city. He found General Trinidad Cervantes to be "a decent kind" who, remarkably, had "not seized or looted anyone's house . . . On this account he is not popular with the military element." The newly appointed governor of the state, Manuel Carlos de la Vega, he found to be "a nice young fellow" who had only recently come to Zacatecas from Sombrerete. De la Vega told Canova the priests had been expelled "because papers had been found in the headquarters of the Federals here in which it appeared they had given Medina Barrón 22,000 pesos for his gallant defense of the town against Natera . . . They had mixed in politics and deserved some punishment." Of the killing of priests De la Vega claimed to know nothing, it having happened before his arrival.

On the night of August 9 Canova and the British consular agent attended a performance in the Calderón Theater which had opened under new management after the death of the gold-toothed Señor Hernández. Canova noted that the theater boxes were occupied by "a spectacular-looking bunch of cut-throats." He particularly noticed one, Colonel Melitón Ortega, chief of arms of Zacatecas. Ortega sat in a box next to the stage, wrapped in a blanket, his skin swarthy, his cheeks unshaven, his hair unshorn, with a huge, heavily ornamented hat on his head. Occasionally he would take a pull from a quart bottle, blot his mouth with the heel of his hand and pass the bottle to his companion, General Santos Bañuelos, who had his velvet-clad, silver-trimmed legs up on the rail for the audience to admire.

Between the acts Colonel Ortega disappeared briefly. He walked a few steps down the street to a cafe. There the political chief of the town, Ignacio Rivera Castañeda, stood watching a game of dominoes. Without a word Ortega pulled out his pistol, put it behind the political chief's ear and fired. He then reholstered his gun and staggered back to the theater for the rest of the show.

Canova did not learn until the next day that Castañeda had been killed. What the quarrel was about he could not discover; he knew only that it was Castañeda who had looted the Church of San Juan de Dios, obtaining a considerable haul of gold and silver ornaments, including a solid silver pedestal on which an image of the Virgin of Guadalupe had stood. It was the sort of thing that could cause jealousy. Canova called on the governor, De la Vega, inquiring into the crime. De la Vega, who had been in office little more than a month, said that he was going away immediately for a vacation, leaving his secretary, Antonio Acuña Navarro, as acting governor. Canova composed a telegram to the Secretary of State:

LAST NIGHT THE CHIEF OF ARMS KILLED THE POLITICAL CHIEF OF THIS TOWN. IT WAS ANOTHER CASE OF MURDER. GOVERNOR DE LA VEGA INTENDS TO LEAVE FOR SAN ANTONIO, TEXAS, FOR A MONTH'S VACATION, LEAVING HIS SEC-RETARY ANTONIO ACTING GOVERNOR, BUT ACCOUNT THIS CRIME AND OTHER LAWLESSNESS OF THE MILITARY ELEMENT HAS REFUSED TO ACCEPT RESPON-SIBILITY OF THE POSITION UNLESS MILITARY ARE AMENABLE TO CIVIL AUTHOR-ITIES AND PUNISHABLE FOR CRIMES. HE STATED ALSO TO ME WILL RESIGN AS SECRETARY IF NECESSARY MEASURES NOT TAKEN TO STOP CARNIVAL CRIMES. VEGA TELEGRAPHED NATERA URGING SUMMARY ACTION. NATERA HAS NOT YET ANSWERED. LAST NIGHT SOUTHBOUND TRAIN DERAILED AND ATTACKED NEAR CALERA AND IT IS SUPPOSED BY SOME OROZCO SYMPATHIZERS. NATERA'S FORCES GONE AGUASCALIENTES; FOR OROZCO IS VERY ACTIVE WITH FOUR THOUSAND MEN IN THAT VICINITY. IT IS SAID THAT IN THE SACKING OF THE TOWN OF LEON, GUANAJUATO, HE OBTAINED AN APPROXIMATION OF TWO MILLION DOLLARS CASH. THE PEOPLE MUCH ALARMED BECAUSE OF LAWLESS CONDITIONS.

Canova was an emotional and at times confused reporter. He had at first identified Colonel Melitón Ortega as General Toribio Ortega, who was dead. He often specified dollars when he meant pesos (less than half the value of a dollar under normal conditions and no one could determine what they were worth at this point). And he frequently contradicted himself. But he was indisputably correct in saying that the people were much alarmed. Zacatecas was a shambles—as were so many other towns and cities over which the Revolution had swept. The civilian population suffered misery and indignity, loss of property and even life, no matter who was in charge.

Frederick Palmer, a Britisher who had both an hacienda and a mine near Zacatecas, wrote to his son about what had happened to him. First had come Natera in his unsuccessful attack. As Natera's troops retreated they killed pigs, took horses and fodder. Four days later federal troops under Medina Barrón appeared at his hacienda—called San Bernabé. They wrecked his house and offices, took his four carriage mules, his carriage, his saddle horses, took the dynamite stored in the nearby mine and "cleaned out everything they could get their hands on." Then the combined forces of Villa and Natera attacked Zacatecas. Federal troops under General Benjamín Argumeda made a stand at the hacienda and were badly beaten by Villa's men, who then proceeded to take what was left at the hacienda—more horses and mules which Palmer had hidden in the mine and some two hundred tons of fodder, so that both hacienda and mine had to suspend operations for want of animals. "I don't make any distinction," Palmer wrote, ". . . between the federals, Villa's troops and Natera's . . . they are all equally bad. None show any consideration of any kind and I feel we are fortunate in having a coat . . . and shoes . . . Plunder, plunder is the main aim of all of them . . . They don't rob me as a foreigner because they rob their own countrymen equally . . . they are impartial . . . Their motto, applicable to both sides alike, clean out everyone that has anything. Doubtless after a short time they will for want of others to rob have to rob each other . . . It does not limit itself to robbery but to outrages of every kind on both men and women. May God be pleased to give us peace soon."

CHAPTER 23

TOWARD PEACE

> "Villa? Obregón? Carranza? What's the difference? I love the revolution like a volcano in eruption. I love the volcano because it's a volcano, the revolution because it's a revolution."
>
> Mariano Azuela, *The Underdogs*

ZACATECAS DESTROYED Victoriano Huerta. Three weeks after the battle he resigned and fled the country. And while it was the greatest victory yet won by the Constitutionalists it was, in a way, a disaster for them, too. For it made the schism in their ranks an irreparable one. The battle had been fought and won in defiance of Carranza's orders.

The First Chief was not long in retaliating against Villa, Angeles, and the other generals of the Division of the North for their insubordination. While Angeles was directing the tactical operations at Zacatecas he received a wire from Carranza: BECAUSE YOU DID NOT RESPOND TO THE TRUST THE FIRST CHIEF PLACED IN YOU AND BECAUSE YOU COMMITTED A GRAVE ACT OF INSUBORDINATION THE FIRST CHIEF HAS DECIDED THAT, EFFECTIVE IMMEDIATELY, YOU WILL CEASE TO BE THE SUBSECRETARY OF WAR, FOR THE GOOD OF THE SERVICE AND THE GOOD NAME OF THE CONSTITUTIONAL ARMY . . . I HAVE COMMUNICATED THIS DECISION TO ALL UNITS IN THE ORDER OF THE DAY.

It made little difference to Angeles. As "Subsecretary of War in charge of the office" in Carranza's cabinet he had had neither responsibility nor respect. The position had been meaningless; so was his dismissal from it—except as an expression of the First Chief's displeasure. Angeles went on with the battle. And when it was over he asked Villa for the command of four brigades. With these troops he proposed to push on to Aguascalientes, the next important city on the route to Mexico

City. Although Medina Barrón's federal forces had been virtually destroyed at Zacatecas there were supposed to be forces under Pascual Orozco operating in the Aguascalientes area. Angeles wanted to go after them. Villa agreed immediately but insisted that Angeles take seven brigades instead of four, and proceed at once.

Before this decision could be put in force, however, it became apparent that Carranza had other—and more effective—means of retaliation. Shipments of arms and ammunition, purchased by Villa and due to be forwarded from Tampico, did not arrive. Neither did supplies of coal from the mines of Coahuila. No trains were coming through. Without fresh munitions a movement to the south would be foolhardy. Without coal to fuel the troop trains there could be no movement at all. The great Division of the North, which had begun as a handful of self-sufficient men on horseback, each with his rifle and cartridge belts, had become a vast military organization dependent upon locomotives and a complicated system of logistics. Villa reluctantly canceled his authorization for Angeles to advance on Aguascalientes.

Villa was puzzled. He knew that insubordination was a serious matter. He would not tolerate it in the men who served under him, and he had shot—or ordered shot—many men to prove it. But he had tried, in his own clumsy, ingenuous way, to reassure Carranza. Was Carranza afraid of him as a rival for the presidency once the Revolution was won? Villa had twice issued statements disclaiming any interest in a political office; he was simply a soldier for the Revolution. Was Carranza jealous of Villa's military victories? Villa had ordered the editor of his paper, back in Chihuahua, to eliminate the name of Pancho Villa from stories of revolutionary triumphs. Now, after the Battle of Zacatecas, Villa insisted that General Pánfilo Natera—whom Carranza had ordered to take Zacatecas but who had failed to do so until Villa took over—send in the official report of the victory. He thus hoped to make it appear, at least in the official records, that Carranza's orders had been carried out in the way Carranza wanted, with Villa doing nothing more than providing reinforcements.

But the shutting off of the coal and munition supplies showed that Carranza was not mollified. Then, in case there remained any doubt as to the state of affairs, Carranza announced military promotions. Both Alvaro Obregón, commander of the army corps of the Northwest, and Pablo González, head of the army corps of the Northeast, were advanced to the grade of divisional generals. Villa, whose military feats outshone both of them, remained a brigadier general, and his Division of the North, larger, more powerful and effective than either of the army corps, remained what it had been, a division.

The generals of González' army corps of the Northeast, concerned with the Villa-Carranza crisis and the danger of an open break which could destroy the revolutionary movement at a time when victory was in sight, sent a delegation to Zacatecas to see what could be done to patch up the feud. Villa, knowing his own shortcomings in matters of argument and logic and not trusting his own temper, appointed Miguel Silva, a doctor in his medical service, to act as his spokesman. Silva explained the Villistas' position. Villa and his generals recognized Carranza as First Chief and were loyal to him. But what was the function of the First Chief of the Constitutional army? It was a title which Carranza had invented himself. It apparently meant whatever Carranza intended for it to mean. Did it mean that he commanded the military forces in the field? If his orders had been followed at Zacatecas there would have been a disaster. The generals of the Division of the North thought that the First Chief should function as the civilian head of the revolutionary movement but should leave military decisions in the hands of the military men. The generals from the Northeast, who were acting with Carranza's knowledge and consent but without his authorization, agreed to a meeting in Torreón to try and close the rift.

Villa, meanwhile, had been trying to persuade Alvaro Obregón to join him in resistance to Carranza. Villa had never met Obregón, but he had followed with interest and respect his successful campaign down the west coast. After those of Villa, Obregón's military victories were the most impressive that had been won by the Constitutionalists.

When Villa and his generals rebelled against Carranza's orders before the battle of Zacatecas, Villa held a telegraphic conference with Obregón, then in Tepic. Villa proposed that the two of them agree on joint operations toward Central Mexico, ignoring the restrictions of Carranza. Obregón, while polite and tactful, offered Villa no encouragement. Instead, a few days later, he sent a wire to Carranza, presumably reporting what had happened (no record was kept), and reaffirming his loyalty to the First Chief.

Obregón had enjoyed Carranza's confidence from the outset and had operated with no interference from the First Chief. He had run his campaign as he saw fit but had done it in a way that permitted Carranza to believe that he, the First Chief, was determining strategy and directing tactics, and he wholeheartedly approved of everything that Obregón did. In mid-May Carranza had sent his splendidly uni-formed former secretary, Alfredo Breceda, now promoted to the rank of general in the Constitutionalist army, to confer with Obregón. Car-ranza, Breceda reported, suspected the intentions of Villa and Angeles. Obregón must advance as rapidly as possible to the center of the country and take the national capital before the Division of the North could do so. This was what Obregón had hoped to do anyway, and he readily agreed.

On June 25, after the Battle of Zacatecas, Villa addressed a "very urgent" telegram to Obregón at Ahualulco, Jalisco. I REGRETFULLY INFORM YOU, Villa said, THAT SENOR CARRANZA CONTINUES TO OBSTRUCT THIS DIVISION'S ADVANCE TO THE INTERIOR OF THE COUNTRY WITH OBSTACLES AND DIFFICULTIES. He reviewed his problems with coal and munitions. He pointed out that Pablo González was keeping his troops in Saltillo and Monterrey, making no effort to move forward. Villa's only course, he told Obregón, was to turn back to the north and await some resolution of the problem. Thus, if Obregón continued his operations toward Central Mexico he would be doing it without the help of either Villa or González, and the operation might be risky. He also told Obregón of the approaching conference in Torreón between representatives of his division and González' corps to discuss matters of "gravity and transcendence," and suggested that Obregón should also be represented.

Obregón replied on July 2, saying that due to rainstorms and washouts Villa's message of June 25 had reached him only that day (he had, nevertheless, received a message from Carranza the previous day informing him of his promotion to the rank of divisional general). Obregón told Villa that he was not fully informed on what was going on between the chief of the Division of the North and Carranza— which was not entirely true. But he cautioned Villa not to act as sole arbiter of what was right and wrong because "you thus endanger not just one man but the entire nation." He conceded that Carranza could make errors, and when he did so it was the responsibility of the military leaders to point them out to him. The solution to the difficulty, he suggested, was not to withdraw recognition from a man the military chiefs themselves had "chosen" as their leader. He hoped that the conference at Torreón would be helpful and regretted that he could not be represented. He invoked Villa's patriotism, urged him to continue his "honorable career," subordinating his feelings to the orders of the First Chief.

Obregón then added a curious note. There would be an opportunity in the future, he said, "to make known to our chief the programs which we believe necessary to guarantee peace for our country." Villa had not raised the question of "programs"; he was for the moment only concerned with military necessity and the discrimination against himself and his division. Obregón, perhaps unconsciously, had touched on the most sensitive, vulnerable aspect of Carranza's Constitutional movement: it had no object other than to oust Victoriano Huerta, to install Carranza in his place and to restore the country to constitutional rule—as Carranza understood constitutional rule. Huerta was beaten—there could no longer be any doubt of this; but the things that Huerta represented—reaction, oppression, military rule, and the ages-old alliance between the wealthy conservatives and the Catholic clergy would not necessarily be eradicated. Carranza had no clear program to deal with these and other problems. The lack was obvious to the cool and calculating Alvaro Obregón, just as it was to the hot-tempered Villa. And it was equally clear to the men who were about to gather in a second-floor suite of the Bank of Coahuila in Torreón and consider the problems between Villa and Carranza.

Villa was represented by two civilians and a soldier: Dr. Silva, who had served as his spokesman in the preliminary negotiations at Zacatecas; Manuel Bonilla, an engineer from Sinaloa who had been a pioneer in Madero's Anti-Reelectionist movement; and General José Isabel Robles. González' representatives were all generals: Cesareo Castro, Luis Caballero, and Antonio I. Villareal, the former Magonista whom Villa had admired at Saltillo.

Villa—leaving Zacatecas in what amounted to a state of anarchy—went to Torreón for the conference. He did not attend the meetings, however, but entertained the delegates at dinner each evening. He avoided mention of the topics being deliberated, but he spoke at length "of the miseries and humiliations of the poor which I had endured."

The conference continued for five days, July 4 to 8. The first item on the agenda was to establish the fact that the Division of the North still recognized Carranza as First Chief of the Constitutionalist army. Without this the delegates knew there was no hope of getting Carranza to agree to anything. It was also agreed that Villa should remain in command of the Division of the North.

There then followed six more points of agreement. Carranza should furnish Villa everything required, included the needed coal and munitions, and Villa should have freedom of action in military and administrative affairs in his area "when circumstances demand," with the proviso that he report his activities to Carranza for "ratification or rectification." A list of names, about equally divided between Carrancistas and Villista intellectuals, was submitted with the suggestion that Carranza choose his cabinet from among them. When Carranza assumed the interim presidency in accordance with the Plan of Guadalupe he should call a convention of representatives of the Constitutionalist military forces, on the basis of one representative for a thousand men, to make plans and set dates for a national election and to formulate a program of government. Carranza should take steps to end the feud in Sonora between the governor and the military. Carranza should be empowered to appoint and remove federal employees in states controlled by the Constitutionalist forces.

And finally, there was clause number eight, the so-called "golden clause," which read: "Inasmuch as the present conflict is a struggle of the poor against the abuses of the powerful, and inasmuch as the country's misfortunes have been caused by pretorianism, the plutocracy and the clergy, the Divisions of the North and the Northeast solemnly commit themselves to fight for a complete destruction of the ex-federal army; to implant a democratic regime in our nation; to secure the well-being of the workers; to emancipate the peasants economically, making an equitable distribution of lands or whatever else is needed to solve the agrarian problem; to correct, punish, and hold responsible those members of the Catholic clergy who, materially or physically, have aided the usurper, Victoriano Huerta."

The "golden clause," probably in large part the doing of General Villareal with the support of the Villista representatives, was far more revolutionary than anything Carranza had agreed to in the past.

There were other points that the representatives of the Division of the North wanted incorporated. But they were issues which almost certainly would antagonize Carranza, and it was deemed expedient to put them in a secret communication to Carranza; the contents would not be made known to the public. One was that Villa should be promoted to the rank of divisional general, equal with Obregón and González, and his Division of the North should be raised to the status of an army corps, like those of the Northwest and Northeast. Felipe Angeles should be restored to the position of Subsecretary of War, from which Carranza had fired him (according to the version Villa related to U.S. special agent George Carothers, it was asked that Angeles be made military commander-in-chief of all Constitutionalist forces, thus leaving Carranza with only civil and diplomatic responsibilities). The coal mines and railroads should be placed under the management of a Villa appointee—thus making certain that Villa would have all the fuel and rolling stock he needed. And "all Constitutional chiefs," i.e. military leaders, should be banned from candidacy for the presidency or vice-presidency after the culmination of the Revolution. This proviso may have been intended to reassure Carranza that Villa would not be a rival for political leadership of the nation (and it echoed the anti-militarist sentiments Alvaro Obregón had expressed to Carranza long before). But it also raised a troublesome question: Was Carranza, the First Chief of the Constitutionalist army, a "Constitutionalist Chief"? If so it would prevent him from holding the office that he obviously wanted. In an attempt to make these suggestions palatable, the generals of the Division of the North who had signed the insubordinate telegram on June 14, apologized and asked that their rude remarks be forgiven.

Carranza replied on July 13. Regarding the formal protocol, he agreed with it in general. On the suggestion of a convention to call elections and determine a program of government, he suggested that state governors (most of whom would be his appointees) also be represented, and that the resolutions of such a body should not interfere with measures which he already was taking for the economic betterment of the Mexican people. But he could not accept clause number eight which was, he said, outside the purpose for which the Torreón conference had been held. It was a curious reservation since he had been careful to avoid giving official sanction to the conference, whatever its purpose might be.

As for the secret communication from the representatives of the Division of the North, he was glad to accept their apologies. But his response to their proposals was negative. It was impossible to restore Felipe Angeles to his post. He declined to promote Villa "for reasons which I have," although he did concede that it might be possible at some future time. Nor could the Division of the North be elevated to a higher category. The division would remain, organizationally, a part of the army corps of the Northwest. With the victory of the Constitutional cause near at hand creation of a new army corps would be pointless since the entire army would soon be reorganized anyway.

Special Agent Canova visited with Carranza immediately after his reply to the proposals of the Torreón conference and found him "very affable." Canova expressed the hope there would be no more hostility between Villa and Carranza. "He assured me," Canova reported, "that so far as he is concerned the incident will never be reopened, but if it was I could depend upon it, some act of General Villa would be responsible. He stated that the difference between he [sic] and Villa was that he was a man of one purpose while General Villa was very impressionable, of deep and sudden passions and very hasty in action. He said he did not believe there would be any more trouble . . ."

Carranza had good reason to be both affable and confident. His political skills had triumphed. If Villa and his generals had persisted in their attitude of defiance Carranza's position of leadership would have been greatly diminished, perhaps destroyed. Carranza was not the sort of man who could personally attract a large and enthusiastic following. But the Villistas, hoping for something in return, had apologized for their behavior and renewed their allegiance to the First Chief. In return, Carranza promised to supply the provisions needed for military operations. Carranza had also made a commitment: the promise of a convention to arrange for a general election and to consider a program of post-revolutionary government. But this was a matter for the future and posed no immediate problem for the First Chief.

Carranza sat in his old state capital, Saltillo—which the Villistas had liberated for him—and looked to the south toward the national capital, Mexico City which he would almost certainly enter victoriously before long. The military news was good. After a decisive battle of Orendáin, Obregón's army corps of the Northwest had taken Guadalajara on July 8. Two thousand federal soldiers died in the defense of Guadalajara; five thousand more were taken prisoner—and the balance, no more than three thousand, fled. Obregón's troops entered the Jalisco capital in triumph and a *corrido* was sung in bars and cafes—

"Everyone wants Carranza to be president— That is all you hear the people say."

Obregón did not linger. He had captured eighteen military trains and thirty locomotives at Guadalajara. He sent part of his troops south into the state of Colima to liberate the port of Manzanillo. He sent other troops eastward to seize Irapuato, an important railroad center in the state of Guanajuato. Here the lines from Guadalajara and the west joined the Mexican Central line that came south from Torreón and Zacatecas.

Meanwhile victories were falling into the lap of Pablo González. He had been making leisurely preparations for a move to the south and an attack on San Luis Potosí. But on July 20 San Luis Potosí was taken without a struggle. One of his columns moved on to the colorful old mining city of Guanajuato and found that federal troops had abandoned it. They then advanced to the industrial town of León, met and defeated the forces of Pascual Orozco. Orozco fled north and crossed the border into Texas. González' troops moved into Querétaro, only 135 miles northwest of Mexico City, and just sixty miles east of Irapuato, which Obregón's troops had already secured. It was now possible for the army corps of the Northwest and the Northeast to join together for the final advance on the capital. The combined forces now had control from the Gulf of Mexico to the Pacific and north to the U.S. border in the east and west. Villa and his Division of the North were bottled up in Chihuahua with no place to go. Carranza ordered Obregón to take charge of the advance to the capital.

Carranza had, meanwhile, been busy on the diplomatic and political front. He had brushed off the suggestion of the ABC mediation conference that he discuss with Huerta the selection of a provisional president acceptable to both sides. He had refused to negotiate anything with Huerta. When Huerta resigned and left the country Carranza was just as unyielding in his attitude toward the interim President, Francisco Carvajal, who attempted to open peace discussions. Carvajal sent a three-man negotiating team to confer with Carranza, to seek an armistice and to suggest the reconvening of the 26th Legislature—the one Huerta had dissolved—so that it could select a provisional president. Carranza avoided them. They went first to Tampico, where Carranza had been, then to Monterrey and finally to Saltillo in search of the First Chief, harassed at every step by Constitutionalist authorities. Finally, in Saltillo, they were told that there was nothing to discuss. The only acceptable basis for peace was unconditional surrender.

Carranza, in addition to demanding a hard peace, had also been clarifying his own future plans. He was opposed to any arrangement for the choice of a provisional president, not even if he himself were chosen for that office. As early as July 6 he had told Special Agent Canova that a provisional president would find it difficult to achieve any program of reform. A provisional president would have to convene Congress and this would impede his freedom of action.

A few days later Carranza had his acting Foreign Minister, Isidro Fabela, send a wire to Rafael Zubaran Capmany, his confidential agent in Washington, on the same subject: A PROVISIONAL PRESIDENT MUST OPERATE ONLY IN ACCORDANCE WITH THE RIGHTS AND OBLIGATIONS CONCEDED TO HIM BY THE CONSTITUTION. THUS HE WOULD BE UNABLE TO DICTATE LAWS WHICH THE MEXICAN PEOPLE NEED AND WHICH SOCIAL NECESSITIES DEMAND WITHOUT PROVOKING OPPOSITION AND BEING SUBJECTED TO ATTACK, POSSIBLY ARMED. INASMUCH AS THE FIRST CHIEF OF THE CONSTITUTIONALIST ARMY IN HIS CHARACTER AS A MILITARY CHIEF IS INVESTED WITH EXTRAORDINARY AUTHORITY, SUPPORTED BY THE ARMS OF SUBORDINATE MILITARY CHIEFS, WHO, WITH THEIR TROOPS, ARE DESIROUS OF CERTAIN SOCIAL REFORMS, HE CAN DICTATE THESE MEASURES. THESE LAWS WOULD BE IN FORCE UNTIL CONSTITUTIONAL ORDER IS REESTABLISHED, AT WHICH TIME THEY WOULD BE RATIFIED OR RECTIFIED BY THE CONSTITUTIONAL CONGRESS . . . A PRESIDENT COULD ACT EFFECTIVELY ONLY WITH THE EXTRAORDINARY POWERS GRANTED BY CONGRESS, BUT IF WE NAMED A PROVISIONAL PRESIDENT THERE WOULD BE NO CONGRESS TO GRANT THESE SPECIAL POWERS; OTHER THAN SENOR CARRANZA I DO NOT BELIEVE THERE IS AT PRESENT ANOTHER PERSON WHO HAS THE SUPPORT OF PUBLIC OPINION, WHO HAS THE KNOWLEDGE OF THE NEEDS OF THE PEOPLE AND WHO COULD FULFILL THIS TRANSCENDENTAL WORK . . .

The Fabela statement gave examples of reforms to be undertaken: abolition of company stores, municipal autonomy, adjustment of tariffs and tax assessments and revision of judicial procedure. There was no mention of agrarian or labor problems.

It was clear that Carranza intended to take over the government, but he would not do it as interim president, which his Plan of Guadalupe had proposed, but as First Chief with dictatorial power. If Carranza permitted himself to be forced into the provisional presidency, the Constitution—which he had promised to restore as the guiding charter of Mexico—would prevent him from succeeding himself as constitutional president.

THE OUTSIDERS

> "Perhaps it is my destiny to win the greatest battles of the war so that other generals may receive the honors of the victory."
>
> Martín Luis Guzmán, *Memoirs of Pancho Villa*

THERE WERE ONLY a few obstacles left between Carranza and the supreme power of Mexico.

The remnants of the federal army were in no condition to resist. They were retreating toward Mexico City and showed no inclination to fight.

Carranza was confident that his regime, once installed, would be recognized by foreign powers, including the United States. With this would come withdrawal of American troops from Veracruz. He would have a free hand to begin the national reconstruction.

But there was still the problem of Villa in the North and Zapata in the South. While Carranza had managed to prevent any union of the two, he could not eliminate them. Nor could he ignore them. Villa was immobilized in Chihuahua, at least for the present. But Zapata and his peasant horde were within striking distance of Mexico City—just as they had been under Díaz, under Madero, under Huerta. Carranza's efforts to communicate with Zapata had come to nothing. Zapata had scoffed at Carranza's Plan of Guadalupe as meaningless since it made no mention of land reform. Anyone wanting Zapata's collaboration must accept the Plan of Ayala.

A year earlier, shortly after Carranza had been forced to flee Coahuila, Zapata sent a letter to a Mexico City newspaper, saying: "According to newspapers from the northern frontier which we receive in our camp I have understood with surprise that the Carrancistas claim that I, as general-in-chief of the revolutionary forces of the South and Center of the republic, have placed myself at the orders of Señor Don Venustiano Carranza and recognized him as chief. This is notoriously false . . . Neither I nor the patriots who follow me in the armed fight on behalf of the people would be capable of joining such a faction . . ."

The next month when General Lucio Blanco expropriated the property of Felix Díaz at Matamoros and divided it up among the peasants, Zapata wrote an enthusiastic letter from Yautepec, applauding his action. Carranza's subsequent punishment of Blanco for his unauthorized act only served to deepen the Zapatistas' suspicions.

Shortly after Villa had captured Juárez in November 1913 he was visited by a representative of Zapata. Although the two leaders, Villa and Zapata, did not know each other, they had much in common. Both were peasants who had become guerrilla fighters. Both were dedicated to the cause of the poor and oppressed. As a result of the meeting in Juárez Villa sent several letters of sympathy and admiration to Zapata.

The following March, while Villa was preparing for the second battle of Torreón, the Zapatistas drew up a resolution defining their attitude toward the Constitutionalist forces. They recognized Carranza only as governor of the state of Coahuila. They proposed court martial proceedings against Carranza for having proclaimed himself First Chief, "naming his government as if he were provisional President of the Republic." Villa, on the other hand, they recognized as "first chief of the army of the North with faculties to operate and advance with his army to lay siege to the capital of the republic in accordance with the Supreme Chief of the Army of the South, General Emiliano Zapata." In addition, Villa was invited to send representatives to a convention which the Zapatistas planned to hold on May 15 in Chilpancingo for the purpose of selecting a junta to govern the nation and arrange for general elections once the Revolution had been won. By that time Villa was too busy with his battles in the North to think of attending a convention but he was aware of the Zapatistas' friendly feeling toward him and their antipathy to Carranza.

In the troubled summer of 1914 the young and brilliant Martín Luis Guzmán was to counsel Villa: "If you find a way to agree with Obregón, nobody can break the unity of our movement, but if you and Obregón do not unite against Carranza . . . [there will be] war with Obregón and González. You must be prepared for this, Señor General. Get the revolutionary men of the South on your side."

But Zapata and his men of the South were far away and there was no communication. Villa, although disappointed by the apparent failure of the pact of Torreón, made a few more conciliatory gestures, trying to patch up his relations with Carranza. He freed some forty-odd Carrancistas whom he had been holding prisoner since the first flare-up with Carranza at Torreón. He also agreed to return to the First Chief a money press which Carranza had left behind in Chihuahua and with which the Villistas had been turning out their own money. With it went some millions of pesos.

Villa may have still entertained some hope that Carranza would permit him to be in on the kill at Mexico City. When Carranza advised him by wire that Obregón had taken Guadalajara, Villa acknowledged the information with elaborate courtesy: "I received with great satisfaction the news which you were kind enough to give me regarding the taking of the important city of Guadalajara by General Obregón's troops . . . I send you my most cordial felicitations for this important triumph which I hope brings us nearer to the end of our noble cause. I salute you very affectionately." When Carranza advised him that he had rejected the peace feelers of Carvajal's envoys, Villa again congratulated him for his attitude and sent him "my most enthusiastic felicitations." But he added, meaningfully: "You can count on 30,000 unconditional adherents of the Division for the campaign against the so-called government of Carvajal. Only operating in this way can we succeed in our efforts to save the country. In accordance with your orders I am preparing to march to the South whenever you indicate, and to be completely ready I need only the munitions which are coming to me from Tampico." It had been three weeks since Carranza, in accepting part of the pact of Torreón, had promised to supply the Division of the North with coal and munitions, and thus far Villa had received only a few carloads of coal.

Despite the polite words, Villa was pursuing his own course. He was strengthening the Division of the North for whatever lay ahead—collaboration with Carranza or an armed showdown with him. Fresh recruits and the incorporation of former federal soldiers were raising the numerical strength of the division to formidable proportions—probably greater than the 30,000 he reported to Carranza. He raised money by confiscation of property of all sorts. Expropriated cattle were driven by the tens of thousands to the border where they could be sold at $15 a head. With these funds he was buying heavily in El Paso where nearly everything was available—more rifles, machine guns, ammunition, dynamite, powder, and the much-needed coal for his locomotives.

He also was holding his own peace discussions—separate but inconclusive—with an envoy from interim President Carvajal.

And he permitted—or perhaps encouraged—his generals and advisers to draw up a manifesto on August 2, criticizing Carranza for his "hostile injustice" toward both the Division of the North and Villa, and expressing lack of confidence in his capacities for "bringing to a happy end the exigencies of the Revolution." "We are convinced," the manifesto concluded, "that in assuming this firm attitude we are acting in the public interest. Without the counterweight of our opinion the popular ideals may be wrecked and we may see erected over the still-warm bodies of our brothers who died to gain liberty and democracy for Mexico, a despotic government with the same absolutism that characterized that of the old dictator." But after the document was drawn up Villa ordered that it be kept secret.

A secretary read to Villa again and again a communication from Secretary of State Bryan relayed to him by Agent Carothers, impressing upon him "the patriotic duty of using his influence to prevent discord among the Constitutionalists. It is of vital importance that they do not allow personal feelings or personal quarrels to jeopardize the victory which they have won. Huerta has gone and the transfer of government can now be secured without further bloodshed. The outlook is bright for peace and prosperity in Mexico, and the President is very anxious that nothing shall occur to delay the reforms needed to restore justice to the people. Villa has played an important part in winning the victory, and the President feels sure that he will use his influence on the side of harmony and cooperation."

But if the President of the United States had faith in Villa, Venustiano Carranza did not. While Obregón and González closed in to claim the capital for the First Chief there was nothing for Villa to do. He accepted an invitation from his *compadre,* Tomás Urbina, to come to his hacienda of Las Nieves in Durango for the christening of his latest child. It was a convenient time for Villa to take a vacation. He left Chihuahua with an armed escort from the Villa brigade, with a musical band equipped with shiny new instruments and with a Chihuahua priest to officiate at the services, priests having become scarce in Urbina's part of the country.

Villa and his large party stopped en route to spend several days in Parral as guests of General Maclovio Herrera and his father, José de la Luz Herrera. The fields of Parral were green and pleasant after the unusually heavy summer rains, and the people came to greet Villa with gifts of flowers, fruit and cheese. There were horse races, cockfights, dances and all manner of social gatherings. Villa then moved on to

Las Nieves and joined Urbina for the christening. Urbina was, in many ways, a wilder, rougher man than Villa himself, in addition to which he was a heavy drinker which Villa was not.*

In addition to the baptismal ceremonies Urbina had arranged many festivities for Villa, just as the Herreras had done in Parral—more horse races, more cockfights and more dancing—to the music of Villa's fine band with its shiny instruments.

During lulls in the festivities Villa and Urbina would withdraw and talk together of the old days with the Parra gang, of the battles against Pascual Orozco and his *colorados,* of the campaigns through Chihauhua and Durango, of the thundering victory at Zacatecas. And they spoke of the troubles with Carranza—the troubles they had already had and the ones that lay ahead. Urbina counseled his old friend: "We must be like hawks, which hover about and never scream. I say only this: be ready for the break . . . there is no help for that. Carranza is waiting to annihilate you, *compadre."*

Outside the band played *La Cucaracha* over and over again, the simple country song about the cockroach who can no longer travel because he has no marijuana. The Villistas were now singing a new verse:

> "With the whiskers of Carranza
> I'll make a new *toquilla* (hatband)
> For the sombrero
> Of my general, Pancho Villa."

Far away in the South the Zapatistas had also adopted *La Cucaracha* and had invented a new verse of their own:

> "With the whiskers of Carranza
> I'll braid a great *reata* (lariat)
> To lasso a horse
> For my general, Zapata."

* John Reed tried, before the second battle of Torreón, to see Urbina at his hacienda which, he said, covered more than two million acres and had previously belonged to a wealthy Spaniard who had fled. Urbina, Reed was told by some underlings, was "A good man, all heart . . . very brave. The bullets bounce off him like rain from a sombrero . . . A few years ago he was just a peon like us; now he is a general and a rich man." A doctor explained to Reed why it was impossible for him to see the general: "There has been some little trouble. The general has not been able to walk for two months from rheumatism . . . and some-times he is in great pain and comforts himself with *aguardiente.* Tonight he tried to shoot his mother. He always tries to shoot his mother . . . because he loves her very much."

CHAPTER 25

PEACEMAKER

> *Quítate tu para ponerme yo.*
> (You get out so that I can get in.)
> Mexican *dicho*

WHILE VILLA MARKED TIME in the North the eighteen-month war came to an end.

By August 9 Alvaro Obregón and his troops had advanced to Teoloyucan, almost to the boundaries of the Federal District. Here he was joined by Pablo González and the army corps of the Northeast. Federal forces lay a little way ahead, at Cuautitlán.

Obregón sent a message to the caretaker President, Carvajal, asking him if he would surrender Mexico City; if Carvajal proposed to fight for it Obregón suggested that all foreigners be ordered out of the city in order to avoid subsequent claims for damages.

Carvajal, who had tried to avoid unconditional surrender, gave up and took the well-traveled road to Veracruz and exile, leaving the governor of the Federal District, Eduardo N. Iturbide, and General José Refugio Velasco, Secretary of War, to arrange the surrender. In his farewell message he complained that there had not been a single conciliatory voice among the revolutionists.

Obregón agreed that federal troops employed in guarding the city against the Zapatistas—who continued to threaten the southern parts of the capital—should remain at their posts temporarily. It was an arrangement that infuriated the Zapatistas. The balance of the federal forces, more than 40,000 men, was divided into small detachments and stationed at intervals along the railroad between Mexico City and Puebla to await disarming and discharge. It was to be the end of the federal army. A few of the federals and many of the *colorados,* volunteers who had served with the federal army, would not accept the terms of surrender. Some, such as the young general, Juan Andrew Almazán, fled into the mountains and later joined forces with Zapata (Almazán had, earlier, fought both for and against Zapata). Others would, eventually, join up with revolutionary troops—and some left the country to fight elsewhere (a force led by General Joaquín Téllez went to the republic of El Salvador).

Obregón, having signed the Treaty of Teoloyucan on the left front fender of a Packard touring car, proclaimed martial law for the city and on August 15 marched in at the head of his troops with his Yaquis, who formed a considerable part of his force, beating on Indian drums. Along the line of march was a banner erected by a workers' organization: *HAIL, GREAT LEADER, EMBLEM OF JUSTICE AND LIBERTY, VENUSTIANO CARRANZA. LONG LIVE THE REVOLUTION.* Carranza, who had yet to be present at any decisive battle or turning point of the Revolution, had remained behind. Obregón went to the National Palace, appeared on the balcony facing the Zócalo, and took possession of the capital in Carranza's name. He forbade the sale of liquor, promised strict order and justice (and shortly thereafter two drunken officers were executed, one for shooting a slow-moving bootblack and the other for shooting a waiter in the Cafe Colón).

One of Obregón's first acts was to make a pilgrimage to the grave of Francisco Madero. A young schoolteacher, María Arias, who had been imprisoned by the Huerta regime, made a little speech: "We weak women, unable to bear arms, could only give our sighs, our tears and our flowers on the grave of the martyr." Obregón removed his pistol and presented it to her; she was thereafter known as María Pistolas.

During the coming weeks there were many memorial services at the graves of Madero and Pino Suárez. The blood-stained clothing of the murdered President and Vice-President was dug up from the cellar of the penitentiary and examined; an investigation was launched into responsibility for the assassinations. And the remains of other victims of the Huerta dictatorship—Belisario Domínguez, Serapio Rendón, and Adolfo Bassó, most of whom had been buried where they were killed, were dug up and reburied ceremoniously.

Carranza did not enter Mexico City until five days after Obregón had claimed it for him. In suburban Tacuba he mounted a superb black horse and, surrounded by his principal generals—with the exception of Pablo González who was jealous of Obregón and refused to ride with him—led a procession into the heart of the city by way of the Paseo de la Reforma and the Avenida Juárez. In front of the Daguerre photographic studio, where Madero had taken temporary shelter on the first of the tragic ten days, he was handed the flag which Madero had waved on that day to rally his followers. He rode on through crowded streets to the National Palace where he was pelted with flowers by a crowd of women waiting there (his wife greeted him when he reached the second floor of the palace). A foreign observer reported that the crowds, while tremendous, packing the Zócalo and all the streets leading to it, seemed more curious than enthusiastic.

The people in the streets of Mexico City were not the only ones who were curious. Woodrow Wilson, who had been so eager to see Huerta ousted, thought that "the final working out of the situation is still a little blind." Francisco Bulnes, a former Díaz collaborator and journalist, predicted that Carranza "will be a future victim of our anarchy . . . the arrogant butcher of today is the humbled beast of tomorrow."

Carranza's generals occupied the city's finest mansions—Obregón in the home of Alberto Braniff in the Paseo de la Reforma, González in the palace of Ignacio de la Torre y Mier, Rafael Buelna in the Calle la Fragua house of Tomás Braniff, and Lucio Blanco in the home of Joaquín D. Casasús. Carranza modestly moved into temporary headquarters in the St. Francis, a small hotel in the Avenida Juárez. He seemed to have had a change of heart regarding Francisco Madero. He took part in one of the many memorial services being held at Madero's grave. And with his authorization the names of two mid-city streets were renamed for Madero and Pino Suárez.

Repeatedly the First Chief said "we now begin the work of peace and harmony." But if his public manner was mild and conciliatory, Carranza's actions were something else. He snubbed the diplomatic corps. He declared Huertista currency worthless and non-exchangeable for Constitutionalist currency, the only legal tender. Business and banking were paralyzed and a good part of the city went hungry. He ordered the printing of 130,000,000 pesos worth of additional Constitutionalist currency, and the cost of living soared. He closed those courts which were open, suspended constitutional guarantees, made no move to reconvene the Congress and kept all administrative authority in his own hands. He dissolved the recently established National Academy of History. Priests were taken into custody as they had been elsewhere—although one, a talented painter, was offered a waiver of his 5000 pesos ransom if he would paint a portrait of the victorious First Chief.

Everything was done "in accordance with the Plan of Guadalupe," but it was apparent that the plan was being revised retroactively by Carranza. It had called for Carranza to assume the interim presidency —as did the Treaty of Teoloyucan, which Obregón had signed for him. Instead Carranza assumed the cumbersome title of "First Chief in charge of the Executive Power," and advised foreign representatives that this was the way in which he should be addressed. Instead of appointing ministers, as a provisional president would have done, he appointed subsecretaries in charge of the various ministries and departments, retaining ultimate—and almost unlimited—authority in his own hands. But with all his power he showed no inclination to act. When a group of workers presented a petition asking for adequate wages, decent housing for workers and suppression of paper money Carranza listened politely and said he would study it. About land reform, the most pressing matter in the minds of the Mexican masses, he did almost nothing. Nor did he make any move to call an election.

Decisions on all such matters, he said, would be made at the junta of generals and governors he had ordered to meet in Mexico City October 1 "in accordance with the Plan of Guadalupe." The plan had made no mention of such a gathering. The meeting had, instead, been suggested to Carranza by the signers of the Pact of Torreón. He had adapted the idea to his own purposes and arranged it so that many of the delegates would be men who owed their appointments to him, which should make for a manageable group.

Carranza's dictatorial behavior did nothing to alleviate the distrust with which he was regarded by the Villistas and Zapatistas. Zapata made no effort to conceal his antipathy. The collaboration between Carranza's troops and the federals in keeping the Zapatistas out of Mexico City was hateful. The Zapatistas continued to fight. When a Constitutionalist force approached the town of Chalco, southeast of Mexico City, it was met by a Zapatista general. He advised the officers to divide into small groups so that they could enter the town without alarming the inhabitants. They did, and as each group entered the town the officers were shot and the men made prisoners. The Zapatistas were holding at least two thousand Constitutionalist soldiers. Carranza, for his part, had arrested two Zapatista agents—although they carried safe-conduct passes from General Lucio Blanco—and threatened to imprison any more he found in the capital.

Zapata had rejected suggestions that he and Carranza meet at a point midway between Mexico City and Zapata's territory. If Carranza wanted to see him he must come to Zapata's headquarters at Yautepec, deep in the state of Morelos.

Carranza commissioned his principal intellectual adviser, Luis Cabrera, and General Villareal to go to Cuernavaca and "explain Constitutionalism" to the Zapatistas. Cabrera and Villareal found the Zapatistas' demands were unacceptable. They insisted that Carranza either step aside or govern with a Zapata man at his side, approving every move; that the Zapatistas should be allowed to occupy Xochimilco, the southeastern suburb which supplied food and water to the capital; and that Carranza's Plan of Guadalupe be scrapped in favor of Zapata's Plan of Ayala.

Carranza went ahead with plans for his junta and also pressed for withdrawal of American troops from the port of Veracruz. The port was vital to his plans: if the Villistas and the Zapatistas should force Carranza out of Mexico City, Veracruz would be a convenient seat for the Constitutionalist government. The U.S. government—for which the occupation of Veracruz had been something of an embarrassment—was agreeable, and on September 15 Woodrow Wilson advised Carranza that U.S. forces would shortly be withdrawn.

Meanwhile a final effort was being made to patch up relations with Villa. Obregón, on the first day after Carranza's entry into the capital, had suggested that he be sent on a peace-making mission to Chihuahua. There was a good excuse. The governor of Sonora, José María Maytorena, who was friendly with Villa, was quarreling violently with Obregón's subordinate officers in northern Sonora, first with Colonel Plutarco Elías Calles and then with General Benjamín Hill, whom Obregón had sent in with the hope of restoring order. Obregón and Villa together might be able to solve the Maytorena-Calles-Hill problem —and in the course of doing so Obregón would try to determine Villa's intentions toward Carranza.

Obregón arrived in Chihuahua City on August 24 and was ceremoniously met at the railroad station by Villa and his principal generals. He was then driven to Villa's residence, passing through streets lined with Villista troops, stiffly at attention. The first meeting between the two most famous and successful soldiers of the Revolution was pleasant. Villa, mercurial in temperament, responded warmly to the man from Sonora, and affectionately addressed him as *compañerito* (little companion).

Villa reviewed his complaints and reservations about Carranza and then "I asked him whether he would agree to unite with me and all mine, just as in Torreón my generals had united with those of Pablo González, to ask Carranza to form a government of the people, to govern, not by caprice of a single man but according to the law of our victory. He answered yes, that he would join us in such petitions, which also represented his desires, and that since we and our troops were the conquerors, Carranza would have to satisfy our wishes." Villa also recorded that Obregón was of the opinion that Villa's division should have the status of an army corps and that Villa was entitled to the rank of general of division—advances in status for both which Carranza had refused to approve. Villa was promoted to divisional general almost immediately after Obregón's return to the capital.

Each man left a different version of these and subsequent proceedings. Obregón's version of the first meeting: Villa was curious about Carranza's reception in Mexico City and eager to know the amount of arms that had been taken from the federal troops. And then: "Look, *compañerito,* if you had come here with troops there would have been much shooting. But as you came alone you have no reason to be uneasy. Francisco Villa would not be a traitor. The destinies of the nation are in your hands and mine. With the two of us united, in less than a minute we would control the country, and as I am an obscure man, you would be president."

With these preliminaries out of the way Obregón and Villa began talk of Sonora where, since May, the followers of Governor Maytorena had been openly rebellious against the military control of Colonel Calles. Now, on the day of the Obregón-Villa meeting, Maytorena, at the head of two thousand of his followers, had attacked and taken the Mexican border town of Nogales. Calles and General Benjamín Hill had been driven back to Agua Prieta and Naco. Some of Maytorena's men wore Viva Villa hatbands. Villa explained that while he had been sympathetic to Maytorena and thought he was a misunderstood man, he, Villa, had not authorized this use of his name.

The two generals boarded a special train to travel to El Paso (where they were greeted by two U. S. Army officers, Brigadier General John J. Pershing and a young lieutenant, George S. Patton, Jr.) and then traveled on the American side of the border to Nogales. Obregón was stiffly and correctly uniformed; Villa wore a loose Norfolk jacket, a Texas hat and a loud bow tie. The meeting with Maytorena was, at first, tense. But an agreement was worked out which was acceptable to the Sonora governor: he would have command of all forces in the state, including those of Hill and Calles, under the supervisory command of Obregón as chief of the army corps of the Northwest.

The next day an inflammatory handbill was circulated in Nogales. Headed "Energetic Protest," it declared that Obregón had violated the state's sovereignty and warned him that "we, the town and army, have decided to rid our state of traitors and assassins who flout our sovereignty and the authority of our government." Obregón and Villa thereupon canceled the previous day's settlement and worked out—without Maytorena's participation—a new solution. Maytorena would be removed from the governorship and replaced by General Juan Cabral, another Sonora military leader, presently on duty in Mexico City. The Hill-Calles troops would be withdrawn to Chihuahua. Meanwhile any violation of the cease-fire would be put down by joint forces of Obregón's army and Villa's division. Villa admitted to Obregón that he had been misled; that while Maytorena was a good man he was surrounded by troublemakers.

Back in Chihuahua the two leaders turned their attention to the complaints of Villa and his men against Carranza. "If you had not come, *compañerito*," Villa said, "we would already be throwing punches." But he now realized that an electoral fight rather than warfare was the way in which Carranza must be defeated. The two men and their aides then drew up, on September 3, a memorandum to the First Chief, in the name of both Villa's division and Obregón's army corps. A preamble expressed "absolute confidence in the patriotism" of Carranza, along with the hope that he would receive "the dearest reward of great men—the gratitude of a people." It then made specific recommendations that the First Chief should assume at once the title of interim president, should appoint a cabinet and arrange for the appointment of judges; that local elections should be held to form town governments and choose delegates to Congress and state legislatures; that the Congress thus chosen should give immediate attention to various constitutional reforms, including disqualification of military leaders for the presidency, governorships, and other elective posts unless they had retired from their commands six months before becoming a candidate; that the interim president should call elections for a constitutional president and governors, elections in which the provisional occupants of these positions were ineligible; and finally, that commissions would be appointed in each state to study the agrarian problem and work out legal solutions.

The document was well thought out and composed and reflected sincere attitudes on the part of both men. Obregón returned to Mexico City, confident of having made progress on both the Maytorena and the Villa problems. Arrangements were made for General Cabral to go at once to Sonora and take charge, and the joint Villa-Obregón memorandum was presented to Carranza. Carranza, surprisingly, said he approved of the first recommendation—regarding assumption of the interim presidency—although he did nothing about it; and he favored the suggestion regarding local elections. But he rejected the document as a whole because these were questions "of such profound importance that they can neither be discussed nor approved by a small group of persons." They would, instead, be considered by the junta of generals and governors he had summoned for October 1.

OBREGON'S ORDEAL

> "And then there were men of good faith
> who were unhappy at seeing that the Rev-
> olutionaries were going to fight among
> themselves . . ."
>
> Martín Luis Guzmán, *Memoirs of
> Pancho Villa*

MEANWHILE Obregón was having a curious exchange of telegrams with Villa. Villa's wires were, at first, friendly and cooperative. Then they became sharp and testy. He urged that Cabral make haste to take over in Sonora, and complained that the Hill-Calles forces were violating the truce agreement, ignoring Villa's orders. When Obregón wired Villa asking him to send a message to the First Chief supporting the latter's efforts to get the United States to evacuate its troops from Veracruz, Villa's first response was cordial and agreeable. Obregón should sign Villa's name to whatever sort of petition seemed suitable. Then came a second message, countermanding the first, asking that Obregón *not* sign Villa's name for reasons which he would explain later. Obregón had by now composed the message to Carranza, signed Villa's name—and the news had been published in the newspapers of the capital. Villa's new attitude toward the First Chief was news of importance.

Villa's changeability stirred doubts in Obregón's mind. He recalled that on the evening of his departure from Chihuahua, after his friendly and apparently constructive meeting with Villa, he had talked with young Luis Aguirre Benavides, Villa's secretary. Aguirre Benavides had said, "Now you see him so tame. But wait. In two hours he will have changed his advisers completely." Obregón suspected that the advisers responsible for Villa's truculence were Tomás Urbina, the unreconstructed bandit, Felipe Angeles, an old personal enemy of Obregón's, and Miguel

Díaz Lombardo, an intellectual lawyer who had been Madero's minister in Paris and who was now associated with the Villista cause.

Obregón decided on a second trip to Chihuahua. His mission may have been one of espionage, to report on the exact strength of the Villista forces. Or it may have been for the purpose of encouraging the Villistas' participation in Carranza's October 1 meeting; he knew that many of Villa's generals were deeply concerned with the danger of war between Villa and Carranza.

With his staff Obregón arrived in Chihuahua City on the morning of September 16, Independence Day. Villa's manner was changed; he was far angrier than before with Carranza, whose rejection of the Villa-Obregón memorandum he had received. But for the moment he was polite with Obregón and arranged for him to stand at his side on a balcony of the Government Palace and review a military parade in honor of the national holiday. Villa said—pointedly, Obregón thought —that the parade would be made up of 15,000 men and sixty cannons. The parade lasted three hours, moving slowly, and Villa spoke almost continuously of the strength of his division, the discipline of his men and the quality of their equipment. Meanwhile Lieutenant Colonel Francisco R. Serrano, Obregón's chief of staff, was carefully observing the parade. He counted 5200 men and forty-five cannon.

Afterward Villa took Obregón to his arsenal and showed him boxes full of new rifles, still unpacked, and case after case of ammunition— and Obregón guessed that of 7-millimeter cartridges alone Villa had at least five million. While he displayed his military might Villa continued to grumble about Carranza and the trouble in Sonora. Obregón concluded several things: Villa apparently had abandoned hope for a peaceful settlement and was preparing for a show of force; not all of the generals of the Division of the North were in complete agreement with him; and, finally, that he, Obregón, and his staff were probably in danger. He took the precaution of sending Major Julio Madero, a younger brother of the late President, to Sonora with a message for General Hill: if any message came to Hill over Obregón's signature but emanating from Villa's headquarters, Hill was to ignore it. Obregón also gave to Major Madero a packet of 20,000 pesos in bank notes. If Obregón and his staff were killed the money was to be distributed to the families of his staff members.

With these precautions out of the way Obregón assumed an air of normalcy. The following morning he ordered members of his staff to arrange a ball for that night in the Teatro de los Héroes to repay the social kindnesses that had been extended to him and his staff on their previous visit to Chihuahua. He then went to visit the quarters of General Raul Madero, still another of the Madero brothers, this one on Villa's staff. Here he sat down to a long midday meal. Just as they were finishing, at 4 P.M., Villa's chauffeur arrived with an urgent summons for Obregón to come to Villa's residence.

Villa obviously was in a fit of temper. There had been news that the Hill-Calles forces had clashed with those of Maytorena. Villa thought Obregón had had a part in it. His eyes were squinted almost closed and his voice was high-pitched and angry.

"General Hill thinks he is playing with me." Villa shouted, and, pointing at Obregón, "You are a traitor and I am going to have you shot." He called in Luis Aguirre Benavides and dictated a wire to General Hill, ordering him to withdraw his troops to Casas Grandes, Chihuahua. The message was to bear the signature of Obregón as commander of the army corps of the Northwest.

Villa turned to Obregón. "Shall we send it?" It was a rhetorical question.

"You can," said Obregón. To argue was pointless.

Villa ordered the secretary to send the wire and also told him to telephone for Major Cañedo and a squad of twenty Dorados (The Gilded Men), gold-uniformed members of Villa's elite escort, who were to come prepared "to shoot this traitor." Obregón remembered Major Cañedo as an officer he had expelled from his own command in Sonora for misconduct—a man who would gladly shoot him.

As calmly as he could he spoke to Villa: "From the moment I placed my life at the service of the Revolution I have never thought I would consider it a misfortune to lose it." He even engaged in some of the wry humor for which he was famous. If Villa ordered him shot, he added, "You will be doing me a personal favor. Such a death will give me a personality—something I have always lacked. And as for you, you will only be the loser." The squad of Dorados arrived and awaited only the order to take Obregón to the bullet-pocked wall of the patio below. Obregón's staff, meanwhile, had been herded into the adjoining bedroom—the room Obregón, as a guest, occupied the night before.

At the entrance to the suite a crowd was gathering. Raul Madero was there, summoned by a frantic call from Luis Aguirre Benavides. So was Rodolfo Fierro, Villa's "butcher." So was a doctor, Felipe Dussart, who, like Cañedo, had formerly been under Obregón's command but had left in disgrace. Dussart's presence was lucky for Obregón. Villa, somewhat incoherently, was repeating again and again his intention of shooting Obregón. Dussart applauded loudly, jumped up and down like a child and shouted: "Bravo! Bravo, my general! That's the way to operate!"

The applause seemed to startle Villa. He wheeled and pointed at

Dussart: "Get out of here! *Bribon* (rascal)! *Fantoche* (nincompoop)! Get out before I kick you out!"

Obregón had begun pacing the room; now Villa fell into step and paced it with him, still muttering that he was going to kill Obregón for his treachery. Then, suddenly, he left Obregón alone with the firing squad—to which he had not yet given instructions—and went to the room in which Obregón's staff was being held, still rambling incoherently. Obregón's chief of staff, Serrano, a man of diminutive stature, stepped in front of Villa and said: "We are all ready to meet the same fate as our chief, but before that you and I should have a few words, as men." Pulling up a chair he added, smiling broadly: "Do me the favor of taking a seat, my general." Villa stopped talking and sat down, watching Serrano closely.

Serrano continued: "Look, my general, when it was known in Mexico City that we were coming to see you everyone told us it was madness to let ourselves fall in your hands . . . But we were always sure that if General Obregón's negotiations with you failed you would permit us to return without harm. Do you know why we had this confidence in you?"

"Why?" Villa asked. His eyes were wide open now and so was his mouth.

"Very simple," said Serrano. "There has never been in the history of the world a case of a man who is as brave as you are who has not respected the life and tranquillity of his guests. I know very well that you, at the head of your troops, would prefer to meet General Obregón at the head of his to fight to the end, like two soldiers, like two great men, disputing the field hand to hand, exchanging life for life, never lacking respect for honor, honor which makes sacred and untouchable the person of a guest in one's house . . ."

Villa gave a wide grin—as if, said one of the staff members, he had found a toy of which he had heard but never seen.

"Colonel," he said, "Pancho Villa is a man! Pancho Villa would like to be in the field with General Obregón, the two of us there alone, with plenty of bullets. But, here, in my house!" He paused and shouted: "Major Cañedo, Major Cañedo!" Cañedo came to the door, smiling, expecting orders for the execution. "Dismiss your squad, immediately," said Villa, and returned to the room where Obregón waited.

Villa sat on a sofa, invited Obregón to sit beside him, and began speaking, using the familiar form of *tu* for "you," instead of the more formal *usted*.

"Francisco Villa is no traitor," he said. "Francisco Villa does not kill defenseless men, and least of all you, *compañerito,* who are my guest. I am going to prove to you that Pancho Villa is a man, and if Carranza does not respect me I know how to fulfill my obligations to my country . . ."

As he went on in this vein tears filled his eyes and finally sobs choked off his voice, and there was a long silence, interrupted only when a servant entered to say the evening meal was served. "Come to eat, *compañerito*," said Villa, throwing a heavy arm around Obregón's shoulder. "It's all over."

Later Villa excused himself from attending Obregón's ball, saying he felt indisposed. Obregón, despite the ordeal he had been through, did go, and danced until the early hours of the morning. Although everyone in the ballroom knew of the afternoon's unpleasantness it was not mentioned.

The next day Villa received a telegram from General Hill saying he would recognize no orders from Obregón that originated from Villa's headquarters. Villa, knowing that Obregón had somehow got word to Hill, lost his temper again and once more prepared to kill his guest. Various of Villa's own men interceded in Obregón's behalf and so did Canova, the American agent. At one point in the discussion Canova told Obregón that they had persuaded Villa to free him and send him to El Paso. Canova offered to accompany him for safety. Obregón declined. If he were a bandit or a traitor, he said, he should be executed without delay; if he were not he insisted that he should be set free to return to Mexico City. While Obregón waited for a final decision he amused himself and his companions in card games, reciting, at the end of a game, the order in which each card had fallen, impressing everyone with his coolness as well as his memory.

The question of life or death for Obregón became sidetracked. Villa and his generals were deep in discussions whether they should attend Carranza's junta of generals and governors. Finally it was decided that some of Villa's generals would attend but Villa would not. A wire was sent to Carranza saying that the consensus of the Division of the North was against the meeting as Carranza had planned it since it had no democratic basis and particularly because the agrarian question, "the soul of the Revolution," would not be discussed. However, "as a testimony of our subordination and respect for the First Chief," the division would participate if it could be assured that the question of calling general elections would be considered. Obregón, meanwhile, had escaped execution again.

Two of Villa's most cool-headed and respected generals, Eugenio Aguirre Benavides, the cross-eyed brother of Villa's secretary, Luis, and José Isabel Robles, were to be sent ahead as an advance party in Mexico City, with the others to follow. Obregón and his staff were put on the same train with the two generals. Obregón became friendly with the two officers on the train and found that they spoke frankly—and critically—of some of Villa's extreme measures.

The train was suddenly halted at the tiny station of Ceballos, about midway to Torreón. Robles entered Obregón's compartment and showed him a wire he had just been handed by the station telegrapher. Villa had ordered the generals to bring Obregón back to Chihuahua. The two Villista generals were ill at ease. They knew this was probably another sentence of death, as did Obregón. Obregón assured them that he would go willingly if they would do their best to save him from abuse or outrage at Villa's hands; if Villa insisted on shooting him, he asked that they try to insure it being done with dignity and without humiliation. Obregón was back in the Chihuahua City railroad station before dawn on the 23rd for one more confrontation with Villa. At 7 A.M. an officer came to take him to Villa's house.

Villa was furious again. His telegraphers had picked up orders which Carranza had sent to Pánfilo Natera, the commander at Zacatecas. Natera was ordered to stop railroad traffic north of Aguascalientes, and, if there was any advance of the Villista troops south of Torreón, to tear up the tracks. Similar orders were sent to Monterrey, to prevent eastbound traffic from Torreón. Villa had telegraphed Carranza, demanding an explanation. Carranza replied that it was none of his business, and asked a question of his own: What had Villa done with Obregón and his staff? Villa had replied: IN ANSWER TO YOUR MESSAGE, GENERAL OBREGON AND SOME GENERALS OF THIS DIVISION LEFT LAST NIGHT FOR THE CAPITAL IN ORDER TO DEAL WITH IMPORTANT AFFAIRS CONCERNING THE GENERAL SITUATION OF THE REPUBLIC. BUT IN VIEW OF YOUR ACTIONS, WHICH REVEAL A PREMEDITATED DESIRE TO PLACE OBSTACLES IN THE PATH OF PEACE WHICH WE ALL DESIRE SO MUCH, I HAVE ORDERED THEIR TRIP HALTED . . . THIS DIVISION WILL NOT ATTEND THE CONVENTION YOU HAVE CALLED. I INFORM YOU OF OUR DISAVOWAL OF YOU AS FIRST CHIEF OF THE REPUBLIC. YOU CAN PROCEED IN ANY WAY YOU SEE FIT.

Obregón was shown the exchange of telegrams and once more was told that he and his staff would be executed. But Villa wavered on giving the order, listening to the arguments of his advisers. His *compadre* Urbina was vociferously in favor of the execution. So were Fierro, José Rodríguez, Manual Banda, Pedro Bracamontes, and Anacleto Girón —the rougher elements of the division. From Sonora, Maytorena sent a telegram urging Villa to go ahead with the execution, saying he was forwarding justifying documents. But a majority of Villa's generals and advisers were opposed, among them the better educated ones, such as Angeles, the Aguirre Benavides brothers, Díaz Lombardo, Chao, Raul Madero, and Roque González Garza. It was one of the peculiarities —and perhaps a saving grace—of Villa that he surrounded himself with men of radically different types, ruffians and gentlemen, hotheads and thinkers, united only in their loyalty to their leader. The interplay of their divergent attitudes contributed to the frequency and rapidity with which Villa changed his mind.

By the evening of the 23rd, Villa, once more in a genial mood, informed Obregón that he was going to send him back to Mexico City after all. His former escorts, Eugenio Aguirre Benavides and Robles, had already been ordered back to their base at Torreón in case the verbal war with Carranza turned into a shooting war. He was to be escorted by Colonel Roque González Garza, the young veteran of the Madero revolution who had been snubbed by Carranza in Sonora and had become an ardent Villista. A military train under General Mateo Almanza preceded Obregón's train. During the night it had to halt on a siding to allow overheated bearings to cool off, and while Almanza slept Obregón's train went ahead. The next day, at the lonely desert station of Corralitos, Obregón's train was flagged to a halt. González Garza was handed a telegram from Villa, ordering him to return—with Obregón and staff—to Chihuahua. But Obregón had had enough. He descended from the train, ordered his staff out, and informed González Garza that he would not go back, that he preferred to die first. Then, to deepen the mystery, still another wire came from Villa, ordering Obregón's train to proceed to Torreón.

At Gómez Palacio, near Torreón, the train was boarded by officers under the command of Aguirre Benavides and Robles. Obregón was given a safe-conduct pass to see him through the remainder of the Villista territory on his way back to Mexico City.

Obregón, in his memoirs, said at this point he learned the details of the latest attempt on his life. Villa, he said, had intended for General Almanza's train to halt him en route and execute him on the spot. Obregón had unknowingly escaped this trap. Villa, hearing this, then sent the message which halted Obregón's train at Corralitos, ordering it back. Telegraphers for Robles and Aguirre Benavides overheard the telegraphic order and then, in a telegraphic conference, persuaded Villa to change his mind. Obregón's train was allowed to proceed. Then, according to Obregón, Villa wired the garrison at Gómez Palacio to stop Obregón's train when it reached that point, remove him from the train and shoot him. Again the telegram was overheard by Robles' telegrapher, and an escort was sent to Gómez Palacio to greet Obregón and protect him from any attempt on his life.

Finally Obregón returned to Mexico City to deny in person published reports of his death before a Villista firing squad.

THE CONVENTION

> "'What I can't get into my head,' ob-
> served Anastasio Montañez, 'is why we
> keep on fighting. Didn't we finish off this
> man Huerta?'"
>
> Mariano Azuela, *The Underdogs*

IN MEXICO in September 1914 one civil war was barely over and another
was about to begin. The one man who could prevent it was Venustiano
Carranza, but Carranza was unable or unwilling to bring together the
dissident factions of the Revolution. He listened to Obregón's firsthand
report on Villa's anger and the awesome buildup of the Division of
the North but did not let it deter him. He proceeded with plans
for his October 1 junta in which neither the Villistas nor the Zapatistas
—more than half of the revolutionary fighting force—would be represented. He was continuing to arrest and hold without trial men suspected of Villista or Zapatista sympathies.

The men around Carranza were alarmed. Some of them—Lucio
Blanco, Rafael Buelna, Ignacio Pesqueira, Julian C. Medina, and Eduardo
Hay—were so concerned that they constituted themselves as a "Permanent
Peace Commission." Obregón, after returning from his harrowing experience in Chihuahua and reporting to Carranza, joined their meetings.
All were loyal to Carranza. But as battlefield veterans they recoiled
from the idea of another war, this one between revolutionary groups
which should be working together. A meeting of all revolutionary
elements seemed called for—not the kind that Carranza planned, with
only selected groups represented, but a democratic meeting in which all
viewpoints could be expressed and a broad-based program of government adopted.

Aguascalientes was tentatively chosen as a site for the meeting. It was comparatively undamaged by the war. It was accessible by railroad from the key areas of the country. And it was about midway between Villa's Chihuahua and Carranza's Mexico City, and would be declared neutral territory. The meeting was called for October 5 with formal sessions to begin October 10. Invitations were sent out to leaders of all factions.

Obregón reported the commission's plans to Carranza. Carranza said he would hold his meeting in Mexico City on October 1 regardless. But he said he had no objection to the Aguascalientes meeting although he was certain nothing could be achieved by it. The Villistas, he insisted, were opposed to any sort of peaceful solution of the nation's difficulties. He would do nothing to obstruct the convention, except that under no circumstances would he deliver the country into the hands of an "ignorant and ambitious" man like Villa.

When the delegates to Carranza's junta gathered in the Chamber of Deputies on October 1 there was a perfunctory air about the proceedings. Practically all the military men present planned to go on to Aguascalientes where the real business would be transacted. Their presence in Mexico City was a courtesy to the First Chief. And although Carranza's civilian supporters—and Luis Cabrera functioned as spokesman for them—tried to whip up enthusiasm there was very little of it.

Carranza, austerely dressed in black frock coat and bowler hat, came to the chamber to address the delegates. "You entrusted to me the command of the army," he said. "You put in my hands the executive power of the nation. I cannot, except at the cost of my honor, turn these sacred trusts over to the hands of some misguided generals and some civilians to whom the nation owes nothing in this struggle. I can only turn them over to the leaders here assembled." Having said this Carranza left, apparently in an emotional state. Had he resigned? No one quite knew. Like so many Carranza statements it was ambiguous. But Carranza's civilian supporters in the assembly, particularly the eloquent Cabrera, made it appear that the First Chief had indeed resigned and it was up to the junta to accept or reject it. Cabrera closed his oration with "Here is my vote for Citizen Carranza." The delegates voted to reject the resignation. But the rejection was hardly a vote of confidence in Carranza. It was, instead, dictated by the fact that any such matter should be considered by the Aguascalientes convention. The only other matter before the Mexico City junta was a motion for adjournment—with the delegates agreeing to reassemble in ten days' time at Aguascalientes.

So, during the second week in October the revolutionary leaders gathered in Aguascalientes, a peaceful agricultural town in the Bajío district of north central Mexico. The limited railroad yards were crowded with locomotives, sleeping cars, cabooses that had become traveling command posts for the revolutionary generals, boxcars for the personal escorts of the *jefes*. Aguascalientes had been officially declared a neutral city, governed by a joint commission representing both Carranza and Villa. All *cantinas* had been ordered closed. But the town swarmed with armed men, their cartridge belts full of ammunition and their bellies full of tequila, roaming the city, firing their guns in the air. Their leaders were more sedate. Dressed in newly tailored uniforms or black civilian suits they moved about with self-conscious dignity and effusive camaraderie, exchanging *abrazos,* back-slapping embraces which demonstrate affection and can also disclose the presence of a concealed gun.

The hotels, of course, were inadequate. Townspeople, knowing that they would have to give up either spare rooms or perhaps their entire houses, went about inviting the better-dressed, better-behaved elements— men like Angeles, Chao, Raul Madero, Eugenio Aguirre Benavides—to share their homes, fearing that they might, instead, end up with the rough, wild men like Tomás Urbina. Urbina was on hand and many others like him. Most of Villa's important officers were there. General Angeles and Colonel Roque González Garza shared duties as spokesmen for Villa, who was encamped with 11,000 of his men at Guadalupe, one hundred miles to the north.

For the Carrancistas Obregón was the leading figure. One of his first acts was to present the convention with a special flag; the Mexican standard with the words MILITARY CONVENTION OF AGUASCALIENTES printed across its face. There were also Villareal, Carranza's military governor of Nuevo León; Juan G. Cabral, a respected general from the army corps of the Northwest; Eduardo Hay, who had lost an eye fighting for Madero at Casas Grandes and who prided himself on being a philosopher and a poet as well as a soldier; and the boyish (age twenty-four) but courageous General Rafael Buelna. Pablo González, second only to Obregón in Carranza's trust and esteem, was represented but was not present in person; instead he was camped with a strong Carrancista force at Querétaro, approximately two hundred miles to the southeast on the main route to Mexico City. Here González maintained a close watch on Villa and his troops at Guadalupe, just as Villa kept a close watch on him.

For the Zapatistas, the third important element in the Revolution, there was at first no representation. The Convention designated Felipe Angeles head of a commission to go to Morelos and press upon Zapata the importance of his participation.

Meanwhile the Convention opened its sessions in the Teatro Morelos, just off the west side of the plaza. It immediately declared its sovereignty.

It was assuming the supreme authority in the nation, not just the consultative role Carranza had been willing for it to play. With much emotional ceremony the delegates came to the platform individually and, while a band played the national hymn, placed their signatures as "armed citizens," in the white mid-section of the flag. Obregón made a fiery speech of loyalty to the Convention, declaring that he was prepared to give up his general's insignia and, with a sergeant's stripes, go to fight anyone who opposed the will of the Convention. Chao, Villista general, said he would march at Sergeant Obregón's side as a plain soldier.

A few days later Villa came down from his encampment at Guadalupe. To the accompaniment of shouts of "Viva Villa" he marched to the platform and, awkwardly as a schoolboy, placed his signature on the flag and took an oath to support and obey the Convention. He was smartly uniformed; even his unruly hair was neatly in place. He made a little speech to the delegates: "You are going to hear sincere words spoken from the heart of an uncultured man. What I want to say to you is that Francisco Villa will not be an embarrassment to men of good conscience, because he will seek nothing for himself . . . I want the destinies of my country to be bright."

When Villa had spoken Obregón came forward and gave his old enemy an *abrazo* while the 150-odd delegates rose from their wicker-seated chairs in the red, white, and gold auditorium and cheered. Villa was moved to add a few more words: "I want you to understand our sentiments. I will not be a shadow over the future of Mexico. History will be able to say who are Mexico's true sons."

"Exactly, Señor," said Obregón, smiling.

Villa returned to his encampment at Guadalupe, touched by the warmth of his reception at Aguascalientes. But he was also beset by troubles. There were many disturbances in Aguascalientes and most of them were being blamed on Villistas. Despite the closed *cantinas* there was much drunkenness. There were quarrels and gunfighting over the few prostitutes available in Aguascalientes, and according to one story the Convention had sent a special train to Guadalajara to bring additional *mercancia* (merchandise) with which Guadalajara had always been bountifully supplied. There were many incidents of Villista soldiers bullying townspeople and even Convention delegates, forcing them at gunpoint to shout "Viva Villa." A Carrancista colonel, García Vigil, complained that he was set upon by a trio of Villistas outside the door of the Hotel Washington in the heart of Aguascalientes. They forced him to cheer for Villa and then made him throw his new Texas hat on the sidewalk and dance on it. Tomás Urbina had ordered his men to seize a Colonel Manuel Manzanera, a delegate representing the

Arrieta brothers, whom Urbina hated. Manzanera was taken to Zacatecas and executed. Villa noted sadly that Manzanera was a brave man; his last act was to request his executioners to deliver a note to his mother: *"Mama, at 12 tonight they are going to shoot me."* Villa considered Urbina's action reprehensible and he was also concerned lest the Convention, whose authority he had promised to obey, would order him to shoot his *compadre*.

The harder Villa tried to play the role of a peaceful, law-abiding citizen, the more things happened to provoke him and destroy the impression. José Bonales Sandoval, a representative of Felix Díaz, once more approached Villa with a suggestion of a Díaz-Villa alliance against Carranza. Villa had spared him on a previous such occasion. This time he ordered him shot immediately. He also ordered the shooting of "The Gaucho" Mujica, an Argentine soldier of fortune who admitted, Villa said, that he had been commissioned by Pablo González to assassinate the leader of the Division of the North. Maclovio Herrera, one of Villa's favorite generals—the one who in the pre-Zacatecas telegraphic conference with Carranza had told the First Chief that he was a sonofabitch—had now deserted Villa for Carranza and was fighting Villa's men in Chihuahua. Villa was directing the campaign and winning—with regret; his affection for Herrera had been great. Only two months earlier Herrera and his father had entertained Villa at a fiesta in Parral.

All these things—fairly normal in his stormy career—now weighed heavily on Villa at a time when he was particularly anxious to create good will and cooperate in the Convention's peace-making efforts. Ironically, to make matters worse, he was suffering from an unprecedented reverse in his career as a lover. In Jiménez, Chihuahua, he had, through the pandering services of an ambitious aunt, made an alliance with a beautiful girl, Conchita del Hierro. But despite the arrangements Conchita regarded him with nothing but loathing. It was upsetting to a man who considered himself irresistible.

The Aguascalientes Convention was, for the present, more concerned with Zapata than it was with Villa and his problems. Zapata had accepted the Convention's invitation and was sending a group of twenty-six representatives, including five generals and a group of civilian intellectuals who had been given military rank for the occasion. Most of the delegation, military and civilian alike, wore either charro suits or the white cotton peasant attire that was a uniform for the Zapatistas. Their train arrived in Aguascalientes and then, surprisingly, kept right on going, steaming north to Guadalupe where the Zapatistas conferred with Villa. Many of the Convention delegates viewed this move with suspicion. Zapata's twenty-six representatives voting with Villa's thirty-seven delegates would not hold a majority of the votes, but they could cause trouble.

The Zapatistas returned to Aguascalientes from Guadalupe and on October 26 entered the Teatro Morelos and were seated. Although there were some notable exceptions, the Zapatistas were provincial and suspicious. They had had difficulty finding lodging in Aguascalientes; they regarded the automobiles, the luxurious accommodations, the splendid uniforms and new civilian suits of Convention delegates with scorn; and, one witness said, they entered the Convention hall as though they were going into battle, wary of ambushes. It was apparent that two civilians would be spokesmen for the group, Paulino Martínez, a journalist, and Antonio Díaz Soto y Gama, a radical lawyer from San Luis Potosí who had adopted the Zapatista cause as his own.

Zapata's representatives announced that they had come to the Convention not as delegates but as a "commission" to learn if the Convention would accept Zapata's Plan of Ayala as its charter. Zapata, it appeared, wanted his representatives to avoid commitment to the Convention until the Convention committed itself to him. But in the meantime he wanted his men to have the right both to speak and vote in the Convention proceedings.

The right to speak was readily conceded. After a reasonable opening statement by Paulino Martínez, the melodramatic Díaz Soto y Gama took the floor and caused an uproar. The special Convention flag which Obregón had presented and which all the delegates had signed, stood at the left of the speaker's podium. Almost every speaker who had addressed the Convention had taken occasion to touch the flag reverently and mention his devotion to it. Díaz Soto y Gama scorned it. In a burst of demagogic oratory, he criticized the Convention as being a military gathering instead of a revolutionary one. He and his comrades had come there with honorable intentions, and he placed more faith in a man's word of honor than he did in a signature on the flag—here he clutched and shook the famous flag. He himself did not intend to place his name on it. There was a growing rumble from the audience but it did not slow down the orator. Still jerking the flag, he referred to it as a "rag" and as "the standard of the clerical reaction headed by Iturbide." "We are waging a great revolution," he went on, "against the lies of history, a revolution which will expose the historical lie this flag represents. What we call our independence was not independence for the Indian, but only for the creoles, the inheritors of the Conquest, so that they could continue laughing . . ."

By this time the rumble had turned into an uproar. "Let go of the flag! Savage! Imbecile! Bastard! Barbarian! Renegade! . . ." Colonel Vigil—the one who had been mistreated by the Villista soldiers—

mounted the steps to the stage and shouted "Get off the platform!" General Villareal, the presiding officer, roared "More respect for the flag!" The shouts from the auditorium and the public galleries grew louder. Delegates pounded their chests, reached for their guns and the black eyes of more than a hundred pistols stared directly at the speaker. Díaz Soto y Gama calmly stood his ground, arms crossed over his chest, his head thrown back, pale but with his eyes shining, apparently pleased with the commotion he had caused. Now the Zapatista representatives, seeing their orator in danger, drew their guns and stood on their chairs, ready to fight back. In the galleries the public was stampeding for the exits. The air was filled with hisses, whistles, catcalls, and oaths. General Villareal pounded on his bell for order.

Finally the Zapatista orator was allowed to continue. He explained that the flag itself was unimportant, since it was only a symbol of the nation. In the case of the flag of the Convention, he insisted that it was being used to conceal selfish, personal ambitions. And he launched into a vitriolic attack on Carranza and his Plan of Guadalupe. He ridiculed the men who surrounded Carranza and were rewarded with palaces, patronage, and money. Many of his listeners looked at Obregón, who scowled. Díaz Soto y Gama concluded: Zapata's Plan of Ayala was the only true expression of the aims of the Revolution.

When he was finished Roque González Garza, spokesman for the Division of the North, rose and said: "I agree with everything Díaz Soto y Gama has said. In principle, the Division of the North accepts as its own the Plan of Ayala." Obregón, still visibly angry, asked if González Garza spoke for the entire division. González Garza turned to his delegation and asked those who agreed with him to rise. Every man in the group got to his feet, and from the galleries there were shouts of "Viva Pancho Villa," "Viva Zapata," "Up the Division of the North," and "Hurrah for the Liberation Army of the South." The alliance between the Villistas and the Zapatistas, an alliance which Carranza and others had feared and tried to prevent, had been accomplished—in sentimental if not in physical terms.

In the following day's debate Paulino Martínez said that on the accepted ratio of one delegate per 1000 men in arms, the Zapatistas should have sixty delegates since they had 60,000 men. Obregón immediately threw a barbed question at the speaker. If Zapata had 60,000 men why had he not taken Mexico City? Why had they waited for Obregón, with a force of only 23,000 to march 4000 kilometers across the republic to capture the capital?

Martínez answered: Obregón had taken the capital only by making compromises with the federal forces, while they, the Zapatistas, had remained clean, having nothing but enmity for the forces of the usurper.

Carranza too had been invited to attend and take part in the Convention. His first reaction was to question the Convention's right to declare itself sovereign. It was a question which struck many delegates as ironic since the legality of Carranza's position was defined only by the Plan of Guadalupe, a document he had drawn up himself and of which he was the only recognized interpreter. He would not attend, nor would he send representatives, since this would be a recognition of the Convention's claim to sovereignty.

Then, after a delegation from the Convention, headed by Obregón, called on him in person to try to persuade him to participate Carranza took a somewhat different course. He recognized the general feeling of the Convention delegates—many of whom were loyal to him—that his resignation was a prerequisite for any kind of peaceful settlement. On October 23 he composed a letter to the Convention—a letter which Obregón read in a closed session on the 29th: "If the Convention of Aguascalientes believes my retirement would be the most effective means of restoring harmony among the revolutionary elements . . . the conditions I would stipulate would not be of a personal character nor would they be for the purpose of preparing for a future return to the position I now occupy . . .

"These conditions would be for the purpose of guaranteeing that my retirement would not be sterile, that I would not merely surrender the field to enemies of the Revolution, to military chiefs with personal ambitions.

"I am disposed to deliver the command of the Constitutionalist army and the executive power of the nation, and, if it is necessary, to leave the country, under the following conditions:

"First, that there be established a pre-constitutional government which, with the support of the Constitutionalist army, will bring about needed social and political reforms before the reestablishment of a constitutional government.

"Second, that General Villa will renounce, not his candidacy for the presidency or the vice-presidency, neither of which has been offered to him, but the military command of the Division of the North, retiring, like me, to private life, abandoning all political influence and leaving the country if the Convention decides that I shall expatriate myself.

"Third, General Zapata will resign the command of his forces, renounce political ambitions, leave the country and put his forces under the command of the Convention.

"This is the formula with which the conflict can be resolved. I am disposed to fulfill it and I submit it for your consideration . . . I am firmly disposed to serve the cause for which I have been fighting. If the junta of Aguascalientes can solve the existing difficulties patriotically I will march in accord with it; but if the moment comes when it is unable to move forward because there are some who do not have my spirit of abnegation and patriotism, then, for the salvation of the country and the triumph of the Revolution, I will call to my side the Constitutionalist army which recognizes me as its chief to fight against the enemies of liberty and the Mexican people."

It was a skilfully worded letter (and the delegates should have paid more attention to the repeated use of "I am disposed") and a masterful political stroke. If the Convention had the authority it both claimed and appeared to have, it could very easily disregard his "conditions" and oust Carranza from his dog-in-the-manger position. It had the allegiance of pro-Carranza generals as well as the anti-Carrancistas. If the generals remained obedient to their oaths to support the Convention Carranza would have few armed forces to support him. He did, however, have two things. He had a circle of able civilian advisers, such as the canny Cabrera. And he occupied—no matter how questionable his claim to it—the only position of supreme authority in the country. The Convention had no such leadership.

The following day the Convention approved by a vote of 112 to 21 a peace-making formula, drawn up by a committee in which Obregón was a principal figure. The resignations of Carranza and Villa were called for. Each man was given a vote of thanks for his services, and Carranza given the rank of general of division, with retroactive seniority back to his proclamation of the Plan of Guadalupe. The Convention would proceed to choose a provisional president to carry out its orders and supervise the return to constitutional government. The commands of the various army corps and divisions—including Villa's Division of the North—would be abolished and their control would be in the hands of the secretariat of war of the interim government. Regarding Zapata, action was deferred until the Zapatistas were represented by regular delegates to the Convention, subject to the Convention's orders.

The Convention next turned its attention to the selection of a provisional president. General Antonio I. Villareal had been serving as president pro tem. An imposing figure of a man with a nobility of manner and revolutionary credentials more impressive than most of the men present, Villareal was considered a certain choice for the provisional presidency. But he was opposed by the Zapatistas on the simple grounds that he had functioned as a spokesman for Carranza in the abortive negotiations immediately after the capture of Mexico City. While the Zapata commissioners were not delegates and could not vote, the Convention was, nevertheless, still hopeful of winning their adherence, and Villareal's candidacy was doomed. In this and other things the Zapatistas, without accepting the authority of the Convention, were able to determine its course. They also insisted, successfully, that whoever was chosen for the provisional presidency should serve only for twenty days, by which time Zapata would be represented by a full and official delegation which would then have the opportunity to accept or reject the provisional president.

The Constitutionalists in the Convention refused to support any of the Villistas—although one of the most acceptable of the lot, José Isabel Robles, was a candidate. Most of the Villistas, knowing they could not elect one of their own, tended to support Juan G. Cabral of Sonora. Eduardo Hay, a Carrancista, had little chance. Lucio Blanco, who was thought to want the position (and who was rumored to be backed by a $50,000 political war chest put up by some adventurous Texans) was not even on hand. If Obregón was ambitious for the post he did not show it. A practical man, he knew he would never be acceptable to the Villistas and Zapatistas. Instead he worked for a comparatively unknown compromise candidate: Eulalio Gutiérrez.

Gutiérrez, a slow-moving, bull-necked, heavy-paunched man was one of the few delegates in the Convention sincerely without any political ambitions. He was a solid, earnest man who had successfully avoided identification with any of the revolutionary factions, and he had presided over Carranza's short-lived junta in Mexico City. He had been municipal president of Concepción del Oro, Zacatecas, and a copper mine foreman. He had joined the Revolution early and became famous as a train dynamiter. Although he had, as a revolutionary leader, operated in or near the Carrancista theater of operations, he was an independent, unimpeded by any ties to the Carrancistas, the Villistas or the Zapatistas, and no commitment except to the Revolution. He was easily elected, with 88 votes out of 128.

FLIGHT

"It could be yes, it could be no, but the
most likely thing is—who knows?"
Mexican *dicho*

GUITIERREZ, AS PROVISIONAL PRESIDENT, named commissions to notify Carranza and Villa of the Convention's actions.

Juan G. Cabral and Martín Espinosa were sent to Guadalupe to inform Villa. Villa's response was brief and to the point: "I accept your decision and await your orders." He also suggested that all problems might be quickly solved if both he and Carranza were sentenced to death before the firing squad (he had earlier proposed a double suicide).

Obregón, Villareal, Hay, Eugenio Aguirre Benavides, and Felipe Gutiérrez de Lara were appointed to the commission to tell Carranza that his conditions had been met and his resignation accepted. When Obregón's appointment was announced there was muttering among anti-Obregón elements of the Convention that if Obregón went to see Carranza he would not return. Obregón told Vito Alessio Robles: "If I do not return I authorize you to spit in my face."* The commission set off and reached Querétaro before they learned that they would be unable to confer with Carranza in Mexico City.

Carranza had been going through some strange maneuvers. When it became apparent that the Convention was going to meet the conditions for his resignation he went to Toluca, capital of the state of Mexico, where Francisco Murguía, a general of unwavering pro-Carranza sympathies, was in charge. Carranza made a speech in which he promised to undertake the reforms Madero had left undone, and received Murguía's

* Six years later Obregón told Alessio Robles: "You now have the right to spit in my face."

assurances of support. He returned to Mexico City and set off on what was supposed to be a sight-seeing trip to the pre-Columbian pyramids at San Juan Teotihuacán, twenty miles northeast of the capital. Instead of returning to the capital he bore to the east, entered the state of Tlaxcala, then moved south and east to Puebla. The Military Governor of Tlaxcala, Máximo Rojas, and the Military Governor of Puebla, Francisco Coss, were both loyal to Carranza, as was Murguía.

Back in the capital Carranza's staff was busy packing up archives, bales of paper money and the presses for printing more. His Subsecretary of Foreign Relations, Isidro Fabela, was hurriedly negotiating with the United States government on the terms under which the already promised evacuation of Veracruz would take place. Carranza had at first been opposed to the United States' insistence upon protection of refugees and amnesty for those who had served the occupation forces. Now, in his eagerness for possession of the port city, he agreed to everything, provided the evacuation was prompt.

When the Convention commission reached Querétaro, General Pablo González, whose army corps blocked the way, informed the commissioners they could go no farther. Obregón, serving as spokesman, held a telegraphic conference with Carranza in Puebla, asking that they be allowed to proceed. Carranza replied that when he had finished some business he had on hand he would come to Querétaro and meet with his old friend. Obregón stressed the urgency of their mission and again Carranza explained how busy he was. Obregón reminded Carranza of the conditions of his proffered resignation and pointed out that Villa had agreed to quit his post. Carranza said it was impossible to discuss the Convention's proceedings by telegraph and that they would discuss everything in person as soon as there was time to do so. Obregón replied that the commission's only concern was to deliver in person the Convention's decision and again asked that they be allowed to proceed. Carranza finally agreed that they could but again said that it might be some time before they could meet.

Two members of the commission gave up and returned to Aguascalientes. The others, Obregón, Villareal, and Hay, proceeded to Mexico City and then to Puebla. By the time they reached Puebla Carranza had gone on to Córdoba in the state of Veracruz. They also found that Generals Coss and Rojas and eighty other Carrancistas from Puebla and Tlaxcala had issued a manifesto reaffirming their loyalty to Carranza and his Plan of Guadalupe. The manifesto declared those generals who supported the Aguascalientes Convention to be in a state of rebellion, "severely punishable under military laws." This, obviously drawn up by Carranza or with his supervision, was the most warlike statement yet in the war of words between the Convention and Carranza. It appeared that Carranza would under no circumstances accept the decisions of the Convention, even if his previously stipulated conditions were met. Carranza made a speech in Córdoba in which he declared that it was not his obligation to turn over executive authority of the nation to "just anyone."

Obregón, Villareal, and Hay, still in pursuit, arrived in Orizaba on November 7 and took rooms in the Hotel Francés. A meeting with Carranza in nearby Córdoba was arranged for the following day, the 8th. The Convention, meanwhile, had set a deadline of November 10 for Carranza to live up to his pledge to resign.

Obregón's own version, in his memoirs, of what he said to Carranza in Córdoba, was: "Señor, I was one of those who voted in the Convention for the retirement of both you and Villa and for the election of General Eulalio Gutiérrez as provisional president of the republic. Now I am obliged to fulfill and to seal with my blood these commitments. If Gutiérrez gets rid of Villa and if the latter leaves the country I have no alternative other than to recognize Gutiérrez. But if he insists on leaving Villa where he is I will be the first to fight him." Carranza's answer, according to Obregón, was: "Gutiérrez would be nothing but a tool of Villa. If Villa retired the difficulties would be solved, because, as I have said, I am entirely disposed to resign as soon as it is certain Villa has done so . . ."

Exactly what Villa was doing was uncertain. He had agreed to give up his command, and had, at least in theory, turned over his troops to José Isabel Robles who was both Secretary of War and Vice-President in Gutiérrez' provisional government. Some of these troops had by now moved into Aguascalientes and this move was interpreted by the Carrancistas as a violation of the neutrality of the Convention city.

The Carrancistas also argued that Villa had not relinquished his command as he had promised to do. They were right. Short of actually leaving the country it was probably a human impossibility for Villa to sever himself from the position he had created. The division was Villa and Villa was the division.

Carranza on November 9 addressed a long telegram to the Convention. He sincerely deplored, he said, THAT THE JUNTA HAD COMMITTED ERRORS WHICH CAN COMPLICATE AND IN FACT ARE COMPLICATING THE SITUATION OF THE COUNTRY, and he thought it was, perhaps, due to a misunderstanding. MY NOTE OF OCTOBER 23 DID NOT, PROPERLY SPEAKING, CONTAIN MY RESIGNATION, BUT ONLY AN EXPOSITION OF THE CONDITIONS UNDER WHICH I WAS DISPOSED TO RESIGN. And, he went on to say, these conditions had not been met.

Eulalio Gutiérrez then, on November 10, the deadline which the Convention had set for Carranza's compliance, held a telegraphic conference with Carranza. GENERAL VILLA HAS LEFT THE COMMAND OF THE DIVISION OF THE NORTH, said Gutiérrez. A COMMISSION HAS BEEN APPOINTED TO RECEIVE ITS ARCHIVES, AND THE FORCES OF THE DIVISION WERE YESTERDAY PLACED UNDER THE COMMAND OF MY SECRETARY OF WAR . . . WE HAVE BEEN AWAITING YOUR DECISION. AS SOON AS YOU INDICATE THAT YOU WILL ACCEPT THE AGREEMENTS OF THE CONVENTION AND RESIGN, GENERAL VILLA WILL RETIRE ABSOLUTELY. I REGRET TO HAVE TO OBSERVE THAT WHILE THE CONVENTION HAS BEEN WORKING FOR HARMONY AND PEACE WE HAVE INTERCEPTED MESSAGES FROM YOUR ADHERENTS ISSUING ORDERS TO DISAVOW AND ATTACK THE CONVENTION. And he warned that if their differences could not be resolved WE ARE GOING TO HAVE THE BLOODIEST CIVIL WAR WE HAVE EVER HAD, AND NOT FOR PRINCIPLE, AS IN THE WAR JUST ENDED, BUT SOLELY BECAUSE OF PERSONAL AMBITION.

Carranza, in his reply, took a somewhat different tack, challenging the legitimacy of Gutiérrez' role as provisional president: I CONSIDER YOUR ELECTION ILLEGAL. IT WAS MADE ARBITRARILY BY THE JUNTA WITHOUT MY HAVING RESIGNED. ALSO, THE JUNTA HAS NO AUTHORITY TO ELECT A PRESIDENT. YOU WILL RECALL THAT I DID NOT CALL MYSELF PRESIDENT, BUT FIRST CHIEF IN CHARGE OF THE EXECUTIVE POWER IN ACCORDANCE WITH THE PLAN OF GUADALUPE. THERE IS NO LAW, NOR A PLAN, NOR A DOCUMENT, NOR A TREATY AUTHORIZING THE JUNTA TO DESIGNATE A PRESIDENT.

Gutiérrez patiently reiterated his points regarding Villa's retirement and the legitimacy of his own position. And he concluded: THIS MORNING I TOLD THE CONVENTION THAT I REFUSED TO BE AN OBSTACLE TO AN AGREEMENT, AND THAT I WOULD RESIGN IF THE CONVENTION THOUGHT MY RESIGNATION WOULD ASSURE PEACE. YOU MAY, IF YOU CONSIDER IT ADVISABLE, ALSO SUBMIT YOUR RESIGNATION TO THE CONVENTION WHICH IS NOW IN PERMANENT SESSION AND CAN RESOLVE MATTERS. I SALUTE YOU COURTEOUSLY AND TAKE MY LEAVE.

Carranza had been given until 6 P.M. on the 10th to resign. He did not. At 6:15 Gutiérrez' Secretary of War, José Isabel Robles, declared Carranza to be in a state of rebellion. He sent a message to the Zapatista forces in Morelos to attack the Carrancista forces in Puebla; this would prevent reinforcements from the state of Veracruz from coming to the aid of Pablo González in Querétaro. Lucio Blanco, in charge of a cavalry division of 15,000 in Mexico City was ordered to attack González' rear.

But the main striking force was the Division of the North which now began to move toward Querétaro, and Villa was in charge. He sent a message to Zapata: THE HOUR HAS COME. IN THE MORNING I BEGIN MY MARCH TO THE CAPITAL. Whatever his status may have been in a technical sense it was clear that he was now in active command of the principal force supporting the Convention.

Villa's move determined Obregón's course. Obregón's allegiance had followed a curious path. He had been a faithful Carranza adherent, but at Aguascalientes he had advanced the candidacy of Gutiérrez and had devised the formula for Carranza's retirement. But between his departure from Aguascalientes and his meeting with Carranza in Córdoba he held a strange conference with General Manuel Diéguez. He trusted Diéguez and had left him, with 6000 troops, in command at Guadalajara. He proposed that his own forces in Mexico City join those of Diéguez and together they would force the resignations of Carranza and Villa. Diéguez refused; he was remaining loyal to Carranza.

In Córdoba Obregón renewed his own fealty to the First Chief. The only logical explanation was that he had become convinced that neither Villa nor Carranza would under any circumstances obey the edict of the Convention, and that of the two evils Carranza was the lesser.

Whatever the reason, he was, by November 10, back in the Carranza camp. On the 11th he sent a message to Villa: I KNOW THE DIVISION OF THE NORTH HAS BEGUN ITS ADVANCE . . . THIS IS THE MOMENT IN WHICH YOU CAN WITH DEEDS PROVE YOUR PATRIOTISM. IF YOU RETIRE AND LEAVE THE COUNTRY TEMPORARILY NOT A SINGLE SHOT WILL BE FIRED AND SENOR CARRANZA WILL SURRENDER THE EXECUTIVE POWER . . . IT WILL BE NO SACRIFICE FOR YOU TO SAVE THE COUNTRY FROM A NEW FIGHT . . . IF YOU PERSIST, YOUR PAST GLORIES AND YOUR PROTESTATIONS OF PATRIOTISM WILL BE FOR NAUGHT . . . CONSULT YOUR CONSCIENCE . . . YOU WILL SAVE MUCH BLOOD. He sent copies of his message to Villa's various subordinate generals in the Division of the North, slyly reminding them that VILLA OWES MUCH OF HIS PRESTIGE TO YOUR VALOR AND PATRIOTISM, and adding: FOR MY PART I WILL, UPON THE RETIREMENT OF GENERAL VILLA, BE IN THE CAPITAL WITH ALL THE FORCES AT MY COMMAND TO GIVE ALL MANNER OF GUARANTEES TO THE CONVENTION AND TO PROVISIONAL PRESIDENT GUTIERREZ, AT WHOSE ORDERS I REMAIN. Obregón sent another message to Gutiérrez: IF YOU SEPARATE YOURSELF FROM VILLA . . . I WILL BE AT YOUR ORDERS; IF NOT, I WILL BE THE FIRST TO FIGHT HIM WITH ALL MY ENERGIES . . . I WILL NOT ABANDON SENOR CARRANZA TO AID A MAN LIKE VILLA.

The Convention recessed and moved to San Luis Potosí, hoping to establish itself later in the national capital. Despite noble efforts to chart a course for the wayward revolution, it had failed. A committee had, it was true, drawn up an agenda of reforms—expropriation and division of land, autonomy of municipalities with no interference from political chiefs appointed by the central government, restrictions on the power of the presidency, reorganization of the judiciary and simplification of laws, minimum wages, education for the poor and so on. But the document was never acted upon.

Francisco Madero had failed—tragically—because his revolution was directed at the person of Porfirio Díaz, not at the things that had made a dictator like Díaz inevitable. The Carranza revolution had ended in nothing but confusion since it was aimed at the person of Huerta and attempted little more than putting Carranza in his place. Now the Convention, the greatest hope, the brightest spot in the tragic course of the Revolution had degenerated into a war of personalities: on one hand the passionate, reckless Villa, and the stubborn and wily Carranza on the other. Both men were patriots; both wanted a better and happier Mexico, but they pursued their ideals along divergent, mutually exclusive paths. Had the Convention had a more inspired, more powerful leader than the well-meaning Gutiérrez—who had not wanted the job—the incompatibility of the two men might have been buried. José Isabel Robles, one of the bravest and most thoughtful of the Villistas, had found a copy of Plutarch's *Lives* in the loot of the second battle of Torreón. He studied it eagerly and lamented that the Convention had not had a Demosthenes. Obregón, in retrospect, said that one of the reasons for the Convention's failure was "our lack of experience in such matters."

Carranza, while he waited for U.S. troops to get out of Veracruz so that he could establish his fugitive capital there, indulged in one more peace-making gesture. On November 15 he addressed a message to General Pablo González suggesting a new formula. He, Carranza, would turn over his command to a "person of confidence," and he specifically suggested González, if Villa would turn over his command to Eulalio Gutiérrez. Then he and Villa would leave the country, both agreeing to be in Havana, Cuba, by November 25. The Convention would then reconvene in Mexico City to select a provisional president. If these conditions had not been met by November 30 Carranza would return to Mexico and resume his position as First Chief of the Constitutionalist army in charge of the executive power.

It was an odd suggestion. Why should the Convention choose another provisional president when it already had one in the person of Gutiérrez? The reassembly of the Convention and the effort to select still another provisional president in these tense days would produce more confusion, more dissension—which would certainly open the way for Carranza to take over again on November 30. Meanwhile Carranza had named Obregón, not González, as his chief of operations. Gutiérrez officially restored Villa to his command, promising to remove him again if Carranza should decide to resign.

Obregón, in charge in Mexico City, announced through the press on

November 19 a declaration of war against Villa and issued one of his remarkably bombastic manifestos, saying it would be preferable for Mexico to become a vast cemetery rather than live infected with the gangrene of the "accursed trinity," of Villa, Angeles, and Maytorena. "Mothers, wives, daughters," he urged, "kneel before the altar of the nation and raise your voices in prayer for your sons, husbands and fathers and curse those who, forgetting honor, raise treacherous hands to stab the Fatherland!"

Obregón had little more than brave words. The troops under his immediate command had been reduced to no more than 4000. General Rafael Buelna and General Juan Cabral had remained with the Convention. It appeared that Lucio Blanco, in charge of a cavalry division of 15,000 men in the capital, was getting ready to desert Carranza. Obregón had enough supplies of artillery, ammunition, and rifles to equip an army of 50,000—but he did not have the men to handle them. The surplus equipment was loaded on trains, ready for retreat. When Veracruz was evacuated by U.S. troops on the 23rd, Obregón ordered a military celebration of the event in front of the Juárez monument in Mexico City—but he could find only two drummers and two buglers to provide martial music. On the 24th Obregón and his reduced forces boarded trains and left the capital, leaving it, by default, in the hands of Lucio Blanco. Blanco, a colorful figure of a man who affected a gold-handled riding crop and a leopard-spotted saddle blanket, ruled the deserted city for two days. Then at the head of his 15,000 men and with his loyalties uncertain, he left, by way of Toluca, for the neutral state of Michoacán.

The capital was, both politically and militarily, a vacuum. But from the south the dark-faced, white-clad soldiers of Zapata, as insistent and silent as drifting sand, took over Xochimilco, then San Angel, then the southern areas of the capital, then the capital itself. And the Division of the North ground steadily forward through Lagos, León, Silao, Irapuato, Celaya, Querétaro. The defending forces commanded by Pablo González were being annihilated; the general who had never won a battle was losing still another one. So easy was the advance to the capital that Villa hardly paid attention to details. In his private car he amused himself doing rope tricks with a new lariat.

NORTH AND SOUTH

"A people ignorant and brave are better
than a people cultured and abject."

María Arias (María Pistolas) at
Madero's grave, August 1914

IN THE LAST WEEK of November 1914 long-suffering dwellers in the
capital were frightened. They remembered the excesses of the Constitutional troops the previous August—looting, seizure of property, aimless violence. They expected the invasion by the Zapatistas to be far
worse, possibly the ultimate in savagery. For years the Zapatistas had
been painted in lurid colors by the press—first under Díaz, later under
Madero, Huerta, and Carranza—as a horde of bloodthirsty barbarians
who would swoop down out of the mountains destroying everything
in their path.

Instead the Zapatistas entered the city quietly. The small dark men
shuffled along in ragged columns, silent, courteous, and with none of
the bravado their predecessors had shown. There were neither blaring
bugles nor rattling drums; only the occasional mournful sound of a
bull horn trumpet. There was no random firing of guns in the air.
These men saved their ammunition. They took over police duties and
the city was calmer and better controlled than it had been since the
days of Don Porfirio. There was no looting, no requisitioning of mansions, horses, or automobiles. There were no victory celebrations. The
invaders with their leathery skins and huge hats would tiptoe cautiously
into Sanborn's, as awed by the waitresses as the waitresses were afraid
of them. They would drink coffee, holding the cup awkwardly, and
when they left they paid, not in paper money, but with crudely coined
silver. Unlike the Constitutionalists who closed churches and punished
priests, the Zapatistas marched behind banners of the Virgin of Gua-

dalupe, went to Masses and doffed their hats to clerics. They wore religious medals pinned to their hats and suspended around their necks—along with love charms and amulets against the evil eye.

When Emiliano Zapata arrived in the city he did it unobtrusively. Instead of occupying one of the great private homes along the Paseo de la Reforma as had the successful generals before him, he took a room in a cheap railroad hotel in the Calle Moneda, close to the San Lázaro station. He made no ringing proclamations, issued no decrees, and he answered journalists' questions with monosyllables. Yes, his men held the capital. No, he did not plan to take up residence. Yes, he supported the Aguascalientes Convention and provisional President Eulalio Gutiérrez. Yes, he would turn the government over to Gutiérrez. He planned to return to Morelos and await the arrival of General Villa and his troops. Before leaving he installed his brother Eufemio as custodian of the National Palace.

Eufemio and his men and horses occupied dingy quarters in the rear of the palace. By twos and threes they would explore the great halls and salons of the palace, their sandal-clad feet moving uneasily over the carpets. They stared in wonder at the brocade walls, the silk draperies, the portraits and statuary. Eufemio kept looking for *la silla presidencial,* declaring he would burn it when he found it. But he could not find it and concluded that Señor Carranza had taken it with him. Later he admitted that he had thought *la silla presidencial* was a saddle (the word *silla* is used for both chair and saddle). The presidential chair was there and was left intact and undamaged by Eufemio and his men, as was everything else in the palace.

While the Zapatistas were establishing their control of the capital Villa and his troops were approaching from the northwest, rolling easily and smoothly on countless railroad trains. They stopped occasionally to repair railroad tracks or build bridges and, less frequently, to skirmish with disheartened Carrancista troops. The division under Francisco Murguía at Toluca, capital of the state of Mexico, had withdrawn toward the west. Obregón's reduced forces had left the capital. The cavalry division of Lucio Blanco, principal defending force for Mexico City, had withdrawn. The only military obstacle to Villa's advance had been the 20,000 troops commanded by Pablo González in the Querétaro area, but these melted away. Battlefield losses and desertion reduced his 20,000 to 3000, and with these survivors González fled into the sierra. Hungry, disorganized, soaked by torrential rains and jeered at by villagers they made their painful way from the high plateaus and mountains of central Mexico down into the *tierra caliente* of the Gulf Coast.

By December 1 when Villa's troops reached Tacuba, a suburb northwest of Mexico City, the military fortunes of that unpredictable warrior were at apogee. He was no longer just the chief of a division, victimized by the jealousy, distrust, and caprices of an inscrutable commander-in-chief. He was undisputed the commander-in-chief of the largest military force in the nation, the military arm of the Convention of Aguascalientes, the sovereign authority of Mexico. In some ways he acted as though he himself were the sovereign authority. He was appointing civil officials in states and cities without bothering to consult provisional President Gutiérrez, the Convention or anyone else. He had issued a decree—over his signature as "general-in-chief of operations of the Convention Army" for behavior of troops in the Federal District—banning looting, confiscations, forced loans, the sale of alcoholic beverages, scandals, outrages, abuses, and hostile manifestations, and inviting civilians to submit any complaints, not to the Gutiérrez government, but to Francisco Villa. He was already functioning as ultimate authority in civil matters. When five men accused of counterfeiting were brought before him he issued a Villa-like judgment: "Try them at once and shoot them the first thing in the morning."

But in some matters he displayed an air of restraint. His principal generals, among them his trusted adviser Felipe Angeles, argued that Villa's forces should drive on toward Veracruz where they could, with ease, push Carranza and his reduced supporters right into the Gulf of Mexico. Villa would not hear of it. The territory to the south and east of Mexico City was the theater of Zapata and his Liberation Army of the South. The privilege of delivering the final blow to Carranza belonged to Zapata. Angeles argued that Zapata was admirable as an agrarian leader but was not a great battlefield commander. Zapata had never won a major battle—nothing like Tierra Blanca, Torreón, Zacatecas. The Zapatistas had only won guerrilla skirmishes. The Zapatistas had never been capable of a sustained drive. They would win a battle and then go back to the cornfields of their *patria chica*. This military opportunity should not be entrusted to such troops, Angeles cautioned.

Had Villa pushed on toward Veracruz he might have had an easy victory. But Villa was obdurate, and his obstinacy on this was one of the pivotal points in the Revolution, determining not only his own fate but the course of the civil war for many years to come.

Villa had never met Zapata, but he had had correspondence with him, had reached an understanding with Zapata's representatives at the Aguascalientes Convention. Zapata's single-minded preoccupation with the plight of the landless Indians, Mexico's disinherited, appealed to Villa's groping idealism as had nothing since the social preachments of Abraham González. Zapata was as relentless a foe of the *chocolateros* and the *perfumados* as Villa was. Villa would do nothing that was not in accord with Zapata. He would not even attempt to occupy Mexico City without Zapata's consent. He remembered Obregón's occupation of the capital and his collaboration with the hated federal troops, in effect making war on the Zapatistas, the revolutionists whose constant pressure on Huerta and the capital had helped make Obregón's victory possible. Zapata had been a forgotten man of the Constitutionalist victory, just as Villa himself had been—ignored, snubbed, even persecuted. Villa did not intend to let it happen again.

Eulalio Gutiérrez arrived at the outskirts of the capital on the day after Villa. Gutiérrez went into the city in an automobile caravan to visit the National Palace and its custodian, Eufemio Zapata. Villa consented to ride in the caravan, but he went only as far as the palace gates. There he left Gutiérrez and sped back to Tacuba where he killed time in his private car with his rope tricks. He sent Roque González Garza with a simple message to Zapata in Cuernavaca: Francisco Villa was eager to give an *abrazo* to his ally and friend.

González Garza, whose aquiline profile, penetrating eyes and close-cropped full beard made him look like a Bedouin tribal chief, found Zapata cordial and receptive. He would indeed like to meet with the great General Villa. But, displaying the Indian caution that was characteristic of the Army of the South, he insisted that the meeting be on Zapata's terrain, in the village of Xochimilco, southeast of the capital. Xochimilco, famous for its flowers, fruits, and floating gardens was as stubbornly Indian as was Zapata himself and had always been Zapatista in its sympathies.

Villa accepted Zapata's invitation. On Friday morning, December 4, he and a small escort set out on horseback for Xochimilco, twenty miles from his headquarters in Tacuba, carefully skirting the heart of the capital which lay between the two points. Villa was not in uniform. He wore an artilleryman's helmet, a heavy brown sweater with a roll collar, khaki trousers stuffed into worn leggings and heavy, scuffed shoes—the sort of garb in which he had won his great victories. He had, by this time, a trunk full of uniforms. One was a gaudy, ill-fitting uniform of white duck—like a bandmaster's—which had been presented to him by American newspapermen who thought a general should not go about dressed as a cowhand. And he had the blue serge dress uniform of a divisional general of the Mexican army, heavy with frogging and gold braid. But this was a time for plain dress and modest behavior.

After the long trip out the Calzada Tlalpan, Villa and his little party were met on the outskirts of Xochimilco by Otilio Montaño, the one-time schoolteacher who had drafted the Plan of Ayala for

Zapata and now served as one of Zapata's secretaries. Villa and his party dismounted. Montaño made a speech of welcome, then led them up the narrow village street to where Zapata waited. Zapata was more colorful in appearance than his visitor. He wore a short black jacket, a brilliant lavender shirt, a blue neckerchief. The seams of his tight-fitting trousers were lined with silver buttons. His short boots were of the Spanish style, sharp-toed and high-heeled. He wore two gold rings; and two gaudily colored handkerchiefs cascaded from his pockets. His face, with the large, dark eyes and the huge black mustaches, was shaded by a wide-brimmed sombrero.

Given the importance and character of the individuals involved—the Centaur of the North and the Attila of the South—a certain barbaric splendor might have been expected. But the meeting was one of homely simplicity. The village band—cornets, a tuba, drums, played the national hymn and popular songs of the Revolution, *Adelita, Valentina,* and *La Cucaracha.* The two principals exchanged an *abrazo* and walked arm in arm to the village school. Here they went to a second-floor room and sat at a large oval table. At Villa's right was Paulino Martínez, the journalist; then Leon Canova, the confidential agent of the United States; then a woman, plainly dressed but with her left hand heavy with brass rings; then Zapata's young son, Nicolás, dressed in plain white peasant clothes (the boy put his head on his arms and slept through most of what followed.) Zapata sat on Villa's left. Next to him was his brother, Eufemio, whom Gutiérrez had dismissed as custodian of the National Palace. Other Zapatistas and Villistas were scattered around the table. The room quickly filled with people. The band stayed in the corridor and continued to play discordantly but loud enough to make it difficult to hear what was said at the table.

At first very little was said. Villa, ruddy-faced, bared his brown teeth in a fixed grin and for once seemed unable to speak. Zapata, his dark Indian face still shaded by the huge hat, seemed expressionless except for the eyes which roamed over his guests with curiosity.

For almost half an hour the two men exchanged rambling, incoherent remarks separated by long silences. The two battlefield veterans acted, one witness said, as shy as two country sweethearts. Their language was rough, idiomatic, ungrammatical, and, at first, meaningless. Villa would say "I was always worried . . . being forgotten . . . I had an obligation to the Revolution. Carranza is a man so shameless . . . he was taking over the Revolution while I waited." And Zapata would say "I have said to all of you, always I said . . . I said, this Carranza is a . . ." Gradually their mutual hatred of Carranza loosened up the dialogue and it began to assume more direction. Villa damned men who went to banquets, slept on soft beds and knew nothing of people who lived in suffering. Zapata would add that these men had, as well, been the people's scourge. Villa told of having fought so that the Carrancistas could come to the capital, and Zapata asked intelligent questions about the battles in the North, appearing to know more about Villa's battles than Villa did about his. They discussed the Convention's demand for Villa's resignation and Villa said he had been willing to retire but decided "it is better to speak first with my General Zapata." They spoke of putting the government in the hands of reliable civilians so that the fighters could be sent where they were needed. Villa said that he had much to do in the North, once things were arranged here in the capital. Would he go back to his old pastures, Zapata asked. Villa answered with a *dicho* of the North: "To handle the bulls of Tepehuanes the horses of Tepehuanes are best."

There was, of course, a discussion of land division. "The people," said Zapata, "love the land. They still don't believe it when you say 'This land is yours.' They think it is a dream. But when they see others growing things on this land, they say 'I'm going to ask for land and I am going to plant it.'" And Villa said, "Now they will see that it is the people who rule and they will see who are their friends . . . I believe there is going to be another life, and if not . . . I have forty thousand Mausers, seventy-seven cannon, and sixteen million cartridges."

Zapata called for cognac and poured it. Villa eyed it uneasily. Zapata raised his glass and drank. Villa, who never drank, did the same. He coughed and wheezed and his eyes reddened, and he called for water. "Well, here I am," he gasped. "I came to meet the true men of the people." Zapata responded: "I congratulate myself for meeting a man who truly knows how to fight." "I've been at it for twenty-two years," Villa said, and Zapata replied, "And I since the age of eighteen."

A glass of water was brought. "Wouldn't you like some water?" Villa asked. "No, go ahead and drink it," said Zapata. Then the two great guerrilla warriors who, between the two of them, might decide the future of the Mexican nation, began admiring each other's headgear —Zapata's a broad-brimmed, high-crowned sombrero, and Villa's cloth-covered, British-type pith helmet. "I never wear any kind but this," said Zapata. Villa said, "I always used to wear that kind, made of palm fiber, but for the past three years I've been wearing these" (which wasn't quite correct; he more often wore a felt hat, the kind Mexicans called a *tejano,* or Texan).

By this time the band in the corridor outside had made conversation impossible. Villa and Zapata and their immediate aides withdrew to another room where they got down to more serious business. They agreed on an alliance between their two armies, one in the North, one in the South, dedicated to the cause of the poor and the defeat of Carrancismo. Villa promised to supply Zapata with needed elements of war. They agreed that Mexico should have a constitutional president who was a civilian identified with the Revolution. They made plans for a triumphal entry into Mexico City of both their armies in a military parade two days later, on Sunday, December 6.

The two men also discussed in matter-of-fact fashion people they wanted killed. Zapata insisted that the Villistas deliver to him for execution Guillermo García Aragón, a one-time Zapatista who was vice-president of the permanent commission of the Convention and who had in recent days been named by Gutiérrez as superintendent of the National Palace—the position Eufemio Zapata had held unofficially. Villa had no liking for García Aragón and agreed readily. In turn he asked Zapata to turn over to him three generals—one of them Juan Andrew Almazán—who had fought for Huerta and had, more recently, joined Zapata's forces. Zapata demurred; they were his guests and he could not do it. But he offered substitutes. Villa, all affability, was willing to accept substitutes. Another man he wanted was Paulino Martínez, the journalist who had sat next to him in the other room. Martínez, in the paper, *La Voz de Juárez,* which he published in Cuernavaca, had been outrageously critical of the late Francisco Madero (as had Zapata himself). Villa, who still regarded Madero as a saint, could forgive this disrespect on the part of Zapata but not on the part of a Zapata underling.

There was, afterward, a banquet of Indian dishes—corn, beans, chiles, roast pork and kid, pulque and beer. Villa made his set speech: "Companions, you are going to hear the words of an uncultured man, sentiments which my heart cherishes . . ." an affirmation of his concern for the suffering of Mexico's poor.

Paulino Martínez—who did not know that he was doomed—also spoke, heaping praise on the two men: "This date should be engraved with diamonds in our history. It is the first day of the first year of the redemption of the Mexican people. It is the dawn of their happiness because two pure men, two sincere men, men without duplicity, men born of the people, know their griefs and fight for their happiness." Finally Villa's spokesman, González Garza, who spoke with a slight lisp, described how the two leaders shared the obligation for the triumph of the Revolution, Villa in the North and Zapata in the South, and he concluded: "May the God of nations guide you in the great roles you play in the grand undertaking destiny has entrusted to you."

Two days later the two armies joined for a gigantic parade through the capital. The Zapatistas marched in from their concentration points south of the city—Xochimilco, San Angel, and Mixcoac—and the Villistas moved in from their encampments near Tacuba. The great mass of men —estimates ran as high as 50,000—formed into a marching column in the Calzada de la Veronica and moved down the Paseo de la Reforma toward the center of the city and the National Palace. Villa and Zapata rode side by side behind a cavalry patrol. Villa wore his dark blue dress uniform with high leather leggings. Zapata was spectacular in a charro outfit—the uniform of a gentleman *hacendado* and Sunday horseman rather than a peasant leader. His deerskin jacket was elaborately embroidered with silk and gold thread, the emblem of the Mexican eagle emblazoned on the back. Instead of the usual straw sombrero he wore a splendid twenty-ounce felt, also heavily worked with gold. The Zapatista troops came next—white-clad foot soldiers, cartridge belts crossing their chests, rifles carried either vertically, horizontally, or in the ready position; then the Zapatista cavalry, mounted on small and thin but quick-footed horses. Some of the officers wore swords which seemed to be in the way. The Villista troops which followed displayed greater uniformity—in dress, equipment, and marching order.

The huge column moved through the city across the north side of the Zócalo to the front of the palace. Here Villa and Zapata dismounted and took positions beside Eulalio Gutiérrez on the palace balcony to review the remainder of the parade. Then, after a session of picture-taking during which Villa lolled smilingly in the presidential chair with Tomás Urbina at his right and Zapata at his left, Eulalio Gutiérrez entertained his guests at a banquet. Both Villa and Zapata were stiff and uneasy in the formal atmosphere.

Eulalio Gutiérrez was uneasy, too. He did not know what to make of the close-mouthed Zapata, and he did not trust Villa. He had, without wanting it, been thrust into a position of almost total dependence on Villa's armed might. It was an uncomfortable position.

CHAPTER 30

DISSENTERS' DISSENSION

> "I don't care whether I live, or die, but I am glad to be going to a world where perhaps I will find neither executioners nor tyrants."
>
> Last words, before execution, of Dionisio Triana

NO ONE WAS MORE AWARE of Gutiérrez' discomfort that Obregón—and no one was readier to take advantage of it.

Obregón had had difficulties and uncertainties of his own. When he left Mexico City with the remnants of his once-great army corps the outlook had been almost hopeless. Most of the country was either with the Convention regime or in a non-committal position under the leadership of local caudillos who waited to see which side offered the greater advantages. Rejoining Carranza in Veracruz, Obregón wanted, at first, to go south to the Isthmus of Tehuantepec. He could embark at the Pacific port of Salina Cruz, come up the west coast and join Diéguez in Jalisco. But Carranza insisted that he remain with him in Veracruz. Under the First Chief's orders he inspected defenses at Jalapa and Perote, points at which he would have to meet the Convention forces if they advanced on Veracruz. He also reconnoitered the country to the south, the escape route if they had to retreat—which seemed a likely possibility.

Meanwhile he published in Veracruz an open letter to Gutiérrez, calculated to aggravate the provisional President's problems.

"Isn't it true," he asked, "that in Aguascalientes on various occasions you stated in the presence of Generals Robles, Chao, Aguirre Benavides, Villareal, and the undersigned that General Villa was a bandit and assassin from whom the country must be saved by whatever means? Isn't it true that you criticized our peace-making efforts, saying that bandits like Villa understood only bullets? Did Villa cease being a bandit when he began making war on honorable men who would not accept him? Have you resigned your status as an honorable man? These things are equally impossible. Those of us who knew General Gutiérrez, the impeccable revolutionist of unstained honor, can explain it only in this way: either Gutiérrez is no longer his own man, or . . . all his virtues have been overcome by vanity. General Gutiérrez: it is never too late to remedy an evil. Get out of that atmosphere that has robbed you of energy and honor and return to the battlefield with your brothers!"

Whatever Gutiérrez may have thought or feared about Villa their relations were, at first, cordial. Villa dutifully reported his military plans to Gutiérrez: Zapata and his army would march on Puebla, the most important point between the capital and Carranza's Veracruz headquarters, while he, Villa, would move to the west and drive the Carrancistas out of Guadalajara. And Villa was behaving well in public. He tearfully attended ceremonies at Madero's grave and, with his own hands, restored the street plaques on the Avenida Madero—formerly the Calle San Francisco—which had been torn down during the last days of the Carrancista occupation of the capital. His public utterances were mild and self-effacing. To a group of foreign correspondents he declared: "My only mission is to restore order in Mexico without resorting to personal vengeance. In this task I will not function as a coarse soldier but as a respectful servant of the government created by the Aguascalientes Convention. I will scrupulously respect property, both national and foreign and I will not intervene in anything except in the interest of order and justice." He frequently spoke of his complete subordination to the Gutiérrez government.

But at the same time Villa kept the railroads under his control—trains did not move in or out of the capital without his orders, and no telegraph messages were sent unless they had been approved by Villa's headquarters. As he had in Chihuahua he now conducted his own diplomacy, negotiating with foreign representatives, making promises and statements of policy as if he and not Gutiérrez were provisional President.

Both Villa and the Zapatistas were administering what they described as justice, with the result that within the first fortnight of the Convention government's rule of the capital approximately 150 persons had been executed. One of the first was Guillermo García Aragón, whom Villa turned over to the Zapatistas for execution. Paulino Martínez, the Zapatista, soon followed. He was summoned from his residence in Mexico City by Villa's executioner, Rodolfo Fierro, supposedly for a conference with Gutiérrez' Minister of War, José Isabel Robles. Instead he was taken to the San Cosme barracks and shot.

One of the next victims was Lieutenant Colonel David Berlanga, an outspoken young journalist and teacher who, while intensely loyal to the Convention government, had been critical of the behavior of the Villistas. He had shamed a group of Villista generals who had dined well in a restaurant and then refused to pay their bill; Berlanga ostentatiously paid the bill himself. Villa ordered Fierro to execute him. Fierro found Berlanga with friends in the Silvain Restaurant, enjoying an after-dinner cigar. Fierro bluntly ordered Berlanga to come with him, that he was going to be executed. Berlanga coolly told his friends goodbye and followed the orders of the heavily armed Fierro. He, too, was taken to the San Cosme barracks and placed against a wall in the courtyard. He continued to smoke his cigar with icy calm, carefully preserving the ash, which grew longer and longer. Fierro watched with fascination. Berlanga took a few more puffs of the cigar, his hand still steady, the cigar ash still unbroken. After a final pull on the cigar he threw it away, extended his arms and announced that he was ready and Fierro uneasily gave orders for the squad to fire. Berlanga's coolness almost undid the tough Fierro, veteran of hundreds of such executions. The next day he visited Martín Luis Guzmán, to whom he told the story of Berlanga. While he talked Fierro puffed at a cigar, anxiously watching the ash—which would break and fall because of the tremor in his hands.

These three executions—each of the victims a member of the Convention—made it appear doubtful that Villa would ever subordinate himself either to the Convention or to Gutiérrez. Villa also menaced Gutiérrez' cabinet. He ordered the new Secretary of Education, José Vasconcelos, to abandon his cabinet post and leave the capital—or be executed. Villa's own explanation of it was that General Juan Banderas, one of Zapata's fiercest killers—who only a few days before had shot down a brother officer in the barroom of the Hotel Cosmos in a dispute over an automobile—had announced his intention to kill Vasconcelos because of an old grievance. Villa insisted he was acting only in the interest of Vasconcelos' safety, but Vasconcelos and Gutiérrez were not convinced.

On the day before Christmas, Gutiérrez sent a circular to generals of the Convention army. The population, he said, was "alarmed to the point of panic" by the wave of kidnapings and assassinations. He had hoped, on assuming the provisional presidency, for the cooperation of his comrades in arms in establishing a strong, honorable, and just government of morality and law. To operate otherwise would give comfort to the enemy who could, then, justly call them bandits, kidnapers, and assassins. And he urged the generals and "chiefs of armed groups, no matter how numerous," to stop taking the law in their own hands and thereby damaging not only themselves but their government.

Secretly he sent messages to his brother Luis Gutiérrez in Saltillo and Antonio I. Villareal in Monterrey, both of whom had remained loyal to Carranza, urging them to give their support to his government and to cooperate in his effort to control Villa.

It was a grim Christmas season in the capital. Food was scarce and charcoal almost non-existent—and the few supplies that were available were prohibitively expensive. The only prosperous business was that of the money exchanges which could somehow determine comparative values of the various kinds of paper money in circulation. Confiscated automobiles, driven by inexperienced—and often drunken—generals, careened through the streets, running down pedestrians and crashing into one another. An outbreak of typhoid threatened to grow into an epidemic.

Villa returned to the capital from Guadalajara, which his troops had taken from Diéguez. He went to the Teatro Colón and, from his box, leered at the leading lady, María Conesa, in *The Girl of the Kisses*. But he had his mind on less agreeable matters. Gutiérrez' circular had been aimed at him and his men. Some members of the Convention became so alarmed by Villa's behavior that they fled from Mexico City, taking with them the flag on which all the Convention generals had taken their oaths and signed their names. Worse, he heard that Gutiérrez was contemplating moving the seat of the government to some place where he would be free from Villa—if such a place existed.

The next afternoon Villa, accompanied by two thousand cavalry under the command of Fierro, went to the Braniff mansion which was Gutiérrez' official residence. The cavalrymen surrounded the building and Villa, pistol in hand, went in to confront Gutiérrez. Villa's eyes were blazing and his voice was high-pitched.

"You are betraying me!" he shouted. "Tell me, what are you trying to do?"

"I'll tell you, General," said Gutiérrez, with remarkable calm. "I'm going." With a steady hand he tossed off a small glass of cognac.

"No you aren't," Villa roared. "I've ordered that no train will leave the city."

"In that case I'll go by burro," said Gutiérrez. He refilled his cognac glass.

Villa, becoming a little calmer, asked for reasons. Gutiérrez reiterated what he had already said in his circular, and mentioned specifically the assassinations of Berlanga and García Aragón and the threats against Vasconcelos. Villa admitted the murder of Berlanga and excused it because Berlanga was a vicious little dog who was nipping at Villa's heels. As for Vasconcelos, Villa was only trying to save his life—Vasconcelos should appreciate it. Gutiérrez said such things were intolerable—and the argument raged on until José Isabel Robles intervened and promised that he would guarantee that his friend Gutiérrez would not leave the capital. Gutiérrez had not retreated from his position, nor had he retracted what he had said, but Villa's temper seemed to burn itself out. He withdrew and also ordered away the guard outside Gutiérrez' residence.

Villa moved from his railroad car headquarters into a handsome house at 76 Calle Liverpool where he lived in splendor. He went to theaters and bullfights and carried on a flirtation with the pretty cashier of the Hotel Palacio. When the manager of the hotel, a French woman, interfered, Villa seized her and locked her in a bedroom in his house, which brought formal protests from the French government. The news that Obregón was advancing from Veracruz with a newly formed army did not bother him; nor did the lassitude of the Zapatistas who, having taken Puebla, were doing nothing about an offensive against the Carrancistas. Villa's own troops, under Angeles, were preparing for a campaign northeastward from Torreón to drive the Carrancistas out of Coahuila and Nuevo León. So confident was Villa that on January 5 he left the capital for the Juárez-El Paso frontier for a meeting with his old friend General Hugh L. Scott. The Maytorena and Calles forces were still fighting on the Sonora-Arizona border; rifle and artillery fire was taking American lives and the United States government was protesting. Villa was pleased that Scott sought his counsel.

On the day Villa left, Obregón and his army moved into Puebla, easily overcoming the Zapatistas who had held it for less than three weeks. Zapata's peasant soldiers, uneasy in any city, had deserted by the hundreds to go back to their own land in the mountains and valleys of Morelos. Their officers, in addition, were having difficulty obtaining necessary supplies from the Gutiérrez government. There was a suspicion that Gutiérrez and his Minister of War, José Isabel Robles, were deliberately obstructing the Zapatista operations.

The suspicion was correct. Gutiérrez was not only withholding supplies, but was also attempting reconciliation with Obregón. Two days after Obregón had taken Puebla, Gutiérrez wrote to him: he and his colleagues—Robles, Lucio Blanco, and Eugenio Aguirre Benavides—suggested that Obregón suspend his advance toward Mexico City while they divorced the Convention government from Villa. Their move to end "the banditry and desolation" of Villa and his followers, he said, had support in the states of Tamaulipas, Coahuila, Nuevo León, and San Luis Potosí. Only a union of all true revolutionists, he said, could save the nation from anarchy and ruin.

The Gutiérrez letter was as important to Obregón as a battlefield victory. But by now he had regained enough strength to feel no need for compromise. On December 13, Carranza named him "general-in-chief of the Army of Operations," with authority over Carrancista military elements in the states of Veracruz, Puebla, Tlaxcala, Oaxaca, and Hidalgo. Within a fortnight he had organized a striking force of 12,000 men—and the first engagement, at Puebla, had been an easy victory.

Obregón's reply to Gutiérrez offered little comfort: Obregón said he was glad to see that Gutiérrez recognized the justification of Obregón's opposition to Villa. But he could not suspend operations against the capital. If Gutiérrez and his colleagues would declare war against Villa he would do all in his power to avoid bloodshed and reestablish peace in the country. He hoped that Gutiérrez would recognize his past error—but said that he would have nothing further to do with him until there was a complete break with Villa.

Gutiérrez was in an untenable position, isolated from the possibility of support from either side. He was guilty of many of the things he criticized in others (he had two flashy diamond rings of questionable origin which he sometimes wore on his left hand, and he was reported to have made a fortune harvesting guayule on other people's land). But his most damaging fault—his perilous alliance with Villa—had been forced upon him by the desertion of his erstwhile friends; he had no other course if he were going to enforce the will of the Convention.

On January 13 Gutiérrez drew up a manifesto addressed to the Mexican people. It was a sad document, a declaration of revolutionary bankruptcy. He reviewed Carranza's intransigence and refusal either to bring about reforms or give up the executive power, the decision of the Convention and the way in which he, as provisional president, had been left with only the support of Villa's Division of the North to enforce the Convention's decisions. He described Villa's incorrigibility and listed the crimes of violence for which both Villa and Zapata had been responsible. Zapata, he said, far from being a pure agrarian revolutionist, was nothing more than a military dictator in the state of Morelos; he had brought about no social reforms, there were no elections and the system of land ownership was being perpetuated. "When I have remarked on these things to Generals Villa and Zapata and their close advisers," Gutiérrez said, "they have told me that these things are necessary steps in the Revolution. I myself am a revolutionist, perhaps not as famous but with as much service as Generals Villa and Zapata. I have on my side elements whose fidelity to the revolutionary cause is indisputable. But we have a different understanding of the Revolution. We cannot conceive of it as a matter of robbery and assassination. We believe that when the Revolution kills it should do so publicly, acting with strict justice; that when the property of others is taken it should be according to law and for the benefit of the nation . . .

"A just government would find ways to resolve our economic problems, would destroy the latifundia, not with the perpetuation of burdens as in Morelos nor with arbitrary usurpation as in Chihuahua . . . but with laws that would regulate property rights for all time and protect the small property owner against all assaults, even the assaults of the revolutionists themselves . . .

"Political liberty, the second most important factor in the Revolution, is at present rarer than at any other time in our history, and this great popular movement will go down in disaster if we cannot shake off the dictatorship of these soldiers of fortune and false leaders . . . The moment has arrived for Mexicans once more to put their citizenship to the test. They can choose between the dictatorship offered them by the caudillos of the North and South and by Señor Carranza, and the liberal, democratic government which was born in the Convention of Aguascalientes which I am both obliged and resolved to sustain.

"The Revolution has traveled a difficult road and achieved little in recent months because of its divisions into factions based on personalities. Those who follow Villa, Zapata, and Carranza are bad revolutionists; they fight for persons, not for principles. Now all good Mexicans must, in these moments of grave crisis, unite in defense of principles.

"I have hesitated in taking this serious step, which may bring even greater bloodshed, because those who oppose the government have great resources. I have thought also of those Carrancistas who continue to support a man who takes advantage of the schism in the legal party in order to continue a war against it. But finally I have chosen to take the road which, if it does not lead to triumph, is at least the path of honor."

Gutiérrez then announced the removal of Villa and Zapata from their commands and once more demanded the retirement of Carranza, inviting the Carrancista military forces to join the forces of the Convention.

The document was not immediately released. Instead Gutiérrez made secret preparations to leave Mexico City, planning to reestablish his government in San Luis Potosí, where he had served as military governor before being elected to the provisional presidency. When day broke on January 16 he was gone. With him went those members of his government who were loyal to him: Secretary of War José Isabel Robles, Secretary of Education José Vasconcelos, Secretary of Government Lucio Blanco, and the troops commanded by Blanco and General Francisco Almanza. He also took 10,453,473 pesos from the National Treasury. Such a large-scale evacuation could have gone unnoticed only under the anarchic conditions which prevailed in Mexico City.

The Gutiérrez party paused in the mining town of Pachuca, fifty miles north of Mexico City, long enough for Gutiérrez' manifesto to be published. A copy earlier had been taken to Obregón by representatives of Gutiérrez. Obregón was as unreceptive as before and the envoys were sent to Veracruz for imprisonment. Gutiérrez sent a separate message to Obregón informing him that Villista troops were leaving for the North and urging him to occupy the capital.

Gutiérrez was counting on nine thousand troops commanded by Eugenio Aguirre Benavides to secure San Luis Potosí as his new capital. He planned then to launch a war of harassment against Villa's troops in the North. But Aguirre Benavides, after vain attempts to win support of the more conservative of the Villista leaders such as Angeles, was driven out of San Luis Potosí by Tomás Urbina. After suffering heavy losses he joined the Gutiérrez party which was traveling somewhat aimlessly from one out-of-the-way village to another. They were sheltered for a while by Saturnino Cedillo and his brothers, independent revolutionists in the state of San Luis Potosí, and then moved on north, the party growing smaller and smaller. Late in May, Gutiérrez, quartered in the village of Ciénega del Toro, Nuevo León, addressed a letter to Robles and Aguirre Benavides, most faithful of his retinue. He discharged them from the posts of secretary and subsecretary of war which they had occupied in his cabinet, authorizing them to act in whatever way their honor might dictate in the growing civil war (both of them later would die before firing squads). Then he composed another manifesto, lamenting the desertion of his followers—"some for want of valor and others for political convenience"—and submitting his resignation "to the Mexican people since I cannot submit it to the Convention, which has disintegrated."

But the Convention had not disintegrated immediately upon Gutiérrez' departure from the capital. Roque González Garza, the presiding officer of the Convention, assumed temporarily the role of acting executive officer of the nation—he objected to being identified as provisional president. He was only twenty-nine years old. He reappointed Villa and Zapata to the commands from which Gutiérrez had removed them. The Convention, or what was left of it, was predominantly Zapatista in character. Zapatista delegates—particularly Antonio Díaz Soto y Gama whose oratory had been so disruptive at Aguascalientes—were as capricious and flighty as their leader was direct and simple. What if Obregón was only a day's march away from the capital? The Convention debated the advantages of a parliamentary system of government for Mexico. What if the people of the capital were starving? What if telephone workers, tramcar drivers, and textile workers were on strike? The Convention listened to long harangues on Danton, Marat, Robespierre, Mirabeau, Kropotkin, Marx, and Bakunin. There was much confusion. When the secretary asked those voting affirmatively on a resolution to stand, everyone stood. When those opposed were asked to stand, everyone stood again.

On January 25 González Garza tried to bring the Convention to a realization of the gravity of the situation. Guadalajara, which the Villistas had taken and held briefly, had been recaptured by Carrancista forces under Diéguez and Murguía. The Villistas' greatest strength was far away in the North, where Angeles held parts of Coahuila and Nuevo León. The Zapatistas informed González Garza that everything was going well on their front but it was not true. Obregón was moving on Mexico City from Puebla, meeting almost no resistance from Zapata's men. González Garza had asked Villa for troops to protect the capital, but Villa could not spare them. Various generals were rebelling against the authority of the Convention. The state of affairs was, in short, disastrous. The enemy, González Garza told the Convention, "advances, advances, advances."

CHAPTER 31

CONVENTION'S END

> " 'What moves us is what men call
> ideals; our action is what men call fighting
> for a principle.'
> " 'Yes . . . yes . . .' said Venancio.
> " 'Hey there, Pancracio,' Macias called,
> 'pull down two more beers.' "
>
> Mariano Azuela, *The Underdogs*

ON THE DAY AFTER González Garza's grim warning of the advancing enemy the Convention government decided to abandon Mexico City and transfer its headquarters to Cuernavaca. By the next day the city was once more a no-man's land, paralyzed, silent, hungry. Government offices were empty, businesses closed.

The retreating Zapatistas had wrecked the pumping machinery at Xochimilco, the city's principal source of water. Crowds of people with clay pots and bottles thronged around those public water taps that still trickled; the few trading stalls still open in the public market were rushed by starving people. No tramcars, no carriages, no automobiles moved through the streets—only the clouds of dust swept in by the chilly, dry-season wind. Men with axes attacked the beautiful trees along the Paseo de la Reforma and in Chapultepec Park, seeking firewood.

On January 28 Obregón and his army entered a dead city. In the Zócalo a few random shots were fired at him from the cathedral bell tower as he rode in at the head of his marching column. Otherwise there was no resistance. Obregón, instead of celebrating his second triumphant entry into the capital, retired to a room in the Hotel St. Francis and nursed a case of laryngitis.

It was the first of a series of bewildering shifts in control of Mexico City. Six weeks later Obregón and his men left again, in search of Villa. The Convention and the supporting Zapatista troops moved back into the city. Four months later Pablo González and his troops came to claim the city again for Carranza. The Zapatistas retreated to the south. A week later González, alarmed by a daring Villista raid led by Rodolfo Fierro, evacuated the city and the Zapatistas came back. In one five day period the Zapatistas occupied the city three times, only to leave again. A fort-night later, with Fierro no longer a threat, González returned to the capital and the Zapatistas and the Convention left for the last time.

It was a time of anarchy and uncertainty. Mexico had four govern-ments simultaneously: Carranza in Veracruz; the Convention shuttling between Mexico City and Cuernavaca; Eulalio Gutiérrez with his diminished following (and most of the national treasury) wandering from village to village in northeastern Mexico; and a separate civil administration set up by Villa in Chihuahua. There was no mail in the capital, no commercial telegraph, no cables to and from abroad except those that the Carrancistas permitted to pass through the cable head at Veracruz. Generals communicated with one another by the railway telegraph system which they controlled, but the public at large hardly knew what was going on in the country. Newspapers were of little help. Military reverses were reported as victories or, more often, not reported at all. The few papers which attempted to report the news were closed; others were suspended for such minor offenses as reporting the rocketing prices of corn and beans. Surviving newspapers played it safe by printing long non-controversial articles on trachoma, the physiology of sleep, and how cats see in the dark.

With each shift in control of the capital there was monetary chaos; the currency of the former occupants would be declared illegal. Mer-chants found it easier to shut up business entirely. The poor, as usual, bore the heaviest burden. Even the lucky ones who received wages would be paid one day with money which would be valueless the next. Supplies of food for the capital were cut off and the little food available was exorbitantly priced.

Rats were trapped for food and crowds swarmed around slaughter-houses, begging for offal. One hungry woman was killed and another wounded by nervous storekeepers fearing mob violence. Children were trampled to death in crowds. Corpses of those who had collapsed and died in the streets from hunger or disease were collected in delivery wagons and taken to the Panteón Dolores for mass cremation. Signs appeared in the windows of mansions offering to trade pianos, furniture, and clothing for food. The stench of unflushed drains was everywhere. There were epidemics of smallpox and typhus. For years afterward 1915 was to be described as "the year of hunger"; one of the theatrical pro-ductions of the year in Mexico City was *His Majesty, Hunger*.

For residents of Mexico City the entire year of 1915 was one of hardship, misery and, frequently, horror. But perhaps the bitterest part of it was the six-week occupation by Alvaro Obregón and his troops in the late winter. Obregón, with Carranza's firm backing, seemed determined to humble the city and its inhabitants. His self-esteem as "the invincible general" had been hurt by his withdrawal from the capital a few months earlier. He may have held the *capitalinos* responsible; it was well known that they had regarded occupation by the Zapatistas as a welcome change after the harshness of Obregón and his Constitutionalists. Or it may have been that he hoped, by making civilian life unbearable, to stimulate recruitment in his army. His efforts to alleviate suffering in the capital were minimal. Small amounts of Constitutional currency were doled out to the poor. But food, needed more than money, was seldom obtainable at any price.

When the foreign colony of Mexico City formed a relief committee and purchased food in rural areas to relieve distress in the capital, Obregón refused to provide railroad trains to haul it into the city, although cars and locomotives were standing idle. Appeals to Carranza in Veracruz did no good. Food products from the rich Gulf Coast were being exported to pay for arms. When foreign agencies shipped food into Veracruz, intending it for the starving people of Mexico City, the cargoes were confiscated by the Carrancistas. Carranza sent missions to Mexico City to strip government offices and move all furniture and equipment to his temporary capital; schools were closed and the teachers ordered to migrate to Veracruz. Carranza decreed that Mexico City was no longer the national capital but was only the capital of a newly created "State of the Valley." He hoped to force diplomats to transfer their chancelleries to the port city. The diplomats made no such move, but continued to report to their governments the alarming actions of Obregón.

Merchants were forced at gunpoint to open their safes and deliver their contents to the occupying forces. Those suspected of hoarding food were made to sweep the streets. Members of the Catholic clergy—whom Obregón accused of having donated 40,000,000 pesos to the Huerta regime—were ordered to raise 500,000 pesos for relief of the poor. When the priests complained that they were as short of money as everyone else, 168 of them were imprisoned. Churches were sacked. Obregón seemed to be inviting violence. If his own children were starving, he said, he would take a knife in his hand and go out in the streets to obtain food any way that he could. If hunger riots broke out, he warned, he would never turn his guns on the starving poor. He would, instead, abandon the city, which was of no military importance anyway, and leave it to the mercy of the mobs. On March 10 he finally evacuated the capital—

after stripping the hospitals of bedding and surgical supplies. He headed north for the inevitable showdown battle with Villa.

The Convention government returned to Mexico City from Cuernavaca. As before, the people were glad to see the *sombrerudos,* the big-hatted men of the South, simpler, gentler, more pious and more considerate than the Constitutionalists. Repairs were made on the pumping system at Xochimilco so that the city could have water again. With the roads no longer blockaded by Zapatista patrols supplies of food began to trickle into the capital. There were distributions of free corn for the poor. When a crowd of impatient, hungry women stormed into a meeting of the Convention, the delegates dug into their own pockets to make up a relief fund (but to avoid a recurrence they did not meet the next day).

If the Convention's mood was benign its performance as a governing body was erratic and inept. It was trying to draft a "program of government" to serve as a socio-political charter for the Revolution, a comprehensive definition of goals and procedures. But progress toward this end was constantly interrupted by growing friction between the Villistas and the Zapatistas.

Although the presiding officer—and acting President of Mexico—Roque González Garza, and a few other key figures were Villistas, a majority of the Convention members left in the capital were Zapatistas. The cordial relations that prevailed at the Xochimilco meeting between Zapata and Villa had all but disappeared. The Villistas had become increasingly critical of the Zapatistas for their failure to attack the Carrancistas in Veracruz and Puebla; now the Zapatistas were again dragging their feet. Although the Villistas urged them to attack Obregón's rear and cut his communications with Veracruz, they did little more than harass the enemy. The Zapatistas on the other hand complained that the Villistas were not providing them adequately with either arms or money—despite the fact that González Garza's meager treasury had been depleted by demands from Zapatista leaders. Rail traffic around the capital was paralyzed by Zapatista chieftains who claimed locomotives and trains as their property and used them for personal transportation. Trusted Zapata henchmen were put into key governmental posts without the consent of and in some cases in spite of the opposition of González Garza who supposedly, as president of the Convention, held executive power. Zapatista orators—particularly the explosive Díaz Soto y Gama —disrupted debates with harangues, denunciations, and pointless discussions of such trivia as the etymology of the word boycott. At one point Villista delegates tried to get the Convention to order a sanity test for Díaz Soto y Gama. They were unsuccessful.

González Garza tried to keep the Convention on an even and productive course. Urged by Villa, he demanded that the Zapatistas take more aggressive military action against the Constitutionalists but only succeeded in stirring up more wrangling. Villa suggested that if the Zapatistas could do nothing against the Constitutionalists militarily the Convention should move its headquarters to either Torreón or Chihuahua where it could be protected by Villista forces. More quarrels ensued. A drunken Zapatista general, Antonio Barona, carousing in the Degollado dance hall, killed a Villista general and Convention delegate, Francisco Estrada. A street fight followed in which more than forty people died. The Zapatista delegates circumvented any disciplinary action by the Convention against Barona. The killing had no political significance, they said, and therefore should be regarded as a meaningless prank.

One of González Garza's most troublesome problems was with Manuel Palafox, whom Zapata had ordered installed as Minister of Agriculture. In this position he could speed the expropriation and division of land, a matter close to Zapata's heart. Instead Palafox, in the manner of so many revolutionists, was enriching himself. When Palafox demanded funds to pay an old bill for uniforms, González Garza, suspecting a *mordida* ("bite"), refused to pay it. Palafox behaved in a menacing fashion and relations between the Villistas and Zapatistas became further strained.

González Garza finally had a showdown with Zapata, who stubbornly insisted that Palafox, insubordinate or not, be kept in his post. Zapata, in a belligerent mood, told González Garza that he was moving from Cuernavaca to Mexico City with all his troops. González Garza, with only a single companion, rode out to meet Zapata at a halfway point. Zapata was drinking and threatened González Garza with his pistol. González Garza stood his ground, insisting that his authority was superior to Zapata's. Finally Zapata agreed to accompany González Garza to the National Palace for further talk. Either because of Zapata's continued drinking or because there was no hope of agreement, the discussion at the National Palace was brief. Zapata rode his horse onto a platform car of the city tramlines which delivered him to Xochimilco. From there he rode over the mountains into Morelos and never again came back to the city.

Nor was the Convention itself to remain much longer in the capital. It was hopelessly divided, bankrupt, and completely unable to cope with the critical food shortages. On June 9 González Garza—who had offered earlier to resign—was voted out of office and replaced by his secretary, Francisco Lagos Cházaro. González Garza gladly went off to fight the Constitutionalist forces of González, which was simpler than fighting his supposed allies.

Lagos Cházaro pledged himself to work for unity and understanding between the Villistas and the Zapatistas. An agreeable and honorable man whose forehead was always creased with worry, he was even less able than González Garza to make the ill-fated Convention function. With Carrancista forces approaching, the Convention held its final Mexico City sessions in July. Then the delegates dispersed. Some of the Zapatista delegates resumed sessions in Cuernavaca; when the Constitutionalists drove them out of Cuernavaca they moved on to the village of Jojutla where the group finally dissolved. Other Conventionists, including the Villistas, moved to Toluca where they continued to work on the Convention's program of government. The program, later adopted and somewhat modified by the Zapatistas, was ambitious and more thorough than anything since the Magonistas' 1906 program of the Liberal party. It called for the destruction of latifundia, creation of small landholdings for everyone who wanted them and return of land and water rights to dispossessed villages; agriculture was to be stimulated with irrigation, roads, agricultural schools and experiment stations and loan facilities for farmers. Mineral exploitation was to be controlled, monopolies banned, and railroad rates standardized. The federal senate and the vice-presidency were to be suppressed and the national government would be parliamentary in form. The judiciary was to be independent. Free public school facilities were to be expanded, more teachers trained and religious control of education abolished. There would be a divorce law and protection for natural children and unwed mothers. The welfare of labor was to be protected by law and the right to organize, strike, and boycott guaranteed. Enemies of the Revolution were to be punished by seizure of their property.

This document, completed on September 27, 1915, almost disappeared in the revolutionary turmoil. In 1916 four former members of the Convention, by then in exile, laboriously reproduced fifty typewritten copies—the only relic of the idealistic Convention.

The Toluca Convention had, by then, long since ceased to exist. Weakened by internal strife and increasingly pressed by Constitutionalist forces, the group finally disbanded. Lagos Cházaro and a few faithful followers fled, going first to the village of Ixtlahuaca in the state of Mexico, then into the state of Hidalgo, through the Huastecas region. Overtaken by Constitutionalists at Gruñidora, Zacatecas, the last members of the group were dispersed. Lagos Cházaro made his way through the mountains to the Pacific Coast and embarked for Central American exile.

General Benjamín Argumedo was not so lucky. Argumedo had been a Madero revolutionist, had fought for Huerta at the Battle of Zacatecas, had later joined Zapata, who was so impressed with his military skills that he refused to turn him over to Villa for execution. He allied himself with the Convention and remained faithful to it to the end, then vanished supposedly carrying 125,000 pesos in gold, the last resources of the Convention government. He made his way to a ranch in the Sierra of Durango, hoping to join Villa, his one-time enemy. A Villista general, Juan B. Vargas, found him there and urged him to come with him to Villa headquarters. Argumedo wanted to but was too ill to mount a horse. He would have to stay, he told Vargas, and he knew he would be both captured and killed by the Carrancistas. "I was one of the first whom Carranza, the Governor of Coahuila, tried to persuade to rebel against President Madero," he told Vargas. "My refusal to do so made me an enemy, and Señor Carranza will neither forget nor forgive." He had fought for Huerta, he said, because as a loyal Maderista he could not serve Carranza.

True to his own prediction Argumedo was captured somewhat later by General Murguía. Murguía received instructions from Carranza by telegram to try Argumedo before a military tribunal. This was done and Argumedo was sentenced to death. Murguía, who respected Argumedo for his military ability and admired his bravery, interceded with Carranza for mercy despite Argumedo's insistence that such an effort was useless. Carranza's response was brief. Shoot him at once. On March 1, 1916, Argumedo took his stand against a wall and gave orders to the firing squad: "I am ready boys, fire!" The 125,000 pesos in gold, if it ever existed, was never found.

Another revolutionary soldier whose career and loyalty was almost as checkered as Argumedo's was Juan Andrew Almazán, who had been a Maderista, an anti-Maderista, a Huertista, a Zapatista, and was, in 1915, fighting for the Convention against the advancing Carrancista forces. On his birthday, June 24, a fiesta was arranged at his encampment east of Mexico City between Chapingo and Texcoco. Scarce foods and liquors were collected and an open-air banquet was spread under the big trees. María Conesa, a flashy and colorful singer from Valencia— and a favorite of Almazán's—was brought out from Mexico City to perform for the general; she not only sang for the general but presented him with a shawl from Jerez to protect him from the chill while sleeping in the open.

After much eating and drinking Almazán and some of his staff made a tour of their forward positions—within a few hundred yards of the Carrancista troops under the command of General Francisco Coss. In the dark someone shouted a challenge, *"Quien vive?"* From Coss's side came a chorus. "Venustiano Carranza." And Almazán and his men roared back "the sovereign Convention." But there was no firefight. Instead, soldiers on both sides began singing together, the

haunting songs of the Revolution, full of longing, love, and death—
songs they had sung together before the Revolution divided and turned
them into enemies. They sang *Adelita:*

> "I'm a soldier and my nation calls me
> To fight in the fields of strife.
> Adelita, Adelita of my soul,
> For the love of God do not forget me.
> If Adelita left me for another,
> I would pursue her endlessly,
> In a warship if she went by ocean,
> In a military train by land."

and *Valentina:*

> "If today I drink tequila,
> Beer and Spanish sherry;
> If today you see me sodden,
> Tomorrow I'll be dead.
> Valentina, Valentina,
> I ask you just this once—
> If they shoot me tomorrow,
> I pray you, come and claim me."

CHAPTER 32

VILLA'S DECLINE

> "We are seduced by death . . . Death revenges us against life, strips it of all its vanities and pretensions and converts it into what it really is: a few neat bones and a dreadful grimace."
>
> Octavio Paz, *The Labyrinth of Solitude.*

BY THE SPRING of 1915 Francisco Villa had virtually divorced himself from the luckless Convention and was functioning as an independent warlord, ranging over most of northern and much of central Mexico. He was accountable to nobody. He ran his army and his civil government in Chihuahua as he saw fit. There was no longer anyone to approve—or disapprove—of his actions. More and more he disregarded the counsel of Felipe Angeles whose advice had been so valuable to him in the past. There was no point in coordinating his campaigns with Zapata who seemed both disinterested in and incapable of a sustained military drive.

Villa had taken Guadalajara effortlessly in December 1914, but the men he left in charge were unable to hold it. Villa had to come back and fight for it, only to lose it again—and meanwhile he had to deploy his forces all the way from Jalisco to the U.S. border.

In April 1915 he was at the railway junction of Irapuato preparing to meet and—he hoped—crush Obregón who, leaving Mexico City unoccupied, had advanced to Celaya, a little more than thirty miles to the east of Irapuato.

Angeles, who was in Torreón recovering from an injury suffered when his horse fell with him, urged Villa to be cautious. Villa was dividing his forces. Angeles wanted him, instead, to concentrate all his troops in Irapuato and wait for Obregón to attack. Obregón would be farther from his supply base, Veracruz, and Villa would be that much closer to his own—and he was already short on ammunition. Angeles insisted that Zapata—whose troops once more controlled Mexico City—should attack Obregón's rear and cut off his supplies and his communications with Carranza. As usual the Zapatistas—aside from a few exercises in harassment—did nothing.

Villa ignored Angeles' advice. He was confident that the sort of tactics he liked best, "the tremendous blow" as he called it, would work again. He would, he thought, capture enough ammunition from Obregón to replenish his own stores. Angeles shrugged and said *"No hay remedio"* ("It can't be helped") and confided to an aide that the day on which Francisco Villa suffered a severe defeat in the field would be the beginning of the end for the great Division of the North.

Obregón, in Celaya, was pursuing the sort of tactics Angeles had urged on Villa. He carefully guarded his supply lines and sent a stream of messages to Carranza in Veracruz to keep ammunition and reinforcements coming. He had ignored Carranza's pedantic advice to study the campaigns of Caesar, Scipio, Frederick the Great, and Napoleon, but he had studied the reports of the great war now being waged in Europe. He had learned, for instance, that mass attacks can be withstood by an army which, well protected by trenches and barbed wire, waits for the enemy to move. The plain of Celaya was well-suited to his purpose. Broad and level and planted to wheat, it afforded excellent visibility in all directions; it also was crisscrossed with irrigation and drainage ditches which could be converted into trenches.

Villa, having sent part of his forces westward into Jalisco against Diéguez and Murguía, had between 10,000 and 12,000 men for the coming clash. He scorned defensive tactics. He urged his brother Hipólito, in Ciudad Juárez, to rush more ammunition to him. Without waiting for it, he formed his infantry and cavalry into a massive force and launched a furious offensive on April 6.

Despite murderous fire from machine-gun emplacements and entrenched infantry Villa's forces, fighting all through the night, advanced into the center of Celaya on the 7th and even rang the church bells in victory. But Obregón's troops reformed and drove the Villistas back with heavy losses on both sides. By the evening of the 7th Villa had withdrawn to Irapuato, disorganized and disheartened but not, as yet, completely beaten; but Obregón, also weakened, was unable to force a decision.

Villa recalled his troops from Jalisco to strengthen his striking force in Irapuato; he sent more urgent messages to Hipólito in Juárez for ammunition. And he sent a message to the foreign consuls in Celaya suggesting that they urge Obregón to come outside the city and fight, thus sparing the non-combatant population. Obregón told the consuls that he considered the intervention of foreigners in a purely Mexican affair unnecessary. When Villa attempted to speak with him by telephone Obregón answered with an obscenity.

On April 13 Villa launched his second attack. He had less than half the artillery he had counted on and most of his artillery shells were defective, useful only at dangerously close range. He had more troops than he had had for the first attack, but his soldiers had only eighteen cartridges apiece, scant supplies for what was to be one of the bitterest battles of the Revolution. Obregón, meanwhile, was receiving trainloads of ammunition from Veracruz. Villa sent charge after charge against Obregón's strongly entrenched infantry west of Celaya. Foot soldiers died in the barbed wire. Obregón's Yaquis disemboweled cavalry horses that attempted to jump their trenches and then used the same bayonets on the dismounted horsemen. The green of the wheatfields turned to red.

Villa was in the midst of the fighting, shouting orders to regroup his units: "Form up, lads, form up my little boys, form up or they will kill you, the sons of bitches!" The struggle went on around the clock, in darkness and in light, with enormous casualties. At the end of twenty-four horror-filled hours the Villistas broke into disorganized retreat. Soldiers threw away their rifles and artillerymen abandoned their fieldpieces.

Villa admitted he had lost 6000 men. Others estimated Villa's losses at 4000 dead and 8000 captured. Obregón, in his official report (in which he referred to "Doroteo Arango, alias Francisco Villa, and his so-called generals"), said that Villa had begun the second battle with 30,000 men and had lost 14,000. Some three hundred captured Villista officers were penned in a goat corral at Celaya and cut down with machine-gun fire; the heaped bodies were then soaked with gasoline and burned. Obregón, not normally given to picturesque behavior, had his photograph taken wearing a full beard and a colorful charro costume.

News of Villa's disastrous defeat was suppressed by the Convention government in Mexico City and by Villa's local government in Chihuahua. A month later Sylvestre Terrazas, Villa's Secretary of Government, sent a message to Villa's confidential agent, in Washington, claiming Celaya had been a glorious victory for Villa, that Obregón's troops, driven by Villa's cavalry, were fleeing toward the south where they would be overwhelmed by the Zapatistas.

Villa retreated to Aguascalientes to reorganize his forces. Felipe Angeles, still on crutches, joined him there and asked what had happened. "They stoned us," said Villa. "I would rather have been beaten by a Chinaman than by that *perfumado,* Obregón." And he told Angeles of his plan to move his troops to León, halfway back to Celaya, for a showdown with Obregón. He urged Angeles to take command of the León operation, leaving Villa free for front-line combat. Angeles objected. Villa's ammunition was still critically short. León would be difficult to defend against a strong, well-equipped enemy. It would be better, he thought, for Villa to retreat toward Chihuahua, destroying rail lines as he went, reorganize and reequip his forces in Chihuahua and then move into the northwestern state of Sonora for a campaign toward the south—in effect an entirely new campaign.

But Villa was still supremely confident and eager for revenge; once more he disregarded Angeles' advice and prepared for another battle.

The battle of León was to last forty days. The Villistas adopted some of Obregón's methods, such as entrenchments, and added some new ones of their own including hand grenades and reconnaissance by airplane (the latter was not successful; the low-flying plane was damaged by rifle fire and crashed). The troops of both sides were miserable. The heat was oppressive. Clouds of green flies buzzed around the wounded and the dead, hordes of rats gorged themselves on the corpses, while the living were infested with lice as large as grains of rice.

Villa planned and executed a spectacular maneuver. He led a cavalry force out of León, through the hills, moving toward the east and seizing the town of Silao where he could cut Obregón's rail communication with the east. For a time Obregón's forces were virtually surrounded. A shell shattered Obregón's right arm and Obregón, crazed with pain, tried to commit suicide with an unloaded pistol.* Temporary command of Obregón's army passed to General Benjamín Hill.

Two days later the Carrancista troops broke through Villa's lines, stretched thin because of his daring move toward Silao, and took León. Again the Villistas were forced to retreat in disorderly fashion. Villa had gone into the battle with a slight numerical superiority—19,500

* In his memoirs Obregón wrote: 'With my remaining hand I took my small pistol from my belt and discharged it against my left breast, hoping to finish the work the shrapnel had begun. But my intention was frustrated since the pistol had no shell in the chamber, my aide, Captain Valdes, having cleaned it the day before. Colonel Garza rushed to me and seized the pistol . . ." Obregón, with grisly humor, later invented a story of how the missing forearm and hand were found. An aide, he said, walked through the piles of dead and broken bodies on the battlefield holding out a ten-peso gold piece. Obregón's hand reached up to grasp the gold piece and was thus recovered. Actually the forearm was amputated on an impromptu operating table by a field surgeon, General Enrique Osornio Camarena, and was preserved in a jar of alcohol. General Osornio Camarena tried several times, unsuccessfully, to present the pickled memento to the Mexican nation. Finally in 1943 President Manuel Avila Camacho accepted it and the relic was placed in the Obregón monument in Coyoacán.

cavalry and 6000 infantry to Obregón's 9400 cavalry and 14,300 infantry. Again he suffered heavy losses—approximately 8000 men. Obregón losses were about one-third of that.

Angeles' prediction that a major battlefield defeat would mean the end of the Division of the North seemed to be coming true. After Celaya and León, Villa withdrew to Aguascalientes. Here he was defeated again and he retreated to Zacatecas, scene of one of his greatest and bloodiest victories. Here he was beaten again. He pulled back to Torreón, which he had won twice before, changing the whole course of the Revolution. Finally he was forced to leave Torreón and return to Chihuahua.

The only variation in the pattern of defeat was when Rodolfo Fierro, Villa's trusted killer, took 4000 cavalry troops and staged a daring raid that carried him almost back to Mexico City.

Fierro sent a telegram over Obregón's signature to the commandant of the Carrancista garrison in León, ordering him to withdraw. Fierro and his troops occupied the town, scene of their recent defeat, without firing a shot. Then with lightning thrusts he moved to the east and south, from León to Irapuato, Silao, Salamanca, Celaya, Querétaro, San Juan del Rio, and finally to Tula, where he destroyed a garrison of 1500 Carrancista troops and was within easy striking distance of the capital. He had torn up the rails of the Central Railroad as he came— so that Obregón's troops in the center of the country could receive supplies only through the seaport of Tampico—which had withstood a Villista attack.

Fierro's drive caused such consternation that Pablo González evacuated his troops from Mexico City. Fierro was joined by troops commanded by González Garza, the recently deposed president of the Convention. But their combined force was too small for an attempt on the capital. Since Fierro's principal purpose, destruction of the railroad, had been achieved, they began to retreat the way they had come. On July 30 they were met by Obregón's troops at Jerécuaro, southeast of Celaya, and badly beaten. Fierro and González Garza, with only a thousand men left, worked their way north to join Villa, having achieved little more than a temporary disruption of Obregón's communications and supply lines. Villa meanwhile was receiving word of other military reverses—in Nuevo León, in Tamaulipas (with its oilfields), in Coahuila (with its coal fields), in San Luis Potosí, in Durango.

The epic struggles between Villistas and Carrancistas made 1915 one of the bloodiest and most disastrous years in Mexico's history—the worst, perhaps, since the Conquest, four centuries before. But in the Conquest there had been a clash of alien peoples and cultures—a few Europeans against a multitude of Indians, Christians against non-Christians, firearms against sticks and sharpened stones. In 1915 there was a parity of numbers, of weapons, even of belief. Both sides believed in the Revolution, in land for peasants, protection for workers, schools for children, and curtailment of the powers of wealth and privilege. On only one thing did they disagree: the leadership and authority of Venustiano Carranza. Because of this Mexicans died by the tens of thousands at Celaya, León, Aguascalientes, Zacatecas, and scores of lesser battles during that sorrowful spring and summer.

Disastrous as were the defeats Villa suffered on various battlefields, the most damaging blow was to come on the diplomatic front and from a country whose favor he had courted: the United States.

Until the summer of 1915 Villa had enjoyed reasonably cordial relations with the United States, due largely to the efforts of Special Agent George Carothers and General Hugh L. Scott. Both Carothers and Scott had treated Villa with consideration. As a result they had been able to get him to moderate his behavior on many occasions and both had obtained from him concessions to U.S. interests unobtainable from any other revolutionary leader. For a time it appeared that if the United States extended recognition to any of the warring factions in Mexico it would be to the one headed by Villa.

But the United States' course in relations with Mexico had been uncertain, and the need for a fixed policy was becoming more pressing in view of the growing European war. By June 1915 it was clear that the Villistas were no longer the dominant military force, and that the Carrancistas, under the generalship of Obregón, were. Frightful stories in the U.S. press about the devastating civil war and the pitiful state of the civilian population—starving, dying of disease, and hopeless —made it apparent that Woodrow Wilson's "watchful waiting" was not enough.

On June 2, 1915, President Wilson addressed a message to all factions of the Mexican struggle. The tone was sympathetic—but it also appeared to threaten intervention if the Mexicans could not somehow work out their own salvation. "For more than two years," it read, "revolutionary conditions have existed in Mexico . . . The leaders of the Revolution, in the very hour of their success, have disagreed and turned their arms against one another . . . unable or unwilling to cooperate . . . Mexico is apparently no nearer a solution of her tragical troubles than she was when the Revolution was first kindled. And she has been swept by civil war as if by fire. Her crops are destroyed, her fields lie unseeded, her work cattle are confiscated for the use of the armed factions, her people flee to the mountains to escape being drawn into unavailing bloodshed, and no man seems to see or lead the way to peace and settled order . . . Mexico is starving and without a government . . . The United States cannot stand indifferently by and do nothing to serve their neighbor. They want nothing for themselves in Mexico. Least of all do they desire to settle her affairs for her, or claim any right to do so. But neither do they wish to see utter ruin come upon her . . . The government of the United States . . . must presently do what it has not hitherto done or felt at liberty to do, lend its active moral support to some man or group of men, if such may be found, who can rally the suffering people of Mexico to their support in an effort to ignore, if they cannot unite, the warring factions of the country, return to the constitution of the Republic so long in abeyance, and set up a government at Mexico City which the great powers of the world can recognize and deal with, a government with whom the program of the Revolution will be a business and not merely a platform . . . If [the factional leaders] cannot accommodate their differences and unite for this great purpose . . . this Government will be constrained to decide what means should be employed by the United States in order to help Mexico save herself and serve her people."

In response to Wilson's statement there was a flurry of messages— from Villa to the Convention government in Mexico City and to Carranza, from Roque González Garza of the Convention government to Carranza and Villa—all showing a disposition to negotiate and arrange an armistice to save the country from destruction and to avoid foreign intervention. Both Villa and González Garza also replied directly to Washington regarding Wilson's statement, indicating a cooperative attitude.

Carranza did not reply immediately. Instead, nine days after the Wilson statement, he published a "manifesto to the Mexican nation" in which he made a case for recognition of his Constitutional regime. He reiterated his old argument about the legality of his course of action and of his position and promised various reforms. But the most telling part of the manifesto was his claim that the Constitutionalists, because of their recent victories over Villa, now controlled seven-eighths of Mexico, that it had organized local government in twenty of the twenty-seven states, that it held all ports on the Gulf and Pacific coasts with the exception of Guaymas, and all ports of entry on the northern and southern frontiers except for Piedras Negras, Ciudad Juárez, and Nogales. In short, the Constitutionalists claimed to govern 13,000,000 of Mexico's 15,000,000 people.

Carranza's statistics might be wrong, but enough of the facts were on his side to make his claim impressive. Although he had previously declared Mexico City no longer the capital and of no military importance, he changed his mind. Knowing that Wilson's insistence on a settlement was in part based on his concern for the people in the stricken capital, Carranza ordered Pablo González to retake the city—which González did shortly afterward.

Early in August the new United States Secretary of State, Robert Lansing, summoned a meeting of Latin American diplomats to discuss the Mexican situation. As a result, on August 11 a message was sent to all factional leaders in Mexico, signed by Lansing and by the Washington-based diplomatic representatives of Brazil, Chile, Argentina, Bolivia, Uruguay, and Guatemala. The revolutionary leaders were urged to arrange a conference at a neutral location "far from the sound of cannon" and to take "the first steps necessary to the constitutional reconstruction of the country—and to issue the first and most essential of them all, the immediate call to general elections."

Villa, Zapata, and the Convention government responded immediately and favorably. The governor of the state of Oaxaca, which had officially declared itself no longer a part of the Mexican republic, offered his state as neutral ground for such a meeting.

A month later, on September 10, Carranza replied, rejecting "any conference with the chiefs of the rebel party." Nor could he, he said, "consent to a discussion of the domestic affairs of the republic by mediation or on the initiative of any foreign government whatever." He was, he said, at the head of an army of 150,000, and the strife was nearing its end. He would agree, he said, to a meeting with foreign representatives at one of the border towns which he controlled, to discuss recognition of his regime as a de facto government.

The strife was far from an end, and Carranza exaggerated his control of the country. Washington representatives of both Villa and the Convention attempted to point out to Secretary Lansing and the Lain American diplomats the fallacies in Carranza's claims and re-iterated their own eagerness to participate in any sort of mediation. But Lansing and his fellow conferees decided, on October 9, that a de facto government must be recognized and that only Carranza's regime was qualified for such recognition. Recognition of Carranza by the United States government followed on October 19; on the same date an embargo was placed on arms shipments from the United States to anti-Carrancista forces.

It was a crippling blow to Villa. Villa apparently had seen it coming. In Ciudad Juárez on October 8, the day before the decision, he had held a press conference.

"My own forces have recently been diminished," he said. "We haven't the men and haven't the money we once had. All the men who have made money out of our cause have left us . . . because they think no more money is to be made out of it. They have gone to other lands where they are living upon the profits which they accumulated by turning the patriots' agony and the widows' and orphans' sorrow into a means of making money. My enemies will tell you that I made money out of the Revolution and I now have stored in banks in foreign countries a large personal fortune . . . a foul slander and a deliberate lie. If any man will tell me where that money is I will instantly write my check on that bank in his favor for the whole amount.*

"I am here in Juárez, but this is as far north as I shall go. Mexico is my country. I shall not run away from it. Here I have lived and here I have fought . . . Here also I shall die, and that probably soon, but I am content. They may kill me in battle or murder me on the highway or assassinate me in my bed, but the cause I have fought for for twenty-two years will live . . . the cause of liberty, of human freedom, of justice . . . I care nothing for myself. I care only for my country, for the millions of poor, oppressed people with whom your great President, Mr. Wilson, recently said he had a passionate sympathy."

Of the possibility of recognition of Carranza, Villa said: "Carranza has no government. He has not even the form of government. He has no cabinet, no civil administration . . . The recognition of such a man and such a government . . . would not bring peace to Mexico. It would bring revolution after revolution, revolution in its worst form . . . To recognize Carranza is to invite anarchy in our country."

He told the interviewers that American lives and property had been respected in the territory under his control, although he conceded that there might have been "some irregularities—war is war." Carranza, he insisted, was "inconsiderate of American interests and insolent toward American authority." He referred to the U.S. government's efforts to get the dissident Mexican factions together for mediation: "Our faction and the Zapata faction gave prompt and complete compliance . . . [Carranza] alone stood in the way of honorable peace in Mexico . . . He alone defeated the suggestion of your honored President. Are we to believe that as a reward for his insolence he is now to be granted recognition?"

General Hugh L. Scott, who had had many dealings with Villa and

* There were rumors that Villa, operating through his brother Hipólito, his agent in Ciudad Juárez, had accumulated a fortune in El Paso and was continuing to sell stolen goods on the American side of the border for his personal benefit. Special Agent Zach Cobb, on October 16, 1915, wired the State Department from El Paso, mentioning Villa's commerce in stolen property and urging that "the port here should be closed outright . . . We must break up the band of commercial thieves operating here who are now the root of the Villa menace . . . and who if not broken up will be conspirators, ammunition smugglers, and managers of new revolts."

the other revolutionary leaders, commented that the decision favored "a man who had rewarded us with kicks on every occasion . . . making an outlaw of the man who had helped us."

It was a blow from which Villa would never fully recover. It was the climax of a year of disaster. Villa had seen his once-invincible Division of the North reduced to a defeated, disorganized, ill-disciplined band of marauders. The *compañeros* who had, under Villa's leadership, made the division great were melting away. Many were dead. Others had deserted or gone into exile. Felipe Angeles had left after the battle of León and gone to Washington to plead with the officials of the United States government; González Garza was there, too, and their efforts had come to nothing. Melitón Ortega had died on a Jalisco battlefield. Maclovio Herrera had been killed at Nuevo Laredo; he and Villa had become enemies but Villa still affectionately regarded him as one of his protégés. Two of his best generals, Eugenio Aguirre Benavides and José Isabel Robles, had deserted him for Eulalio Gutiérrez. Now Aguirre Benavides had been killed by the Carrancistas; Robles had escaped but had decided to join the enemy.

Tomás Urbina, Villa's companion of so many years, had run out of luck. He had failed utterly in his campaign against Jacinto B. Treviño at El Ebano. In a Villa-like gesture Urbina had sent a message to Treviño lamenting the loss of life on both sides and suggesting that they settle the issue in personal combat, just the two of them. When this failed he set fire to a tank full of asphalt which then ran flaming through Treviño's trenches. Even this did not save Urbina. He was forced back farther and farther until, finally, he abandoned his command. With a personal escort he retired to his hacienda, Las Nieves, in Durango, fortifying it and, supposedly, burying the treasure in gold and silver he had taken with him. There was a suspicion that he planned soon to go over to Carranza. In September, Villa with a mounted escort of two hundred men under the command of the trusted Fierro made a surprise attack on Las Nieves. There was a gunfight within the compound of the hacienda and Urbina was wounded. Villa helped him to his feet and the two old friends talked in private. Villa then issued orders for Urbina to be taken back to Chihuahua for hospitalization. Fierro objected; he reminded his chief that his orders had been to kill Urbina. Villa admitted that this was true and told Fierro to go ahead and shoot Urbina, which he did.

It was the last of Fierro's many executions. Although his bloodthirstiness was an occasional embarrassment to Villa (he had recently killed all his prisoners at Jalisco) he had remained a favorite through loyalty and steel-nerved bravery; his great cavalry raid toward Mexico City was only one of many exploits. He was the kind of man Villa understood and appreciated. Villa soon lost him, too. Ironically, Fierro's death was to involve neither gunfire nor courage. Shortly after his killing of Urbina, Fierro was marching toward Sonora with Villa's troops. Near Casas Grandes he became impatient with delays and took a short-cut across what appeared to be a dry lake bed. His horse became mired in quicksand. The horse sank out of sight, and Fierro, struggling to free himself from the stirrups, sank with him. It was said that one reason he could not escape was that his pockets were loaded with gold.

Villa's movement toward Sonora was in belated compliance with advice that Angeles had given him much earlier—to move into the Northwest, consolidate his forces with those of Maytorena, and then drive south again—in effect starting a new revolution. The advice might have been good when Angeles offered it, but now it was too late. Villa's own forces were greatly reduced. He had no more than 6000 men. This by itself was not the problem. He had, in 1913, entered Mexico with only eight men and increased his following to 30,000 or more. But his men were tired, poorly equipped, disheartened. Winter weather had come early and the crossing of the sierra was perilous and painful. On November 1, Villa reached Agua Prieta, held by General Plutarco Elías Calles. Villa had lost many men in the Sierra crossing and those who remained were ill, starved and nearly dead with fatigue. Calles' troops were fresh, and with reinforcements he had recently received—due to Carranza's recognition the reinforcements were permitted to come by rail on the U.S. side of the border—he had 6500 troops ready for combat. Villa made a poor showing against them; he lost about six hundred men either dead or wounded and another four hundred through desertion. Villa complained bitterly that during a night attack searchlights from the American side of the border had blinded the attacking forces and made them easy targets for Calles' fire. Villa moved on to the west, and then south toward the state capital of Hermosillo. Hermosillo was held by General Diéguez. Villa and Diéguez fought a damaging but inconclusive battle at Alamito on November 18. Then, on November 22, Villa launched a fierce, thirty-hour attack on Diéguez' troops in Hermosillo. Villa's troops were virtually wiped out. At the same time a young cavalry colonel, Lázaro Cárdenas, had inflicted a painful defeat on the Maytorena troops at Nogales, forcing the ex-governor, last of Villa's allies, to flee to the United States for safety.

Villa, having suffered losses of almost 90 percent, limped back toward the sierra and into Chihuahua. But Chihuahua was no longer safe. The border garrison of 4000 men at Ciudad Juárez had surrendered to the Carrancistas. Arriving back in Chihuahua City, Villa told the four-hundred-odd men who were still with him that they were at liberty to leave and do whatever they saw fit. One of those who left for exile was General José Delgado, a former federal officer whom Villa had put in charge of his currency factory (Villa's *bilimbiques,* which had been worth 60 cents U.S., were now worth only two cents). Villa went to bid Delgado farewell at the railroad station, and as a parting gift pressed on him a bundle of his own currency. Delgado thanked him. But as he opened his overcoat to put the currency in his pocket a torrent of gold coins spilled out of another pocket. Without saying a word Villa drew his pistol and shot him.

Villa addressed a formal statement to those officers who had, in various parts of Mexico, remained faithful to him. "Companions: Our struggle to recoup our losses has failed completely . . . effective proof that the people support Carranza, although erroneously. The nation needs peace, and I will not stand in the way. I want to go back into the sierra with only my escort . . . If, within six months, Carranza has not pacified the country and established a government, I will rise again, more fiercely than before. Meanwhile, do whatever you like. If at the end of this period there is no peace I hope you will again heed my call to arms. I give you sincere thanks and I wish you happiness."

On the day before Christmas, Villa and his small personal following disappeared from Chihuahua City. The United States had indicated that Villa could take refuge across the border if he complied with the laws. Villa did not answer. He was angry with the United States and eager to revenge what he considered an injustice.

No one knew exactly where Villa had gone and there were many rumors: that he had been killed, that he had gone insane, that he was planning an invasion of the state of Sinaloa, that he had gone into exile in Cuba.

By January 1, 1916, General Jacinto B. Treviño had occupied Chihuahua City for the Carrancistas and prepared a report on the Villistas who had laid down their arms: 44 generals, 347 chiefs, 3648 other officers, and 11,118 soldiers.

CHAPTER 33

HUERTA'S LAST VICTORY

> "Every moon, every year, every day,
> Every wind comes and goes
> And all blood reaches its final
> resting place."
>
> *Chilam Balam* (Mayan
> prophecies)

THE YEAR 1915, now closing, was a dividing point in the Revolution. The struggle which had begun as a rebellion against dictatorship and degenerated into a civil war had, for a time, ended. New characters were emerging, and the old ones were disappearing.

Porfirio Díaz, whose thirty-year rule brought Mexico's chronic ills to a wild and destructive climax, died peacefully in Paris in the summer of 1915. For days the old man—he was now eighty-four—had sat in the window of his apartment at No. 28 Avenue du Bois, staring out. When his wife and his son, Porfirito, spoke of the war in Europe and of the little they knew of conditions in Mexico the old man seemed to pay no attention. He would interrupt, feebly, with "What news is there of Oaxaca?" He would comment "In other years at this time the sugar cane was this high," and he would extend a trembling hand. When his body was entombed in the cemetery of Montparnasse it was accompanied by a crystal urn containing a handful of earth from his native Oaxaca.

It was also the last year in the turbulent life of Victoriano Huerta. But Huerta's end was not to be as tranquil as that of Díaz.

After fleeing Mexico on the German ship *Dresden,* Huerta had taken up residence in Barcelona. He found a cafe called the Colón, as was his favorite in Mexico City, and the waiter soon knew enough to bring him cognac without waiting for an order. But the cognac lacked savor and the old soldier brooded about ways to return to Mexico. Then, providentially, he was sought out by a German spy-saboteur, Captain Franz von Rintelen—who also went by the names of Gasche, Gibbons, and Hansen.

Rintelen promised German support if Huerta would return to Mexico and take control. It was a move that would benefit both parties. Huerta would again have power—and probably vengeance. For Germany it would mean distraction of American attention from the deepening European conflict—and might prevent America's entrance in it.

Early in April 1915, Rintelen arrived in New York. Ten days later Huerta followed. Huerta was on his best behavior. He avoided alcohol and in public took only soda water. He went to baseball games and to the theater. He was politely evasive in answering reporters' questions about the murder of Francisco Madero: "This is a professional secret. I am a soldier. Why can't soldiers have professional secrets?" But, he added, "I know that I was not to blame for Señor Madero's death. Time and history will justify me." He stayed, at first, in the Hotel Ansonia. Then, a few weeks later, his family arrived from Spain—thirty people including wife, children, grandchildren, in-laws, servants, governesses, tutors, and more than a hundred trunks. It took five automobiles to move just the people. After a night in the Ansonia they moved to the estate of Paul Lecroix at Forest Hills, Long Island, which Huerta had leased. Huerta posed for news photographers implausibly mowing the lawn, a typical householder.

Huerta the family man was also playing a furtive role. He attended a series of secret hotel room meetings with Rintelen and other German agents. Large sums of money were changing hands and orders for arms and ammunition were being placed. There were communications with Felix Díaz somewhere in Mexico and Pascual Orozco at El Paso, both eager to launch another counterrevolution.

The United States Department of Justice knew of the meetings and began to keep a close watch on Huerta as well as the German agents. On Thursday, June 24, Huerta and his large retinue closed the mansion at Forest Hills, leaving only one servant as custodian. Someone identified him when he stepped from his Pullman car to stretch his legs in Kansas City. He said he was going to visit the Panama-Pacific Exposition in San Francisco. On the 27th he again left his car, this time at a lonely station twenty miles north of the Mexican border at El Paso. Pascual Orozco was there to meet him with an automobile, ready to take him into Mexico. So were U.S. authorities from El Paso, accompanied by a squad of soldiers. Huerta and Orozco were arrested for violation of neutrality laws and taken to jail in El Paso.

El Paso was buzzing with conspiracy. Representatives of Felix Díaz had set up a junta in El Paso to cooperate with the Huerta movement.

A cousin of Pascual Orozco's said their movement had the backing of the Clerical party of Mexico. Exiled Mexicans were streaming into the border city from all directions. El Paso, which had been so close to the confusion and anarchy of post-Huerta Mexico, was to a large extent sympathetic with the tight-lipped old soldier. The mayor, Tom Lea, agreed to serve as his attorney.

Huerta was released on bond. But after Orozco jumped bail (subsequently to be shot by Texas Rangers) Huerta was rearrested. Because of the explosive feelings in El Paso, Huerta was removed to the U. S. Army post, Fort Bliss, where he was guarded by armed soldiers. There he fell ill. He was released to his family, living in a rented house in Stanton Street. The U.S. government wanted to avoid the embarrassment of having him die as a prisoner. He recovered and was taken back into custody. He became ill again and once more was released to his family. His ailment was variously diagnosed as poisoning, jaundice, gallstones, and cancer. Huerta received a sympathetic wire from the former American ambassador to Mexico, Henry Lane Wilson, expressing hope that his illness had not been caused by the treatment he had received from U.S. authorities. Wilson also expressed confidence that in time Huerta's "humane and sympathetic attitude" toward Americans would be brought to light. In the Stanton Street house he underwent surgery without anesthetic. On January 13, 1916, he died.

On the night of Huerta's death El Paso was tense—not because of Huerta but because of his old enemy, Francisco Villa. Fugitive Villistas had attacked a train at Santa Isabel, Chihuahua, and massacred the passengers. The bodies of sixteen American victims arrived in El Paso and a mob formed, carrying posters denouncing President Wilson and urging the public to Remember the Alamo. They were preparing to march into the Mexican section of the city with torches, guns, and knives when U.S. troops dispersed them.

The lives of Huerta and Villa had been intertwined for almost five years. Huerta's final conspiracy had brought about Villa's undoing without either of them quite realizing what was happening.

The United States government had known for months of Huerta's complicity with the German spy ring. In December U.S. authorities had let it be known that Germany had spent between $27,000,000 and $30,000,000 in the United States for sabotage, espionage, and conspiracy. Of this amount about $12,000,000 reportedly had been spent to mount a counterrevolution in Mexico which Huerta was to lead. Most of the money had gone for arms, but $800,000 was said to have been deposited to Huerta's account in Havana. Felix Díaz was to march from the south, Pascual Orozco was to subvert the border garrisons, and Huerta was to take command. The United States would be forced to intervene and would soon find itself fighting a German-supported enemy on its southern border. There were promises that German U-boats would unload additional supplies of arms on the Mexican coast.

Knowledge of this plot had been a key factor in U.S. recognition of Venustiano Carranza. Continuation of the civil war in Mexico could only facilitate the Huerta-German plot. One of the warring factions in Mexico must be granted recognition, helped and strengthened in order to avoid even more horrible chaos than before. So, the willingness of various revolutionary factions, and particularly of Villa, to cooperate in the idealistic President Wilson's hopes for achieving peace in Mexico, had to be ignored. Instead, recognition had to be extended to Carranza who had shown no inclination to cooperate, who had voiced strong resentment of foreigners meddling in Mexican affairs. At the moment, thanks to the battlefield achievements of Alvaro Obregón, Carranza had unquestioned military superiority in the war-ridden nation.

The strange twist of events was to turn Francisco Villa, an erstwhile friend, into an implacable enemy of the United States.

RECOGNITION

> "The best thing that can happen to one
> of those so-called [Latin American] re-
> publics is to get as soon as possible a dic-
> tator who will keep order . . ."
>
> Lord Bryce to Woodrow Wilson, 1913

ON OCTOBER 19, 1915, Venustiano Carranza was staying in the Hotel Salvador in Torreón when his director of telegraphs, Mario Méndez, handed him a wire from his Washington representative, Eliseo Arredondo. Arredondo informed the First Chief that U. S. Secretary of State Robert Lansing had announced the de facto recognition of the Carranza regime. Recognition was also being granted by Argentina, Bolivia, Brazil, Colombia, Guatemala, and Uruguay. The United States would, accordingly, exchange diplomatic representatives with Mexico and resume normal relations. More important, an arms embargo would be applied to anti-Carrancistas.

Carranza, showing more emotion than usual, read the telegram to his companions at the Hotel Salvador. But, quickly recovering his composure, he said only, "I expected it," and then retired for a siesta. Everything was working out as he had planned.

Less than a year before Carranza had come very close to political oblivion. His resignation—which he insisted he had never really offered —had been accepted. His Plan of Guadalupe, by which he set such store, had been rejected as useless. His great and powerful Constitutionalist army, which had ousted Huerta from power, had disintegrated and all but disappeared. He had set up his "capital" in Veracruz with his back to the sea, ready to retreat into exile if things got any worse—as they almost certainly would.

But then he began doing the right things. He placed Obregón in charge of the loyal remnants of the Constitutionalist army. Obregón, a genius at organization as well as strategy and tactics, quickly shaped them into a powerful and effective new army—smaller than before but well-armed. With this new army he swept inland—Puebla, Mexico City, and on to the whole series of shattering victories over Villa in central Mexico. Carranza had the wisdom not to interfere; he merely saw to it that Obregón had the supplies and reinforcements he needed.

Next he turned his attention to the shortcomings of the Plan of Guadalupe, the revolutionary agenda which he had always insisted was adequate but which obviously was not. The fervor with which not only the Zapatistas and the Villistas but even the more "respectable" elements of the Revolution embraced the need for land reform had finally broken through his conservative notions about land. The cry of *Tierra y Libertad* was a much more effective political weapon than the dull organizational prose of the Plan of Guadalupe. Whether he liked it or not Carranza was faced with political realities. Accordingly, soon after his arrival in Veracruz he issued a manifesto declaring that while the Plan of Guadalupe was still in effect and in accordance with it he would continue to serve as First Chief in charge of the executive power, he would soon, nevertheless, make some amendments to it. These amendments would, he said, "satisfy the economic, social, and political needs of the country," and would include "agrarian laws to encourage the creation of small landowners."

On January 6, 1915, he published his agrarian decree. It was the work of Luis Cabrera, who had long interested himself in the land problem. It also reflected the thought of Andrés Molina Enríquez, whose book, *The Great National Problems,* published in 1909, had thoroughly explored the agrarian question which had plagued Mexico for centuries. The Carranza decree did not attempt to solve the whole, complicated agrarian problem, but it made a start. It declared null alienation of Indian village communal lands or ejidos by local and state authorities dating back to 1856 and by federal authorities since 1876. Provision was made for Indian communities which had been thus deprived to reclaim enough land to reestablish their traditional ejidos. A national agrarian commission was to oversee these restitutions. Within four months General Cándido Aguilar, Governor of Veracruz (and Carranza's future son-in-law), had begun distributing land to peasants at Medellín, a village just to the south of Veracruz.

It was not the sort of thoroughgoing measure that would satisfy the radical *agraristas* but it was, nevertheless, a step that Carranza had previously been unwilling to take.

He also issued decrees governing the exploitation of natural resources, legalizing divorce, guaranteeing municipal freedom and "efficiency" of suffrage, promising minimum wages. He ordered that the San Juan Ulúa fortress no longer be used as a prison, and suppressed lotteries and bullfights. He also promised to summon a congress to which he would submit his decrees for ratification or amendment; the congress also would call a presidential election.

Having attended to military and political matters Carranza then turned his attention to diplomacy. Neither his nor any other revolutionary regime could hope for stability and control without diplomatic recognition. Since most of the world powers and the sister republics of Latin America would tend to follow the leadership of the United States, his greatest efforts were directed at Washington. There he had been represented by a series of confidential agents, the most recent and ablest being Eliseo Arredondo. But Arredondo was working under difficulties. The gravest of these was the dislike with which Carranza was regarded by President Woodrow Wilson and his Secretaries of State, first Bryan and later Lansing. Before his series of military disasters in 1915 Villa was more favored in Washington than was Carranza. But after Celaya it was clear that Villa no longer was in a position to control the country.

Aside from a few conciliatory gestures in the early phases of the Constitutionalist movement, Carranza had been unyielding in his attitude toward the United States—or at least he appeared to be. He voiced no support of the United States in its quarrel with his enemy Huerta, he opposed the occupation of Veracruz (as most Mexicans did) and he virtually ignored the efforts of the ABC mediators to solve the Mexican crisis. And in the spring of 1915 he seemed indifferent to Wilson's efforts to bring the various Mexican revolutionary factions together—although both Villa and González Garza were receptive.

Secretly, however, Carranza was pursuing an entirely different course aimed at coming to terms with the American President.

In February 1915, two months after he had set up his capital in Veracruz, Carranza sent three representatives on a confidential mission which he hoped would bring about U.S. recognition. The envoys—Jorge Orozco, the Carrancista consul in El Paso; Rafael Múzquiz, a nephew of the First Chief; and Roberto V. Pesqueira, who had served as Carranza's first confidential agent in Washington—traveled to California to confer with Richard H. Cole of Pasadena. Cole was widely acquainted in Mexico and also was said to have good connections in Washington. According to Cole he was asked to become Carranza's personal representative in the effort to come to terms with President Wilson. Financed by the Carrancistas, Cole enlisted the services of Richard Lee Metcalfe, who had recently served as civil governor of the Panama Canal Zone. Metcalfe also had for many years been a close associate of Secretary of State Bryan, serving both as his secretary and as editor of Bryan's newspaper, *The Commoner*. Metcalfe made a

trip to Veracruz for conference with Carranza and reported his findings
to Washington, where other pro-Carranza forces were being mobilized.
Among them were John Lind, the former governor of Minnesota who
had been President Wilson's personal envoy to Mexico during the Huerta
usurpation; Joseph Folk, former governor of Missouri; and Charles
Douglas, a Washington attorney retained by Carranza.

With information supplied by Metcalfe, Cole, and Arredondo, the
group drew up a declaration of Carranza's program and policies aimed
at convincing the United States government that Carranza alone, of all
the Mexican factions, was deserving of U.S. recognition and support.

A preliminary draft of the document was drawn up in Folk's office
on April 16, 1915. The date was significant. It was the day after Obregón
had decisively defeated Villa at Celaya; from this point on serious
consideration of Villa as the strongest figure in the Revolution declined.

The preliminary document was taken to Secretary Bryan who, in
turn, took it to President Wilson. The President studied it, suggested
certain changes, and the document was returned to Carranza's Washington strategists for revision. When these changes had been made the
document was sent to Carranza in Veracruz. Cole said receipt of the
document was acknowledged in a wire to him from Carranza: YOUR
ATTENTIVE MESSAGE RECEIVED. PROCLAMATION WILL BE ISSUED AT OPPORTUNE
TIME. I SALUTE YOU ATTENTIVELY.

On June 11, 1915, Carranza issued a "Manifesto to the Mexican
People" apparently based on the document drafted in Washington and
amended in accordance with President Wilson's suggestions. It complained that he and his movement had been misunderstood abroad because of misrepresentation in the United States press. It reviewed the
origin and course of the Constitutionalist movement and a legalistic justification for Carranza's assumption of the role of First Chief. More to
the point was the claim that he now controlled seven-eighths of Mexico.
Because of "the recent definite victories of our army" he was now in de
facto possession of the sovereignty of the country. There followed a series
of points intended to reassure foreign interests. Foreigners residing in
Mexico would have, under his regime, "all the guaranties to which
they are entitled" and would receive ample protection for "their lives,
their freedom and the enjoyment of the rights of property" as well as
"indemnities for the damage which the Revolution may have caused
them . . ." Carranza further promised that peace would be restored and
that "in due time amnesty would be declared." No one, he said, would
"suffer in his life, freedom and property because of his religious beliefs,"
and there would be "no confiscations in connection with the settlement
of the agrarian question."

The reassuring clarification of Carranza's position came at a time when the United States, increasingly involved in the European crisis and worried by Germany's efforts to inflame anti-U.S. feeling in Mexico, was eager for some sort of resolution of the chaos in Mexico. Secretary of State Lansing, who had succeeded Bryan on June 25, arranged a series of Washington meetings of Latin American diplomats to discuss the Mexican problem.

By October 11 Carranza felt sufficiently confident that he abandoned his base in Veracruz. He boarded the Mexican gunboat *Bravo* and sailed up the coast to Tampico. It was the beginning of a casual, aimless tour through the parts of Mexico that were firmly held by Constitutionalist forces—although he avoided Mexico City which was too vulnerable to raids by the Zapatista guerrilla fighters.

In Tampico, Carranza was greeted by Obregón, the man who had made it all possible. Beside the well-groomed Carranza and the smartly uniformed members of his staff, Obregón seemed shabby in his baggy trousers and his bulldog-toed shoes. Instead of a medal-laden military tunic he wore an old shawl-collared sweater with the empty right sleeve flapping in the wind. Often he wore his fedora backwards; he was not yet accustomed to doing things with his left hand.

The Carranza party moved slowly through north central and northeastern Mexico. After receiving word in Torreón of U.S. recognition, Carranza was interviewed by newspapermen. As usual there was confusion over Carranza's title. President? General? Carranza explained once more that he was the First Chief of the Constitutionalist army in charge of the Executive Power and would remain so during the "pre-constitutional" period. And, he said, he was also governor of the state of Coahuila—a peculiar addition since his term as governor had long since expired and he had appointed a trusted underling in his place. There was, he said, no law prohibiting his election to the presidency of Mexico. He did not know whether he would be a candidate for the office but might be if the public demanded it.

He acted very much like a candidate. Traveling most of the time on the presidential train he went from Torreón to Saltillo, to Piedras Negras, to Monclova, to his home town of Cuatro Ciénegas, to the hacienda of Guadalupe where his famous Plan had been formulated, to Monterrey and Nuevo Laredo where he met Texas Governor Jim Ferguson in the middle of the International Bridge, to San Luis Potosí. Sometimes he spoke on international matters (all nations were equal in the "universal concert"), sometimes on internal Mexican matters (he urged his supporters to follow him to the completion of the work they had begun). In the visitors' book at Dolores Hidalgo, the home of Father Hidalgo, he wrote a note in memory of the old priest who had launched the independence movement more than a century before: *"We will know how to preserve the independence of the nation in which you believed."*

The trip was leisurely and festive. Since there was no schedule he took time out to enjoy the thermal baths at Hermanas, Coahuila, and had a fortnight's vacation at the hacienda of Ciénega del Toro, property of friends. There were dances, concerts, banquets, picnics, and patriotic fiestas. His fifty-sixth birthday was celebrated aboard the presidential train on December 29. On the last day of the year he arrived in the pleasant old colonial city of Querétaro and announced that Querétaro would become both his residence and the capital of Mexico. Here Mexico's struggle against the French intervention had ended with the execution of the Emperor Maximilian on the nearby Hill of Bells. Now, Carranza said, Querétaro would "see the end of the greatest revolution in our history."

CHAPTER 35

COLUMBUS

"Villa was the incarnation of the virtues
and the defects of our people . . . He delivered himself to the Fatherland as he
was."

Roque González Garza

THE WORK OF RECONSTRUCTION which Carranza promised to undertake
in Querétaro was not to proceed in tranquillity, largely due to Carranza's old enemy, Villa. Villa had been beaten on the battlefield,
discredited in the world of diplomacy and officially declared an outlaw
in Mexico—to be shot on sight. But, like a wild animal which becomes
even more dangerous when wounded, he could—and did—cause infinite trouble. His depredations during 1916 cast serious doubts on the
extent to which Carranza controlled Mexico.

After his disappearance from Chihuahua in December 1915 Villa
returned to a life of banditry, stealing horses to ride, cattle to eat or
trade, and money to replenish his supply of arms and ammunition.
On January 10, 1916, some Villistas, led by Pablo López and Rafael
Castro, attacked a train near Santa Isabel, Chihuahua. The train
carried a party of American miners and engineers bound for the Cusi
mine; they had been assured in Chihuahua City by the newly installed
Carrancista governor that it was perfectly safe to travel to the mine.
The train was stopped, the passengers robbed and then sixteen of them
were lined up outside the train and shot. The robbery could be explained: Villa and his men needed money. The mass murder could
only be interpreted as an expression of Villa's fury against the United
States.

The same motive—revenge—may have played a part in the Villista
raid, two months later, on the border town of Columbus, New Mexico.
There were various explanations, none of them wholly logical. One

was that Villa was angry with the town's principal merchants, Sam and Louis Ravel, for non-delivery of arms for which he had paid. Another was that two of Carranza's advisers, Luis Cabrera and Roberto Pesqueira, were returning from Alvaro Obregón's Sonora wedding. They were due to pass through Columbus on the El Paso-bound train—and Villa hoped to capture them (he did not). Still another was that the U. S. 13th Cavalry was stationed at Columbus and had in abundance the things the Villistas needed—rifles, machine guns, ammunition, horses, mules, clothing, and food. Or it may have been that in both the Santa Isabel massacre and the Columbus raid Villa wished to demonstrate to the United States that Carranza, whom they had recognized, could not bring peace to Mexico.

Whatever the reason, Villa and 485 men crossed the lonely and lightly guarded border at a point several miles west of Columbus in the early morning hours of March 9. Villa, who once proudly rode at the head of his troops, had remained behind at the Santa Isabel massacre and he did the same at Columbus. The Villistas rode into the sleeping town shortly after 4 A.M., their hoofbeats muffled in the drifted sand. Then, with shouts of "Viva Villa" and "Viva Mexico" they attacked the 13th Cavalry encampment and set fire to some of the town's business establishments. The cavalrymen, completely surprised by the attack, retaliated at first in a confused and disorderly fashion. The raiders, meanwhile, looted without opposition, raiding stores, demanding money, and shooting civilians without provocation. By daybreak the Villistas had begun retreating across the border. They took with them more than a hundred of the 13th Cavalry's horses and mules along with a heavy load of rifles and machine guns—but they paid dearly for them. At least a hundred Villistas either were killed in the raid or died later from wounds. Eighteen Americans, ten of them civilians, had been killed and eight others were wounded.

The Columbus raid was a foolhardy and costly exercise in brigandage on Villa's part. But the raid put Villa's name in headlines around the world (the news was followed with particular interest in Germany). In the United States, where President Wilson's policy of "watchful waiting" had long been regarded with some distrust, there was an immediate demand for retaliation. A small party of American cavalrymen had pursued the retreating Villistas across the border on the morning of the raid.

There were international complications. Venustiano Carranza had been embarrassed by Villa's action and he would gladly have seen Villa captured and killed by anyone, Mexican or American. But there were other considerations. One was the traditional Mexican suspicion of the United States, dating back to the war with Texas in 1836 and the war of 1846–48—struggles which had cost Mexico half of its national territory. The presence of American troops on Mexican soil, whatever the reason, was an affront to Mexican sovereignty. Another factor was that Villa's outrages and his freedom of movement seemed to negate Carranza's claim that he controlled Mexico, a claim that had been important in winning the de facto recognition from the United States. Villa's daring once more made him a popular figure in many parts of Mexico. The resurgence of Villa's popularity was a threat to Carranza's precarious hold on the affections of the Mexican people. By cooperating with the forces that were pursuing Villa, Carranza ran the danger of heightening public sympathy for his enemy.

On the day after the Columbus raid, March 10, 1916, the United States announced that "an adequate force" would be sent in pursuit of Villa in order to put "a stop to his forays." It would be done in cooperation with Mexican authorities and with "scrupulous respect for the sovereignty of that Republic."

Carranza's Foreign Secretary sent a message to the State Department expressing regret over the "lamentable occurrence" at Columbus and suggesting, as an implausible reason for it, the pressure which Carrancista forces had exerted on Villa within Mexico. The message recalled that in the 1880s Indians from U.S. reservations had crossed the border and raided in Mexico. In this instance, the message pointed out, there was an agreement between the governments of Mexico and the United States that the armed forces of either country "might freely cross into the territory of the other to pursue and chastise those bandits." It was then suggested that "Mexican forces be permitted to cross into American territory, if the raid effected at Columbus should unfortunately be repeated at any other point on the border."

It was a curious message. Carranza seemed to suggest collaboration in the pursuit of Villa and reciprocal rights to cross the border, but only if there was another raid. This condition was either overlooked or ignored, and the United States went ahead with its retaliatory plans.

By the next day Carranza had adopted a more belligerent tone. He spoke of the United States waging an "unjust and outrageous war" on Mexico, and warned that "if the government of the United States does not take in consideration the mutual permission for Mexican and American forces to cross into the territory of one another in pursuit of bandits and insists in sending an operating army into Mexican soil, my government shall consider this act an invasion of national territory." Mexican officers along the border were ordered to repel any invasion.

Carranza seemed to ignore two key facts. His insistence on the right of Mexican troops to operate on U.S. soil was meaningless since Villa was not hiding in the United States but somewhere in Chihuahua.

Furthermore, the United States had already demonstrated a willingness for Mexican troops to cross the border. Only five months earlier four thousand Carrancista troops had entered the United States at Eagle Pass, Texas, and had traveled by railroad to Douglas, Arizona. There they had recrossed the border and, under the command of Calles at Agua Prieta had inflicted a telling defeat on Villa—a defeat which Villa attributed in part to the collaboration of American authorities.

On March 15 two columns of U.S. troops crossed the New Mexico border into Chihuahua—the beginning of the Punitive Expedition. Although intervention-minded U.S. newspapers proclaimed that Villa was going to be taken "alive or dead," the expedition's orders were only to pursue and destroy Villa's band. President Wilson issued assurances that the U.S. military operations would not in any way violate Mexican sovereignty nor would they be permitted to expand into intervention into Mexican affairs. Obregón, whom Carranza hastily installed as Minister of War to handle the crisis, issued orders to governors of states along the U.S. border to instruct military commanders "to act in accord with the military authorities of the American Army in order that the pursuit of these bandits may give the best results."

The multiple misunderstandings—between the United States and Carranza, between Carranza and his new Minister of War and, subsequently, between U.S. and Mexican field commanders—were to bring the two neighbor nations to the brink of war. Carranza grew increasingly critical of the operations of the Punitive Expedition. Meanwhile, his own forces, which the year before had been devastatingly effective against Villa when the latter had tens of thousands of troops, now seemed wholly unable to cope with a Villa who had only a handful of followers. One frustrated and weary Carrancista general, pressed for a progress report on his operations in Chihuahua, replied by wire: I HAVE THE HONOR TO INFORM YOU THAT ACCORDING TO ALL RELIABLE DATA I HAVE FRANCISCO VILLA IS CURRENTLY EVERYWHERE AND NOWHERE.

Villa played hide-and-seek with his pursuers. After the Columbus raid he and his men moved into southern Chihuahua, frequently skirmishing with Carrancista troops and frequently beating them—without making any attempt to hold territory—his force was too small for that. During a battle with Carrancistas under General José Cavazos at Ciudad Guerrero, Villa was wounded in the right leg, a soft lead bullet from an old-fashioned Remington entering four inches below the knee and breaking the tibia. Unable to stand or mount a horse, he was placed in a wagon and headed for the sierra. He gave orders: his followers were to disperse in small groups. They were to spread the word that Pancho Villa was dead. If Villa should, in fact, die, his body was to be cremated so that his enemies would never know for certain.

But if he survived, he and all his followers would meet again on July 6 at San Juan Bautista, on the border between Chihuahua and Durango, territory Villa had known well since his bandit days.

The wagon carrying the wounded Villa crept deeper and deeper into the sierra. After the wagon was overturned and wrecked, Villa's followers, now reduced to only a few, fashioned a litter of saplings and blankets and carried him farther, trudging through the snow that was falling heavily in the mountains. Finally they came to a cave in which they hid themselves. The entrance to the cave was overgrown with brush but from within there was a clear view of the slopes below. Villa's wound had become infected. He was feverish and delirious. The supply of permanganate of potash which a doctor in Guerrero had given him to clean the wound was exhausted. His companions squeezed pus from the infected leg and saw bits of bone emerge from the wound. Then they dressed it with peeled blades of the nopal cactus, a favorite folk remedy.

Pursuing troops, both Mexican and American, passed so near the mouth of the cave that their conversations could be heard. Villa said later he heard Americans singing *It's a Long, Long Way to Tipperary*. He also heard soldiers talking of a 50,000 peso price being on Villa's head, and he commented "so many pesos, so little head."

One of his commanders, Pablo López, a slender, hot-blooded guerrilla fighter, was less successful. López had directed the Santa Isabel massacre and was a leader in the raid on Columbus, where he was wounded in both legs. Unable to follow the retreating Villa, he had returned to his home town of Satevó. Pursued by Mexican and American forces he then took refuge in a cave in the Sierra de la Silla. One of his two companions was sent back into Satevó for food and medicines. He was recognized and, under the threat of execution, revealed López's hiding place. López, in his cave and half dead from his wounds, hunger, and thirst, heard troops approaching. Seizing his carbine he crawled from the cave shouting: "Well, here I am. If you are Mexicans I will give myself up. But if you are gringos I will never surrender."

His Mexican captors, much as they admired his spirit, took him as a prisoner to Chihuahua City. There he was treated in a hospital and, a little later, tried and condemned to death. Hobbling before the firing squad on his crutches, he was asked if he had a last request. He did. There was an American in the crowd gathered to watch the execution. López insisted that he be ordered to leave; he did not want a gringo to witness his death. When the American had left López announced that he was ready. He dropped his crutches and stood at attention on his crippled legs while the firing squad performed its duty.

The anti-American feeling that made Pablo López a folk hero was making things difficult for the Punitive Expedition. The American soldiers found their pursuit of Villa hampered by Carrancista forces which, like themselves, were supposed to be chasing Villa, and also by the fierce antipathy of the civilian population. In April 1916 American forces camped in the town of Parral were attacked by townspeople, including women and children, all shouting "Viva Villa" and "Viva Mexico." Three Yankee soldiers were killed in the melee and seven were wounded.

The Expedition's only engagement which in any way resembled a battle was fought, not with Villa, but with the Carrancistas. The Carrancista military authorities had warned the American troops that any movement to the east, south, or west—in short any movement other than a withdrawal toward the border—would be considered a hostile act. General John J. Pershing ignored the order. On June 20, 1916, Troops C and K of the 10th Cavalry were reconnoitering in the direction of Villa Ahumada, Chihuahua, where there was a concentration of Carrancista forces. As the American cavalrymen, 84 in number, were advancing toward Villa Ahumada they halted outside the village of Carrizal, eighty miles south of Juárez. General Felix U. Gómez, commander of the Carrancista garrison, came out to meet Captain Charles T. Boyd, and warned him that any advance would be forcefully opposed. After an unproductive parley General Gómez withdrew. The Americans dismounted and prepared to go forward on foot. Firing broke out and General Gómez was killed, the first of seventy-four Mexicans to die in the engagement. Captain Boyd fell a few minutes later in a burst of machine-gun fire from the Mexican side. Boyd's second in command was also killed. The Americans retreated, minus eight dead and twenty-three prisoners. Mexican-American relations, long strained, reached the crisis stage. Only by the narrowest of margins did the United States escape being embroiled in a continental war which might have precluded entrance into World War I the following year.

The Carranza government, two weeks after the Carrizal battle, suggested that the differences between the two countries might be settled either by mediation or negotiation. The United States readily agreed and negotiations were begun first in New London, Connecticut, and later in Atlantic City, New Jersey. They were to continue, for six months, accomplishing nothing. Carranza's representatives were not authorized to bargain but only to repeat Carranza's demand: complete, immediate, and unconditional withdrawal of the Expedition. The Americans, on the other hand, refused to accept the Mexicans' claim that order had been restored since incursions by unidentified Mexican bandits continued all along the frontier.

Meanwhile, Villa, the man who had caused it all, recovered from his wound enough to leave his hiding place. He submitted to surgery without anesthetic for removal of the bullet from his leg. For a while he could walk only with a heavy cane, and he rode in a carriage instead of on horseback. But he kept his July 6 appointment with his men in San Juan Bautista. With his following increased to a thousand men he began moving northward. There were clashes with Carrancista troops and raids for the sake of arms and ammunition. In small groups his cavalry would make their way into towns and seek out blacksmiths to shoe their horses. Finally, on September 15, the eve of Independence Day, Villa and a few of his companions, wearing disguises, entered the state capital of Chihuahua and studied the disposition of the Carrancista troops commanded by General Jacinto B. Treviño. Treviño was said to command a force of 30,000 men in the state. At 3 A.M. the next day the Villistas had infiltrated the city in force and began shooting. Within minutes they had seized the Government Palace and the state penitentiary where many political prisoners, most of them Villistas, were freed. Villa appeared on the balcony of the Government Palace. He made a brief speech, expressing his affection for the people of Chihuahua and promising to return soon. Then he left the city, along with sixteen automobiles loaded with rifles and cartridges and followed by 1500 new recruits for his army— a number of them from the personal escort of General Treviño. The departing Villistas were cheered with shouts of "Viva Villa."

From San Andrés, Chihuahua, Villa issued a manifesto, labeling Carranza and his followers as traitors for having permitted "the barbarians of the North" to enter Mexico. He also called for a presidential election, promised legal reforms, nationalization of railroads and mines, a closing of the United States border and a prohibition of foreigners—in particular North Americans and Chinese—from owning property in Mexico. Villa had always hated the Chinese; he had in recent years ordered countless Chinese killed for no greater offense than being Chinese.

He took Chihuahua City for a second time that year on November 23 but held it only for a week. On December 1 he was badly beaten in a punishing seven-hour battle on the plains of Horcasitas by Murguía. He abandoned a trainload of provisions and retreated to Satevó. But he was soon ready to launch another furious attack on Torreón, the city he had taken twice before at critical junctures in his career as a revolutionary leader. He attacked the city from three sides and swept all the defenses. Two Carrancista generals were killed and a third committed suicide. He raised a forced loan and went on the warpath again. Torreón was back in Carrancista hands by the first of the year and Villa's victories were diminishing in scale and frequency. The Centaur of the North was becoming a minor character in a drama that was becoming more political than martial.

NEW CHARTER

"Men may be mutilated and sacrificed
for principles, but principles must not
be . . . sacrificed for men."

Alvaro Obregón, message to Constituent Congress, Querétaro, December
12, 1916

AFTER AN ABSENCE OF a year and a half Venustiano Carranza suddenly
returned to Mexico City on April 14, 1916. By Carranza's reasoning,
i.e. that the capital of the nation was wherever he, the First Chief,
happened to be, Mexico City was once more the capital of Mexico. The
Carrancistas had been in control of the city since the previous summer
when Pablo González drove the Zapatistas out for the last time. Carranza could have returned at any time, but instead he had wandered
about the country, receiving homage and holding court, finally establishing himself in Querétaro where the misery and chaos of the civil
war was less apparent than they were in the traditional capital. But
the crisis in relations with the United States, brought on by Villa, had
forced a number of changes. He had installed his most successful
general, Alvaro Obregón—who had just returned from his honeymoon—
as Secretary of War, and Cándido Aguilar, a trusted ally from Veracruz,
as Secretary of Foreign Relations. Now he took the most radical step
of all: he came to Mexico City himself.

Carranza seldom went anywhere without elaborate preparations. He
was partial to parades, music, festive dress, floral wreaths, banners of
greeting and patriotic oratory. His staff was adept at arranging public
demonstrations of affection, enthusiasm, and respect. But this time
Carranza arrived without preparation. There was no crowd to greet
him, no music, no bunting. A lone newspaper reporter happened to
be at the station when his special train arrived. Normally Carranza

would have had a lengthy statement for the press. Now his only statement was: "It is better to work than to talk." Not since Benito Juárez had returned from his forced wanderings, dressed in severe black clothes and riding in a plain black carriage, lonely in his great responsibility, had Mexico City seen a chief of state arrive in such unpretentious fashion.

The First Chief seemed to be cultivating parallels between himself and Juárez, whom he was fond of quoting. Both had had the problem of governing a nation torn by civil war and divided by apparently irreconcilable loyalties. Both tried to protect their countries from foreign intervention—Juárez from the French, Carranza from the United States. Both were civilians in a conflict dominated by military men. And both had been political fugitives (Veracruz and Querétaro had served both men as temporary capitals).

Juárez was above all revered in Mexico as a man of law. He had played a key role in formulation of the Constitution of 1857—the charter which was still the basic law of the land although it had been long ignored. He had also drafted the radical Reform Laws, separating church and state, nationalizing church properties, declaring marriage, birth and death to be civil rather than ecclesiastical matters, abolishing monastic orders and guaranteeing freedom of religious belief.

Carranza, too, had been functioning as a lawgiver. In his recent amendments to the Plan of Guadalupe he had belatedly added provisions for social change and reform that both his loyal followers and rival revolutionists had been demanding from the outset. Then Carranza began to think in larger terms. As early as February 3, 1915, he had hinted that he might find it necessary to draft an entirely new constitution for Mexico. He wired his Washington agent, Arredondo, that WHEN PEACE IS REESTABLISHED I WILL SUMMON A CONGRESS WHICH WILL BE CONSTITUENT IN CHARACTER IN ORDER TO RAISE TO CONSTITUTIONAL STATUS THE REFORMS DECREED DURING THE STRUGGLE.

There was irony in this. Carranza had, from the beginning, described his revolutionary movement as Constitutionalist, dedicated to the restoration of Mexico's Constitution of 1857. While Carranza and his revolutionary followers were still designated as Constitutionalists there was no constitutional provision for the position of "First Chief in charge of the Executive Power" which Carranza had assumed. Carranza's role was an extemporization. This being the case, there was no constitutional authority for the decrees which he had been issuing. Carranza had, accordingly, invented the term "pre-constitutional" to describe the period in which he was functioning as chief executive. To return the country to its constitutional government would invalidate both his role and the decrees he had been issuing on questionable authority. A new constitution, drafted on Carranza's orders and in accordance with his ideas, would solidify the First Chief's position in the history of Mexico, just as the Constitution of 1857 and the Reform Laws had done for Juárez.

His propagandists began describing him as "the eponym of the Revolution" (also as "the divine breath of the fatherland" and "the arbiter of our future destinies"). They carefully avoided the contradiction of a man who had gone to war to restore one constitution now wanting to replace it with another. Most prolific of the propagandists was Felix Fulgencio Palavicini, a former surveyor who had become an enthusiastic supporter of Carranza and, as a consequence, publisher of the newspaper *El Universal*. Two other supporters, José Natividad Macías and Luis Manuel Rojas, began to work on a rough draft of the proposed constitution.

Negotiations with the United States for withdrawal of the Punitive Expedition dragged on. Villa continued to be a menace. So did Zapata. And Felix Díaz, the nephew of the old dictator and a perennial rebel, was back in Mexico. With the help of Juan Andrew Almazán—who had fought for and against almost everyone in the Revolution, he was trying to stir up trouble in Oaxaca. In Mexico City the masses of people were miserable and angry. Workers were paid in Carrancista currency which, they said, became worthless before they could get it in their pockets. Food was scarce and prices were marked not in Carrancista currency but in gold.

There was also labor unrest. The organized workers of Mexico City and particularly the Casa del Obrero Mundial (House of the World Worker) had, until now, been friendly to Carranza. Largely through the blandishments of Obregón they had even raised "red battalions" to fight for Carranza in the critical period of 1915. Now hungry and hopeless, they became disenchanted. Late in May 1916 the electrical workers and street railwaymen went on strike, demanding living wages. A slight adjustment of the pay scale was granted, but the value of the currency continued to decline and they were worse off than before.*
At the end of June the federation of labor syndicates of the Federal District called a general strike. The capital was paralyzed. Carranza ordered strike leaders imprisoned and declared they would be tried on the basis of the hated and overworked Juárez law of January 25, 1862. Finding that this harsh law—intended to punish those who aided the enemy—was hardly applicable to striking workers, Carranza, on August 1, dictated an even harsher decree of his own, imposing the death penalty for those who incited strikes in factories or industrial

---

* The value of the Mexican peso had declined from 0.4748 (U.S. currency) at the fall of Porfirio Díaz to .0255 in the spring of 1916, and it continued to diminish.

plants providing public services—and for those who even discussed the strike. Troops occupied the headquarters of the electrical workers, the restaurant workers, and the Casa del Obrero Mundial. The strike was broken. One of the strike leaders, Ernesto Velasco, was sentenced to death. He remained in prison for the next year and a half, awaiting execution but was finally freed.

By September 1916, Carranza had issued a call for election of deputies—or delegates—to the constituent congress which would meet December 1 in Querétaro. The call was so drafted as to exclude anyone who was not a member of Carranza's Constitutionalist movement. Zapatistas, Villistas, and other considerable segments of the Mexican population would not be represented. The congress would be, in effect, a convention of the Carrancista party, which would assume the responsibility of writing a constitution for all Mexicans, Carrancistas and anti-Carrancistas alike.

The choice of Querétaro as a meeting place for the convention instead of Mexico City where it would logically have been held, was explained as an effort to free the delegates from the political intrigues of the capital. There was also the fact that Carranza operating from the National Palace in Mexico City wore all the trappings—if not the title—of an interim president. An interim president was ineligible for election as the constitutional president. Carranza had fully made up his mind that he would be a candidate for the presidency: Constitutional President Carranza would succeed First Chief Carranza.

By October, Alvaro Obregón and Pablo González were holding a series of meetings—garden parties at the luxurious Tacubaya mansion González had appropriated for himself and more businesslike meetings in the Jockey Club—to promote Carranza's candidacy. It was Obregón's decision that the Carranza organization should be known as the Liberal Constitutionalist party. Early in November, Carranza was permitting Palavicini to say in *El Universal* that while Carranza was a candidate for the presidency he would not relinquish his position as First Chief. At a fiesta in the Arbeu Theater in honor of the Constitutionalist army Pablo González presented to Carranza a red, white, and green sash, identical with the sash of office worn by Mexican presidents on ceremonial occasions.

On November 17, 1916, Carranza left for Querétaro. As he had done on other occasions, he made the journey something of a spectacle by going on horseback. Accompanied by his staff, a cluster of generals and a party of journalists, he took a leisurely excursion through the countryside, now turning gray and yellow in the first month of the winter drouth. Arrangements were made in advance for his fine black horse to be well-brushed daily and there were always freshly pressed uniforms and bouquets of flowers for the First Chief at the prearranged stops.

They covered the 135 miles to Querétaro in eight days. Householders in Querétaro had been told of the First Chief's imminent arrival and instructed to decorate their homes "in the most spontaneous manner," the alternative to spontaneity being a fifty-peso fine. One of the accompanying journalists told of the arrival in Querétaro as a "scene of indescribable enthusiasm . . ." with more than ten thousand persons lining the principal streets. With Carranza in residence Querétaro was once more proclaimed to be the capital of the republic.

If the polite and obedient townspeople of Querétaro were indescribably enthusiastic, the reception of Carranza's proposed draft of a new constitution was something less than that. The revolutionary movement which had divided itself so many times before—Zapata against Madero, Villa against Carranza, the Convention against Carranza, and Gutiérrez against Villa and the Convention—was about to undergo another division —although the seriousness of it was not immediately apparent.

Outwardly there was an ostentatious display of loyalty to the First Chief; but sharp political lines were being drawn. All members of the constitutional congress proclaimed themselves to be liberals, but they were of varying hues of liberality. The moderates proclaimed themselves to be "classic liberals." Their critics, however, described them as *renovadores* (renewers) since some of them were suspected of collaboration with the Huerta regime. Many of Carranza's closest collaborators were, rightly or wrongly, identified as *renovadores*.

Obregón—who during most of the convention stayed in Mexico City attending to his responsibilities as Secretary of War—was the idol of the more radical delegates to the congress. He not only had been the outstanding military figure of the Carrancista movement—having successively overcome the forces of Huerta and Villa. He also—despite his middle-class background—had become an exponent of radical reform. Before the battles of Celaya he had organized his officers into political discussion groups to study the aims of the Revolution.

The radical delegates—battlefield veterans for the most part—were referred to by the moderates as leftists and, more frequently, as Jacobins. The moderates held the chairmanship of the congress and thus controlled the order of speaking. They also controlled the stenographic service, the printing of texts, and Palavicini chronicled the proceedings of the congress in *El Universal* with a pro-moderate, anti-radical slant (he described the radical wing as "narrow and sterile," the liberal or moderate wing as "conscientious, ample, and fecund"). Proceedings of the congress, as a result, tended to be reported with a pronounced bias. But the truth was that on almost every issue the Jacobins both outtalked the moderates and outvoted them, often by ratios of four to one.

Carranza's approach to the problem of constitutional revision had been generalized, even vague. In his opening speech, in the Iturbide Theater late in the afternoon of December 1, he said that the old Constitution of 1857 was composed of "abstract formulas based on scientific conclusions which were of great speculative value but from which it has been possible to derive little or nothing of positive usefulness." He followed this with proposals for rewriting specific parts of the constitution. Some of his proposals were just as abstract, possibly more abstract than the constitution which he proposed to replace.

The radical delegates insisted on putting teeth into the new constitution. Perhaps the most outspoken of the Jacobins was Francisco J. Múgica, a diminutive, thirty-two-year-old firebrand who had been with Madero in San Antonio, had been a signer of the Plan of Guadalupe, had helped Lucio Blanco make the Revolution's first distribution of land in Matamoros and had served as governor and military commander of Tabasco. Múgica emerged early as a spokesman for the radical wing of the congress and was principally responsible for the controversial nature of Article 3. Carranza had proposed only that there be full liberty of teaching (a repetition of the Constitution of 1857) and that instruction in public educational institutions be secular. Article 3 as written, due largely to Múgica's influence, specifically forbade "religious corporations" and "ministers of any cult" to establish or conduct schools, a blow at the control the Catholic Church had held over education in a country in which free public schools had always been inadequate.

Even more controversial were Articles 27 and 123, dealing respectively with property and with the rights of labor. Article 27 established an entirely new concept of property rights. All land, water, and minerals were subject to the dominion of the federal government which had authority to sell them or grant them in concessions or, on the other hand, to expropriate and redistribute them. Subsoil resources, however, inalienably belonged to the nation and could be exploited only through concession. Contracts drawn and concessions granted since the first years of the Díaz era were to be reviewed and would be subject to nullification. This, at one stroke, could destroy most of the fortunes and great landholdings that had been built up in Mexico during the past forty years, a blow at the landholding classes of which Carranza himself was a representative, and at foreign entrepreneurs and capitalists who had become rich in Mexico. Church properties were to be nationalized, and there was provision for redistribution of land by federal and state governments on either a community or individual basis.

Many parts of the constitution were a hybrid of native Mexican radicalism and of advanced European ideas. This was true in Article 123, the labor code, which borrowed from English and European laws but made them even more advanced in the light of peculiarly Mexican needs. The result was, in total, perhaps the most advanced labor code in the world, highly detailed as to the rights and privileges of labor, governing hours, wages, employment of children, overtime pay, maternity care (and time for working mothers to nurse their children), payment in legal tender (instead of credit at the company store), the right to strike, the responsibility of employers for accidents and occupational diseases and so on—a comprehensive, if somewhat Utopian, document. All that Carranza had asked for was that the federal government be empowered to enact labor legislation. As in almost everything, the congress went far beyond his wishes.

Article after article in the new constitution placed strictures on religious activity, directed principally at the Catholic Church which historically had favored and aided conservative regimes.

Article 120 spelled out the relations between organized religion and the state—although these had been touched on in the articles dealing with education and property rights. Marriage was declared to be a civil contract; ministers were recognized only as professional men, subject to the laws governing their profession; they must never criticize the laws of the land or the authority of the government; ministers must be native-born Mexicans—thus outlawing the numerous European Catholic priests—mainly Spanish—in Mexico. States were given the authority to limit the number of priests or ministers within their borders.

In everything, religious matters and others, the authority of the nation was supreme. Human rights were recognized not as inherent but as creation of the nation.

Much of the Querétaro Constitution was an expression of revolutionary philosophy rather than a precise chart for action, an expression of aspiration rather than achievement, but it was still the most concrete ideological achievement of the struggle Madero had launched more than six years before. It went far beyond anything Madero had dreamt of— and certainly beyond Carranza's conservative plans.

Nevertheless, Carranza accepted the document, swearing to obey and enforce it. He was by this time fully started on his campaign for election to the constitutional presidency of Mexico and it was no time for another break in the revolutionary ranks. He had remained detached from the lively debates between the *renovadores* and the Jacobins. Much of his time was spent amiably in posing for photographs with individual state delegations. Behind the scenes, however, he was cautiously maneuvering to make certain he would not be opposed for the presidency. Although both men had been outwardly loyal to him he suspected presidential ambitions on the part of both Alvaro Obregón and Pablo González, and he particularly feared Obregón.

Carranza enlisted the aid of Adolfo de la Huerta, provisional governor of Sonora, who had long been closely associated with Obregón. It was De la Huerta who, when the Constitutionalist movement was just beginning, had told Carranza that Obregón was the most able and promising of the emerging revolutionary leaders in Sonora. Now Carranza confided his fears to De la Huerta. He had suffered greatly, he said, because of the uncontrollable excesses of various revolutionary leaders—presumably including Obregón. He, the First Chief, bore the historical responsibility for everything that happened. Very soon a constitutional government would be elected. Carranza thought that he should be at the head of that government in order, according to De la Huerta's memoirs, "to demonstrate to the world that I am a man of order and government and not the figure painted by enemies because of the errors of some of my military chiefs." Carranza wanted De la Huerta to dissuade Obregón and González from standing in his way.

De la Huerta accepted the mission. The next day he sat on a park bench with Obregón in the central alameda of Querétaro, talking of the political future for four hours while Carranza nervously paced the floor of his headquarters. No one could tell just how serious a threat Obregón posed to Carranza's hopes; but he was an ambitious, willful man, conscious of his abilities and flattered by his popularity among the revolutionists. De la Huerta argued that Obregón, unlike Carranza, was still a young man, that there would be much political opportunity for him in the future. The argument was successful—so successful that the next day Obregón had decided he wanted to get out of politics immediately and altogether—and presented his resignation from the post of Secretary of War. Carranza persuaded him to stay on until after the presidential election.

The constituent congress completed its work January 31, 1917, the deadline Carranza had arbitrarily set for it. The document was signed with the same pen that had been used for the Plan of Guadalupe, almost four years earlier. The Jacobins who had had their way in drafting the most significant parts of the new charter, issued a statement damning Carranza's closest collaborators as reactionaries, adulators and obstructionists who had opposed the true revolutionists' intention of "finishing completely with capitalism, economic slavery, clericalism and ignorance." But, on the other hand, they praised Carranza himself for his "strong and tranquil spirit."

A banquet was held that night in the Centro Fronterizo to celebrate the completion of the constitution. Carranza made a conciliatory speech commending the work of the delegates and reminding them that he had imposed his will on no one and had, instead, allowed the delegates to work with complete liberty. And although the new constitution "in some aspects goes beyond our social medium," it did, nevertheless, defend not only the rights of Mexicans but of all humanity, and he pledged himself to uphold it.

A young delegate from Sonora, Juan de Dios Bojorquez, who later was to write a history of the constituent congress, did not attend the banquet. Instead he went carousing with young officers from the staffs of Obregón, Hill, and Diéguez. They drank quantities of beer on the private railway car of General Hill. Then they left the Central Railroad station, marched in ragged military formation through the narrow old streets, shouting and singing the *Marseillaise,* and entered the Salon Verde, a saloon across the street from the Centro Fronterizo where the banquet was being held. There was more beer, emotional recitations of revolutionary poetry and sentimental singing of *Adelita* and *Valentina.* At midnight they made their way across the street and noisily entered the Centro Fronterizo. Bojorquez found himself standing near the speakers' table where Carranza was making his statement about the delegates working in complete freedom. Bojorquez drunkenly interrupted: "Bravo! The First Chief is a real Jacobin!" Later in the night Bojorquez was given a bed in Obregón's private railway car. The next morning, bleary-eyed and remorseful, he saw a laughing Obregón at breakfast. "What a yank you gave to Don Venustiano's whiskers last night," said Obregón.

Carranza ordered promulgation of the new constitution on February 5, 1917—the anniversary of the Constitution of 1857. The date had another significance. On the same day the last troops of the U. S. Punitive Expedition were withdrawn from Mexico in accordance with an order signed two weeks earlier by President Wilson. It had been an inconclusive military operation. The U.S. government finally followed the advice of Consul General Philip Hanna who had suggested that withdrawal "would place responsibility for restoring order . . . on the de facto government, where it belongs." The only practical result of the military venture for the United States was field experience for 12,000 American troops and for their commander, General Pershing, which would prove useful in the European war in which they were soon to be engaged. Carranza, meanwhile, had profited politically. His opposition to the expedition and his refusal to negotiate on any basis but complete and unconditional withdrawal won admiration, even among his enemies.

During the eleven-month stay of U.S. troops in Mexico, Carranza had, as "pre-constitutional" head of the government, been pursuing a complicated foreign policy. He was assiduously cultivating the friendship of other Latin American nations. Their national holidays were observed, their diplomatic representatives honored. Streets in the old section of Mexico City were renamed as a gesture of amity (San Agustín became Uruguay, Santo Domingo became Brasil), and Carranza spoke vaguely of a union of Latin American nations in which he, as the man who had the courage to talk back to the United States, would inevitably be the leader. In this and other schemes he was encouraged by the German Minister to Mexico.

Germany, long expert at turning other nations' problems to its own advantage, was interested in Mexico. Early in the century the Kaiser had sought unsuccessfully to buy or lease Magdalena Bay on the west coast of Mexico's Baja California peninsula—a natural naval base. He also dreamed of a war between the U.S. and Japan, to be fought on Mexican soil. Any involvement of the United States with Mexico would further German commercial and strategic interests in the New World. Germany's backing of the exiled Victoriano Huerta in 1915 had achieved nothing. But in 1916 German agents were dealing with both Carranza and Villa, both of whom had been enemies of Huerta, both of whom now hated the United States, and both of whom hated each other. German secret societies existed throughout Mexico. Officers of either German birth or descent were prominent in the military—with Villa as well as with Obregón. German entrepreneurs were eagerly buying up property—notably mines—which had been abandoned by revolution-weary Americans. Carranza sent one of his closest advisers, Rafael Zubaran Capmany, as his Minister to Germany. Zubaran spoke no German but he became very friendly with the German Foreign Secretary, Alfred Zimmerman, and did not even bother to make a duty call on the American Ambassador.

In Mexico the German Minister, von Eckhardt, diligently cultivated Mexico-German friendship (he was able, through cajolery and bribery, to send coded messages over the Mexican telegraph system, forbidden to others). There began a flow of cordial messages between the two countries. In October 1916 Eckhardt advised his government that Carranza was now "openly friendly" to Germany and was "disposed, if it becomes necessary, to give aid to our submarines in Mexican waters." On November 3 another message describing Carranza's attitude reached Foreign Secretary Zimmerman: Germany was the only great power with which Mexico—as represented by Carranza—would like stronger economic and political ties; Mexico's sympathies in the European war were with Germany; in return, Mexico wanted help from Germany in the way of arms and naval equipment.

On January 16, 1917, Zimmerman sent a history-making telegram to Eckhardt. The latter was informed that Germany planned to begin unrestricted submarine warfare on February 1. In the likely event that the United States should become a belligerent as a result of this move, Germany proposed an alliance with Mexico. The two countries would be allies in war and peace. Mexico was to be encouraged to attack the United States and "to reconquer" Texas, New Mexico, and Arizona.* Eckhardt was instructed to suggest that Carranza invite Japan into the conspiracy. Eckhardt consulted with Carranza's Foreign Minister, Cándilo Aguilar. On February 24 Aguilar was a guest of honor at a banquet in the Japanese legation and had a long private conversation with the Japanese Minister, Tameksichi Ohita, possibly about the suggested alliance although Aguilar later denied it.

An indication of where Carranza's sympathies were in the European struggle came on February 13 when the First Chief issued a call for neutral countries to cooperate in the reestablishment of peace and to embargo war materials destined for belligerents in the war—a move which would have hurt England. In the United States Carranza was caricatured as a wooden puppet manipulated by a Prussian officer.

The famous Zimmerman message had been intercepted and decoded at the time of transmission by British Naval Intelligence. Its contents were splashed on front pages around the world on March 1, considerably embarrassing the Germans, hastening the United States toward an open declaration of war, and making Carranza a figure of suspicion in Allied capitals. Germany continued to try to open up a Mexican front. As late as April 13 Zimmerman was still promoting a New World battlefront. On this date Eckhardt was asked how much money Carranza wanted. But the next day Eckhardt advised Zimmerman that Carranza had decided to remain neutral, the proposed alliance having been made impractical by premature publication of Zimmerman's scheme.

Mexico, so crippled and scarred by its own civil war, escaped being made a battlefield of World War I. Students of Carranza's actions suggest that he was pursuing a course of defensive nationalism rather than an outright commitment to German imperialism. Mexico, in the past, had suffered at the hands of Germany's enemies—Britain, France, and the United States—and, by contrast, had had little trouble with Germany. But, practical man that he was, Carranza could have entertained little hope—even with Germany's help—of "reconquering" the territory lost to the United States in the nineteenth century.

Whatever the reason, Carranza had begun to retreat from his pro-

* In an interrogation in the Reichstag on March 5 regarding the prudence of his Mexican proposal, Zimmerman admitted being doubtful that Mexico could succeed in any such venture in "reconquest." But, he added, "I was looking toward a definite objective. I would set new enemies on America's neck . . . By holding up these American states as bait I would urge Mexico to invade the United States as quickly as possible and so keep the American army busy."

German position soon after the withdrawal of the U. S. Punitive Expedition from Mexico in February 1917. He had a more immediate and pressing matter on his mind: the coming election.

Shortly after the close of the Querétaro congress he had issued a call for an extraordinary election to be held on March 11, an election in which he would be the principal candidate for the presidency. But he did not return to Mexico City; there was still the awkwardness of sitting in the National Palace, holding the reins of government while an election was held to legalize his grip on those reins. Accordingly, he began traveling again, this time to the west. Except for the arrival of the newly appointed American Ambassador, Henry P. Fletcher, who presented his credentials to Carranza in Guadalajara, it was an uneventful and idle trip. News was so scarce that the correspondent for *El Universal* was reduced to reporting that, in Ahualulco, Jalisco, Carranza visited the municipal presidency and enjoyed a glass of cool water.

The election was almost as uneventful. Although 3,000,000 Mexicans were qualified to vote and although Carranza's headquarters claimed that 1,500,000 ballots were cast for the First Chief, fewer than 250,000 citizens bothered to go to the polls. Of these, 197,385 were for Carranza. Most of the rest were cast either for Obregón (40,008) or Pablo González (11,615), neither of whom had campaigned for the office.

Finally, after a four-month absence, Carranza returned to the capital once more, the first legally elected president since Madero—although the legality of Carranza's election was disputed by his enemies.

On May 1, escorted by his favorite generals and those signers of the Plan of Guadalupe who were available and in good favor, he went by open carriage from the National Palace to the Chamber of Deputies to be formally installed as President. As the procession moved through the Zócalo the bells in the cathedral rang and thousands of doves were released; fluttering behind the doves were red, white, and green ribbons with the words *"Viva Carranza—26 March 1914–1 May 1917."* Carranza wore a tall silk hat, had the tricolor sash of office across his chest. The afternoon sun shone brightly on his blue-tinted spectacles and his carefully brushed white beard. The streets were lined with spectators and the crowds were thick around the Chamber of Deputies, where there had been a steady flow of generals, politicians, and diplomats. Von Eckhardt, the stiff German Minister, had been cheered enthusiastically. For the new American Ambassador, Fletcher, there were hisses and whistles.

At 5:21 P.M. Carranza took the oath of office. With his right arm extended straight before him he promised to "obey and enforce the political constitution of the United Mexican States . . . If I do not do so the people may demand it of me."

The Revolution was over. Or was it? Villa and Zapata were still fighting. But these "reactionary bandits"—the official description of anti-Carrancistas—would in time be overcome. Other bandits were respected generals. Old generals became cabinet members and state governors. Young officers who had stayed close to the First Chief became new generals. Friendly intellectuals became newspaper publishers or diplomats. There was something for all—except one.

On the day of the inauguration Obregón, who had wanted to do so long before, resigned as Secretary of War. "Constitutional order has been restored," he said. "Since I do not have the vocation for a permanent military career I have resigned my military rank in order to assume my rights as a simple citizen, retiring to private life."

Obregón had never been and could never be a "simple citizen." He was a talented, complex man, sure of himself and of the men who followed him so loyally. He and Pancho Villa were the most powerful figures of the Revolution. Together they might have brought the struggle to a quick and merciful close. Instead they had become mortal enemies and had, in their struggle, nearly destroyed not only each other but also the country they both loved. Now Obregón was weary and disillusioned. He distrusted many of the men around Carranza. Some he identified with the Huerta regime, or even with *porfirismo*. Few of them had played any part in the bloody struggle that had almost cost him his life. Their weapons were servility and flattery, and they used them well. In the inevitable round of farewell banquets Obregón's moon face became more and more expressionless. Finally he left for Sonora—to join his children and his new wife, to become a garbanzo grower again—and an object of much curiosity: a man who had won a revolution and then divorced himself from public life.

CHAPTER 37

'MILIANO

> "Men in Mexico are like trees, forests that the white man felled . . . But the roots are deep and alive . . . What else it needs is the word, for the forests to begin to rise again. And some man among men must speak the word."
>
> D. H. Lawrence, *The Plumed Serpent*

DURING 1916 Pablo González appeared, for once, to be having some success as a military commander. Laughingly called "General Sidewalk" because of his avoidance of battlefields and "General Horserace" because of his unmatched speed in retreating, González was actually doing something about the Zapatistas.

From his appropriated mansion in Tacubaya, González issued orders deploying his Army of the East through the states of Mexico, Morelos, Puebla, and Guerrero. The largest forces were directed into Morelos, the home state of Zapatismo. By May 2, 1916, the Army of the East had taken Cuernavaca, the state capital. Two days later they were in Cuautla and Yautepec, Zapatista strongpoints. By May 6 they had taken Jonacatepec and Villa Ayala. On May 25 Jojutla fell—and the last remnant of the Convention government, which had fled there from Cuernavaca, disappeared for good. By mid-June the Carrancistas had taken Tlaltizapán, Zapata's hideaway to the south of Cuernavaca. Zapata himself barely escaped.

But González could not manage the unfriendly territory. Zapata's guerrillas raided supply dumps to get ammunition—and they went on fighting. They ambushed careless Carrancista troops. They blew up trains. They cut communications. By the end of the year, weakened by malaria and frustrated by uncertainty, González' army was withdrawn from Morelos. Early in 1917, just when the finishing touches were being put on the new constitution in Querétaro, the Zapatistas were back in Cuernavaca and Zapata was once more directing operations from Tlaltizapán.

Zapata was also waging a paper war against Carranza. In January 1917 he issued a manifesto denouncing Carranza as an autocrat, an impostor and a tyrant, and his followers as a military rabble bent on robbery, rape, and assassination. The Carrancista troops had pillaged the state during their brief occupation. They had burned villages, confiscated cattle and work animals, taken villagers' precious corn to feed their horses and mules—or simply destroyed it to keep the peasants from eating and planting another crop. They had molested women and destroyed mountainside forests to deprive the people of fuel. And González was credited with wrecking sugar mill machinery—which the Zapatistas had been careful to spare—and tearing up hacienda railroad tracks, all of it to be taken to Mexico City and sold as scrap iron on his own account.

That the Zapatistas should be fought so vigorously at this late date was strange since the Carrancistas appeared to have come around to Zapata's way of thinking. Carranza's Veracruz decree of January 6, 1915, had accepted agrarian reform as a national necessity; and Article 27 of the new Querétaro Constitution provided for expropriation and distribution of land—and this was what Zapata had been fighting for. But the fighting continued. Whatever comfort Zapata, the agrarian reformer and peasant leader, may have taken from the government's adoption of his goals was obliterated by his profound distrust of Carranza and his conviction that Carranza, having put words on paper, would do nothing further. Carranza was a prosperous middle-class landowner who had accepted the imperatives of the Revolution only reluctantly. He was also a consummate politician. Zapata and his people distrusted him both as landowner and politician.

Zapata, trying to rally his diminishing forces and raise their morale, issued more and more manifestos and pronouncements excoriating Carranza, the Carrancista troops and their atrocities. These documents, although they bore the name of Zapata, were, as usual, the work of others. Zapata no longer had the services of Otilio Montaño, author of the Plan of Ayala and the journalist Paulino Martínez, both of whom had been executed. Manuel Palafox, another intellectual (nicknamed "the ulcer of the South") had deserted and, to the delight of the Carrancistas, was spreading tales of Zapata's alleged personal fortune in land and cattle. But Zapata still had the loyalty and talent of Díaz Soto y Gama and Gildardo Magaña. Politically sophisticated and far more radical than Zapata—whose sole aim remained the recovery of land for the peasants—Díaz Soto y Gama larded Zapata's statements with unlikely allusions. He had Zapata expressing solidarity with the revolutionists of Russia and making references to Agrippina and Nero, to Louis XVI and the guillotine, all equally remote from Zapata's ken (although one fellow revolutionist had suggested the use of the guillotine as a means of saving ammunition). But when Díaz Soto y Gama dealt with Carranza there was no doubt that he was expressing Zapata's sentiments.

In March 1919, Díaz Soto y Gama composed his masterpiece, an "open letter" to Carranza for Zapata's signature. It said:

"As a citizen, as a man with a right to think and speak aloud, as a peasant aware of the needs of the humble, as a revolutionary caudillo who knows the bitterness and hopes of the national conscience, with the rights given me by my nine years of rebellion, I address myself to you, Citizen Carranza, for the first and last time. I am not talking to a president whom I do not recognize, nor to a politician whom I distrust. I speak to you as a Mexican, as a man of feeling and reason. I am going to speak bitter truths.

"From the time when you first had the idea of revolution . . . and named yourself chief of a movement which you maliciously called 'constitutionalist' . . . you proceeded to turn the struggle to the advantage of yourself and the friends and allies who helped you climb and then shared in the booty—riches, honors, business, banquets, sumptuous fiestas, bachanals of pleasure, orgies of satiation, of ambition, power and of blood. It never entered your mind that the Revolution was for the benefit of the great masses, for the legions of the oppressed whom you stirred up with your harangues. In order to avoid popular commotion— a dangerous, two-edged weapon, you turned against those whom you used; in order to obstruct the people, now half liberated and feeling their strength, you took justice in your own hands and created a dictatorship which you gave the name of 'revolutionary.'"

The letter was a catalog of charges against Carranza both as a revolutionary leader and as President: banks sacked, reckless issuance of paper money, commerce disorganized by monetary fluctuation and exhausted by forced contributions, mining and agriculture dying for want of guarantees, the poor reduced to misery through uncertainty and the high cost of living, labor organizations made meaningless by political intervention. Far from returning land to the people (Carranza had actually made several minor distributions of land) the haciendas had been given to favorite generals—"the old latifundistas have been replaced by modern landowners in epaulets and kepis, with pistols in their belts."

"Does freedom of suffrage exist?" asked the letter. "It is a lie! In most of the states the governor has been imposed by the central government. The senators and deputies in the Congress are creatures of the executive power. In the matter of elections you have mastered and surpassed your old chief, Porfirio Díaz." As President, it was charged Carranza was systematically violating the constitution, operating with no legislative approval for his budget, establishing and abolishing taxes and tariffs at will, operating the Ministries of War, Treasury and Government according to personal whims, making appointments without bothering to inform the Congress. Carranza's troops—"the scourge of the towns and countryside"—had robbed and burned the homes of peasants, killed the innocent, speculated in stolen livestock. There was specific mention of the "Gray Automobile Gang," an organized group of marauders in Mexico City "whose ferocious deeds go unpunished because the leaders are allied with you or occupy positions in the army" (a reference to General Pablo González who was rumored to have connections with the gang).

Carranza was even rebuked for his conduct of foreign policy. "Foreign nations remember your conduct during the great war and have nothing but resentment, disconfidence and hostility for you. You swore you were neutral but you conducted yourself as a rabid pro-German; you permitted and stirred up propaganda against the Allied powers; you protected German espionage; you obstructed the interests of foreigners who were hostile to the Kaiser. With your blindness and tortuous movements, with your false steps and disloyalties, you are the cause of Mexico being deprived of aid from the triumphant powers. If any international complications result you alone will bear the blame."

Carranza's course, it was charged, had alienated the best Mexicans—"the intellectuals, the idealistic youth, unblemished, uncorrupted people . . . [all] unhappily separated from public life."

"Give the public back its liberty, Citizen Carranza," the letter concluded. "Abdicate your dictatorial powers. Allow the sap of a new generation to flow. It will purify, invigorate and save the country. If you, as a simple citizen, can collaborate in the work of reconstruction and concord you will be welcome. But, for the sake of responsibility, honor, humanity and patriotism, resign the high post you occupy and from which you have presided at the ruin of the Republic . . . Retire from the so-called first magistracy in which you have been so noxious and prejudicial, so ill-fated for the Republic."

The letter to Carranza might have passed as nothing more than routine polemic had it not been for a single, stinging sentence: "The revolutionists of the Constitutionalist faction, those whom you offered to unite, are each day more disunited; this much you admitted in your latest manifesto."

The reference was to a statement of Carranza's two months earlier in which he had urged the public not to be hasty in affiliating with presidential candidacies which were beginning to take shape for the 1920 election. Political rivalries were emerging. Obregón, in retirement in Sonora, was a strong man and a hero and would be a natural popular choice. Carranza wanted to choose his own successor.

Carranza had already been informed that Zapata had sent word to Obregón that he would be willing to discuss an anti-Carranza alliance. He knew that with Obregón's ability and general popularity and Zapata's appeal to the masses of Mexicans this would be a dangerous combination. Since it was clear he could do nothing about Obregón, Zapata must be eliminated. Carranza some time earlier had made a proposition to a free-lance revolutionist, Manuel Sosa Pavón. Sosa Pavón had fought for Zapata, then for Felix Díaz and was now seeking the favor of the Carranza government. Carranza asked him to go to Morelos, to rejoin the Zapatistas and then either capture or kill Zapata. Sosa Pavón objected: Zapata had been his friend and benefactor. He could not do it. Sosa Pavón was imprisoned.

González was eager to put an end to Zapata. He was afraid of Obregón and knew what a Zapata-Obregón combination could mean to his own political hopes. If he could deliver the final blow to Zapata and Zapatismo it would brighten his own tarnished reputation. And, more important, it might win for him the political blessing of Carranza.

Zapata's forces had dwindled to the point where he could no longer be considered a serious military threat. His old leaders were gone— deserted, killed in action or executed for treachery. His brother Eufemio had been killed by a Zapatista who was preparing to go over to the enemy. But, even in this reduced state, Zapata's very existence was a danger. His appeal was too strong for too many people. And he was elusive. He could ambush superior forces and fade away into the hills and be unheard of until his next manifesto or his next surprise attack. Capture or defeat in battle appeared impossible.

The Carrancistas found their answer in a dashing young colonel with upswept mustaches, a reputation for ruthlessness and a burning hatred for agrarians—a hatred he had demonstrated against peasants in the state of Michoacán. Colonel Jesús María Guajardo became the central figure in an intricate plot. One of Zapata's generals, Eusebio Jáuregui, had been captured. Instead of being shot, as were most captured Zapatistas, he was allowed the freedom of González' headquarters in Cuautla—enough freedom to overhear Guajardo complaining of his treatment by his new commander, criticizing the Carranza regime and muttering darkly about "making a somersault," i.e., changing sides. Jáuregui, a novice at espionage, smuggled the information out to be relayed to Zapata—just as his captors planned.

Zapata, wanting any kind of ally, took the bait. On March 21, 1919, he addressed a letter to Guajardo: "Although I do not know the reasons I understand that you have had some difficulties with Pablo González and that you have been threatened unjustly. This, and the firm and serene conviction that the arms of the Revolution will soon triumph, leads me to write this letter making a formal and frank invitation to you to join our troops. Among us you will be received with the consideration which you merit . . . Our movement is perfectly unified and pursues a great end—the betterment of the great Mexican family."

The Carrancista governor of Morelos, José G. Aguilar, composed a reply for Guajardo to send to Zapata: "I inform you that due to the great difficulties I have had with Pablo González I am disposed to collaborate with you if I am given sufficient guarantees for myself and my men, improving my circumstances as a revolutionist . . . I have sufficient elements of war—munitions, weapons and cavalry under my orders as well as other elements ready to follow me, awaiting only my decision. I await your letter; please keep this delicate matter absolutely secret."

The letters flowed back and forth between the two, Zapata writing from various hiding places, Guajardo answering from the hacienda of San Juan Chinameca. Most of the communications were carried by an itinerant photographer. Zapata, perhaps because he so badly needed allies and reinforcements, seemed to have shed the distrust of strangers and outsiders. He had excellent reports about Guajardo as a revolutionist, he said, that he was frank and sincere, a man of his word and a gentleman. He suggested that Guajardo's first step be to attack and overcome Victoriano Bárcenas, a Zapatista who had deserted and gone over to the Carrancista side with his troops. This step should be taken on Thursday, April 3. The troops should be disarmed and held at Guajardo's headquarters, Chinameca, while Bárcenas and his staff should be sent on to Zapata at the Rancho de Tepehuaje for disposition —presumably execution.

Guajardo replied that it would be impossible to comply with the order on Thursday. Bárcenas had been called to Pablo González' headquarters in Cuautla, leaving only a skeleton force behind. In addition, headquarters owed Guajardo ten thousand pesos in cash and twenty thousand cartridges; these were to be delivered between April 6 and 10 and it would be a shame to lose them. To soften whatever disappointment this might cause Zapata he offered to send him food and other supplies which he might need. He also mentioned that he had daily mule trains operating between Chinameca and Cuautla, bringing supplies. Would Zapata instruct his men not to interfere with the mule trains? (In retrospect it appeared certain that, in addition to supplies, the mule trains were bringing Guajardo instructions in the plot against Zapata and carrying his reports back to Cuautla.)

Zapata replied that he would be glad to get the supplies, and that he was instructing his men not to interfere with the mule trains.

The time had come for Guajardo to make a convincing demonstration of his apostasy. On April 8 he launched an "attack" on the town of Jonacatepec. The place was defended by a small body of Carrancista troops. Their commander had been informed by both González and Guajardo as to what to expect. A sham battle was fought. Both sides were supposed to use blank ammunition—but in the confusion some mistakes were made. Twelve of the defenders and seven of Guajardo's men were killed. Later the same day Guajardo had an opportunity to make an even more persuasive show of his supposed switch in allegiance. At a place called Mancornadero he was approached by a group of campesinos who complained to him of outrages committed by troops commanded by Bárcenas, the Zapatista-turned-Carrancista. Remembering Zapata's hatred of the turncoat, Guajardo had fifty-nine of Bárcenas' troops lined up and shot.

A little later Zapata received Guajardo and his officers at Pastor station, about fifteen miles south of Jonacatepec. Zapata had already heard of Guajardo's simulated victory at Jonacatepec and of the shooting of Bárcenas' men at Mancornadero and was pleased. Guajardo introduced each of his officers to Zapata and then had them all mount their horses and ride slowly past their new commander. He invited Zapata to take his choice of the horses and to accept it as a gift. Zapata chose a fine sorrel and offered "my sincere felicitations to General Guajardo." Guajardo the Carrancista colonel thus became a Zapatista general.

Arrangements were made for Zapata to make a visit on April 10 to Guajardo's headquarters at Chinameca. Guajardo wanted to offer him a fiesta in honor of their alliance.

Zapata withdrew to Tepalcingo. Here he was visited by a woman who had just returned from Cuautla where she had heard rumors of a plot against Zapata's life. There had been many attempts on Zapata's life and he was by nature wary and suspicious. But if he had any fears he apparently did not associate them with Guajardo. Guajardo's demonstration the day before—shooting his erstwhile companions in arms—had been convincing.

Zapata spent the night "with the woman he loved," according to his imprecise biographers. It was a restless night. Zapata, normally a sound sleeper, had nightmares, and so did his companion. Zapata rose at 3 A.M., saddled and mounted the new sorrel horse, and set off for Chinameca, followed by 150 of his men. It was a pleasant time of year; the night air was cool and fresh with a hint of moistness. The rains would begin in a few more weeks; in a less troubled time Zapata and his men would have been preparing their fields.

They arrived at Chinameca mid-morning. Guajardo met Zapata at the wide gate to the hacienda of San Juan Chinameca. They spoke briefly but were interrupted by a messenger with news that Carrancista troops were approaching. Zapata went out to reconnoiter. He knew the area well. In 1911 he had been surrounded by federal troops at the Piedra Encimada, a towering rock outcrop, and saved his life by fleeing through the canebrakes. Now, surveying the countryside from the same rock, he could see no approaching troops. Nevertheless he left most of his troops to guard against a surprise attack and returned to the hacienda for the fiesta Guajardo had promised. He entered the gate a second time, now accompanied by only ten companions. Guajardo's men were standing at attention in the patio, their weapons in the present arms position. A bugle sounded three times just as Zapata passed through the shadow of the gate into the patio, and on the third note Guajardo's men raised their rifles and fired at Zapata and his followers. Zapata turned his horse, his pearl-handled pistol still in its holster. He stood in the stirrups with his arms outthrust and then crashed to the ground. His companions fell with him. Inside the hacienda Feliciano Palacios, one of Zapata's aides, was with Guajardo, waiting for Zapata. Hearing the shooting, he asked Guajardo what it was. "This," said Guajardo, and pulling his pistol he shot Palacios. Most of the Zapatistas who had been left at the Piedra Encimada were also killed.

Zapata's body, with the white shirt and dark charro trousers soaked with blood, was tied to a horse like a sack of corn and taken to Cuautla. The body was laid on the ground floor of the Municipal Palace so that the people of Morelos could see that their hero was dead. Eusebio Jáuregui, whose bungling espionage had innocently furthered the plot, was asked to identify the body as that of his commander. This Jáuregui did. His statement was included in the official report. Then, having served his enemies well, he was shot.

Pablo González reported to Carranza: "With the greatest satisfaction I have the honor of informing you that Colonel Jésus Guajardo and his forces have just arrived bringing the cadaver of Emiliano Zapata who, for so many years, was chief of the Revolution in the South and the irreducible rebellion in this region." All of this, he pointed out, was the result of plans which had earlier been communicated to Carranza orally.

Carranza replied: "I received with satisfaction your report telling of the death of Emiliano Zapata as a result of the plan executed so well by Colonel Jesús M. Guajardo . . . Because of Colonel Guajardo's conduct I have dictated . . . a promotion in grade for Colonel Guajardo and his officers . . ." Guajardo received not only his generalship but also a cash reward of fifty thousand pesos.

Morelos peasants streamed into Cuautla by the thousands to see Zapata's body, now dressed in a clean gray charro suit. One by one they would kneel and cross themselves and then stare closely into the dead face, looking for the mole on the right cheek, just above the thick mustache, and for the little crescent scar by the left eye. The identifying marks were important. Couldn't the Carrancistas have killed another man and made him look like 'Miliano, just to discourage the *campesinos?* Even having seen the mole and the crescent scar many of them were unconvinced. For years afterward they insisted that on dark nights 'Miliano could be seen back in the hills, dressed in white peasant clothes and riding—not the sorrel on which he had been killed—but a fine, white horse of the earlier, happier days. And with quavering voices they would sing *La Triste Despedida de Emiliano Zapata,* the corrido written on the night of Zapata's death by Marcianito Silva, a guitarist who had often played for 'Miliano:

> Adios, forest of Ajusco,
> Adios, hills of Jilguero,
> Adios, you caves and mountains.
> That knew our *guerrero.*

AGUA PRIETA

"All the men of the Mexican Revolution were, without a single exception, inferior to its demands."

Daniel Cosío Villegas,
Mexico's Crisis

EVEN IN A TIME when the value of human life in Mexico was being depreciated at a dizzy pace, the callous killing of Emiliano Zapata sent shock waves of reaction through the war-weary country. For the peasants of the southern states it was the death of a messiah. For fellow revolutionists it was a grim warning. For those Mexicans who were neither revolutionary nor political it appeared to be a confession of the desperate straits of the Carranza government. Zapata was, perhaps, no more than a zealous peasant who had been guilty of atrocities himself. Jesús María Guajardo, the executioner, was a run-of-the-mill killer, a type that was becoming sickeningly familiar. His immediate superior, Pablo González, was living proof that men of slight ability could become rich and famous in the Revolution if they were sufficiently ruthless. González was now frequently described as the *Bandido con Corbata* (Bandit with a Necktie).

But the lines of responsibility did not end with González and Guajardo. Instead they led directly to the white-bearded patriarch who sat in the National Palace, the man who had promised that he would bring an era of peace, unity and Utopian contentment to Mexico. That Don Venustiano had been unable to cope with Zapata with any means other than treachery—which involved the killing of some of his own loyal followers—was an admission of helplessness.

If the Zapata murder had ended the last element of resistance to the Carranza regime it might have been better understood. But there was belligerent opposition on all sides. Farther to the south, the important state of Oaxaca, under the leadership of Guillermo Meixueiro, had seceded from the central government, declared its own sovereignty and its adherence only to the Constitution of 1857; although Meixueiro surrendered in August 1919, Oaxaca remained questionable in its loyalty. In the remote peninsula of Yucatán there was great unrest; the Mayan peasants had taken literally the provisions of the 1917 Constitution. In the state of Veracruz, Felix Díaz, the indefatigable counterrevolutionist, was rallying dissident elements.* Farther north in the oilfields of Veracruz and Tamaulipas General Manuel Peláez had an autonomous revolutionary regime of his own, receiving regular tribute from the foreign oil companies, most of whom would have liked to see him in the presidency. In the far northwest there was a separatist movement in the territory of Baja California. In Sonora, home state of so many influential revolutionists, including Obregón, there was a deep resent- ment of Carranza's efforts to assert the federal government's authority over use of the valuable water of the Sonora River. In the north-central states of Durango, Chihuahua, and Coahuila, Francisco Villa continued his hit-and-run war, taking cities, looting them and then disappearing again.

Felipe Angeles, long absent in the United States, rejoined Villa late in 1918, representing the Alianza Liberal, a group of revolutionary exiles. With Villa's help they hoped to establish peace in Mexico. Villa and Angeles attacked and took the border city of Juárez, presumably the first step in another revolutionary drive down through the center of the country. U.S. troops again crossed the border, drove Villa out— and again stretched Mexican-U.S. relations to the breaking point. Angeles was subsequently captured by the Carrancistas, taken to Chihuahua City and shot. Carranza ordered that the death sentence be carried out despite widespread protests, Angeles being one of the most re- spected figures of the Revolution. Before going before the firing squad Angeles wrote his own epitaph: "I know that my death will further the cause of democracy, because great causes are enriched by the blood of martyrs." Villa went on with his marauding.

Carranza appeared to be indifferent to all of this. He was surrounded by "unconditionals," men whose loyalty to him personally was stronger than any loyalty to either the nation or to the Revolution which had

* Among those supporting Díaz was General Aureliano Blanquet. Blanquet was supposed to have been a member of the firing squad that executed Maximilian at Querétaro in 1867. He was involved in the betrayal and killing of Madero, was Minister of War in Huerta's cabinet and went into exile when Huerta left Mexico. In April 1919, while serving with Díaz's "National Reorganization Army," he was surrounded by Carrancista troops near Huatusco, Veracruz. He died of injuries when he fell into a ravine. His head was severed and exhibited publicly in Vera- cruz.

put him in power. Most of the old revolutionists had disappeared from his official family. The few who remained, such as Pablo González, were busy with personal enrichment (although it was subsequently proven that Carranza himself did not profit personally from the widespread corruption of his administration and, in fact, died in modest circumstances). The rest were either civilians or new young generals whose experience in the Revolution was slight. The lavish scale on which some of the "unconditionals" were enjoying the fruits of the Revolution was strangely at variance with Carranza's own puritanical character, but the First Chief appeared to be wholly insulated by his belief in his own infallibility and righteousness. Thieves went unpunished because of official connections. Widows had to surrender a portion of their pensions to bureaucrats in order to receive anything.

The liberal Constitution of 1917 which Carranza promised to obey and enforce was to a large extent a dead document. A few small parcels of land had been distributed to peasants, it was true, but there was nothing like the wholesale division of land the constitution had promised. Organized labor—far from realizing the promises of the constitution—was controlled by generals and state governors. The free education which the constitution had pledged was almost non-existent; there were fewer schools in operation than before. The federal ministry of education was abolished and Carranza pushed the responsibility for schools back on the municipalities, and the municipalities, having no money to operate them, simply closed them. In the Federal District teachers went on strike for unpaid wages and still more schools were shut down. In the Federal District, which was better supplied with schools than the other parts of the republic, it was estimated that no more than 45 percent of the school age children were receiving any kind of instruction.

Although the press was theoretically free it was to a large extent subsidized and controlled by the government. When a few independent journals printed the truth about Villa's victories in the north the responsible editors were seized, locked in a railroad caboose and taken on a forced tour of the state of Chihuahua to see for themselves that the state was not in Villa's hands. Less daring writers were kept busy turning out authorized biographies of Carranza. The fee for such hack work was 25,000 pesos.

In the area of foreign relations the Carranza government also had difficulties. The Allies of World War I would never forgive him for what they could only interpret as pro-German sympathies. In the United States oil interests, alarmed by the new constitution's regulation of subsoil rights, pressed hard for military intervention. Each new incident along the border was played up in the U.S. press as further evidence of

Carranza's inability to govern Mexico. In Washington there was gossip as to whom the United States would appoint as governor-general of an occupied Mexico. Senator Albert B. Fall, an outspoken and powerful ally of the oil industry and a proponent of intervention, launched a congressional investigation into Mexican affairs. Witnesses such as Henry Lane Wilson, the former ambassador, painted Mexico, the Revolution, and Carranza particularly in the worst possible light. Woodrow Wilson, whose idealism had done so much to tangle Mexican-U.S. relations, was too preoccupied with other matters to come to the aid of the man whom he had, in desperation, recognized as head of the Mexican government.

These pressures, far from forcing Carranza into a conciliatory posture, seemed, instead, to strengthen his attitude of stubborn independence in foreign relations. He had, in the years since the landing of American troops in Veracruz, developed a three-point anti-interventionist policy: (1) that all nations are equal and should mutually respect the laws, institutions and sovereignty of each other; (2) that no nation should intervene in the internal affairs of another; and (3) that foreigners could expect no special rights or privileges from a host country. Whatever Carranza's shortcomings as a statesman were his countrymen respected —and continue to respect—him in his role of defender of Mexico's national interests, so long preyed upon by foreigners and their governments.

He still played the role of a promoter of unity among the Latin American nations, a protector of their interests against encroachment from abroad, particularly by the United States. In his annual message to Congress on September 1, 1919, he assailed the United States' cherished Monroe Doctrine. Mexico, he declared, did not recognize it "inasmuch as it establishes, against the will of all the people of America, a rule and a situation upon which they have not been consulted . . . That doctrine attacks the sovereignty and independence of Mexico and would create a forced tutelage over all the nations of America."

When statements such as this caused an international uproar Carranza would go solemnly and calmly about his business, following a strict routine. He would rise early each morning, dress in his dove gray gabardine uniform, take a cup of black coffee and go for a canter on his favorite black horse. Later he would have a hearty Coahuila style breakfast of beef, beans, flour tortillas, and more coffee. Then, dressed in a well-tailored civilian suit and bowler hat he would go to the National Palace to dictate correspondence and legislative projects in labyrinthine prose and to hear reports from members of his cabinet and staff. Pressing matters tended to be buried under the avalanche of compliments and pleasantries from his young aides such as General

Juan "Juanito" Barragán, twenty-nine, his dashing Chief of Staff, and General Francisco Urquizo, twenty-eight, his Subsecretary of War. On receiving visitors the President would place himself before a window so that the sun shone in the visitor's eyes, while he sat back, running his fingers through his beard, occasionally rubbing his nose—swollen and multicolored from broken veins—and adjusting the dark glasses. When he spoke it was with confidence and authority with no hint that his fortunes—and Mexico's—were in a precarious state.

But if Carranza was oblivious to the state of the nation, helpless in restoring internal peace and indifferent to the mandates of the new constitution, he was deadly earnest about the matter of presidential succession. His legal term would end in 1920. Even before the beginning of this term he had recognized that his greatest political rival would be the genuinely popular Alvaro Obregón. Carranza had, earlier, suggested that Obregón hold his political ambitions in check until 1920. Shortly thereafter, Obregón retired from public life and returned to his garbanzo farming in Sonora.

In the meantime Carranza had become convinced that what Mexico needed as its next president was another civilian like himself. Election of a general—and Obregón was still considered a general although he had retired from the army—would lead to quarreling among other generals. In addition, a military president, particularly a strong one like Obregón, accustomed to command decisions, would want to run the country with no interference. Carranza wanted to be an elder statesman, subtly directing national policy from a cabinet post in the administration of a man he would designate for the job.

There was, perhaps, another reason for Carranza to fear Obregón. Almost from the beginning of its troubled existence as an independent nation, Mexico had a tradition of military leaders turning against the men they had helped to install as head of the government. There had been Vicente Guerrero against Guadalupe Victoria, Anastasio Bustamante against Guerrero, Santa Anna against Bustamante, Mariano Paredes y Arrillaga against Santa Anna and so on. In more recent times, Pascual Orozco had no sooner won the 1911 struggle for Madero than he turned against his chief; Madero placed his faith in the military skills of Victoriano Huerta to protect him from Orozco. This Huerta did, only to turn around and oust Madero from office and arrange to have him assassinated. As early as 1916 the cynical Francisco Bulnes had predicted "with almost mathematical precision" that Carranza would inevitably be overthrown by Obregón, the military genius who had put him in power. Carranza was an ardent student of history and perhaps foresaw matters as clearly as Bulnes.

Whatever the reason, he picked as his successor Ignacio Bonillas, his ambassador to Washington. It could be argued that Carranza, worried about the state of his relations with the United States, wanted a man who might be able to improve them. Bonillas was well-liked in Washington, an intelligent, sober man of pleasant manners. But he was wholly unknown within Mexico. It was rumored that he had actually made application for citizenship in the United States, that he had once served as sheriff in some unidentified U.S. county—charges which Bonillas denied. Mexicans, who love nicknames, referred to him as "Meester" Bonillas, and *Flor de Té* (Tea Flower), after a popular Spanish song which told the story of a homeless little shepherd girl who did not know her name, where she had come from or where she was going.

Carranza insisted that Bonillas was well-known and indeed very popular, but he found it necessary to spend approximately two million pesos in scarce government funds promoting his candidacy. Obregón had known Bonillas since childhood—Bonillas was also from Sonora—and conceded that he was "a nice fellow . . . reliable, conscientious and hard-working. The world has lost a first class bookkeeper."

On June 1, 1919, Obregón issued a manifesto from Nogales, Sonora, formally announcing his candidacy for the presidency. He criticized the Carranza regime for its inability to pacify the country and declared that "the First Chief's historical personality will suffer if he does not permit the country to liberate itself from its liberators."

Pablo González also had his eyes on the presidency but was less decisive than Obregón, hoping for Carranza's blessing. González had been, before the Revolution, a poorly paid factory worker in Monterrey. Now, in 1919, he was one of the ranking generals in Carranza's army, despite his poor military record. He had also become one of the wealthiest men in Mexico, a dapper man with thick black eyebrows and mustache and eyes shielded by dark glasses (like the First Chief's). In January 1920 he accepted the presidential nomination of the Democratic League. But he still thought he might persuade Carranza to withdraw his backing of the "imposition" candidate, Bonillas, and did not fully break with the First Chief until later. Some of his supporters were less hesitant. General Guajardo, the officer who had killed Zapata on González' orders, hearing that two other officers were secretly in favor of Obregón, sternly ordered them to shout "Viva González" in public. When they refused Guajardo pulled his pistol and shot them both.

Carranza, who had once thought González "so respectable," began to change his mind about his formerly favored general. He subsequently described him as "the most unfit man of all. Not only do I know his personal unfitness to handle government money but also his moral and civil weakness . . . [he] came to me saying that if I would give him command of the army and repay the money he had spent in the

election campaign he would be loyal and would take the field against
Obregón . . ."

Obregón expected no help from Carranza and he campaigned vigorously and independently. He and his followers were subjected to harassment from the outset. Army officers and government officials suspected
of favoring Obregón were dismissed from their positions. State governors
were summoned by Carranza to a meeting in Mexico City where they
were instructed to work against Obregón. In provincial cities Obregón
workers were hanged and shot. Others were merely arrested on vague
charges and held incommunicado. Obregón found frequently that the
train on which he was traveling would be shunted onto a siding without explanation and held long enough for him to miss his next speaking
engagement. In Mexico City where an elaborate official welcome was
arranged for the arrival of "Meester" Bonillas at Buenavista station,
Obregonistas infiltrated the crowd throwing confetti mixed with sneez-
ing powder; forty of them were arrested.

Obregón continued campaigning, not so much against Bonillas as
against the men around Carranza, "unscrupulous men of ambition,
who would turn justice into a source of speculation . and make our
national dignity a rag." He joked frequently and coined catchy phrases
and never hesitated to take advantage of his reputation as a national
military hero. When Carrancistas charged that he was, in his speeches,
insulting the President and the Mexican army, Obregón waved the
stump of his right arm and said, "Me, injure the army? Would my
remaining arm betray the one I lost defending the rights of the people?"
He knew that he was in danger. If something happened to him, he
wrote to his wife, she should "offer up your grief as a sacrifice to
the Fatherland. Under no circumstances shall you sue any of my executioners for mercy, for they would but deride your sufferings . . . they
have long since hardened their consciences against any noble sentiment."

The Carranza government worked out a complicated stratagem. Various rebels had been surrendering to the government under amnesty. One
of them was a Colonel Roberto Cejudo, one of Felix Díaz's men.
Cejudo's surrender was at first accepted and he was set free. Then
he was arrested. It was alleged that he had communicated with Obregón
his willingness to join in an anti-Carranza uprising. The government
held correspondence—subsequently proved to be forged—to prove that
Obregón was conspiring with Cejudo. Obregón was ordered to come
to Mexico City to testify at the proceedings against Cejudo.

Although his aides sensed a plot and advised against it, Obregón
obeyed the order and came to Mexico City. At his first court appearance
—in which he denied knowing Cejudo or having any correspondence

with him—the judge was so nervous that he put the lighted end of his cigar in his mouth.

Obregón was ordered to remain in the capital for a further appearance in court—an appearance that he well knew might send him to the firing squad. Instead of going to his usual hotel, the St. Francis, Obregón stayed in the home of a friend. The house was under constant police guard. When he went out his automobile would be followed by motor-cycle policemen. Nevertheless he continued to move about. He was not without friends. Only a few days before a group of senators and deputies favoring Obregón had published a manifesto condemning Carranza for converting the executive branch of the government into a militant political party in defiance of the constitution, and of using government funds to support "the exotic candidate," Bonillas.

Pablo González had, by this time, finally broken with Carranza, and on the night of April 11, in the Chapultepec Restaurant, Obregón and González had a long dinner meeting to discuss their respective efforts against Carranza's imposition. The following day Obregón lunched with the Spanish novelist, Vicente Blasco Ibañez. Blasco Ibañez was in Mexico hoping to do a book on Carranza, but Carranza—who had subsidized many lesser writers—refused to meet his price, said to be $100,000 (dollars) instead of the usual 25,000 pesos. Obregón regaled Blasco Ibañez with tales about Carranza. He said that when a new minister from Spain had arrived Carranza had honored him with a banquet at Chapultepec. Midway in the meal the minister discovered his watch was missing. He looked suspiciously at Obregón, who was seated on his left—but Obregón's right arm was missing, so he could not have stolen the watch. He looked to his right: there sat Cándido Aguilar, Carranza's son-in-law but Aguilar's left hand was paralyzed, so he could not have taken it. The minister angrily shouted: "This is no government, but a den of thieves!" Whereupon Carranza, who was sitting across the table, reached in his own pocket, removed the missing watch and handed it to the minister, saying "take it and be quiet." The minister's anger was replaced with admiration: "Ah, Señor President, this is why they call you the First Chief."

"You see," Obregón added, "here we are all a little inclined to thievery, but I have only one arm."

But Obregón knew there was not much more time for joking. The police that were following him everywhere were increasing in numbers and were heavily armed, apparently waiting for a signal. That night he went for an automobile ride with two friends. The car was, as usual, followed by motorcycle police. Obregón slouched in the seat, traded his white Panama hat for the felt hat of one of the friends. Then, as the car turned past a park he jumped from the car and hid behind the trees. The police continued to follow the white Panama hat in the car.

Obregón was picked up by two friends. During the night, dressed as a railroad worker and with an overcoat draped over the stump of his right arm, he boarded a freight car bound for the state of Guerrero where he had friends in power. He was accompanied by another of the Sonora generals, Benjamín Hill.

Carranza's relations with the state of Sonora had, meanwhile, reached the crisis stage. Sonora, a large and wealthy state far removed from the capital had always had a spirit of tough independence. It was Sonora which had provided refuge for Carranza at the beginning of his career as a rebel in 1913, and *sonorenses*—Obregón notable among them, who had given him his first significant military victories. But in 1919 Sonora had stubbornly resisted Carranza's attempt to assert federal sovereignty over the Sonora River, and the situation had steadily deteriorated.

In the fall of 1919 Carranza had chosen Plutarco Elías Calles, who had just retired as governor of Sonora, to be his Minister of Industry, Commerce, and Labor—apparently in an effort to patch up relations with Sonora. But Calles did not fit into the Carranza family. In labor disputes he sided with labor, and he was shocked by what he later described as "the most corrupt administration in the history of Mexico." He was particularly angered by the operations of Carranza's Chief of Staff, the youthful General "Juanito" Barragán who, he said, headed a "corrupt camarilla . . . They speculate with everything, they sell offices and concessions, authorize thefts from the national treasury . . ." If Carranza expected the Calles appointment to appease Sonora it did quite the opposite. On February 1, 1920, Calles resigned, explaining that he had political commitments, i.e. to Obregón. Anti-Carranza feeling was building up rapidly. The federal government had perpetrated electoral frauds in the states of Guanajuato, San Luis Potosí, Querétaro, Nuevo León, Tamaulipas, Nayarit, and in the government of the Federal District— all adding to the discontent. Clearly a showdown was coming between Carranza and the state governments.

Returning to Sonora, Calles was named Chief of Military Operations in the Northwest by Governor De la Huerta. Carranza, deeply suspicious, ordered General Manuel Diéguez, also a Sonora man but one loyal to the First Chief, to mobilize his forces and prepare to move into Sonora. The Sonora legislature responded by voting extraordinary authority to the state government to confront the "notoriously hostile" attitude of the Carranza government. Calles told newspapermen that any attempt by Carranza to interfere with Sonora sovereignty would mean revolution. On the day after Obregón's flight from Mexico City the state government issued a manifesto all but declaring war on the central government.

Obregón, meanwhile, had some bad moments. While still on the train he heard that the governor of Guerrero, Francisco Figueroa, and the Chief of Operations in the state, General Fortunato Maycotte, had affirmed their loyalty to Carranza. Abandoning the train near Mezcala, Guerrero, he stretched himself on the ground to rest and went to sleep. He awoke to find himself face to face with General Maycotte. He shrugged. "I am at your orders." "No, Señor," said Maycotte. "I am at your orders."

With Maycotte, Obregón went on to the state capital in Chilpancingo where Governor Figueroa assured him of his friendship and support and showed him an exchange of telegrams between Carranza and Maycotte. THE PRESIDENCY, Maycotte had been told, HAS INFORMATION THAT GENERALS OBREGON AND HILL ARE TRAVELING ON THE BALSAS TRAIN IN A STATE OF REBELLION. STOP THE TRAIN AND APPLY THE FULL RIGOR OF THE LAW TO THE AFOREMENTIONED GENERALS" ("full rigor of the law" was a euphemism for summary execution). To this Maycotte replied that he would indeed apply the full rigor of the law to THESE TURN-COATS OF THE REVOLUTION. Maycotte then changed his mind and when General Barragán sent a wire to Maycotte asking his attitude toward the fugitives Obregón and Hill, replied: TELL DON VENUSTIANO WE ARE TIRED OF ALL THE PUPPETS WHO SURROUND HIM, SUCH AS YOU . . . AND TELL HIM THAT GENERALS OBREGON AND HILL HAVE ARRIVED AND HAVE PLACED THEMSELVES AT THE HEAD OF THE TROOPS AND WILL ADVANCE ON MEXICO CITY. When Obregón heard of the exchange he commented: "We shall see who kills whom."

Obregón, who had let his beard grow out just as he had before the battles of Celaya, issued on April 30 from Chilpancingo a manifesto: "It is impossible to continue the political campaign; it is indispensable that we once more take up arms and reconquer those things which they are by force trying to take away from us."

Calles, meanwhile, issued the Plan of Agua Prieta, disavowing Carranza as President, naming Governor De la Huerta as supreme chief of the "Liberal Constitutional Army," and invited other states to follow Sonora's lead. The plan promised that once the movement had triumphed De la Huerta would summon Congress to designate a provisional president, replacing Carranza, and that the provisional president would call for election of a president and national Congress.

By the end of the month rebellions against the central government had broken out in the states of Nayarit, Nuevo León, Veracruz, Michoacán, San Luis Potosí, Chihuahua, Hidalgo, Oaxaca, Morelos, Chiapas, Zacatecas, Tabasco, and Mexico. By May 4 Pablo González declared himself in revolt in the state of Puebla. Carranza could count on his fingers the generals who remained loyal.

CHAPTER 39

TLAXCALANTONGO

> "Social changes are not made by bread-crumb pellets; they are effected by bayonets and gunpowder."
>
> Alberto Morales Jiménez,
> *The Permanent Revolution*

AT DAWN ON May 5, 1920, Mexico City was awakened by cannonading from the Ciudadela, the thick-walled old arsenal in the heart of the city which had so often been the scene of momentous and tragic events in Mexican history. The nervous city dwellers were convinced that the new revolution, which they knew was coming, had erupted. Then they remembered: it was the national holiday commemorating the victory over the French at Puebla in 1862, and the cannons were firing a 21-gun salute.

President Carranza issued a manifesto urging the public to help prevent the government falling into the hands of "the military caudillos who would bloody the Fatherland." Then, wearing his sash of office, he presided over the memorial services in the Pantheon of San Fernando. During the ceremony he received a report that General Francisco Murguía, whom Carranza had made Chief of Operations for the Valley of Mexico, was fighting rebel forces at Otumba, thirty miles outside the city. General Benjamín Hill was approaching the city from the south at the head of Zapatista troops. Obregón was someplace behind him. González, the general who had received more from Carranza that any other, was preparing to move on the capital from Puebla.

Communications were erratic but it appeared that most of the nation was up in arms against the government. Carranza decided to do what he had done once before: go to Veracruz. His son-in-law, General Aguilar, was influential there, and General Guadalupe Sánchez, on whom Carranza had showered many favors, was Chief of Military Operations. He wired Sánchez inquiring his attitude. PRESIDENT AND FATHER, Sánchez replied, THOUGH EVERYONE ELSE BETRAY YOU, I SHALL NOT . . .

With amazing calm Carranza began issuing orders for the greatest evacuation of the Revolution. The treasury was emptied of coin, currency, gold, and silver bullion, and the dies from the mint. Printing presses, cartridge-making machinery, and airplanes were disassembled and crated. Furniture from the National Palace was boxed, and the national archives were packed for shipment. Horses and forage were prepared for the journey. All loyal Carrancistas collected wives, children, mistresses, and household furnishings. There were ten thousand people—less than half of them men. Bales, bundles, crates, and luggage were piled in mountains on the platforms of the Buenavista and Colonia stations. Trains were assembled—passenger cars, Pullmans, freight cars—and the presidential Gold Train. There were difficulties. Many of the cars lacked air brakes. Some of the locomotive were short of both water and fuel. There were not enough engineers. Most railroad men and train crews were Obregonistas and the work had to be done with inadequate numbers of workers.

Carranza, whatever his shortcomings as a leader and administrator might have been, was behaving with dignity and composure. He had little to be cheerful about. His wife had died six months earlier. Generals whom he had made rich and powerful were turning their backs on him. The office he had dreamed of and finally won was about to be wrested from him. Here he was, a sixty-year-old man with a huge paunch and defective eyesight, forced to give up everything and start all over again on the crooked path to power. But, pacing splendidly up and down the railroad station platforms, he encouraged everyone with cordial greetings, reassuring them that the convoy would soon be ready to move. Making a final visit to his house in Calle Lerma he told a nephew: "I am not fleeing into exile like Díaz, nor resigning like Madero. I will return to my house, either in victory or in death."

Finally, less than forty-eight hours after Carranza had given the order for evacuation, the giant convoy began to move out—more than fifteen miles of trains. It was a hazardous journey from the beginning. At Villa de Guadalupe a locomotive charged with dynamite was set loose by unfriendly railroad workers. It crashed head-on into a train carrying part of an infantry regiment, killing two hundred. The survivors from this train and in the trains behind it were then attacked by a cavalry troop led by General Jesús María Guajardo—the officer whom Carranza had promoted to general and rewarded with 50,000 pesos for killing Zapata. The trains behind the wreck were stopped; they carried most of the artillery, the cartridge-making machinery, a thousand soldiers of the same regiment, four hundred members of the presidential guard and a number of cars of horses, including two of Carranza's own.

When the convoy—which Carranza had by this time named the Expeditionary Column of Legality—reached the railroad junction of Apizaco in the state of Tlaxcala—a halt was called and stock was taken. Aside from the civilians, women, and children, the column now consisted of 3000 infantry, 1100 cavalry, and only two artillery pieces. Some reinforcements were received overland from Mexico City and from Puebla, and skirmishes were fought along the route which crossed the state of Tlaxcala and entered the state of Puebla. The convoy was attacked at San Marcos, and the cadets of the Military College fought a valiant rear guard action to permit Carranza's trains to move on. The cadets, some of them beardless boys, were obligated by oath to defend the President of Mexico, and they had come with Carranza in a body. The convoy moved on to Rinconada, Puebla, where, at dawn, there was even heavier action, and Carranza's troops beat off the attackers. During the Rinconada battle Carranza, who had so often in the past avoided military action, mounted a horse and patrolled the battle lines in a rain of fire until his horse was finally shot out from under him.

Carranza had received a message from Obregón offering him safe conduct to Veracruz where he would be placed on a ship to go into exile. He ignored it. Now, at Rinconada, he received a message from General Jacinto B. Treviño whom Obregón and González had jointly named chief of operations in the pursuit of Carranza. Treviño gave Carranza four hours to remove himself and all civilians from the convoy to a place out of the danger zone. At the end of that period a full scale attack would be launched. Carranza read the message, gave a meaningless smile, and again did not reply. The convoy moved on, diminishing in size. As locomotives ran out of water, bucket brigades were organized to bring water from the nearest wells.

On the morning of May 14 the convoy was halted near the station of Aljibes. The fugitives were informed that the rail lines beyond Aljibes were destroyed. Treviño's troops were closing in from the rear. And the convoy was being attacked from the front by cavalry led by Guadalupe Sánchez, the general from Veracruz who had addressed Carranza as "President and Father" in assuring him of his loyalty.

With Veracruz in rebel hands the convoy could go no farther. After a breakfast of scrambled eggs, beans, and weak coffee Carranza met with his generals. His troops were retreating, surrendering, and the attack was so close that bullets were shattering windows and clanging against the wheels of Carranza's car. The generals insisted that they must flee. At first Carranza refused, stubbornly maintaining he was going to stay. Finally they persuaded him and the First Chief, with maddening slowness, descended from the car. Then he remembered that his horse had been killed the day before. General Urquizo loaned him his. Carranza calmly mounted, decided the stirrups were too short, dismounted while they were lengthened, remounted, remembered he'd left some papers in the car, sent for them and waited placidly while they were brought. A bonfire was made of the archives. At last the party, generals, cabinet members, a few troops—including the cadets from the Military College—and some civilians, including Ignacio Bonillas, whom Carranza had hoped to make President of Mexico, abandoned the battlefield and the trains. All were on horseback. Additional supplies—bedding and a portable typewriter for Carranza—were carried by pack mules. There was little food. And they had to leave behind in the train 3,733,704.50 pesos in gold and 58,000 pesos in silver.*

With Veracruz out of the question Carranza now planned to lead his party through northern Puebla, the states of Hidalgo and Querétaro, into San Luis Potosí until a place could be found for a reorganization of his forces. He already was talking of sending a commission to the United States to secure supplies for a new military campaign.

The northern part of the state of Puebla is one of the roughest terrains in Mexico. Here the great central plateau has its eastern boundary, an awesome barrier of precipitous mountains, running north and south, shrouded in clouds and cold mist. The sierra is cut by chasms through which course streams draining the central highlands and flowing toward the Gulf of Mexico. In the late spring—this was mid-May—the rainy season is just beginning; the rains are of cloudburst proportions and the streams in the canyons become torrents, all but impassable. The route that Carranza chose was, in short, one of the most difficult in Mexico, but it had the virtue of isolation.

The trip was at first fairly easy, through Zapatepec, Santa Lugarda, and Temextla where the party was put up at an hacienda. The next night they slept at the side of the road near the village of Zitlacuautla. In the morning they rode on to the settlement of Cuautempan where Carranza, long hungry, was given a meal in a tiny hut. Here he ordered the cadets of the Military College to return to Mexico City as best they could (he had ordered most of his civilian followers—many of them senators and deputies—to remain behind at Zacatepec). The Expeditionary Column of Legality was now reduced to approximately a hundred men. Horses and mules had been lost through lameness. Supplies had been abandoned. Food was scarce. Indian villagers, with that strange sense of impending trouble bred into them through centuries

---

* The money was recovered for the government by a young major, Adolfo Ruiz Cortines, who thirty-two years later was elected President of Mexico.

of persecution, would flee as they approached, leaving cooking fires smoldering, but no food. The mountains grew steeper and the rivers rose higher under the incessant rain. Carranza uncomplainingly led the column on, often dismounting to get his horse past danger spots on the path. On the night of May 19 Carranza and his reduced party spent the night at the miserable *rancheria* of Tlaltepango, cold, wet, and hungry.

The following morning Carranza and his party crossed the Río Necaxa and halted at the village of La Unión to discuss where they should go next. Here they were joined by a local guerrilla fighter, Rodolfo Herrero. Herrero had been a partisan of Manuel Peláez, the caudillo from Veracruz, but two months before had surrendered to Carranza's forces under a promise of amnesty and had been allowed to keep his rank of general.

Herrero counseled Carranza and his group that the course they were following would surely expose them to attack. Instead he proposed to take them to a place where there was shelter, food, and pasturage for the horses. There they would be secure until they could continue their journey to the north. Some of Carranza's followers distrusted Herrero; a man who had changed sides once could do so again. But Carranza accepted. With the affable Herrero riding beside him, talking volubly, complimenting the First Chief, helping him off and on his horse, they rode off into an even higher and more remote part of the sierra. The rain came down harder and the gloom deepened.

Their destination was a tiny settlement called Tlaxcalantongo, a village perched on a ledge with the towering mountains on one side and a steep barranca on the other. The mountains on the west shut off what little there was left of the gray afternoon light when the Carranza party arrived. The village was empty. The Indians had, as usual, fled. There were no solid structures; only huts of wattle, earthen floors and leaky thatch roofs. On one of the mud walls was crudely lettered Muera Carranza (Death to Carranza).

There was no food (although one of Carranza's aides caught a sickly chicken and prepared it for the First Chief's supper) and no pasture for the horses. Herrero led Carranza to one of the largest huts and said grandly: "This is the best house. Here you can pass the night. For the present it is your National Palace." He watched as Carranza spread his saddle blanket on the damp floor. Herrero excused himself. His brother had been wounded in a skirmish, he said, and he had to return to help him. Carranza insisted that Herrero be supplied with bandages and disinfectants. Herrero thanked him and disappeared in the dark.

Some of Carranza's party, still suspicious of Herrero, urged that they not stay but move on in the hope of finding a more comfortable stopping place. But Carranza ruled against it. It was 7 P.M., pitch dark. The horses were exhausted as well as hungry. And it was raining harder than before. Carranza stretched on his pallet and talked to his aides of his boyhood in Coahuila. The only light was a stub candle. Finally it was extinguished and the men tried to sleep.

At midnight there was a noise at the door. The stub candle was lighted again. The visitor was a Totonac Indian who said he had a message that he must place in Carranza's hands. He was shown in. The message was from General Francisco Mariel, whom Carranza had sent on to Villa Juárez to see if it was safe for the Expeditionary Column of Legality to proceed in that direction. The message said that everything was arranged. The Indian refused Carranza's invitation to stay in the hut, out of the driving rain. It seemed curious that Mariel should have chosen this man for a messenger, and that, with his mission accomplished, the Indian should have insisted on leaving in such weather. The candle was put out again and Carranza went to sleep.

At about 4 A.M., Friday, May 21, the black silence of Tlaxcalantongo exploded with gunfire. There was much running and yelling. Most of the shooting seemed to be coming from in back of the hut Carranza occupied. There were shouts of "Viva Obregón" and "Muera Carranza." One of the first shots struck Carranza high on the left thigh, close to the hip joint, and Carranza was heard to complain that he could not move because his leg was broken. There were more shots, and Carranza could be heard breathing stertorously. Then he was silent.

The gunfire, the shouting and the confusion continued. Some of Carranza's followers attempted to return the fire, but no one knew for certain who or where the enemy was; others fled through the rain and mud. Then the shooting stopped. At daybreak the attackers—they were Herrero's men—returned to take prisoners and to loot the "national palace," taking Carranza's portable typewriter, his pistol, his watch, and his tinted spectacles.

Carranza's body was placed in a rough coffin and carried by Indians down out of the mountains to Villa Juárez, where an autopsy was performed. In addition to the wound in the left thigh there were three chest and abdominal wounds, all on a trajectory from left to right and on a downward course. There was also a wound in the index finger of the left hand.

Nevertheless, Rodolfo Herrero, director of the strange events that ended in Carranza's death, maintained that the victim, after receiving the leg wound, shot and killed himself.

Herrero was ordered into Mexico City by Obregón, who accused him of "treason and vulgar assassination." Herrero was brought into the capital on a military train by General Lázaro Cárdenas, commander of a nearby sector. In the capital Herrero was questioned at length but not held. Seven months later he was confined for a week in the military prison of Santiago Tlaltelolco. He was deprived of his military rank, removed from the army rolls and then allowed to go free.*

Herrero's brother Ernesto and Major Herminio Márquez Escobedo, both of whom were believed to have been in the attacking party at Tlaxcalantongo, were also brought in for questioning. They too insisted that Carranza had killed himself. Herminio Márquez was particularly suspect. In 1915, a trainload of Carrancista officials returning from Veracruz to Mexico City, had been dynamited with heavy loss of life. On July 30, 1915, Carranza outlawed Emilio Márquez, brother of Herminio, for the deed. Two years later, on August 16, 1917, Emilio and two other Márquez brothers, Esteban and Gaspar, were killed by Carrancista troops at Otatlan, Puebla. Their bodies were put on public display, and Herminio was said to have sworn vengeance on Carranza. But after questioning in Mexico City, Ernesto Herrero and Márquez were also given their freedom.

The true circumstances of Carranza's death were buried under charges and counter charges. Among them was an accusation that Obregón had been responsible for Carranza's death warrant. In December 1920, General Alberto Basave y Piña, who had been Herrero's immediate superior, sent a letter to the Mexican Supreme Court from a hiding place in southern Mexico. He said that he had relayed to Herrero a message from Obregón which said "Attack Carranza's party and render a report that he died in combat." It was believed that Basave y Piña's version, apparently inspired by the die-hard Carrancistas, among them Carranza's son-in-law, Aguilar, who was also in hiding, was nothing more than an attempt to embarrass Obregón, whose way to the presidency was now clear.

* Herrero was subsequently reinstated as a general, serving under the government of Obregón, and was again dismissed from service during the presidency of Lázaro Cárdenas (1934–40) as being "unworthy of the army." In retaliation he later attempted to show—with forged documents—that Cárdenas had ordered Carranza killed.

CHAPTER 40

A LITTLE PEACE

> "I hadn't caused any of these popular ex-
> plosions . . . I was a man of peace, con-
> cord and brotherhood . . . with this and
> good luck I was able to achieve my goal—
> the pacification of the country."
>
> Adolfo de la Huerta, *Memorias*

THE TEMPEST OF DISCONTENT, resentment, and revolutionary frustration which swept Carranza to his death in the lonely sierra of Puebla was the most powerful and decisive Mexico had seen in ten years of civil war. Francisco Madero's movement had followed a desultory course and triumphed not so much through its own momentum as through the debility of the Díaz regime. Carranza's Constitutionalist crusade had beginnings just as inauspicious as Madero's and, handicapped by factional strife, advanced erratically.

But the anti-Carranza revolution had moved with lightning-like speed, beginning with the Plan of Agua Prieta on April 23, 1920, and ending with Carranza's death, less than a month later. More remarkable was the fact that virtually all of Mexico was united in the movement.

This unanimity seemed to promise a period of peace and good feelings. Sonora Governor Adolfo de la Huerta, designated by the Plan of Agua Prieta as chief of the Liberal Constitutionalist army, seemed determined to achieve it. He issued a call on May 13 for federal senators and deputies to meet in Mexico City and elect a provisional president. On May 24, three day after Carranza's death, the special session of Congress chose De la Huerta provisional president by 224 votes to 28 for General Pablo González, the closest contender.

As provisional president De la Huerta immediately scheduled a national election for September 5, at which time a constitutional president

would be chosen. There was no doubt that the principal candidate and
certain winner would be Alvaro Obregón—whose political ambitions
Carranza had tried to thwart.

Earlier it had appeared that Pablo González would oppose Obregón
for the presidency. They were the two most powerful generals in the
country and nominally allies, but they were not friends. Obregón was
scornful of González as a general and impatient with his reluctance in
recognizing the Plan of Agua Prieta. González was jealous of Obregón,
who had been so successful as a soldier and was more popular. But
González avoided a test. Even before the election of the provisional
president, in which he ran second to De la Huerta, he declared that he
would not be a candidate for the constitutional presidency. In the
statement issued from his Puebla headquarters on May 15, González
said there was no hostility between him and Obregón, and he was
withdrawing only to preserve harmony. Shortly thereafter provisional
President De la Huerta's newly appointed Secretary of War, Plutarco
Elías Calles, granted González an unlimited release from the army.
González made another statement, announcing his return to private
life and reviewing his recent actions in a favorable light. Then he returned to his home in Monterrey.

Jesús María Guajardo, who had done so much of González' dirty
work, was transferred to northern Mexico to fight Villa. On July 2 at
Gómez Palacio, Durango, he rebelled against the central government
and with his troops began moving toward the northeast. The next day,
trying to stop the desertions which were cutting into his force, he
told his troops that General Pablo González was also rebelling against
the De la Huerta government.

In Monterrey there was an uprising, and Secretary of War Calles
ordered the arrest of González. González was found hiding in the
basement of his Monterrey home, and imprisoned. The following day
Guajardo was found in Monterrey in the company of his beautiful young
wife. He was seized on a charge that he planned to bring about a
garrison revolt and liberate González. He was arrested at 6 P.M. one
day, and, on the order of the state government, was executed at 6:30 A.M.
the next, calmly smoking a cigar.

González went before a court-martial and was found guilty of inciting
to rebellion. But, instead of being shot, he was set free on the specific
orders of Calles. In his message freeing González Calles said "the government feels itself sufficiently strong, supported by public opinion and
confident of its honor and rectitude that it has no fear that General
González might continue being a threat to the stability of this administration . . . place him at absolute liberty."

The reprieve for González was not so much a reflection of the good will of Calles as it was of De la Huerta's opposition to capital punishment.*

De la Huerta was an honest, forthright man, noted for his sincerity, good humor, and excellent singing voice (he had had operatic ambitions). His manner was frankly conciliatory, and during the six months of his provisional presidency there was more harmony between the various revolutionary factions than there had ever been before. The Zapatistas were at peace with the central government. Rebels in southern Mexico were pacified. Most of Felix Díaz's followers accepted amnesty and Díaz was allowed to go into exile. Followers of the anarchistic Ricardo Flores Magón, some of them expatriates for almost two decades, finally returned to Mexico. Francisco Lágos Cházaro, last president of the ill-fated Convention government, came back from exile.

Of all the dissident revolutionary factions only Francisco Villa was still a belligerent. In the years since the Punitive Expedition he had continued to fight a war peculiarly his own. Much of the time it seemed to be a war for war's sake. A city would fall to one of Villa's thundering cavalry attacks. A forced "loan" would be imposed. Old enemies would be sought out and killed, often with Villa's own gun. He personally executed the father and two brothers of his one-time comrade and later enemy, Maclovio Herrera. His followers were reduced in number but they were as violent as ever. Baudelio Uribe specialized in cutting off his captives' ears. In Santa Rosalía de Camargo, where a federal garrison had been surprised and wiped out, the Villistas executed the *soldaderas,* the soldiers' women and their children. One of the *soldaderas* had insulted Villa. Some said thirty were killed, some said more than two hundred. News concerning Villa was always variable. There continued to be lurid stories about Villa and his love affairs. In Jiménez he was said to have burned the feet of Ignacio Rentería in order to win possession of his daughter, Austroberta. At Satevó, where a fifteen-year-old girl was said to be bearing Villa's child, the parish priest was forced to confess paternity, abandon his vows and marry the girl. In Valle de Allende, Villa's roving eye fell on a twenty-two-year-old beauty, Soledad Seañez. The apprehensive villagers, made nervous by Villa's mere presence, were summoned to the plaza where Villa spoke to them. He told them he planned to do nothing in Valle de Allende but get married. He was carried away with emotion; his simple statement became a harangue. He told his past history as a revolutionist and how

* The Constitution of 1917, in Article 22, had prohibited capital punishment "for political offenses; it can only be imposed for high treason committed during a foreign war, parricide, murder that is treacherous, premeditated or committed for profit, arson, abduction, highway robbery, piracy, and grave military offenses." Like many other parts of the constitution it had been ignored.

he had always fought for the ideals of the people. He wept as he spoke. He then appointed a village elder to function as judge and perform the civil ceremony. Afterward Villa organized an impromptu fiesta to celebrate the event and ordered all to be joyous.

He fought a notable series of battles with Francisco Murguía, Carranza's commander in Chihuahua, sometimes winning, sometimes losing. The people of Chihuahua insisted that the government troops were not really trying—that they could annihilate Villa if they only would, but if Villa were gone they would have nothing to do.

The fruitless American Punitive Expedition had not deterred Villa. He continued to operate along the border, seizing Americans and holding them for ransom, thus creating ticklish diplomatic situations for the Carranza government. Twice in 1917 he had attacked the Mexican border town of Ojinaga, driving Carrancista troops out of Mexico and across the border. In the second attack on Ojinaga he captured a train said to be carrying silver bullion to the United States. The bullion, if it existed, disappeared (supposed caches of Villista loot in Chihuahua and Durango have excited generations of treasure hunters).

His attack on Juárez in June 1919 was one of his last grand gestures. With this as a base he had hoped to drive his newly organized army down into central Mexico, just as he had once done with his Division of the North. But American troops crossed the international boundary and drove the once invincible guerrilla fighter out of the border town and into obscurity again.

From time to time Villa had issued manifestos denouncing Carranza and his government. At one point he even planned to go to Mexico City in disguise and kidnap the President during his morning horseback ride in Chapultepec Park. But after the Juárez debacle he forgot such ambitious undertakings. He limited his operations to minor ventures, striking whatever targets promised enough booty to support him and his followers who, depending on circumstances, might number from a few hundred to a thousand or so.

The mortality rate was high among his favorite officers. In September 1919 Martín López, younger brother of the gringo-hating Pablo López, was shot in the stomach during a hopeless attack on El Chorro station, Durango. Villa had regarded young López almost as a son and had been delighted by his exploits—such as riding his horse up the stairs of the Government Palace in Chihuahua City the last time they had captured it. He wept when young López died of his wound.

And he wept when he heard, a few months later, of the execution of Felipe Angeles who had worked so hard to make Villa both a military tactician and a gentleman—succeeding in one rather more than the other.

In his desolation Villa, a teetotaler all his life, now occasionally took a pull from a bottle of *anis*. He would snip out newspaper pictures of his enemies, nail them to a tree and, for amusement, shoot at them with his pistol. If his military luck was bad his marksmanship was as good as ever: it was said that he could, at twenty paces, fire a bullet into an empty cartridge shell of the same caliber. Otherwise he seemed a little less bloodthirsty than before. In February 1920 he told a guest at his camp in the sierra of Chihuahua that he no longer liked to kill people and was, at present, studying mathematics. A few weeks later he stopped a train from Tlahualilo searching for a landowner who was not on the train. While his followers politely bought and paid for the train vendor's stock of beer Villa conversed pleasantly with the passengers. One day soon, he told them, he would make another attack on Torreón, but he promised that he would inflict no hardships on the townspeople.

When the anti-Carrancista rebellion came into the open with the proclamation of the Plan of Agua Prieta, Villa offered his aid—and did cooperate in the taking of Chihuahua City April 28 and 29. There were efforts to arrange a meeting between Villa and Calles, but neither trusted the other. Villa sent word to Calles that he and his men would put themselves at Calles' disposal if their military ranks would be recognized and if Villa could be given an hacienda on which he could live and work honorably. Calles' response was to suggest that he could offer such things only if Villa would leave Chihuahua and come and settle in Sonora, where he had neither friends nor enemies. Villa made no further move.

General Ignacio C. Enríquez, whom the Agua Prieta rebels had installed as governor of Chihuahua, then tried his hand at making peace with Villa. With his troops he approached Valle de Allende, where Villa was camped. Both generals rode out and met on neutral ground between the two forces—and Mexico City papers printed photographs of the two men sitting on the ground and talking in friendly fashion. But the talk came to nothing. Enríquez withdrew his forces. Then, at night, he made a surprise attack on Villa's camp. He found campfires burning and a few horses tethered. But the Villistas were all gone. Villa had expected treachery. A few days later Villa retaliated, attacking Enríquez' forces in Parral, causing a heavy loss of life. He almost captured the commander, General José Gonzalo Escobar, whom he had once defeated at Juárez and whom he hated for having presided at the court-martial which sentenced Felipe Angeles to death.

On July 2 Provisional President De la Huerta received a letter from Villa, written at the hacienda of Encinillas, Chihuahua, and carried by Elías L. Torres, an engineer and writer who had assumed the role of peacemaker. *"In writing to you,"* said Villa, *"I am guided solely by love of country . . . In order to achieve a definite pacification of the country . . . I am disposed to give a brotherly embrace to you, and Generals*

Obregón, Calles, and Hill. If you are ashamed to be my friends, reject me. I am ready to fight against injustices, without fear of the danger or the number of the enemy; I will listen and follow the voice of justice. If you would deal honorably with me, send me a letter signed by all of you and we can begin to discuss the well-being of the republic. Meanwhile I am suspending hostilities . . . A brother of your race who speaks with his heart, Francisco Villa."

Although De la Huerta was ill when he received Villa's message he was pleased with the news. "What a proud thing it will be for my government," he told Torres, "to bring to order the most feared guerrilla, the only one still in arms. I will be able to turn over the government . . . with the country entirely pacified." De la Huerta was eager to make peace with Villa on any honorable terms and addressed a cordial letter to him for Torres to deliver—Villa's whereabouts being kept secret. Calles, the Secretary of War, and General Benjamín Hill signed a separate letter, pledging themselves to observe guarantees made to Villa by De la Huerta. Obregón, however, urged De la Huerta not to come to terms with Villa.

Torres, en route back to Villa's secret encampment, encountered, at Saucillo, Chihuahua, government troops commanded by General José Gonzalo Escobar. They were admittedly searching for Villa on orders from Secretary of War Calles. When he reached Villa's camp Torres found that Villa was aware of Calles' treachery, having intercepted a telegram giving orders to Gonzalo Escobar to find Villa and attack him.

Villa and the men who were with him saddled their horses—Villa was riding a favorite mare, the almost legendary Siete Leguas (Seven Leagues). He sent a message to De la Huerta saying he would get in touch with him later. They struck off toward the east in the fierce summer heat, riding night and day across the Bolsón de Mapimi, the cruelest desert in Mexico. They were searching for a location from which Villa could communicate directly with De la Huerta by telegraph without harassment or interference by government troops.

At 1 A.M. on July 22 the weary horsemen, after a hard ride of 250 miles under impossible conditions, saw the lights of Sabinas, Coahuila. They destroyed the railroad lines north and south of Sabinas to prevent any sudden approach of government troops, and then rode into the town, wearily shouting "Viva Villa."

When daylight came Villa went to the railroad telegraph office and dictated another message to De la Huerta: I AM AT YOUR ORDERS, SENOR PRESIDENT. THE INTRANSIGENCE OF ONE OF YOUR CHIEFS FORCED ME TO TAKE THIS CITY. IT WAS DONE IN PERFECT ORDER. THE PEOPLE HAVE SUF-

FERED NO HARM. THERE HAS NOT BEEN A SINGLE DEATH . . . I AM READY
TO CONTINUE THE INTERRUPTED NEGOTIATIONS . . .

While his men sprawled on the ground in the cool shade of the
cypress trees for which Sabinas is famous Villa stayed at the telegraph
office, listening to the messages coming fom De la Huerta in Mexico
City. He dictated his replies to his personal telegrapher, Gómez Moretín.
The government's offer was generous. An hacienda was to be deeded
to Villa. Other land was to be granted to his men. All of Villa's troops
were to receive one year's pay. Those who wished to do so were invited
to join the federal army and preserve their present rank. Villa could
maintain a personal escort of fifty men; the rest would be disbanded,
and all would lay down their arms. There were nine generals, 56
captains, 75 lieutenants, 64 sergeants, 14 corporals, and 480 soldiers. Villa
swore on his honor never to take up arms against the government,
and General Eugenio Martínez, acting for De la Huerta, promised
to see that all guarantees were carried out.

The hacienda deeded to Villa by the government was Canutillo, a
25,000 acre estate in the northern part of Villa's native state of Durango,
close to the Chihuahua border. It was remote from the capitals—and
politics—of both states. During the past decade it had been deserted
except when occupied by some revolutionary force. Tomás Urbina
had once used it as his headquarters. Villa had fought one of his
battles with Murguía's artillery here and heavy shells had blasted through
the thick adobe walls in several places. Although long neglected and
now overgrown with weeds it was good land for cattle and grain.

The government offered a train to take Villa and his men to Durango,
but they preferred to go the way they had come, on horseback. For
Villa it might be his last opportunity to ride at the head of a column of
men. They rode unarmed and at peace, and in town after town in
Coahuila and Chihuahua they were greeted, cheered, and stared at with
curiosity. At Cuatro Ciénegas, Carranza's home town, the town council
came out in a body to meet them and offer them official hospitality.

The same happened in San Pedro de las Colonias, Francisco Madero's
town. Here Villa received cordial letters from De la Huerta, Calles,
and General Hill. But there was nothing from Obregón, the man
who would be the next president of Mexico. To a newspaperman Villa
commented: "I love Don Adolfo de la Huerta like a brother. As for
General Obregón, well . . . to tell the truth I have no confidence in
him."

In Parral, Chihuahua, quite near the hacienda that would be his home,
he was again warmly welcomed. He made an emotional speech about
the new life he was going to lead. With General Martínez, to whom he
had surrendered, and General Gonzalo Escobar, whom he had fought

here in Parral only a few months earlier, he faced a group of Mexican and American newspapermen. With an arm around each general Villa said to the reporters: "Now you see, gentlemen, we are going forward united, honorable gentlemen and bandits together." He summoned his men, thanked them for their services, wished them well, and assured them that the government would lead the nation along the path of peace and prosperity. He closed with "Viva Mexico!" Then he and his fifty-man escort, chosen from the elite Dorados, mounted their horses and rode south to Canutillo.

At Canutillo Villa poured his great energies into rehabilitating the hacienda. With the pension he had received from the government—reputedly 500,000 pesos—he ordered quantities of farm machinery, tractors, harrows, plows, threshing machines—and blooded stock. The Dorados and Villa, all used to the saddle, now mounted tractors, cleared the land, put it back in production. Two-thirds of the property was reserved for Villa's men, who farmed it with modern equipment.

The big house was put back in order—new windows and doors replacing those that had been destroyed or carted away. Adobe walls were patched and whitewashed.

A school was built for the children of the hacienda and Villa regularly visted the classes to make certain the children were learning. He did his own studying at night in his office, decorated with a portrait of Madero and a bronze bust of Angeles, under the direction of his secretary, Colonel Miguel Trillo, "Trillito." He studied arithmetic and plodded his way through books dealing with economics and history, mouthing the words as he read but forgetting nothing.

The hacienda had medical facilities, a store, a telegraph office, and a chapel. Villa arranged a collective marriage ceremony to regularize the common law marriages of his men, many of whom were living with the *soldaderas* who had followed them in the campaigns. And Villa took still another wife: Austroberta Rentería, the young and pretty woman from Jiménez whose father had undergone torture in a vain effort to keep his daughter away from Villa. There were two other wives still living, Luz Corral in El Paso and Soledad Seañez whom Villa, according to local gossip, had installed in a house in Parral where he visited her regularly. Villa was proud of the brood of six children he had with him at Canutillo and hoped to have many more.

He also had a cote of white doves at Canutillo. When he whistled the doves would come and perch on the hands, arms, and shoulders of Villa, the man of peace.

Although he was seldom without a pistol at his belt Villa scoffed at rumors that he had stockpiled weapons at Canutillo against the day when he and his men would go to war again. He stayed out of political discussions and tried to avoid interviews with newspapermen who invariably got on the subject of politics. To journalists who wrote to him he would reply politely, using his imported English stationery with a partially clad female figure of justice in the upper left hand corner: "From the beginning I have abstained from any sort of participation, direct or indirect, in political matters and for this reason I cannot grant your wish. I have retired completely to private life, dedicated in body and soul to work. After a long career of fighting this is the best way to contribute truly to the reconstruction and enrichment of my country!"

On the rare occasions on which he did grant interviews he preferred to talk about non-political matters. To the American journalist Frazier Hunt he said: "Poor, ignorant Mexico. Until she has education nothing much can be done for her. I know. I was twenty-five before I could sign my own name . . . And I know what it is to try to help people who can't understand what you are trying to do for them. I fought ten years for them. I have a principle: I fought . . . so that poor men could live like human beings, have their own land, send their children to school and have human freedom. But it wasn't much use. Most of them were too ignorant to understand the ideas. That's why I quit fighting. I fought as long as the traitor Carranza was in power, but now that Obregón is at the head I'd be doing more harm than good, so I stopped . . . Nothing much can be done at all until the common people are educated."

THE PRACTICAL MAN

> "My comrades are generals, governors,
> even presidents . . . rich, famous . . .
> while I am poor, unknown, sick . . .
> branded as a felon . . . My old comrades
> were practical men."
>
> Ricardo Flores Magón, Prisoner No.
> 14596, Leavenworth Penitentiary,
> 1923

WHEN THE FORTY-YEAR-OLD Alvaro Obregón donned the tricolor sash of office in midnight inauguration ceremonies on November 30, 1920, he became the twelfth President of Mexico in less than a decade.

In ten years of struggle and suffering the Mexican Revolution should have achieved its goals. The old order had been destroyed; a charter for the new order had been drafted in the 1917 Constitution. The death of Carranza had been a macabre climax to destructive factionalism, to the furious aimlessness into which the revolutionary movement had drifted. Mexicans by the hundreds of thousands had died or disappeared.* Mexico had had enough of suffering.

Now Obregón, a strong, popular man, noted for his common sense and practicality, had the responsibility for bringing about the fundamental changes which his old mentor, Carranza, had been unwilling or unable to effect.

He had the advantage of the air of good feeling De la Huerta had brought about. Zapatistas, Villistas and other dissident elements

---

*In the 1900 census the population had been 13,607,000; in 1910 it was 15,160,000, an increase of 11.4 percent in the decade. But in the next census, 1921, it had dropped to 14,335,000—an apparent net decrease of 825,000. Mexican census figures for the first quarter of the century are unreliable, however. But it is certain the population dropped sharply, perhaps by one million.

were collaborating with the government. Even Antonio Díaz Soto y Gama, Zapata's fiery orator and ideologue, was an Obregón supporter. Obregón was easy to like, easy to work with. In a nation of emotional people he was wholly unsentimental. On the day the body of his old leader, Carranza, was returned to Mexico City he had planned to go to the bullfight and would have gone had not his friend Miguel Alessio Robles convinced him that it would not look right. Although his public pronouncements tended to be platitudinous, his private observations of men and politics were extremely frank ("Any upheaval such as ours," he said, "leaves a residue of men who refuse to live by their labor, who . . . offer up incense to those on their way to power"). Mexico City swarmed with at least five hundred generals, most of them men of humble origin who had once had nothing but a gun and a horse and now had flashy uniforms, limousines, mistresses and no cares. The days of revolutionary banditry were over, Obregón said, because he had brought all the bandits with him to the capital to keep them out of trouble.

Obregón had long believed that military men should be kept out of politics, that government should be entrusted only to civilians. In this he had agreed with Carranza. But he, as a soldier, had gone against his beliefs in assuming the presidency. He had also violated the constitution which his supporters had drafted at Querétaro. Article 82 of the constitution excluded from the presidency anyone who had "taken part, directly or indirectly, in any uprising, riot or military coup" against the established government. This Obregón had done against the established government of Carranza. Shortly after Obregón's assumption of office an effort was made to sidestep this legal embarrassment. Eduardo Neri, the Attorney General, told the Mexican press that Carranza, at the time of his death, had not legally been President of Mexico—without explaining just why.

"The framing of laws in the belief that these can abolish evil and right every wrong" was futile, Obregón insisted. What Mexico needed was "honest and intelligent men to apply good laws." As President he set about getting both the laws and the men he needed.

He gave freedom and encouragement to organized labor. He distributed land to the landless—almost ten times as much as had been distributed under Carranza—although Obregón was more cautious than some of his radical collaborators. He argued that land distribution should, if possible, be preceded by instruction in the economics and techniques of farming.

His greatest accomplishments were in the field of education, and they were due largely to his choice of José Vasconcelos as his Minister of Education. Vasconcelos was one of the most brilliant men in Mexico, a facile writer, a man of culture and scholarship. He had served with Madero, Villa, and in Eulalio Gutiérrez' short-lived Convention government he had also been Minister of Education. Under De la Huerta he had recently served as rector of the National University. He was a man of romantic ideas and behavior (his love affairs were notorious), but he also had vision and energy. The Ministry of Education, which Carranza had abolished, was reestablished by Obregón for Vasconcelos.

Under the idealistic leadership of Vasconcelos the ministry turned out hundreds of young, idealistic teachers. Zealous as missionaries, they were sent into the most remote Indian villages, to build schools with their own hands and to teach Mexico's neglected and illiterate majority. Vasconcelos organized normal schools to train more teachers, agricultural schools, schools for every sort of specialization. He also promoted festivals of music, dancing, art, and poetry. A lover of classical learning (he was an authority on Pythagoras), he told Obregón "What this country needs is to sit down and read the *Iliad*. I am going to distribute a hundred thousand Homers in the schools . . ."

Vasconcelos, with Obregón's backing, began publishing cheap, sturdy editions of the classics for free distribution. Green clothbound copies of Homer, Aeschylus, Euripides, Plato, Dante, and Goethe began to be shipped out to schools all over Mexico. Vasconcelos had hoped to distribute a hundred classical titles in this way but only got as far as number seventeen. In the process he suffered the criticism of teachers who complained that they needed more practical things, and of revolutionary intellectuals who said it was an aristocratic gesture.

Obregón regarded Vasconcelos' venture with amused patience. One day, he said, he walked along the railroad platform while his train was halted at a station in Guanajuato. Among the many food vendors was a dirty and ragged old man with a tin tray balanced on his head. Obregón asked what he was selling. The old man said he was selling *pepitas* (toasted pumpkin seeds).

"Would you like some, my chief? Five centavos a measure."

"How much do you make in a day?"

"Thirty to forty centavos, chief."

"And you live on this?"

"Why yes, señor. It is enough to buy my food in the market stalls. I sleep free in the house of a niece."

"If you spend everything you make on food, how do you replace your stock?"

"It costs nothing, little chief. I gather the seeds where the people who preserve pumpkin throw their garbage. To toast them I gather other rubbish and build a fire under this very tray."

Obregón turned to his secretary, Fernando Torreblanca, and said:

"Give this old man five pesos and tell Vasconcelos to send him a collection of the classics." (In another version as Obregón told it—as with many story tellers, his tale varied with each telling—the man destined to receive the books was a poor Indian who did not know the name of the village where he had lived all his life, never having had occasion to refer to it.)

But Vasconcelos was proud of his accomplishment: "Among all the fine things that the Ministry of Education produced in my time . . . [this] gives me the most pride and joy . . . the best propaganda for Mexico . . . the good it has done for humble readers."

He was also to be remembered, not only in Mexico but around the world, as the man responsible for the spectacular renaissance in mural painting. In the process of refurbishing old colonial buildings, notably the church and convent of San Pedro y San Pablo and the National Preparatory School, Vasconcelos hired Mexican artists to decorate the walls. What the Minister of Education had in mind was illustrations from his beloved classics. What he got, from painters so eager to paint that they worked for unskilled laborers' wages, was an explosive expression of Mexican nationalism, first in terms of allegory, later as folk art and finally as epic history. Roberto Montenegro and Gerardo Murillo ("Dr. Atl") were among the first muralists to go to work for Vasconcelos. Diego Rivera, who was to become the most vocal of the revolutionary painters although he had seen nothing of the Revolution, was lured back from Europe and given a wall in the National Preparatory School to paint. Around him clustered young painters, including Revueltas, Alva, Leal, Cohero, and Charlot—who came to be known as *Dieguitos* ("Little Diegos"). They often had to paint with pistols in their belts to protect themselves from assault and their work from mutilation by self-appointed critics.

David Alfaro Siqueiros—who had actually been a soldier of the Revolution and was the most truly revolutionary of the lot—was also summoned back from Europe where he had been studying and painting on a government stipend. Siqueiros became the most militant and articulate of the artists of the Revolution, a powerful painter and a front line fighter for causes in which he believed. And finally, José Clemente Orozco, a silent, lonely man who had been best known for his cartoons brimming with the horror and brutality of the Revolution, was given walls to fill with his apocalyptic visions of his tormented country.

These painters, and many who were to follow them, converted Mexico's bloody history, its vivid landscape and oppressed people into a new, startling, and genuinely American art. The painting was often didactic and polemical in tone, but it spoke directly to a people most of whom were unable to learn of their country's past and present from reading books. And it was in the Mexican tradition; unknown Mexican craftsmen had been painting temple walls for a thousand or more years.

Vasconcelos at times became impatient with the stridency of his painter-protégés and weary of the interminable Indian faces and Indian themes, but he had—perhaps without realizing the extent to which it would go—initiated one of the great art movements of the twentieth century.

It was a time of enthusiasm, of new hopes and pride, for clearing away the wreckage. Historians, journalists, and novelists began sorting the tangled history of the Revolution. Anita Brenner, one of the most sympathetic observers of the scene, wrote: "Poets wrote lyrics about high tension cables. Peasants hung necklaces of flowers on tractors and invented Indian nicknames for steam shovels."

In September 1921 the nation celebrated the centennial of the achievement of Mexico's independence. In the National Stadium an operatic company presented *Aida* in honor of the national army (*Aida* had also been staged during Porfirio Díaz's celebration, eleven years earlier, of the beginning of the struggle for independence). Common soldiers sat in the bleachers with their *soldaderas,* watching and listening with incomprehension. It was typical of Mexico's high and frequently unrealistic ambitions. There were 112 other elaborate events—banquets, balls, diplomatic receptions. A military parade followed the route that in 1821 had been followed by Agustín Iturbide and the Army of the Three Guarantees.

But peace was illusory in Obregón's Mexico as it had been in Iturbide's. For all the well-dressed, well-fed generals enjoying the good life in Mexico City there were still many regional caudillos left behind, resentful that they were not enjoying the spoils of the Revolution and jealous of those who were. There were also many die-hard Carrancistas, some in outlying parts of Mexico, some waiting in neighboring countries for the day when they could fight again.

There was increasing strife between radicals and Catholics. Bombs exploded in the residences of the archbishops in Mexico City and Guadalajara. There was bloody street fighting in Morelia after Socialists raised their red and black flag on the tower of the cathedral. Another bomb blasted the altar of the Basilica of Guadalupe, Mexico's most venerated shrine. Tension and fear mounted. In the capital a crowd gathered in front of the Municipal Palace to protest a water shortage (the water supply had been cut off in a political dispute). Nervous guards, excited by the flash of a photographer's magnesium powder, fired into the crowd, killing many. The mob then stormed the palace and set it afire.

Obregón found it necessary to deal summarily with the growing unrest in the country. "People are pacified with laws," he said, "and laws are defended with rifles." Government troops were kept busy controlling brushfire rebellions. There were disturbances in Hidalgo, Puebla, Michoacán, Oaxaca, Chiapas, Tabasco, Yucatán, and Nuevo León. Week after week rebels, or supposed rebels, went before firing squads at the army rifle range in Mexico City or in garrison compounds in remote parts of the republic.

But the list of dissident generals continued to grow: General Miguel Alemán (father of a later President of Mexico) who had forces in Veracruz and Puebla; General Domingo Arrieta in Durango; General Lindoro Hernández in Hidalgo; General José V. Elizondo in Nuevo León; and General Carlos Greene who had troops in Tabasco, Campeche, and Yucatán. In June 1922 Juan Carrasco, a tough old general from Sinaloa, publicly disavowed Obregón's presidency and declared his adherence, as had others, to General Francisco Murguía as "supreme chief of the Revolution."

Murguía, one of the ablest and most faithful of Carranza's generals, had been arrested during the investigation into the Tlaxcalantongo disaster but had been released from custody shortly after Obregón took office. He had gone into exile in the United States where he maintained communication with other Obregón enemies.

In August 1922 Murguía crossed the border near Brownsville, Texas, hoping to find a rebel army waiting for his leadership. Instead he was met by only a handful of men. Undaunted, he went ahead, and from Zaragoza, Coahuila, addressed an open letter to Obregón, signed "your loyal enemy." Murguía reviewed the alleged illegality of Obregón's presidency and said this would not matter if Obregón were governing justly and peacefully. But, he said, Obregón's government was one "born of crime and sustained by crime," and he accused Obregón of responsibility for the assassination of Carranza. "Your jails," he said, "contain no political prisoners because you have shot all of them." He appended a grisly list of 121 Mexicans, both soldiers and civilians, who had been killed since Obregón's accession—a few after summary court-martials on the charge of "considering rebellion" but most shot with no trial at all or through application of the old *ley fuga*.

Included on the list was the name of General Lucio Blanco, who, after Carranza's assassination, had taken refuge in Laredo, Texas. Blanco had been lured with a friend to a supposed assignation. The next day the bodies of Blanco and his friend, handcuffed together, were found in the Rio Grande, the victims, it was believed, of Mexican government agents who suspected Blanco of "considering rebellion."

There was little response to Murguía's call to arms. With his "Army of

Replevin," consisting of only seventy men, he tried to take refuge in a church at Tepehuanes, Durango, where he was captured, quickly tried by a court-martial, taken to the local cemetery and shot. He was offered the option—a courtesy usually extended to generals—of calling out orders to the firing squad, but he declined. He refused, he said, to commit suicide. He died shouting "Viva Carranza."

Although he considered war "essentially immoral, a temporary lapse into savagery," Obregón did not hesitate to wage what amounted to civil war to maintain security while he got on with the work of reconstruction. Similarly, although he believed in democratic procedures, he was taking preliminary steps to guarantee that the choice of a candidate to succeed him in the presidency would rest in his hands alone.

The political scene was one of confusion. Party organization was loose and impermanent. The Liberal Constitutionalist party, whose candidate Obregón had been in 1920, broke up in political wrangling. Political factions under various names—labor, agrarian, cooperative, Socialists, even Communists, shifted from one alliance to another. The only stable political factor was in the person of the President, Obregón. But Plutarco Elías Calles, who had been Minister of War in De la Huerta's cabinet and was now Minister of Government for Obregón, began to emerge as the strong man, with substantial backing from both labor and agrarian sectors, and, more important, the support of Obregón. A close second was De la Huerta, who had become Obregón's Secretary of the Treasury. De la Huerta insisted that he had no interest in the presidency but instead favored Calles. Calles made no such disclaimer; he was very definitely interested in becoming President.

CHAPTER 42

DEATH AT PARRAL

> Fly, fly little dove,
> Perch among the castor beans
> And tell all the gringos—
> Francisco Villa's dead.
>
> *Corrido* on the death of
> Villa

FRANCISCO VILLA HATED CALLES. The hatred dated back to the Battle of Agua Prieta in which Calles, a not particularly distinguished soldier, inflicted a stinging defeat on Villa and the remnants of the Division of the North.

And he was very fond of Adolfo de la Huerta, to whom he referred as his "little brother" and, affectionately, as Fito, the diminutive for Adolfo.

As rivalry between Calles and De la Huerta for the presidency began to appear likely Villa occasionally broke his self-imposed restriction not to talk politics. To some American newspapermen he said that the only circumstances under which he would again take up his arms would be an American attack on Mexico or if De la Huerta needed his help for any reason. And to a Mexican newspaperman he said: "Fito is a very good man. If he has faults they come from his goodness. He is one politician who would like to conciliate the interests of everyone, and he who does this does good for the fatherland. He is good, intelligent, and patriotic, and wouldn't look bad in the presidency."

But Villa showed no serious intention of again becoming involved in politics. His business was growing larger. Canutillo was prosperous. He had bought the Hotel Hidalgo in Parral, useful when he was in town with all of his men. He had also organized a bank through which small farmers could get low-interest loans. He improved the road from Canutillo to Parral, and often drove back and forth in a Dodge automobile.

He rode horseback every day, but he no longer lived in the saddle as he once had. The great mare, Siete Leguas, which had carried him on the desperate ride across the Bolsón de Mapimi, was gone; Villa had sent her as a present to De la Huerta (who subsequently gave her to General Lázaro Cárdenas). His other great horses, Taurino and Príncipe Tirano, were becoming dim memories.

He still loved cockfights. On a Sunday in April 1923 he was, as usual, at the cockfight pit in Parral and lost several hundred pesos to Melitón Lozoya, a cattle dealer from the village of La Cochinera. On the road back to Canutillo Villa grumbled about his loss, and one of his companions told him something of Lozoya he had not known. The hacienda of Canutillo, now Villa's, had once belonged to the Jurado family. Like so many *hacendados* they had fled to Mexico City at the beginning of the Revolution, abandoning Canutillo. They then had written to Lozoya, authorizing him to collect all the stock at the hacienda and also all the farming equipment, household furnishings, and everything else that could be moved, to sell it all and retain half for himself.

This had all transpired long before Villa had acquired Canutillo. But it threw him into one of his fits of irrational anger. He summoned Lozoya the next day and with his eyes blazing in the old way told him that he had thirty days in which to restore to the hacienda everything that had belonged to it. Otherwise he would kill him. Lozoya admitted having sold the stock but said he would not have done so if he had known that Villa would be the future owner. Villa, unmoved, repeated the threat. Lozoya withdrew to La Cochinera, summoned some friends and began to make plans to kill Villa. The thirty days of grace came and went without Villa molesting Lozoya, but the plotting went on. So went one version of what happened.

There had been several unsuccessful attempts on Villa's life since he had established himself at Canutillo. He had, at first, never gone abroad without a heavily armed escort, but by the summer of 1923 he was beginning to be less cautious.

Early in June 1923 Villa received a letter from one of his old soldiers, Sabas Lozoya—not related to Melitón—who had settled at the village of Rio Florido, east of Parral, asking him to be a godfather at the christening of a new son. Villa agreed. He planned at first to go on horseback at the head of his troop of Dorados; the sentiment of the occasion seemed to call for such a show. Trillo, however, dissuaded him. Sabas Lozoya was a poor man. He would be unable to feed so many men or provide pasturage for their horses. It would be an

embarrassment for their old comrade. Villa concurred, and plans were
made to make the trip in the Dodge touring car with only a few
companions.

The christening was a happy event. Afterward Villa and his men
returned to Parral and Villa paid an overnight call on a woman friend
in the Calle Zaragoza.

Two blocks away where the Calle Juárez joins the Calle Gabino
Barreda, eight men led by Melitón Lozoya were hiding in a two-room
house, each armed with a new repeating rifle and a large caliber pistol.

They had camped here before, awaiting an opportunity. They knew
Villa's movements well. They knew that he often stayed in the house
in the Calle Zaragoza; that upon leaving he usually drove his car
down the Calle Juárez, past the Plaza Juárez, then turned right in
the Calle Gabino Barreda to cross the bridge over the Rio Parral and
head for Canutillo, 47 miles away.

They had missed on two occasions. On one the sunlight reflected
from the windshield of Villa's car made it impossible to shoot. On
the other a procession of school children—among them an adopted
child of Lozoya's—came into range at the critical moment.

On the morning of July 20, 1923, Villa was ready to return to
Canutillo. The conspirators in the house in the Calle Gabino Barreda
knew his schedule. They had eavesdropped on conversations of members
of his escort. The Parral garrison of federal troops had left town on
field maneuvers—a move which was later interpreted as meaningful.
It was a clear, hot summer morning—the kind on which townspeople
rose early to get to work. But on this day few people moved about;
the streets were empty.

At a little after seven Villa left the house in the Calle Zaragoza.
He decided to take the wheel of the Dodge himself. The faithful
Trillo, a paunchy, adenoidal man who always played Sancho Panza
to Villa's Quixote, seated himself beside Villa. At Trillo's feet was a
satchel containing 20,000 pesos to be used for payrolls at Canutillo.
Rosalío Rosales, the regular chauffeur, rode on the running board. Four
other Villa men, Daniel Tamayo, Claro Hurtado, Rafael Medrano, and
Ramón Contreras, chief of the escort, rode in the rear.

Villa was in high spirits, laughing and joking with his men. In
his career as a guerrilla he had always avoided love on the night
before a battle—just as bullfighters are supposed to do. But that was
long ago. Today he was relaxed and happy, foreseeing nothing. Only
minutes before he left the house on Zaragoza an old friend had come
to warn him that the town was full of rumors of a coming attempt
on his life. Villa brushed it off. "The man hasn't been born who can

lay a hand on Pancho Villa," he said. He had had many such warnings and had disregarded all of them.

The durable but noisy Dodge—the rough roads of Durango and Chihuahua had produced a variety of rattles—moved down the Calle Juárez at 7:20 A.M. At the edge of the Plaza Juárez stood a vendor, his tray of candies, gum, and trinkets ready for the school children who would be passing a little later in the morning. As the car approached he peered closely, then raised his hand in a salute and shouted "Viva Villa." Villa glanced at him, waved and drove on. The man took a bandanna from his pocket and, glancing toward the end of the street, mopped his face. It was a signal.

The door and two street-facing windows of the house on Gabino Barreda swung open and four rifle barrels appeared in each window. Villa's car approached the intersection, began to make the turn, and the rifles roared, first four from the window on the left, then the other four, then the first four again. Villa's car swerved wildly and crashed head-on into a tree. The firing continued. The men ran out of the house, still firing, using pistols now.

Villa, although he received multiple wounds, two of them in his head, had succeeded in pulling his pistol in the split second of life that remained and fired it, killing one of the attackers, Ramón Guerra. Trillo appeared to have been killed outright; in a death spasm his body catapulted two-thirds of the way out of the right side of the Dodge. Rosalío Rosales, the chauffeur, fell from the running board in the first blast of fire. The assassins continued firing. One of them, Librado Martínez, said later, that he emptied his rifle twice and his pistol three times, a total of thirty-three shots.

The men in the back seat of the car, all wounded, tumbled out and returned the fire. One of them, Ramón Contreras, with one arm shattered and a gaping hole in his abdomen, managed to escape into the Parral River bottom. He went to a hospital to have his stomach wound sewed up, then, distrustful of Parral, started back to Canutillo on foot.

The assassins surveyed the six dead men, then mounted horses and calmly rode away, apparently confident that they would not be molested.

The bodies of Villa and his men were displayed in the hall of Villa's Hotel Hidalgo. Pictures of Villa's shattered body were soon being hawked all over Mexico with the caption "the forty-seven wounds of Pancho Villa"—although there were only thirteen.

It was common knowledge in the states of Chihuahua and Durango that Melitón Lozoya and his friends had been the assassins, and that they had been paid three hundred pesos apiece for their work. By whom?

Jesús Salas Barraza, a Durango politician and a relative of two of the men in the assassination party, was generally suspected. He was well-connected with business and political interests in Durango, Chihuahua, and Mexico City. He had been heard frequently expressing his hatred of Villa, to whom he referred as "the animal" and "the dog." Salas Barrazas had often talked of hoping to take Villa's life as a matter of "social vengeance." And he had spent some time with the assassination party in their rented house on the Calle Gabino Barreda before the assault.

A week after the massacre President Obregón told the press that "the mysterious assassination of Francisco Villa will soon be clarified." The next day a Mexico City newspaper commented: "Despite the time that has elapsed no one knows a relevant thing. All conjectures point to numerous assassins. It is curious that none of them has committed an indiscretion which would provide a clue to the plot." Two days later another Mexico City paper said that within a week the Ministry of War would know the identity of the assassins . . . "but up to the moment nobody knows anything." On August 1 a special investigative commission appointed by the Chamber of Deputies returned from Parral: the commission's only findings were that the bullets used in the assassination were the same kind used by the federal army, and that the assassination was "probably political."

On August 9 more than two weeks after the murder, capital newspapers printed a story that Jesús Salas Barraza had admitted being the "intellectual author" of the assassination. Salas Barraza wrote a letter confessing the crime; the letter was forwarded to President Obregón, who turned it over to the chief prosecutor for the state of Chihuahua. In the letter Salas Barraza referred to the victim as Doroteo Arango, whose "innumerable crimes deserved just punishment," and said that nine participants were "satisfied with the result we had hoped for: the death of the hyena." There was also a curious statement: he was making his confession "to save the good name of the government and to prevent suspicion falling on certain public functionaries."

Two days later Salas Barraza appeared in the capital, apparently of his own volition. He was shut up in the penitentiary where he was made easily available to journalists and seemed eager to talk of the assassination. Among other things he said that he understood that the state of Chihuahua had authorized a reward of 100,000 pesos for the killer of Villa. The reward had nothing to do with his action. If the reward was offered to him he would use it for a fund to benefit the children of Villa's victims.

At the end of August Salas Barraza was taken in custody to Parral to explain details of the crime. Somewhat later he was again jailed, this time in the state penitentiary of Chihuahua. But on April 4, 1924, less than a year after the event, he was pardoned by the Chihuahua governor, Ignacio C. Enríquez, who had himself tried to destroy Villa in a surprise attack after their truce talks in 1920. Salas Barraza took a commission in the federal army, later served in the national Congress, and until his death in 1951 still maintained that it was he who planned and directed the assassination—although he was wrong on some of his facts (he claimed, for instance, that he had fired four pistol shots into Villa's head as a *coup de grâce;* yet there were only two head wounds).

More than a year after the killing a Mexico City journalist, Justino N. Palomares, spoke with Colonel Felix C. Lara, who commanded the military garrison of Parral, the garrison which had gone on maneuvers the day of the slaying. Lara told Palomares that several months before the event he had been summoned to Mexico City by Calles. Calles had given him instructions to eliminate the "Cincinatus of Canutillo," who was described as a grave danger to the peace of the country. Lara returned to Parral and began interviewing Villa's numerous enemies. This, although Lara did not say so, apparently led to the contact with Melitón Lozoya and, subsequently, to Salas Barraza. It may have explained how the assassins happened to have new weapons and government issue ammunition. Lara added that after the killing he temporarily sheltered the assassins in his quarters and spread false stories that he was pursuing them.

There was, of course, nothing completely certain, any more than there had been in the killing of Madero and Carranza. A cartoon of the period showed two men in the street, one asking the other "Who killed Villa?" and the other answering *"Calle . . . se, amigo,"* a phrase which, in the beginning sounds like "Calles" but, after a pause, means "Shut up, friend."

The question of guilt in Villa's murder was not the last mystery about the dead guerrilla fighter. Two and a half years after his death his grave at Parral was broken open, the head severed from the cadaver and taken away. There were various stories: that the U.S. government had offered a reward of $100,000 for Villa's head as proof that he was really dead; that a soldier of fortune had stolen it and planned to take it on tour, charging admission to see it; that an American scientific institution wanted to obtain Villa's cranium for scientific studies to determine the reasons for Villa's strange combination of genius and madness.

CHAPTER 43

THE SONORA SCHISM

> ". . . in Mexico all men of advanced
> thought are called Bolsheviks. I also, nat-
> urally."
>
> Plutarco Elías Calles, 1924

IN THE LITERATURE OF the Mexican Revolution Obregón is usually referred to as *el general invicto* (the unconquered general), and Calles as *el estadista* (the statesman).

More familiarly, Obregón was called *el manco* (one-arm), and Calles *el Turco* (the Turk).

Calles was not a Turk but his antecedents and early history were somewhat vague.

In the flood of denunciation later directed at him by Catholics it was alleged: (1) that he had been born in Arizona and was thus ineligible for the presidency of Mexico; (2) that he was the son of a Yaqui Indian woman and a Syrian peddler, and that as the son of an alien he was ineligible for the presidency; and (3) that he was a Jew. Records are scarce, but as nearly as can be determined he was the natural son of María de Jesús Campuzano and Plutarco Elías, member of a politically prominent Sonora family of supposedly Lebanese antecedents. He was born in the municipality of Guaymas, Sonora. He was born Plutarco Elías but subsequently took the name Calles.*

* Two standard Mexican biographical collections make no mention of Calles. The *Diccionario Biográfico Revolucionario* of Francisco Naranjo carries a biographical sketch but no details of his early life or parentage. *Mexico Before the World*, which carries Calles' name as author (New York: The Academy Press, 1927) contains two biographical essays which presumably met with Calles' approval. One, by General José Monje Sánchez, says that Calles was a great-grandson of Manuel Elías Pérez, a native of Spain who settled in Sonora and was the founder of a town and a man of property. Calles' father, says Monje Sánchez, was Plu-

As a young man Calles was a schoolmaster. Later he worked as town treasurer and then was employed as a bartender and manager of a saloon in the Hotel Gambrinus in Guaymas. The saloon had gambling tables and Calles' observation that drinking and gambling didn't go well together is said to have made him an ardent prohibitionist (many years later as interim governor of Sonora he made the manufacture and sale of intoxicants a capital offense). When the saloon and hotel burned to the ground he had a brief career managing a flour mill belonging to a relative.

After the triumph of the Madero revolution Calles became police commissioner in the border town of Agua Prieta. He was an active and enthusiastic revolutionist, first as a Maderista and later in Carranza's Constitutionalist movement. He was somewhat inept as a field commander of revolutionary troops, but his political skills made up for his military shortcomings. He was a forceful speaker and an able maneuverer and he rose rapidly in the ranks—colonel, general, military governor, and finally, a cabinet post under Carranza. He did not stay with Carranza long. He resigned, returned to Sonora and soon thereafter issued the anti-Carranza Plan of Agua Prieta. Actually the plan was the work of Gilberto Valenzuela, who subsequently was to accuse Calles of the same wrongdoings that Calles had attributed to Carranza.

He was tall and powerfully built. His face was one that delighted caricaturists: it appeared to have been roughly hewn from a block of wood—both eyes and mouth tight slits in the rugged surface. He rarely smiled. He usually stood with his heavy shoulders in a slouch and was seldom without a cigarette.

Obregón was genial, affable, gregarious—and Calles was none of these. Obregón loved to tell stories and jokes; Calles did neither. Obregón was regarded with affection by the men around him and with respect by his enemies. Calles received awed respect from the one, loathing from the others. Obregón was often ruthless, but he was also consistent. Calles

---

tarco Elías Lucero, who inherited considerable properties near Fronteras, Sonora, and "had numerous sons who devoted themselves to various activities." Monje Sánchez does not account for the Calles name. Another biographer in the same volume, Manuel Becerra Acosta, speaks of the poverty of Calles' background and says that he was the son of Plutarco Elías and María de Jesús Calles. He also says that Calles' mother died when he was young and that he was reared by a maiden aunt, Manuela Calles and that, in gratitude, "her nephew added to his name that of the self-sacrificing woman who had been a second mother to him." Fernando Torreblanca, who was both secretary and son-in-law to Calles, says that Calles' mother died when he was very young and that he was supported by his uncle, Juan Calles, husband of his mother's sister, María Antonia Campuzano de Calles. The future president changed his name from Plutarco Elías to Plutarco Elías Calles in honor of the uncle, according to Torreblanca.

was inconsistently ruthless. He upheld the rights of the Indian masses but he was an oppressor of the Yaquis. He formed strong political ties with organized labor, but he had machine-gunned workers who went on strike at the mine of a friend in Sonora. He was a rich man but he hated the rich. He was a large landowner but he condemned landowners as a class. In two things he was consistent. One was his abiding enmity for the Catholic Church. The other was the zeal with which he put down real or suspected opposition.

Anti-Calles elements in 1923, foreseeing Calles' probable succession of Obregón, began to promote the candidacy of Adolfo de la Huerta, Secretary of the Treasury in Obregón's cabinet. De la Huerta, close to both Obregón and Calles, gave them no encouragement.

In the spring of 1922 Treasury Secretary De la Huerta, who had been a bank clerk in Sonora before he became involved with revolutionary politics—made a trip to New York and Washington to try to find a solution to Mexico's crushing financial problems. He entertained often and well aboard his private car, the Hidalgo, serving liquors and wines to Prohibition-parched American financiers and politicians. In Washington he conferred at length with President Warren G. Harding and his Secretary of State, Charles Evans Hughes. The result was the De la Huerta-Lamont agreement by which Mexico agreed to resume service on its bonds and to acknowledge an indebtedness of approximately one billion pesos ($500,000,000 in U.S. currency). De la Huerta was convinced that diplomatic recognition, badly needed by the Obregón administration, would follow in due course.

The United States, however, had already suggested, apparently as a prerequisite to recognition, a treaty of friendship and commerce which would cover not only the question of indebtedness but also foreign-owned oil properties and compensation for land expropriations. The De la Huerta-Lamont agreement did not cover all these questions and, as a result, a conference was arranged between Mexican and U.S. representatives in Mexico City in the summer of 1923. The conference meetings were held in an old mansion in the Calle Bucareli, and the resulting document—whether it was a treaty or merely an agreement was a matter of dispute—was known as the Bucareli pact. Mutually satisfactory agreements were reached on such difficult matters as the retroactivity of the 1917 Constitution regarding oil concessions, adjustment of the debt, land expropriation and the multitude of claims against the Mexican government for damages dating back to the beginning of the Revolution. These would be adjusted by a mixed, i.e. Mexican and American, claims commission. Formal recognition of the Obregón government followed almost immediately. De la Huerta objected from the outset that the Bucareli pact was a treaty and that it was being imposed as a condition of recognition—which he interpreted as an affront to Mexico's sovereignty.

Within three weeks after the announcement of resumption of U.S.-Mexican relations De la Huerta resigned as Secretary of the Treasury. Although the immediate reason appeared to be a dispute over the appointment of a state governor, the basic disagreement was in regard to the Bucareli pact. De la Huerta's separation from the government caused widespread concern. He was well-liked for his peace-making efforts during his interim presidency. As Minister of the Treasury he had managed the nation's finances carefully and well under difficult circumstances. Perhaps most remarkable of all, he had not enriched himself. He was still a comparatively poor man. When he left Chapultepec Castle at the end of his interim term he had moved into a government-owned house on which, it was noted with amazement, he paid rent once a month.

Although De la Huerta had repeatedly disavowed any interest in the presidency, his friends, including a number of conservatives who regarded him as a more reasonable man than most of his colleagues, applied pressure to get him to reconsider. That De la Huerta did, finally, change his mind was probably more due to the action of his successor as Secretary of the Treasury, Alberto J. Pani. Pani reported, upon taking over De la Huerta's post, that the nation's finances were in a disastrous state and placed the responsibility on De la Huerta. De la Huerta boosters staged a mass demonstration, a huge crowd carrying banners marching from the Zócalo to De la Huerta's residence. This was followed shortly by a statement from Obregón, blaming the nation's financial plight on his old friend De la Huerta. At this point De la Huerta reversed himself and decided that he would, after all, be the presidential candidate of the National Cooperative party.

De la Huerta's candidacy was announced on November 23, 1923. It was apparent that the government would throw all its power behind Calles, who had resigned his cabinet post in order to campaign.

By November 30 General Rómulo Figueroa, an old friend and ally of Obregón, had declared himself in rebellion in the state of Guerrero, protesting the government's position in regard to the presidential succession.

From Guadalajara General Enrique Estrada, commander of the 2nd Division, wrote to Obregón: "I have the honor of disavowing Alvaro Obregón, the backslid revolutionary, the President who has violated the Magna Carta he swore to uphold, the soldier who has failed in his duty by becoming the principal sponsor of an imposed candidacy." Estrada's defection was particularly annoying to Obregón who had only recently loaned him money so that he could get married.

From Tiquicheo, Michoacán, José Rentería Luviano, a veteran revolutionist who had supported Obregón in the rebellion of 1920 wrote: "I have the honor to inform you that I am in this place. My attitude is frankly rebellious. But I have not yet begun to mobilize my forces. For the last time I appeal to the patriotism you have proven on other occasions. A new war would mean the ruin of the country and the complete discredit of the Revolution . . . I implore you, don't follow this road."

De la Huerta, a man who loved art and music and who, aside from revolutionary ideals, had little in common with the military men who controlled Mexico, decided to flee. On December 4 he secretly boarded a train for Veracruz, the port city which had so often served as a base for political fugitives. In addition to its strategic and fiscal advantages, it was controlled by General Guadalupe Sánchez, the man who had betrayed Carranza and who now supported De la Huerta. From Veracruz De la Huerta issued a manifesto, on December 7, accusing Obregón of the same misdeeds for which Obregón and his followers had turned against Carranza.

Approximately 60 percent of the federal army rebelled and declared for De la Huerta. Some of the defections were embarrassing. General Fortunato Maycotte, the man who switched his loyalty from Carranza to Obregón in the spring of 1920, changed sides again. Maycotte came to Mexico City from Oaxaca, where he was in charge of federal troops, to pick up 200,000 pesos to finance the campaign he was to wage against the Delahuertistas; having obtained it he then went over to the De la Huerta side.

But if the rebel forces had greater military strength the government retained the loyalty of organized labor and peasants; also, because of the recent diplomatic recognition Obregón was able to procure quantities of war matériel, including 11 De Havilland aircraft, 32 new machine guns, 15,000 Enfield rifles and five million rounds of ammunition, which more than overcame the government's numerical inferiority.

It was a short, sad war and a bloody one: at least seven thousand men lost their lives, and survivors were pursued with cruel vengeance.

By February De la Huerta and his skeleton government were forced to leave Veracruz and take refuge in Frontera, Tabasco. On March 12 De la Huerta left the country, fleeing to Key West, which he entered in disguise. From there he made his way to Los Angeles where he became a singing teacher and remained for many years (under the presidency of Lázaro Cárdenas he was invited back to Mexico and became a functionary in the Ministry of Foreign Relations).

Few of De la Huerta's fellow rebels fared as well. Manuel Diéguez, who had begun his revolutionary career as a strike leader at Cananea and had become one of Obregón's earliest and most trusted collaborators, was pursued into the southernmost Mexican state Chiapas, captured and executed. Salvador Alvarado, the one-time pharmacist who had, as Military Governor of Yucatán, become one of the most radical and picturesque of the revolutionists, also was a victim. Defeated in the field he had managed to escape to the United States. Then he made his way back to southeastern Mexico, apparently intent on starting all over again. He and his handful of followers were captured near the ancient Mayan ceremonial city of Palenque and shot. Ramón Treviño, a lawyer, was tried by a court-martial for rebellion. He protested that since he was a civilian the court-martial had no authority. Secretary of War Francisco Serrano solved it with a terse telegram: Treviño was appointed a general of the army, and General Treviño was to be shot at once. Manuel Chao, who had been both an ally and rival of Francisco Villa in the early days of the Revolution, was shot as a Delahuertista rebel in Chihuahua. José Rentería Luviano, who had informed his old friend Obregón that he was "frankly rebellious," escaped the firing squad by committing suicide. Rafael Buelna, the pint-sized general who was affectionately called "the little nugget of gold" (and of whom Martín Luis Guzmán wrote: "He reflected not the enthusiasm of the Revolution but its sadness . . . conscious of the tragedy . . .") was lucky: he died in battle.

Fortunato Maycotte, who had changed sides so often, was less fortunate. Maycotte had crowded much combat into his thirty-six years, and had continued to fight after the De la Huerta cause was already obviously lost. With a constantly diminishing force Maycotte retreated from Puebla to Oaxaca. In the Mixteca mountains he divided his remaining two hundred men into small groups so that they could travel faster and attract less attention. With a dozen men he headed south for the coast. They were captured at San Pedro Mixtepec, Oaxaca, but bribed their captors and went on to the Pacific Coast, a short distance away. With only three followers Maycotte moved southeastward along the coast. The government meanwhile had sent ships and troops to the ports of Puerto Angel and Salina Cruz. They also circulated rumors that Maycotte carried a vast sum in gold. Maycotte and his men periodically left the beach to climb back into the mountains and escape pursuit. In fording a river he was bitten by an alligator. He managed to buy a horse from an unsuspecting rancher and pushed on, hoping to find refuge in Salina Cruz. After having been without food or water for days and half delirious he approached a group of civilians. He was tortured, relieved of a money belt containing 2500 pesos and a gold watch, and turned over to military authorities. On May 14, a little more than a month since the beginning of his agonizing retreat, he was shot at Arenal, Oaxaca.

One of the grievous losses for the government was the young governor of Yucatán, Felipe Carrillo Puerto, a militant Socialist popularly known as "the red Christ of the Maya." He had organized at least one-third of the population of Yucatán in "resistance leagues" which took the names of such Mexicans as Madero, Zapata, and Flores Magón and such non-Mexicans as Karl Marx and Maxim Gorky. The leagues fought for the socialization of all industry, suppression of Catholicism, for "rationalistic education," and prohibition of gambling, alcohol, and tobacco. Carrillo Puerto, a large, green-eyed man who claimed descent from a Mayan king named Nachi Cocom, would read the 1917 Constitution to his followers in the Mayan language, and, cynics said, his greatest fault was that he believed it. His romantic attachment to Alma Reed, a young newspaperwoman from San Francisco—for whom he commissioned the popular song *La Peregrina* to be written—was one of the few pleasant interludes in the annals of the Revolution.

When the De la Huerta rebellion broke out Carrillo Puerto remained loyal to Obregón and Calles. Troops stationed in Yucatán rebelled in favor of De la Huerta and the young governor was forced to flee from Merida, the capital. With a few followers he retreated toward the east, being joined by armed peasants. He took whatever funds there were in the treasuries of villages he passed through, but there would be only a few pesos in one, even fewer in the next. He refused to tear up railroad tracks behind him—even though he knew rebel troops were pursuing him; the tracks belonged to the people and should not be damaged. At the very tip of the Yucatán Peninsula Carrillo Puerto and his party boarded a small boat, hoping to escape into the territory of Quintana Roo or into Guatemala. Their boat went aground and they were captured. Carrillo Puerto and his companions were returned to Merida. During the early hours of January 3, Carrillo Puerto and twelve associates, including his five brothers, were taken to the cemetery and shot. It was an execution that caused consternation on both sides in the seemingly senseless renewal of the civil war.

CHAPTER 44

THE CRISTEROS

> "Mexico will sacrifice much, but Mexico
> will be free."
>
> Handbill in support of Mexican Cath-
> olic boycott, 1926

DON NICOLAS ZUNIGA Y MIRANDA was a man of many distinctions. He was
very tall and thin and stood out in any crowd. He wore a silk top hat
and frock coat and carried a cane. He was both a geologist and a lawyer,
a man of much erudition. He was also an eccentric. He was called "the
eternal candidate." He had quixotically run for the presidency of Mexico
against Porfirio Díaz, Francisco Madero, Venustiano Carranza, Alvaro
Obregón, and, in 1924, against Plutarco Elías Calles. He always lost.
And in 1925 he died, in poverty and from natural causes—either of
which circumstance was a distinction for a Mexican with political ambitions in those years.

The other candidate who had opposed Calles was General Angel
Flores of Sinaloa (he received, according to the official canvass, 250,500
votes to 1,340,634 for Calles). Soon afterward he died in Mazatlán—apparently of arsenic poisoning.

Calles took the oath of office on November 30, 1924, in the newly
completed National Stadium before a crowd estimated at 30,000, the
largest ever gathered for an inauguration. The size of the crowd was a
tribute to the organizing ability of the military hierarchy, the labor
leaders and the agrarian groups, all of whom supported Calles and
who were, in turn, rewarded by him. The number of top rank military
men in good standing had been sharply reduced by the De la Huerta
rebellion. Those who remained were well-rewarded and also, for the
first time since the beginning of the Revolution, brought under tight
control by the central government.

To keep the agrarians happy Calles began expropriating and distributing land at a record-breaking rate. By the end of his administration he would have distributed 3,088,000 hectares (7,630,448 acres), compared with 971,000 hectares under Obregón and 132,000 under Carranza. The land distribution was accompanied by an unprecedented program of construction of highways, bridges and—most important in an arid land —dams for irrigation. Calles spent his leisure time at the controls of a tractor, plowing his own considerable land holdings, claiming that this was better relaxation than the pursuits of many of his colleagues— motoring, polo, even golf. The extent of his holdings—in Nuevo León, Tamaulipas, Sinaloa, Morelos, and the Federal District—was the subject of much rumor and disagreement, but it was substantial.

Of his various political alliances, Calles' attachment to the labor move- ment—and particularly to Luis Morones, the paunchy, heavy-jowled workingman's czar—was the strongest. Morones, an electrical worker by trade but a born organizer and manipulator, had been in the Mexican labor movement for many years. He was active in the Casa del Obrero Mundial and had been a leader in the paralyzing Mexico City utility strike in 1916, a strike which pushed Carranza to the extreme of threaten- ing strikers with capital punishment. He organized the Socialist Worker party in 1917 and the powerful Regional Confederation of Mexican Workers (CROM) the following year. Membership in the CROM grew from 40,000 at its beginning to approximately 100,000 in 1920 when Obregón took office. Early in Calles' term it claimed to represent a million workers and within a few years it had almost doubled this figure.

With sure political foresight Morones allied himself with Obregón during the Carranza administration; when Obregón was forced to flee from Mexico City in the spring of 1920, a move which led directly to the rebellion that overthrew Carranza, Morones played a key role in arranging the escape.

When Obregón became President Morones became director of the National Military Manufacturing Establishments, a vital industry in the nation. Morones was by now an internationally known labor figure and an important Mexican politician. He dressed elaborately, wore many diamonds and was driven about in limousines. He spent long hours in the Sonora-Sinaloa club—hangout for the men of the Northwest who were the political masters of Mexico—and was host at many drink- ing and gambling parties at his mansion in suburban Tlalpan.

Morones' relations with Obregón cooled, but by now he was very wealthy and powerful and was a leader of the radical wing of Congress. He was always involved in the stormiest debates, was once wounded during a particularly boisterous session, and was blamed for the as- sassination of Francisco Field Jurado. Field Jurado, a senator from Campeche, was opposed to ratification of the General Claims Convention which Obregón's representatives had worked out with the United States. Morones demanded a war without quarter against legislators like Field Jurado. Field Jurado wrote a note advising Morones and his agents where he could be found at various times of the day "awaiting you with the attentions you deserve." A few days later Field Jurado, upon leaving the Senate, was shot in the street. Three other senators were kidnaped. One of the Field Jurado killers was hidden in Morones' office. Among members of the government there was no doubt as to Morones' complicity. Vasconcelos threatened to resign unless Morones was brought to trial. Obregón wrote a stiff letter to Morones indicating that he planned to separate Morones from his administration. Morones made a court appearance and declared his complete innocence of any wrongdoing.

If relations between Morones and Obregón were chilled—and there was later to be actual enmity—the Calles-Morones alliance seemed to grow stronger. There were rumors that just before Calles' inauguration the President-elect made a series of promises to Morones and the CROM in return for their support. Morones would become Minister of Industry, Commerce, and Labor in the Calles cabinet (which he did). The CROM would receive both favors and financial support from the incoming government. And, finally, that within a year, the federal army would be dissolved to be replaced with workers' battalions. The replacement of the army with workers' battalions, if it was actually considered, did not come about, but Morones and CROM staunchly supported Calles anyway.

Gilberto Valenzuela, one-time close associate of Calles but later a bitter enemy, said that in 1925, when he was serving as Calles' Secretary of Government, he became aware that Calles was gradually turning over to Morones "all the vital forces, all the sources of influence of the country." Calles was giving at least some consideration to Morones as his successor in the presidency. That there was a working relationship between the President and the portly labor leader was obvious. In 1921 under Obregón there were 310 strikes in Mexico; under Calles the number steadily decreased until, in 1928, labor syndicates found it necessary to go on strike only seven times.

While labor leaders were being elevated to a commanding position in Mexico the Catholic Church which for many centuries had been the single most powerful social force in the country underwent a crisis period. The conflict between church and state in the mid-1920s became one of the most hatred-filled chapters in the Revolution.

The Catholic Church had played a key role in Mexican history from the moment of the Conquest. Priests accompanied the conquerors, seeking souls to convert. They rooted out, or attempted to root out, both pagan beliefs and a pagan culture of considerable richness. They destroyed temples, idols, records, and artifacts (except for those which contained gems or precious metals). Often well-established Indian deities were converted to Christian objects of worship. The Aztec shrine of Tonantzín, the mother of gods, for example, became, after authentication of a miracle, the shrine of the Virgin of Guadalupe, patroness of Mexico.

Some of the priests, notably Bartolomé de las Casas, Bishop of Chiapas, became famous for protecting the Indians from the rapacious Spaniards. Others, such as the Franciscan friar, Bernardino de Sahagún, did distinguished work in translating Indian languages and preserving both Indian history and traditions. But in the main the role of the Church was an oppressive one for the Indians and mestizos.

The Church became the wealthiest landlord in Mexico. In 1790, shortly before the outbreak of the struggle that would in time sever the ties with Spain, it was reckoned that four out of every seven houses in Mexico City were owned by the Church. The same pattern of ownership was reflected in rural land holdings. For this reason if for no other it was natural for the Church to be on the side of the royalist conservatives and landowners in the war for independence. Hidalgo and Morelos, the leaders, were both priests, and they remained fervent Catholics until their tragic ends. Both were "people's priests," more concerned with the humble than with the aristocrats. Both had gone against the Church's edicts. Hidalgo was a naïve idealist. Morelos was a more practical sort. Both deeply believed in the sovereignty of the people although the Inquisition in 1808 had damned this idea as "manifest heresy." Nevertheless, the insurgent priests remained faithful, and the rag-tag armies that followed them marched behind the standard of the Mexicanized Virgin of Guadalupe (the aristocratic, Spanish and rival Virgin of the Remedies was officially declared a general in the royalist army). When Morelos drew up his Constitution of Apatzingán in 1814 it specifically guaranteed the sanctity of Roman Catholicism as the only religion to be tolerated in Mexico.

Both of the visionary priests were excommunicated and both were executed. Morelos was declared to be "a heretic, a propagator of heresy, pursuer and disturber of the ecclesiastical hierarchy, profaner of the holy sacraments, schismatic, lascivious, a hypocrite, irreconcilable enemy of Christianity, traitor to God, King and Pope."

When independence came to Mexico the official status of Catholicism as the state religion was confirmed in Iturbide's Plan of Iguala, and it was reconfirmed in the Constitution of 1824. Despite this, Pope Leo

XII issued an encyclical ordering Mexican priests to preach obedience to Ferdinand VII of Spain.

Before the War of the Reform it was estimated that the Church, directly or indirectly, controlled 70 percent of the wealth of Mexico. This was, perhaps, an exaggeration, but the Church's wealth was vast, and the threatened loss of much of it through enactment of the Reform laws once more made bitter enemies of the Church and the Mexican government. In the civil wars that followed the Church was an active participant. The Archbishop Lázaro de la Garza y Ballesteros declared that anyone who swore allegiance to the Mexican Constitution of 1857 was to be denied the sacraments; priests who ignored the order and administered sacraments anyway were suspended and, in some cases, executed.

When Archduke Maximilian and his wife Carlota were recruited to go to the New World and rule over the Mexican "empire" Pope Pius IX, in giving them his blessing, reminded them that "Great are the rights of the people, and it is necessary to satisfy them, but still greater and more sacred are the rights of the Church." The Church later condemned the unlucky Maximilian for his genuine streak of liberalism and compassion for his Mexican subjects.

Porfirio Díaz was, early in his career, a practicing anti-clerical and a Mason, but during his long reign over Mexico he chose to disregard the anti-clerical aspects of the Constitution of 1857 (along with many other of its provisions). Long before he was driven into exile Don Porfirio had come to be regarded as a staunch friend of the Church, and the Church's wealth under the *Porfiriato* was estimated at 800,000,000 pesos ($400,000,000 in U.S. currency). Perhaps for this reason the Church was opposed to the Madero revolution—although the mild Madero was as tolerant of Catholicism as was Don Porfirio. Nevertheless, when Madero was assassinated, prayers of thanksgiving were said in at least one church, and Victoriano Huerta, who was generally credited with responsibility for the murder, became, as President, the recipient of the Church's sympathy and support.

Alvaro Obregón maintained that the clergy had bolstered the Huerta regime with a gift of 40,000,000 pesos. After Huerta's overthrow Mexico City papers published a letter said to have been written by Archbishop José Mora y del Rio on July 11, 1913, to Huerta's Minister of Government assuring him that all priests would do everything possible to achieve peace and tranquillity. Apologists for the archibishop said that the prelate had given nothing to Huerta. Huerta, they said, had appealed to Mora for a loan for the defense of Mexico City against the revolutionists. Archbishop Mora had then raised 25,000 pesos from wealthy Catholics to prevent the destruction of the city. The truth probably lay somewhere in between the extreme figures of 40,000,000 and 25,000 pesos—the spread of variation was typical of pro- and anti-Church feelings of the time. But that the Church looked with more favor on the hard-drinking Huerta than it did on the inoffensive Madero who preceded him or the self-righteous Carranza who followed was beyond question.

All of these things contributed to the anti-clerical fury that swept Mexico during the Constitutionalist revolution. Many of the revolutionists knew their Mexican history and the Church's part in it. Many had been indoctrinated with freemasonry. Some were veterans of the old Liberal party, seasoned Church haters. Some knew only that they were fighting the established order and the Church was part of that order. And there was, of course, looting of churches and extortion of priests as an added inducement. The churches with their gold and silver ornaments, the churchmen with their rich vestments, fine jewelry and their well-fed look invited both.

One of the most spectacular looter-extortionists was the brutal Tomás Urbina. His sacking of the churches of Durango in March 1914 caused an international outcry. For many years afterward treasure hunters sifted the earth of his hacienda looking for the vast treasure said to be hidden there, most of it supposedly from churches. But it was doubtful that Urbina knew much about the Church or its place in Mexican history; he was driven not by ideological hatred but an insatiable hunger for wealth.

The years 1914–16 were studded with outrages against Catholicism and its priests by revolutionists: Villareal in Monterrey, Obregón in Tepic and later in Mexico City, Villa in Zacatecas, Diéguez in Guadalajara, Gertrudis Sánchez in Morelia, Calles in Sonora, Eulalio Gutiérrez in Querétaro and San Luis Potosí, Alvarado in Yucatán. Bishops were imprisoned or held for ransom; some priests were killed; others, with nuns, were sent away by cattle car; libraries were burned; ecclesiastical vestments draped the weary bodies of camp followers; candelabra were melted for precious metal; soldiers and horses were quartered in temples and sanctuaries.

Anti-clerical feeling showed up in article after article of the Querétaro Constitution of 1917, restrictions far more stringent than those contained in the Constitution of 1857. But, as with so many other provisions of the radical constitution, Carranza did little in the way of enforcement. To the contrary he proposed to Congress that Article 130 of the constitution be amended to permit greater religious freedom (no action was taken). Although Carranza had, on occasion, had harsh words for the Church he was not by any means a militant anti-clerical as were so many of his revolutionary colleagues.

Obregón was not extreme in his anti-clericalism. He considered himself more bound to the spirit of the 1917 Constitution in matters pertaining to the Church than had Carranza, but he was also a practical man, willing to compromise when this could be done without injury to principle. He was also, as President, hoping for recognition by the United States and knew that moderation might be rewarded. His followers, notably among the Socialists and organized labor, had no such restraint, however. In the second year of Obregón's administration there were many outbreaks of violence—bombings, street fights, desecration of churches.

The Catholics began to organize. There were associations of Catholic youth, Catholic workers, Catholic journalists, and Catholic women. An apostolic delegate, Monsignor Eugenio Ernesto Filippi, arrived in Mexico. On January 11, 1923, Monsignor Filippi took charge of the laying of the first stone for a monument to Christ the King on Cubilete Hill near Silao, Guanajuato, geographical center of Mexico. The ceremony brought delegations from dioceses in all parts of Mexico and thousands upon thousands of faithful, praying, walking on their knees, shooting off firecrackers, and shouting vivas for Christ the King. It was a violation of a specific prohibition of the 1917 Constitution: the holding of religious services outside a church. The government moved quickly. Monsignor Filippi was ordered to leave the country within seventy-two hours. Further work on the monument on Cubilete Hill was prohibited. Obregón urged the bishops not to interfere with the government's "essentially Christian and humanitarian" program. But from this point on tensions between Obregón and the Catholics grew, and when the De la Huerta rebellion broke out much Catholic sentiment was on the side of the insurgents.

It was not until the administration of Plutarco Elías Calles, however, that the conflict between the Catholics and the government began to assume the proportions of a civil war. Although Calles had participated in the Catholic Church wedding of his daughter, Hortensia, to his secretary, Fernando Torreblanca, he was a far more unrelenting anti-Catholic than Obregón. The first demonstration of it came in his support of the schismatic Mexican Catholic Apostolic Church, an ill-defined organization led by José Joaquín Perez, who assumed the title of "patriarch" and declared independence from the Holy See. The sacraments would be administered free, tithing would be abolished along with the vows of celibacy for the clergy. The schismatics seized control of the three-hundred-year-old Soledad de Santa Cruz Church, but when they tried to hold services there a riot broke out. Calles decreed that the church could be used by neither the original congregation nor the schismatics. But to the schismatics, for use as their "cathedral," he presented the lovely old colonial church of Corpus Christi, just across Avenida Juárez from the Alameda, in the heart of the city.*

The schismatics were important only in the anger and resentment they aroused among orthodox Catholics. The anger was mounting anyway. In January 1926 the archbishops and bishops in Mexico signed a letter stating that the Constitution of 1917 "wounds the most sacred rights of the Catholic Church," and disavowed it. The various states, acting on authority given them by the constitution, had begun limiting the number of priests. In Aguascalientes there was to be one priest for 5000 inhabitants, in Chihuahua one for 9000, in Sonora one for 10,000, and in Tabasco one for 30,000—provided that that one priest be forty years or more of age and married.

Organized resistance by the Catholics increased, and on June 24, 1926, an angry Calles issued a penal code activating the anti-Catholic provisions of the 1917 Constitution. Ministers, i.e. priests, must be native Mexicans. The ministration of sacraments and making of doctrinal pronouncements were forbidden, also religious instruction in primary schools. Religious vows were banned. Monasteries and convents must be disbanded. Criticism of the constitution, the laws or public authorities must not be voiced by ministers nor by the religious press. Religious garb must not be worn in public. Any acts of worship must take place within church buildings, not in the open. All church buildings were property of the government which could regulate their use. The "Calles law," as it was called, was posted on the doors of all churches.

In retaliation the Mexican Catholic hierarchy, with the backing of the Holy See, suspended church services throughout Mexico on July 31. There was a desperate rush to have marriage, baptism, and confirmation ceremonies before the deadline. In a nation that was predominantly and devoutly Catholic, the ecclesiastical strike was a powerful weapon. Public unrest grew. Next a boycott was organized. Catholics were urged to buy nothing except absolute necessities, to employ no services, to use no vehicles or electric current, to buy no lottery tickets, to attend no entertainment. Signs were posted: Do You Want to Die without a Priest to Help You? Then Support the Boycott.   Young Lady, If You Use Powder, Rouge or Perfume You Are Damaging the Boycott.   You Lose Absolutely Nothing If You Do Not Buy Lottery Tickets.   Do You Have to Go Some Place? Go On Foot.   Do You Want Your Children to Be Godless? Avoid It! Your Weapon Is the Boycott. The boycott resulted in a slowdown of the economy, and caused some hardships among the poor. A sign

---

* The church was originally part of a convent established for the purpose of giving Aztec girls of noble birth instructions in religion, Spanish, and deportment. It now serves as a government-operated museum and sales room for Mexican folk arts.

was painted on the wall of the cathedral in Guadalajara: WORKERS: RICH CATHOLICS MAKE THE BOYCOTT. WE, THE POOR OF ALL CREEDS, ARE THE ONES WHO SUFFER.

There were many polemics against the Catholics. A general, Manuel Navarro Angulo, published a "liberal doctrine": "The slaves of conscience who do not know how to live as free men frequently ask me with horror if I am not a Catholic, if I am a heretic, if I have no religion, and to all I answer: My religion is the fatherland, reason my deity, truth my dogma, and Morelos, Juárez, and Madero my trinity. My saints are Cuauhtémoc and Hidalgo . . . the Pope is my Lucifer, the priests my demons, the nuns my temptation. My temple is the universe, majestic on a serene night. Viva Mexico! Viva the Reform! Viva the ragged ones! Death to the Catholics! Death to the traitors! Viva Juárez! Viva Calles, who carries on the work of Juárez!"

Pope Pius XI, in an encyclical, condemned Mexico's "great perversion of public authority," and Mexico was severely criticized around the world. But Calles pursued his course and on September 1 reported in a message to Congress that 129 Catholic colleges and schools, seven convents and seven propaganda centers had been closed and that 185 foreign priests had been deported. Neither the closing of the churches nor the boycott was deterring the government from its course.

By the end of the year the Catholics were taking more militant measures. Units of the League for the Defense of Religious Liberty had been formed throughout the country. Los Altos, the mountainous back country of Jalisco, became a center of Catholic guerrilla activity, led, at first by Anacleto González Flores, a Catholic activist who had been inspired by the struggle of the Maccabees against the Greeks and of the Irish against the English. In January 1927 guerrilla warfare broke out. A few months later González Flores was captured and shot. He was succeeded by General Enrique Gorostieta who had had both a West Point education and experience in the federal army. Under him the guerrilla army became known as the National Liberating Army, but they were better known—from their cry of *Viva Cristo Rey,* as Cristeros. In many parts of Mexico women purchased ammunition in small lots—to avoid suspicion—and shipped it to the Cristeros in Los Altos in bags of feed or boxes of soap. A federal commander in the area, hard pressed by gambling debts, sold 20,000 rounds of ammunition to the Cristeros whom he was supposed to be pursuing and fighting.

It was not a war of massed armies. Small parties of Cristeros swept out of the hills, attacked army garrisons, burned buildings, dynamited trains and then retreated back into the hills. Labor leaders, when they could be found, were favored targets. So were Protestants. The destruction of government-built schools was widespread, and in many cases the young teachers sent into primitive areas by the federal government were tortured and killed, often by villagers incited by the local priest. At Villa de Refugio, Zacatecas, a young woman teacher came out of her school when she heard mounted men approaching. She was lassoed, then dragged feet first over miles of rocky ground until there was almost nothing left for her friends to bury. She was one of many who died in lonely places.

Cristero activity was greatest in the states of Jalisco, Colima, Zacatecas, Michoacán, Aguascalientes, San Luis Potosí, Guanajuato, and Querétaro. Railroad trains were attacked frequently. On March 20, 1927, Cristeros attacked the Laredo-Mexico City train near San Miguel Allende, killed the conductor and guards and took a reported 100,000 pesos in government funds. On this occasion the passengers were unharmed.

A month later near La Barca, Jalisco, the train from Guadalajara to Mexico City was attacked. The train crew were killed as were 113 passengers. Many of them, wounded, were burned to death when the rebels set fire to the cars. The government charged that the four hundred attackers were led by three priests, and shortly afterward all remaining bishops and archbishops were expelled from the country. One of them, Archbishop José María González y Valencia, later sent a pastoral letter from Rome, saying that he had consulted that city's "sagest theologians" regarding the Cristero movement and advised them: "Be tranquil in your conscience and receive our benedictions."

The League for the Defense of Religious Liberty acknowledged the horror of the train assault in a bulletin, but pointed out: "if the misfortune has caused grief in the hearts of all well-born persons, this sentiment is exceeded by the just indignation of all society against the government which is truly responsible for the bloodshed . . . [a government] which refuses to hear the public's demand for its most legitimate rights . . . We protest . . . against Calles, who twists the facts in order to damage the noble cause of Catholicism and the people."

Reprisals by government troops were harsh. Cristeros, or suspected Cristeros, were strung up by the dozens to telegraph poles along the railroad lines. Hundreds more were marched to execution walls and shot. Forty-odd people were machine-gunned to death in a Guadalajara church. To add to the horror, bandit gangs became self-appointed executioners of the government's anti-Catholic policy, raiding and pillaging, destroying farms and ranches for whatever loot there might be. Property owners who had taken no part in the rebellion would find "Viva Cristo Rey" painted on their doors and then be punished—and robbed —as Cristeros. As was so often the case during the revolutionary struggles the non-partisans, the innocents, suffered more than anyone. The whole of the Los Altos region of Jalisco, some 8000 square miles, was scourged, the inhabitants driven from their land to take uncertain refuge in the towns and cities.

CHAPTER 45

LAST BATTLE, FIRST DEFEAT

> ". . . unfortunate land where each gener-
> ation must destroy its masters . . ."
>
> Carlos Fuentes, *The Death of
> Artemio Cruz*

BY MID-SUMMER OF 1927 the Cristero rebellion was at least temporarily under control—although there were to be outbreaks for many years to come. Meanwhile public attention was again being distracted by the question of presidential succession. The election would be held in July 1928, and Calles' first term would end November 30 of that year.

Calles seemed, at first, to favor Morones, the high-living labor leader. Morones, he felt, was sufficiently experienced in government and identified with the working class which, under his administration, had become a more important part of the electorate than ever before. His second choice was believed to be General Arnulfo Gómez, who had played a major role in quelling the De la Huerta rebellion.

But Morones was acceptable neither to Obregón nor to the powerful bloc of Obregonistas among the federal deputies and senators. Obregón's first choice for the presidency was General Francisco Serrano. Serrano had been Obregón's chief of staff and court jester. A diminutive, dapper man, he claimed to have worked, during his youth, as a clown in a circus and as a violinist in a bordello. He was affable, literate, full of jokes, and had a weakness for liquor, gambling, and women. Obregón did not drink, smoke, or gamble although he was a skilled card player, and he was a devoted family man. Nevertheless he was very tolerant of Serrano's weaknesses. When Serrano lost 75,000 pesos gambling with the bullfighter Rodolfo Gaona, Obregón, then President, made up Serrano's loss. At the end of his term he sent Serrano on a European study mission in the belief it would straighten him out and prepare him for the presidential candidacy in 1928. He owed Serrano much; Serrano's nimble wits had helped save him from being executed by Villa.

Obregón changed his mind. Serrano, he became convinced, could not handle the responsibility of the presidency. Calles' choice, Morones, was unthinkable. His election to the presidency would only aggravate the religious controversy, for Morones was more anti-Catholic than Calles. He was also disliked by the military.

On leaving office in 1924 Obregón had said: "I will be alert for whenever the nation calls me." He had then returned to his large farm at Cajeme, Sonora (the town, named for a Yaqui hero, was later to be renamed Ciudad Obregón). Here he plunged into large scale farming on his estate, Nainari (Yaqui for louse), irrigation projects, development of new crops, establishment of a canning factory to handle produce, and development of shipping facilities. He seemed serenely happy with his life. He went about in work clothes and unshaven. A Japanese diplomat who came to award him a decoration said: "I did not know you, Señor, in your disguise." "This is my natural state," said Obregón. "It was when I was in the National Palace that I wore a disguise."

But there was continual pressure on him to return to politics. Old comrades, political and military, made pilgrimages to Nainari in increasing numbers. The chaotic religous conflict was growing. The Obregonistas in the capital did not like the men around Calles. Only the firm hand of the hero of Celaya could save Mexico and the Revolution. By June 1927 Obregón had been persuaded. He announced that he would again be a candidate for the presidency.

His supporters in Congress pushed through an amendment to the constitution's ban on reelection: a former president could be reelected to the office after the interval of one term. The presidential term was extended from four years to six, just as it had been in 1904, on Díaz's orders. This was widely interpreted as a Calles-Obregón deal: Obregón would succeed Calles and Calles would succeed Obregón. It was a violation of one of the basic precepts of the Revolution: no reelection. The justification was that democratic ends could only be achieved by undemocratic means, that the achievements of the Revolution were not yet secure enough to permit the luxury of literal interpretation of its goals. Obregón's tone in explaining his decision was one of regret. He preferred, he insisted, the satisfaction of life as a private citizen, but he spoke of the "imperative of my duty," and "my inescapable obligation."

Francisco Serrano, whose presidential hopes had been encouraged by Obregón, and Arnulfo Gómez, who had been led to think he might be supported by Calles, did not see it that way. Both became candidates for the presidency, the former for the National Revolutionary party, the latter for the National Anti-Reelectionist party. Both men were from Sonora, as was their old leader, Obregón (although Serrano had been born in Sinaloa). At about this time a third floor was being added to the National Palace. The venerable building was encased in scaffolding. Men in the street joked that the palace was being crated up for shipment to Sonora.

The three candidates met as old friends and agreed that it should be a gentlemanly contest. But the air of friendship was quickly dissipated. Serrano and Gómez were not running against each other so much as they were running against Obregón and "reelectionism." Soon there were rumors that the Serrano-Gómez forces were planning rebellion. Serrano and Gómez disappeared from Mexico City, Serrano going to Cuernavaca where he planned to celebrate his birthday, and Gómez to the state of Veracruz where he had been chief of military operations and where he might be expected to get armed support.

On October 2 military maneuvers were scheduled for Balbuena Park, just to the east of Mexico City. They were to be directed by General Eugenio Martínez, chief of operations in the Valley of Mexico. President Calles, presidential candidate Obregón and General Joaquín Amaro were to sit in the reviewing stand. Word leaked out that a coup was about to begin. At the last moment General Martínez was given orders for one of the familiar "study missions" in Europe and was bundled aboard a train for Laredo. Calles and Obregón stayed away from the maneuvers. Approximately a thousand men, elements of the 48th and 50th Battalions and the 25th and 26th Regiments rebelled under the leadership of General Hector Ignacio Almada and took the road to Veracruz where, apparently, they intended to join Arnulfo Gómez. There was talk of blockading Mexico City.

Calles, with Obregón sitting at his side in Chapultepec Castle, issued incisive orders. In Cuernavaca the fun-loving Serrano was arrested with thirteen friends. With their hands tied behind their backs with barbed wire they were loaded into automobiles which then started on the mountainous road for Mexico City. Near Huitzilac, where the low-lying clouds keep the groves of pine and oak in perpetual gloom, the 14 men were taken from the cars and shot. The bodies were then loaded back in the cars and hauled to a hospital in Mexico City where they were turned over to their families. There is an apocryphal story that one of the victims was still alive on reaching the hospital and was finished off with a doctor's scalpel.

The bloody scene on the Cuernavaca road was not the end of it. In Torreón General Agapito Lastra was arrested and shot; so were Lieutenant Colonel August Manzanilla and all officers of the 16th Battalion. In Mexico City Generals Luis Hermosillo and José C. Moran were executed. So were Generals Alfredo Rodríguez and Norberto Olvera in Zacatecas and Generals Pedro Medina and Alfonso de la Huerta (a brother of Adolfo de la Huerta) in Sonora. Arturo Lasso de la Vega was killed in Pachuca. General Luis Vidal, governor of Chiapas, was executed by his own troops.

Many of the thousand soldiers who marched away from the capital on the night of the maneuvers surrendered to loyal troops at San Juan Teotihuacán. The remainder went on to the state of Veracruz hoping to join General Arnulfo Gómez. Gómez, fearing a trap like the one in which Zapata had been slain, fled into the mountains and, with two companions, hid in a cave. The man who was supposed to deliver food to them revealed the hiding place. Gómez was ill and dispirited. He was so weak that he had to be tied to the execution wall.

Vito Alessio Robles, who had resigned his diplomatic post in Sweden to return to Mexico and run Gómez' campaign, delivered a bitter funeral oration for his old friend: "May your memory be our shield in the struggle for vindication! May the tomb in which you lie be the altar on which we say the prayer for liberty and sacrifice for the good of all!" He promised that the campaign against reelectionism would go on.

Obregón continued campaigning as though nothing had happened, as though he still had opponents.

On Sunday, November 13, Obregón had just returned from a campaign trip and was riding in his Cadillac limousine in Chapultepec Park with two friends. They planned to go to the bullfight at 4 P.M. Meanwhile they were killing time on a bright and sunny day, watching the streams of cars, carriages, mounted charros, pedestrians and vendors of balloons, flowers and trinkets who had swarmed to the lovely old park for the weekly promenade. For the moment Obregón may have been able to forget the aftermath of the Serrano-Gómez rebellion in which many of his old comrades had been executed on government orders.

Suddenly a small Essex car with license number 10-100 pulled alongside of Obregón's Cadillac and two bombs were thrown at Obregón. A pistol was fired. The bombs exploded simultaneously, shattering glass and denting the metal panels of the larger car but, surprisingly, causing only minor injuries to the occupants (Obregón, after washing and changing clothes, continued to the bullfight as though nothing had happened).

The Essex wheeled around in the crowded street and sped away, followed by two carloads of Obregón's escorts, shooting wildly. The pursuit went through Avenida Chapultepec and into Insurgentes Sur.

The Essex was disabled. Two of the occupants fled, leaving two companions behind, one mortally wounded and the other with his clothing covered with his companion's blood, so that he was quickly captured.

One of the young men who escaped was Luis Segura Vilchis, an engineer with the electric company. After leaving the Essex he boarded a tramcar loaded with people bound for the bullfight. At the bullring he boldly approached Obregón and congratulated him for his escape from the assassination attempt—which might have provided him with an alibi. But on the next day he was taken to police headquarters where he readily admitted his part in the dynamite attack and claimed full responsibility for it.

Segura had been active in the League for the Defense of Religious Liberty, gathering food, clothing and munitions for the Cristero guerrillas in Jalisco. He also became a bomb maker, determined to kill Obregón. He rented a house at Alzate 114-A as headquarters for his plot. The League provided him with the Essex automobile which had also been used by and had been licensed in the name of Humberto Pro, another League worker. He was assisted in his bomb making by Nahum Lamberto Ruíz. They laid plans to dynamite a train on which Obregón was traveling, but a change in train schedule foiled the plot. On the morning of the 13th they went to the Colonia station, where Obregón was arriving from his campaign trip, hoping to kill him there, but the welcoming crowd was too large; they could not get near their intended victim. They followed Obregón from the station to the Hotel St. Francis, then to his residence, Avenida Jalisco 185. There they waited in the crowded street, hoping for a chance. Failing in this, they then trailed Obregón's car to Chapultepec Park where the bombs were thrown.

Of the four occupants of the attack car, Lamberto Ruíz had been fatally wounded, Juan Tirado captured, and Segura Vilchis, in custody, refused to identify the fourth man, the driver, who had escaped. Detectives said that the dying Lamberto Ruíz implicated not only Segura Vilchis but also the Pro brothers, Humberto—in whose name the car had been registered, Roberto, and Father Miguel Pro, a Jesuit priest who had been active in Catholic undercover work, saying clandestine Masses, hearing confessions, performing marriages, baptizing children. The three Pro brothers were arrested. They denied any part in the attack and had alibis for the time in question.

Ten days after the attack on Obregón's car the accused men, without having been tried, were executed. One by one they were led out of their cells in the police headquarters building—where the National Lottery building now stands—and taken to the execution yard in the patio. Here they took positions between the bullet-shredded wooden dummies that had been used for target practice by the firing squads.

Father Pro was the first to go. He refused a blindfold. He extended his arms at right angles so that his body formed a cross. As the command was given for the squad to fire he shouted *Viva Cristo Rey* and fell to the ground, still in the same position. Journalists in the crowd, most of whom had seen many executions and many examples of ultimate courage, were awed. Father Pro, according to his biographer, had "long since abandoned fear as other men . . . abandon hope. For at least a year he had prayed that he might be accepted as a sacrifice for the Faith in his country."

The others followed in quick order: Segura Vilchis, Humberto Pro and Juan Tirado. Roberto Pro was reprieved at the last moment and sent into exile.

Among the witnessing journalists there was talk that General Roberto Cruz, the inspector of police who had been in personal charge of both the investigation and execution, had urged that the accused men be tried before being killed. But Calles had insisted that they be shot without any bothersome court proceedings; it would set an example for other militant Catholics.

But the Cristero disturbances went on. A bomb exploded in the men's room of the Chamber of Deputies. A week later another bomb wrecked Obregón's campaign headquarters in the Avenida Juárez. Obregón asked his campaign director, Aarón Sáenz, to study means of ameliorating the religious conflict and went on with his unopposed campaigning. The election—which was no more than a ratification of the choice of Obregón for the next presidential term—took place the first Sunday in July 1928. On July 15 Obregón returned to Mexico City and promised a government for the next six years that would be "morally and materially strong."

Two days later the federal deputies from the state of Guanajuato arranged a luncheon for the President-elect in San Angel at the garden restaurant of La Bombilla, a large, airy, thatch-roofed pavilion.

Obregón had begun to seem older. The last year had been a difficult one. His hair was still dark, but his mustache had turned gray. His body, always stocky, had become thicker. He wore eyeglasses most of the time. Once chronically sloppy in his dress, he now wore well-tailored suits of expensive cloth, the right sleeve neatly cut to elbow length. His wit and his camaraderie were as lively as ever; so was his memory for names and faces. But he moved with a certain weariness. Obregón took his seat at the head table between Federico Medrano and Aarón Sáenz. The mariachi band of Esparza Oteo played *El Limoncito,* a popular song, and there was much jocularity as the politicians prepared to eat. The speeches would come later.

On the outskirts of the crowd was a young man with a sketch pad.

His name was José de León Toral, age twenty-seven, occupation uncertain, although he sometimes worked as an art instructor. He was
slightly built. His expression was one of frowning intensity. Toral,
mild-mannered in most things, was fanatically loyal to the League for
the Defense of Religious Liberty. He had known and admired Humberto
Pro and Luis Segura Vilchis. He frequented a clandestine Catholic outpost operated by Concepción Acevedo de la Llata, otherwise known as
Madre Conchita, a militant nun. Madre Conchita had been director of a
convent at Tlalpan until it was closed by the government. Her new
headquarters in the Calle Chopo housed some of her nuns, served as an
impromptu chapel for sub rosa religious services and was a center of
conspiracy. Among the plots concocted there was one in which a poison-
filled hypodermic syringe was to be hidden in a young girl's bouquet.
The girl hoped to lure General Obregón into dancing with her at a
fiesta; she would then plunge the flower-hidden syringe in his back.
This did not work, nor did some of the other fanciful schemes.

Toral was deeply moved by Madre Conchita's avenging fervor. At
her house he met such zealots as Carlos Castro Balda, an amateur bomb
maker (it was one of his bombs that exploded in the Chamber of Deputies) and Manuel Trejo Morales who was also implicated in various
Cristero bombings. Toral, peaceful by nature, became convinced that it
was his mission to kill Obregón and to become a martyr for his religion. He borrowed a pistol from Trejo, practiced shooting it on the
outskirts of the city (and discovered that he was a poor marksman at
any range beyond a few feet).

On July 15, the day of Obregón's return to Mexico City, Toral began
shadowing his intended victim, looking for an opportunity to shoot.
First he was at the railroad station where Obregón's train arrived, just
as Segura Vilchis and his friends had been. Again there were too many
people. Then he waited in the Paseo de la Reforma—the bulge in his
jacket concealed by a beribboned rosette welcoming Obregón. Again he
could not get close enough. He hung around the Obregonista headquarters in the Avenida Juárez, went with the crowd to the Parque
Asturias where there was a victory celebration, then mingled with the
crowd outside Obregón's residence in the Avenida Jalisco, watching and
waiting for the opportunity that he was confident would come. He
systematically made notes of things—the street number of Obregón's
house, 185, and the license number of his car, 8596 (he got it wrong;
it was 6985). He read newspapers for hints of the President-elect's
movements, and occasionally ate in a nearby pastry shop from which
he could observe activity around the Obregón house. He interrupted his
vigil for a visit with Madre Conchita. She had by this time moved her

residence to the Calle Zaragoza where only close associates were admitted.

At noon on the 17th, Toral noticed various cars leaving the Obregón residence and turning south in the Avenida Insurgentes. He guessed at first that they were going to the Trépiedi Restaurant and went there. Discovering his mistake he went on to La Bombilla. Here he drank a beer in the bar, then got out his sketchbook and began making drawings. Free-lance caricaturists are commonplace at such gatherings and little notice was taken of him. First he drew a cartoon of the orchestra leader. Gradually he moved closer to the head table. He made a quick sketch of Obregón; then one of Aarón Sáenz, seated at Obregón's left; then a more careful sketch of Obregón, done from only a few feet away. He showed his sketchbook to Deputy Ricardo Topete, three chairs away from Obregón, then to Sáenz. Then he offered the sketchbook to Obregón, extending it with his left hand. When Obregón reached for it Toral thrust his right hand into his jacket, pulled out the pistol and fired directly into the President-elect's face. As Obregón slumped down in his chair and then onto the floor Toral continued to fire the borrowed pistol. At this close range he couldn't miss.

Obregón, the last of the major figures of the Revolution, was gone— a victim of violence as had been the others—Madero, Zapata, Carranza, Villa. And of the three men who had aspired to the presidency in 1928—Francisco Serrano, Arnulfo Gómez, and Alvaro Obregón—there was now no one left.

END OF VIOLENCE

> "Progress without justice is not progress.
> But justice without progress is not justice,
> either. These, I believe, are the fundamen-
> tal lessons that the Revolution has be-
> queathed to us."
>
> Antonio Carrillo Flores

THREE MEN were to occupy the presidential chair during what would have been Obregón's six-year term: Emilio Portes Gil, Pascual Ortiz Rubio and Abelardo Rodríguez. In the slang of the period they were called *peleles,* straw men. Ultimate authority still rested with the man who held it at the time of Obregón's assassination: Plutarco Elías Calles.

No sooner had Calles left office, on November 30, 1928, than his colleagues began to refer to him as the *jefe maximo,* the maximum chief of the Revolution, and the press called him "the strong man of Mexico." Although Calles repeatedly announced his withdrawal from political authority and responsibility, his was a power which he could not easily drop, even had he wanted to. Again and again Calles insisted that what Mexico needed was a government of institutions, not of personalities. The more often he made the point the more important became his personality as maximum chief, the greater his reputation as a political wizard, the greater his indispensability as the nation's elder statesman.

He made his services available to the nation and performed well both as Minister of Finance (and founder of the Bank of Mexico) and, during a time of strife, as War Minister. But with or without a position of authority, his advice, assistance—and even permission—were sought continually on matters ranging from practical political details to the philosophy of the Revolution. The net result was an extra-official dictatorship, well-intended for the most part, but a dictatorship nevertheless.

In Mexico City Calles' headquarters was his mansion in the Anzures district, near the official presidential residence in Chapultepec Castle. During the unhappy residence there of Ortiz Rubio someone painted on the castle walls: HERE LIVES SENOR PRESIDENTE, BUT THE BOSS LIVES ACROSS THE WAY. In Cuernavaca Calles' *palacete* was in a cluster of Hollywood-type *palacetes* belonging to his henchmen; the luxurious colony was known as the Street of the Forty Thieves. His hacienda of Santa Barbara, on the road from Mexico City to Cuautla, was a rural retreat. For greater seclusion he went to his El Tambor ranch in the state of Sinaloa. But wherever he went there was little privacy; always there were throngs of political hangers-on, faithful, unquestioning, and grateful.

The man who would ultimately end Calles' domination of Mexican politics was, until almost the very last, both faithful and grateful to the maximum chief. Lázaro Cárdenas had been Calles' youthful protégé in both military and political matters. Despite his youth Cárdenas had a formidable reputation as a soldier (although he would later describe his military career as an accident of the times; he would have preferred being either a teacher or a farmer). He was a skilled fighter and battle-field commander with a cold courage that put some of his flamboyant companions to shame. He was sober, puritanical, and soft-spoken. He would walk, alone and unarmed, into an enemy's camp and persuade him to give up. He never shot his prisoners. Instead he would tell them to go home and quit fighting—even, in many cases, permitting them to keep their weapons. When he was in need of money he would impose a forced loan, as did other revolutionists. But Cárdenas would always pay it back, to the centavo. At the end of military campaigns he would return unused funds to the war ministry—an unprecedented thing. He won general rank at the age of twenty-five, and even his enemies conceded that whatever else he might be he was *muy hombre* (much man) and not an assassin—something of a distinction in that atmosphere.

Cárdenas was totally disinterested in wealth and privilege. This atti-tude—an eccentricity in a time when the mark of the successful revo-lutionist was an instant fortune—could have brought distrust, hatred, even violence. But Cárdenas was also indifferent to power. He wanted no one's job. Although interested in politics as the medium through which the aims of the Revolution must be achieved, he had little in-terest in being a politician. He served a short period—three months— as interim governor of his home state, Michoacán—in 1920. With this taste of authority he might have gone into politics immediately. Instead he returned to military life (and almost lost his life fighting for the government in the Delahuertista rebellion). Later he began to think of retirement from the army and considered running for mayor of his home town, Jiquilpan, a remarkably modest ambition for a successful revolutionary general. Friends persuaded him that he should run for the governorship of the state. Calles gave Cárdenas his blessing and the other two candidates withdrew. Cárdenas was elected governor in July 1928—the same election in which Obregón won the presidential term.

Cárdenas took office in September at a time of great contention and bitterness. Obregonistas, still outraged by the murder of their chief, were quarreling with Callistas and even hinting that Calles bore a share of the guilt for the assassination. They argued that Calles had knowingly aggravated the religious conflict in order to make the more conciliatory Obregón's term as president a difficult one; the aggravation had resulted in the fanaticism which in turn ended in the killing of Obregón.

In his annual message to Congress on September 1, 1928, Calles made a gesture toward restoring peace. He said there must be an end to *caudillismo,* the rule of political and military bosses; that the Congress must select an interim president and set a date for election of a constitutional president to complete Obregón's period of office; and he announced that he would, at the end of his own term, retire from politics for good. A few weeks later, after much consultation with Calles, the Congress elected as interim President Emilio Portes Gil, a stocky, Indian-faced lawyer from Tamaulipas.

Meanwhile, in Michoacán, Cárdenas, the newly installed governor, seemed to have turned his back on the national political turmoil. He was zealously putting into effect an ambitious program, building schools and roads, draining flooded land and developing irrigation projects, distributing land and encouraging peasants, laborers and students to unite in a revolutionary front.

At least three-fourths of the population of Michoacán was dependent upon agriculture, but less than 3 percent of them owned the land they worked. The state's fertile land was owned by sixty-odd *hacendados,* whose holdings ranged from 5000 to almost 400,000 acres apiece. Much of the peasantry was so submerged in feudalism that when, at last, expropriated land was given to them they were afraid to accept it (in one instance Cárdenas persuaded them to accept land only after threatening to bring in peasants from other states who would eagerly accept the expropriated properties).

But, in addition to its timid peasantry, Michoacán had a reputation as a spawning ground for advanced political thought and unrest. As early as 1767 Michoacán had been the scene of a peasant revolt, with scores of villages declaring themselves independent of Spain. Father Hidalgo was a provocative teacher in the College of San Nicolás in

Valladolid (later Morelia). The state's most famous son had been Father Morelos, the priest who, like Hidalgo, became a martyr to the independence movement (as governor, Cárdenas constructed a gigantic statue of Morelos on the lovely island of Janitizio in Lake Pátzcuaro). Cárdenas' own town, Jiquilpan, was a center of the struggle—so much so that when a Spanish cavalry unit occupied the town a hundred of its citizens were lined up in the town square and every fifth man executed as an example to the rest.

In the twentieth century Jiquilpan had many secret followers of Ricardo Flores Magón, many readers of scarce copies of *Regeneración*. Later there was substantial support for Madero and his Anti-Reelectionist movement. This was the atmosphere in which Cárdenas grew up. His father, Dámaso, had been the proprietor of a small store with a billiard hall annex—called "The Reunion of Friends." The family, neither wealthy nor poor, lived in a modest adobe house in the Calle San Francisco (destroyed during the Cárdenas administration to make way for a highway). The father was highly regarded in the town and was a skilled practitioner of folk medicine, using the herbs Indians had used for centuries. He saw to it that Lázaro and the other children had the best education he could afford—elementary school. One of Cárdenas' heroes was his teacher, Hilario Fajardo, who had a reputation locally as a poet and as "a radical but not a *comecuras* (priest eater)." To the philosophically liberal but pedagogically strict instruction of Fajardo Cárdenas added instruction in the Second Reserve, a sort of youth militia, and much historical lore learned from the town tailor, Modesto Estrada. Even as a child he had an air of seriousness and austerity. Upon completion of his elementary schooling at eleven he went to work for the local tax collector who also owned a small printshop. He was fifteen years old when the Madero revolution began. He was the oldest son in a family of eight children. He became the head of his household at sixteen, when his father died. Cárdenas became a printer's devil and, somewhat later, set type for the revolutionary proclamation of José Rentería Luviano, a Michoacán rebel. Although finished with formal education he read widely in everything available—novels, poetry, geography, biography and, above all, history—of the world, of the French Revolution, of Mexico, of Michoacán. The unhappy history of the victimization of the Tarascan Indians helped shape his lifelong preoccupation with the plight of Mexico's indigenous masses.

At eighteen he became a soldier in the Revolution. At the time when Carranza in Coahuila, Villa in Chihuahua, Obregón in Sonora, and Zapata in Morelos were rising against the Huerta government, various local leaders were taking up arms in Michoacán. Cárdenas, a slender young man with outthrust, elongated ears, was temporarily serving as town jailer of Jiquilpan. He freed his own prisoners and with them made his way to Apatzingán in the hot country of western Michoacán. There he joined the forces of Guillermo García Aragón, a former Zapatista general who had fallen out with his old leader and formed a revolutionary group of his own (Zapata later ordered the execution of his old comrade). Cárdenas, having had both military training and an education, was commissioned as a second captain and became pay-master for García Aragón and secretary to the general. His first en-gagement, at Purépero, ended in defeat; the García Aragón forces were dispersed and Cárdenas returned to Jiquilpan where he was forced to go into hiding. Gradually the revolutionary forces in Michoacán began to prevail; they moved toward the north, Cárdenas with them, and joined Obregón's army in Jalisco. Cárdenas was by this time a seasoned soldier. He took part in the liberation of Guadalajara and then advanced toward Mexico City. He was soon campaigning in the mountains surrounding the capital against the guerrillas led by Zapata—with whom, ironically, Cárdenas had more in common than he did with most of his comrades in arms.

In the confusion following the Aguascalientes Convention Cárdenas was, at first, aligned with the pro-Convention—i.e. anti-Carranza—forces. Under the command of General Federico Morales, Cárdenas, by now a lieutenant colonel, was ordered to the north, to be under the command of Villa. General Morales was somewhat uncertain as to what to do. Cárdenas was not. After discussing matters with his staff he decided to place himself at the orders of Plutarco Elías Calles, who had remained loyal to Carranza. This he did at Agua Prieta on March 27, 1915.

Calles was very impressed with the young (then twenty) officer whom he referred to as *el chamaco* (the kid), and whom he soon promoted to full colonel. Calles' military dispatches were normally laconic, bare facts, no elaboration, no adjectives. But so taken was he with Cárdenas both as a battlefield leader and as a civil administrator that he frequently referred to him as "this brave chief." Cárdenas' combination of valor, modesty, and decency made friends for him among his own soldiers, civilians, and even among the many prisoners whom he spared from the usual punishment, the firing squad. His only enemies were saloon keepers; in any town he took he put them out of business.

By 1920 when Calles issued the Plan of Agua Prieta launching the revolt against Carranza, Cárdenas was stationed in the Huasteca region of Veracruz. He, like virtually everyone else in the army, went over to the rebel side, and was soon thereafter promoted to general rank— the youngest in the Mexican army. During the Delahuertista revolution he suffered the greatest military defeat of his career, at Teocuitcatlán, was severely wounded, captured and barely escaped execution. In the mid-

1920s he was stationed in the oil-producing area of Tampico where he observed closely the operations of foreign-owned oil companies. It was from here that he returned to Michoacán and the governorship in 1928.

His administrative duties were frequently interrupted by military assignments—campaigns against the Cristeros in 1928 and 1929, and the quick, decisive war against the rebels led by General José Gonzalo Escobar in 1929.

While Cárdenas was engaged in his administrative and military responsibilities in Michoacán a development took place in Mexico City which was to have great importance in his future. This was the formation of an official party, a move which Obregón had seen the need for. Heretofore parties had existed, but were active only at election time. They usually revolved around the candidate, rather than the candidate being put forward as a representative of an established policy. With the candidate elected, defeated, dead or exiled the party became dormant.

Calles realized the need for a permanent party, even if such a party meant the end of the firm and highly personal control he held over Mexican politics. On December 1, 1928, the same day on which he left office and Portes Gil took over as interim president, Calles and his friends announced formation of the Partido Nacional Revolucionario (PNR). It was the same name that had been used by followers of the ill-fated Francisco Serrano the previous year, but there was no connection. This was to be a party of "definite principles and permanent life."

Although the manifesto regarding the formation of the PNR called for the establishment of "parties," the resources and influence of the government went into the establishment of the single, official party. The name of the party has since changed—from PNR to Partido de la Revolución Mexicana (PRM) in 1938 and to Partido Revolucionario Institucional (PRI) in 1946—but its domination of Mexican politics has never been relinquished. At the time of its formation many Mexicans saw in it an effort by Calles to perpetuate his personal control over Mexico.

First order of business for the new party was nomination of a candidate for the presidency. The choice was Pascual Ortiz Rubio, a colorless engineer from Michoacán whose credentials as a revolutionist were in good order but whose philosophy was sufficiently flexible that he was acceptable to all factions.

Principal opposition to Ortiz Rubio came from José Vasconcelos, Obregón's Minister of Education, who returned from abroad to campaign. The Vasconcelistas—one of them was a bright young student named Adolfo López Mateos who would be elected President of Mexico twenty-nine years later—suffered obstruction, indignities and persecution. On

Election Day nineteen persons were killed in Mexico City alone and there were disturbances in all parts of the country. The official count gave Ortiz Rubio nearly 2,000,000 votes and only 110,979 to Vasconcelos. Vasconcelos, who had campaigned more against Calles than against Ortiz Rubio, charged fraud and insisted, from exile, that he was the president-elect. He called for a rebellion and claimed that the "official" results of the election had been announced in Wall Street on Election Day hours before the polls had closed in Mexico.

Violence did not end with Election Day. On the day of Ortiz Rubio's inauguration, February 4, 1930, an obscure young man emptied his pistol at the new President, wounding him, his wife, and a niece. A month later a hungry dog scratched open a shallow grave near the village of Topilejo on the Mexico City-Cuernavaca road. Villagers found other impromptu graves and dug up more than a hundred bodies, all thought to have been Vasconcelos partisans and all victims of strangulation.

There was widespread consternation and fright. No one was more frightened than the new President, Ortiz Rubio, who was recovering from his wounds. It was reported that he suspected Calles of everything, including the attempt on his life. While he was being driven to the hospital after the shooting the car bounced over rough streets and Ortiz Rubio complained "*Qué calles!*" which meant "what streets," but should, many insisted, be translated "that Calles." He ordered an armored car for his personal use and talked darkly of enemies in the government. He shifted his cabinet constantly and seldom left his official residence, Chapultepec Castle.

Ortiz Rubio's government was, at first, dominated by Calles' men. But they were withdrawn and finally none of them, on Calles' orders, would collaborate with the luckless President. Finally after less than three years of his term he resigned, to be replaced by General Abelardo Rodríguez, a tough man from the Northwest who had at one time been a professional baseball player and had, through gambling concessions and farming operations in Baja California become one of the twelve richest men in Mexico (Vasconcelos wrote that Rodríguez spoke English poorly and Spanish even worse). A stronger, more decisive man than Ortiz Rubio, Rodríguez even went so far as to object to Calles' meddling in the government. Calles' power was, however, still both real and effective.

Meanwhile the governor of Michoacán began to rise in the political world. In October 1930 he was chosen chairman of the PNR, the official party—a position which was not technically a government post but which made him one of the strong figures in the government. In addition to his impressive record as governor (in two years he had more than doubled the number of schools in his state and was spending 47 percent of his budget on education) Cárdenas was close to both Ortiz Rubio and to Calles, between whom a dangerous gulf was widening.

Soon after Cárdenas assumed leadership of the party Luis Cabrera, the old revolutionist who had been Carranza's principal adviser and also his Minister of the Treasury, celebrated the twentieth anniversary of the beginning of the Madero Revolution by declaring the Revolution a failure. He ticked off the aims of the Revolution: "Liberty, equality, justice, effective suffrage, no reelection, autonomy of authority, free municipalities, state sovereignty, international independence . . . words, words, words! The Revolution has solved none of the political problems of the country. Nor can it solve them so long as these problems are studied with hypocrisy . . . In order for there to be political liberty there must be economic and social equality . . . This is a country of superimposed strata, of unequal racial and economic classes. One cannot speak of constitutional equality nor of equality before the law."

Cárdenas, as head of the official party, was compelled to answer. He interrupted the relief work he was doing in the party's name in the state of Oaxaca where there had been a devastating earthquake. "The reason that moves these men to disturb the tranquillity that reigns in the Republic this year," he replied, "is the longing to reconstruct political situations that would be favorable to influencing the public mind and win for themselves a political following." Cabrera briefly went into exile to escape punishment for his remarks (although by the following January he was back in Mexico and dared to say that there was not a single public official in Mexico who had been elected by the people). Cárdenas returned to his work with the PNR, which he was trying to expand from mere political management into an instrument of social service which would, in time, remedy some of the very shortcomings Cabrera had criticized. In his concern for social inequalities Cárdenas was, in reality, much closer to the views of his political enemy, Cabrera, than he was to those of his political mentor, Calles.

For Calles seemed to be retreating steadily from his original radicalism. Some of it may have been the natural consequences of age and wealth. Or it many have been the result of the unconventional diplomacy of the new United States Ambassador, Dwight W. Morrow. Morrow was a partner in the J. P. Morgan & Co. banking firm whom President Calvin Coolidge assigned to Mexico in 1927. Morrow, impatient with the protocol and obliqueness of orthodox diplomacy, delighted Calles with his warmth, directness, and friendliness and soon the two men were breakfasting together regularly and talking freely—the closest relationship of its sort since the unfortunate liaison between Henry Lane

Wilson and Victoriano Huerta. Morrow was able, as a result, to bring about a friendlier attitude toward U.S. business in Mexico—particularly the oil companies, an easing of tension between the Mexican government and the Catholic Church (church services were resumed on a limited basis June 30, 1929), and in sounder Mexican fiscal policies. The extent to which Morrow altered Calles' political philosophy is a matter of debate, but the maximum chief's philosophy was shifting. At the end of the Escobarista rebellion, during which he had temporarily served as Minister of War, Calles once more announced that he was retiring to private life and took the occasion to observe that the Revolution had been a "political failure." He shortly thereafter went on a European trip and upon his return to New York made a speech in which he said that Mexico was going ahead with its plan to create a class of small peasant landowners but that "it is not the intention of the government to split up large estates for this purpose." In Mexico, to which he returned in mid-December 1929, the land distribution program had been proceeding at a rapid rate under the interim presidency of Portes Gil. But now, with Calles declaring that agrarianism had failed, the program was slowed almost to a halt. In 1929 nearly 2,500,000 acres had been distributed. By 1932 the rate of distribution had dropped to one-third of that.

Calles was, perhaps, following the path of all old revolutionists, knowing that social upheavals are initiated and carried out by radicals but consolidated by conservatives. Whatever his reasoning, he was on a collision course with Lázaro Cárdenas.

Cárdenas, after ten months as head of the PNR, was shifted to the Ortiz Rubio cabinet, taking over the Ministry of Government. After holding this post briefly he resigned and returned to the governorship of Michoacán to finish up the term which he had never relinquished. It was work more to his liking, closer to the problems of the common people. Whatever his feelings were about the inept administration of Ortiz Rubio and the Machiavellian control by Calles, he kept them to himself. His demeanor had been proper. He had been respectful to Ortiz Rubio and obedient to Calles. But on his home ground he was more independent. After Calles had forced Ortiz Rubio's resignation Cárdenas received a message from the maximum chief instructing him to take over the Ministry of War in the interim cabinet. He refused to do so. As a result of his insubordination he was denied the customary privilege of helping select his own successor, and was replaced in the governorship by General Benigno Serrato, a pro-Catholic conservative and an enemy of the agrarian projects Cárdenas had launched. After being ignored temporarily Cárdenas was given command of the military zone of Puebla. He had to borrow money to move his household goods to Puebla. Having been a general, a state governor, head of the official party and a cabinet minister, he was still a poor man.

After a few months in Puebla Cárdenas was forgiven and was appointed to the cabinet of Abelardo Rodríguez as Minister of War. Soon there began to be talk of Cárdenas as a candidate for the presidency in the next election. His friendly relationship with Calles had been resumed, and two of Calles' sons became active workers for Cárdenas' candidacy. Calles' own position was unclear; his personal philosophy, increasingly conservative, and that of Cárdenas were far apart. But, being a political realist above everything else, Calles was aware of widespread feeling that the rightward swing of the revolutionary family had gone too far and that anti-Calles feeling was rising.

Calles supported Cárdenas after the latter received the nomination of the PNR at the party's convention in Querétaro in December 1933. Cárdenas accepted the nomination, promised to seek the counsel of leaders of the party (which many listeners interpreted as a guarantee of Calles' continued control), but added that he alone would bear responsibility for his actions. He also promised to uphold the Six Year Plan, a program of government drafted by the PNR convention as a guide for the administration of the next president.

No one had any serious doubts that Cárdenas would win and do so by the vast margin characteristic of Mexican presidential elections. Mexico's carefully managed elections produce an electorate which goes to the polls with the same enthusiasm with which it goes to the bullfights, and with equal certainty as to the outcome. All of this Cárdenas knew; but he nevertheless campaigned with a vigor and fervor that had never been seen before. He visited all twenty-eight Mexican states and traveled more than 17,000 miles, going by train, automobile, on horseback and afoot. He did not confine himself to the well-staged, well-organized meetings of political enthusiasts and favor seekers, but went into remote Indian pueblos, from the mountains of Chihuahua and Sonora in the northwest down into the jungles of Tabasco and the arid plains of Yucatán. He explained the Six Year Plan, translating that wordy document into simple terms that his listeners would understand. He had three main proposals of his own: the ejidos restored through a strong agrarian program to combat the outmoded domination of the haciendas; modern schools administering education based on socialism to combat the "fanaticism" of the Church; and workers' cooperatives to combat industrial capitalism. Above all he pleaded for peasants, workers and students to form a united front. Cárdenas' manner was simple and unassuming. At times his low-pitched voice was inaudible. Some of his ideas were too abstract for his listeners. But his manner was always sincere and convincing. So wrapped up did he become in his highly personal campaigning that he continued it even after the election, the official canvass of which showed him winning 98.19 percent of the votes, the highest figure since Madero in 1911 except for Obregón's uncontested victory in 1928.

Cárdenas as President also set new patterns. He was inaugurated in a plain business suit. He announced that he would not live in Chapultepec Castle. He reduced his own salary by half and cut off the entertainment allowance the government customarily gave to the President's wife. He closed gambling establishments which had been operating openly and enriching their revolutionary proprietors—including some men highly placed in previous regimes. He talked of national prohibition. He ordered the national telegraph system to accept free for one hour each midday messages from anyone, no matter how humble, who wished to take up problems with the President. At the National Palace the waiting rooms were thronged with peasants wishing to talk to the President about the land program, the village school or, simply, a sick cow. The country people, some of them barefoot, and workers in overalls were invariably ushered into the presidential suite while generals, politicians and businessmen waited outside. Even when Cárdenas could do nothing to solve the problems of the common people he was attentive and sympathetic. "When people have suffered in silence for so many centuries," he would explain, "the least I can do is listen to what they say." Nor did he listen only at the National Palace. At every opportunity he got out of the capital, leaving his cabinet members to deal with crises in foreign relations, economics, labor, and legislative matters, and went out among his beloved *campesinos,* distributing parcels of land at an unprecedented rate, studying their problems firsthand and listening. The Indians of Michoacán referred to him as Tata (Daddy) Lázaro, and Indians in all parts of the country regarded him with love and trust.

While Cárdenas was concerned with the most primitive areas and peoples of Mexico, the capital was displaying more civilized splendor than ever before. The gigantic steel skeleton which Porfirio Díaz had intended as a national legislative palace had been converted into a monstrously impressive monument to the Revolution. The grandiose National Theater, also begun by Díaz, was finally completed and became the Palace of Fine Arts. The fearsome old prison of Belem was finally razed and replaced by a school—the Centro Escolar Revolución. A monument to Obregón was erected at the spot where he was assassinated.

Old revolutionists became rich, luxury-loving civilians. "You want us to have the honesty of angels?" a fictionalized ex-general says in Carlos Fuentes' novel, *Where the Air Is Clear.* "Because of what we went through we are entitled to everything. Because we were born in dirt-floored shacks we have the right to live in mansions with high ceilings and stone walls, with a Rolls-Royce at the door." Carriages had disappeared from the streets, and horses were—in the city—used mainly on bridle paths and polo fields. Joaquín Amaro, a dark-skinned Indian general who had given up the gold earring he once wore in his right ear, had learned table manners and was a splendid polo player (he lost an eye in one game).

Cárdenas' behavior was conspicuously different. He dressed and lived modestly. He forbade buglers at the National Palace to give the usual fanfare when he arrived there each morning. He arrived like any other citizen going to work except that he was much earlier than most. He banned the display of presidential portraits in public buildings; only Madero before him had issued such a ban and no president has done it since. One ambitious politician commissioned a sculptor to do a bust of Cárdenas and then ordered fifty replicas cast in bronze. These he proposed to distribute to schools throughout the country. Cárdenas concealed his dismay and politely asked that the fifty busts be brought to the National Palace so that he could inspect them. This was done; then, overnight, they disappeared, never to be seen again.

Cárdenas' personal modesty was not the only departure. His regime was—and still is—regarded as the most radical in Mexican history. But it was a *sui generis* radicalism. Cárdenas, far more than any of his predecessors, tried to govern by both the letter and intent of the Constitution of 1917, and his application of these somewhat Utopian principles was shaped by a regard for the sort of primitive communism that had prevailed in Mexico before the Spanish Conquest. He admired the efforts of the late Felipe Carrillo Puerto to establish a Socialist state in Yucatán and he was, for a while, influenced by the even more extreme program executed in Tabasco by Tomás Garrido Canabal and his Red Shirt followers (one of their leaders had business cards identifying him as "personal enemy of God"). He named Garrido Canabal to his cabinet as Minister of Agriculture, but later became disillusioned and replaced him with a more conservative man.

Zealous young teachers, imbued with the ideals of Socialist education, clashed with conservatives and Catholics in all parts of the country. Organized workers, conscious of the greater freedom under the new regime, launched an unprecedented number of strikes, by oil workers, electrical workers, tramline crews, railroad workers, taxi drivers, and there were general strikes in the states of Puebla and Veracruz. There were 642 strikes in 1935, more than twice the number there had been in all the preceding six years (and the average for Cárdenas' six years in office was to be 478 strikes per year, more than ever before or since). Feminist movements were launched, sex education for all children was promoted (complicating the already difficult conflict with the Catholics), and obsolete cannons and other military equipment were being converted into plows and agricultural tools.

Calles felt that much of what his former protégé was doing was a refutation of Callismo. In the national Congress there soon was a division between Cárdenistas and Callistas.

In June 1935 Calles released a statement deploring radicalism and the factional division of the Congress and castigating the labor movement for disrupting the country's progress. Although Calles insisted that he and Cárdenas were friends, he referred ominously to the fate of Ortiz Rubio. The statement was interpreted as a threat to overturn the Cárdenas government. Cárdenas responded with a mild statement re-affirming his faith in the Revolution. But he acted more decisively than he spoke. He asked for the resignation of all his cabinet members—and in appointing a new cabinet carefully avoided those of Callista sympathies. Callista members were expelled from the Chamber of Deputies. Cárdenas carefully checked the attitudes of state governors. Army units of known loyalty were concentrated near the capital.

Calles retreated. Once more he announced his retirement from politics and flew to the United States. Three months later there were rumors he was coming back. Cárdenas, asked about it, said that Calles could return any time he liked. Calles returned, accompanied by Luis Morones, the labor leader. He established a small paper for the express purpose of voicing his concern over the radical tendencies of the Cárdenas government. He aired his disapproval in the foreign press. Labor and agrarian groups loudly demanded that Calles be expelled from the country. Cárdenas, in a carefully worded speech, said that there was no need for expulsion of Calles and his allies since they constituted no threat either to the government or the people, and that it was better that they should remain in Mexico where they would "feel the shame and weight of their historical responsibility." But the outcry against Calles continued to grow. A group of militant women even went to his hacienda of Santa Barbara insisting that Calles divide *his* land among the peasants. The clamor against Calles increased as did the rumors of a Calles-inspired rebellion. Finally Cárdenas acted. On the night of April 9, 1936, a party of twenty soldiers and eight police headed by General Rafael Navarro, chief of the army garrison of the Valley of Mexico, surrounded the hacienda of Santa Barbara. Navarro walked into Calles' bedroom. The maximum chief, who had been suffering from grippe, was in bed, covered with a red silk spread. He wore blue and white silk pajamas and was reading a Spanish translation of Hitler's *Mein Kampf.*

"By orders of the President of the Republic you are arrested," said Navarro.

"I am at your orders," said Calles. And he asked the reason for the action.

"The condition of the country demands it," said Navarro, and explained that a special plane would fly the maximum chief to the U.S. border. The next morning, which was Good Friday, Calles and seven companions—Morones among them—were loaded aboard a Ford trimotor plane. After they were already in the air the government called the U. S. Ambassador, Josephus Daniels, and asked him to arrange for the Calles party to land at Brownsville, Texas; there had not been time for the usual visa arrangements.

But if Cárdenas had acted harshly with Calles, he was kindly disposed to others who had been forced abroad. José Vasconcelos came back, as did Adolfo de la Huerta, the former interim president, José María Maytorena, the ex-governor of Sonora, Gilberto Valenzuela, Enrique Estrada, Felix Díaz, Pablo González, José Gonzalo Escobar, and other rebels against the government—and Porfirio Díaz, Jr. The list of returning exiles was long and impressive. Calles did not return to Mexico until Cárdenas' term had ended. By that time Cárdenas had long since expropriated Calles' extensive land holdings and distributed them to peasants (he had also turned over most of his own property to either local peasants or to the nation).

There was to be only one more rebellion in the revolutionary family, the last of the many schisms that littered the path of the wayward Revolution.

Its leader was Saturnino Cedillo, the caudillo of San Luis Potosí. Oddly enough he was, or had been, a close friend and admirer of Cárdenas and had been an important factor in the selection of Cárdenas as the official candidate for the presidency.

Cedillo had been a revolutionary leader since the first Madero uprising in 1910. His record, by revolutionary standards, was good. He had followed Carranza against Huerta, had followed Obregón and Calles in their rebellion against the First Chief. In the progress he had profited enormously. His vast ranch of Las Palomas in San Luis Potosí was the headquarters not only for his ranching and farming operations but also the base of what amounted to a private army. He was more conservative than most revolutionists, and was a good Catholic. He not only had a private chapel at Las Palomas but also, as boss of the state, permitted the Catholic Church to operate with comparative freedom. Of the 275 Catholic churches open and functioning in Mexico, approximately one-fourth were in the state of San Luis Potosí.

When Cárdenas found it necessary to fire his ultraradical Minister of Agriculture, Tomás Garrido Canabal, he did a political about-face and named the conservative Cedillo to the post. The appointment was applauded by conservatives, much of the army, the Catholics and both Mexican and foreign business interests. Cedillo was also popular with the Gold Shirts, a Mexican fascist organization, and as his personal adviser he had a hard-faced German artillery officer. Several things became apparent. Cedillo was in disagreement with Cárdenas over the latter's distribution of land to peasants on a collective basis. Also he had presidential ambitions—either as a duly elected successor to Cárdenas in 1940 or as the leader of a coup. His agents were soliciting funds from U.S. business interests and there was a remarkable build-up in the arsenal at Las Palomas—weapons, bombs, even airplanes and high-powered radio facilities.

A showdown came when students at the government agricultural school at Chapingo, east of Mexico City, objected to the man Cedillo appointed as head of the school. Cedillo ceremoniously offered his resignation to the President and Cárdenas accepted it. The Ministry of War then assigned Cedillo as commander of the military zone of Michoacán—which would have enabled Cedillo to save face. Cedillo excused himself for health reasons, returned to San Luis Potosí, and soon thereafter the state legislature announced that it no longer recognized the federal government. It was clear that Cedillo was launching the rebellion everyone had long feared.

Federal troops were sent into the state of San Luis Potosí, and Cárdenas personally went to the state capital. Cedillo had retreated back into the mountains, but the city of San Luis Potosí was full of his armed supporters. Cárdenas made a speech in which he condemned Cedillo for his actions but promised that he would be unharmed, and that his followers would not be punished. Cárdenas' peace-making gestures and the successful operations of the federal forces in outlying parts of the state soon reduced Cedillo's following to no more than a few dozen men.

From his rebel camp Cedillo issued statements maintaining his state's sovereignty and his own position as commander of the state's "constitutionalist army" and also criticizing Cárdenas for collectivizing agriculture and trying to implant a Soviet regime.

Cárdenas stayed in San Luis Potosí long enough to promise more schools, roads, and water systems and to divide up some land among the peasants. Then he returned to Mexico City. Months later a federal patrol found Cedillo's hideout at a place called Biznaga. During early morning fog the two groups exchanged shots and Cedillo was shot and killed while trying to mount his horse.

It was a sad affair for Cárdenas, the man who never killed his enemies; he considered Cedillo not so much an enemy as a friend who had gone astray. The matter was further complicated by Cedillo's apparent involvement in the greatest crisis of Cárdenas' administration: his dispute with the foreign-owned oil companies. Cedillo had denied any connection with the oil companies but his denial was not widely accepted. Foreign interests—particularly oil interests—were believed to be potential backers of a Cedillo counterrevolution.

Mexico, as one of the world's oil-rich nations, had been having trouble with oil companies ever since the days of Porfirio Díaz—during whose regime the oil interests had operated peacefully and profitably. But after Díaz the oil question became a seesaw proposition. The oil companies objected strenuously to a very modest tax proposed by Madero. Huerta, during his period of usurpation, received friendly treatment from Great Britain because of Britain's need for Mexican oil for her ships; American oil interests tended to side with Carranza. Nevertheless, the Constituent Congress which Carranza called, wrote, in Article 27, a provision that subsoil resources belonged to the nation—which the oil companies regarded as a hateful innovation although it actually reflected Spanish colonial law and was in line with the laws of several other Latin American nations. Obregón, in his eagerness to achieve U.S. recognition, agreed to certain ameliorations of the oil companies' conditions; and Calles, although he was at first very severe with foreign mineral exploiters, softened his position toward the oil companies under the influence of Ambassador Morrow.

Cárdenas, while stationed as a military zone commander in the Gulf Coast oil region in the 1920s, had formed a sour opinion of the foreign oil companies. Part of it was based on the way in which Mexican workers were treated as inferiors, in wages as well as working conditions. Part was because of the oil companies' employment of "white guards" to harass the workers under the guise of maintaining security. And part of it came from the oil interests' unsuccessful efforts to bribe him—with a new automobile according to one story, with a case of champagne and a check for 50,000 pesos according to another.

But far more important than Cárdenas' personal feelings was the new militancy of the Mexican labor movement under the leadership of such men as Vicente Lombardo Toledano, far tougher and more radical than the discredited Morones.

The changed attitude was nowhere more apparent than among the oil workers. Oil workers had gone on strike soon after Cárdenas took office. In 1935, with the encouragement of the Cárdenas government which wanted uniform conditions and pay throughout the oil industry, the twenty-one oil workers organizations were merged into one large syndicate. This syndicate subsequently demanded wage increases which would have raised the companies' labor costs by 133 percent and many additional benefits such as paid vacations of three to eight weeks per year. The oil companies refused; they probably would have refused any concession, and these were inordinately heavy demands. Cárdenas intervened and arranged a series of employer-labor conferences, hoping for settlement. Before more than one-tenth of the items on the agenda had been covered the oil workers voted a general strike. A prolonged strike could have been disastrous for all concerned—the unions, the companies, and Mexico. Accordingly the union finally agreed to arbitration. An investigating commission, headed by the noted economist-diplomat-historian, Jesús Silva Herzog, looked into the economics of the oil industry and recommended wage increases of only about one-fourth the amount originally asked by the workers. The union accepted the recommendation. So did the Mexican court of arbitration and conciliation. The oil companies did not. They appealed the decision to the supreme court of Mexico. The court ruled against them. The oil companies then announced that they would not only ignore the court's ruling but that they also would ignore Section XXI of Article 123 of the constitution (which provides that if a company refuses to submit to arbitration or refuses to abide by an arbitration decision the labor contract is terminated and the company must pay the workers three months wages—which in this case would have cost the companies 100,000,000 pesos).

Cárdenas held a grim meeting with his cabinet to discuss the oil companies' defiant attitude. At its conclusion he went on a national radio network at 10 P.M., March 18, 1938, to announce the nation's response: expropriation of the foreign-owned oil companies.

"The sovereignty of the nation," he said, "is thwarted by foreign capitalists who, forgetting that they have formed themselves into Mexican companies, now attempt to elude the mandates and avoid the obligations placed upon them by the authorities of this country . . . I call upon the whole nation to furnish such moral and physical support as may be needed to face the consequences . . ." A few days later he addressed a mammoth crowd in the Zócalo, telling them that Mexico would honor its foreign debts—the bill for the newly nationalized oil industry would be large—and adding: "We place ourselves on a high legal and moral plane so that our country may be great and respected . . . Is our task dangerous? Must sacrifice be demanded of the country? There is no doubt about this . . . [but] The Revolution, having come into power, will, with the fullest support of all patriots, save the honor of Mexico."

Cárdenas was not underestimating the problem. Mexico's economy, weakened by so many years of civil war and further damaged by the world-wide depression of the 1930s, was near collapse. Cárdenas' programs of land distribution and public works were costly, and the government's account in the Bank of Mexico was overdrawn. The peso took a sharp drop in value and threatened to go even lower. The United States government, which already had put purchases of Mexican silver on a month-to-month basis, suddenly cut them off altogether after oil expropriation. Diplomatic relations with Great Britain were broken. The markets for Mexican oil were cut off. The dispossessed oil companies mounted an effective propaganda campaign to discredit Mexico and Mexican leadership in the eyes of the world.

Strangely, in the face of all these adverse factors, the Mexican people, so long divided on the many issues of the Revolution, so cynical toward the successive governments the Revolution had given them, responded with almost unanimous support. Fund-raising committees were formed throughout the country. Politicians whose sources of illicit income Cárdenas had cut off pledged their aid. Wealthy ex-revolutionists wrote fat checks. Government workers turned back part of their pay. Fashionable women stripped off earrings, necklaces, even wedding rings and threw them into collection urns. Peasant women straggled into the city carrying live chickens as their donation. Except for foreigners and a few wealthy Mexicans who talked darkly of revolution, popular support of the government in the time of crisis was strong and broadly based. Even the Catholic Church, so long embattled, endorsed the nation's position. Archbishop Luis Martínez declared: "I pray to God that Catholics in this hour of proof will know how to comply with their duty as citizens."

Cárdenas' concern for the integrity and sovereignty of Mexico and for the well-being and dignity of Mexicans as a people had unified the nation so long victimized by exploitation—alien and native—and so weary of civil war.

Settlement of the debt to the foreign oil companies was to be onerous. And operation of newly nationalized industry, oil and others, was to be difficult, hampered by bureaucracy and inexperience. This was to be true of many of Cárdenas' innovations. The government gave over management of the nationally owned railroads to the railroad workers' syndicate; after a period of operational chaos it had to take them back again. The land distribution program continued apace; Cárdenas distributed more than twice as much land as had his last seven predecessors in the presidency (44,200,000 acres against 18,900,000 acres). But often the parcels were too small or non-productive, or the recipients lacked the required skills or financing was unavailable. Socialist education, on which so much store had been set as a weapon against "fanaticism" was something less than successful and was later abandoned as a matter of official government policy.

But if some of his measures ended in disappointment Cárdenas nevertheless left a mark on Mexico, a more enduring mark than any of his predecessors. He made the welfare of peasants and workers—the long neglected masses of Mexico—an important force in the dynamics of government instead of the revolutionary rhetoric it had been.

He also overhauled the huge and awkward structure of the official party to make it function in a more democratic manner. Agrarian, labor, and army sectors were formed to insure the broadest sort of popular representation.

And although the incumbent President of Mexico had—and still has —overwhelming influence in the selection of his own successor, Cárdenas carefully refrained from abusing this power. As the time approached for consideration of candidates for the presidential election of 1940 it was assumed that Cárdenas would throw his support to General Francisco Múgica, a close friend and collaborator who had also been his Minister of Communications. Múgica had written some of the most controversial provisions of the Constitution of 1917 and could be expected to carry on and perhaps intensify Cárdenas' radical governmental policies. He was suspected of being a Communist although he denied it. Múgica, backed by some labor and agrarian groups, hoped for the official party's nomination..

Conservative forces were pushing a candidate of their own: General Juan Andrew Almazán, the veteran revolutionist of many loyalties who had now become a very wealthy industrialist in Monterrey. Middle-of-the-road sentiment was behind General Manuel Avila Camacho, Cárdenas' Minister of War. Avila Camacho, a heavy-jowled man of amiable manners and conciliatory disposition, had had a respectable but unspectacular background as a military man. As soon as the campaign was under way he was nicknamed "the unknown soldier."

Cárdenas offered no help to his old friend, Múgica, and Múgica withdrew his candidacy. With no interference from the President the official party gave its nomination—tantamount to election—to the mild-mannered Avila Camacho. Cárdenas' friends, in trying to understand his actions (newspapers had begun to refer to him as "the Sphinx") reasoned that support for and election of the leftist Múgica would surely have provoked the ultraconservative forces backing Almazán into an armed rebellion.

Avila Camacho was announced as the winner of 93.89 percent of the vote in the 1940 election. Almazán fled to Cuba and then to the United States, fulminating against alleged election irregularities. Although there were some disturbances by Almazanistas in northern Mexico, Cárdenas said they were of no importance. He did not, he said, consider that Almazán and his supporters were in revolt against the government, and they were free to return to Mexico any time they liked. This

Almazán soon did, renouncing his political ambitions and returning to private life.

The installation of the new President was peaceful and, in a way, a landmark. It had been almost exactly thirty years since Madero issued his first call to rebellion. In the three decades of revolution, counter-revolution and civil strife each transfer of power had been accompanied by political upheavals. Now Avila Camacho, a political moderate and a Catholic, took office with no disturbance whatsoever. It became popular to say that the Mexican Revolution ended in 1940. It wasn't quite true. Much remained to be done. But the period of violence and divisiveness had come to an end.

The man who, of all the revolutionists, had done the most to make this possible, left Mexico City with no fanfare. There was a sharp change in the political climate. Avila Camacho admitted that he was a Catholic; many army officers now openly attended Mass—something they had not dared to do for many years. Management of the railroads was taken away from the workers. Politically radical textbooks were withdrawn from the schools. At each step toward the right political observers predicted that Cárdenas would not stand for it, that he would return. He did not. He had confided to friends that he would not interfere with his successor, nor with his successor's successors. He had returned to Michoacán. Reporters from the capital pursued him but Cárdenas, while he was courteous to them, would not talk. He was supervising the remodeling of his modest country house at Lake Pátzcuaro. The reporters wrote stories that it was being expanded into a *palacete,* a little palace worthy of an ex-president. Finally Cárdenas explained what he was doing: he was equipping the house to be a free clinic for the Indians of the region.* As for politics, he had no intention of mixing in them. "I am," he said, "no longer the governor, but the governed."

* The house was subsequently given to UNESCO by Cárdenas for use as a teacher training center.

UNENDING STRUGGLE

"For the first time in our history, we are
contemporaries of all mankind."

Octavio Paz, *The Labyrinth
of Solitude*

LÁZARO CÁRDENAS, the last truly revolutionary president of Mexico, was succeeded by Manuel Avila Camacho, who was also a general. Mild in both his manner and his commitment to revolution, he acknowledged his Catholicism quite openly. The first in a series of Presidents (Miguel Aleman, 1946–1952, Adolfo Ruíz Cortines, 1952–1958, Adolfo López Mateos, 1958–1964) to hold office during a period of economic growth, he gave high priority to stabilizing and stimulating the economy while promoting social programs.

Despite prosperity, during the presidency of Gustavo Díaz Ordaz (1964–1970) serious questions began to be raised about the Revolution and the extent to which it had met its goals. Population was gaining at a yearly rate of more than three percent and soon outstripped the job market. Mexico City was becoming one of the world's largest cities, and an alarmingly large part of its population was unemployed and living in the dismal slums that had sprung up on its outskirts. Despite agrarian reform and land redistribution, many peasants were still without land. Some of those unable to make a living from farming clandestinely crossed the border to work as undocumented aliens in the United States, while more still swarmed into the already teeming packing box slums of the cities.

There was growing cynicism regarding the continued rule by the official party, the Partido Revolucionario Institucional (PRI), a political monolith that incorporated business, professional, labor, military, bureaucratic, and peasant elements in its complex and powerful structure. Although it had undoubtedly given Mexico a degree of political stability rare in Latin America, at the same time it smothered any striving toward true democracy. Opposition parties were tolerated but kept ineffective.

Students and intellectuals in the Díaz Ordaz era were becoming sharply aware of the shortcomings of the PRI, and dissent became both visible and vocal. A rising number of minor demonstrations and scuffles with the police culminated in a mass demonstration at the Plaza of Three Cultures at Tlatelolco. On this historic site where Cortés and his men had crushed the last resistance of the Aztecs, students organized a protest observed by thousands of bystanders on October 2, 1968. While military helicopters circled overhead, the police and soldiers who ringed the Plaza opened fire without warning. Estimates of the number of students and bystanders killed ran as high as 325. Hundreds of others were imprisoned on vague charges. The sinister shadow thrown across the accomplishments of the Revolution domestically was heightened by the pall the event threw over the 19th Olympic games, in which Mexico had hoped to present itself to the international community as a mature and sophisticated nation. Historians tend increasingly to regard the massacre as a watershed in Mexico's economic and political fortunes.

Díaz Ordaz had chosen as his successor Luis Echeverría Alvarez, a modest bureaucrat of supposedly conservative views. As secretary of the interior, in charge of internal security, he had, at least technically, borne some of the responsibility for Tlatelolco—a handicap he needed badly to overcome as president (1970–1976). The alienation of many students and intellectuals from the government coincided with an upsurge of both urban and rural guerrilla activity—ambushes, bank robberies, and kidnappings whose victims were either ransomed for cash or bartered for the release of other political prisoners.

Echeverría worked hard to establish his credentials as a man of the left. He freed most of the student protesters from incarceration and opened prison doors for political prisoners. In accordance with guerrilla demands, many were allowed to fly to Cuba. He promoted populist measures aimed at defusing social unrest, cultivated friendships with Third World nations, and proclaimed the establishment in Mexico of a University of the Third World. Late in his administration he energetically (but unsuccessfully) campaigned to succeed Kurt Waldheim to the secretary-generalship of the United Nations.

Echeverría's Third World stance led to trouble. He backed an Arab-inspired resolution in the United Nations General Assembly condemning Zionism for its "racism and racial discrimination." Israel and the international Jewish community, both of which had long enjoyed cordial and mutually profitable relations with Mexico, were outraged. The resulting boycott against Mexican tourism was highly effective and damaged Mexico's second-largest source of foreign exchange to the point where Echeverría was forced to modify his stand.

He also indulged in impassioned rhetoric about the Mexican peasants' right to land—a Revolutionary aim that had never totally been fulfilled and perhaps never could be. As a result, emboldened peasants in the northwestern states, Mexico's most prosperous agricultural area, marched onto private lands and occupied them, becoming, in the Mexican idiom, *paracaidistas* (parachutists)—i.e., squatters. Some of the seizures were legally validated ultimately, but many were declared illegal by Mexican federal courts. Thus Echeverría was caught between the rising tide of peasant demands and the complaints of landowners whose success in agriculture had been a strong prop of the Mexican economy and whose political power could not be ignored.

Although the newly discovered oil fields in southern Mexico promised future prosperity, Echeverría's populist agenda, his public works, and his program of "shared growth" reduced revenues and forced a devaluation of the peso. The peso, one of the most stable currencies of the hemisphere, which for 22 years had remained steady at 12½ to the dollar, fell to 27 to the dollar—and in the closing months of Echeverría's administration fell still lower, producing country-wide economic distress. Echeverría, meanwhile, had chosen as his successor José López Portillo, his finance minister and a lawyer, teacher, and novelist.

The nation that had been in deep trouble when Echeverría had taken over as president was in even worse condition when López Portillo assumed stewardship. A weakened peso resulted in 30 percent inflation and a foreign debt of $20 billion. A program of austerity reduced subsidies and government payrolls. Promises were made to eradicate graft and corruption, always a drain on the Mexican economy but particularly so in recent administrations.

The peso responded by a slight recovery, but far more significant was the discovery of major oil fields in southern Mexico. Mexico was thus projected into the position of fourth-largest oil producer in the world—after Russia, Saudi Arabia, and the United States—with vast reserves that placed it second only to Saudi Arabia.

Mexico's oil wells pumped 2.5 million barrels daily during 1981 and earned the nation $14 billion. Austerity was virtually forgotten. López Portillo launched grand plans for bolstering the economy which included public works, government-subsidized enterprises, construction of a score of nuclear reactors, establishment of a basic support system for agriculture, and funding for both light and heavy industry. These programs necessitated heavy borrowing, and international bankers were only too happy to oblige a country as oil rich as Mexico appeared to be.

With the influx of billions in newly borrowed capital came a sharp rise in the degree of corruption at all levels. Oscar Flores Tapía, governor of the border state of Coahuila, was expelled from both his office and the PRI for "inexplicable enrichment," allegedly obtained by brokering contracts for relatives and friends. Jorge Díaz Serrano, a former ambassador to the Soviet Union, was ejected from the Senate and jailed on allegations of skimming $34 million from Pemex shipbuilding contracts. Meanwhile the management of the largest Mexican labor union, representing Pemex workers, was rocked by charges and countercharges regarding misappropriation of some 20 billion pesos over a ten-year period. Salvador Barragan Camacho, secretary general of the union, and Joaquín Hernandez Galicia, its political counselor, were accused by the union's director of education and welfare, Hector García Hernandez, while he was under investigation for an alleged $6.5 million theft of union funds.

Simultaneous with these revelations came a worldwide oil glut and recession. Mexico, saddled with her new foreign debt, refused to reduce oil prices or to limit production. Contracts for delivery of Mexican oil were canceled, and the nation slid rapidly into the most severe economic crisis since the worst days of the Revolution. The peso slipped to 50, to 100, and kept on sliding. Inflation reached 100 percent. Wealthy citizens, despairing of the stability of their own currency, transferred their fortunes to equities, bank accounts, or real estate investments abroad. Although the government condemned them as *sacadolares*, or dollar movers, and talked of prosecution, the drain did not stop. It appeared that Mexico might have to default on its foreign debts—about $80 billion —and go into bankruptcy. Late in his administration López Portillo, who wryly described himself as a "devalued president," imposed strict exchange controls and took the bold step of nationalizing domestic private banks, which he blamed for a major role in the nation's predicament. It was perhaps the most radical government action since Cárdenas expropriated the oil properties.

When he assumed the red, white, and green sash of office on December 1, 1982, López Portillo's chosen successor, Miguel de la Madrid, took charge of a country deep in trouble—far deeper trouble than either Echeverría or López Portillo had faced. In some ways there was as much misery as there had been three-quarters of a century earlier in the last days of the iron rule of Porfirio Díaz. No solutions were in sight for the problems of overpopulation, unemployment, and official corruption. The role of the PRI as national stabilizer was dependent on doling out the privilege that goes with power, and any serious attack on the cancer of corruption would weaken that role.

In foreign affairs Mexico was in an uncomfortably ambiguous position, heavily dependent on historical, racial, and commercial relationships with the United States yet deeply and sympathetically involved with revolutionary aspirations in Central America and the Caribbean, whose struggles echoed Mexico's past.

There was much speculation in foreign capitals about Mexico's ability to continue as a free and democratic nation. Answering these doubts is Mexico's proven ability to survive—until now—in its long struggle to overcome what López Portillo, in a memorable phrase, described as "the old structure of injustice."

PRINCIPAL CHARACTERS

Aguirre Benavides, Eugenio: Villista general, later a supporter of Eulalio Gutiérrez; executed.

Aguirre Benavides, Luis: Secretary to Francisco Villa.

Alemán, Miguel: Veracruz revolutionary leader; his son of same name President of Mexico 1946–52.

Almazán, Juan Andrew: Veteran revolutionary soldier of many loyalties; unsuccessful candidate for presidency in 1940.

Alvarado, Salvador: Pharmacist from Sinaloa and important general in the Sonora group; Socialist governor of Yucatán; against Obregón in the De la Huerta rebellion; executed.

Angeles, Felipe: Professional soldier, loyal to Madero; alienated by Carranza, then a close associate of Villa in his greatest military victories; executed.

Argumedo, Benjamín: Revolutionist with Madero, later a general under Huerta, then a supporter of Convention government; executed.

Avila Camacho, Manuel: President of Mexico 1940–46.

Blanco, Lucio: Cavalry officer noted for first distribution of land in the Revolution, at Matamoros in 1913; murdered.

Blanquet, Aureliano: Plotter against Madero and close associate of Huerta; killed in action in counterrevolutionary attempt.

Bonillas, Ignacio: Carranza's Ambassador to Washington and his choice for succession to the presidency in 1920.

Buelna, Rafael: Revolutionary general from Sinaloa, noted for youth, small size (*Granito de Oro*) and integrity; killed in rebellion against Obregón.

Cabrera, Luis: Lawyer and intellectual adviser to Carranza.

Calles, Plutarco Elías: Revolutionary soldier and politician from Sonora; President 1924–28, thereafter the *Jefe Maximo* until expelled from country in 1936.

Canova, Leon: Special agent of the United States.

Cárdenas, Francisco: Officer in charge of the party which killed Madero and Pino Suárez; suicide.

Cárdenas, Lázaro: Revolutionist from Michoacán; President of Mexico 1934–40.

Carothers, George: Special agent of the United States.

Carranza, Venustiano: "First Chief" of the Constitutionalist movement; President of Mexico 1917–20; assassinated.

Carrillo Puerto, Felipe: Socialist leader of Yucatán; loyal to government in De la Huerta rebellion; executed.

Carvajal, Francisco: Jurist; peace negotiator for Díaz in 1911; interim president of Mexico after Huerta's resignation.

Cedillo, Saturnino: Conservative caudillo from San Luis Potosí; first a collaborator and then a rebel against Cárdenas government; killed in skirmish with government troops.

Cepeda, Enrique: Confidant of Huerta and his appointee as governor of Federal District; mysteriously killed at San Juan de Ulúa.

Corral, Ramón: Vice-President under Díaz.

Creel, Enrique Clay: Son-in-law of powerful Terrazas family; governor, ambassador and Foreign Minister under Díaz.

De la Barra, Francisco León: Foreign Minister under Díaz; interim president between Díaz and Madero.

De la Huerta, Adolfo: Sonora governor; interim president 1920; rebel against Obregón.

De la Madrid, Miguel: President of Mexico 1982–

Díaz, Felix: Politically ambitious nephew of Porfirio Díaz; a plotter against Madero and rebel against later governments.

Díaz, José de la Cruz Porfirio: Usually referred to as Don Porfirio; dictator of Mexico from 1876 to 1911; died in exile in Paris 1915.

Díaz Ordaz, Gustavo: President of Mexico 1964–1970.

Díaz Soto y Gama, Antonio: Intellectual lawyer from San Luis Potosí prominent in early radical circles; adviser and orator for Zapata; later a supporter of Obregón.

Diéguez, Manuel: A leader of the strike at Cananea in 1906; later a successful revolutionary general loyal to Carranza; against Obregón in De la Huerta rebellion; executed.

Domínguez, Belisario: Chiapas Senator and critic of Huerta; assassinated.

Echeverría Alvarez, Luis: President of Mexico 1970–1976.

Escobar, José Gonzalo: Leader of an anti-government rebellion in 1929.

Fierro, Rodolfo: Villa's chief executioner; died in quicksand.

Flores Magón, Ricardo: Revolutionary journalist, liberal at first and later an anarchist, whose writing and agitation helped pave way for Madero's revolutionary movement; died in Leavenworth.

Garrido Canabal, Tomás: Radical caudillo of Tabasco and leader of Red Shirts; briefly Minister of Agriculture under Cárdenas.

Gómez, Arnulfo: General active in suppression of De la Huerta rebellion; nominated for presidency in 1927; executed.

González, Abraham: Maderista leader and revolutionary mentor of Villa; governor of Chihuahua; assassinated.

González, Pablo: Carrancista general noted for military reverses; aspirant to presidency in 1920; later an exile.

González Garza, Roque: Villista; successor to Eulalio Gutiérrez as presiding officer of Convention government.

Guajardo, Jesús María: Director of ambush in which Zapata was killed; rebel against De la Huerta government; executed.

Gutiérrez, Eulalio: Provisional president chosen by Military Convention of Aguascalientes.

Guzmán, Martín Luis: Chronicler of Revolution.

Herrero, Rodolfo: Director of ambush in which Carranza was assassinated.

Huerta, Victoriano: Professional soldier; plotter against Madero and his successor in presidency, 1913–14; died in El Paso 1915.

Lagos Cházaro, Francisco: Last president of the Convention government.

Lascuráin, Pedro: Madero's Foreign Minister and, upon his forced resignation, his successor in presidency for less than one hour.

Limantour, José Yves: Díaz's Secretary of Treasury, leader of the *científico* group.

López Mateos, Adolfo: President of Mexico 1958–64.

López, Pablo: Villa lieutenant and key figure in Santa Isabel massacre and raid on Columbus, New Mexico; executed.

López Portillo, José: President of Mexico 1976–1982.

Madero, Francisco Ignacio: Leader of the Anti-Reelectionist movement and initiator of the Revolution in 1910; elected President 1911; assassinated.

Madero, Gustavo: Brother of Francisco and his political strong arm; executed.

Madero, Julio: Brother of Francisco; active in Carrancista ranks.

Madero, Raul: Brother of Francisco; a member of Villa's staff.

Martínez, Paulino: Zapatista journalist and spokesman; executed.

Mata, Filomena: Independent journalist much persecuted by Díaz regime.

Maycotte, Fortunato: General loyal first to Carranza, later to Obregón, still later to De la Huerta against Obregón; executed.

Maytorena, José María: Governor of Sonora at time of Madero's overthrow; later an ally of Villa and enemy of Obregón.

Molina Enríquez, Andrés: Author whose study of Mexico's land question, *The Great National Problem* (1910) was great influence in agrarian reform.

Mondragón, Manuel: Professional soldier and leader in plot against Madero.

Montaño, Otilio: Intellectual adviser to Zapata and author of Plan of Ayala; executed.

Morones, Luis: Labor leader and political figure under Carranza, Obregón and Calles.

Morrow, Dwight: Partner of J. P. Morgan & Co., appointed Ambassador of the U.S. to Mexico in 1927; a strong influence on Calles.

Múgica, Francisco: Leader of the radical "Jacobin" group in drafting the Constitution of 1917; collaborator in Cárdenas government and aspirant to presidency in 1940.

Murguía, Francisco: General loyal to Carranza and leader in 1922 of an abortive rebellion against Obregón; executed.

Obregón, Alvaro: *El invicto*, the unconquered general; most important of Carranza's supporters, later his enemy; President 1920–24; reelected in 1928 but assassinated before taking office.

Orozco, Pascual: Guerrilla fighter for Madero; later leader of anti-Madero rebellion; killed by Texas Rangers.

Ortiz Rubio, Pascual: Engineer and revolutionary general from Michoacán; elected President 1929; resigned from presidency in 1932 because of interference by Calles.

Palafox, Manuel: Zapatista intellectual; installed as Minister of Agriculture in Convention government on Zapata's orders; later an enemy of Zapata.

Palavicini, Felix Fulgencio: Journalist and adviser to Carranza.

Pino Suárez, José María: Madero's Vice-President; assassinated.

Portes Gil, Emilio: Lawyer and politician from Tamaulipas; provisional president from end of Calles term until election of Ortiz Rubio.

Reyes, Bernardo: Governor and military boss of Nuevo León; aspirant to presidency; plotter against Madero; killed on first day of *Decena Trágica*.

Robles, José Isabel: Villista general; Minister of War under provisional presidency of Eulalio Gutiérrez; executed.

Rodríguez, Abelardo: Chosen in 1932 to serve balance of Ortiz Rubio's presidential term.

Ruiz Cortines, Adolfo: President of Mexico 1952–58.

Serdán, Aquiles: First martyr of the Madero Revolution.

Serrano, Francisco: Staff officer under Obregón, later his Secretary of War; nominated for presidency in 1927; executed.

Terrazas: Wealthy landowning family of Chihuahua.

Urbina, Tomás: Former bandit; close associate of Villa; later his victim.

Valenzuela, Gilberto: Political leader from Sonora; author of Plan of Agua Prieta; Secretary of Government under Calles; later his enemy.

Vasconcelos, José: Intellectual and writer; Secretary of Education under Obregón and patron of Mexican revolutionary muralists; aspirant to presidency in 1929.

Vázquez Gómez, Emilio: Lawyer; Minister of Government in De la Barra cabinet and an opponent of discharge of revolutionary troops; later an enemy of Madero.

Vázquez Gómez, Francisco: Physician; first a political ally, later an enemy of Madero.

Villa, Francisco (Doroteo Arango): Most famous guerrilla fighter of the Revolution; assassinated.

Villareal, Antonio I.: Early collaborator of Ricardo Flores Magón; later with Madero, still later with Carranza.

Wilson, Henry Lane: U. S. Ambassador to Mexico under Díaz, De la Barra, Madero and Huerta; accused of complicity in overthrow of Madero; relieved during administration of Woodrow Wilson.

Zapata, Emiliano: Peasant leader from Morelos and most consistent champion of land reform; killed in ambush.

CHRONOLOGY

1900 Founding of *Regeneración,* revolutionary journal of Ricardo Flores
   Magón. First published in Mexico City, later in San Antonio, Texas,
   St. Louis, Mo., and Los Angeles, Calif.

1906 Strike at Consolidated Copper Company, Cananea, Sonora; 23 dead;
   first of series of pre-Revolution labor disturbances.

   Publication of program of Liberal party by Mexican exiles in St.
   Louis, Mo.; forerunner of all the "plans" of the Mexican Revolution.

   First attempt (September-October) of Flores Magón to launch rebellion in Chihuahua and Sonora.

1907 Strike in mills at Rio Blanco, Veracruz; 200 killed.

1908 Publication in *Pearson's Magazine* of James Creelman's interview with
   Porfirio Díaz in which latter says he would welcome formation of
   opposition party.

   Second attempt of Magonistas to launch a revolution; Liberal party
   members arrested throughout Mexico.

   Francisco I. Madero finishes writing *The Presidential Succession in
   1910,* but does not distribute it until following year.

1909 Publication of *The Great National Problems* by Andrés Molina Enríquez, a thorough study of land question.

1910 Madero nominated for presidency by Anti-Reelectionist party.

   Halley's comet interpreted as evil omen.

   Madero arrested, imprisoned; 5000 of his supporters arrested.

   Celebration of Centennial of war of independence.

   Mexican Congress declares Porfirio Díaz elected for eighth term.

   Madero flees to Texas, publishes Plan of San Luis Potosí calling for
   revolution; first attempt at revolution fails.

1911 Victory of Madero's forces at Juárez.

   Díaz resigns, goes into exile; Francisco León de la Barra provisional
   president.

   Madero assumes presidency after winning 99 percent of vote in
   free election.

   Emiliano Zapata breaks with Madero, publishes Plan of Ayala.

   Bernardo Reyes fails in effort to launch counterrevolution.

1912 Pascual Orozco rebels against Madero, is defeated by Victoriano Huerta.

Abortive rebellion of Felix Díaz against Madero government.

1913 *Decena Trágica,* a reign of terror in Mexico City, ends in Huerta's takeover of presidency, murder of Madero and Vice-President José María Pino Suárez.

Venustiano Carranza assumes leadership of resistance to Huerta, draws up Plan of Guadalupe as charter for Constitutionalist movement.

After military reverses in Coahuila Carranza goes to Sonora to lead revolutionary movement there, already progressing under military direction of Alvaro Obregón.

Francisco Villa has series of great victories at Torreón, Juárez, Tierra Blanca and Ojinaga.

1914 United States lifts arms embargo, thus aiding rebels.

Carranza leaves Sonora for Chihuahua; beginning of rift with Villa.

Villa retakes Torreón.

U.S. troops landed at Veracruz; 19 Americans and 300 Mexicans killed; shipload of German munitions for Huerta escapes interception; ABC conference (Argentina, Brazil, Chile) attempts to solve Mexican-U.S. crisis.

Villa's victory at Zacatecas and Obregón's at Guadalajara seal fate of Huerta's army.

Huerta resigns; Francisco Carvajal becomes interim president. Torreón conference tries to heal Villa-Carranza split.

Obregón takes control of Mexico City.

Carranza assumes title of First Chief in charge of the executive power, summons a junta of generals and governors to plan future.

Military Convention of Aguascalientes elects Eulalio Gutiérrez provisional president, calls for Carranza's resignation; Villa becomes military arm of Convention.

Carranza flees Mexico City, makes Veracruz—just evacuated by U.S. troops—his capital; Obregón commands Carranza's forces.

Villa and Zapata control Mexico City.

1915 Carranza acknowledges need for land reform, issues moderate agrarian decree.

Eulalio Gutiérrez, unable to control Villa, flees Mexico City.

Obregón takes Puebla, then Mexico City, then defeats Villa in battles of Celaya; Villa suffers further defeats at León, Aguascalientes, Zacatecas, Agua Prieta, Hermosillo, and by end of year is no longer a major military force.

Convention government is dissolved.

Carranza, claiming control of seven-eighths of Mexico, is recognized on de facto basis by U.S.

1916 Villa, with Santa Isabel massacre and raid on Columbus, N.M., provokes crisis; U.S. sends Punitive Expedition into Mexico.

Carranza calls constituent congress in Querétaro.

1917 Querétaro congress finishes new constitution with radical provisions for land reform, labor welfare, education, control of Catholic Church and state ownership of resources.

German foreign minister's efforts to enlist Mexico on side of Germany cause international scandal. Carranza decides to remain neutral.

Carranza elected.

1919   Zapata lured into ambush and killed; his killer rewarded by Carranza. Carranza chooses Ambassador Ignacio Bonillas as his successor.

Obregón announces his candidacy, has difficulty campaigning.

1920   Obregón flees into Guerrero and calls for rebellion. Calles issues Plan of Agua Prieta disavowing presidency of Carranza.

Carranza, deserted by most of his followers, flees Mexico City hoping to reestablish his capital in Veracruz. He is ambushed and killed at Tlaxcalantongo.

Under interim presidency of Adolfo de la Huerta there is period of reconciliation among revolutionary factions: Villa accepts amnesty, retires to Canutillo.

Obregón elected President.

1922   Secretary of Treasury De la Huerta goes to New York, negotiates Lamont agreement regarding Mexican debts.

1923   Obregón recognized by U.S. after completion of Bucareli pact dealing with debts, land expropriation and oil.

Villa assassinated at Parral.

De la Huerta, supported by conservatives and much of army, rebels against government, shortly afterward goes into exile.

1924   Calles becomes President, inaugurates ambitious program of land distribution, public works and fiscal reform.

1925   Calles supports schismatic Mexican Catholic Apostolic church.

1926   Calles issues anti-Catholic decrees; Catholics in retaliation suspend church services throughout Mexico.

1927   Catholics launch guerrilla war.

Obregón decides to run for presidency again; his supporters amend constitution to permit reelection, also extending presidential term from four to six years.

Presidential aspirants Francisco Serrano and Arnulfo Gómez and their followers are executed.

Four men accused of bomb attempt on Obregón's life are executed without trial, among them Miguel Pro, a Jesuit priest active in the Catholic underground.

Dwight Morrow, new U.S. ambassador, exercises strong influence on Calles.

1928   Obregón, only candidate and winner in presidential election, is assassinated at La Bombilla Restaurant by José de León Toral, a Catholic zealot.

Emilio Portes Gil named provisional president; Calles, out of office, retains great influence as *Jefe Maximo*.

Formation of Partido Nacional Revolucionario (PNR).

1929   Calles, increasingly conservative, declares both agrarianism and the Revolution failures.

Pascual Ortiz Rubio elected to complete Obregón's presidential term; opposed by José Vasconcelos.

1930   Attempt on life of Ortiz Rubio on his inauguration day.

More than 100 bodies of followers of Vasconcelos, all victims of strangulation, found in shallow graves at Topilejo.

1932   Ortiz Rubio, discouraged by interference of Calles in his administration, resigns and leaves Mexico. Abelardo Rodríguez, a businessman-general, is appointed to complete term.

1934   PNR adopts Six Year Plan as a program of government.

Lázaro Cárdenas, young but experienced revolutionary general from Michoacán, is nominated by PNR, campaigns vigorously and wins presidency.

1936   Calles expelled from Mexico for interference with Cárdenas administration.

1938   PNR becomes PRM (Partido de la Revolución Mexicana).

Cárdenas expropriates foreign-owned oil companies.

Saturnino Cedillo, last of the caudillos, rebels against government, is killed in skirmish with federal troops.

1940   Election of Manuel Avila Camacho; Cárdenas sets precedent by retiring completely from exercise of authority and power.

1946   PRM becomes PRI (Partido Revolucionario Institucional).

Election of Miguel Alemán.

1952   Election of Adolfo Ruiz Cortines.

1958   Election of Adolfo López Mateos.

1964   Election of Gustavo Díaz Ordaz.

1970   Election of Luis Echeverría Alvarez.

1976   Election of José López Portillo.

1982   Election of Miguel de la Madrid.

ACKNOWLEDGMENTS

THE NAMES of many sources cannot be recalled; such as the old porter at the St. Francis hotel who, long ago, was full of tales of revolutionists who had stayed there; and an old Villista who was left for dead on the battlefield and later came back to claim a pension from the government. Others, all direct participants in or close observers of the struggle, are readily identifiable—such as Juan Andrew Almazán, the Avila Camacho brothers, Ramón Beteta, Luis Cabrera, Lázaro Cárdenas, Francisco Castillo Nájera, Adolfo de la Huerta, Emilio ("el Indio") Fernández, Martín Luis Guzmán, Amada ("la coronela") Muzquiz, José Clemente Orozco, Felix F. Palavicini, Diego Rivera, Abelardo Rodríguez, David Alfaro Siqueiros, María Tapía de Obregón, Fernando Torreblanca, José Vasconcelos. Many others, not participants but well-informed and concerned, were helpful with comments and observations; such as Albert Almada, Arturo Arnaiz y Freg, Federico Bach, Anita Brenner, Alejandro Carrillo, Antonio Carrillo Flores, Hal Croves, Rose Elena Luján, Rafael Muñoz, Adolfo Orive Alba, Alma Reed, and Ethel Duffy Turner. They should not, however, be held accountable for the contents of the book since the author in many instances went counter to their counsel. Valuable help came also from old friends such as Tom Lea, Rafael Delgado Lozano, Juan Guzmán, Ida Novi and Jane Scholl. The regents of the University of California are due thanks for the granting of a sabbatical and leave of absence in which part of the research was done. The author is indebted to helpful staff members of the UCLA Research Library, the Bancroft Library at Berkeley, the Los Angeles Public Library, the El Paso Public Library, the Latin American Collection of the University of Texas Library, the National Archives in Washington, and the Hemeroteca Nacional and Biblioteca Nacional in Mexico City.

BIBLIOGRAPHY

Ackerman, Carl W. *Mexico's Dilemma*. New York: George H. Doran Co., 1918.

Aguirre Benavides, Adrián. *Madero el inmaculado; historia de la Revolución de 1910*. Mexico City: Editorial Diana, 1962.

Aguirre Benavides, Luis and Adrián. *Las grandes batallas de la División del Norte al mando de Pancho Villa*. Mexico City: Editorial Diana, 1964.

Alamán, Lucas. *Historia de Méjico*. 5 vols. Mexico City: 1849.

Alessio Robles, Miguel. *Historia política de la Revolución*. Mexico City: Ediciones Botas, 1946.

———*Ideales de la Revolución*. Mexico City: Editorial Cultura, 1935.

Almada, Francisco R. *Diccionario de historia, geografía y biografía Sonorenses*. Chihuahua, Chih. No date.

———*La Revolución en el estado de Chihuahua*. Vol. I. Chihuahua: Biblioteca del Instituto Nacional de Estudios Historicos de la Revolución Mexicana (BINEHRM), 1964.

Amaya, Juan Gualberto. *Venustiano Carranza, caudillo Constitucionalista*. Mexico City: 1947.

Anaya Ibarra, Pedro María. *Precursores de la Revolución Mexicana*. Mexico City, Secretaria de Educación Pública, 1955.

Anguiano Equihua, Victoriano. *Lázaro Cárdenas: su feudo y la política nacional*. Mexico City: Editorial Eréndira, 1951.

Arciniegas, Germán. *Latin America*. Translated by Joan MacLean. New York; Knopf, 1967.

Arenal, Angélica: *Biografía humana y profesional de José David Alfaro Siqueiros*. Mexico City: Instituto Nacional de Bellas Artes, 1947.

Arenas Guzmán, Diego. *Del Maderismo a los tratados de Teoloyucan*. Mexico City: BINEHRM, 1935.

———*La consumación del crimen*. Mexico City: Ediciones Botas, 1935.

Arnaiz y Freg and others. *Mexico y la cultura*. Mexico City: Secretaria de Educación Pública, 1961.

Azuela, Mariano. *The Underdogs*. Translated by E. Munguía, Jr. New York: New American Library, 1963.

———*Two Novels of Mexico. The Flies. The Bosses*. Translated by Lesley

Byrd Simpson. Berkeley and Los Angeles: University of California Press, 1956.

Baerlein, Henry. *Mexico, Land of Unrest.* Philadelphia: Lippincott, 1914.

Baker, Ray Stannard. *Woodrow Wilson; Life and Letters.* Vols. 4 and 6. Garden City: Doubleday Doran & Co., 1931.

Baltierra Rivera, Leonardo. *Breve analisis de la evolución constitucional de Mexico.* Thesis for law degree, National Autonomous University of Mexico, 1945.

Bancroft, Hubert Howe. *History of Mexico.* 6 vols. San Francisco: A. L. Bancroft. 1881–1888.

Barragán Rodriguez, Juan. *Historia del ejército y de la Revolución Constitucionalista.* 2 vols. Mexico City: Antigua Librería Robredo, 1946.

Barrera Fuentes, Florencio (ed.). *Crónicas y debates de las sesiones de la Soberana Convención Militar.* Mexico City: BINEHRM, 1964.

Beals, Carleton. *Civil War in Mexico.* New Republic July 6, 1927.

——*Mexico's Coming Election.* New Republic August 17, 1927.

——*Porfirio Diaz, Dictator of Mexico.* Philadelphia: Lippincott, 1932.

Bell, Edward I. *The Political Shame of Mexico.* New York: McBride, Nast & Co., 1914.

Beteta, Ramón. *Camino a Tlaxcalantongo.* Mexico City and Buenos Aires; Fondo de Cultura Económica, 1961.

Blaisdell, Lowell L. *The Desert Revolution.* Madison: University of Wisconsin Press, 1962.

Blanco Moheno, Roberto. *Crónica de la Revolución Mexicana.* 3 vols. Mexico City: Libro Mex Editores, 1961.

Blasco Ibañez, Vicente. *Mexico in Revolution.* New York: Dutton, 1920.

Bojórquez, Juan de Dios (pseud. Djed Bórquez), *Crónica del Constituyente.* Mexico City: Ediciones Botas, 1938.

——*Forjadores de la Revolución Mexicana.* Mexico City: BINEHRM, 1960.

——*Lázaro Cárdenas.* Mexico City: Imprenta Mundial, 1933.

——*Obregón: apuntes biográficos.* Mexico City: Ediciones Patria Nueva, 1929.

Boletín oficial del Consejo Superior de Gobierno del Distrito Federal, vols. XIV–XVIII. Mexico City, 1910–1912.

Bonilla, Manuel, Jr. *El régimen Maderista.* Mexico City: Editorial Arana, 1962.

Booth, George C. *Mexico's School-Made Society.* Stanford: Stanford University Press, 1941.

Bosques, Gilberto. *The National Revolutionary Party of Mexico and the Six-Year Plan.* Mexico City: PNR, 1937.

Braddy, Haldeen. *Pancho Villa at Columbus. The Raid of 1916.* Southwestern Studies Monograph No. 9. El Paso: Texas Western College, 1965.

Brandenburg, Frank. *The Making of Modern Mexico.* Englewood Cliffs, N.J.: Prentice Hall, 1964.

Breceda, Alfredo. *Don Venustiano Carranza: rasgos biográficos escritos en 1912.* Mexico City: Talleres Gráficos de la Nación, 1930.

————*Mexico revolucionario 1913–1917.* Madrid: Tipografía Artística Cervantes, 1920.

————*Mexico revolucionario 1913–1917,* vol. II. Mexico City: Ediciones Botas, 1941.

Brenner, Anita. *Idols Behind Altars.* New York: Payson & Clarke, Ltd., 1929.

————and Leighton, George R. *The Wind that Swept Mexico.* New York: Harper, 1943.

Bulnes, Francisco. *The Whole Truth about Mexico.* Translated by Dora Scott. New York: M. Bulnes Book Co., 1916.

Cabrera, Luis. *El pensamiento de Luis Cabrera,* ed. by Eduardo Luquín. Mexico City: BINEHRM, 1960.

————*La herencia de Carranza, por el lic.* Blas Urrea [pseud.] Mexico City: Imprenta Nacional, S.A., 1920.

————*Obras politicas.* Mexico City: Imprenta Nacional, S.A., 1921.

————(pseud. Blas Urrea). *Veinte años despues.* Mexico City: Ediciones Botas, 1938.

Calderón de la Barca, Fanny. *Life in Mexico.* Edited and annotated by Howard T. and Marian Hall Fisher. Garden City: Doubleday & Company, 1966.

Callcott, Wilfrid Hardy, *Liberalism in Mexico, 1857–1929.* Stanford: Stanford University Press, 1931.

Calles (see Elías Calles, Plutarco)

Castellanos Tena, Fernando. *Nuestras constituciones.* Thesis for law degree, National Autonomous University of Mexico, 1944.

Carrillo, Alejandro. *Causas y programa de la Revolución Mexicana.* Mexico City, 1963.

————*Defensa de la Revolución en el parlimento.* Mexico City: Chamber of Deputies, 1943.

Carrillo Flores, Antonio. *Revolución y pragmatismo en el México moderno.* Speech before Cleveland, Ohio, Council on World Affairs, March 9, 1962.

Casasola, Gustavo. *Historia gráfica de la Revolución Mexicana.* 4 vols. Edición comemorativa. Mexico City: Editorial F. Trillas, S.A., 1964.

Castillo Torre, José. *La luz de relámpago. Ensayo de biografía subjetiva de Felipe Carrillo Puerto.* Mexico City: Ediciones Botas, 1934.

Castle of Chapultepec. Mexico City: Instituto Nacional de Antropología, 1963.

Cejas Reyes, Victor. *Yo maté a Villa.* Mexico City: Populibro La Prensa, 1960.

Cervantes, Federico. *Felipe Angeles en la Revolución.* Mexico City, 1964.

————*Francisco Villa y la Revolución.* Mexico City: Ediciones Alonso, 1960.

Charlot, Jean. *The Mexican Mural Renaissance, 1920–1925.* New Haven and London: Yale University Press, 1963.

50 años de la Revolución Mexicana en cifras. Mexico City: Presidencia de la Republica, 1963.

Clendenen, Clarence C. *The United States and Pancho Villa. A Study in Unconventional Diplomacy.* Ithaca: Cornell University Press, 1961.

Cline, Howard F. *The United States and Mexico.* New York: Atheneum, 1963.

Cole, Richard R. Statement to Los Angeles *Times* September 17, 1916 re his work for U.S. recognition of Carranza.

Compendio estadística de los Estados Unidos Mexicanos, 1962. Mexico City: Secretaria de Industria y Comercio, 1963.

Correa, Eduardo J. *Balance del Cardenismo.* Mexico City: Talleres Acción, 1941.

Creelman, James. *Diaz, Master of Mexico.* New York and London: Appleton, 1916.

――――*President Diaz: Hero of the Americas. Pearson's Magazine,* March, 1908.

Cumberland, Charles C. *Mexican Revolution. Genesis under Madero.* Austin: University of Texas Press, 1952.

De Fornaro, Carlo. *Carranza and Mexico* (with chapters by Colonel I. C. Enríquez, Charles Ferguson and M. C. Roland). New York: Mitchell Kennerly, 1915.

――――*Diaz, Czar of Mexico.* Philadelphia: International Pub. Co., 1909.

De la Huerta, Adolfo. *Memorias de don Adolfo de la Huerta, segun su propio dictado: Transcripción y comentarios del lic.* Roberto Guzmán Esparza. Mexico City: Ediciones Guzman, 1957.

De María y Campos, Armando. *Episodios de la Revolución. De la caida de Porfirio Díaz a la decena trágica.* Mexico City: Libro Mex Editores, 1958.

――――*La Revolución Mexicana a través de los corridos populares.* Mexico City: BINEHRM, 1962.

――――*Vida de Gral. Lucio Blanco.* Mexico City: BINEHRM, 1963.

De Valle-Arizpe, Artemio. *Historia de la ciudad de Mexico segun los relatos de sus cronistas.* Mexico City: Editorial Pedro Robredo, 1946.

Díaz Babio, Francisco. *Un drama nacional.* Mexico City: Imp. M. León Sánchez, 1939.

Dillon, E. J. *President Obregon. A World Reformer.* London: Hutchinson & Co., 1922.

Dromundo, Baltasar. *Vida de Emiliano Zapata.* Mexico City: Editorial Guaranía, 1961.

Dulles, John W. F. *Yesterday in Mexico: A Chronicle of the Revolution 1919–1936.* Austin: University of Texas Press, 1961.

Elías Calles, Plutarco. *Mexico Before the World,* ed. by Robert Hammond Murray. New York: Academy Press, 1927.

――――*Partes oficiales de la campaña de Sonora rendidos por el gral. P. Elías Calles.* Mexico City: Talleres Graficos de la Nación, 1932.

Escobedo, José G. *La batalla de Zacatecas, 32 años despues.* Mexico City, 1946.

Espinosa, Gonzalo, with Piña, Joaquín and Ortiz, Carlos. *La Decena roja.* Mexico City, 1913.

Ethics in Action; Porfirio Díaz and His Work, by a Soldier of the Old Guard. Mexico City: Imprenta de Hull, 1907.

Fabela, Isidro, ed. *Revolución y régimen Constitucionalista (Documentos históricos de la Revolución Mexicana).* 4 vols. Mexico City: Fondo de Cultura Económica, 1960, 1962, 1963.

――――*Revolución y régimen Maderista (Documentos históricos de la Rev-*

olución Mexicana). 3 vols. Mexico City: Fondo de Cultura Económica, 1964, 1965.

Ferrer de Mendiolea, Gabriel. *Historia de la Revolución Mexicana.* Mexico City: Ediciones de El Nacional, 1956.

——*Historia del Congreso Constituyente, 1916–1917.* Mexico City: BINEHRM, 1957.

Flores Magón, Ricardo. *Epistolario y textos. Prólogo, ordenación de notas, Manuel González Ramírez.* Mexico City and Buenos Aires: Fondo de Cultura Económica, 1964.

——*Semilla Libertaria (articulos).* 2 vols. Mexico City: *Grupo Cultural "Ricardo Flores Magón,"* 1923.

Foix, Pere. *Pancho Villa.* Mexico City: Ediciones Xochitl, 1950.

Foreign Relations. Papers Relating to the Foreign Relations of the United States, 1909/10 on. Washington: Government Printing Office. Note: this has been supplemented from the 812 files, on deposit in the National Archives, particularly for the otherwise unpublished dispatches of Leon Canova and George Carothers.

Fuentes, Carlos. *Where the Air Is Clear.* Translated by Sam Hileman. New York: Ivan Obolensky, Inc., 1960.

——*The Death of Artemio Cruz.* Translated by Sam Hileman. New York: Farrar, Strauss & Co., 1964.

Fuentes para la Historia de la Revolución Mexicana. Vol. I, *Planes políticos y otros documentos* (1954). Vol. II, *La caricatura política* (1955). Vol. III, *La huelga de Cananea* (1956). Vol. IV, *Manifiestos políticos* (1957). Vol. V, Alvaro Obregón: *Ocho mil kilómetros en campaña* (1959). Mexico City: Fondo de Cultura Económica.

Gamez, Atenedoro. *Monografía historica sobre la genesis de la Revolución en el estado de Puebla.* Mexico City: BINEHRM, 1960.

Gamiz Olivas, Everardo. *La Revolución en el estado de Durango.* Mexico City: BINEHRM, 1963.

García Rivas, Heriberto. *150 biografías de Mexicanos ilustres.* Mexico City: Editorial Diana, S.A., 1964.

González-Blanco, Edmundo. *Carranza y la Revolución de México.* Valencia: Prometeo Sociedad Editorial, 1914.

González-Blanco, Pedro. *De Porfirio Díaz a Carranza.* Madrid: Imprenta Helénica, 1916.

González Casanova, Pablo. *La democracia en México.* Mexico City: Ediciones Era, 1965.

González Ramírez, Manuel. *La Revolución social de México.* Mexico City and Buenos Aires: Fondo de Cultura Económica, 1960.

——*México, litografía de la ciudad que fue.* Mexico City, 1962.

Gruening, Ernest. *Mexico and Its Heritage.* New York: Appleton-Century-Crofts, 1928.

Guzmán, Martín Luis. *The Eagle and the Serpent.* Translated by Harriet de Onis. Garden City: Doubleday, 1965.

——*Febrero de 1913.* Mexico City: Empresas Editoriales, 1963.

——*Memoirs of Pancho Villa*. Translated by Virginia H. Taylor. Austin: University of Texas Press, 1965.

——*Muertes históricos*. Mexico City: Cia. General de Ediciones, S.A., 1963.

Hannay, David. *Diaz*. London: Constable & Company Ltd., 1916.

Hannsen, Hans Peter. *Diary of a Dying Empire*. Translated by Oscar Osburn Winther. Bloomington: Indiana University Press, 1955.

Herrera, Celia E. *Francisco Villa ante la historia*. Mexico City, 1939.

Herring, Hubert and Weinstock, Herbert (ed.). *Renascent Mexico*. New York: Covici Friede, 1935.

Huerta, Victoriano. *Memorias*. Mexico City: Ediciones Vértice, 1957. (Although written in first person it apparently was the work of Joaquín Piña, a journalist close to Huerta).

Hunt, Frazier. *One American and His Attempt at Education*. New York: Simon and Schuster, 1938.

Investigation of Mexican Affairs. Preliminary Report and Hearings (September 8, 1919 to May 28, 1920) of the Committee on Foreign Relations, U. S. Senate. 2 vols. Washington: Government Printing Office, 1920.

Inman, Samuel Guy. *Intervention in Mexico*. New York: George H. Doran Co., 1919.

Junco, Alfonso. *Carranza y los orígenes de su rebelión*. Mexico City: Ediciones Botas, 1935.

Kelley, Francis Clement. *Blood-Drenched Altars*. Milwaukee: Bruce Publishing Co., 1936.

Lamicq, Pedro (pseud. Crater). *Madero, por uno de sus íntimos*. Mexico City: Editorial Azteca, 1914.

Lansing, Robert. *War Memoirs*. Indianapolis and New York: Bobbs Merrill, 1935.

Langle Ramírez, Arturo. *El ejército Villista*. Mexico City: Instituto Nacional de Antropología e Historia, 1961.

Leon-Portilla, Miguel. *Aztec Thought and Culture*. Norman: University of Oklahoma Press, 1963.

Link, Arthur S. *Woodrow Wilson and the Progressive Era 1910–1917*. New York: Harper, 1954.

Madero, Francisco I. *La sucesión presidencial en 1910* (3rd ed.). Mexico City: La viuda de C. Bouret, 1911.

——*Madero y su obra; documentos ineditos*. Mexico City: Talleres Gráficos de la Nación, 1934.

——*Manual espírita, por Bhima (pseud.)*. Mexico City: Tip Artística, 1911.

Magaña, Gildardo. *Emiliano Zapata y el agrarismo en México*. Vols. I–II (1951), Vols. III–IV (1952). Mexico City: Editorial Ruta.

Maldonado R., Calixto. *Los asesinatos de los señores Madero Y Pino Suárez, como ocurrieron; recopilación de datos historicos*. Mexico City, 1922.

Mancisidor, José. *Historia de la Revolución Mexicana*. Mexico City: Libro Mex Editores, 1964.

Márquez Sterling, Manuel. *Los últimos dias del presidente Madero*. Havana: El Siglo XX, 1917.

Martínez Nuñez, Eugenio. *La vida heróica de Praxedis G. Guerrero.* Mexico City: BINEHRM, 1960.

——*La Revolución en el estado de San Luis Potosí.* Mexico City: BINEHRM, 1964.

Martínez de la Vega, Francisco. *Heriberto Jara, un hombre de la Revolución.* Mexico City: Ediciones Diálogo, 1964.

Maytorena, José María. *Algunas verdades sobre el gral. Alvaro Obregón.* Los Angeles: Imprenta El Heraldo de México, 1919.

McCullagh, Francis. *Red Mexico.* New York, London and Paris: Brentano's Ltd., 1928.

McNeil, Norman Laird. *Corridos de Asuntos Vulgares.* Unpublished M.A. thesis, University of Texas. Austin, 1944.

Medina Ruiz, Fernando. *Calles, un destino melancólico.* Mexico City: Editorial Jus, S.A., 1960.

Melgarejo, Antonio D. *Los crímenes del Zapatismo; apuntes de un guerrillero.* Mexico City: F. P. Rojas y Cia., 1913.

Mellado, Guillermo. *Crímenes del Huertismo.* Mexico City, 1916.

Mena, Mario. *Alvaro Obregón. Historia militar y política 1912–1916.* Mexico City: Editorial Jus, S.A., 1960.

——*Zapata.* Mexico City: Editorial Jus, S.A., 1959.

Mena Brito, Bernardino. *Carranza, sus amigos, sus enemigos.* Mexico City: Ediciones Botas, 1935.

Mendieta Alatorre, María de los Angeles. *La mujer en la Revolución Mexicana.* Mexico City: BINEHRM, 1961.

Mendoza, Vicente T. *El corrido en la Revolución Mexicana.* Mexico City: BINEHRM, 1956.

Mexico: cincuenta años de Revolución. Vol. I, *La economía.* Vol. II, *La vida social.* Mexico City: Fondo de Cultura Económica, 1961.

Moctezuma, Aquiles P. *El conflicto religioso de 1926.* 2 vols. Mexico City: Editorial Jus, S.A., 1960.

Molina Enríquez, Andrés. *Los grandes problemas nacionales.* Mexico City: Imprenta A. Carranza e Hijos, 1909.

Morales Jiménez, Alberto. *1910. Biografía de un año decisivo.* Mexico City: BINEHRM, 1963.

——*Historia de la Revolución Mexicana.* Mexico City: Instituto de investigaciones políticas, económicas y sociales del Partido Revolucionario Institucional, 1951.

——*Hombres de la Revolución Mexicana. 50 semblanzas biográficas.* Mexico City: BINEHRM, 1960.

Moreno, Daniel. *Francisco I. Madero, José Ma. Pino Suárez, el crímen de la embajada.* Mexico City: Libro Mex Editores, 1960.

——*Los hombres de la Revolución.* Mexico City: Libro Mex Editores, 1960.

——*Venustiano Carranza, Alvaro Obregón, Plutarco Elías Calles.* Mexico City: Libro Mex Editores, 1960.

Muñoz, Ignacio. *Verdad y mito de la Revolución Mexicana relatada por un protagonista.* 3 vols. Mexico City: Ediciones Populares, 1960–61–62.

444 *Bibliography*

Murray, Robert H(ammond). *Huerta and the Two Wilsons.* Harper's Weekly, March 25, April 1, 8, 15, 22 and 29, 1916.

Naranjo, Francisco. *Diccionario biográfico revolucionario.* Mexico City: Editorial Cosmos, 1935.

Nicholson, Harold. *Dwight Morrow.* New York: Harcourt, Brace and Co., 1935.

Obregón, Alvaro. *Ocho mil kilómetros en campaña.* Paris and Mexico City: Bouret, 1917. (Also see *Fuentes.*)

Olea, Hector R. *Breve historia de la Revolución en Sinaloa.* Mexico City: BINEHRM, 1964.

O'Shaughnessy, Edith. *A Diplomat's Wife in Mexico.* New York and London: Harper, 1916.

————*Intimate Pages of Mexican History.* New York: George H. Doran Co., 1920.

Palavicini, Felix F. *La estética de la tragedia Mexicana.* Mexico City: Imprenta Modelo, 1933.

————*Mi vida revolucionaria.* Mexico City: Ediciones Botas, 1937.

Palomares, Justino N. *Anecdotario de la Revolución.* Mexico City: Ediciones del autor, 1954.

Parkes, Henry Bamford. *A History of Mexico.* Boston: Houghton Mifflin, 1938.

Paz, Octavio. *The Labyrinth of Solitude. Life and Thought in Mexico.* Translated by Lysander Kemp. New York: Grove Press, 1961.

Plenn, J. H. *Mexico Marches.* Indianapolis: Bobbs Merrill, 1939.

Poniatowska, Elena. *Massacre in Mexico.* New York: Viking Press, 1975.

Portes Gil, Emilio. *Quince años de política Mexicana.* Mexico City: Ediciones Botas, 1941.

Prida, Ramón. *La culpa de Lane Wilson en la tragedia Mexicana de 1913.* Mexico City: Ediciones Botas, 1962.

Puente, Ramón. *La dictadura, la Revolución y sus hombres.* Mexico City: Manuel León Sánchez, 1938.

————*Pascual Orozco y la revuelta de Chihuahua.* Mexico City: E. Gomez de la Puente, 1912.

————*Villa en pie.* Mexico City: Editorial Mexico Nuevo, 1937.

Quirk, Robert E. *The Mexican Revolution 1914–1915.* New York: Citadel Press, 1963.

Ramírez Plancarte, Francisco. *La ciudad de México durante la Revolución Constitucionalista.* Mexico City: Ediciones Botas, 1941.

Ramos, Samuel. *Profiles of Man and Culture in Mexico.* Translated by Peter G. Earle. Austin: University of Texas Press, 1962.

Reed, Alma. *Orozco.* New York: Oxford, 1956.

Reed, John. *Insurgent Mexico.* New York and London: Appleton, 1914.

Reyes, Alfonso. *Mexico in a Nutshell and Other Essays.* Translated by Charles Ramsdell. Berkeley and Los Angeles: University of California Press, 1964.

Rippy, J. Fred. *Mexico* (American Policies Abroad); with José Vasconcelos and Guy Stevens. Chicago: University of Chicago Press, 1928.

Roeder, Ralph. *Juarez and His Mexico.* New York: Viking Press, 1947.

Rojas, Luis Manuel. *La culpa de Henry Lane Wilson en el gran desastre de México*. Mexico City: Cia La. Verdad, S.A., 1928.

Romero Flores, Jesús. *Historia de la Revolución en Michoacán*. Mexico City: BINEHRM, 1964.

——*La Revolución como nosotros la vimos*. Mexico City: BINEHRM, 1963.

Ross, Stanley R. *Francisco I. Madero. Apostle of Mexican Democracy*. New York: Columbia University Press, 1955.

——(ed.) *Is the Mexican Revolution Dead?* New York: Knopf, 1966.

Royer, Fanchon. *Padre Pro. Modern Apostle and Martyr*. New York: P. J. Kenedy & Sons, 1954.

Saenz, Moises and Priestley, Herbert I. *Some Mexican Problems* (lectures of the Harris Foundation). Chicago: University of Chicago Press, 1926.

Sánchez, Azcona, Juan. *Apuntes para la historia de la Revolución Mexicana*. Mexico City: BINEHRM, 1961.

——*La etapa Maderista de la Revolución*. Mexico City: BINEHRM, 1960.

Sánchez Lamego, Miguel A. *Historia militar de la Revolución Constitucionalista* (Vol. I, February-June 1913; Vol. II, *Documents,* February-June 1913; Vol. III, July-December, 1913; Vol. IV, *Documents,* July-December, 1913; Vol. V, January-August 1914). Mexico City: BINEHRM, 1960.

Santamaría, F. J. *Diccionario de Mejicanismos*. Mexico City: Editorial Porrua, 1959.

Schlarman, Joseph H. L. *Mexico, a Land of Volcanoes. From Cortés to Alemán*. Milwaukee: Bruce Publishing Co., 1950.

Scott, Hugh Lenox. *Some Memories of a Soldier*. New York: Century, 1928.

Sherman, William L. and Gruen, Richard E. *Victoriano Huerta; A Reappraisal*. Mexico City: Imprenta Aldina, 1960.

Silva Herzog, Jesús. *Breve historia de la Revolución Mexicana*. 2 vols. Mexico City and Buenos Aires: Fondo de Cultura Económica, 1964.

——*Colección de folletos para la historia de la Revolución Mexicana; la cuestion de la tierra*. 3 vols. Mexico City: Instituto de Investigaciones Económicas, 1961.

——*Trayectoría ideológica de la Revolución Mexicana 1910–1917*. Mexico City: Cuadernos Americanos, 1963.

Simpson, Eyler N. *The Ejido: Mexico's Way Out*. Chapel Hill: University of North Carolina Press, 1937.

Simpson, Lesley Byrd. *Many Mexicos*. Berkeley and Los Angeles: University of California Press, 1959.

Sotelo Inclán, Jesús. *Raíz y razón de Zapata*. Mexico City: Editorial Etnos, 1943.

Starr, Frederick. *Mexico and the United States*. Chicago: The Bible House, 1914.

Stephenson, George M. *John Lind of Minnesota*. Minneapolis: The University of Minnesota Press, 1935.

Tannenbaum, Frank. *Mexico, the Struggle for Peace and Bread*. New York: Knopf, 1950.

——*Peace by Revolution. Mexico after 1910.* New York and London: Columbia University Press, 1966.

Taracena, Alfonso. *La verdadera Revolución Mexicana.* 16 vols., first nine in *Figuras y Episodios de la Historia de México* series, remainder in *México Heroico* series. Mexico City: Editorial Jus, S.A., 1960–1966.

——*Venustiano Carranza.* Mexico City: Editorial Jus, S.A., 1963.

Terrazas, Sylvestre. Collection of miscellaneous papers relating to Villa, Madero, Carranza, Flores Magón and the Revolution in Chihuahua. Bancroft Library, University of California, Berkeley.

Timmons, Wilbert H. *Morelos of Mexico. Priest, Soldier, Statesman.* El Paso: Texas Western College Press, 1963.

Toor, Frances. *A Treasury of Mexican Folkways.* New York: Crown, 1947.

Torres, Elías L. *Como murió Pancho Villa.* Mexico City: El Libro Espanol, 1963.

——*La Cabeza de Villa y 20 episodios mas.* Mixcoac: Editorial Tatos, 1938.

——*Vida hazañas de Pancho Villa.* Mexico City: El Libro Espanol, 1951.

Townsend, William Cameron. *Lazaro Cardenas: Mexican Democrat.* Ann Arbor: George Wahr, 1952.

Tuchman, Barbara W. *The Zimmerman Telegram.* New York: Dell, 1965.

Turner, Ethel Duffy. *Ricardo Flores Magón y el partido liberal Mexicano.* Traducción de Eduardo Limón G. Morelia, Mich.: Editorial Erandi, 1960.

Turner, John Kenneth. *Barbarous Mexico.* Chicago: Charles H. Kerr & Co., 1911.

——Under Fire in Mexico. Semi-Monthly Magazine, May 13, 1913.

Turner, Timothy G. *Bullets, Bottles and Gardenias.* Dallas: South-West Press, 1935.

Ugalde, R. *Vida de Pascual Orozco, 1882–1915.* El Paso, (1915 ?).

Urquizo, Francisco Luis. *Asesinato de Carranza.* Mexico City: Populibros La Prensa, 1959.

——*Carranza el hombre, el politico, el caudillo, el patriota.* Mexico City, 1959.

——*Mexico-Tlaxcalantongo, Mayo de 1920.* Mexico City: Editorial Cultura, 1932.

——*Origen de ejército Constitucionalista.* Mexico City: BINEHRM, 1960.

——*Páginas de la Revolución.* Mexico City: BINEHRM, 1956.

——*"Recuerdo que . . ." Visiones aisladas de la Revolución.* Mexico City: Ediciones Botas, 1934.

Valadés, José. *Imaginación y Realidad de Francisco I. Madero.* 2 vols. Mexico City: Antigua Librería Robredo, 1960.

Vasconcelos, José. *A Mexican Ulysses; an autobiography.* Translated and abridged by W. Rex Crawford. Bloomington: Indiana University Press, 1963.

——*Breve historia de México.* Mexico City: Editorial Polis, 1944.

——*El desastre.* Mexico City: Ediciones Botas, 1951.

——*La caida de Carranza. De la dictadura a la libertad.* Mexico City: Imp. Murguía, 1920.

Vera Estañol, Jorge. *Carranza and his Bolshevik Regime.* Los Angeles: Wayside Press, 1920.

Weyl, Nathaniel and Sylvia. *The Reconquest of Mexico.* New York: Oxford, 1939.

Whetten, Nathan L. *Rural Mexico.* Chicago: University of Chicago Press, 1948.

Wilson, Henry Lane. *Diplomatic Episodes in Mexico, Belgium and Chile.* Garden City: Doubleday, Page & Company, 1927.

Wolfe, Bertram D. *The Fabulous Life of Diego Rivera.* New York: Stein and Day, 1963.

Zuño, José G. *Historia de la Revolución en la estado de Jalisco.* Mexico City: BINEHRM, 1964.

SOME NOTES ON SOURCES

THE FOREGOING BIBLIOGRAPHY is incomplete (standard bibliographies are readily available to the serious student). No attempt has been made except in the text to cite newspaper and periodical sources. And no attempt could be made to credit all the human sources—many of them participants in or witnesses to the events here treated—accumulated during thirty-odd years of journalism.

This listing attempts two things. It acknowledges some of the author's debts. And it is a guide to the wealth of material recently published in Mexico dealing with this period.

Particularly noteworthy:

The series of monographs, memoirs, essays, biographies and regional histories published by the Biblioteca del Instituto Nacional de Estudios Históricos de la Revolución Mexicana (herein referred to, for brevity's sake, as BINEHRM). And two series published by the Fondo de Cultura Económica: The *Documentos históricos de la Revolución Mexicana,* published under the direction of the late Isidro Fabela, including three volumes on the *Revolución y régimen Maderista* and four volumes on the *Revolución y régimen Constitucionalista;* and the five volumes of *Fuentes para la historia de la Revolución Mexicana.* These series contain much material that has heretofore been either unavailable or inaccessible.

The author owes a special obligation to two remarkable publications. To point out the number of times they were used for guidance, illumination and clarification would be burdensome since they were consulted repeatedly in virtually every chapter.

One is the four volumes of the *Historia gráfica de la Revolución Mexicana* compiled by the Casasola family whose members were and are photographers with a sense of history. The most recent edition, commemorating the first half-century of the Revolution, tells the story in pictures—supplemented by text—from 1900 up to the 1960s, in strong, clear visual terms.

The other is Alfonso Taracena's 16-volume *La verdadera Revolución Mexicana.* It is a day-by-day record of the revolutionary period, a chronicle of social and political upheavals, diplomatic crises, battles, scandal, gossip, otherwise unavailable correspondence, even theatrical attractions and literary controversies. It is a huge and impressive expansion of the work he did in his earlier *Mi vida en el vértigo de la Revolución,* which served generations of researchers.

Other sources consulted, chapter by chapter:

CHAPTER 1: Beals, *Díaz;* Cumberland, *Genesis under Madero;* Bell, *Political Shame; Boletín oficial;* Bulnes, *Whole Truth;* Creelman, *Hero of the Americas;* De Fornaro, *Czar of Mexico;* Morales Jiménez, *Año decisivo;* O'Shaughnessy, *Intimate Pages;* Rippy, *Mexico;* Romero Flores, *Como nosotros la vimos;* Starr, *Mexico and the United States;* J. K. Turner, *Barbarous Mexico.*

CHAPTER 2: Alamán, *Historia de Méjico;* Bancroft, *History of Mexico;* Leon-Portilla, *Aztec Thought and Culture;* Parkes, *History of Mexico;* Roeder, *Juarez;* Timmons, *Morelos;* Vasconcelos, *Breve historia.*

CHAPTER 3: Beals, *Díaz;* Cumberland, *Genesis under Madero;* Morales Jiménez, *Año decisivo;* Rippy, *Mexico;* Romero Flores, *Como nosotros la vimos;* Terrazas collection, Liberal Party correspondence; E. D. Turner, *Flores Magón.*

CHAPTER 4: Blaisdell, *Desert Revolution;* Flores Magón, *Epistolario;* also, *Semilla Libertaria; Huelga de Cananea (Fuentes para la historia* v. 3); Hannay, *Díaz;* Martínez Nuñez, *Praxedis Guerrero;* Morales Jiménez, *Año decisivo;* also, *Hombres de la Revolución;* Senate Hearing, Mexican Affairs; Silva Herzog, *Breve historia;* Terrazas collection, Liberal Party correspondence, Enrique Clay Creel correspondence; E. D. Turner, *Flores Magón.*

CHAPTER 5: Bell, *Political Shame;* Bonilla, *Régimen Maderista;* Cabrera, *Obras Políticas; Manifestos políticos (Fuentes para la historia* v. 4); Madero, *Manual espírita;* also, *Sucesión;* Mendoza, *El corrido;* O'Shaughnessy, *Intimate Pages;* Ross, *Madero;* Valadés, *Imaginación.*

CHAPTER 6: Beals, *Díaz;* Bell, *Political Shame;* De Fornaro, *Czar of Mexico;* Foreign Relations 1910–1911; Mendoza, *El corrido;* Parkes, *History of Mexico;* Rippy, *Mexico;* Romero Flores, *Como nosotros la vimos;* Ross, *Madero;* Sánchez Azcona, *Apuntes;* also, *Etapa Maderista;* Senate Hearing, Mexican Affairs; Silva Herzog, *Trayestoría;* T. Turner, *Bullets;* Valadés, *Imaginación.*

CHAPTER 7: Aguirre Benavides, *Inmaculado;* Almada, *Revolución en Chihuahua;* Bell, *Political Shame;* Cumberland, *Genesis under Madero;* Foreign Relations 1911; Puente, *Pascual Orozco;* Sánchez Azcona, *Apuntes;* E. D. Turner, *Flores Magón;* T. Turner, *Bullets.*

CHAPTER 8: Bell, *Political Shame;* Cumberland, *Genesis under Madero;* Muñoz, *Verdad y mito* v. 1; O'Shaughnessy, *Intimate Pages;* Reyes, *Nutshell.*

CHAPTER 9: De María y Campos, *Episodios;* Magaña *Zapata* v. 1; O'Shaughnessy, *Intimate Pages;* Sánchez Azcona, *Etapa Maderista.* Madero-Zapata interchange, from Magaña, *Zapata,* v. 1, p. 132. Cabrera, analogy to surgery, from Cabrera, *Pensamiento de Luis Cabrera,* p. 148. Description Madero women, from O'Shaughnessy, *Intimate Pages,* p. 131.

CHAPTER 10: Aguirre Benavides, *Inmaculado;* Dromundo, *Zapata;* Gruening, *Heritage;* Magaña, *Zapata* vols. 1 and 2; Mena, *Zapata;* Silva Herzog, *Trayectoría;* Simpson, *Ejido;* Sotelo Inclán, *Raíz y razón;* Valadés, *Imaginación;* Whetten, *Rural Mexico.*

CHAPTER 11: Aguirre Benavides, *Inmaculado;* Almada, *Revolución en Chihuahua;* Bell, *Political Shame;* Blanco Moheno, *Crónica* v. 1; *Boletín oficial;* Bonilla, *Régimen Maderista;* Cumberland, *Genesis under Madero;* Foreign Relations 1911, 1912; Prida, *Culpa;* Puente, *Pascual Orozco;* Reyes, *Nutshell;* Ross, *Madero;* Senate Hearing, Mexican Affairs; Silva Herzog, *Breve historia;* Simpson, *Ejido;* T. Turner, *Bullets;* Ugalde, *Pascual Orozco;* Valadés, *Imaginación.*

CHAPTER 12: Aguirre Benavides, *Inmaculado;* Baerlein, *Land of Unrest;* Bell, *Political Shame;* Bonilla, *Régimen Maderista;* Bulnes, *Whole Truth;* Cervantes, *Felipe Angeles;* Cumberland, *Genesis under Madero;* De Valle-Arizpe, *Historia de la ciudad;* Espinosa, *Decena roja;* Foreign Relations 1913; Guzmán, *Febrero de 1913;* Huerta, *Memorias;* Maldonado R., *Asesinatos;* Márquez Sterling, *Ultimos días;* Murray, *Huerta and Two Wilsons;* O'Shaughnessy, *Intimate Pages;* Reyes, *Nutshell;* Ross, *Madero;* Sánchez Azcona, *Apuntes;* also, *Etapa Maderista;* Valadés, *Imaginación;* Wilson, *Episodes.*
Description Madero in intendancy, from Márquez Sterling, *Ultimos Días,* p. 538

CHAPTER 13: Aguirre Benavides, *Inmaculado;* Baker, *Woodrow Wilson* v. 4; Bell, *Political Shame;* Bonilla, *Régimen Maderista;* Cumberland, *Genesis under Madero;* Foreign Relations 1913; Gruening, *Heritage;* Guzmán, *Febrero de 1913;* Lamicq, *Madero;* Márquez Sterling, *Ultimos días;* Moreno, *El Crímen;* Murray, *Huerta and Two Wilsons;* Prida, *Culpa;* Rippy, *Mexico;* Rojas, *Culpa;* Ross, *Madero;* Sánchez Azcona, *Apuntes;* Senate Hearing, Mexican Affairs; E. D. Turner, *Flores Magón;* J. K. Turner, *Under Fire;* Vasconcelos, *Ulysses;* Wilson, *Episodes.*
"Don't be smelted . . ." from Bell, *Political Shame,* p. 173.

CHAPTER 14: Bell, *Political Shame;* Bonilla, *Régimen Maderista;* De María y Campos, *Episodios;* Espinosa, *Decena roja;* Foreign Relations 1913; Murray, *Huerta and Two Wilsons;* Maldonado R., *Asesinatos;* Sánchez Azcona, *Apuntes;* Valadés, *Imaginación.*
Madero "unsound . . ." from H. L. Wilson, *Episodes,* p. 287. "An ambassador who should not have been there," from Bell, *Political Shame,* p. 416.

CHAPTER 15: Aguirre Benavides, *Inmaculado;* Baker, *Woodrow Wilson* v. 4; Blanco Moheno, *Crónica* v. 1; Bell, *Political Shame;* Bonilla, *Régimen Maderista;* Bulnes, *Whole Truth;* Cline, *U.S. and Mexico;* Cumberland, *Genesis under Madero;* Guzmán, *Febrero de 1913;* Huerta, *Memorias;* Magaña, *Zapata* v. 1; Mellado, *Crímenes;* O'Shaughnessy, *Intimate Pages;* also, *Diplomatic Wife;* Quirk, *Revolution;* Ramírez Plancarte, *Ciudad durante;* Ross, *Madero;* Sherman, *Reappraisal;* Silva Herzog, *Breve historia;* Simpson, *Ejido;* Stephenson, *Lind;* Tuchman, *Zimmerman Telegram.*
"Why, it is good, fighting," from Reed, *Insurgent Mexico,* p. 37. "Look at that stone," from Azuela, *Underdogs,* p. 147. "Cultivate friendship," from Baker, *Wilson,* v. 4, p. 66. "Submerged 85 percent," from interview by Samuel G. Blythe, *Saturday Evening Post,* May 23, 1914. "That scoundrel," from Baker, *Wilson,* v. 4, pp. 266, 273.

CHAPTER 16: Aguirre Benavides, *Inmaculado;* Amaya, *Carranza;* Blanco Moheno, *Crónica* v. 1; Bonilla, *Régimen Maderista;* Breceda, *Carranza;* Bulnes,

Whole Truth; Cumberland, *Genesis under Madero;* Foreign Relations 1913; Guzmán, *Eagle and Serpent;* Junco, *Carranza;* Quirk, *Revolution;* Fabela (ed.), *Revolución y régimen Constitucionalista* v. 4; Ross, *Madero;* Sánchez Azcona, *Apuntes;* Senate Hearing, Mexican Affairs; Taracena, *Carranza;* Vasconcelos, *Ulysses.*

CHAPTER 17: Aguirre Benavides, *Inmaculado;* Almada, *Revolución en Chihuahua;* Amaya, *Carranza;* Blanco Moheno, *Crónica* v. 1; Bonilla, *Régimen Maderista;* Cervantes, *Villa;* Fabela (ed.), *Revolución y régimen Constitucionalista* v. 4; Foix, *Villa;* Guzmán, *Eagle and Serpent;* also, *Memoirs of Villa;* Herrera, *Villa;* Quirk, *Revolution;* Reed, *Insurgent Mexico;* Tannenbaum, *Peace by Revolution;* Taracena, *Carranza;* Torres, *Cabeza de Villa;* also, *Vida y hazañas;* T. Turner, *Bullets;* Ugalde, *Pascual Orozco.*

"Here is one rich man," from Guzmán, *Memoirs of Villa,* p. 38.

CHAPTER 18: Aguirre Benavides (Luis and Adrián), *Las grandes batallas;* Cervantes, *Felipe Angeles;* also, *Villa;* Guzmán, *Memoirs of Villa.*

"Never do violence," from Guzmán, *Eagle and Serpent,* p. 310.

CHAPTER 19: Almada, *Diccionario* (of Sonora); Amaya, *Carranza;* Blasco Ibañez, *Revolution in Mexico;* Bojórquez, *Forjadores;* Cervantes, *Felipe Angeles;* De María y Campos, *Lucio Blanco;* Dillon, *Obregon;* Guzmán, *Eagle and Serpent;* Junco, *Carranza;* Maytorena, *Algunas verdades;* Mena, *Obregón;* Obregón, *8,000 kilómetros;* Reed, *Insurgent Mexico;* Taracena, *Carranza;* Urquizo, *Origen;* Vasconcelos, *Ulysses.*

Letter to son Humberto, from Obrégon, *8,000 kilómetros,* p. 32. "If, through some monstrosity," Obregón, p. 74. "I immediately began," Obregón, p. 104.

CHAPTER 20: Amaya, *Carranza;* Bojórquez, *Forjadores;* Cervantes, *Felipe Angeles;* also, *Villa;* Foix, *Villa;* Guzmán, *Memoirs of Villa;* Senate Hearing, Mexican Affairs; Taracena, *Carranza;* Vasconcelos, *Ulysses.*

Angeles-Velasco-Villa telephone conversation, from Guzmán, *Memoirs of Villa,* p. 149; also Cervantes, *Villa,* appendix 6, p. 676.

CHAPTER 21: Blanco Moheno, *Crónica* v. 1; Cervantes, *Felipe Angeles;* also, *Villa;* Foix, *Villa;* Guzmán, *Memoirs of Villa;* Junco, *Carranza.*

Carranza to Barrón, from Taracena, *Verdadera Revolución,* v. 7, p. 198. Angeles to Barrón, from Taracena, *Carranza,* p. 231; also Cervantes, *Villa,* p. 132. Ortega to Carranza, from Taracena, *Carranza,* p. 235; also Cervantes, *Villa,* p. 129. Telegraphic exchange with Carranza, from Cervantes, *Villa,* appendix 7, p. 701; also Guzmán, *Memoirs of Villa,* p. 213; also Amaya, *Carranza,* p. 119. Herrera incident, from Blanco Moheno, *Crónica,* v. 1, p. 202.

CHAPTER 22: Azuela, *Underdogs;* Cervantes, *Felipe Angeles;* also, *Villa;* Escobedo, *Zacatecas;* Guzmán, *Memoirs of Villa;* Gruening, *Heritage;* Muñoz, *Verdad y mito* v. 2; Torres, *Vida y hazañas.*

Cervantes' battle description, from Cervantes, *Villa,* appendix 9, p. 719. Ancheta incident, from Torres, *Cabeza de Villa,* p. 64. Canova reports, from DOS files, National Archives, 812.00/12826, 12888, and 12979.

CHAPTER 23: Cervantes, *Felipe Angeles;* also, *Villa;* De María y Campos, *Lucio Blanco;* Guzmán, *Memoirs of Villa;* Mena, *Obregón;* Obregón, *8,000 kilómetros;* Puente, *Villa;* Quirk, *Revolution;* Taracena, *Carranza;* Vasconcelos, *Ulysses.*

Carranza to Angeles, from Taracena, *Carranza*, p. 238. Villa-Obregón messages, from Guzmán, *Memoirs of Villa*, p. 246; also Obregón, *8,000 kilómetros*, p. 127; also Amaya, *Carranza*, p. 107.

CHAPTER 24: Cervantes, *Villa*; Guzmán, *Memoirs of Villa*.

Guzmán advice to Villa, Guzmán, *Memoirs of Villa*, p. 269. Description of Urbina, from Reed, *Insurgent Mexico*, pp. 18, 25.

CHAPTER 25: Amaya, *Carranza*; Baker, *Woodrow Wilson* v. 4; Blasco Ibañez, *Mexico in Revolution*; Cervantes, *Villa*; Guzmán, *Memoirs of Villa*; Maytorena, *Algunas verdades*; Obregón, *8,000 kilómetros*; Quirk, *Revolution*; Ramírez Plancarte, *Ciudad durante*.

Villa-Obregón meetings, from Guzmán, *Memoirs of Villa*, p. 288 ff.; also Obregón, *8,000 kilómetros*, p. 168 ff.

CHAPTER 26: Amaya, *Carranza*; Blanco Moheno, *Crónica* v. 1; Cervantes, *Villa*; Obregón, *8,000 kilómetros*; Quirk, *Revolution*.

CHAPTER 27: Amaya, *Carranza*; Barragán, *Ejército Constitucionalista*; Barrera Fuentes, *Crónicas y debates*; Blanco Moheno, *Crónica* v. 1; Cervantes, *Villa*; Guzmán, *Eagle and Serpent*; also, *Memoirs of Villa*; Obregón, *8,000 kilómetros*; O'Shaughnessy, *Intimate Pages*; Quirk, *Revolution*; Ramírez Plancarte, *Ciudad durante*; Vasconcelos, *Ulysses*.

CHAPTER 28: Amaya, *Carranza*; Cervantes, *Villa*; De María y Campos, *Lucio Blanco*; Guzmán, *Eagle and Serpent*; also, *Memoirs of Villa*; Obregón, *8,000 kilómetros*; Quirk, *Revolution*.

CHAPTER 29: Barragán, *Ejército Constitucionalista*; Cervantes, *Villa*; Junco, *Carranza*; Morales Jiménez, *Hombres de la Revolución*; Quirk, *Revolution*; Ramírez Plancarte, *Ciudad durante*; Vasconcelos, *Ulysses*.

Villa-Zapata meeting, from Cervantes, *Villa*, p. 367; also Guzmán, *Memoirs of Villa*, p. 376; also Ramírez Plancarte, *Ciudad durante*, p. 261; also Canova, 812.00/14048.

CHAPTER 30: Cervantes, *Villa*; De María y Campos, *Lucio Blanco*; Guzmán, *Eagle and Serpent*; also, *Memoirs of Villa*; Obregón, *8,000 kilómetros*; Ramírez Plancarte, *Ciudad durante*.

Obregón letter to Gutiérrez, from Obregón, *8,000 kilómetros*, p. 238. Fierro-Berlanga incident, from Guzmán, *Eagle and Serpent*, p. 347. Villa-Gutiérrez confrontation, from Guzmán, *Eagle and Serpent*, p. 355. Gutiérrez manifesto, from Cervantes, *Villa*, appendix 15, p. 764. Gutiérrez farewell message, from María y Campos, *Blanco*, p. 176.

CHAPTER 31: Amaya, *Carranza*; Barragán, *Ejército Constitucionalista*; Blanco Moheno, *Crónica* v. 2; Bojórquez, *Forjadores*; Cervantes, *Villa*; Guzmán, *Memoirs of Villa*; Quirk, *Revolution*; Ramírez Plancarte, *Ciudad durante*.

Argumedo-Carranza emity, from Amaya, *Carranza*, p. 340.

CHAPTER 32: Barragán, *Ejército Constitucionalista*; Cervantes, *Villa*; Clendenen, *U.S. and Pancho Villa*; Dillon, *Obregon*; Foix, *Villa*; Link, *Wilson and Progressive Era*; Obregón, *8,000 kilómetros*; Scott, *Memories of a Soldier*; Terrazas collection, correspondence of Villa and S. Terrazas.

Villa statement in Juárez from El Paso *Morning Times*, Oct. 9, 1915.

CHAPTER 33: Bulnes, *Whole Truth;* Guzmán, *Muertos históricos;* Huerta, *Memorias;* Link, *Wilson and Progressive Era;* O'Shaughnessy, *Intimate Pages;* Senate Hearing, Mexican Affairs; Tuchman, *Zimmerman Telegram.*

CHAPTER 34: Barragán, *Ejército Constitucionalista;* Callcott, *Liberalism in Mexico;* Cervantes, *Villa;* Cole, statement to L.A. *Times;* Fabela (ed.), *Revolución y régimen Constitucionalista* vols. 1 & 4; Lansing, *War Memories;* Link, *Wilson and Progressive Era;* Mancisidor, *Historia de la Revolución;* Molina Enriquez, *Grandes problemas;* Quirk, *Revolution;* Silva Herzog, *Breve historia;* Simpson, *Ejido;* Taracena, *Carranza;* Tuchman, *Zimmerman Telegram.*

CHAPTER 35: Blanco Moheno, *Crónica* v. 2; Braddy, *Villa at Columbus;* Cervantes, *Villa;* Clendenen, *U.S. and Pancho Villa;* Foreign Relations 1916; Torres, *Vida y hazañas.*

CHAPTER 36: Amaya, *Carranza;* Baltierra Rivera, *Breve analisís;* Barragán, *Ejército Constitucionalista;* Blanco Moheno, *Crónica* v. 2; Bojórquez (Bórquez), *Crónica;* Bulnes, *Whole Truth;* Callcott, *Liberalism in Mexico;* Castellanos Tena, *Nuestras constituciones;* Clendenen, *U.S. and Pancho Villa;* De la Huerta, *Memorias;* Dillon, *Obregon;* Fabela (ed.), *Revolución y régimen Constitucionalista* v. 4; Ferrer Mendiolea, *Congreso constituyente;* Hanssen, *Dying Empire;* Inman, *Intervention in Mexico;* Morales Jiménez, *Hombres de la Revolución;* Plenn, *Mexico Marches;* Silva Herzog, *Breve historia;* also, *Trayectoría;* Tannenbaum, *Peace by Revolution;* Taracena, *Carranza;* Tuchman, *Zimmerman Telegram.*

Bojórquez-Carranza incident, from Bojórquez (Bórquez), *Crónica del constituyente,* p. 674.

CHAPTER 37: Dromundo, *Zapata;* Magaña, *Zapata* vols. 1–4; Melgarejo, *Crímenes del Zapatismo;* Mena, *Zapata;* Naranjo, *Diccionario biográfico revolucionario* (appendix); Ramírez Plancarte, *Ciudad durante;* Silva Herzog, *Trayectoría;* Sotelo Inclán, *Raíz y razón;* Whetten, *Rural Mexico.*

Zapata letter to Carranza, from Dromundo, *Zapata,* p. 260. Carranza-Sosa Pavón incident, from Taracena, *Verdadera Revolución,* v. 5, p. 215. Zapata-Guajardo correspondence, from Dromundo, *Zapata,* p. 269; González-Carranza correspondence re death of Zapata, from Naranjo, *Diccionario biográfico,* p. 233 (n).

CHAPTER 38: Blasco Ibañez, *Revolution in Mexico;* Callcott, *Liberalism in Mexico;* De la Huerta, *Memorias;* Dillon, *Obregon;* Dulles, *Yesterday in Mexico;* Gruening, *Heritage;* Priestley (with Saenz), *Mexico Problems;* Rippy, *Mexico;* Romero Flores, *Como nosotros la vimos;* Tannenbaum, *Peace by Revolution;* Urquizo, *Carranza;* Vera Estañol, *Carranza;* Vasconcelos, *Breve historia;* also, *Caida de Carranza.*

CHAPTER 39: Amaya, *Carranza;* Blanco Moheno, *Crónica* v. 2; Dillon, *Obregon;* Dulles, *Yesterday in Mexico;* Gruening, *Heritage;* Guzmán, *Muertos históricos;* Taracena, *Carranza;* Urquizo, *Carranza;* also, *Mexico-Tlaxcalantongo;* Vasconcelos, *Caida de Carranza.*

CHAPTER 40: Amaya, *Carranza;* Ceja Reyes, *Yo maté a Villa;* Clendenen, *U.S. and Pancho Villa;* De la Huerta, *Memorias;* Hunt, *One American;*

Dillon, *Obregon;* Dulles, *Yesterday in Mexico;* Puente, *Villa;* Torres, *Cabeza de Villa;* also, *Como murió Pancho Villa.*

Villa-De la Huerta correspondence, from Torres, *Vida y hazañas,* pp. 168, 184. Villa letter to journalist, from Terrazas collection. Villa statement to Hunt, from Hunt, *One American,* p. 232.

CHAPTER 41: Arenal, *Siqueiros;* Blanco Moheno, *Crónica* v. 2; Blasco Ibañez, *Revolution in Mexico;* Bojórquez, *Forjadores;* Brandenburg, *Making of Modern Mexico;* Brenner, *Wind that Swept Mexico;* Charlot, *Mural Renaissance;* Dillon, *Obregon;* Dulles, *Yesterday in Mexico;* González Ramírez, *Alvaro Obregón, estadista (appendix to the Fuentes para la historia* edition of *8,000 kilómetros*); McCullagh, *Red Mexico;* Mena, *Obregón;* Obregón, *8,000 kilómetros;* Reed, *Orozco;* Taracena, *Carranza;* Vasconcelos, *Ulysses;* Wolfe, *Fabulous Life.*

CHAPTER 42: Ceja Reyes, *Yo Maté a Villa;* Foix, *Villa;* Guzmán, *Eagle and Serpent;* Herrera, *Villa;* Palomares, *Anecdotaria de la Revolución;* Puente, *Villa;* Torres, *Cabeza de Villa;* also, *Como murió Pancho Villa.*

Lara on Villa assassination, from Palomares, *Anecdotaria,* p. 163.

CHAPTER 43: Bojórquez, *Forjadores;* Calles, *Mexico Before the World;* Cline, *United States and Mexico;* Dulles, *Yesterday in Mexico;* Guzmán, *Eagle and Serpent;* Gruening, *Heritage;* Medina Ruiz, *Calles;* McCullagh, *Red Mexico;* Mena, *Obregón;* Royer, *Padre Pro;* Schlarman, *Mexico, Land of Volcanoes;* Vasconcelos, *El desastre.*

CHAPTER 44: Barragán, *Ejército Constitucionalista;* Beals, *Civil War in Mexico;* Calles, *Mexico Before the World;* Cervantes, *Villa;* Dulles, *Yesterday in Mexico;* Gruening, *Heritage;* Guzmán, *Memoirs of Villa;* Kelley, *Blood-Drenched Altars;* Moctezuma, *El conflicto religioso* vols. 1 and 2; O'Shaughnessy, *Diplomatic Wife;* Quirk, *Revolution;* Romero Flores, *Como nosotros la vimos.*

CHAPTER 45: Beals, *Mexico's Coming Elections;* Blanco Moheno, *Crónica* v. 2; Bojórquez, *Forjadores;* Dulles, *Yesterday in Mexico;* Gruening, *Heritage;* McCullagh, *Red Mexico;* Mena, *Obregón;* Royer, *Padre Pro.*

CHAPTER 46: Bojórquez (Bórquez), *Cárdenas;* Bosques, *National Revolutionary Party;* Cabrera (Blas Urrea), *Veinte años despues;* Carrillo, *Defensa de la Revolución;* Correa, *Balance del Cardenismo;* Anguiano Equihua, *Cárdenas, su feudo;* Dulles, *Yesterday in Mexico;* González Casanova, *Democracia en Mexico;* Herring and Weinstock, *Renascent Mexico;* McCullagh, *Red Mexico;* Morales Jiménez, *Hombres de la Revolución;* Medina Ruiz, *Calles;* Nicolson, *Dwight Morrow;* Portes Gil, *Quince años de política Mexicana;* Romero Flores, *Revolución en Michoacán;* Schlarman, *Land of Volcanoes;* Simpson, *Ejido;* Townsend, *Cardenas;* Vasconcelos, *Ulysses;* Weyl, *Reconquest of Mexico.*

"Because of what we went through," from Fuentes, *Where the Air Is Clear,* p. 87.

INDEX